THE STRUCTURE OF
HUMAN PERSONALITY

THE STRUCTURE OF
HUMAN PERSONALITY

H. J. EYSENCK

Professor of Psychology, University of London;
Director, Psychological Dept., Institute of Psychiatry
Psychologist, Maudsley and Bethlem Royal Hospitals

METHUEN & CO. LTD.
11 NEW FETTER LANE, LONDON, E.C.4

First published August 27, 1953
Second Edition 1960
Third Edition 1970
SBN 416 16420 x

First published as a University Paperback 1970
SBN 416 18030 2

PRINTED IN GREAT BRITAIN BY
JOHN DICKENS AND CO LTD NORTHAMPTON

Distributed in the U.S.A.
by Barnes & Noble Inc.

To

L. L. THURSTONE

In Profound Admiration

If there are some subjects on which the results obtained have finally received the unanimous assent of all who have attended to the proof, and others on which mankind have not yet been equally successful; on which the most sagacious minds have occupied themselves from the earliest date, and have never succeeded in establishing any considerable body of truths, so as to be beyond denial or doubt; it is by generalizing the methods successfully followed in the former enquiries, and adapting them to the latter, that we may hope to remove this blot on the face of science.

J .S. MILL.

CONTENTS

INTRODUCTION

IN SPITE OF the great interest that psychologists, psychiatrists, and psycho-analysts have shown in the subject, no detailed account appears to exist of those natural phenomena on which our views of the organization or structure of personality are based. There are, it is true, many professions of faith; thus we are assured that "personality is an emergent 'gestalt' phenomenon whose organization cannot be accounted for in terms of atomistic concepts", and that "the unique totality of personality determines the very nature and meaning of the individual sub-wholes or 'parts'; it is not determined by them". Proof of such far-reaching asseverations is hardly ever attempted; occasionally recourse is had to philosophical deduction (which is irrelevant) or analogy with perceptual phenomena (which is improper), but, by and large, reliance is placed more on intuitive agreement than on scientific demonstration. Such demonstration, including the demand for proof which it implies, is indeed often declared to be superfluous; clinical experience and phenomenological observation are believed to be able to take its place. This view is maintained, even although it would appear to make impossible any rational choice between opposing experiences and observations, by explicitly denying the very principles of scientific method on the basis of which one expert's views might be shown to be correct and another's to be faulty.

It consequently appeared worth-while to bring together in one volume some of the major theories of personality organization, and to comb the literature for empirical studies either undertaken with the aim of testing deductions from these hypotheses or at least having some direct bearing on them. The first chapter represents an attempt to set forth these theories in broad outline, and to discuss some of their implications; the remainder of the book is devoted to a critical presentation of the evidence, arranged according to the technique employed—rating, self-rating, objective testing, constitutional assessment, autonomic measurement, and so forth. Also discussed in the first chapter is the problem of a proper statistical model for the investigation of personality organization, and an attempt is made to show that at the present moment the method of factor analysis alone enables us to represent the known facts in terms of a strictly quantitative conceptual schema.

There are three main criticisms of such a conclusion which merit at least a brief answer. (Criticisms based essentially on a misunderstanding of factor analysis, either with respect to its aims or its methods, will not be dealt with here. They are deplorably prevalent in the literature, so much so that it might be wise to follow psychoanalytic practice and lay it down that criticism of factor analysis should be confined to those who had themselves been factor analysed!)

The first point often made is a denial of the importance of the problem which factor analysis attempts to tackle. Essentially, types, traits, syndromes, and the various other concepts which psychology and psychiatry have elaborated in their attempts to describe the organization of personality, all of which are in principle similar to factors by virtue of their derivation on the basis of consistencies of behaviour similarities, are said to be artefacts which are used to imprison the unique personality, a veritable bed of Procrustes which distorts the essence of the phenomena under observation. That these concepts are artefacts is of course undeniable, as by definition all concepts are artefacts; the concepts of extraversion, hysteria, or suggestibility are artefacts in precisely the same sense that an electron, magnetism, or an ohm are artefacts. Spearman's "g" (general intelligence) is in the same position as Newton's "g" (gravitational force). Science attempts to bring order into the multiplicity of phenomena; it does so by introducing concepts which have no counterpart in the world of reality. These concepts may be useful or worthless; their value must be decided on other grounds than that of their being "artefacts"

Granted, then, that such concepts are unavoidable for the solution of our problem, is the problem itself worth-while? In all sciences we find a division between "statics" and "dynamics", between attempts to create taxonomies, classifications, or nosologies, and attempts to derive causal laws and developmental sequences. The table of the elements of chemistry, the dimensional analysis of physics, the taxonomic principles of flora and fauna in biology—these are all examples of the "static" type of analysis. To deny the importance of either type of approach is an admission of prejudice, because the history of science shows over and over again the essential dependence of these two types of approach on each other, and the fact that advances in one may lead to important advances in the other. Both are vital to the development of science, and there appears to be no reason why psychology should be a solitary exception to this general rule. We may conclude, therefore, that the "static" approach implied in the study of *organization* has its valid place beside the "dynamic" approach implied in the study of *development*.

It is here that the second objection comes in. How, it is maintained, can we study organization without detailed knowledge of development? Physical diseases are classified in terms of their causes, i.e. by reference to development; without such knowledge of causes we may be gravely mistaken in our principles of nosology. Must not the same apply in psychiatry, and with reference to mental disorders? Biological classification proceeds by way of evolutionary concepts, i.e. again in terms of development; should psychology be an exception?

There are two answers to this point. The short answer is that while principles of organization derived from firmly established principles of development are, of course, infinitely preferable to principles of organization established in any other way, psychology cannot be said to have a choice in the matter because these firmly established principles of development are completely missing. In the absence of any knowledge of the causes of mental disorders, we must needs fall back on some other method of classification; in the absence of any knowledge of the determinants of personality development in general, we clearly cannot base our system of organization on these non-existing principles. In other words, although no one would deny the advantages of being able to base one's principles of organization on principles of development, some other method is called for at the moment in view of the conspicuous lack of the latter. (There is, of course, no lack of theories; quite on the contrary, there is such a multiplicity of theories regarding development, none of them based on firm scientific ground of proof and verification, that any choice between them becomes a matter of temperament rather than of reason.)

A somewhat longer answer may be made in terms of historical considerations. If we take botany as our example, we find that taxonomy began with the Greeks; Theophrastus may be considered to have been the first to classify plants and to describe them accurately (300 B.C.). Like more recent attempts in psychology, "the writings of the Greeks embodied too few observations on what plants are and too much philosophizing as to how they might be expected to be" but, nevertheless, their attempts at classification were an indispensable preliminary to later work which superseded theirs. There is no need to trace the development of systems of taxonomy through the work of Bauhin, Ray, Linnæus, Jussieu, Candolle, Endlicher, and others who preceded the publication of Darwin's *Origin of Species* in 1859; the important point to note is that the principle of evolution could not have been established, or even conceived, without these previous attempts at taxonomy, and that its establishment gave a new foundation to taxonomy but did not change its general outline as much as might have been anticipated. "After the first wave of excitement was over, systematists quite generally accepted the doctrine and began to revise their systems to fit the new principle of phylogenetic relationships. Fortunately, much that had already been done was usable, for all but the morphological systems had been pretty much eliminated from botanical taxonomy, and *morphology has proved the best single criterion of phylogeny*" (Swingle, D. B., *A Textbook of Systematic Botany*, 1946).

Thus, in botany, and in zoology as well, it has proved possible to work out natural groupings on the basis of morphology, i.e. on the basis of correlational clusters of surface characteristics, which adumbrated rather closely the "true" relationships as established on the basis of developmental (phylogenetic) principles. Morphology in botany corresponds to the study of behavioural acts in psychology, and the rather non-rigorous methods used by the earlier workers to establish "natural groupings" are based on precisely the same principle as is factor analysis. It is to be hoped that in due course principles of development will be found in psychology which correspond to that of evolution in biology; it seems reasonable to expect that here also such new discoveries may lead to an improvement in, but not a complete change of, the principles of organization already developed.

The third objection, which is often raised against factorial methods, refers to the subjectivity of choice between one system of factor axes and another, and to the apparent and often acrimonious disputes between factor analysts. Where practitioners of the same methodology arrive at contradictory findings, it is often said there must be some vital flaw in the method used. Let us consider these points in some detail. There is of course a certain subjectivity implied in all dimensional work; this is true in physics as much as in psychology. As the physicist Bridgman points out, "there is nothing absolute about dimensions . . . they may be anything consistent with a set of definitions which agree with the experimental facts". To object to such subjectivity is to misunderstand altogether the nature of science and its methodology. Where there are alternative solutions to the problem posed by a set of experimental facts, these solutions are mathematically convertible into one another, or else give rise to different deductions which can be experimentally checked. Thurstone's disproof of Spearman's original contention regarding the sufficiency of "g" and "s" as the only factors to account for the intercorrelations between cognitive tests may be quoted here as an example of such experimental check.

What, then, about the alleged disagreements? These occur in all sciences, and are often much more fundamental than those which have arisen in the brief history of factor analysis. The fundamental opposition in mathematics between Kronecker and Weierstrass; the continuing difficulties implied in reconciling the theories of light advanced by Newton and Huyghens in physics; the antagonism between Engler and Prantl on the one hand and Bessey and Hallier on the other in botany; the differences between Fisher and Pearson in statistics; the heated disputes between Glover and Klein in psycho-analysis—should these lead us to discard mathematics, statistics, physics, botany, and psycho-analysis as unworthy of our attention? Indeed, factor analysis, at the moment, appears to have reached a point in its development where there are hardly any fundamental issues on which agreement is not fairly complete; Thurstone's brilliant development of his system to embrace oblique and second-order factors has led to a reconciliation of opposing viewpoints which leaves room only for very minor disagreements.

The history of this book itself may illustrate the influence of these developments. A collection of references was undertaken first in connection with the preparation of *Dimensions of Personality*, and then again in connection with *The Scientific Study of Personality*; but in view of what appeared to be marked contradictions between results reported by different writers, no attempt was made to work these references up into some connected whole. The development of Thurstone's system in terms of second-order factors, and an opportunity for the writer to discuss some of the resulting problems with Thurstone personally, changed the somewhat pessimistic outlook, and a reassessment was begun which resulted in the present book. The reader will be able to judge for himself to what extent the results summarized may be said to give a congruent picture; to the writer himself the amount of agreement found was a revelation.

It is the writer's hope, as it presumably is that of all the students whose work is reported here, that from these studies there should arise a system of taxonomy, or classification, or nosology, which may be regarded as firmly based on biological reality, and which will find considerable support in principles of ontogenetic development when these are established, as well as aid in its turn in the discovery of these principles. Even if these hopes should be judged ill-conceived, however, and even if the reader be unwilling to admit the writer's contention regarding the importance and value of the factorial technique, nevertheless there is here a store of facts regarding human behaviour which any theory which attempts to cover the total human personality must account for. Most psychological theories only blossom in a climate of their author's devising, and die of inanition when exposed to the sharper winds of facts gathered outside the sanctified circle; here is a set of facts on which the theoretician may try out the inclusiveness of his hypotheses. The test is a very clear and simple one: does his theory help him predict the observed cor-relations? Is his picture of personality organization inclusive enough to permit of cross-checking with the data here recorded? If the answer be no, then the theory is clearly segmental only and does not cover the whole of personality. Nor would it be adequate to claim that the facts recorded are unimportant or uninteresting. In science we cannot pick and choose; the theory of gravitation must account for all the facts subsumed under it, and even such minor deviations as the slight eccentricity of Mercury's motion, or the minute bending of light rays when passing the sun, were sufficient to dethrone what used to be the most strongly established theory in the history of science.

One word regarding the method of presentation adopted. It ap-peared useless to present to the reader a simple summary of all rele-vant research, uncritical and undigested. Instead, the writer has adopted a highly critical attitude, and has not hesitated to point out flaws in experimental design, method of analysis, or even in calcula-tion which reduce the value of a given paper. These are fairly objec-tive matters, on which agreement would be reasonably high among competent judges. It is to be feared that other judgments are less objective; while the writer has made an attempt to keep the book clear of purely personal preferences, he has no illusions regarding the success of this undertaking, and can only hope that the reader will be a charitable judge of any deviations from this ideal. It is perhaps a matter of personality, but to the writer it appears better to err in the direction of excess of critical rigour than in the opposite direction of eclectic acceptance of good and bad indiscriminately—a tendency exemplified in so many of our text-books on personality.

While only primary sources were used for the preparation of this book, acknowledgment should be made to several authors whose writings have exerted some influence on the presentation. The most important of these are probably G. W. Allport, whose book on *Personality* has been more influential perhaps than any other in the development of this branch of study; A. A. Roback, whose *Psychology of Character* is the most learned historical introduction, as well as the most lucid; P. E. Vernon, whose *Assessment of Psychological Qualities by Verbal Methods* is a masterpiece of condensation and critical evaluation; C. Spearman, whose *Abilities of Man* has a place secure in the history of psychology; and L. L. Thurstone, whose *Multiple Factor Analysis* is the foundation-stone on which all later workers may securely build. As without his brilliant unification of apparently antagonistic elements this book could not have been written, it is most fittingly dedicated to him as a small token of indebtedness.

INSTITUTE OF PSYCHIATRY,
  Maudsley Hospital.
    30*th Dec.*, 1951.

INTRODUCTION TO THE THIRD EDITION

THE SECOND EDITION of this book, coming seven years after the first, had been changed and amplified in many ways. Two new chapters were added, dealing with methods of analysis (albeit briefly and probably inadequately) and with projective techniques. Over a hundred new references were added and for the sake of simplicity the terminal bibliography was given up and instead lists of references printed at the end of each chapter. In spite of these additions, the main argument did not seem to require any change; if anything, work done in the intervening years had strengthened the foundations on which it rested.

The third edition, appearing another ten years later, has been changed primarily by adding a chapter dealing with casual theories of personality structure, and detailing some of the hypothetico-deductive chains of evidence linking these theories with experimental and observational evidence accruing over the years; an attempt was made in particular to give preference to articles and books which had appeared quite recently. The ever-increasing flow of literature in this field has made it even more necessary than before to be selective and critical in one's choice of experiments; a simple survey of the 5,000 or more articles in my files would be of very little use to the reader who rightly demands from an author that he should organise the field for him, and present him with certain guide-rails, however tenuous, to help him in traversing it. There is of course no gainsaying the fact that in making such provision the writer is departing from the ideal (if it be a proper ideal, rather than an "idol of the market place") of complete impartiality; he inevitably introduces value judgments both into his selection of what to include and what to exclude, and into his evaluation. Such value judgments, as Polanyi among others has so strongly emphasised in his writings, are in fact of the essence of science; the Psychological Abstracts are an invaluable tool for the practicing scientist, but they do not provide a proper example for writers of scientific books. The need for personal commitment in providing structure for a field of scientific endeavour is sometimes underplayed; readers who prefer a completely impersonal and non-commital account are accordingly warned that they are likely to be disappointed.

It is a particular feature of this book that a large number of figures are reproduced in the text; this is essentially a consequence of the writer's belief that diagrammatic representations are better suited to the transmitting and remembering of information than are words or numbers. There is little precise information on this point, unfortunately, and one has to go by experience; all the same, it would be surprising if this generalisation were to be disproved. The reader must of course be his own judge, and the possibility arises that different personality types prefer different information media. In any case, there are also many Tables, and a considerable body of Text, for those who do not share my preference for visual displays.

The study of personality is becoming more and more recognised as an essential complement of the experimental investigation of any particular human function, be it learning, conditioning, memory, perception, sensory thresholds, or any other of the hallowed title-headings of psychological textbooks. As the reader will discover, phenomena are not independent of the type of person who is being studied; verbal learning, to take but one example, shows reminiscence over time in introverts, forgetting in extraverts; these contrary trends cannot be reconciled by simple averaging. To resort to averaging simply sweeps the problem under the carpet; it does nothing to solve the difficulty of bloated error terms. Personality study in an integral part of experimental psychology, simply because the subject of the experiment is a person. This ineluctable truth is finally dawning on many experimentalists who had hoped to eliminate from their experiments just that feature of their field of expertise which is in fact central to it—man. It is in the interplay between experimental psychology and personality study that I see the greatest hope for the development of both into truly scientific disciplines, and it is in the hope of furthering this desirable development that this book has been written.

ACKNOWLEDGEMENTS

The author wishes to acknowledge his indebtedness to authors and publishers who permitted the reproduction of tables and figures. A detailed list of copyright holders who agreed to such reproduction follows below:

The McGraw-Hill Book Company; Harper Brothers; Paul B. Hoeber; Cornell University Press; The World Book Company; The Harvard University Press; The Macmillan Company; University of Chicago Press; Stanford University Press. *The Journal of Personality; The Journal of Mental Science; The British Journal of Social Medicine; The Journal of Genetic Psychology; Child Development; Educational and Psychological Measurement; The American Journal of Psychiatry; Psychologische Rundschau; Journal of Psychology; Personnel Journal; The Journal of Applied Psychology; The Journal of the Royal Statistical Society; The Canadian Psychiatric Journal*, and the journals of the American Psychological Association, particularly *The Journal of Experimental Psychology* and *The Journal of Abnormal and Social Psychology*.

THEORIES OF PERSONALITY ORGANIZATION

"EXPERIMENT WITHOUT theory is blind; theory without experiment is lame." There is perhaps no field in psychology where this saying of Kant's applies with greater force than in the study of the structure of personality. Observers have been struck again and again by the fact that what should be a unitary field of study is cleft in two; that instead of an harmonious co-operation between theory and experiment, we have, on the one hand, an experimental school which investigates in the minutest detail processes having only the most tangential relevance to personality or to any plausible theoretical orientation, and, on the other, theoretical schools of the "dynamic" type whose theorizing proceeds without any proper basis in ascertained fact and without any consciousness of the need for verification. Most psychologists would agree that this division of labour has been carried to such extremes that it is threatening the very conception of "personality" as a legitimate field of scientific study.

Corresponding to this division into "experimentalists" and "theoreticians", there are a number of other divisions among students of personality hardly less deep and hardly less acrimoniously debated. Yet to the onlooker it often appears that while both sides are right in their positive claims, they are wrong and one-sided in their condemnation of what other schools and other points of view have to contribute. Few would seriously argue that experiment could fruitfully be carried on without theory or theory lead to important advances without the check of experimentation. Similarly, most of the other disputes which appear so formidable in cold print seem amenable to compromise when each side's arguments are carried to their logical conclusion.

As an example, we may take the very definition of the term "personality" itself. Here we find immediately an apparently irreconcilable opposition between those who lay stress on *behavioural acts* and those who lay stress instead on *dynamic concepts*. As an example of the behavioural type of definition, we may quote Watson (1930), according to whom personality is "the sum of activities that can be

1

discovered by actual observation over a long enough period of time to give reliable information". As an example of the dynamic type of definition we may quote Prince (1924), according to whom "personality is the sum-total of all the biological innate dispositions, impulses, tendencies, appetites, and instincts of the individual, and the acquired dispositions and tendencies".

It is obvious that the concepts which enter into one kind of definition—observable behavioural acts—play no part in the other, which deals entirely with dynamic concepts—impulses, dispositions, instincts, and the like. Yet the opposition clearly cannot be as complete as it appears. We have no direct knowledge of instincts, dispositions, and impulses; they are abstract conceptions created to unify and make intelligible the observable behavioural acts from which they are abstracted. Without these behavioural acts the concepts would have no assignable meaning: all we can know about human behaviour must ultimately derive from observations of behaviour. Yet such observation of behaviour by itself is not enough. We must have concepts which denote aspects of behaviour common to a number of situations; science cannot exist without abstractions based on common properties. Both definitions therefore are one-sided; a proper definition must stress both the empirical source of our data and the theoretical nature of our unifying concepts.

For the purposes of this book, we shall adopt the following definitions: Personality is the more or less stable and enduring organization of a person's character, temperament, intellect, and physique, which determines his unique adjustment to the environment. Character denotes a person's more or less stable and enduring system of conative behaviour ("will"); Temperament, his more or less stable and enduring system of affective behaviour ("emotion"); Intellect, his more or less stable and enduring system of cognitive behaviour ("intelligence"); Physique, his more or less stable and enduring system of bodily configuration and neuro-endocrine endowment. It will be noted that this definition, which owes a great deal to Roback (1927), Allport (1937), and McKinnon (1944), stresses very much the concept of *system, structure,* or *organization*; in this it goes counter to the doctrine of *specificity of behaviour,* which held almost complete sway in American research from the early nineteen-twenties until quite recently. A few words may therefore be said regarding this issue of specificity versus generality, particularly as from one point of view all the experimental work reviewed in this book is intimately related to this problem.

Common-sense psychology unhesitatingly describes and explains behaviour in terms of traits, such as persistence, suggestibility, courage, punctuality, absent-mindedness, stage-struckness, "being one for the girls", stuck-upness, and queerness, or posits the existence of types, such as the dandy, the intellectual, the quiet, the sporty, or the sociable type. For the greater part, orthodox psychology has taken over these concepts, and has presented us with traits such as ascendance-submission, perseveration, security-insecurity, and with types such as extraversion-introversion, schizothymia-cyclothymia, or Spranger's *Lebenstypen*. This easy acceptance of these concepts has been challenged, however, by a number of critics, who hold that "there are no broad, general traits of personality, no general and consistent forms of conduct which, if they existed, would make for consistency of behaviour and stability of personality, but only independent and specific stimulus-response bonds or habits".

This theory of specificity has its roots deep in the experimental tradition, and its *à priori* improbability should not prevent us from glancing at the main sources from which it draws its strength. The first of these sources is the Thorndikian type of learning theory prevalent around the first decades of this century. Learning is conceived in terms of S-R (stimulus-response) bonds after the manner of the reflex or the conditioned reflex, and these bonds are, of course, conceived to be entirely specific. If the organization of personality is largely a matter of learning—and here the great majority of writers have favoured an anti-hereditarian view, without however basing themselves on any convincing experimental evidence—then the specificity of the learning process should be mirrored in the final product of learning, i.e. the adult personality. And while S-R theories in the field of learning have been challenged by S-S (sign-significate) theories which maintain that learning is part of a larger problem of organization, particularly perceptual organization, these non-specific theories came into the field more recently, have been somewhat less influential historically, and have not carried over into the field of personality description to the same extent as the specificity theories.[1]

A second source, not unrelated to the first, has been the vast volume of work done on the problem of "transfer of training". It used to be assumed that certain specific acts (learning verses by

[1] For a review of experimental studies of these theoretical issues, see Hilgard (1948), Hilgard and Marquis (1940), and the appropriate chapters in S. S. Stevens (1951).

heart, or doing problems in arithmetic, or writing out French irregular verbs) would in the course of time lead to improvement in
general abilities or faculties (memory, will-power, logical ability,
and so on). James and Thorndike showed in a number of investigations that this easy assumption had little empirical foundation. When
two groups of subjects were equated for their ability in a given task,
such as learning poetry by heart, for instance, and one group subjected to a period of training in memorizing material which might
even be closely similar to that on which they had been tested, while
the other group was not given any training, then the predicted
superiority of the former group over the latter on a repetition of the
original task was not observed. Learning, apparently, is relatively
specific: there is no general effect on the hypothetical faculties
which such training was supposed to improve. Any transfer effects
which might be observed were considered to be due, not to the
action of broad mental "faculties", but to the fact that the original
and the practised activities had certain elements in common. This
theory is known as the "theory of identical elements"; in Thorndike's (1903) own words, "a change in one function alters any other
only in so far as the two functions have as factors common elements.
. . . To take a concrete example, improvement in addition will alter
one's ability in multiplication because addition is absolutely identical
with a part of multiplication, and because certain other processes—
e.g. eye movements and the inhibition of all save arithmetical impulses—are in part common to the two functions." Development of
personality, no less than of linguistic or numerical skills, is therefore
seen as specific training of individual association, never as generalized
improvement of larger mental units or "faculties".[1]

A third source of the specificity theory of personality organization,
equally influential as the other two, has been the direct experimental
attack on the problem by Hartshorne and May (1928, 1929, 1930).
These writers carried out a large-scale project, described in some
detail on a later page, in which many hundreds of children were
given the opportunity to behave in a dishonest, deceitful manner
under conditions which apparently made discovery impossible, but
which in reality were completely under experimental control. Other
types of behaviour (persistent, moral, charitable, impulsive, and self-
controlled behaviour, for instance) were also investigated by means
of ingenious and largely novel techniques. The statistical treatment

---

[1] A recent review of the voluminous literature on "transfer of training" is given
by Gagné, Foster and Crowley (1948).

of the data was beyond cavil, and in view of the brilliance of the design and the technical excellence of the execution, this study has rightly been regarded as crucial in respect to the theory of specificity. When therefore Hartshorne and May found very low intercorrelations between their tests, and discovered that children who were honest, or persistent, or co-operative, or charitable in one test-situation were not always honest, or persistent, or co-operative, or charitable in another, their conclusion that these alleged qualities were "groups of specific habits rather than general traits" was very widely accepted as finally settling the issue in favour of the theory of specificity.

This powerful and imposing theoretical structure was subject to a variety of damaging criticisms, however, and none of the three sources on which it bases itself has remained unscathed. We have already mentioned that S-R theories were opposed by writers whose outlook was formed or at least influenced by Gestalt notions; Köhler, Koffka, Tolman, Adams, Zener, and others have developed theories which account for the observed facts without invoking the specific connections posited by the followers of Thorndike, and, indeed, Thorndike himself has admitted concepts into his system which are incompatible with a completely specifist point of view. There is no sign of any decision in this battle of learning theories, but it is already clear that if one's theory of personality organization must be determined by one's learning theory, then there is still freedom of choice between a "specific" and a "general" type of learning theory. It would seem to follow that a direct attack on the problem of specificity in the field of personality itself would be more promising than a somewhat lengthy wait for a decision in the field of learning theory.

Much the same must be said about the conclusion to be drawn from investigations into the problem of "transfer of training" and of "identical elements". Allport's (1937) brilliant criticism of the specifist contention is probably too well known to need repetition. By showing that the very notion of an "element" is completely ambiguous in the writings of those who support the Thorndikian view, and that the alleged "identity" of these elements is merely an *a posteriori* justification of the observed phenomena, without any value in predicting and without any possibility of verification, he has succeeded in throwing great doubt on the tenability of this whole view. When his criticisms are seen in the light of experimental work, which fails to show the theoretically predicted correspondence between improvement after practice, and the similarity between original task and practised task, we can only conclude that regardless of the eventual outcome of the argument regarding "transfer of training" and the theory of identical elements, our decision with regard to the question of specificity in the field of personality must rest on direct evidence from that field, rather than in deductions from principles of such uncertain validity.

We are thus led to a re-examination of the results of the Hartshorne-May study. While the detailed results are presented in a later chapter, we may here note certain doubts regarding the interpretation of their perfectly valid results made by these two authors. Let us examine first of all their finding that a child who behaves in a dishonest manner in one situation does not necessarily behave in a dishonest manner in another situation; their conclusion is that honesty is not a general trait but specific to the two situations. But this would assume that the two situations made equal demands on the hypothetical honesty of the child, a view for which there is no evidence at all. A child may fail a difficult item in an intelligence test and pass an easy one; because he passes one and fails on another, we do not argue that he is not behaving in a consistent manner! A child may tell what he considers a white lie, but balk at cheating; or he may cheat, but balk at stealing. To imagine that an advocate of the view that a general trait of honesty existed would necessarily deny the existence of degrees of temptation, or of degrees of immorality as between one act and another, is quite unrealistic, and there is no such implication in the "generality" theory. Related to the first point is a second, made by Hartshorne and May, and by many other writers since, namely that while some children do show the postulated trait, i.e. are always honest or persistent, and while others are consistent in never showing it, i.e. being always dishonest or lacking in persistence, the majority sometimes show the trait and sometimes not. Thus the trait is supposedly applicable only to a few cases, i.e. those who demonstrate it consistently, and not to others. By a similar argument it might be maintained that the concept of intelligence is applicable only to those who never fail an item or to those who fail every item! If we conceive of honesty as constituting a continuum, then the most honest should indeed never cheat and the least honest always; intermediate grades of honesty should be reflected in action by cheating when temptation is strong or when the immorality involved is rather slight, and by not cheating when temptation is weak or the immorality involved strong. For a given degree of temptation and immorality of the act, we would then be able to predict with as much accuracy for the intermediate child as for the extreme, just as we can predict for the child of average intelligence as easily as for the genius or the dunce whether he will succeed or fail with any given problem.

As a third argument, Hartshorne and May advance the view that the very low intercorrelations between the different tests for each one of the various personality qualities measured—honesty, persistence, self-control, and so on—make the assumption of the existence of such qualities very unlikely. Yet on the specificity theory these correlations should be zero; in actual fact they are almost in every case positive. Thus it is reported that "the twenty-three tests used in securing our total character score, for example, intercorrelate $+ \cdot 30$ on the average". Such intercorrelations are admittedly lower than those found between intelligence tests, but we must be careful not to compare an intelligence test, composed of fifty to a hundred items, with a single test of honesty, or persistence, which in truth would correspond rather to an item in a much larger test battery for the measurement of honesty, or persistence, made up of fifty or a hundred such items. We shall see, in our discussion of the detailed results of this experiment, that reliabilities and validities approaching and sometimes even exceeding values of $\cdot 85$ and $\cdot 90$ are found in Hartshorne and May's own work for such batteries of "honesty" or "persistence" tests. Such results are inconceivable on any strict specificistic hypothesis, and must therefore be held to controvert that position.

In the fourth place, we must take into account the fact that Hartshorne and May used social and ethical concepts as the qualities whose specificity or generality was to be investigated. Now, even if the chosen qualities had been shown to be entirely specific, it would not follow that because certain socio-ethical qualities lacked generality, therefore more genuinely psychological qualities would also be found to be specific; as Watson (1933) points out, the experiment may beg the question by selecting the wrong type of quality to investigate. We may find consistency in the habits of frequenters of library by observing whether they choose books from the fiction, science, history, or poetry racks; our failure to observe such consistency when we direct our attention to the colour of the binding of the books selected does not prove the specificity of the choices!

In the fifth place, the preceding argument appears to apply with particular strength when children constitute the experimental population, as they did in these studies. Socio-ethical concepts are clearly not innate; they are acquired through social learning. The young child has only had insufficient time to integrate the teaching he has received from a variety of sources into some kind of general *set*, some standard which he or she can apply to a variety of different situations; integration should hypothetically be incomplete in the young child and progress as the child advances in age. Such is indeed the fact, as demonstrated in Hartshorne and May's own data, and McKinnon's (1933) later work with adult subjects. This latter writer found considerable consistency in the honest and dishonest behaviour of his subjects, and even succeeded in predicting their reactions to the test on the basis of a five minutes' interview. We may therefore with some confidence assert that in part at least the lowness of the correlations found by Hartshorne and May was due to the youth of their subjects; if the investigations were to be repeated with older subjects, higher coefficients could confidently be expected.

It may be asked whether Hartshorne and May were not aware of some at least of these criticisms. The answer must be that they were, and that they recognized the difficulties raised for their hypothesis of specificity by the observed correlations, low as they were. Their reply was not to deny the observed correlations, but to explain them in terms of "identical elements". As we have seen, they speak of "groups of specific habits rather than general traits". But in doing so they have given up what is most significant about the theory they hold, namely the complete specificity of conduct, and have admitted at least the partial generality of behaviour. Their explanation, it is true, is in terms of specific S-R bonds, but, as we have seen above, little faith can at the moment be placed in any explanation in terms of learning theory, in view of the lack of agreement between different investigators. We are left, therefore, with a very clear admission of the existence of generality in behaviour. A child who is honest, or persistent, or co-operative in one situation does tend to be honest, or persistent, or co-operative in another situation, although prediction is very far from perfect. Our task, then, must be to enquire into the *degree* of generality manifested in human conduct, and to construct a theoretical model which will faithfully represent the facts in so far as they have been established by experimental enquiry. In doing so we will do well to bear in mind that although Hartshorne and May have failed to show that human conduct is completely specific, they have shown conclusively that it is far less general than we tend to imagine, and far more strongly determined by the specific situation in which it occurs than used to be thought at one time. There is truth in the contentions of the adherent of the theory of specificity, as well as in those of the adherent of the theory of generality; the problem ceases to be a theoretical one, and becomes instead quantitative and empirical.

In looking for a model for our description of personality organization, we find two claimants in the field, two concepts which have for a long time been used by those who have theorized about the mechanics of consistent and congruent behaviour—the concepts, namely, of "trait" and "type". The former of these has found a particularly warm champion in Stern (1921), who writes: "We have the right and the obligation to develop a concept of trait as a definitive doctrine; for in all activity of the person, there is besides a variable portion, likewise a constant purposive portion, and this latter we isolate in the concept of trait." And how are these traits to be discovered? According to Allport (1937), who has done much to popularize this concept in the Anglo-Saxon countries, "traits . . . are discovered not by deductive reasoning, not by fiat, not by naming, and are themselves never directly observed. They are discovered in the individual life—the only place where they can be discovered—only through an inference (or interpretation) made necessary by the demonstrable consistency of the separate observable acts of behaviour". And again: "Traits are not directly observable; they are inferred (as any kind of determining tendency is inferred). Without such an inference the stability and consistency of personal behaviour could not possibly be explained. Any specific action is a product of innumerable determinants, not only of traits but of momentary pressures and specialized influences. But it is the repeated occurrence of actions having the *same significance* (equivalence of response) following upon a definable range of stimuli having the same personal significance (equivalence of stimuli) that makes necessary the postulation of traits as states of Being. Traits are not at all times active, but they are persistent even when latent, and are distinguished by low thresholds of arousal."

It will be clear from these quotations that the notion of *trait* is intimately connected with the notion of *correlation*. Stability, consistency, repeated occurrence of actions—all these terms, when translated into more rigorous and operationally definable language, refer to co-variation of a number of behavioural acts. Such co-variation, as we shall see, may refer to correlations between tests, correlations between persons, or even to correlations between different occasions of measurement within the same person. A trait may be defined as a co-variant set of behavioural acts; it appears thus as an organizing principle which is deduced from the observed generality of human behaviour.

The concept of *type* has fared very badly at the hands of psychologists in the Anglo-Saxon countries; they mostly seem to share Stagner's (1948) belief that "the shift from type to trait conceptions

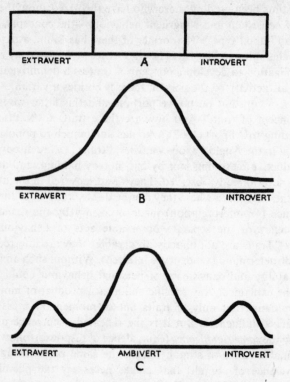

Fig. 1.—Three Conceptions of the Type Theory.

has generally paralleled the progress of psychology as science". As the same writer points out: "There are at least three different conceptions of psychological types, as they appear in the writings of various authors. These have been diagrammed in Fig. 1. Some writers still seem to think of types as pigeon-holes, mutually exclusive classifications with clear dividing lines, into which people can be segregated (Fig. 1, A). Others use the type concept as more or less equivalent to a trait, contrasting types defining the end of a continuum between which people are distributed according to the normal curve (Fig. 1, B). A third usage proposes that true types differ from traits, in that the distribution is multimodal, with people clustering at certain points which approximate a pure type (Fig. 1, C)."

Stagner's discussion leaves out of account two points which may be important in coming to a conclusion regarding the value of the "type" concept as a model for personality organization. In the first place, as will be seen from Fig. 1, B and C, these two different concepts of type are related to the hypothetical distribution of the population with respect to the alleged type, i.e. either unimodal or multimodal. But no knowledge of the form of distribution of any kind of mental quality is possible without the prior determination of a scientifically meaningful *metric*. We can plot raw scores on tests or questionnaires, but not even the veriest tyro in statistical analysis will assume that such scores give us any knowledge regarding the distribution of the hypothetical underlying trait—particularly when, as is usually the case, our measuring instrument measures more error than true variance! Until a proper metric is proposed, no argument from the form of distribution can be regarded as relevant; as no such metric has hitherto even been suggested in the field of personality measurement, it does not appear possible to argue the merits of the "type" concept on this basis.

In the second place, the distinction drawn between continuous and discontinuous distributions (Fig. 1, A, as opposed to B and C) is perfectly valid, but it does not in any way reflect the theories and hypotheses of those whose concepts have been most influential in creating modern typology, namely Jung and Kretschmer. They do reflect a widespread misconception of the views held by these writers, and by many others who have worked in the same tradition. These misconceptions have become so widely accepted that a brief outline of the correct position is imperative.

If we consider Jung's (1921) position first, we note that in his view "every individual possesses both the mechanism of introversion and that of extraversion, and it is only the relative strength of the one as compared with the other which creates the type. . . . A rhythmic alternation of these two psychic functions characterizes the normal course of life. . . . External circumstances and inner dispositions frequently favour one mechanism and impede or restrict the other. This quite naturally leads to the dominance of one of the mechanisms. If this dominance should, for whatever reason, become chronic, then we would be faced with a *type*, i.e. the habitual dominance of one mechanism. . . . Type never denotes more than the relative dominance of the one mechanism. . . . It follows that there can never be a pure type in the sense that the one mechanism is completely dominant to the exclusion of the other." These quotations could be multiplied many times, but they will suffice to show that Jung was very far from conceiving of all human beings as being either extraverted or introverted. Rather, he considered that most of them were characterized by a balance between the extravertive and the introvertive mechanisms; a relatively small number he considered to be unbalanced and characterized by the more or less marked dominance of one function or the other. Nothing is farther from his thoughts than the hypothesis of discontinuity; stress is laid again and again on the notion of complete continuity and balance. Admittedly his description is in terms of ideal types, i.e. of completely introverted or extraverted individuals, but he emphasises repeatedly that these are abstractions, in the same sense that Newton's laws of motion are idealized abstractions, not to be found in actual experiment.

What, then, is at the basis of his concept of type? We may answer this question by quoting a passage from Kretschmer (1948), who seems to hold a view of typology similar to that of Jung, and who has discussed this concept with admirable lucidity. According to him, "the concept of type is the most important fundamental concept of all biology. Nature . . . does not work with sharp contrasts and precise definitions, which derive from our own thought and our own need for comprehension. In nature, fluid transitions are the rule, but it would not be true to say that, in this infinite sea of fluid empirical forms, nothing clear and objective could be seen; quite on the contrary. In certain fields, groupings arise which we encounter again and again; when we study them objectively, we realize that we are dealing here with focal-points of frequently occurring groups of characteristics, concentrations of correlated traits. . . . What is essential in biology, as in clinical medicine, is not a single correlation but groups of correlations; only those lead to the innermost connections. It is daily experience in the field of typology, which can be deduced quite easily from the general theory, that in dealing with groups of characteristics one obtains higher correlations than with single characteristics. . . . What we call, mathematically, focal-points of statistical correlations, we call, in more descriptive prose, constitutional types. . . . A true type can be recognized by the fact that it leads to ever more connections of biological importance. Where there are many and ever-new correlations with fundamental biological factors . . . we are dealing with focal-points of the greatest importance."

A type is defined, then, as a group of correlated traits, just as a trait was defined as a group of correlated behavioural acts or action tendencies. According to this view, then, the difference between the concepts of *trait* and *type* lies not in the continuity or lack of continuity of the hypothesized variable, nor in its form of distribution, but in the greater inclusiveness of the type concept. The relationship between the two concepts is presented diagrammaticaly in Fig. 2,

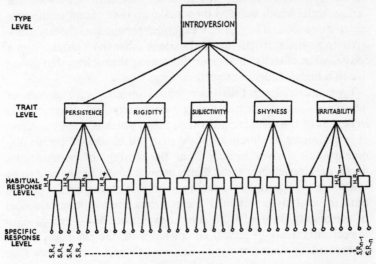

Fig. 2.—Diagrammatic Representation of Hierarchical
Organization of Personality.

taken, as is the explanatory text, from Eysenck (1947). "We are dealing with four levels of behaviour organization. At the lowest level, we have specific responses, $S.R._1$, $S.R._2$, $S.R._3$, . . . $S.R._n$. These are acts, such as responses to an experimental test or to experiences of everyday life, which are observed once, and may or may not be characteristic of the individual. At the second level, we have what are called habitual responses, $H.R._1$, $H.R._2$, $H.R._3$, . . . $H.R._n$. These are specific responses which tend to recur under similar circumstances; i.e. if the test is repeated, a similar response is given, or if the life-situation recurs, the individual reacts in a similar fashion. This is the lowest level of organization; roughly speaking, the amount of organization present here can be measured in terms of reliability coefficients, i.e. in terms of the probability that on repetition of a situation behaviour will be consistent.

"At the third level, we have organizations of habitual acts into traits T_1, T_2, T_3, ... T_n. These traits—irritability, persistence, rigidity, etc. —are theoretical constructs, based on observed intercorrelations of a number of different habitual responses; in the language of the factor analyst, they may be conceived of as group factors.

"At the fourth level, we have organization of traits into a general type; in our example, the *introvert*. This organization also is based on observed correlations, this time on correlations between the various traits which between them make up the concept of the type under discussion. Thus in our example, persistence, rigidity, subjectivity, shyness, irritability, and various other traits would form a constellation of traits intercorrelating among themselves, thus giving rise to a higher-order construct, the type."

Type and trait are thus both defined in terms of a pattern of intercorrelations; the question of continuity or distribution is irrelevant to the distinction between them, which is merely in terms of inclusiveness. It should be noted that this model of personality organization derives directly from the writings of psychologists like Jung, Kretschmer, and Allport, none of whom can be said to be orientated very positively towards psychometric techniques in general or factor analysis in particular. Nevertheless, this hypothetical model of personality deduced from clinical experience and acute psychological insight fits in almost completely with the statistical model elaborated by factor analysts. Factorial theory distinguishes four types of factor: error factors, which are present only on one occasion, but not on others; specific factors, which are peculiar to a single test or trait whenever it occurs; group or primary factors, common to certain of the tests or traits, but absent in others; and general or second-order factors, common to all the tests or traits used in an investigation. "It will be noted that the four levels of personality organization correspond closely to the four types of factor. . . . An 'habitual response' is merely a 'specific response' divested of its error component and made into a specific factor; a 'trait' is a system of 'specific responses' divested of its error and specific variance; a 'type' is a system of 'specific responses' which has lost its error, specific, and group-factor variance." (Eysenck, 1947.)

The remainder of this chapter will deal with the outstanding type theories suggested in the literature; the remainder of the book will deal with empirical attempts to verify theories regarding the existence and interrelationship of traits, and of the hypothesized types. But before dealing with these attempts to apply the methods of factor analysis to psychological theories of personality organization, it may be worth while to draw attention to a feature of the scheme illustrated in Fig. 2 which has caused a great deal of difficulty to many psychologists in their endeavours to follow the arguments presented by factor analysts. This difficulty results from the fact that we have two main alternative ways of approaching our problem, namely the ways identified respectively with the names of Spearman and Thurstone, and that superficially their two methods sometimes appear to give different or even contradictory results. This apparent contradiction has been most apparent in the field of intellectual ability, where the debate regarding the existence of Spearman's "g" has attracted a good deal of attention; it is equally noticeable, however, in the non-cognitive areas of personality research.

Let us assume that our main interest lies in the type-factor of introversion, and that we use Spearman's technique in order to test our hypothesis. We would choose one test of persistence, one test of rigidity, one test of subjectivity, one test of shyness, and one of irritability; we would then correlate these tests over our experimental population and discover the existence of a general factor ("introversion") which satisfied our statistical criteria, such as the vanishing of the tetrad differences. We might also be led to the (erroneous) conclusion that group factors, or traits, did not exist because they did not emerge in our analysis. If group factors did appear, we might be tempted to discount their existence on the plea that the tests which gave rise to them were "too similar" and consequently that these group factors were really only "overlapping specifics".

On the other hand, let us assume that our main interest was in the traits, or group factors, and that we used Thurstone's technique in order to test our hypotheses regarding these factors. We would choose a number of tests of persistence, of rigidity, of subjectivity, and so on, intercorrelate them over our experimental population and discover the existence of a number of group factors, identified in in terms of our traits, which satisfied our statistical criteria, such as simple structure. By forcing these factors to remain orthogonal and uncorrelated, we would make it impossible to discover from our analysis the existence of any higher-order concepts, such as introversion, based on these proscribed inter-trait correlations. Thus the results reached by adherents of one school might be entirely different from those of the other, and apparently quite irreconcilable.

Recent years have brought a solution of this conflict. It became clearer and clearer that Spearman-type hypotheses could no longer be maintained, either in the cognitive or in the orectic field, because the statistical criteria were hardly ever satisfied when the number of cases studied was large enough to make sampling errors relatively unimportant. Similarly, it became clear that Thurstone-type hypotheses could no longer be maintained because the demands of simple structure and those of orthogonality of factor structure were found to be irreconcilable. As is well known, Thurstone finally achieved a solution which enabled a reconciliation to be effected in terms of oblique factors and second-order factors. Such a solution still emphasizes interest in the trait-level type of hypotheses, and extracts primary factors from the matrix of intercorrelations first of all, to go on to the investigation of type-level hypotheses only as a second step, by extracting second-order factors from the intercorrelations of the primary factors. Followers of Spearman still retain a prime interest in "general factors", as they call Thurstone's second-order factors, and extract these first of all; they no longer deny, however, the existence of "group factors", as they call Thurstone's primary factors, and proceed to deal with them after the extraction of the general factor. It is debatable whether one procedure is preferable to the other (the present writer has a distinct preference for Thurstone's method), but it can hardly be doubted that the differences which have remained are of detail only, and in no way preclude complete agreement on the general outline of the model offered.

This agreement on matters so fundamental is of course welcomed by all those who felt somewhat disturbed by what seemed to be the eternal differences of opinion between different schools of factor analysis. However, in a survey of the experimental literature such as the present, we shall be dealing with many articles and books written before reconciliation was effected, and, indeed, the great majority of our sources will be seen to fall into that period. This has necessitated a somewhat detailed discussion of several researches, as well as the reinterpretation of others. On the whole, however, the writer was surprised and delighted to see what large measure of agreement there was between writers who saw themselves as protagonists of opposed doctrines, and who in their more argumentative moments would have left their opponents hardly an intellectual shred to cover their nakedness. Ultimately the facts asserted themselves, and demanded that factors at all levels of complexity of organization be taken into account. Our discussion will throughout proceed on the basis of such recognition of the hierarchical structure of personality, and will deal very fully with the experimental evidence in favour of this position.

So far we have discussed almost exclusively the *formal* properties of the hypotheses which are going to be discussed in these pages. We must now turn, at least briefly, to their *content*. In doing so, we shall not attempt to duplicate the admirable historical account of theories of personality and character given by Roback (1927), nor shall we follow Jung (1921) in tracing these concepts through the writings of poets and philosophers. We shall, instead, restrict ourselves to those theories which have influenced and in large measure determined the empirical studies described in the following chapter; without some brief acquaintance at least with the theories of Jordan, Gross, Heymans, Wiersma, Jung, Spearman, and Kretschmer no adequate understanding is possible of the factorial studies set up to test these theories.

Of mainly historical interest, but nevertheless still very instructive, is the four-type theory popularized by Galen, Kant and Wundt. According to this theory there are four temperaments classified according to reaction type, as shown below:

	Strong	Weak
Quick	Choleric	Sanguinic
Slow	Melancholic	Phlegmatic

These types were conceived of as being quite separate; as Kant says in his *Anthropologie*: "There are four and only four simple temperaments." However, we can redraw this scheme as in Fig. 3, and it will be obvious from simple inspection that we can shift our attention from the four *quadrants* which constitute the four types of these earlier authors to the two *co-ordinates* or dimensions, i.e. the quick/slow and the strong/weak continua. If we do that we immediately shift to a much more modern conception implying not four completely separate types but rather two orthogonal (independent) dimensions which are continuous and along which the position of any particular person can be plotted. Thus a person with strong emotional reactions could also be quick, in which case he would be called "choleric" by Galen; he could be slow, in which case he would be called melancholic; but he could also be intermediate in the speed of his reactions, in which case none of the four type concepts

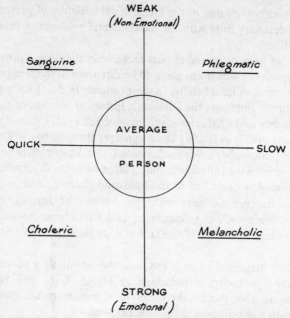

Fig. 3.—The Galen-Kant-Wundt system of personality description, illustrating both the *categorical* form (four discrete types in four quadrants) and the *continuous* or *dimensional* form (quick-slow and weak-strong dimensions).

would fit him. Similarly, a person who was quick might also have strong emotional reactions, weak emotional reactions or emotional reactions intermediate in strength. Indeed, it would appear quite likely that the majority of people would be intermediate on both continua, thus being placed somewhere near the point of intersection of our two dimensions; only relatively few would be high or low on two dimensions. We would expect therefore that not very many people would be easily characterized as cholerics, melancholics, sanguines, or phlegmatics, and, of course, this is precisely what we do in fact find.

This transfer of interest from the quadrants to the coordinates, or from a categorical to a continuous typology, or from qualitative to quantitative measurements, has been a lengthy and drawn-out affair and even nowadays remnants of the old view still linger, particularly in psychiatry, where diagnosis and classification are still categorical. Nevertheless, the evidence in favour of the modern treatment is overwhelming as we shall see throughout the remainder of this book. Granted the admissability of this transformation, it will be seen that modern experimental work gives some support to

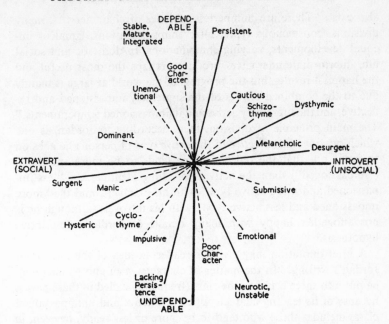

Fig. 4.—Diagram of relations between main personality dimensions according
to Vernon (1953).

such a claim as that presented above. Fig. 4, which is taken from
Vernon's review of modern personality theories (1953), shows a
picture not essentially unlike that given in Fig. 3. If we can identify
extravert and introvert respectively, with the quick and slow reactors
of Galen, and the neurotic, unstable, undependable type of person
with the strong, emotional reactor, as opposed to the stable, de-
pendable kind of person, who would be the weak, unemotional
reactor, then we might claim a certain continuity from the early
Greek theories of temperament to the most modern. Such an
identification is probably only warranted to a very limited degree;
it is easy to read into historical writings what one wishes to see, and
particularly to interpret ancient terms in line with modern connota-
tions. Nevertheless, there do appear to be certain similarities
providing a continuity between these early speculators and the more
modern work summarized in this book.

Jordan (1890) may perhaps be considered with some justification
the first of the modern theorists. He posits two antithetical types,
without of course losing sight of the fact that intermediate gradations

also exist. "There are numberless varieties of character . . . many divisions, conspicuous types, intervening gradations, equal or unequal developments, varying combinations. In domestic and social life, intermediate characters produce perhaps the most useful and the happiest results, but the progress of the world at large is mainly due to the combined efforts of the supremely impassioned and reflective, and the supremely active and unimpassioned temperaments." The main principle of division, then, according to Jordan, is one which opposes the *reflective* to the *active* type of person; he goes on to point out that the reflective type tends to be more emotional ("impassioned") than the active type. Jung identifies the "less impassioned and more active type" with his extravert, and the "more impassioned and less active type" with his introvert, although he is not altogether happy with many details of Jordan's descriptive hypothesis.[1]

A brief quotation may give the reader an idea of the flavour of Jordan's writing. "In the matter of character men and women may be put into three classes. One class (frequently called in these pages, because of its leading characteristics, the active and unimpassioned class) includes those who tend to be more or less ready, or even, in some instances, restless, busy, and quick; who tend, in their extreme varieties, wittingly or unwittingly, to imitation, affectation, and love of notice; who may also be fitful, or uncertain in mood, manner, greeting, and conduct; and who, while self-conscious, self-asserting, and self-approving, are given, so far as others are concerned, to discontent, disparagement, and candid criticism or censorious comment. . . . The men and women of this class, in addition it may be to other high qualities, have, not rarely, generous sympathies, emotions, and affections. These sympathies, emotions, affections are not usually deep, but when they are associated with high mental gifts and are helped out by strong reasoning powers, the resulting character is often altogether admirable. Sometimes the emotions and affections appear to be almost, if not entirely, absent; and if, at the same time, the mental gifts are but poor, the resulting

---

[1] The implied opposition between visceral and motor outlet has been verified by Jones (1930), who showed that even in infants disturbing stimuli produced *either* striped-muscle behaviour *or* visceral (autonomic) responses, the one tending to preclude the other. MacFarlane (1939) has drawn attention to a similar opposition between "internalizing" and "externalizing" children. Cf. also Himmelweit's (1952) analysis of Ackerson's data on p. 164, and Freeman and Pathman (1942). Jordan's observation cannot therefore be dismissed too easily as "armchair theorizing".

character is not pleasing. The men and women of quite another class (called here, from its leading characteristic, the more reflective and more impassioned class) are those who tend to repose, tranquillity, gentleness, and who, under a placid demeanour, possess deep—if sometimes sleeping—sympathies, affections, and passions. These passions are sometimes worthy, and sometimes marked by turbulence or indolence, or sensuality, or moroseness, or cruelty." Jordan devotes a whole chapter to the "Bodily Characteristics of Temperament", pointing out that, in addition to many other features, "the more impassioned women and men also have, on the whole, a greater tendency to be lean". This tendency for introversion and leptomorphic body-build to go together we shall encounter again in several experimental studies summarized later on.

Far more influential than Jordan, whose work has been almost completely neglected until Jung devoted a whole chapter of his *Psychologische Typen* to it, was the Austrian psychiatrist Otto Gross, whose two books on *Die Zerebrale Sekundärfunktion* (1902) and *Über psychopathologische Minderwertigkeiten* (1909) introduced the concepts of "primary" and "secondary" function. These concepts are basically physiological, and refer respectively to the activity of the brain cells during the production of any form of mental content, and to the hypothetical perseveration of the nervous processes involved in this production. Thus a nervous process which succeeded in arousing an idea in the mind was supposed to perseverate, although not at a conscious level, and to determine the subsequent associations formed by the mind. Gross also postulated a correlation between the intensity of any experience and the tendency for that experience to persist secondarily and to determine the subsequent course of mental associations. Most intense and energy consuming, in his view, were highly affective and emotional experiences and ideas, and these would therefore be followed by a long secondary function, during which the mental content would still be influenced and in part determined by the perseverative effects of the primary function. (There is an obvious similarity between the concept of "secondary function" and that of "refractory period".)

According to the liability of a person to develop strong emotions, Gross then distinguishes two types—the deep-narrow and the shallow-broad. In the deep-narrow type we find characteristically a primary function which is highly charged with emotion and loaded with affect, involving the expenditure of great nervous energy, and requiring a lengthened period of restitution during which the ideas involved in the primary function go on reverberating and perseverating (long secondary function). In the shallow-broad type, on the other hand, a much less intense primary function, necessitating the expenditure of comparatively little energy, is followed by a short period of restitution (short secondary function).

Certain personality characteristics follow from the type hypothesis briefly described above. In the broad-shallow person, the short secondary function enables a much greater frequency of primary functions to take place within a given time; this constant readiness for brief actions and reactions suggests a certain superficiality, a distractibility, as well as a prompt reaction to external events (Jordan's "activity"). In the deep-narrow person, the long perseverative secondary function makes the integration of different sets of what Gross calls "themas" (sets of emotions, associations, determining tendencies, complexes, and sentiments centred around one idea which is the object of a primary function) more difficult, and leads to a sejunctive (dissociated) type of personality. (This concept of dissociation will be taken up in more detail in connection with Kretschmer's account.) Dissociation leads to a damming up of the available libido, to inhibition, and on the behavioural level to absorption in thought and social shyness.

Jung readily identifies the broad-shallow type with the extravert, the deep-narrow type with the introvert; his main difference from Gross lies in the stress he lays on the intensity of the primary function, whereas Gross stresses the length of the secondary function. "Introversion is characterized by general tension, an intensive primary function and a correspondingly long secondary function." Jung summarizes Gross's contribution by saying: "Gross deserves considerable praise for being the first to put forward a simple and unified hypothesis concerning the origin of these types."

One great advance of the formulation given by Gross over that given by Jordan appears to be that it lends itself extremely well to experimental verification. The first investigators to attempt such a verification were two Dutch psychiatrists, G. Heymans and E. Wiersma, who based a rather more complex system of typology on the notion of primary and secondary function, and who attempted to use objective tests of perseveration as measuring devices. They may be said to have anticipated the two main lines along which modern attempts at the verification of "type" hypotheses have proceeded. As will be shown in Chapter II, they used the method of intercorrelation of traits to demonstrate those sets of correlated qualities we have agreed to call types, and, as shown in Chapter IX, they used the method of objective test construction according to the dictates of hypothesis for the measurement of the functions allegedly underlying the sets of observed correlations. In their work they have slightly expanded and altered the descriptive account given by Gross; as Roback points out, what characterizes the "shallow-broad" type for these writers "is *change*, lightness, lack of endurance and ready susceptibility to objective stimulation", while the concept of the "deep-narrow" type "entails the qualities of seriousness, solidity, endurance, and great susceptibility to ideational stimulation". As a much more detailed account of the work of Heymans and Wiersma will be given below in connection with their experimental studies, no more need be said here.

Spearman (1927) took up the concept of perseveration and made it into a fundamental law, his famous "Law of Inertia": *Cognitive processes always both begin and cease more gradually than their (apparent) causes.* In this law he tried to combine the theoretical contributions of writers such as Gross (1902) and Jung (1921), and the experimental studies of perseveration by Müller (1900), Wiersma (1906), Heymans and Brugman (1913), and others. As his treatment cannot be divorced from the experimental studies on which his law is based, we must postpone consideration of his contribution to a later page, where the empirical studies of "perseveration" will be reviewed in detail.

We must now turn our attention to Jung (1921), whose views have already been alluded to many times. Basing himself on the work of Jordan and Gross, Jung sees the main cause of typological differences in the extraverted or introverted tendency of the libido, i.e. in the tendency of the individual's instinctual energies to be directed mainly towards the outer world (objects), or towards his own inner mental states (subject). "When we consider a person's life-history, we see that sometimes his fate is determined more by the objects which attract his interest, while sometimes it is influenced rather by his own inner, subjective states. ... Quite generally one might characterize the introverted point of view by pointing to the constant subjection of the object and objective reality to the ego and the subjective psychological processes. ... According to the extraverted point of view, the subject is considered as inferior to the object; the importance of the subjective aspect is only secondary."

Jung gives very extensive descriptions of the personality traits which characterize the introvert and the extravert respectively; these descriptions agree to a considerable extent with those of Jordan and Gross. The extravert emerges as a person who values the outer world, both in its material and in its immaterial aspects (possessions, riches, power, prestige); he seeks for social approval and tends to conform to the mores of his society; he is sociable, makes friends easily, and trusts other people. He shows outward, physical activity, while the introvert's activity is mainly in the mental, intellectual sphere. He is changeable, likes new things, new people, new impressions. His emotions are easily aroused, but never very deeply; he is relatively insensitive, impersonal, experimental, materialistic, and tough-minded. He tends to be free from inhibitions, carefree and ascendant. This brief description makes no pretence at being anything more than the most superficial summary of some of the characteristics of the extravert; they form a bare statement of a list of those traits which in Jung's opinion correlate together to define the extravert type. Our main interest will be in the empirical verification of Jung's conception, rather than in its detailed statement.

Jung links his description of extraversion-introversion with the distinction between the main neurotic disorders as given by Janet (1894, 1903). As is well known, Jung believes that the extravert in cases of neurotic breakdown is predisposed to *hysteria*, the introvert to *psychasthenia*. "It appears to me that much the most frequent neurotic disorder of the extraverted type is hysteria. . . ." On the other hand, speaking of the introvert, he maintains that "his typical neurotic disorder is psychasthenia, a disorder which is characterized on the one hand by marked sensitivity, on the other by great exhaustion and constant tiredness." Nowadays we would probably refer to "anxiety state", or "reactive depression" rather than to the obsolescent term "psychasthenia", which also held overtones of obsessional and compulsive tendencies. On the basis of a factorial study of 700 neurotics, referred to in the next chapter, Eysenck (1944) suggested the term "dysthymic" as a more modern equivalent to cover this syndrome of correlated affective disorders. (In literal translation, this term means mood-disorders, and appears to single out the hypothetical underlying emotional dysfunction or hyperfunction posited by Gross, Jordan, and Jung.)

Although Jung never formally elaborated this part of his hypothesis, it can be seen quite clearly that implicit in his scheme is a second factor additional to, and independent of, that of extraversion-introversion. This factor we may provisionally call "abnormality" or "neuroticism"; it is identified as that particular quality which hysterics and psychasthenics have in common as compared with normal persons. The independence of introversion and neuroticism is especially stressed by Jung: "it is a mistake to believe that introversion is more or less the same as neurosis. As concepts, the two have not the slightest connection with each other". If we wish to represent Jung's complete scheme, then, we must have recourse to two orthogonal factors or axes, one of which represents the extravert-introvert continuum, the other the normal-neurotic continuum. This additional factor of abnormality is also implicit in both Jordan and Gross; it is explicitly mentioned by Heymans and Wiersma, as will be shown later. Consequently there is considerable agreement here also between the authors so far considered.

Like Jung, Kretschmer (1948) took his prototypes from the psychiatric field, but unlike Jung he turned to the psychotic forms of disorder rather than the neurotic. Following Kraepelin and Bleuler, he distinguished two main psychotic syndromes or groups of symptoms: the schizophrenic on the one hand, the manic-depressive or cyclic type of psychotic on the other. Unlike most other psychiatrists, however, Kretschmer considered these disorders not as in any way qualitatively different from normal mental states, but merely as the extremes of a continuum, as exaggerated forms of behaviour patterns characteristic of normal persons. This hypothesis may per-

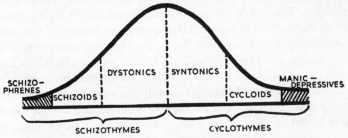

Fig. 5.—Diagrammatic Representation of Kretschmer's Theory.

haps be illustrated in terms of Fig. 5, showing the hypothetical distribution of the whole population in terms of a normal curve of distribution, ranging from one extreme (schizophrenia) to the other (manic-depressive insanity). All persons left of the mean would be *schizothymics*, meaning by that merely that their personality make-up had in common certain elements which are grotesquely exaggerated in those psychotic patients whom we label schizophrenics, whereas all those to the right of the mean would by *cyclothymics*, meaning by that that their personality make-up had in common certain elements which are grotesquely exaggerated in manic-depressive patients. Persons who are definitely abnormal but not yet psychotic Kretschmer would call schizoid or cycloid respectively, according to the side on which they fell, whereas the large number of persons in the centre of the distribution he would call syntonic if they were on the cyclothymic side, and dystonic if they were on the schizothymic side. (It is possible that Kretschmer would object to the use of a normal curve to depict the relation between schizothymes and cyclothymes, but little importance can in any case be attributed to the form of distribution when the underlying metric is unknown.)

Kretschmer's description of the cyclothyme has certain similarities to the types already considered. Like the extravert, the active-unimpassioned, and the broad-shallow type, the cyclothyme is objective, realistic, sociable, optimistic, hedonistic, trustful, co-operative, and frank; he is also subject to mood-changes without apparent cause. The schizothyme, like the introvert, the passive-impassioned, and the narrow-deep types, shows the opposite qualities to these. Kretschmer is suggesting, then, a definite dimension of personality similar to, but probably not identical with, those considered above. It would also seem to follow from his writings that another dimension is also implied, ranging from normality to psychotic disorder, and orthogonal to the cyclothymia-schizothymia dimension. Thus, as in the case of Jung, Kretschmer's theory would best be represented in terms of two orthogonal factors or axes, one measuring cyclothymia-schizothymia, the other normality-psychotic abnormality, or "psychoticism". (Indeed, if we were to follow him faithfully, we would have to add another two dimensions, namely the diathetic and the psychasthetic scales. In his view, cyclothymes vary among themselves on a scale ranging from humorous, vivacious, quick-witted, to the quiet, calm, serious—the so-called diathetic scale; whereas schizothymes vary from shy, nervous, sensitive, to dull, stupid, torpid—the so-called psychasthetic scale. As, however, there is no experimental evidence in Kretschmer's work regarding these scales, and as he makes little use of them and does not define their relation to each other in any way, we shall not deal with these scales in detail. In a similar manner, and for similar reasons, we have not discussed Jung's amplification of his theories in terms of the four functions of feeling, thinking, sensation, and intuition. Little is gained by a discussion of refinements when the major structures themselves are in doubt.)

Kretschmer's approach is more experimental than that of any of his predecessors, and a review of some of the empirical studies carried out by him and his students has been presented by Eysenck (1950). As his attempted proofs do not make use of the correlational or factorial methods, they will not here be considered in any detail; such factorial studies as have been carried out by psychologists outside his immediate circle will be mentioned in later chapters. Two points, however, call for notice. In the first place, Kretschmer attempts to anchor his typology on the firm facts of biological constitution, relating personality types and psychotic syndromes to types of body build. The schizophrenic, and accordingly the schizoid and dystonic person also, is believed to show in the majority of cases an asthenic, leptosomatic type of body-build; the manic-depressive, and accordingly the cycloid and the syntonic person also, is believed in most cases to show a pyknic, thick-set type of body-build. A review of factorial studies of body-build, and an evaluation of this claim, will be found in a later chapter; the hypothesis of this body-mind correlation had to be mentioned at this point because no account of Kretschmer's work could be complete without what he would consider his main contribution.

The second point to be considered relates to Kretschmer's psychological theories regarding the dynamic causes underlying the typology advanced by him. Kretschmer holds that the concept of *dissociation* (Spaltung) is of fundamental importance in understanding the mentality of the schizothyme, just as its opposite, integration, is important for the understanding of the cyclothyme mentality. By *Spaltung* he means "the ability to form separate and partial groupings within a single act of consciousness; from this results the ability to dissect complex material into its constituent parts". This concept of dissociation is very reminiscent of Gross's long secondary function leading to dissociation of "themas", and giving rise to the "sejunctive" type of personality. Kretschmer has added, and this is a most important contribution, a whole series of experimental tests for the measurement of this hypothetical trait of "dissociative ability". Unfortunately these tests have not yet been subjected to factorial study, and consequently their functional unity must remain unestablished; the extensive evidence reviewed by Eysenck (1950) suggests strongly, however, that the majority of these tests succeed in differentiating the cyclothyme from the schizothyme and the leptosomatic from the pyknic type of person.

The apparent similarity between the concepts of schizothymia and introversion, and between cyclothymia and extraversion, has led many psychologists and psychiatrists to identify the respective schemes of Jung and Kretschmer. In doing so, they have often overlooked certain consequences which are implicit in such an identification, but which are seldom if ever brought out in the purely semantic process employed in carrying out such identification. Fig. 6 gives a diagrammatic picture of some of these implications. It will be seen, in the first place, that in accepting such a view we are committed to

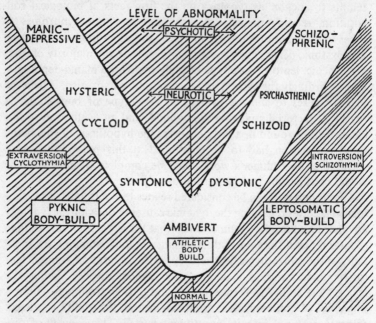

Fig. 6.—Diagrammatic Representation of Combined Jung-Kretschmer Theory.

the proposition that psychotic and neurotic disorders lie along one and the same continuum of "abnormality", a view explicitly held, among others, by Freud, who advances his hypothesis of "psychosexual regression" to account for differences in psychiatric patterns. In the normal person, there is hardly any regression to infantile patterns of psychosexual adjustment. In the conversion-hysteric, and even more so in the anxiety-hysteric, there is a considerable amount of such regression, while in the manic-depressive, and particularly in the schizophrenic, regression is almost complete. This hypothetical axis of "regression" would correspond quite well to the ordinate in our diagram. A similar assumption to Freud's is made by Kretschmer, although he does not invoke the concept of regression; for him also psychosis is merely a more advanced stage along the same road along which neurosis is an intermediate resting-place. Jung is less explicit in his views, but would probably not be found to differ essentially from the other writers mentioned.

One further assumption implied in Kretschmer's and probably also in Jung's system is indicated in Fig. 6 by cross-hatching certain parts of the diagram. If psychosis is the characteristic of persons at the *extreme* positions on the cyclothyme-schizothyme continuum, as Kretschmer appears to believe, then it should be impossible to find a psychotic whose position on the cyclóthyme-schizothyme continuum was intermediate; conversely, it should be impossible to find a normal person whose position on this continuum was very far away from the centre. The regression of abnormality on cyclothymia-schizothymia, therefore, would be curvilinear, as indicated in the non-hatched part of the diagram; no actual cases should be found in the cross-hatched part of the diagram. The same argument would apply to Jung's view at the neurotic level.

There are, however, formidable obstacles to the easy acceptance of this view. These have been reviewed in detail by Eysençk (1952), who summarizes the available evidence and comes to the conclusion that experimental findings are solidly opposed to the hypothesis of one single dimension of abnormality, and that two such dimensions,

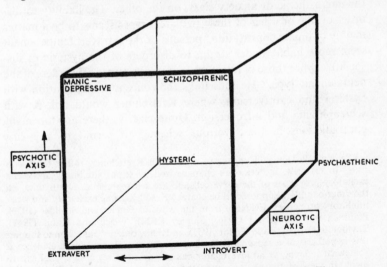

Fig. 7.—Alternative Model of Combined Jung-Kretschmer Theory.

orthogonal to each other and dealing respectively with neurotic and psychotic disorders, are required. Some of this evidence will be considered on a later page, but we may note that these experimental studies are in good agreement with orthodox psychiatric opinion, which is opposed to the "single continuum" hypothesis.

This objection may not be quite fatal to the identification of the two schemes. It might be possible to rotate the psychotic axis away from collinearity with the neurotic axis, while preserving the projections of points on both axes on the extraversion-introversion axis. Fig. 7 illustrates how this might be done. However, even this rotation does not do away with a second difficulty inherent in any attempt to bring the two schemes together. Jung speaks of an "essential relationship" between psychasthenia and schizophrenia; Kretschmer, on the other hand, links up schizophrenia with hysteria; "there is no doubt whatever that there are many 'nervous' and 'hysterical' individuals ... who are biologically nothing but schizoids".[1] A glance at Figs. 6 and 7 will show that there is a clear contradiction here between the Jungian and the Kretschmerian schemes which no amount of rotation can resolve. McDougall (1926) adds to the confusion when he writes: "There are ... two great categories of disorder under one or other of which we may attempt to place many of the cases, though without confidence in respect to many of them. ... These two categories are the dissociative or the hysteric class, on the one hand; the neurasthenic or anxiety class, on the other. The liability to disorder of one or other of these two great types seems to be a matter mainly of innate constitution; persons of the extravert temperament seem more liable, under strain, to disorders of the hysteric or dissociative type; those of introvert ... temperament to disorders of the neurasthenic type." He thus links the concept of dissociation with hysteria and extraversion, where Kretschmer would link it with schizophrenia and introversion. Quite clearly, there are too many contradictions in these various schemes to permit of any easy

---

[1] Pavlov (1941) would appear to agree with Kretschmer, rather than with Jung. In his view, hysterics are characterized by strong inhibitory and weak excitatory properties of the nerve cells; so are schizophrenics. Dysthymics, on the other hand, are supposed to be characterized by strong excitatory and weak inhibitory properties. Evidence from the work of Bender and Schilder (1930), Pfaffman and Schlosberg (1936), Shipley (1934), Welch and Kubis (1947), Taylor (1951), Spence and Taylor (1951), and many others would seem to support this hypothesis at a reasonable level of confidence. However, the evidence is somewhat indirect, as no investigator has attempted to set up a crucial experiment. In view of the obvious importance of the problem, and the objective nature of the test, such diffidence is difficult to understand.

identification; we must turn to deductions which may be made from the various typologies, and the experimental testing of these deductions. Where clinical writers disagree so profoundly, even the most convinced advocate of the clinical approach may find it difficult to arrive at a rational conclusion without the aid of the hypothetico-deductive method.

The next theory to be considered will be dealt with only briefly, partly because it is widely known, and partly because some of the details will be dealt with later when we discuss the empirical evidence. The theory in question is that of Freud and his followers, and is essentially a typological theory derived from a hypothesis about the child's stages of development. Freud defines the stages of development through the first years of the child's life in terms of the *modes of reaction* of particular parts of the body. The first or *oral* stage is concerned with the mouth as the main area of dynamic activity. This stage, which lasts for about a year, is followed during the second year by the *anal* stage which centres around the eliminative functions. This stage in turn is followed by the *phallic* stage. Freud believes that certain definite character traits and behaviour patterns are related to, and derived from, each of these stages. Accordingly he and his followers posit certain types corresponding to these stages. The precise hypotheses regarding the particular character traits associated with these stages will be stated later on; here let us merely note in addition that Freud also posits a mechanism of mental disorder, namely that of *regression*. The growing child invests a certain amount of libido at the various stages of his progress; when he runs into emotional difficulties, he regresses to the earlier stages, very much like an Army falls back on a prepared position when it encounters superior forces. The depth of regression is directly related to the severity of the disorder; the greater the amount of regression, the worse the disease. Schizophrenia is characterized as presenting an almost complete regression to the womb, neurosis presents a relatively mild degree of regression only. Freud may, therefore, be said to have held a unidimensional theory of mental disorder differentiating between neurosis and psychosis only in terms of their severity.

About the Freudian as well as about all the other theories so far mentioned, it might be said in the words of Thomas Aquinas which he applied to the geocentric hypothesis *"non est demonstratio sed suppositio quaedam"*; none of these theories are based on experimental evidence and all attempt to rationalize their point of view by anecdote and argument. Clearly only experiment can decide between so many divergent claims.

ADDENDUM

In describing the typological schemes of Jordan, Gross, Jung, and Kretschmer in the text, no mention has been made of two further schemes which have exerted a considerable influence on Continental psychologists, and which have given rise to a considerable body of experimental investigation. It seemed better not to disrupt the argument by making reference to the work of Pfahler (1936) and Jaensch (1938), which stands somewhat outside the direct succession of the writers mentioned in the text. Also, while factorial evidence is available in connection with the work of Jung and Kretschmer, none has yet appeared which would make it possible to judge that of Pfahler and Jaensch. However, no account of "typology" would be complete without brief mention at least of the contribution of the two last-named authors, and consequently the present note has been added.

Pfahler posits several dimensions orthogonal to each other as his major descriptive constants; it is the position of each person on these continua which determines his "type". These dimensions are: (1) *Apperceptive Mode*. This ranges from one extreme—"crystallized" apperception (objective, analytic, discrete, narrow, fixed range of attention, strong perseveration)—to the other ("fluid" apperception-subjective, synthetic, and global, wide, fluctuating range of attention, weak perseveration). (2) *Emotional Strength*. This dimension opposes strong emotionality to weak emotionality; in Pfahler's account it is somewhat mixed up with what should essentially be quite an independent component, namely (3) *Pleasure-Unpleasure*. He conceives of this polarity as constituting a definite tendency, one person's emotionality responding much more easily to pleasant, another person's to unpleasant stimuli. (4) *Vital Energy*. This concept resembles the Freudian libido, and may be considered to range from weak to strong.

By combining these dimensions as indicated in Table 1, Pfahler finally arrives at twelve types which he describes in great detail. It should be noted, however, that he also does not hold the concept of type criticized by so many American writers; he specially lays stress on the point that "man sich z.B. an Stelle der Rubriken A und D eine unendliche Kette ineinandergreifender Rubriken vorzustellen hat, deren Entfernung von A und Annäherung an D ein allmähliches Abnehmen des Grades der vitalen Energie bedeutet. Irgendwo in einer Rubrik diesser Kette ist der Ort für die nach ihrem Erbgut zu charakterisierende Person". He thus clearly puts forward a theory of continuity of distribution, and nowhere makes any assumption regarding the form of that distribution.

TABLE 1

Classification according to Apperceptive Mode:	Crystallized Apperception (Narrow, fixed attentive range, strong perseveration)		Fluid Apperception (Wide, fluctuating attentive range, weak perseveration)	
Strong pleasurable emotivity.	A	D	G	K
Strong unpleasurable emotivity	B	E	H	L
Weak emotivity	C	F	I	M
Classification according to energy function	Strong vital energy	Weak vital energy	Strong vital energy	Weak vital energy

Pfahler: *Typological Scheme*

Pfahler's dimensions strongly resemble concepts already discussed. Vital energy would appear to mark the opposite pole to neuroticism; the pleasure-unpleasure polarity would seem to correspond to extraversion-introversion; fixed as opposed to fluid apperceptive mode would correspond closely with Kretschmer's description of the schizothyme as compared with the cyclothyme. Of major interest in Pfahler's system are the attempts at experimental description and measurement of his various dimensions; as a detailed account of these would be out of place here, the interested reader must be referred to the original.

Much the same must be said of the system elaborated by the Jaensch brothers. Here also the experimental methods developed are of greater interest than the formal properties of their system, but it is the latter which will here be very briefly described. In doing so we can hardly do justice to all the changes and refinements which this system has undergone; only a rough outline is attempted. The main dimension around which Jaensch (1930, 1934, 1938) orders his typology is one of *integration*; human personality can be found to range from the pole of complete integration to the opposite pole of complete disintegration. However, again there is continuity—"zwischen den beiden Polen als Granzfällen stehen die manning-

fachen Übergänge des Lebens". Secondary to this principle of differentiation is one of introversion and extraversion, i.e. a tendency to
emphasize the inner or the outer world. (Jaensch himself does not
use these Jungian terms, but the similarity of the concepts is clear.)
A third dimension is indicated by the polarity of feeling and thinking.
Various combinations of these three dimensions give rise to seven
types, which are referred to by Jaensch in terms of capital letters and
numerical subscripts. Four types are "integrated": B, J_1, J_2, and J_3.
The first three types constitute a series going from the exaggeratedly
integrated (B) through the normally integrated (J_1) to the partly and
occasionally integrated (J_2); these are all orientated towards the outer
world. J_3 is fully integrated, but orientated towards the inner world.

Of the three "disintegrated" types, S_1 and S_2 show failure of integration either unredeemed (S_1) or compensated by a hyperdevelop-
ment of intelligence which takes over functions rightly performed by
feeling, as in the J types (S_2). A third type, called Svital by Jaensch,
appears to occupy a position intermediate between the J types and
the two S types on the integration scale, and is the only S type not
considered degenerate. While a given person would be considered by
Jaensch to have affinities to one or the other of these ideal types, he
would also maintain that the natural development of any person is
characterized by *phases* dominated by these type-concepts. Thus at
the age of 4 the child goes through an S phase, from 6 to 12 through
a J_1 phase, from 14 to 17 through a J_2 phase, to be followed by another
S phase at 18, and finally by a J_3 phase.

While Jaensch's concepts often resemble those of other typologists
—his concept of integration is very similar to Kretschmer's concept
of dissociation, and attention has already been drawn to his debt to
Jung's introversion-extraversion principle—and while he has originated many interesting and worth-while experimental procedures in
his attempts to prove the correctness of his concepts (his stress on
eidetic imagery as a typological test is probably best known here), his
whole system is much less well structured than any of those discussed
so far. The occasional brilliance which now and then penetrates the
confused semantic diarrhœa of his writings indicates how much
psychology might have gained from Jaensch's work had it not been
for the mental illness which was his personal tragedy.

The reader may feel somewhat confused by this array of putative
dimensions, and echo the feeling of Giese (1939) who writes: "Für
die Typologie, deren Breitenwirkung heute eine besonders grosse und
bei psychologischen Auslesen und Begutachtgaben auch praktisch sehr

bedeutsame geworden ist, kann es nur förderlich sein, wenn wir an Stelle von Typologien *eine* Typologie bekommen". This demand for *one* typology instead of a whole collection of different typologies is, in essence, a demand for a scientific methodology which will enable us to test the claims advanced for any specific system; the essential incompleteness of the typologists' achievement lay in their failure to provide a technique of verification by means of which their claims could be subjected to genuine scientific validation. It is only through the method of factor analysis that such verification can come, and it may be surmised that a combination of the intuitive and often brilliant insight of the "typologists" and the precise and rigorous work of the statistician will in due course lead us to this *one* typology. The work described in the following chapters may serve as an indication that such a hope is at least not unreasonable.

REFERENCES

Chapter I

ALLPORT, G. W. *Personality. A Psychological Interpretation.* London: Constable & Co., 1937.

BENDER, L., and SCHILDER, P. Unconditioned and conditioned reaction to pain in schizophrenia. *Amer. J. Psychiat.*, 1930, **87**, 365–384.

EYSENCK, H. J. *Dimensions of Personality.* London: Kegan Paul, 1947.
Types of personality—a factorial study of 700 neurotics. *J. ment. Sci.*, 1944, **90**, 851–861.
Cyclothymia-schizothymia as a dimension of personality. I. Historical review. *J. Pers.*, 1950, **19**, 123–153.
The Scientific Study of Personality. London: Routledge & Kegan Paul, 1952.

EYSENCK, H. J., and HIMMELWEIT, H. T. An experimental study of the reaction of neurotics to experiences of success and failure. *J. genet. Psychol.*, 1946, **35**, 59–75.

FREEMAN, G. L., and PATHMAN, J. H. The relation of overt muscular discharge to physiological recovery from experimentally induced displacement. *J. exp. Psychol.*, 1942, **30**, 161–174.

GAGNE, R. M., FOSTER, H., and CROWLEY, M. E. The measurement of transfer of training. *Psychol. Bull.*, 1948, **45**, 97–130.

GIESE, F. *Lehrbuch der Psychologie.* Tubingen: Mohr, 1939.

GROSS, O. *Die Cerebrale Sekundärfunktion.* Leipzig: 1902.
Über Psychopathologische Minderwertigkeiten. Leipzig: 1909.

HARTSHORNE, H., and MAY, M. A. *Studies in Deceit.* New York: Macmillan, 1928.
Studies in Service and Self Control. New York: Macmillan, 1929.

HARTSHORNE, H., and SHUTTLEWORTH, F. K. *Studies in the Organization of Character.* New York: Macmillan, 1930.

HEYMANS, G., and BRUGMAN, H. Intelligentz Prüfungen mit Studierenden. *Ztschr. f. angew. Psychol.*, 1913, **7**, 317–331.

HILGARD, E. R. *Theories of Learning*. New York: Appleton-Century-Crofts, 1948.

HILGARD, E. R., and MARQUIS, D. G. *Conditioning and Learning*. New York: Appleton-Century-Crofts, 1940.

HIMMELWEIT, H. T. A comparative study of the level of aspiration of normal and neurotic persons. *Brit. J. Psychol.*, 1947, **37**, 41–59.

A Factorial Study of "Children's Behaviour Problems". *Unpublished MS.*, 1952.

JAENSCH, E. R. *Neue Wege der Menschlichen Lichtbiologie*. Leipzig: Bart, 1930.

Eidetische Anlage und Kindliches Seelenleben. Leipzig: Bart, 1934.

Der Gegentypus. Leipzig: Bart, 1938.

The galvanic skin reflex. *Child Development*, 1930, **1**, 106–110.

JANET, P. *L'état Mental des Mystériques*. Rueff, 1894.

Les Obsessions et la Psychasthénie. Paris: Alcan, 1903.

JORDAN, F. *Character as seen in Body and Parentage*. London: 1890.

JUNG, C. G. *Psychologische Typen*. Zürich: Rascher & Cie., 1921.

KRETSCHMER, E., and ENKE, W. *Die Personlichkeit der Athletiker*. Leipzig: Thieme, 1936.

KRETSCHMER, E. *Körperbau und Charakter*. Berlin: Springer, 1948.

MacFARLANE, J. W. The Guidance Study. *Sociometry*, 1939, **2**, 1–23.

McDOUGALL, W. *Outline of Abnormal Psychology*. New York: Scribner, 1926.

McKINNON, D. W. *The violation of prohibitions in the solving of problems*. Ph.D. Thesis. Massachusetts: Harvard Univ. Lib., 1933.

The Structure of Personality. In: *Personality and the Behaviour Disorders*, Vol. I. (Ed. Hunt, J. McV.) New York: Ronald Press, 1944.

MILLER, D. R. Responses of psychiatric patients to threat of failure. *J. abnorm. soc. Psychol.*, 1951, **46**, 378–387.

MÜLLER, G. E., and PILZECKER, M. Die Perseverationstendenzen der Vorstellungen. *Ztsch. f. Psychol.*, 1900.

PAVLOV, I. P. *Conditioned Reflexes and Psychiatry*. London: Lawrence & Wishart, 1941.

PFAFFMAN, C., and SCHLOSBERG, H. The conditioned knee jerk in psychotic and normal individuals. *J. Psychol.*, 1936, **1**, 201–208.

PFAHLER, G. *System der Typenlehren*. Leipzig: Bart, 1936.

PRINCE, M. *The Dissociation of a Personality*. London and New York: Longmans, 1924.

ROBACK, A. A. *The Psychology of Character*. London: Kegan Paul, 1927.

SHIPLEY, W. C. Studies of Catatonia, VI. Further Investigation of the Perseverational Tendency. *Psychiat., Q.*, 1934, **8**, 736–744.

SPEARMAN, C. *The Abilities of Man*. London: Macmillan, 1927.

SPENCE, K. W., and TAYLOR, J. Anxiety and Strength of the UCS as Determiners of the amount of Eyelid Conditioning. *J. exp. Psychol.*, 1951, **42**, 182–188.

STAGNER, R. *Psychology of Personality*. New York: McGraw-Hill, 1948.

STERN, W. *Differentielle Psychologie*, 1921.

STEVENS, S. S. *Handbook of Experimental Psychology*. New York: Wiley, 1951.

TAYLOR, J. A. The relationship of anxiety to the conditioned eyelid response. *J. exp. Psychol.*, 1951, **41**, 81–90.

THORNDIKE, E. L. *Educational Psychology*. New York: Teachers' College, 1903.

VERNON, P. E. *Personality Tests and Assessments*. London: Methuen, 1953.

WATSON, G. B. Next Steps in Personality Measurement. *Charact. Pers.*, 1933, **2**, 66–73.

WATSON, J. B. *Behaviourism*. London: Kegan Paul, 1930.

WELCH, L., and KUBIS, J. Conditioned P.G.R. (psychogalvanic response) in states of pathological anxiety. *J. nerv. ment. Dis.*, 1947, **105**, 372–381.

The effect of anxiety on the conditioning rate and stability of the P.G.R. *J. Psychol.*, 1947, **23**, 83–91.

WIERSMA, H. Die Sekundärfunktion bei Psychosen. *Z. f. Psychol. u. Neurol.*, 1906, **8**, 1–24.

CHAPTER II

METHODS OF DIMENSIONAL ANALYSIS

IN THIS CHAPTER there will be given a very brief and elementary explanation of some of the methods of the analysis of inter-dependence, their logical basis and their psychological purpose. This is done because few undergraduate courses on personality include techniques such as factor analysis in their curriculum,. and even among graduates knowledge of these techniques is not always found. This is unfortunate because modern methods of component analysis are as important and as fundamental in psychological research as are techniques like analysis of variance and covariance. It is not intended, of course, to go into the actual mathematical techniques here; the aim is merely to give the reader an understanding of the logical basis of these methods.

We may begin by dividing, as Kendall (1950) has done, all the methods of multivariate analysis into *analysis of dependence* and *analysis of interdependence*. "In the latter we are interested in how a group of variates are related among themselves, no one being marked out by the conditions of the problem as of greater prior importance than the others, whereas in the analysis of dependence we are interested in how a certain specified group (the dependent variates) depend on the others. The distinction is perhaps seen at its simplest in the bivariate case: correlation between two variates is a matter of interdependence, and is a symmetrical relationship between them; the regression of one on the other is a matter of dependence and is not a symmetrical relationship—the regression of x on y is not the same as the regression of y on x." The relations between these two methods of analysis are illustrated in Fig. 8.

These two types of analysis permit us to make and test two different kinds of deductions from personality theories.

These two kinds may be termed *direct* and *relational*, respectively. *Relational deductions* are based on the hypothesized system of inter-correlations which defines the alleged type, and involve the calculation of correlations between traits, and the factor analysis of the resulting matrix of intercorrelations. The deduction is verified if the hypothesized pattern of correlations is actually found, and a factor clearly corresponding to the alleged type is actually extracted. It is with this type of evidence that we shall in the main be concerned in the following pages. Verification of deductions in these terms does not of course *prove* the correctness of the hypothesis, because such proof is never possible in terms of the scientific method; all we are entitled to say is that the results support the hypothesis.

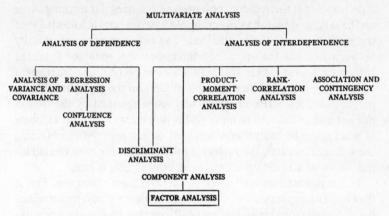

Fig. 8.—Relationships between different types of multivariate analyses according to Kendall (1950).

Direct deductions are seldom made by psychologists, although their verification is much less arduous, and much more convincing, than that given by relational deductions. In any complete investigation of personality organization, both methods should go hand in hand, and it may be helpful to give one or two illustrations of precisely what is meant by this "direct" type of verification.

Let us take as our starting-point Jung's hypothesis that the conduct of extraverts is more determined by objects and relations in the external world, while the actions of introverts are more determined by their inner subjective states. In order to test this hypothesis directly, we must do two things; we must obtain a group of extraverts and a group of introverts, and we must obtain a test of "objectivity-subjectivity" which should in terms of the hypothesis differentiate between our two groups in the predicted direction. We can find our two groups by reference to a subsidiary hypothesis of Jung's according to which he identifies hysterics with extraverts, and psychasthenics (dysthymics) with introverts. If we took groups of hysterics and dysthymics respectively, then we should be able to observe the predicted differentiation with special clarity.

As regards the test required, there is no dearth in the literature of measures which would satisfy Jung's definition; let us choose for our purpose the Level of Aspiration technique. In this test, a task (T) is presented to the subject who is made thoroughly acquainted with the requirements of this task. The score may be in terms of time taken, in terms of errors made, or in terms of number of correct solutions; it is desirable that there should be a marked but irregular learning curve on the task, and that the subject should have no certain knowledge of the score he has actually obtained. The tests are repeated, usually between five and ten times, and three measures obtained from the subject each time. These are: (1) his aspiration (A), i.e. a statement of the score he thinks he is going to obtain on the next trial; (2) his performance score (P), i.e. the actual score obtained by the subject but not communicated to him; (3) his judgment (J), i.e. his estimate of what score he has actually achieved on the trial. After obtaining these three measures, the subject is told his score (he may be told his true score or a made-up score), and the next trial is begun.

Two compound scores are calculated from these raw scores. One is the Goal Discrepancy score, in which the subject's actual performance is subtracted from his aspiration (A-P), so that he obtains a positive score if his aspiration outstrips his performance; and a Judgment Discrepancy score, in which the subject's judgment of his performance is subtracted from his actual performance (P-J), so that he obtains a negative score if he underestimates his own performance. It is known that normal people (non-neurotics, neither extravert nor introvert, i.e. neutral from the point of view of our hypothesis) tend to have slightly positive goal discrepancy scores and slightly negative judgment discrepancy scores. From these facts we are enabled to make up a very definite prediction regarding the scores of hysterics and dysthymics respectively; this hypothesis is represented diagrammatically in Fig. 9. The extravert is supposedly determined in his conduct by external objects and relations; consequently his discrepancy scores (i.e. his deviations from external reality, as represented by his actual P scores) should cluster around zero. The introvert is supposedly determined in his conduct by internal states rather than by objective fact; consequently his discrepancy scores should be considerably removed from zero. Normal persons should be intermediate between these two extremes.

There is ample experimental evidence to show that in its essentials this deduction is borne out. Eysenck, Himmelweit and Miller (cf. Table 40), using different tests and working in different countries, have testified to the correctness of the pattern illustrated in Fig. 9. Other deductions have also been verified in connection with the Level of Aspiration experiment; thus the lack of

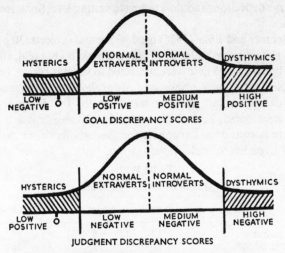

Fig. 9.—Relationship between Level of Aspiration
Test and Temperament.

objective reference of the introvert's behaviour should lead him to act in a rather rigid, non-adaptive manner of making his aspiration and judgment estimates, while the close objective reference of the extravert's behaviour should lead him to a completely non-rigid conformity of his estimates with his objective scores. This prediction also has been shown to be borne out by experimental studies on hysterics and dysthymics.

One further example of this type of verification may be given, this time from the Kretschmerian system. Let us start with the hypothesis that schizothymes have an intense primary and a long secondary function. Again what is required is the selection of two groups, corresponding to the terms "schizothyme" and "cyclothyme", and a measure of primary and secondary function. The former may be found, according to Kretschmer's subsidiary hypothesis, by paying attention to the body-build of our subjects; pyknics should be predominantly cyclothyme, leptosomatics essentially schizothyme, and athletics intermediate between the others. As a test for the measurement of primary and secondary functions we may use the psychogalvanic reflex, a phenomenon believed to be closely related to strength of emotional arousal. We would predict, on the basis of the hypotheses outlined in the first part of this chapter, that pyknics would show slight deflections on the P.G.R. and quick return to resting level (short secondary function), while leptosomatics would show large deflections and slow return to resting level (long secondary function).

Kretschmer and Enke (1936) used 90 normal subjects, 30 of whom were of pyknic body-build, 30 of leptosomatic body-build, and 30 of athletic body-build. These were subjected to various stimuli (pleasant and unpleasant odours, pricks, and pistol shots), and the amount of P.G.R. deflection and the time taken for the P.G.R. to return to normal were noted. The results are given in Table 2; it will be seen that there is considerable support for the hypothesis, or rather the chain of hypotheses, under investigation.

TABLE 2a

(*Maximum Deflection in mm.*)

	Pyknics	Athletics	Leptosomatics
Pleasant odour . .	17	18	33
Unpleasant odour . .	12	19	26
Prick	36	22	28
Pistol shot . . .	29	38	64

TABLE 2b

Return to Resting Level (in secs.)

	Pyknics	Athletics	Leptosomatics
Pleasant odour . .	61	93	101
Unpleasant odour . .	54	63	87
Prick	121	98	149
Pistol shot . . .	118	129	192

Many other examples of the direct method of investigation could have been given; a few will be found in the chapter dealing with tests of perseveration, persistence, suggestibility, and the like; others, dealing specifically with Kretschmer's views, have been summarized elsewhere (Eysenck, 1950). It is probable that a more determined effort to pursue this line of approach would have given us a considerable body of evidence on the basis of which to judge the various theories advanced; unfortunately the great theorists have seldom considered it necessary or even desirable to support their speculations with experimental proof, and experimentalists have tended to fight shy of the considerable difficulties involved in work of this sort.

How about the relational type of deduction and the analysis of interdependence? At its simplest, of course, we find this whenever a single coefficient of correlation is calculated. Freud's hypothesis of the anal retentive character predicts that children brought up in a certain way will be both obstinate and stingy. One test of such a hypothesis would be to take a group of children brought up by very strict and repressive mothers who insisted on early toilet training, in order to determine whether these children were more stingy and obstinate than children brought up under less restrictive conditions. This would be a direct deduction requiring an analysis of dependence. Another test of the hypothesis would be to take a random group of children, some of whom presumably would have been brought up strictly, while others would have been brought up much less strictly. If the hypothesis under investigation were true, we would expect to find that the children who were obstinate would also be stingy—in other words, we would expect these two personality traits to be correlated with each other. This would be a relational deduction requiring analysis of interdependence. Both deductions follow from the hypothesis and must be verified if the hypothesis is to be retained. Verification of either or both deductions does not, of course, prove the hypothesis to be correct; alternative hypotheses can be advanced which predict the same outcome.

However, single correlations are seldom used in modern analysis of interdependence, and the tendency is more and more to use whole tables or matrices of correlations between large numbers of tests. These can be analysed in much more detail than a single correlation and are consequently much more informative. The logic underlying the analysis of such tables of correlations is essentially this (Eysenck, 1957). A given cause A, which may be an ability, a personality trait, an attitude, a habit, or in brief a factor, determines a person's performance on tests $A_1, A_2, A_3 \ldots A_n$. Similarly, factor B determines his performance on $B_1, B_2, B_3 \ldots B_n$, and so on for any number of factors and tests. Because of their dependence on a common cause, $A_1, A_2, A_3 \ldots A_n$ will now be found to correlate with each other to an extent which is proportional to the degree to which they are affected by A. Similarly, for the effect of B on tests $B_1, B_2, B_3 \ldots B_n$. We now reverse the argument and say that *because* tests $A_1, A_2, A_3 \ldots A_n$ are correlated, *therefore* they have a common cause, to wit, factor A. Once this argument is accepted, it is a simple matter statistically to calculate the degree to which the subject's success on each test is determined by a given factor.

Nor is this all. Success on a given test may be determined by more than one factor, and factor analysis allows us to sort out the degree to which different factors are active in causing success in any given test. These "factors" are not usually assumed to have any direct physical reality; they are artefacts in the same way that all scientific concepts are artefacts. No one has ever seen an ability or trait, any more than anyone has seen an energy. The abstract nature of concepts such as these is inevitable and does not expose factor analysis to any criticism which it does not share with all other scientific methods.

An example may make clear the kind of thing that factor analysis does. In Table 3 are given 12 questions from a personality inventory (Eysenck, 1959).

TABLE 3

Questions	*Key*
A. Do you sometimes feel happy, sometimes depressed, without any apparent reason?	N
B. Do you have frequent ups and downs in mood, either with or without apparent cause?	N
C. Are you inclined to be moody?	N
D. Does your mind often wander while you are trying to concentrate?	N
E. Are you frequently "lost in thought" even when supposed to be taking part in a conversation?	N
F. Are you sometimes bubbling over with energy and sometimes very sluggish?	N
G. Do you prefer action to planning for action?	E
H. Are you happiest when you get involved in some project that calls for rapid action?	E
I. Do you usually take the initiative in making new friends?	E
J. Are you inclined to be quick and sure in your actions?	E
K. Would you rate yourself as a lively individual?	E
L. Would you be very unhappy if you were prevented from making numerous social contacts?	E

For various reasons, it was hypothesized that the first six questions, marked with an "N" in the key, would be measures of neuroticism, while the second set of six questions, marked with an "E", would be measures of extraversion. It was further postulated that extraversion and neuroticism were quite independent of each other, i.e. not correlated. The questions were given to a quota sample of the population consisting of 1,600 men and women and their answers correlated with each other. The outcome of this experiment is shown in Table 4.

A simple look at this table will show that the hypotheses are to some extent verified. The average intercorrelation of the first six

TABLE 4

| | Intercorrelations | | | | | | | | | | | | Factor Loadings | |
	1	2	3	4	5	6	7	8	9	10	11	12	E	N
1	—	·65	·48	·38	·29	·50	−·04	·08	−·04	·09	−·07	·01	·01	·75
2	·65	—	·60	·35	·27	·46	−·01	·02	−·10	−·11	−·10	·05	−·06	·74
3	·48	·60	—	·30	·25	·45	−·04	·02	−·06	−·15	−·15	·08	−·09	·71
4	·38	·35	·30	—	·50	·31	·03	−·08	−·04	·17	−·04	·06	·02	·58
5	·29	·27	·25	·50	—	·32	−·04	−·09	−·14	−·14	−·17	·02	−·06	·58
6	·50	·46	·45	·31	·32	—	·02	·12	·04	·02	·07	·13	·09	·63
7	−·04	−·01	−·04	·03	−·04	·02	—	·40	·12	·17	·20	·16	·48	·00
8	·08	·02	·02	−·08	−·09	·12	·40	—	·19	·38	·26	·21	·59	−·04
9	−·04	−·10	−·06	−·04	−·14	·04	·12	·19	—	·08	·44	·53	·59	−·06
10	·09	−·11	−·15	·17	−·14	·02	·17	·38	·08	—	·42	·13	·49	−·04
11	−·07	−·10	−·15	−·04	−·17	·07	·20	·26	·44	·42	—	·41	·68	−·02
12	·01	·05	·08	·06	·02	·13	·16	·21	·53	·13	·41	—	·64	·09

questions is ·41, that of the last six questions is ·27. Thus, in each set, we have a certain amount of covariance. The average of the inter-correlations between the questions of one set and those of the other, is — ·01, i.e. almost exactly zero. We thus have two independent sets of questions and we see that the members of each set share something in common. This can be shown even more clearly if we carry out a formal factor analysis. This has been done and the results are shown in the last two columns of correlations of Table 4. The columns headed "E" and "N" are the factors of extraversion and neuroticism extracted from the Table by means of the statistical method of factor analysis. The numbers in each of these two columns represent the correlations of each of our questions with these two factors. We can see from these figures that Question 11 is the best measure of extraversion while Question 10 is the worst. Similarly, Question 2 is the best measure of neuroticism and Question 5 is the worst.

These results have been plotted in Fig. 10, where two axes drawn

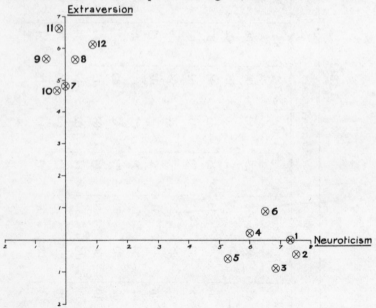

Fig. 10.—Relative position in two-dimensional space of six neuroticism and six extraversion questionnaire items.

at right angles to each other represent the factors and the degree of correlation is indicated on each axis. This geometrical method of representing factors is a very useful one because it shows at a glance the relationships obtaining between tests. The general rule of converting tables of correlations into positions on the geometrical system of co-ordinates, is rather simple. The correlation between A and test B is equal to the cosine of the angle between the lines joining the positions of each test to the origin, multiplied by the product of the distances of the tests away from the origin. The co-ordinates themselves are plotted at right angles to indicate complete independence or a correlation of zero, because the cosine of an angle of 90° is zero.

There are quite a number of restrictions on the use of factor analysis. Data must be normally distributed, tests must have linear regressions on each other, and so forth. When all these conditions are fulfilled, the final solution presents in a very economical manner a very large number of relationships. There are 66 correlations in Table 4; these are adequately represented by the 24 factor loadings of the 12 tests on the two factors. With small tables of correlations like this, the saving is perhaps not too obvious, and the relationships in the original table clear enough even without formal analysis. However, much larger tables of correlations are normally analysed, and then the saving becomes very obvious indeed. The questions here analysed were taken from a larger battery of 48 questions. When these are intercorrelated with each other, they give rise to 1,128 correlations, all of which can be adequately represented by two factors, each having 48 correlations. This is an immense saving, and it is doubtful whether any inspection of the original table, however prolonged, would easily have revealed the pattern shown by factor analysis.

Do factors necessarily have psychological meaning? It may be agreed that they constitute a useful device for reducing the complexity of the data before us, without necessarily implying any belief in the psychological meaningfulness of these data. Such a question misunderstands the nature of statistical analysis. Factor analysis should not be regarded as a kind of sausage machine into which all sorts of rubbish may be thrown in the hope of miraculously receiving back some succulent salami. Like all statistical techniques, factor analysis simply performs a routine function; it does not itself formulate hypotheses, and it does not improve the data which are fed into it. Appropriate data collected in line with a specific hypothesis, will usually give a fairly clearcut answer when treated by factor analysis; data collected at random and with no specific hypothesis in mind are likely to result in factors that cannot be interpreted and have no psychological meaning. In this factor analysis is not different from any other technique, and it should certainly not be regarded as a last resort when all other methods have failed to make sense out of a nonsensical body of data.

Factor analysis, very much like qualitative analysis in chemistry, only gives back what you put into it. In the analysis shown in Table 4 there was no factor of intelligence. This does not mean that intelligence does not exist, but merely that it was not measured by any of the tests intercorrelated. Similarly, if the chemist analysed a mixture of gold and iron, he will not find any carbon; this does not mean that carbon does not exist, but merely that it was not contained in the particular sample of metals analysed. All this is so obvious that it hardly required saying, but so many critics have stated this fact as if it were a criticism that it seemed desirable to make a brief reference to this point.

Perhaps what the critics have in mind is the obverse, to wit, that whatever you think you have put into a factor analysis, then that is what you will get out of it. This, however, as every factor analyst will have found out to his cost, is by no means true. In the experiment mentioned above, six questions were selected for the measurement of extraversion and six other questions for the measurement of neuroticism; this selection represents a hypothesis which can be right or wrong. In this particular case the hypothesis was correct—indeed if it had not been, this example would hardly have been chosen as an illustration! But this is by no means the only conceivable outcome. Among several possibilities are the following.

1. All the intercorrelations might have been zero.

2. There might have been the predicted two groups of correlations, but the mean correlation between the two groups might have been much higher than zero.

3. There might have been only one factor rather than two in the table of correlations.

4. There might have been three or more factors in the table of correlations, instead of just two.

5. There might have been two factors, but they might have been made up in a manner quite different from that predicted.

Any of these outcomes would have been empirically possible, and factor analysis certainly cannot guarantee that the desired outcome would be the one actually found. Most factor analysts will ruefully agree that analyses which clearly verify the hypotheses they are designed to test are the exception rather than the rule. The criticism stated at the beginning of the last paragraph, therefore, is seen to be without foundation. In Chapter III a number of examples are given to illustrate the various possibilities.

There are, however, certain difficulties which factor analysts cannot close their eyes to. One of these relates to the question of interpretation. We have labelled the two factors in Table 4, extraversion and neuroticism. Should they perhaps be called sociability and emotionality, or would some other names be even more appropriate? Up to a point this is a pseudo-question. We can give the term "extraversion" an operational definition in terms of the operations performed in the experiments; this would be one way of getting out of the difficulty, but not perhaps one which would receive universal approval. An alternative method would be by arguing that the tests defining extraversion and neuroticism in this experiment had been deduced from the general theory of extraversion and neuroticism, and that this theory had received support from the experiment to such an extent that the factors could be appropriately called by these names. This also is only a partial answer, and the truth probably is that factors will only be appropriately labelled when they become part of the general body of postulates and laws which is modern psychology. This point has been argued extensively elsewhere (Eysenck, 1957); it implies in essence that *the interpretation of a factor should take into account not only the particular relationships observed in this one single experiment, but instead should try and relate the factor causally to relevant parts of general and experimental psychology.*

The same argument may also be applied to the last problem we shall have space to discuss here, namely that of rotation. If we look back at Fig. 10 it will be seen that the positions of the twelve tests relative to each other are invariant—in other words they are determined by the cosines of the angles between the lines linking them to the origin, and the lengths of these lines. The position of the two factor axes which we have drawn does not affect this invariance. They could be rotated into any alternative position in the plane of the paper without affecting the position of the twelve tests themselves. There is thus a certain subjectivity attendant upon the position of these factors which has caused a good deal of trouble in factor analysis. In the present example the position is fairly obvious and corresponds with what Thurstone has called "simple structure", i.e. a position in which there are as many zero correlations as possible with each factor. (This is a very rough way of stating the criterion of simple structure but it will serve to give an indication of

Thurstone's line of reasoning.) Unfortunately, the position is not always as clear as this, and even when simple structure can be achieved, it has never been obvious to the writer why this should guarantee a position of maximum psychological meaningfulness.

One particular difficulty which often arises with simple structure is the so-called case of oblique factors. Let us assume that in the experiment which we are discussing, the extraversion tests and the neuroticism tests have been correlated to the extent of ·2 with each other. In order to preserve simple structure, we would then have to draw our axes at an angle somewhat less than 90°, that is such that the cosine of the angle would be equal to ·2 rather than zero. But this means that the factors themselves would be correlated, and indeed Thurstone has made out a good case for allowing correlated factors in factor analysis. However, the use of correlated factors implies also a further analysis of the correlations between these factors, and the extraction of what Thurstone calls *second order factors*. Many workers have used correlated factors, but have not gone on to extract second order factors, thus leaving their analysis incomplete and difficult to interpret.

So much then for factor analysis. It is probably the most widely used type of analysis of interdependence, and in spite of its many difficulties and shortcomings, it must be considered to have a secure place among the working methods of psychologists. There is, however, another method of considerable interest which has recently come to the fore and which in certain cases may be preferable to factor analysis. Reference is here to the methods of *multiple discriminant function* and of *canonical variate analysis*. These new methods can be applied whenever our population can be grouped into diagnostic categories, social classes, sex groups, occupational categories and so on. In this these methods are differentiated from factor analysis which applies to one undifferentiated conglomerate of subjects to which a battery of tests is applied, and where no prior grouping of subjects is attempted.

Discriminant function analysis may be exemplified in Fig. 11 (Pickrel, 1958). Here two tests, A and B, have been applied to two groups of subjects; the members of one are identified by crosses, and the members of the other are identified by noughts. Each subject's position in the co-ordinate system produced by the two tests indicates his score on these tests. It is clear that there is considerable overlap of scores between the two groups on either of the two tests. We can try and combine scores on the two tests in such a way that maximum discrimination is achieved. Line x in the diagram illustrates one such combination which clearly is far from optimal as it gives considerable overlap. Line y on the other hand gives an optimum separation between the two groups. "It maximizes the ratio of the variance between groups, to the variance within the groups, for the scores projected on to the discriminant."

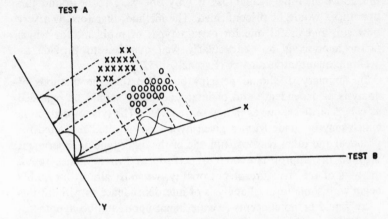

Fig. 11.—Combination of test scores of two groups of individuals on two tests in such a way as to obtain optimum discrimination between them. (Pickrel, 1958.)

Does this line have psychological meaning in the same way that a factor has? The answer here, as in the case of factors, depends entirely on the content of the tests and the nature of the groups, as well as on the hypothesis under investigation. If the two groups are random samples of neurotic and normal people, and tests A and B are hypothetical measures of neuroticism, then one might tentatively identify line y with the factor of neuroticism. One would, of course, feel happier about this if more groups and more tests had been employed in the experiment, but in principle psychological interpretation of such discriminant functions cannot be ruled out. Very little work has so far been done with analyses of this kind, which are rather technical and more complex than factor analysis, but the results have been very promising and will be reviewed in their appropriate place. The technique is particularly useful in determining the number of dimensions required to discriminate between any number of groups which have been subjected to a given number of tests. Thus, for instance, let us assume that groups of normals, neurotics and psychotics have been given a battery of tests, and that we have performed a multiple discriminant analysis on the data.

The Freudian hypothesis of a single dimension of regression would require a single significant discriminant only; if more than one were to be found, this would disconfirm the hypothesis. Conversely, the writer has postulated the two factors of neuroticism and psychotism as being independent determinants of abnormal behaviour (Eysenck, 1957). This hypothesis would require two significant latent roots in the above-mentioned analysis; if only one were to be found this hypothesis would be disconfirmed. The method, therefore, is a very powerful and useful one for certain types of problems for which factor analysis is not particularly well qualified to provide an accurate quantitative answer (Eysenck, 1957).

In summary, it should perhaps be added that the methods of analysis of dependence and of interdependence should be regarded as *complementary*, not as in any sense rivals. The type of deduction which may be made from a given hypothesis is often restricted for practical and other reasons, and one or the other type of experiment may be the appropriate one to perform. When it comes to an analysis of the structure of personality, we must almost inevitably begin with some form of analysis of interdependence as without this there would be no concepts to experiment upon, and no hypotheses to investigate. However, it is the writer's view that as soon as possible experimentalists should try and use methods of experimentation involving the analysis of dependence because it is only by accumulating information along both these lines that we can hope to overcome the limitations inherent in either approach alone.

REFERENCES

Chapter II

EYSENCK, H. J. Cyclothymia-schizothymia as a dimension of personality. I. Historical review. *J. Pers.*, 1950, **19**, 123–153.
    Dynamics of Anxiety and Hysteria. London: Routledge & Kegan Paul, 1957.
    Manual, Maudsley Personality Inventory. London: Univ. Press, 1959.
KENDALL, M. G., *et al.* Factor analysis. *J. Roy. Stat. Soc.*, 1950, 60–94.
KRETSCHMER, E., and ENKE, W. *Die Persönlichkeit der Athletiker.* Leipzig: Thieme, 1936.
PICKREL, E. W. Classification theory and techniques. *Educ. Psychol. Measmt.*, 1958, **18**, 37–46.

PERSONALITY TRAITS AND THEIR MEASUREMENT

A S WAS POINTED out in the first chapter, traits are the building stones of higher-order concepts in the analysis of personality. The number of traits which has been investigated by psychologists along experimental lines is legion, and it is not the purpose of this chapter to give any kind of exhaustive summary of the findings, such as is presented, for instance, by Cattell (1946). A few traits have been selected for discussion because they illustrate certain important points in the application of factor analysis to trait measurement, because they are of exceptional historical interest, or because they play an important part in discussions to follow in later chapters. Indeed, most of the traits discussed here are included for two or even three of these reasons.

1. *Spaltungsfähigkeit* (Ability to dissociate)

We have already encountered Kretschmer's theory regarding the existence of a personality dimension of schizothymia/cyclothymia. Kretschmer holds that the concept of dissociation (Spaltung) is of fundamental importance in understanding the mentality of the schizothyme, just as its opposite, integration, is important for the understanding of the cyclothyme mentality. His concept of dissociation goes further than that of Warren (1934): "The breaking up of a combination of any sort into its constituents." He means by it "the ability to form separate and partial groupings within a single act of consciousness; from this results the ability to dissect complex material into its constituent parts". This tendency towards dissociation characterizes the schizothyme and when exaggerated puts the *schiz* into *schizophrenia*! The absence of this ability to dissociate leads to a concrete, synthetic way of looking at the mental content which characterizes the cyclothyme and, in exaggeration, the manic-depressive.

In looking at the kind of evidence presented by Kretschmer and his followers, and in discussing the type of objective test which he uses as an operational definition of his concept, we must bear in mind a further feature of his theory which will be discussed in much greater detail in a later chapter dealing with the analysis of physique. Kretschmer holds that there is a strong correlation between schizothymia and what he calls leptosomatic or asthenic bodybuild (long, lean, thin); conversely, there is an equally strong relationship between cyclothymia and what he calls pyknic bodybuild (stocky, thickset, fat). Persons of athletic build are an intermediate group. In his experimental work he and his followers used correlations between tests of *Spaltungsfähigkeit* and bodybuild, and correlations between these tests and psychiatric diagnoses, as alternative methods of testing the underlying hypotheses of a greater degree of dissociative ability on the part of the leptosomatic/schizothyme, as opposed to the pyknic/cyclothyme.

There is a very large experimental literature in this field which has been reviewed in English by Eysenck (1950) and in German by Brengelmann (1954). Compared with the work of other typologists, Kretschmer is very much more objective and experimental in his outlook, and he has always stressed the importance of objective psychological tests as measures of personality traits. This makes it possible to test his hypothesis along rigorous hypothetico-deductive lines—something which would be impossible with most of the Continental type theories. In the next few paragraphs eight typical tests of dissociative ability as used by Kretschmer will briefly be described to give the reader an idea of the kind of approach used by this important Continental School.

(1) An experiment carried out first by Van der Horst (1916) and then repeated by Kibler (1925) may be quoted as contributing to the operational definition of this concept, and also as showing most clearly the methodological use of different groups in Kretschmer's work. In a complex reaction time experiment the disturbing effect of various agents was measured in the case of normal pyknics, normal leptosomatics, schizophrenics, and manic-depressives. It was found that the influence of distracting stimuli lengthened the reaction time of normal pyknics and of the manic-depressives much more than those of normal leptosomatics or of schizophrenics. The curves of manic-depressives and normal pyknics coincide, as do the curves of normal leptosomatics and schizophrenes. The greater ability of leptosomatics and schizophrenics to withstand disturbing stimuli is explained in terms of their dissociative ability, i.e. concentration of one aspect of the total situation to the neglect of any other.

(2) In an experiment by Enke (1928) the subject has to remember

the number of differently coloured squares on a card which he himself is pushing at his own speed into an envelope, the theory underlying the experiment being that the schizothyme with his dissociative ability would easily be able to carry in his mind the number of different categories into which to classify these various coloured squares, so that he would be quicker and more accurate in the total task. When the experiment was carried out on normal subjects, pyknics made 32·4 errors on the average, athletics 15·3, and leptosomatics 6·7. The pyknics, on the average, took 75·3 seconds, athletics 71·4, and leptosomatics 66·6. The results thus bear out the hypothesis.

(3) In an experiment by Kibler (1925), coloured groups of non-sense syllables are shown to the subject in a tachistoscope, under instruction to observe either the colour or the letters. The hypothesis underlying the experiment would require the schizothyme, with his higher abstractive ability, to be able to observe what is required and to pay no attention to other features of the stimulus, whereas the cyclothyme would remember more of what he was not asked to observe and less of what he was asked to observe. Kibler found that highest dissociative ability, i.e. complete failure to notice or remember what was not asked for, occurred in 20·7 per cent. of leptosomatics and schizophrenics, but in only 4·5 per cent. of pyknics and manic-depressives. Again, the hypothesis is borne out.

(4) Enke (1928) presented tachistoscopic exposures of long, unfamiliar words, which were being shown ten times so as to facilitate reading of the word, which could not be completed at one exposure. He found that there were two ways of getting at the meaning of the word: firstly, the abstractive, analytic, dissociative method, in which the total word was built up by reading successive letters and syllables and constructing a whole from these parts: and secondly, by getting a single impression and elaborating that in successive exposures, i.e. a synthetic method of procedure. Among his subjects he found that the ratio of dissociative over synthetic approaches was 3·3 over 5·1 for the pyknics; 5·7 over 3·0 for athletics; and 6·0 over 2·0 for leptosomatics, showing a great preponderance of the dissociative method for leptosomatics, of the synthetic, integrative method for pyknics, with athletics intermediate. In view of the obviously greater appropriateness of the dissociative method in this case, it is not surprising to find that pyknics had 75 per cent. failures, athletics 40 per cent., and leptosomatics 42 per cent. In these

experiments, differences between pyknics and the other two groups are significant at the P < ·01 level.

(5) The obverse of this advantage is shown, however, in another series of tachistoscopic experiments carried out by Van der Horst (1924) and Kibler (1925) in which pyknics and manic-depressives were shown to be able to take in more letters simultaneously than leptosomatics and schizophrenics. Enke (1928) failed to verify these results, and in any case, it is not clear to what extent such a finding would support the general theory. Kretschmer (1948) appears to think that the synthetic mode of apperception of the cyclothyme would give him the advantage in experiments of this type, but this argument is not very convincing.

(6) In a rather different modality lies the ergographic work of Enke (1930), who showed the effects of mental addition of 20 numbers on the regular rhythm of the ergograph. There were disruptions of this regular rhythm for pyknics in 27 per cent. of the cases, for athletics in 14 per cent. of the cases, and for leptosomatics in 8 per cent. of the cases. This inability to keep two different tasks separate definitely bears out the dissociative hypothesis, as does also the fact that the correct answer to the mental addition was given by 27 per cent. of the pyknics, 35 per cent. of the athletics and 50 per cent. of the leptosomatics, while the time taken over the task was 48 seconds by the pyknics, 45 seconds by the athletics, and 38 seconds by the leptosomatics. Results are significant at the P < ·01 level.

(7) Enke (1927), using the Rorschach Test, showed that when a comparison is made between the number of whole versus detailed answers, pyknics give 20 per cent. of whole answers and leptosomatics 58 per cent. This is interpreted in terms of the higher abstractive ability of the leptosomatics. The difference is significant at the P < ·01 level.

(8) An experiment by Van der Horst (1924) can, perhaps, also be classified in this connection. He shows that in the word reaction experiment, apparently senseless and remote associations are given by a larger number of leptosomatics (3·1 per cent.) than of pyknics (0·2 per cent.). Little faith, however, is felt in the interpretation that more remote associations are a sign of greater abstractive ability.

While Kretschmer uses the concept of correlation very extensively in his writings, there is no record in the literature of any correlations actually being calculated between the various tests suggested by him as measures of Spaltungsfähigkeit; he relies throughout on differences between criterion groups (schizophrenics vs.

manic-depressives; leptosomatic normals vs. pyknic normals) for his proof. This, of course, is a very dangerous type of procedure. If we compare working class and middle class people we find that the former have lower I.Q.s and fewer natural teeth at any given age; this does not mean that intelligence is the same thing as number of teeth. Schizophrenics and manic-depressives may differ in a large number of ways and we cannot postulate the existence of a single trait em-

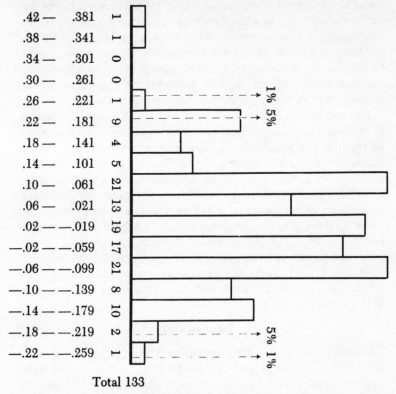

Total 133

Fig. 12.—Distribution of intercorrelations between different tests of dissociation, taken from Payne (1954).

bracing different tests just because these tests all differentiate between manic-depressives and schizophrenics. The concept of correlation is fundamental to the establishment of a trait, and the evidence adduced by Kretschmer and his followers fails to convince because it lacks this important addition.

This gap was filled by the work of Payne (1954, 1955). He tested 100 subjects, equally divided between the sexes, between the ages of

18 and 46, and very heterogenous with respect to intelligence. These subjects were administered 18 tests, 17 of which were tests of Spaltungsfähigkeit and one a test of intelligence. All the tests were scored in such a way that positive correlations would be predicted between them on the basis of Kretschmer's hypothesis.

The results of this experiment are very convincing and are shown in Fig. 12. The mean correlation was ·0096, which is precisely what would be expected if no relationship at all existed between any of the tests and any other. In addition, the distribution of observed correlations around zero is precisely what would have been expected on the basis of chance. Of all the correlations, 66 are negative and 67 positive, again demonstrating that there is in this experiment no evidence whatsoever to support Kretschmer's hypothesis which would lead us to expect positive correlations throughout.

This experiment is important in more ways than one. It appears to contradict as conclusively as can be the hypothesis it was designed to test; this is important in view of the wide currency which Kretschmer's theories have achieved on the Continent. It also demonstrates a point made in the last chapter, namely, that it is by no means certain that what the experimenter thinks he is putting into a table of correlations, he will be able to extract by means of factor analysis. The experimenter had fully expected to extract a general factor of *Spaltungsfähigkeit* running through most of the tests used, if not all; the outcome, of course, was quite different from expectations. In the face of a demonstration such as this, it is difficult to see how critics can still claim that factor analysis, as it were, begs the question.

2. PERSEVERATION

Probably the most widely investigated trait of all those dealt with in this chapter is that of perseveration. Although this term was not coined until 1894 by Neisser, observations of some of the phenomena giving rise to the term can be found as early as Newton, Herbart, Hartley, Malebranche, and even Aristotle. The fundamental property common to all the phenomena concerned has been phrased by Spearman (1927) in terms of general mental law of inertia, which reads "Cognitive processes always both begin and cease more gradually than their (apparent) causes". This law he believes to summarize the varied experimental findings, to be discussed below, while individual differences with respect to mental inertia are hypothesized to underly the various typologies considered in the first chapter, and, indeed, the similarity of the concepts of secondary function and of perseveration is very noticeable.

Let us consider some of the phenomena which have given rise to the various measures of perseveration used. First of all there is what might be called *ideational perseveration*. This phenomenon, according to Aristotle, "occurs when a name or a town or a sentence has come to be much on one's lips; after one has stopped, and without one intending it, one is prompted again to sing or to speak". Allied to this is probably what might be called *emotional perseveration*, which also is described by Aristotle in terms very closely resembling Gross and his theory of secondary function: "Those feel the vexation most who happen to have fluid in the region of the sensory organ, for once the fluid substance is set in motion it is not easily brought to rest until the object sought for returns to mind and the process resumes its direct course. Hence, when they have set something in agitation, emotions of anger and fear, owing to the reaction of these organs, do not come to rest; on the contrary they react once more on them."

Third, in order of historical appearance, is probably the phenomenon of *sensory perseveration*. This is described as follows by Newton: "If a burning coal be nimbly moved round in a circle, with gyrations continually repeated, the whole circle will appear like fire; the reason of which is, that the sensation of the coal, in the several places of that circle, *remains impressed on the sensorium*, until the coal returns again to the same place." The fourth type of perseveration, which we may call *motor perseveration*, appears first in the work of Heymans and Brugman (1913), who compared speed of writing with speed of writing in reverse, on the assumption that high perseverators would be penalized on the second of these tasks. Motor perseveration was later on found to be of two separate kinds, which are called by Cattell (1935): (*a*) creative effort perseveration, shown in tests such as the one just mentioned, and (*b*) alternation perseveration, in which two activities such as writing H and ∞ at maximum speed, first separately and then one alternating with the other, are used, the hypothesis being that perseveration will interfere in this process of alternation.

We must now look a little more closely at the various measures used for these detailed types of perseveration, their intercorrelations and their relationship with other personality variables. As regards ideational perseveration, the work of Muller and Pilzecker (1900) and Foster (1914) showed that there were considerable individual differences in the tendency of subjects to respond incorrectly in an attempt to recall nonsense syllables just learned by responding with syllables that were correct for a series previously learned. In other words, the previously learned syllables apparently perseverated and disturbed the later memory process. Probably much of the later work on such topics as retroactive inhibition might be mentioned here, but in spite of its promise, this approach has not been followed up, and interest has been centred on general laws to the exclusion of individual differences.

Emotional perseveration has not fared very much better. We have already mentioned in the first chapter the work of Kretschmer and Enke (1936), showing great individual differences in the length of time taken by the P.G.R. to return to the normal resting level after an emotional disturbance, and we have also noted the *recovery quotient* originated by Freeman. These appear to be measures of what is usually referred to as emotional perseveration, but, again, hardly any factorial work has been done on them. For the main part, investigators have followed the easier way initiated by Lankes (1915), who used a questionnaire to cover these alleged phenomena.

Most experimental work has been done on sensory and motor perseveration, with only isolated data on the other varieties available. The earliest work reported in the literature is that of Wiersma (1906) and Heymans and Brugman (1913), all of which dealt with phenomena of sensory perseveration. Wiersma used four tests: firstly the persistence of dark adaptation after a period of exposure to light; secondly, the amount of interference caused by an electric shock on electric stimulus threshold measurements; thirdly a phenomenon akin to the "glowing coal" experiment mentioned by Newton, namely the number of electric sparks per second required to be perceived by the subject as a continuous line rather than as separate sparks; and fourthly, the phenomenon of flicker fusion, which is, of course, akin to that of the sparks and of Newton's "glowing coal". Using very small groups of manics, normals, and melancholics (a group apparently also containing some paranoid patients), Wiersma found a very marked tendency on all tests for the manics to show less perseveration than the normals, and for the melancholic-paranoid group to show more perseveration. Wiersma did not actually use correlations in his work, a fault remedied by Heymans and Brugman (1913), who used six tests including two of motor perseveration. Although their results are less important than they might have been because of the small number of cases involved, the correlations reported by them are, nevertheless, reproduced below

(Table 5) because they constitute the first example in the history of psychology of an attempt by means of correlational methods to prove the unitary nature of a hypothetical mental function outside the cognitive field. On the whole, the values are positive, some of them significantly so, while only three values are negative, none of them significant.

TABLE 5

Tests	2	3	4	5	6
1. Colour mixture	·42	·23	·06	·59	·72
2. Flicker fusion	—	— ·12	— ·19	·06	·52
3. Dark adaptation interference . .		—	·66	·47	— ·07
4. Sound threshold interference . .			—	·26	·14
5. Writing forward and in reverse order .				—	·45
6. Mistakes in "tongue-twisters" . .					—

Heymans and Brugman tried to link up their experimental results with independent ratings of primary and secondary function, and found that "we can already go so far as to say that it will be possible to use the after-effects of sensations as a reliable measure of the degree of development of the secondary function". It is interesting to speculate what might happen if their pioneering work had been followed up either on the Continent or in America, both with respect to their method of defining a trait by means of correlational analysis, and also with respect to their attempt to investigate the phenomena of abnormal psychology by means of objective tests. It appears to the present writer that such a course would have led to more important advances than the hundreds of thousands of man-hours devoted to the analysis of questionnaire data and the subjective interpretation of "projective" tests, so called. However, Continental psychologists pursued the whip-poor-will of *Verstehende Psychologie*, and hardly spared one glance of icy contempt for those who would try to attack nature's secrets in such utterly non-philosophical ways, and American psychologists also paid scant attention to this work, although probably for slightly different reasons. It fell to a number of British writers to take up the search, which turned out to be very much more complex and difficult than was at first anticipated.

At Spearman's suggestion, Wynn-Jones carried out four tests of motor perseveration on 77 children, obtaining an average intercorrelation of ·492.[1] The four tests used were (1) writing an S, first repeatedly in the usual way and then as it would appear in a mirror; (2) writing digits, first in the usual way and then making the stroke backwards; (3) mirror drawing; (4) first copying prose in the usual way, and then doing so without dotting the i's or crossing the t's. Wynn Jones used the method of tetrad differences to show that the quality common to those four tests was essentially different from that common to a number of tests of intelligence. Spearman concludes that "the evidence that some group factor or factors pervading these tests of perseveration leaves nothing to be desired". Wynn Jones guarded against the possibility that the intercorrelation between the tests might be due to their all being measures of motor dexterity by showing that some tests of motor dexterity, not involving perseveration, had quite negligible correlations. He also (1929) applied his tests to normals, manics, and melancholics respectively, a total of about 50 subjects, with results which threw some doubt on Wiersma's conclusions. (It should be noted, however, that while Wiersma worked with sensory tests of perseveration, Wynn Jones worked mainly with motor tests. If, as we shall show later on, these two types of perseveration are independent of each other, there is no reason to expect duplication of results. Wynn Jones was working on the hypothesis that motor and sensory tests of perseveration were measuring the same mental function.)

The first writer to use a relatively large number of rather varied tests was Lankes (1915), who explicitly set out to test three types of phenomena: (1) the persistent after effect of a sensory experience; (2) the spontaneous recurrence of an experience; and (3) the subconscious continuance of the effects of past experiences. His tests include examples of sensory, motor, ideational, and emotional perseveration. Also included were estimates of "w", the hypothesis being that perseveration might supply a measure of the functions underlying the persistence of motives and the structure of character denoted by the term "will". The number of subjects (33 students in the preliminary, 47 in the final experiment) was not large, and the intercorrelations are very small. Indeed, most of them are insignificant, although out of 36 only 2 are negative. The correlation of

[1] The results of this research were published a good deal later, and from the point of view of date of publication, the work of Lankes (1915) would precede that of Wynn Jones. We are here following the order given by Spearman (1927), under whose direction all these researches were carried out, rather than the date order of publication.

the pool of tests with a questionnaire turned out to have the respectable size of ·41, so that we do seem to have here a certain amount of evidence for the functional unity of the phenomena considered. The correlation between perseveration as measured by these tests and "w", however, turned out to be the opposite of what was expected. The value is $-$ ·26, which on being corrected for attenuation rises to $-$ ·40. The original hypothesis, according to which a positive correlation was expected, would seem to have mixed up perseveration and persistence, and several later studies have confirmed Lankes' finding of a negative correlation between "p" and "w".

The next investigator to study perseverative phenomena was Bernstein (1924), who gave 10 tests to 130 children and who, in addition, made careful observations of the perseveration shown by the children in their ordinary school work. The correlations between the tests were even lower than in the case of Lankes, although still predominantly positive; each of the tests, however, correlated positively with Bernstein's personal estimates of perseveration based on observation, the correlation of the pool of the tests with the estimates being as high as ·51. This value, which is almost unaffected by the elimination of "g", appears high enough to indicate again a certain amount of functional unity in the tests.

Hitherto, although correlations between different tests tended to be rather low, the evidence still favoured the existence of a general factor of perseveration. The two following studies, however, are completely negative with respect to such a general factor. In the first of these two studies, Hargreaves (1927) discovered a factor of fluency of associations (f) manifested in such tests as completing pictures, completing stories, saying disconnected words, and seeing objects in ink-blots. He attempted an explanation of the intercorrelations found in terms of "p", on the hypothesis that those subjects who were more fluent were less hampered by perseveration. Not only did this prove impossible, but he also found that there was no functional unity at all in the tests of perseveration employed by him.

The evidence of Jasper (1931) is even more damaging, as his is probably the most thorough of the studies mentioned so far. He used 16 tests altogether, including a questionnaire, five measures of sensory perseveration, six measures of motor perseveration, and four measures of ideational perseveration. On 80 subjects, the average intercorrelation turned out to be $-$ ·021, a value which seems to justify his conclusion that "the results of the attempt to measure the perseverative tendency in various kinds of behaviour processes . . . fails to support the hypothesis of a broad group factor of 'perseveration' or 'mental inertia' ''. He did find some evidence for the existence of a narrow group factor of motor perseveration underlying a number of tests requiring a more or less rapid shift from one pattern of response to another pattern within the same general type of response. He also gave a warning which is an implicit criticism of much of the earlier work by pointing out that "it is necessary that measures of perseveration be developed which will be sufficiently specific for perseveration to eliminate the masking of the perseverative tendency by the many other factors which might influence the score before any absolutely definite conclusions can be arrived at as to the nature or existence of the hypothetical functional unity of 'perseveration!' ''.

One of these "many other factors" was found in a study by Rangachar (1932), comparing differences in perseveration among Jewish and English boys. Taking 38 Jewish and 35 English boys, he gave them 7 tests of motor perseveration, having reliabilities from ·76 to ·92, and factor analysed the two tables of intercorrelations obtained from the two groups of boys separately. Out of 14 saturations only one was very slightly negative, all the others were positive. He found a high correlation between speed and perseveration due to the formula he used, $H = n_1 - n_2$, i.e. perseveration (hindrance) = the original activity (n_1) — unusual activity (n_2).[1] Correlations decreased, but were still positive when corrected for speed in the n_1 activity. The Jewish boys were found to be quicker but not more perseverative than the English boys.

The next experiment to be mentioned, that of Pinard (1932), is not based on a factorial study, but supplies some evidence for the functional unity of at least some of the traditional perseveration tests by showing a certain amount of correlation between the mean of the test scores and an outside criterion. Using 194 subjects (mainly orphanage school children), he found a distinctly curvilinear correlation between "p" and ratings on various "w" qualities, as is shown in Fig.14 on p.118 in diagrammatic form. His actual results are shown below in Table 6. These figures are quite unequivocal, as are similar figures later found by him in 160 adults patients in a mental hospital.

Howard (1932) used four tests on 100 children, found a rather low average intercorrelation of ·110, and supported Pinard's finding

---

[1] The n_1 activity might be writing S, writing the alphabet, writing the figure 4, or drawing △. The n_2 activity correspondingly would be writing ƨ, writing aAbBcCdD, writing 4 reversing the direction of the stroke, and drawing ▽.

that the children showing the highest degree of neuroticism tended
to be found among those having very high "p" scores; he did not,

TABLE 6
Number of Cases Rated to have each
Trait

Total No. of Cases in Group	Degree of "p" indicated by Test	Difficult	Self-controlled	Retiring	Sociable	Persevering	Unreliable
46	very high	36	12	16	32	10	38
52	moderately high	10	37	14	33	32	15
46	moderately low	14	33	19	29	33	15
50	very low	39	8	13	32	9	37

however, find any such tendencies among children having very low
"p" scores. Two further studies of a similar kind are quoted by
Spearman (1927), namely those of Maginess and Clarke. The former
is said to have found high "p" scores to be associated with poor self-
control, lack of concentration, lack of physical energy, and low "w".
The latter concluded, on the basis of a questionnaire estimates made
by teachers, that "the results of the questionnaire are in agreement
with Pinard's finding that the difficult child is frequently an extreme
perseverator. The extreme non-perseverator, though appearing
among the difficult children more frequently than the average
perseverator, does not emerge from the questionnaire analysis with
anything approaching the clearly marked traits of the extreme
perseverator."

Stephenson (1932) claims to have found average intercorrelations
of ·40 between "p" tests, and to have shown that these intercorrelations satisfy the tetrad criterion, but no detailed figures are given·
He also claims to have found a correlation of − ·26 with "g" and
to have found a weighted and combined test of "p" to possess a very
high reliability. His clinical data in general support Wiersma's
findings regarding the manic and depressive illness; in addition,
Stephenson claims a very high correlation between "p" and in-
accessibility in præcox cases. Cattell's work, which also lends support
to the hypothesis of a curvilinear regression of "p" on "w" is
quoted below (p. 118).

In a slightly later study, Cattell (1935) pointed out that the notion
of motor perseveration involved two separate processes. One of these
he called "inertia of mental processes", which is assumed to show
itself in the alternation type of test, i.e. in a test where the subject
switches to and fro between two interfering alternate ways of per-

forming a task which are otherwise equivalent, such as, write a row of AAAA's, a row of BBBB's, and then a row of ABABAB's. "Here the X and Y activities, as we may call them, *must follow in rapid temporal succession*, producing interference by their momentum, inertia, or after effect." The other concept he calls "inertia of structural disposition", or "disposition rigidity". "This shows itself in 'creative effort' tests in which the score is measured as the difference between performing a task in some old, accustomed fashion and performing it in some new (but not intelligence-demanding) fashion, e.g. writing a row of SSSS's and then a row in which each S is written backwards (ƧƧƧƧ). Here immediate temporal contiguity of the X and Y tasks is not essential, i.e. there is no question of 'inertia of *functioning process*'." This distinction is important but invalidates a good deal of previous work which did not differentiate between these two principles. If we take as an example of disposition rigidity the factor of writing SSSS's, followed by that of writing ƧƧƧƧ's, the relative speed of the second process is used as a measure of perseveration. If, however, we use S and Ƨ as the alternating processes in the "alternation" test type of procedure, then the writing of S and Ƨ separately becomes a measure of the straightforward process. In other words, the number of Ƨ's written may appear either in the numerator or in the denominator of the fraction which defines a "*p*" score! This failure to differentiate between these two functions may thus lie at the basis of the many inconclusive results reported. Cattell himself, using six tests on 52 adults, found moderate positive correlations between them; when the tests were applied to 53 ten-year-old children and repeated on 50 fourteen-year-old children, approximate zero correlations were observed. This finding is inexplicable, as previous writers had not found correlations between children lower than correlations between adults. (Other writers who have dealt with the question of scoring of perseveration tests are Darroch (1938) and Walker, Staines, and Kenna (1943), whose writings should be consulted on this rather complex subject.)

Immediately following upon Cattell's study was the work of Shevach (1937). His main interest lay in the field of sensory perseveration, and from the point of view of adequacy of test procedure, his study is probably unequalled. His tests deal with negative after-movement, electric shock sensitivity, cube reversal, adaptation to sound, light, and various other similar measures. Using these on 17 adult subjects, he found an average intercorrelation of ·195 between five of the tests. In a second experiment on 11 students, "the results showed that the same tests might intercorrelate positively when applied to one group of Ss and might yield insignificant or even negative correlations when applied to another group of Ss". Shevach tried to reconcile results by means of the following hypothesis. "The tests yield equivocal results, not because they lack reliability or validity, but because in every group of Ss there are a few in whom perseveration, high or low, is not a general characteristic but varies from one situation to another. The degree of positive intercorrelation between tests of perseveration for a given group would thus depend upon the nature of Ss composing the group." In a third experiment 13 Ss, well known to the experimenter, were subjected to a group of tests, the intercorrelations between which this time averaged ·012· When the variability of Ss was established, it was found that the most variable individuals "are usually in a state of general tension; consider a simple sensation as a world event; cannot rid themselves of gnawing ideas; suffer from excrutiating emotions; are 'nervous' and labile; have moods fluctuating between the extreme poles of pleasantness and unpleasantness. . . . The less variable individuals were those who possessed stable personalities free from intricacy or elaboration." Results obtained from the Woodworth Personal Data Sheet, the Thurstone Personality Schedule, and the Bernreuter Personality Inventory supported these ratings, giving correlations of ·32, ·57, and ·67 respectively between variability and neuroticism. "The personality tests thus indicated that there was a definite relationship between variability and psychoneurotic tendencies." (The test-retest reliability for the variability score was ·73 over a period of three weeks.[1])

In a third experiment, Shevach, using 12 children, verified the existence of a correlation between variability and neuroticism, and also found a correlation of − ·54 between neuroticism and lack of perseveration. "This correlation suggests that when perseveration is manifested as a general characteristic, the greater this degree the less the degree of neuroticism; or that stability is not only a primary condition of the elicitation of perseveration as a general characteristic but also of its degree. The more stable the individual the greater the functional unity of perseveration and the greater the degree of perseveration." Thus, if this correlation based on only 12 cases can be taken seriously, we would have to conclude that sensory persevera-

---

[1] These results fit in well with many others summarized in a later section on "variability" as a personality trait, showing variability to be an excellent measure of neuroticism.

tion shows a negative correlation with neuroticism where motor perseveration shows a positive correlation. In another experiment still, 12 subjects with particularly low neuroticism scores were given the "p" tests, and were again found to show a correlation between variability and neuroticism. It was predicted, on the basis of the relationship between neuroticism and variability, that with these non-neurotic subjects overall variability should be lower and, consequently, correlations between the tests higher. This was not found to be so, the average intercorrelation being — ·015.

Taking together all the findings from this study, we must conclude that they are suggestive but far from conclusive. Even if we disregard the somewhat disingenuous remarks of the author regarding correlations between the same tests being positive in one group and negative in the other (a phenomenon surely not unexpected when the groups consist of so very few cases!), hardly any general conclusions seem to be warranted. The results suggest that sensory perseveration has a slight degree of functional unity, and that variability, with respect to performance on these tests, is correlated with neuroticism. This experiment could well be repeated with a much larger number of subjects. In the absence of such a repetition it is impossible to arrive at any rational conclusion. (It seems possible that considerable progress might be made in the study of perseveration if existing tests were improved in the way that Biesheuvel (1938) improved on the method of flicker threshold measurement used by previous investigators. Obtaining ratings on a questionnaire dealing with personality traits believed to be connected with perseveration, he selected two groups of perseverative and non-perseverative children respectively, who were shown to differ very significantly with respect to flicker threshold.)[1]

It will have been noticed that most recent students of perseveration have tended to restrict their work either to sensory or to motor tests. A notable exception is the work of Notcutt (1943), who used measures of sensory perseveration, motor perseveration, of both the creative effort and the alternation type, and associative perseveration. Using altogether 15 tests on 50 adults who also supplied self-ratings, he found a complete lack of intercorrelation between his tests of sensory perseveration as well as between his tests of associative

---

[1] The careful work of Weisgerber (1951), who used a similar method of approach to that of Biesheuvel, disproved the hypothesis that conscious perseveration (as measured by questionnaire) was related to the tendency of the autonomic to persist in functioning.

perseveration. With respect to motor perseveration (creative effort type) his results were inconclusive, whereas with motor tests of the alternation type he found an average intercorrelation of ·181. When scores were calculated for each of the four alleged types of perseveration respectively, their intercorrelations were all almost exactly zero. Notcutt concludes: "Of all the four types of perseveration discussed in the literature two appear to be non-existent and the remaining two appear to be unrelated to one another."

Cattell (1946) returned to the attack on this puzzling problem of the generality of perseveration by giving seven tests involving entirely the "creative effort" principle, and confined largely to motor performance of 100 women students. The intercorrelations, as usual, are rather low, averaging about ·20, but when a factor analysis was carried out a factor was extracted which, according to Cattell "is clearly the general disposition rigidity factor, highest in reverse writing of letters and numbers, but present also in a perceptual speed test—words written backwards". In a second paper published in the same year, Cattell used perseveration scores derived from this battery and correlated them with ratings of the 100 women students on 10 of his personality factors. Disposition rigidity was found to correlate negatively with dominance ($-$ ·44) and with character integration ($-$ ·34). He goes on to say: "A similar study of 200 adult men . . . shows among personality factors that E factor (dominance) correlated most highly (negatively) with disposition rigidity measures, followed by G (character integration)." Cattell goes on to show that in view of the other observed correlations it is reasonable to consider "p" as a measure of his second-order factor (neuroticism) and that the regression of "p" on this second-order factor is curvilinear as found previously by him, Pinard, and others.

In 1949 Cattell and Tiner carried out an experiment on a rather larger scale, administering 17 tests to 100 male college students. The tests included the following: "(a) a test of intelligence and of spatial ability to deal with the ability aspect of rigidity in the tests used for rigidity; (b) tests of the fluency factor, verbal and nonverbal, which we have given reasons for believing also operates in general rigidity situations and problem solving; (c) tests of the 'classical' rigidity factor (p-factor), specifically including tests to discover whether it extends beyond the field of motor performance; (d) some tests coming under other concepts of rigidity discussed above; (e) some tests considered in recent research to be measures of rigidity, but which we consider probably misleading in this rôle".

The first factor to be extracted from this battery is called "disposition rigidity" (perseveration). This identification does not appear too well justified, as a measure of high motor perseveration, which was the average of four tests of the creative effort type previously used, had a saturation of only ·30, which was not much higher than the saturation of a fluency test (·23). Flicker fusion had a much higher saturation on this factor, as had two tests, one of distraction, one of hidden objects, which appear to have little in common with the usual concepts of perseveration. Cattell's second factor is one of spatial intelligence, his fourth is one of fluency, and his third is difficult to interpret. This research is no doubt on the right lines in using a great variety of measures to test their relationship to tests of rigidity and other concepts which may be related to perseveration, but the results are not at all clear in their interpretation.

The complexity of perseveration is brought out even more clearly in the two most recent studies by Rim (1954) and Weisgerber (1954, 1955). The former used a battery of the classical perseveration tests and factor analysed the intercorrelations. His conclusion was that "The first hypothesis, that perseveration is a unitary factor of personality, has been disproved. The matrix of intercorrelations could be accounted for by at least three factors of perseveration and a factor of alternation or speed." Rim identified the perseveration factors as disposition rigidity, creative effort rigidity and ideational or cognitive rigidity. These results are rather similar to those of Cattell and Tiner (1949) and give support to their main conclusions.

Weisgerber analysed the intercorrelations between questions in a questionnaire of perseveration and also extracted four factors which were "tentatively identified as: (I) tendency to aimless perseveration, (II) perseveration of sensory and imaginal impressions, (III) perseveration of emotions and feeling states, and (IV) a tendency to worry."

In the last decade or so, the concept of perseveration has ceased to attract much attention and in its stead the trait of *rigidity* has been widely studied. The similarities between perseveration and rigidity have already been hinted at in the Cattell and Tiner study, and quite generally it must be said that the fate of rigidity has been rather similar to that of perseveration. Conceived as a unitary trait at first, it has been found to be nothing of the kind, and the more rigorous the attempts made to define it operationally, the lower have been the correlations between different tests of rigidity.

One of the early experiments is a factorial study of tests of rigidity by Oliver and Ferguson (1951), which seems to follow logically from Cattell's attempt to explain the relation of perseveration to tests of this type. Included in the battery were five tests which were thought to measure rigidity in non-motor processes. One of these was a measure containing 60 simple arithmetic problems involving the addition, subtraction, division and multiplication of simple digits. The subject's instructions were that, for the purpose of this test, a plus sign meant subtract, a minus sign meant add, a multiplication sign meant divide, and a dividing sign meant multiply. Another test required the subject to write the letter of the alphabet which came two, three, or four before the one listed, depending on the number written after the letter; for example, M-3 means that the subject must write the letter in the alphabet that is three letters before M. The other three tests were of a similar nature. Also included were the Gottschaldt Figures Test, which had been shown by Thurstone (1944) to be a good measure of his factor of flexibility of closure, and numerical problems test used by Luchins (1948), in which the subject has to solve arithmetical problems involving the measuring out of a given number of pints of water by means of three measures, none of which gives correctly the right amount required. In the first part of the experiment, a set is created leading the subject to use a particular sequence of moves; in later problems an easier solution is possible if the subject can break the set produced in the first few problems.

Ninety-eight students in all were tested and three factors extracted. Two of these factors were considered impure and of no great interest. One of them, however, could "be identified clearly as a rigidity factor, although it may be more appropriate to speak of it as a habit interference factor. This factor has significant loadings on the arithmetic test, alphabet test, opposites test, and on same-opposites. Analysis of the first three of these tests shows clearly that they all involve tasks which are performed against the interfering effects of culturally induced modes of behaviour." Both the Gottschaldt Figures Test and the Luchins Numerical Problems Test were found to have zero saturations on this factor. This paper may be said to have made an important beginning in the factorial study of rigidity.

Many more recent studies (Kleemeier and Dudek, 1950; Scheier and Ferguson, 1952; Scheier, 1954; Pitcher and Stacey, 1954; Philip, 1958; Fink, 1958), have pursued the concept of rigidity into its hypothetical component. The most striking finding perhaps is that even very similar tests constructed on identical principles failed to show significant correlations. Fink (1958), who has provided some of the most impressive evidence in this connection, has summarized the position in the following way: "The question of whether rigidity effects tend to be generalised throughout most aspects of the individual's mental behaviour remains confused. The present study . . . simply reinforces the position of Luchins (1951) and others (Applezweig, 1954; Brown, 1953) that rigidity is too complex and poorly defined at this stage to encourage any expectation of conclusive evidence concerning consistency effects."

Much the same may be said with respect to yet another variable, intolerance of ambiguity, which has played a large part in recent psychological writing and which appears to be closely related to rigidity and through it to perseveration. Already in 1949 Frenkel-Brunswik pointed out that the evidence for the generality of this hypothetical trait was only suggestive and stated that "A much wider array of both techniques and population samples would be necessary to establish this generality with an adequate degree of definiteness." The comment by Kenny and Ginsberg (1958) on this remark is very apposite: "While the array of techniques for assessing intolerance of ambiguity has increased, there unfortunately has been no corresponding demonstration that the various measures intercorrelate." Kenny and Ginsberg intercorrelated thirteen suggested measures of intolerance of ambiguity and found that "only seven of the 66 correlations among measures of intolerance of ambiguity were significant at the ·05 level, two of these having a relationship opposite to those predicted." Here again, therefore, there is no clear evidence to suggest the existence of a trait confidently postulated. This review of work on the concept of perseveration has purposely been given in some detail to show the reader the complexity of the issues involved and the slow and gradual process of clarification which takes place in the course of experimental and factorial work. Starting out with a very definite, far-reaching hypothesis, it was shown quite clearly that the alleged general factor of perseveration broke down into a number of relatively independent factors, such as sensory perseveration, motor alternation perseveration, and disposition rigidity. This apparently complete lack of inter-relationship between these different types of perseveration makes it meaningless to use the general term at all, seeing that no functional unit of behaviour corresponds to it. Thus, factorial studies have disproved the original hypothesis, and have put in its place a number of rather less far-reaching hypothesis, which in turn are subject to verification or, more likely, alteration. In spite of the apparent simplicity of the original concept, certain difficulties have appeared, both in the construction of tests and in their scoring, which have invalidated many of the other earlier researches. Nevertheless, there appear to be certain trends running through numbers of different studies which cannot easily be dismissed. Observation of a curvilinear relationship between neuroticism and disposition rigidity; the correlation between variability on tests of sensory perseveration and neuroticism; the constant tendency for tests within one of these groups to show slight but definitely positive intercorrelations—all these cannot easily be brushed aside; yet it cannot be claimed either that the position at the moment is a very satisfactory one. The same experimenter using the same technique will often get different results from different samples. From one point of view, this merely illustrates the general difficulty which always occurs in personality research, i.e. the difficulty of unambiguously defining the properties of the sample one is dealing with, or the conditions under which testing takes place. Yet, while this difficulty is universal in personality research, it appears to be particularly crucial in this field, and strictly experimental work seems called for to establish the conditions which are responsible for these changes in test results. On the whole, modern investigators are less optimistic than Spearman (1927), who considered perseveration "the greatest of all the faculties, if by this may be signified the one which has been the most lavish of promise for individual psychology". A more sober judgment would be that while none of the tests used are ready for employment in clinical or industrial practice, and while the notion of a general factor of perseveration has had to be given up, there is little doubt that some relationship does exist between certain groups of so-called perseveration tests and certain personality traits, and that in due course it may be possible to obtain reliable and valid measures of these personality traits by means of the relatively simple and objective tests described in this chapter.

3. Persistence

It will be remembered that Hartshorne and May, in their studies in service and self-control, used a number of persistence tests, although they carried out no factorial analyses of the intercorrelations. This pattern has been followed by a number of other writers, who may be mentioned before we turn to proper factorial studies. Cushing (1929) used as a measure of persistence the time an individual persisted in a line of activity, finding an average intercorrelation among different tests of ·42. Howells (1933) used as measures of persistence the subject's response to pain and fatigue, and reported positive correlations between his various tests. He also found persistence to correlate positively with intelligence (·10) and with University grades (·44).

Another prefactorial study is that of Crutcher (1934), who used six tests in all. "Certain difficult tasks were set the subjects, and the time they continued to work at these tasks was taken as evidence of their persistence." The tasks selected called upon quite diverse skills— mechanical, manipulative, numerical, artistic—well suited to the 83 children who formed the experimental group, and almost independent of I.Q. The intercorrelations between the six tests are set out in Table 7. A Spearman-type analysis of the data by means of tetrad differences showed "overlapping of specifics", but, on the whole, Crutcher concluded that "the presence of a general factor is indicated", a conclusion which appears well justified.

TABLE 7

	2	3	4	5	6	Factor Saturations
1. Card houses (manual dexterity) .	·45	·56	·48	·49	·49	·73
2. Bolt and nut puzzle (mechanical skill)	—	·71	·37	·29	·41	·71
3. Three nags puzzle (mechanical skill)		—	·47	·23	·50	·76
4. Addition sums (number facility) .			—	·33	·64	·70
5. Copying a picture (artistic ability) .				—	·30	·51
6. Cancellation of f's (routine activity)					—	·72

(Factor saturations calculated by present writer.)

These studies are typical of many others reviewed by Ryans (1939), most of which appear to support the following conclusions: (1) tests of persistence tend to intercorrelate positively to the extent of between ·2 and ·3; (2) tests of persistence tend to correlate with ratings for persistence; (3) persistence usually correlates positively, but only to a slight extent, with intelligence, and rather more highly with school grades. This last fact has led many writers to identify persistence with the "X" factor found by Alexander (1935) in his analysis of ability and school grades. Of this "X" factor, which was found to run through all the school subjects but through none of the ability measures, Alexander said: "We are suggesting that X must be interpreted as a character factor which exercises an important influence on success in all school subjects. If we were to attach a name to this factor, we should be inclined to call it persistence."

The first factorial study of the hypothetical trait underlying various persistence tests used was carried out in 1938 by Ryans, who gave 18 tests to 40 college students. These tests included examples of all the main types of persistence tests, which may be subsumed under the following groupings: (1) *Ideational Persistence*: (*a*) Persistence against time. (Time spent on word building, i.e. making up words from a set of given letters; insoluble puzzles, i.e time spent on tasks which have no solution, and so forth.) (*b*) Persistence against difficulty. (Difficult writing, i.e. continuing reading of a story where the printing is so arranged that the difficulty of reading becomes greater and greater, e.g. by printing alternate letters in capitals, by omitting punctuation, by running words together, and so on; working against distraction, i.e. reading a text interspersed with interesting pictures, etc.). (2) *Physical Persistence*: (*a*) Persistence against boredom. (Persistence in some physical task which is not in itself painful or creative of discomfort but which is devoid of any intrinsic interest.) (*b*) Persistence against pain, discomfort and fatigue. (Holding one's breath as long as possible, pulling a dynamometer at two-thirds maximum strength as long as possible, or enduring an electric shock as strong as possible, etc.)

Tests of these various types, as well as ratings on persistence, scholastic achievement, self-ratings on persistence, and intelligence measures were intercorrelated by Ryans and three factors extracted. The first factor accounted for 22 per cent. of the variance, and was interpreted by Ryans as a persistence factor. It had high saturations on persistence ratings, scholastic achievement, and a variety of persistence tests, including the amount of time spent on the solution of anagrams and on code deciphering, and on continuous mental work, as well as a test of physical endurance. Ryans' second factor accounted for 11 per cent. of the variance, and was clearly a factor of intelligence.

Ryans concluded that "there appeared . . . seeming evidence of a general factor of persistence . . . (which) seemed to be relatively independent of such other capacities as intelligence and perseveration". In later studies, Ryans (1938, 1939) showed that a battery of three tests measuring persistence as defined by his factor was relatively unrelated to intelligence, but showed correlations of between ·4 and ·5 with success in school. He also found persistence to be related to emotional stability as measured by the Bernreuter Inventory.

Thornton (1939) criticized Ryans' findings because of the small number of cases used, and reported a study of his own, using 189 college students. His tests included ten objective measures of persistence, two ratings, and various measures of intelligence, speed of work and physical ability. A multiple factor analysis of the resulting intercorrelations was carried out and the following five factors isolated: (1) withstanding discomfort to achieve a goal; (2) keeping at a task; (3) sex-strength; (4) feeling of adequacy; (5) mental fluency. Clearly the first two factors correspond to the physical and the ideational types of persistence respectively, outlined in our discussion of types of persistence tests on *a priori* grounds. The "physical" factor is characterized by such tests as maintaining dynamometer grip, endurance of shock, length of time breath is held, and length of time pain is endured. The ideational factor is measured by such tests as the time spent on word building, on difficult reading material, practice on an aiming test, and so forth. There is some overlap between these two factors, some tests being identical to both, and in view of the fact that Thornton did not use oblique and second-order factors, we cannot regard these two factors as in any sense independent or as disproving the existence of a general factor of persistence.

A more recent study by Rethlingshafer (1942) used 38 college students as subjects. The tests included six of those which Thornton found to have the highest loadings on his ideational factor, three tests of the physical factors, as well as measures of strength, perseveration, interrupted activities (Zeigarnik affect) and intelligence. Seven factors were obtained by her, namely (1) the habit of keeping on at a task once it is started; (2) a perseveration or physiological inertia factor; (3) a willingness and/or ability to endure discomfort; (4) a sex-strength factor; (5) intelligence; (6) a radical-conservative continuum; (7) natural tempo.

Not too much attention can be paid to these results, as the number of subjects is too small to justify the extraction of so many factors. Superficially, factors 1 and 3 resemble the ideational and physical types of persistence task respectively, but breath-holding was found to have a positive loading of over ·3 on the former and actually a negative loading on the latter. Consequently, no certain conclusions can be drawn from these data. It is, however, interesting to see that both tests of interrupted activities have loadings above ·4 on Rethlingshafer's first factor, a finding which would apparently link this type of task with persistence.

Much more convincing is Kremer's (1942) study, in which 156 boys between eight and fifteen were subjects. Kremer obtained ratings on 17 traits and scores on six persistence tests, four of which were group tests (word-building, magic numbers square, cutting test, and mechanical puzzle), while two were individual tests (total time spent in interpreting ink-blots). In addition to the six persistence tests and the seventeen ratings, mental age and school grades were included in the matrix of intercorrelations, from which six factors were extracted by means of Thurstone's method. After rotation, Kremer named these as follows: (1) will; (2) stability of character; (3) sense of inferiority; (4) intelligence; (5) will to community; (6) reliability. The first factor accounts for 15 per cent. of the total variance, and includes the general average of school marks, as well as persistence ratings. All six persistence tests have positive loadings on this factor, ranging from ·81 to ·24. The second factor is made up entirely of ratings, and may therefore be regarded as a kind of reputation factor; the persistence tests, with one exception, have near zero loadings on the factor. Neither the third nor the fourth factors have any loadings on persistence tests. The fifth factor, however, is of particular interest. The loadings of the persistence tests are negative for the four group tests, but zero for the two individual tests; ratings having positive loadings above ·4 on this factor are: Does he do what everybody else is doing just because they are doing it? and, Is he easily led by others? The suggestion, therefore, is that here we are dealing with a factor contrasting persistence under group pressure with persistence in isolation ("will to community").

Kremer's battery of persistence tests had a reliability of ·85, and the hierarchical arrangement of the coefficients of correlations suggested the presence of one underlying general factor operative in the entire persistence battery. Correlations with intelligence were positive throughout, but very low. Correlations with school marks averaged about ·22.

Interesting though the preceding studies are, they are subject to a number of criticisms. Factors such as age and intelligence were neither experimentally controlled nor partialled out; consequently their influence on the actual intercorrelations of persistence tests is difficult to estimate. The scores used in the tables of intercorrelations were not always, or even usually, experimentally independent; often several scores were derived from the same test procedure, which is of doubtful admissibility in factorial work. The number of cases used was not always sufficient to make the analyses convincing. None of the studies summarized so far is free from some of these faults.

The most recent study by MacArthur (1951, 1955) is much more satisfactory technically, and it is interesting to note that in its major conclusions it agrees with the best of the previous studies. After carrying out a pilot study on 45 boys of between 14 and 16 years of age, a large battery of individual and group tests was chosen for administration. These included all the traditional tests, as well as measures of intelligence, school grades, age, self-ratings, peer ratings, and ratings by teachers. The subjects of the investigation were 120 boys. Twenty-one measures of ability were available in all, and these were intercorrelated and factor analysed. The factors were identified as (1) intelligence, (2) verbal ability, (3) spatial-practical ability, (4) numerical ability, and (5) age-strength. Factor scores were derived for these five factors and the factor scores correlated with the persistence measures. Next, the influence of the mental components underlying the five intellectual factors was removed by partialling out these five factors from the table of intercorrelations between the persistence tests, so that we are finally left with the relationships between 22 experimentally independent measures of persistence after the influence of the main abilities which might be expected to be related to performance on these measures had been removed. 132 correlations are significantly positive, 216 are non-significantly positive, and 114 are non-significantly negative. Thus, 29 per cent. of the correlations are significant, and 75 per cent. are positive.

A Thurstone analysis with rotation was carried out and a good fit to simple structure obtained. MacArthur gives the following interpretation of the factors extracted: (1) general persistence factor. The highest saturations on this factor are obtained by the peer ratings (·603); time spent on the magic square (·584); teacher's rating (·574); time spent on Japanese Cross (·525); time spent on chess-board puzzle (·515); word building (·472), and maintained handgrip (·432). School marks, study time, self-ratings, and various other persistence measures complete the definition of this very clearly marked factor. It may be noted that this general persistence factor runs through both the ideational and the physical measures.

Factor (2) is bipolar; positive loadings are given in those tests in which the subjects had no knowledge as to the performance of their class-mates, while negative loadings are given by tests in which the subjects were well aware of the performance of their class-mates. This factor is interpreted by MacArthur as contrasting individuality with prestige suggestibility in situations requiring persistence, and he considers it to bear a close relationship to Kremer's factor, which he called "will to community".

Factor (3) is also bipolar and contrasts measures of reputation for persistence with objective measures of the time which an individual is willing to spend at a task. It may thus be interpreted as a reputation factor analogous to that found by Kremer. The measures which are opposite in sign to this reputation score are all very similar to those which defined Thornton's ideational factor.

Factor (4) is made up of physical tests (holding foot over chair, maintained hand-grip, breath time, arm extension) and closely resembles Thornton's "withstanding discomfort to achieve a goal", and Rethlingshafer's "willingness and/or ability to endure discomfort".

We thus emerge from this study with a fairly clear picture of a general factor of persistence running through all the tests, ratings, and self-ratings, and four group factors dealing respectively with ideational tests, physical tests, reputation, and what might be called "group prestige persistence". All these group factors, as well as the general one, had been found by one or other of the previous investigators. Their rediscovery in this technically more perfect, methodologically more complete, investigation clarifies the psychological traits underlying persistence to a considerable extent.

MacArthur calculated a persistence score by combining eight of the tests having the highest communalities, taking care to balance the different group factors. This battery of eight tests was found to have an index of reliability of ·9, which may thus be regarded as the theoretical validity of these tests. A measure having that degree of validity must be regarded as important and promising in a psychological description of personality, and there is little doubt that further improvement and shortening of the component measures can lead to even higher factor saturations and greater practical usefulness of the battery suggested. As one example of the possible practical usefulness of this score, MacArthur shows that it correlates to the extent of ·3 with school marks when intelligence is partialled out. This finding of an improved prediction of school achievement through the use of persistence tests may in due course lead to considerable improvement in our measures for student selection.

In summary, we may say that the evidence is fairly conclusive that persistence constitutes an important trait in our culture; that this trait is of a relatively unitary nature and can be measured to the extent indicated by a validity of ·9. In addition to this general factor of persistence, we find groups of activities which cluster together and define more specific types of persistence, such as persistence in physical tasks or persistence in ideational tasks. These smaller and less important factors also are subject to measurement with a degree of validity probably not much below general persistence itself. Persistence, as measured by tests, is fairly closely related to persistence as rated by others, and can be said to predict performance in life situations to a definitely significant extent. Persistence tends to show slight correlations with intelligence, more impressive ones with "w" or lack of neuroticism, and with introversion.[1]

[1] For experimental evidence to substantiate the claim that persistence measures both "w" and extraversion-introversion, cf. Eysenck (1947, 1952).

4. VARIABILITY

It is one of the commonplaces in psychological testing that individuals vary in almost any task from their "true" performance, i.e. from the mean of a large number of trials. Variability may be of two kinds. It may either manifest itself in short-term oscillation, occupying only a few seconds, or in long-term fluctuation, over periods of days, weeks, or even months. The former might be manifested, for instance, in the number of letters crossed out, the number of additions performed correctly, or the number of taps made in successive five-second intervals. The latter might become apparent on repetition of the same task after a lengthy period of time had elapsed. We shall call these two different aspects of variability "oscillation" and "fluctuation" respectively, although in the literature there has not been any consistent use of these terms. It may be surmised that variability would be a function of personality integration or "w", in the sense that the more stable, integrated personalities would be less variable in their conduct. Evidence for this view has already been presented in the work of Hartshorne and May (cf. their integration score) and of Shevach (1937) in connection with his studies of perseveration. Further evidence to be quoted now supports this hypothesis to a considerable extent.[1]

The first experiment demonstrating functional unity in oscillation was published by Hollingworth (1925), who showed that oscillation in tests of tapping, co-ordination, steadiness, substitution, and colour naming produced intercorrelations to an average extent of ·20; variability of pulse-rate showed no relationship with oscillation. Flugel (1929, 1934), whose work had been independent of Hollingworth's, used rather larger numbers of subjects, and found considerable correlations on oscillation scores between eight tests (crossing out figures, cancellation, crossing out words and circles, and doing arithmetical subtraction). All the intercorrelations between the eight tests used were positive and averaged around ·20. Examinations by means of tetrad differences showed that a general factor of oscillation described the pattern of intercorrelations very well; this factor was also shown to be independent of "g" and perseveration.

With respect to fluctuation, Ash (1933) appears to have been the first to show that this aspect of variability is a unitary function. Combining results of various small groups, he found that on learning trials, separated by twenty-four hours, fluctuations in different tasks showed an average intercorrelation of ·31. Neither his data nor those of any later investigator permit us to say anything about the relationship between oscillation and fluctuation, as never so far have the two types of variability been combined in the same investigation.

Walton (1936, 1939) also presented evidence regarding the unity of the oscillation factor, using 55 children in his first and 90 children in his second experiment. Four and seven tests respectively were employed, having reliabilities of ·4 on the average. Also available were ratings of steadiness of character given by two teachers for each child. The average intercorrelation of the tests in Walton's first paper was ·22; in his second it was ·30. On carrying out a factor analysis, he found that one factor accounting for 32 per cent. of the variance was sufficient to reproduce all the correlations within the limits of sampling error. In both papers he obtained significant correlations between the "w" estimates obtained from the teachers and mean score on the tests of oscillation. The most trustworthy of these correlations is one of − ·275 (with age eliminated), showing a slight but significant tendency for oscillation to be higher in the less stable, less steady sort of child.

A similar result is reported by Cummings (1939), who used four tests on 18 girl students. In addition to variability, she also measured the amount of error and time required for each of the tests, but concluded that "variability has here been found to be a much more valuable source of enquiry than the other measures . . . it has been found that the subjects who are variable on one test tend to be

---

[1] Physiological variability also appears related to "w", as shown for instance in the pioneering study by Hammett (1921), but as there has been no factorial study of this important field little is known about the functional unity of this type of variability, cf. also Herrington (1942).

variable in two very different tests. . . . A consistently positive correlation shows that there is a tendency for lack of variability to be associated with . . . measures of 'persistence' and 'w'. . . . The four best correlating traits are in fact the very ones selected, quite independently, . . . to represent 'w'. The traits correlating negatively, on the other hand, are also easily recognizable as non-'w' traits."

Cattell (1943), dealing with fluctuation rather than oscillation, also found considerable support for the hypothesis that variability is less in the more stable individual. Using 60 children and 40 women students, he applied three and five sets respectively of 12-item questionnaires dealing with self-concept, deeper sentiments, superficial attitudes, etc. These questionnaires were re-applied one day and one month later, and personality ratings by peers obtained. Scores were calculated representing amount of change on the questionnaires, and these appear to give good, split-half reliabilities of ·61 and ·77 for children and adults, respectively, after one day, and ·68 and ·79 after one month. Variability after one day and variability after one month correlated ·47 and ·77 respectively for children and adults. Correlations between oscillation and "w" were astonishingly high, giving values of ·71 and ·40 for children and adults respectively after one day and ·49 and ·64 respectively after one month.

The studies of Madigan (1938) and Weber (1938) lend support to the generality of the concepts of oscillation and fluctuation, but only the latter appears to relate variability to personality trends. Weber (1938) specifically follows McV. Hunt (1936), who had shown schizophrenic patients to be considerably more variable than normals. Using 44 subjects, Weber derived a measure of variability from five tests administered to all subjects once a week for six successive weeks. In addition, these subjects were given an intelligence test, the Allport Ascendance-Submission Questionnaire and the Social Shyness and Emotionality parts of the Guilford Personality Inventory. A combined measure of variability was obtained for these subjects, and it was found that the more variable subjects were significantly more ascendant and significantly less emotional than were the more submissive and the more emotional subjects respectively. No connection was found with intelligence. The small number of subjects used and the sole reliance on questionnaires as outside criteria are features which make this study suggestive rather than conclusive.[1]

Cattell (1946) concludes his discussion of tests of oscillation and fluctuation by saying: "The correlations of 'O' with character integration and stability are lower than those of fluctuation, suggesting that these two factors are related but not identical." It is difficult to come to any conclusion regarding the two questions raised here. In the first place, the studies reporting correlations between "w" and oscillation and fluctuation respectively have been too dissimilar to allow of any direct comparison; in the second place, both oscillation and fluctuation might be negatively correlated with "w" without necessarily showing any functional similarity one with the other. It might be reasonable to regard Cattell's summary as a hypothesis worthy of investigation, and indeed the possible use of variability scores as measures of neuroticism or "w" appears to be a very tempting one in view of the ease with which these scores are obtainable.

5. FLUENCY

This factor was isolated first by Hargreaves (1927) in his studies of "the faculty of imagination". He found that a number of tests calling for a large number of imaginative responses tended to correlate together with an average intercorrelation of ·3. These correlations fulfilled the demands of the tetrad criterion and were shown not to be identical with "g". Some of the tests included were: number of things seen in an ink-blot, number of words written, number of different completions to an incomplete picture, and so forth. This "f" factor was considered at first as being the reverse of perseveration, but Hargreaves disproved this hypothesis fairly conclusively.

Cattell (1934) took up fluency tests, and found them to have a low but positive correlation with his surgency factor as rated ($r = ·30$) when the reliability of the test was ·57. In 1936, Cattell reported a more clinical study of a number of maladjusted and delinquent children and came to the following conclusion. "There is a preponderance of extremely high and low 'p' among children referred for delinquency or nervous difficulties. . . . Similarly, there is a preponderance of high and low rather than middling 'fluency of association' scores." This hypothesis of curvilinear regression has not been confirmed by later writers.

The tendency of extraversion (surgency) to correlate with "f" has found some slight report in Notcutt's study (1943), who gave five fluency tests which showed an average intercorrelation of ·45. Score on fluency was found to correlate $- ·24$ with introversion.

---

[1] Chorus (1943) and Gray (1942) also bring forward evidence to support the correlation between variability and emotional lability.

Much stronger support for the hypothesis comes from the studies of Gewirtz (1948), who used "f" tests on 38 children between the ages of 5 and 7. Correlations between these tests ranged from ·08 to ·70 and averaged much the same as the tests reported previously. Gewirtz suggested that the "f" factor might split up into two. "Different patterns of relationships were found between the tests of word fluency and two types of vocabulary tests, one a recall vocabulary test and the other a recognition-definition vocabulary test. The intercorrelation of the word fluency tests and their correlations with mental age and two types of vocabulary tests seem to indicate that there were two abilities involved in word fluency: one involving the rate of word association where there is some restriction imposed, and the other involving the rate of word association where there is little restriction."

In correlating the "f" tests with ratings made by the use of the Fels Child Behaviour Scales, she found a distinct tendency for the signs of the correlations of the various "f" tests to be identical when correlating these tests with each particular item of the Fels scale. There thus emerges a distinct tendency for the child with high fluency scores to receive high ratings on curiosity, gregariousness, originality, aggressiveness, competitiveness, and cheerfulness, and negative ratings on social apprehensiveness and patience. These results would seem to support very strongly the hypothesis of a positive relation between "f" and extraversion, although failure to partial out intelligence and age renders the results less conclusive than one might have wished.

About the existence of such a correlation, there can be little doubt. Benassy and Chauffard (1947) found correlations between intelligence and "f" in the neighbourhood of ·32 when Cattell's "f" test was administered to 282 children and 231 adults. They confirmed, however, that the correlations on which the "f" factor is based are partly independent of "g", and in the main their results of comparing fluency scores with ratings of temperament bear out the general hypothesis that fluency is a valid measure of extraversion.

In addition to the few studies mentioned, all of which have regarded the "f" test as a measure of personality, there are a number of studies in which fluency is related to purely cognitive tests, and as these have been dealt with in some detail by Vernon (1950), the main results only will be mentioned. The work of Thurstone (1938), Johnson and Reynolds (1941), Carroll (1941), Taylor (1947), and Fruchter (1948) tends to bear out the early findings of Holzinger

(1934, 1935) that fluency tests have comparatively high saturations on "g" and "v" (intelligence and verbal ability), but that in addition they have something in common, which gives rise to a separate factor. Thurstone's distinction between his "V" (understanding of verbal material) and "W" (word fluency) underlies this distinction; in more recent years he has added another factor, "F" (ideational fluency with words), to the other two.

Various sub-factors within this general context have been identified by some of the writers mentioned above. Thus, Taylor distinguishes: (1) verbal versatility or ability to express an idea by several different combinations of words; (2) word fluency, involving no reference to the meaning of words; and (3) ideational fluency, or production of words from meaningful associations.

Carroll split Thurstone's "W" factor into: (1) speed of word association in restricted context; (2) rate of production of syntectically coherent discourse; (3) naming or ability to attach appropriate names to stimuli.

It seems likely to the present writer that some at least of these distinctions within the "f" context will be verified in later work, but factors based on these fine distinctions are not likely to contribute much to the total variance. As far as the relation of "f" to personality is concerned, there is no evidence that groupings such as those suggested by Carroll and Taylor are likely to correspond in any way to personality differences. Considering the importance attached to "f" tests by many psychologists who have used them as measures of personality (Cattell, Stephenson, Studman, and others), it seems curious that the number of relevant factorial studies is so small. However, it is possible that the recent interest shown by American writers in the cognitive aspects of "f" will generalize to the orectic aspects.

One fundamental criticism of all the studies of fluency mentioned so far is that the scores which are being analysed can be shown to be compound rather than simple. It has been shown by Bousfield and Sedgwick (1944) that raw output scores could be rationalized in terms of two semi-independent concepts, C, or total supply of relevant words and m or rate of depletion of this total store. The exponential equation $N = C(1 - e^{-mt})$, where N is the number of words produced, t is the time over which the test is carried out and e is the base of the natural logarithms, was shown to fit adequately the rate of output during the test. This finding, if it were to be supported, could revolutionize the factorial study of fluency; we should drop the practice of intercorrelating raw scores and use C and m scores instead.

This possibility was specifically tested by Rogers (1952, 1956), who carried out factor analyses of fluency measures, both raw scores and derived scores, and also correlated them with measures of intellectual ability and of personality. His results from the analysis of raw scores lend support to the existence of a verbal fluency factor, and there appears to be some evidence also for a relationship between fluency and extraversion. The expectation that derived scores would give better results than raw scores was, however, not fulfilled. "Our solution leads to the conclusion that mathematically derived constants, C, and m, do not furnish higher orectic correlations than the raw score data from which they were determined. For all practical purposes the derived scores are of little value as reliable predictors of temperamental qualities. . . . On the other hand, the C constants may furnish higher g loadings than some of the ordinary fluency tests but our evidence on this point, although consistent, is incomplete."

The results obtained by Hofstaetter *et al.* (1957) are equally disappointing. They also used three different tasks, and estimates of a variety of temperamental traits. They found very high correlations between C and m, in the sense that the "larger the reservoir, the slower the discharge". They also found that "the hypothesized relationship between the discharge rates (m) and temperamental traits such as 'activeness', 'impulsiveness' and 'reflectiveness' has not been found. The subject's performance in a task of restricted association is, therefore, highly task-specific. In view of the very high positive correlations between the total number of associations produced in 12 minutes and the inferred size of the reservoirs (C), the use of the former variable in future research was suggested." While these negative results are not decisive, they do suggest that early hopes of improved results through the use of derived scores may have been premature, and that the original type of fluency score was as efficient and effective as the more complex types of score.

6. SUGGESTIBILITY

The close relationship between suggestibility and qualities of temperament and character has been posited by so many writers that there is hardly any call to mention them specifically. A detailed review of the literature has been given by Eysenck (1947), who finds that two hypotheses have been entertained by large numbers of psychiatrists and psychologists, the first linking suggestibility to hysteria (and consequently to extraversion), the second linking suggestibility to neuroticism. All these theories, of course, assume some functional unity of the alleged trait of suggestibility, a unity the existence of which has been doubted by many psychologists, whose judgment has been based largely on the pioneer studies of Brown (1916). This writer, who carried out his experiments on 54 women and 29 men, applied a large number of tests of what might be called sensory suggestibility, in which the subject was put into what appeared a normal laboratory situation involving the establishment of sensory thresholds for odours, touch, heat, brightness, pitch size, motion, etc.; supra-liminal stimuli were then followed by ready signs not accompanied by the expected stimulus; quite frequently the subject would report the expected stimulus, although objectively no such stimulus was present. The number of times the suggestion was effective was considered the score of the person on the particular test in question. Correlations were calculated separately for the men and the women. For nine tests, the average intercorrelation for the men was ·204; for the women it was only ·054. Brown adds: "It is understood that these correlations involve a possible error, in that the work was done by different experimenters, so that the ranking of the individual subject's record may be influenced by the amount of the personal influence of the experimenter." While the amount of intercorrelation between these tests is certainly not very large, and while factors such as intelligence have not been partialled out as they should have been, the crudeness of the experimental methods and the difficulty of having several different experiments, mentioned above by Brown, make it difficult to derive any firm negative conclusions from his data. If anything, they might be taken to indicate the existence of a rather weak factor of sensory suggestibility, but as later investigators have found sensory suggestibility to be correlated with intelligence, even this conclusion cannot be regarded as definite.

Brown also investigated correlations between illusions, æsthetic judgments, and their subjective estimates when suggestions were made to the subjects as to a general standard of judgment, using the amount of change induced as a measure of suggestibility. Seven experiments of this type give average intercorrelations of ·095 and ·003 for men and women respectively; these data suggest a complete absence of functional unity for this type of suggestibility.

In their rather more recent study, Aveling and Hargreaves (1921) came to a conclusion quite opposite to the negative one of Brown. They used in the main six tests, some of which were similar to

Brown's, namely the Illusion of Warmth Test and the Binet Progressive Weights and Progressive Lines. They also included, however, two tests of quite a different type, called hand-rigidity and hand-levitation, in which the motor reaction of the subject to a direct suggestion was measured. Using two samples, one of 32 children and one of 56 children, they found a good deal of variation in correlations. Most of these correlations appeared to be as small as those in Brown's work. The only exception to this rule was a correlation between the two motor suggestibility tests which rose to the striking value of ·73. Aveling and Hargreaves conclude from their study that "there is evidence which points to a general factor of suggestibility complicated by group factors", but their material is not extensive enough to prove this point.

A paper by Eysenck (1943) was designed to test two hypotheses: the first that there were two main factors of suggestibility, one of them sensory, the other motor; and the second, that suggestibility had an intimate relation with hysteria. Sixty subjects in all were used, 15 men and 15 women suffering from conversion hysteria, and 15 men and 15 women who were also neurotic but did not show any signs of conversion symptoms, hysterical personality, etc. Four sensory tests and four motor tests were used, the latter including the Chevreul Pendulum, the Hull Body Sway Test, and two levitation tests.

None of the eight tests differentiated between hysterics and non-hysterics, thus effectively disproving the hypothesis of a special link between hysteria and suggestibility. A factor analysis of the inter-correlations between the tests disclosed two orthogonal factors, one having projections on the four sensory tests, the other having projections on the four motor tests. In order to avoid biasing the interpretation of these factors by giving them names like sensory and motor suggestibility, which would pre-judge more detailed enquiry into their nature, the terms "primary suggestibility" (for tests like Body Sway, Arm Levitation and the Chevreul Pendulum), and "secondary suggestibility" (for tests like the Binet, Progressive Lines and Weights, and the type of test used by Brown) were suggested.

In a later study, Eysenck and Furneaux (1945) attempted to clarify the nature of these tests by increasing the number of procedures used to twelve. Sixty neurotics constituted the sample; all of these had I.Q.s between 90 and 110. Part of the battery of tests consisted of a hyponotizability scale in which different hypnotic suggestions carried out by the subject were given points according to the difficulty of the suggestion. Six of the tests were designed to be measures of primary suggestibility; these intercorrelated to the extent of ·50. The other six tests were selected so as to be representative of secondary suggestibility; these intercorrelated to the extent of ·15. The average intercorrelation of the tests of primary suggestibility with those of

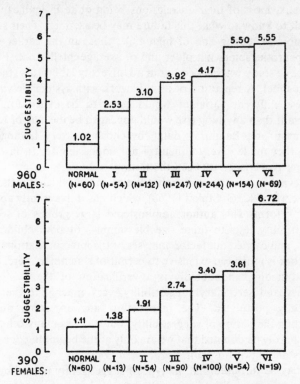

Fig. 13.—Average Suggestibility of Normals and Neurotics, showing increase in Suggestibility correlated with increase in "Neuroticism".

secondary suggestibility was ·02. Two independent factors of primary and secondary suggestibility consequently emerged from the analysis. The highest saturation for primary suggestibility were obtained in the Body Sway Test (·92) and the hypnosis scale (·89); the highest saturations for secondary suggestibility were obtained in an ink-blot and in an odour-suggestion test. A detailed scrutiny of the tests giving rise to these two factors and of their saturations suggested that primary suggestibility was essentially due to ideo-motor tendencies within the individual, whereas secondary suggestibility was essentially of the indirection kind ("gullibility").

Benton and Bandura (1953) carried out a factorial study of various tests of primary and secondary suggestibility on 50 undergraduate students. They failed to duplicate the findings of Eysenck and Furneaux, most of their correlations being quite insignificant. It is difficult to know to what this failure may be ascribed. Their subjects were normal, young and of high I.Q.; those in the earlier studies were neurotic, somewhat older and of average intelligence. Furthermore, one study was carried out in a University laboratory, the other in a hospital. A repetition of all this work with systematic variation of these different variables would seem to be called for. More important than anything else would appear to be the lack of *variance* in Benton and Bandura's data; by chosing a very homogeneous group they made it very difficult if not impossible for themselves to discover *co-variance* between the tests.

Relevant to this apparent contradiction in the evidence is the large-scale work of K. G. Stukat (1958), which has only recently appeared in book form. This author administered large groups of so-called suggestibility tests to quite sizeable samples of both children and adults, and carried out factor analyses of the intercorrelations found. His work is much too extensive to permit of a summary here, but the main outcome undoubtedly is a verification of the existence of primary and secondary suggestibility, very much like the factors originally postulated. The report thus answers some questions regarding the nature of suggestibility, but it raises many others, and it can hardly be doubted that we are only at the beginning of a proper understanding of this trait.

It may be surmised that the type of suggestibility related by many writers to personality is essentially of the ideo-motor type, because of the close relation usually posited between suggestibility and hypnosis; in the experiment outlined above, no connection was observed between hypnotizability and secondary suggestibility, but a very close connection between hypnotizability and primary suggestibility (Furneaux, 1946). Several further studies failed to show any relationship between primary suggestibility and hysteria, so that this hypothesis seems to be definitely disproved. A very close connection, however, was found between neuroticism and primary suggestibility (Eysenck, 1947, 1952). Typical of the findings is a set of figures presented diagrammatically in Fig. 13, in which is shown the amount of body sway in response to the suggestion "You are falling.

you are falling forward . . ." of 960 men and 390 women of whom some were normal, while others were inmates of an Army Neurosis Centre and had been rated on a six-point scale for degree of neuroticism by psychiatrists independently of the experiment. It will be seen that there is a perfect monotonic relation between degree of neuroticism and increase in suggestibility, a finding which has been verified in a number of subsequent studies. There appears little doubt, therefore, that suggestibility is a useful measure of neuroticism, but that it fails to differentiate between extraverts and introverts. This conclusion has since been strengthened by the work of Ingham (1954, 1955), Connor (1952), Eysenck, Granger and Brengelmann (1957), Cattell (1957) and many others.

7. TENSION

The concept of tension, which presumably originated in connection with physiological phenomena, has been used so widely and so frequently in connection with psychological states that it comes with something of a shock to realize how very little experimental evidence there is for any identification of these two meanings of the term. Almost the only relevant work here is that of Duffy (1930, 1932, 1946), who has carried out a number of investigations designed to discover the degree of generality of the physiological phenomena, and to discover the relation of these phenomena to personality and behaviour. The hypothesis underlying her work was stated by her as follows: "Relative degree of tension is a fundamental characteristic of the individual varying . . . with changes in circumstance but varying around a central tendency which is different for different individuals." Working with college students, she used three measures of tension: (1) pressure exerted on a rubber bulb or tube held in the unused hand; (2) pressure exerted by the used hand; and (3) amount of pencil pressure indicated by the penetration of a number of sets of carbon papers. Her subjects were given various tasks, such as colour naming, tapping, crossing out digits or lines, adding numbers and tracing mazes. "Twelve measures of muscular tension and four measures of fluctuation in tension obtained while the subjects were performing a wide variety of tasks were subjected to factorial analysis. These measures were secured on three separate occasions, the first separated from the second by three months; and the second separated from the third by one week." One general factor was found which "is interpreted as representing a general-tension factor. This factor incorporates a variety of tasks, three techniques of tension measurement, and three experimental sessions". Duffy interprets this tension as an indicator of energy mobilization, an interpretation similar to that of Freeman and of Wenger, whose work has been summarized in a previous chapter.

In another study (Duffy, 1932) 18 children between the ages of 3 and 4 showed a correlation of ·63 between tension as evidenced by strength of grip on a rubber ball, and pressure. Tension was found to correlate with ratings of excitability and school adjustment to the extent of ·52 and ·58. A similar correlation was found in yet another study (1930), when 11 children aged from 4 to 5 were assigned a task (of pressing a key whenever a red light appeared), and during the performance of this task a kymographic record was made of the degree of tension in the muscles of the unused hand. The correlation between tension and excitability ratings was ·56, and it was also found that under disturbance (sound of a klaxon horn) there was a greater rise in tension in those who were already tense.

Duffy (1932) sums up her findings of the relation between tension and personality in the following words: "Tension . . . frequently found expression in stammering, enuresis, temper tantrums, and restless movements of various kinds; tense children had fewer physical contacts on the playground (and established fewer voluntary contacts) than children who were more relaxed; tension decreased during successive performance of the same task, but showed an increase when the subject returned to school after an attack of whooping-cough; and various other forms of behaviour and even aspects of health appeared to be related to the characteristic tension level of the individual. It was also shown that habitual grip pressure (the tension measure used) was not a product of a muscular strength since it showed no correlation with dynamometer scores. From these various findings it was concluded that 'tension level' represents a significant aspect of the individual's personality." Duffy appears to be right in her insistence on tension level as an important psychological variable; it is unfortunate that the number of cases used by her is too small to make definite assessment of the relationship between tension and other personality factors possible.

The only writer apart from Duffy who has attempted to study tension by means of factorial techniques is Wenger (1943), whose work on autonomic functioning has been reviewed in a previous chapter. In these studies Wenger found, in addition to the autonomic factor, another which he provisionally identified as one of muscular tension. As he points out, these studies suffered in offering no clear definition of the factor: "It was believed that if at least one test could be added to the battery which was unquestionably a test of generalized muscular tension, it would serve to define and validate (or invalidate) the postulated factor of muscular tension. Since no one test is available which all observers would agree constitutes the valid measure of general muscular tension, and since this concept at present is a subjective one with but little objective support, it was decided to employ a rating scale. If it were found that observers could agree on a definition of muscular tension and then reliably rate behaviour indicative of that trait, there would be available a critical test for use in defining a muscular factor." Wenger accordingly developed a rating scale of muscular relaxation which was shown to have adequate reliability for the purpose in hand by means of inter-correlating 8 observers. Seventeen physiological variables and the rating scale were then intercorrelated, using measures derived from 74 children. Of the two main factors extracted, the first was found to be similar to the autonomic factor found in several other analyses. The second factor, which has its highest loading on the rating of muscular relaxation $(- \cdot 54)$, just discussed, is in many ways similar to the original factor which was labelled by Wenger muscular tension, and the fact that the rating included in the battery has such a relatively high saturation for this factor bears out Wenger's original interpretation. A regression equation was then set up by Wenger involving six tests; this equation gives the best available estimate of the factor score for individual children. Correlations were run between ratings on 9 personality traits, the tension factor score, and the results obtained from the rating scale; these are reproduced in Table 8. It will be seen that the two series of coefficients are almost perfectly correlated, showing that the rating and the factor score measure very much the same underlying trait. Both methods show that the tense child tends to be energetic, emotional, restless, and impulsive, whereas a relaxed child is fatigable and emotionally controlled. These results should only be taken as suggestive; while we may regard existence of the factor of muscular tension as established, a great deal of work will be required before its relationship to various traits and types of personality can be regarded as proven.

We may perhaps note from the purely technical point of view the use made by Wenger of the hypothetico-deductive method. Having obtained from his original analysis a factor the identification of which with "tension" might be regarded as somewhat far-fetched, he then proceeded to make certain deductions regarding the factorial

8

composition of an additional measure which would be crucial to his interpretation: the resulting experiment bore out his hypothesis at a high level of confidence, and we may therefore consider his original interpretation of the factor justified. It is only rarely, unfortunately, that factorial studies follow this course; only too frequently a doubt-

TABLE 8

The Relationship of nine Personality Ratings to two Measures of Muscular Tension for forty-four Children

Personality Traits	Correlations with	
	Factor Score	Rating
Energeticness . .	·46	·46
Fatigability . .	− ·35	− ·24
Frequency of emotion .	·46	·47
Restlessness . . .	·48	·50
Sensitiveness . .	− ·10	− ·02
Emotional Control .	− ·33	− ·32
Distractability . .	·19	·17
Impulsiveness . .	·35	·41
Carelessness . . .	·22	·21

ful or unclear interpretation is allowed to stand without being submitted to further control experimentation. Wenger's study may serve as an illustration of the proper integration of factorial and experimental methods.

8. LEVEL OF ASPIRATION

The concept of level of aspiration has already been mentioned on a previous page, and an excellent summary of the work done with this type of test has been given by Lewin *et al.* (1944). Some evidence of generality of this factor is given by Heather (1942) and Gardiner (1940), but the main burden of proof rests on a paper by Gould (1939), who gave six tests (synonyms, steadiness, additions, symbol-digits, cancellation, and target) to 82 subjects. He found a median intercorrelation of ·29, and very high reliability for the individual aspiration discrepancy scores. The actual correlations found by him are given below in Table 9; it will be seen that they lend very strong support to the notion that level of aspiration is a generalized trait extending over a number of very different types of activity. Correlations between performance and aspiration were found to be negligible; similarly, correlations between performances were found to be negligible.

TABLE 9

	1	2	3	4	5	6
1. Synonyms test .	(·95)	·36	·25	·35	·29	·23
2. Steadiness . .		(·96)	·26	·24	·25	·04
3. Additions . .			(·99)	·44	·40	·28
4. Symbol-digit .				(·96)	·34	·35
5. Cancellation .					(·97)	·34
6. Target . .						(·97)

There can be little doubt that this generalized trait is related both to introversion-extraversion and to neuroticism. Diagrammatic representation of the type of relationship indicated by a number of research papers has been given on p. 41 and will not be repeated here. Most of the data on which these diagrams were based were taken from experiments in which a single test was used; Gould's data indicate that much better discrimination could be achieved if several tests were used and the aspiration scores averaged.

9. PERSONAL TEMPO

There is a large and flourishing literature connected with the concept of personal tempo. The main protagonist in this field perhaps is Frischeisen-Köhler (1933), who used preferred rate of tapping, and preference for metronome speed, as measures of this alleged quality. She demonstrated that monozygotic twins are more alike with respect to personal tempo thus measured than were dizygotic twins and siblings, while these, in turn, were more alike than unrelated persons.

The work of Allport and Vernon (1933) threw a good deal of doubt on the alleged generality of this trait, however, and the studies of Harrison (1941) and Harrison and Dorcus (1938) seem to indicate a rather high degree of specificity in measures of this type. In the first of these studies, 49 subjects were used and subjected to a number of tests, including cranking, tapping, arm and body movements, coordination, walking, etc. From the intercorrelations of these tests they concluded that "the intercorrelation of speed measurements indicates no unitary speed trait which is characteristic of various spontaneous movements or motor adjustments of an individual".

This lack of generality cannot be attributed to the unreliability of the constituent measures because it was found that "individuals tend to perform at a fairly consistent rate from one time to another". Harrison's later experiment gave rather more positive findings from the point of view of generality. Using 50 students, he gave them 12 tasks to do at their preferred (voluntary) speed and another set of 12 partly identical tasks to do at maximum speed. The average inter-correlations of the voluntary speed tests was ·20. That of the maximum speed tests was ·15. The tasks included in both series correlated on the average, ·37. Between personal tempo, as measured by the whole battery, and the subject's self-estimate of his own personal tempo, a correlation of ·51 was found. These results appear to favour the hypothesis that a certain amount of generality does exist in the field of personal tempo, but the number of tests used is too small to come to any definite conclusion.

More definitive is the work of Rimoldi (1951), who used 59 tests altogether on 91 male university students. Reliabilities appeared to be fairly satisfactory, and 9 factors were obtained from the inter-correlations. The first factor appeared to be related to the spon-taneous speed with which large body movements (swinging arm, swinging leg, ergograph, bending body, etc.) were performed. The second factor "is defined by tests involving simple movement. These movements are performed by the distal muscles of the limbs and seem to be independent of site of the body and of the muscular groups involved". The third factor appears to be related to feet movements, the fourth to hand movements, the fifth appears to be related to speed of reading, the sixth to reaction-time tests, the seventh factor appears to be one of cognitive speed, the eighth is a metronome doublet, and the ninth is not interpretable. These factors are not independent but show moderate correlations. Thus, the first and second factors cor-relate ·51 with each other. Second-order factors were accordingly extracted from the correlations between the primaries. "As a result of our second-order analysis, it seems possible to isolate the following variables: α-speed of all motor activities; β-speed of perception; γ-speed of cognition; δ-reaction time." This set of factors closely resembles a set presented by Eysenck (1947) on the basis of a review of the literature, and may be considered a reasonable estimate of the present position of this concept of "personal tempo" which could, presumably, be identified with Rimoldi's α factor. Little is known, unfortunately, about the correlates of personal tempo, as most writers have been content to use only one or two tests instead of the larger number required for getting adequate factor measurements. In view of the many claims for this type of test made in the literature, it seems likely that important personality correlates will be found, but it would be idle to speculate at this stage as to precisely what they might be. Indications are to hand (Eysenck, 1947), that personal tempo may be related to "*w*", but the evidence is not extensive enough to enable us to go further than that.[1]

In recent years there has been a growth of interest in work on personal tempo and its relation to the EEG alpha rhythm in the South African National Institute of Personnel Research. Biesheuvel and Pitt (1956) demonstrated high intercorrelations between different test performances in their study of speed and tempo of behaviour in relation to primary and secondary function, and Mundy-Castle (1956) found a positive and significant correlation between rate of key tapping and the frequency of the EEG alpha rhythm; on the basis of his results Mundy-Castle suggested a hypothesis that alpha frequency was a determiner of the speed of "unstructured motor activity". A more recent study by Herberg (1958) failed to support this conclusion but suggested the relationship of eye movement speed to various behavioural measures of personal tempo. These findings are too recent and too contradictory to make possible any definite conclusion; they do suggest, however, that interesting relationships may yet be discovered in relation to this trait.

GENERAL COMMENT

The studies quoted in this chapter illustrate a number of points which appear very important for the study of personality. It is obviously very easy to postulate the existence of large numbers of hypothetical traits of personality in terms of which the psychologist, or the layman, can interpret behaviour *ex posteriori*. With a certain amount of ingenuity it is also reasonably easy to construct tests of moderate or even high reliability which allegedly measure these alleged traits. It is, however, extremely difficult to demonstrate that different measures of the same trait do in fact correlate together and do in fact define one and the same factor. We have seen time

[1] Another study that may be relevant to the concept of "personal tempo" is the factor analysis by Carpenter (1941) of 14 measures taken on 128 boys and 125 girls. She extracted a "velocity" or speed factor which was characterized by various running and hopping activities.

and time again how the very attractive hypotheses of even the most eminent psychologists were shown to be lacking in any factual foundation, and it is clear that much greater care should be exercised by psychologists in postulating the existence of personality traits. Before such claims can be taken seriously, some form of factor analytic demonstration should be undertaken to prove that the trait in question has some degree of functional unity in terms of the measures suggested for the purpose of its assessment. Where this is not done, we have the absurd situation that a given trait, such as rigidity, or intolerance of ambiguity, or Spaltungsfähigkeit is measured by ten different people with ten different tests, none of which intercorrelate significantly with any of the others. Clearly, the confusion which arises from such unwarranted postulation of traits and trait measures, in the absence of adequate proof, reduces the whole field of personality study to complete chaos. If the student carries away nothing else from the perusal of this book, but the firm realization and resolve that *traits must not be postulated without adequate proof*, the writer will feel well rewarded.

The second point which emerges from this discussion relates to the usefulness of factor analysis as a hypothetico-deductive technique. Most psychologists think of it as a means of suggesting principles of classification in a hitherto obscure and rather neglected field; they do not on the whole regard it as a useful method for disproving erroneous hypotheses. Yet in the majority of the studies quoted, it will be seen that factor analysis did in fact have this very important function of disproving theories firmly held by many well-known workers in this field. Further examples of this use of factor analysis will be encountered later on in this book, but attention may with advantage be drawn to it here as it is nowhere clearer than in relation to the analysis of trait measurements.

REFERENCES

Chapter III

ALEXANDER, W. P. Intelligence, concrete and abstract. *Brit. J. Psychol., Monogr. Suppl.*, 1935, **19**, 177.

ALLPORT, G. W., and VERNON, P. E. *Studies in Expressive Movement.* New York: Macmillan, 1933.

APPLEZWEIG, D. G. Some determinants of behavioral rigidity. *J. abnorm. soc. Psychol.*, 1954, **49**, 224–228.

ASH, E. E. An experimental study of variability in learning. *Arch. Psychol.*, 1933, **22**, 1–54.

AVELING, F., and HARGREAVES, M. Suggestibility with and without prestige in children. *Brit. J. Psychol.*, 1921, **12**, 53–75.

BENASSY, M., and CHAUFFARD, C. Le Test F de Cattell est-il un Test Objectif de Tempérament? *L'année psychol.*, 1947, **43–44**, 200–230.

BENTON, A. L., and BANDURA, A. "Primary" and "secondary" suggestibility. *J. abnorm. soc. Psychol.*, 1953, **48**, 336–340.

BERNSTEIN, E. Quickness and intelligence. *Brit. J. Psychol., Monogr. Suppl.*, 1924, **3**, 1–55.

BIESHEUVEL, S. The measurement of the threshold for flicker and its value as a perseveration test. *Brit. J. Psychol.*, 1938, **29**, 27–38.

BIESHEUVEL, S., and PITT, D. R. The relationship between secondary function and some aspects of speed and tempo of behaviour. *Acta Psychol.*, 1955, **2**, 373–396.

BOUSFIELD, W. A., and SEDGWICK, C. M. W. An analysis of sequences of restricted associative responses. *J. genet. Psychol.*, 1944, **30**, 149–165.

BRENGELMANN, J. C. Spaltungsfähigkeit als Persönlichkeitsmerkmal. *Z. exp. u. angew. Psychol.*, 1954, **2**, 455–494.

BROWN, R. W. A determinant of the relationship between rigidity and authoritarianism. *J. abnorm. soc. Psychol.*, 1953, **48**, 469–476.

BROWN, V. Individual and sex differences in suggestibility. *Univ. Calif. Publ. in Psychol.*, 1916, **2**, 291–430.

BÜHLER, C., BÜHLER, K., and LEFEVER, D. W. *Development of the basic Rorschach score with manual of directions.* California: Copyright, 1949.

CARROLL, J. B. A factor analysis of verbal abilities. *Psychomet.*, 1941, **6**, 279–308.

CATTELL, R. B. Temperament Tests: II. Tests. *Brit J. Psychol.*, 1934, **24**, 20–49.

On the measurement of perseveration. *Brit. J. educ. Psychol.*, 1935, **5**, 76–92.

Fluctuations of sentiments and attitudes as a measure of character interpretation and temperament. *Amer. J. Psychol.*, 1943, **56**, 196–216.

The Description and Measurement of Personality. London: Harrap & Co. Ltd., 1946.

The riddle of perseveration: I. "Creative effort" and disposition rigidity. II. Solution in terms of personality structure. *J. Pers.*, 1946, **14**, 229–267.

Personality and Motivation Structure and Measurement. London: Harrap & Co. Ltd., 1957.

CATTELL, R. B., and TINER, L. G. The varieties of structural rigidity. *J. Pers.*, 1949, **17**, 321–341.

CHORUS, A. H. J. Le rythme personnel (das Persönliche Tempo) et le rythme de travail des enfants instables. *Z. Kinderpsychiat.*, 1943, **10**, 2–8.

CONNOR, D. V. *The effect of temperamental traits upon the intelligence performance of children.* Ph.D. Thesis, Univ. London, 1952.

COX, S. M. A factorial study of the Rorschach responses of normal and maladjusted boys. *J. genet. Psychol.*, 1951, **79**, 95–115.

CRUTCHER, R. An experimental study of persistence. *J. appl. Psychol.*, 1934, **18**, 409–417.

CUMMINGS, J. D. Variability of judgment and steadiness of character. *Brit. J. Psychol.*, 1939, **29**, 345–370.

CUSHING, H. M. A perseverative tendency in pre-school children: a study of personality differences. *Arch. Psychol.*, 1929, **17**, 55.

DARROCH, J. An investigation into the degree of variation in the score of a motor perseveration test. *Brit. J. Psychol.*, 1938, **28**, 248–262.

DUFFY, E. Tensions and emotional factors in reaction. *Genet. Psychol. Monogr.*, 1930, **1**, 1–79.

The measurement of muscular tension as a technique for the study of emotional tendencies. *Amer. J. Psychol.*, 1932, **44**, 146–162.

Muscular tension as related to physique and behavior. *Child Development*, 1932, **3**, 200–206.

Level of Muscular Tension as an aspect of personality. *J. genet. Psychol.*, 1946, **35**, 161–171.

ENKE, W. Die Konstitutionstypen im Rorschachschen Experiment. *Z. ges. Neurol. u. Psychiatr.*, 1927, **108**, 645–674.

Experimental-psychologische Studien zur Konstitutionsforschung. *Z. ges. Neurol. u. Psychiatr.*, 1928, **114**, 770–794.

Die Psychomotorik der Konstitutionstypen. *Z. angew. Psychol.*, 1930, **36**, 237–287.

Die Persönlichkeitsradikale, ihre soziologische und erbbiologische Bedeutung. *Arch. Psychiat.*, 1934, **102**, 314–336.

EYSENCK, H. J. Suggestibility and hysteria. *J. Neurol. and Psychiat.*, 1943, **6**, 22–31.

Dimensions of Personality. London: Kegan Paul, 1947.

Cyclothymia and Schizothymia as a Dimension of Personality. I. Historical Review. *J. Pers.*, 1950, **19**, 123–152.

The Scientific Study of Personality. London: Routledge & Kegan Paul, 1952.

EYSENCK, H. J., GRANGER, G. W., and BRENGELMANN, J. C. Perceptual processes and mental illness. *Maudsley Monogr. No. 2*, Instit. Psychiat. London: Chapman & Hall, 1957.

EYSENCK, H. J., and FURNEAUX, W. D. Primary and secondary suggestibility. An experimental and statistical study. *J. exp. Psychol.*, 1945, **35**, 485–503.

FINK, P. R. Negative evidence concerning the generality of rigidity. *J. abnorm. Psychol.*, 1958, **57**, 252–254.

FLUGEL, J. C. Practice, fatigue and oscillation. *Brit. J. Psychol. Monogr. Suppl.*, 1929, **7**, 13.

Recent studies in oscillation. *Indian J. Psychol.*, 1934, **1**.

FOSTER, W. S. On the perseverative tendency. *Amer. J. Psychol.*, 1914, **25**, 393–426.

FRENKEL-BRUNSWIK, E. Intolerance of ambiguity as an emotional and perceptual variable. *J. Pers.*, 1949, **18**, 108–143.

FRISCHEISEN-KÖHLER, I. The personal tempo and its inheritance. *Char. and Pers.*, 1933, **1**, 301–313.

FRUCHTER, B. The nature of verbal fluency. *Educ. Psychol. Measmt.*, 1948, **8**, 33–47.

FURNEAUX, W. D. The prediction of susceptibility to hypnosis. *J. Pers.*, 1946, **14**, 281–294.

GARDINER, T. V. The relation of certain personality variables to level of aspiration. *J. Psychol.*, 1940, **9**, 191–206.

GEWIRTZ, J. L. Studies in word fluency. I. Its relation to vocabulary and mental age in young children. *J. genet. Psychol.*, 1948, **72**, 165–176.

GOULD, R. An experimental analysis of "Level of Aspiration". *Genet. Psychol. Mon.*, 1939, **21**, 3–115.

GRAY, S. W. The relation of individual variability to intelligence. *Psychol. Bull.*, 1942, **39**, 579.

HAMMETT, F. S. Observations on the relation between emotional and metabolic stability. *Amer. J. Physiol.*, 1921, **53**, 307–311.

HARGREAVES, H. L. The "faculty" of imagination. *Brit. J. Psychol.*, *Monog. Suppl.*, 1927, **10**, 74.

HARRISON, R., and DORCUS, R. M. Is rate of voluntary bodily movement unitary? *J. genet. Psychol.*, 1939, **18**, 31–39.

HARRISON, R. Personal Tempo and the interrelationships of voluntary and maximal rates of movement. *J. genet. Psychol.*, 1941, **24**, 343–379.

HEATHER, L. B. Factors producing generality in the level of aspiration. *J. exp. Psychol.*, 1942, **30**, 392–406.

HERBERG, L. J. Eye-movements in relation to the EEG alpha rhythm, speed of work and intelligence score. *J. nat. Inst., Personnel Res.*, 1958, **7**, 98–103.

HERRINGTON, A. In: McNemar, Q., and Merrill, M. A. *Studies in Personality*. New York: McGraw-Hill, 1942.

HEYMANS, G., and BRUGMANS, H. Intelligentz Prüfungen mit Studierenden. *Ztschr. f. angew. Psychol.*, 1913, **7**, 317–331.

HOFSTAETTER, P. R., O'CONNOR, N., and SUZIEDELIS, A. Sequences of restricted associative responses and their personality correlates. *J. genet. Psychol.*, 1957, **57**, 219–228.

HOLLINGWORTH, H. L. Correlations of achievement within an individual. *J. exp. Psychol.*, 1925, **8**, 190–208.

HOLZINGER, K. J. Preliminary Report on Spearman-Holzinger Unitary Trait Study. No. 1. Raw Correlations, Reliabilities, Means, and Standard Deviations for 78 Variables, using a Sample of 118 Cases. Chicago: Stat. Lab., Dep. Educ., Univ. Chicago, 1934.

Preliminary Report on Spearman-Holzinger Unitary Trait Study. No. 2. Intercorrelations from Reasoning Tests, Correlations with "g" means, and Standard Deviations for Boys and Girls, Preliminary Analysis of Speed and Verbal Tests, using Thorpe Data, 118 Cases. Chicago: Stat. Lab., Dep. Educ., Univ. Chicago, 1934.

Preliminary Report on Spearman-Holzinger Unitary Trait Study. No. 3. Raw Correlations, Correlations corrected for Age, Reliabilities, Means, and Standard Deviations for Mooseheart Sample of 100 Cases. Comparison of Thorpe and Mooseheart Reliabilities, Age Correlations, with Basic Tetrads for Correlations with "g". Chicago: Stat. Lab., Dep. Educ., Univ. Chicago, 1935.

Preliminary Report on Spearman-Holzinger Unitary Trait Study. No. 4. Factor Patterns and Residual Correlations for Thorpe and Mooseheart Data. Chicago: Stat. Lab., Dep. Educ., Univ. Chicago, 1935.

Preliminary Report on Spearman-Holzinger Unitary Trait Study. No. 5. Introduction to Bi-factor Theory: Solid and Hollow Staircase Patterns for Sets of Data from Mooseheart. Chicago: Stat. Lab., Dep. Educ., Univ. Chicago, 1935.

Preliminary Report on Spearman-Holzinger Unitary Trait Study. No. 6. Chicago: Stat. Lab., Dep. Educ., Univ. Chicago, 1935.

VAN DER HORST, L. Constitutietypen bij Geesteszieken en Gezonden. Zutphen (Holland). *Nauta u. Comp.*, 1924.

Experimentell-psychologische Untersuchungen bei männlichen und weiblichen Mittelschülern. *Z. angew. Psychol.*, 1916, **11**, 441–486.

HOWARD, C. *Perseveration*. Unpublished Thesis. Referred to by Walker, G. V., 1944.

HOWELLS, T. H. An experimental study of persistence. *J. abnorm. soc. Psychol.*, 1933, **28**, 14–29.

HSÜ, E. H. The Rorschach responses and factor analysis. *J. genet. Psychol.*, 1947, **37**, 129–138.

HUGHES, R. A factor analysis of Rorschach diagnostic signs. *J. genet. Psychol.*, 1950, **43**, 83–103.

HUNT, J. McV. Psychological experiments with disordered persons. *Psychol. Bull.*, 1936, **33**, 1–58.

INGHAM, J. C. Body-sway suggestibility and neurosis. *J. ment. Sci.*, 1954, **100**, 432–441.

Psychoneurosis and suggestibility. *J. abnorm. soc. Psychol.*, 1955, **51**, 600–603.

JASPER, H. N. Is perseveration a functional unit participating in all behavior processes? *J. soc. Psychol.*, 1931, **2**, 28–52.

JOHNSON, D. M., and REYNOLDS, F. A factor analysis of verbal ability. *Psychol. Rec.*, 1941, **4**, 183–195.

KENNY, P. T., and GINSBERG, R. The specificity of intolerance of ambiguity measures. *J. abnorm. soc. Psychol.*, 1958, **56**, 300–304.

KIBLER, M. Experimentalpsychologischer Beitrag zur Typenforschung. *Z. ges. Neurol. u. Psychiatr.*, 1925, **98**, 525–544.

KLEEMEIER, R. W., and DUDEK, F. J. A factorial investigation of flexibility. *Educ. Psychol. Measmt.*, 1950, **10**, 107–118.

KREMER, A. H. The nature of persistence. *Stud. Psychol. and Psychiat.*, 1942, **5**, 40.

KRETSCHMER, E. *Körperbau und Charakter*. Berlin: Springer, 1948.

KRETSCHMER, E., and ENKE, W. *Die Persönlichkeit der Athletiker*. Leipzig: Thieme, 1936.

LANKES, W. Perseveration. *Brit. J. Psychol.*, 1951, **7**, 387–419.

LEWIN, K., DEMBO, T., FESTINGER, L., and SEARS, R. S. *Level of Aspiration*. In: *Personality and the Behavior Disorders*. (Ed. Hunt, J. McV.) New York: Ronald Press, 1944.

LUCHINS, A. S. *An Examination for Rigidity of Behavior*. Copyright by Luchins, 1948.

On recent usages of the Einstellung-effect as a test of rigidity. *J. consult. Psychol.*, 1951, **15**, 89–94.

MACARTHUR, R. S. An experimental investigation of persistence in secondary school boys. *Canad. J. Psychol.*, 1955, **9**, 47–54.

MADIGAN, M. E. A study of oscillation as a unitary trait. *J. exp. Educ.*, 1938, **6**, 332–339.

MÜLLER, G. E., and PILZECKER, M. Die Perseverationstendenzen der Vorstellungen. *Ztsch. f. Psychol.*, 1900.

MUNDY-CASTLE, A. C. The electroencephalogram in relation to temperament. *Acta Psychol.*, 1955, **11**, 397–411.

NEISSER, C. 65 Sitzung des Vereins Ostdeutscher Irren Artzte. *Allg. Ztsch. f. Psych.*, 1894, **51**.

Perseveration and fluency. *Brit. J. Psychol.*, 1943, **33**, 200–208.

OLIVER, J. A., and FERGUSON, G. A. A factorial study of tests of rigidity. *Canad. J. Psychol.*, 1951, **5**, 49–59.

PAYNE, R. W. *An investigation into the possibility of defining "Dissociation" as a personality trait by means of objective tests*. Ph.D. Thesis, Univ. Lond. Lib., 1954.

Experimentelle Untersuchung zum Spaltungsbegriff von Kretschmer. *Zeitschr. f. Experiment. u. angew. Psychol.*, 1955, **3**, 65–97.

PHILIP, B. R. An elementary linkage analysis of perceptual rigidity. *Canad. J. Psychol.*, 1958, **12**, 115–120.

PINARD, J. W. Tests of Perseveration: I. Their Relation to Character. *Brit. J. Psychol.*, 1932, **23**, 5–19.

PITCHER, B., and STACEY, C. L. Is Einstellung rigidity a general trait? *J. abnorm. soc. Psychol.*, 1954, **49**, 3–6.

RANGACHAR, C. Differences in perseveration among Jewish and English boys. *Brit. J. educ. Psychol.*, 1932, **2**, 199–211.

RETHLINGSHAFER, D. The relationship of tests of persistence to other measures of continuance of activities. *J. abnorm. soc. Psychol.*, 1942, **37**, 71–82.

RIM, Y. Perseveration and fluency as measures of introversion-extraversion in abnormal subjects. *J. Pers.*, 1954, **23**, 324–334.

RIMOLDI, H. J. A. Personal tempo. *J. abnorm. soc. Psychol.*, 1951, **46**, 283–303.

ROGERS, C. A. *A factorial study of verbal fluency and related dimensions of personality*. Ph.D. Thesis, Univ. London Lib., 1952,
The orectic relations of mathematically derived fluency scores. *J. gen. Psychol.*, 1956, **55**, 85–102.
The orectic relations of verbal fluency. *Austral. J. Psychol.*, 1956, **8**, No. 1, 27–46.

RYANS, D. G. An experimental attempt to analyse persistent behavior. I. Measuring traits presumed to involve persistence. *J. genet. Psychol.*, 1938, **19**, 333–353.
The meaning of persistence. *J. genet. Psychol.*, 1938, **19**, 79–96.
A study of the observed relationships between persistence test results, intelligence indices, and academic success. *J. educ. Psychol.*, 1938, **29**, 573–580.
The measurement of persistence: an historical review. *Psychol. Bull.*, 1939, **36**, 715–739.
A note on variations in "Persistence" test scores with sex, age, and academic level. *J. soc. Psychol.*, 1939, **10**, 259–264.
"Persistence" test scores of students compared to the nativity of the male parent. *J. genet. Psychol.*, 1939, **54**, 223–227.
A tentative statement of the relation of persistence test scores to certain personality traits as measured by the Bernreuter Inventory. *J. genet. Psychol.*, 1939, **54**, 229–234.

SANDLER, J. *An experimental investigation into some factors entering into the Rorschach test*. Ph.D. Thesis. London: Univ. London Lib., 1949.

SANDLER, J., and ACKNER, B. Rorschach content analysis: an experimental investigation. *Brit. J. med. Psychol.*, 1951, **24**, 180–201.

SCHEIER, I. H. An evaluation of rigidity factors. *Canad. J. Psychol.*, 1954, **8**, 157–163.

SCHEIER, I. H., and FERGUSON, G. A. Further factorial studies of tests of rigidity. *Canad. J. Psychol.*, 1952, **6**, 18–30.

SEN, A. A statistical study of the Rorschach test. *Brit. J. Psychol.*, Stat. Sect., 1950, **3**, 21–39.

SHEVACH, B. J. Studies in perseveration: I. A survey of researches in perseveration. *J. Psychol.*, 1937, **3**, 223–230.

SPEARMAN, C. *The Abilities of Man*. London: Macmillan, 1927.

STEPHENSON, W. Studies in experimental psychiatry. II. Some contact of p-factor with psychiatry. *J. ment. Sci.*, 1932, **78**, 318–330.

STUKÁT, K. G., *Suggestibility: a factorial and experimental analysis*. Stockholm: Almquist & Wickerell, 1958.

TAYLOR, C. W. A factorial study of fluency in writing. *Psychomet.*, 1947, **12**, 239–262.

THORNTON, G. R. A factor analysis of tests designed to measure persistence. *Psychol. Monogr.*, 1939, **51**, 1–42.

THURSTONE, L. L. *A factorial study of perception.* Chicago: Univ. Chicago Press, 1944.

Primary Mental Abilities. Chicago: Univ. Chicago Press, 1938.

VERNON, P. E. *The Structure of Human Abilities.* London: Methuen, 1950.

WALKER, K. F., STAINES, R. G., and KENNA, J. C. P-tests and the concept of mental inertia. *Charact. & Pers.*, 1943, **12**, 32–45.

WALTON, R. D. The relation between the amplitude of oscillations in short-period efficiency and steadiness of character. *Brit. J. Psychol.*, 1936, **27**, 181–188.

Individual differences in amplitude of oscillation and their connection with steadiness of character. *Brit. J. Psychol.*, 1939, **30**, 36–46.

WARREN, H. C. *Dictionary of Psychology.* Boston: Houghton Mifflin, 1934.

WEBER, C. O. Function, fluctuations and personality trends of normal subjects. *Amer. J. Psychol.*, 1938, **51**, 702–708.

WEISGERBER, C. A. Conscious perseveration and the persistence of autonomic activity as measured by recovery from the psychogalvanic response. *J. genet. Psychol.*, 1951, **43**, 83–93.

The relationship of perseveration to a number of personality traits and to adjustment. *J. genet. Psychol.*, 1954, **50**, 3–13.

Factor analysis of a questionnaire test of perseveration. *J. genet. Psychol.*, 1955, **53**, 341–345.

WENGER, M. A. An attempt to appraise individual differences in level of muscular tension. *J. exp. Psychol.*, 1943, **32**, 213–225.

WIERSMA, H. Die Sekundärfunktion bei Psychosen. *Z. f. Psychol. u. Neurol.*, 1906, **8**, 1–24.

WITTENBORN, J. R. A factor analysis of Rorschach scoring categories. *J. consult. Psychol.*, 1950, **14**, 261–267.

WYNN-JONES, L. Individual differences in mental inertia. *J. Nat. Inst. Ind. Psychol.*, 1929, **4**, 282–290.

THE ANALYSIS OF RATINGS

THE PRECURSOR OF the large number of factorial rating studies which have been carried out in the last fifty years is a *Massenuntersuchung* carried out by two Dutch psychologists, G. Heymans and E. Wiersma (1909). This study differs somewhat from most of those which succeeded it in two ways. In the first place, it was based on a definite hypothesis; in the second place, it used statistical methods which, while they resemble factor analysis in their import, were yet rather simpler and more easily understood by the non-mathematical.

Both the hypothesis to be investigated and the method used are clearly brought out in what is essentially a preliminary paper separate from the main work. In this paper, Heymans (1908) analysed biographical material derived from 110 historical persons about whom a great deal was known. These persons were rated on a large number of traits which were considered to be interrelated in such a way as to give rise to three main factors, dimensions, or principles. These three principles are, first of all, *emotionality*, or emotional instability, secondly, *activity*, or general drive, and, thirdly, what we would now call a bipolar factor opposing dominance of the *primary function* to dominance of the *secondary function*.

This scheme was later on applied by Heymans and Wiersma (1906a, 1906b, 1907, 1908a, 1908b, 1909) to a rating study in which 3,000 doctors in the Netherlands were asked each to pick one family and rate each member of it by a simple method of underlining or double-underlining of a large number of traits. Four hundred doctors responded and sent in material on altogether 2,523 individuals. Most of the papers analysing this material are concerned with the interpretation of intra-familial similarities in terms of hereditary hypotheses; as such an interpretation is clearly arbitrary, and as in any case it is not germane to our own subject, nothing will be said here about it. It is in the last paper that we find a detailed analysis and justification for the threefold classificatory system adopted by the authors.

It is clear that if we consider each person to be either above or below the average with respect to each of the three factors, then there are eight possible combinations which might be considered to create separate types. This general scheme is shown in Table 10, together with a number of cases which were found by the authors to fall into each of the eight types.[1]

TABLE 10

	1 *Emotionality:*	2 *Activity:*	3 *P- or S-Function*	*Type:*	*N:*
1	−	−	P	Amorphous	98
2	−	−	S	Apathetic	94
3	+	−	P	Nervous	174
4	+	−	S	Sentimental	113
5	−	+	P	Sanguine	95
6	−	+	S	Phlegmatic	439
7	+	+	P	Choleric	257
8	+	+	S	Passionate	597
	Impossible to Classify :				656
	Total:				2,523

TABLE 11

Heymans and Wiersma	Ribot	Malapert	Queyrat	Martiny	Jung
Apathetic	Humble	Tempered	Equilibrated	Plastic	Sensitive introvert
Amorphous	Apathetic	Amorphous	Amorphous	Gregarious	Intuitive introvert
Phlegmatic	Active apathetic	Apathetic	Apathetic	Materialistic	Intuitive extravert
Sanguine	Active	Sensitive	Emotional	Primitive	Sensitive extravert
Passionate	Alive	Passionate	Passionate	Practical	Thinking extravert
Choleric	Calculating	Voluntary	Spontaneous	Social	Feeling extravert
Sentimental	Emotional	Affective	Sentimental	Aesthetic	Feeling introvert
Nervous	Contemplative	Calculating	Intellectual	Speculative	Thinking introvert

It may be helpful to quote the actual descriptions of the traits on the basis of which subjects were assigned a plus or a minus for the various factors. The score on the first factor was based entirely on the rater's answer to a single question regarding the emotional in-

[1] This eight-type scheme links up with the French rather than with the German and Austrian typologists. Table 11 shows its correspondence with the work of Ribot (1892), Malapert (1897), Queyrat (1896), and Martiny (1948). As the last-mentioned points out, it has certain affinities also to Jung's model when the four "functions"—sensation, intuition, thinking, feeling—are combined with the extravert-introvert dichotomy.

stability of the subject under investigation. The score on the second factor was, in fact, the average of the rater's endorsement of three traits; namely, (1) "Is always active in office, job, school, or household"; (2) "Usually busy in his spare time"; (3) "Usually attacks duties immediately and without delay". The subject's standing on the third factor was decided on the basis of the average of ten traits: (1) "Is quickly comforted"; (2) "Is easily reconciled"; (3) "Changeable in his likes"; (4) "Interested in new impressions and friends"; (5) "Easily talked around"; (6) "Desirous of change"; (7) "Easily changes job or subject of study"; (8) "Often busy with magnificent plans which come to nothing"; (9) "His actions are mainly determined by consideration of immediate results"; (10) "Often acts contrary to his own principles".

It should be noted that these three factors do not appear to be independent of each other. In Table 12, which gives percentages of cases showing various combinations of factors, it will be seen that emotionality and activity are relatively independent, but that strength of primary function is correlated with emotionality and lack of activity, whereas strength of secondary function is correlated with lack of emotionality and activity. (Note the bearing of these results on Jordan's hypotheses.)

TABLE 12

	A +	A −	
E +	75%	25%	$r_{tet} = + 0.020$
E −	74%	26%	
	P	**S**	
E +	38%	62%	$r_{tet} = - 0.205$
E −	27%	73%	
	P	**S**	
A +	25%	75%	$r_{tet} = - 0.500$
A −	57%	43%	

N = 1,867

The next step in the analysis consists of a detailed tabulation of percentage ratings of each of the whole list of traits submitted to the raters for members of the eight "type" groups. This shows which of these new traits belongs with each of the sets of traits on which the original choice of "type" was made, and while a correlational analysis would have been simpler and more straightforward, the method used is quite adequate for its avowed purpose. Thus, three larger sets of traits, sharing a certain type of "belongingness", are built up from the original hypothetical clusters.

These new and enlarged descriptions of the hypothetical factors will not be given in detail; they illustrate all too clearly that even without the aid of factor analysis, it was possible for psychologists to group together sets of adjectives, the psychological connections between which are very far from being apparent. Thus, while it may seem reasonable for the active person to be fond of movement, practical, self-reliant, abstemious, and courageous, it is not quite clear why he should be miserly, punctual, a collector of things, and patriotic and radical at the same time! [1]

Although the cluster of traits grouped around the "activity" factor does not therefore appear to have very much consistency, the same cannot be said of the other two factors, which we will find recurring again and again throughout this book. Without forcing their interpretation too much, we may say that *emotionality* resembles closely the factor of emotional instability, immaturity, or neuroticism, so frequently encountered, while *primary* and *secondary function* denote extraversion and introversion respectively. To illustrate this correspondence we may set down some of the traits found by Heymans and Wiersma to be characteristic of persons in whom the primary or the secondary function predominated. Those with predominantly primary function are impulsive, give up easily, are always on the move, jocose, superficial, vain, demonstrative, tending to exaggerate, given to public speaking, to telling jokes, and to laughing a lot. On the other hand, the person with predominant secondary function is quiet, persistent, grave, shut-in, reliable, given to introspective thinking, laughs little, has depressive tendencies, and is not given to indulge in the pleasures of the body.

---

[1] We do not intend to suggest that "activity" is not a useful descriptive variable in the psychology of personality; indeed, we will encounter it again in Guilford's factorial studies of inventory responses. We merely doubt whether the term can usefully be extended as widely as Heymans and Wiersma have done; in our view, this factor is located at the trait level, whereas "emotionality" and "primary" and "secondary" function are located at the type level. More will be said later about the difficulties of keeping these levels apart and the dangers resulting from mixing them up.

If our identification of these two factors is correct, we should expect that the emotional person, with predominant primary function (i.e. the *nervous* type of Heymans and Wiersma), would show the characteristics of the neurotic extravert, which if carried to an extreme would result in the diagnosis of hysteria, whereas the emotional person with predominant secondary function (the *sentimental* type) would resemble the neurotic introvert, or in its extreme manifestation the person suffering from anxiety and reactive depression, i.e. the dysthymic. We may quote, in somewhat free translation, the picture given by Heymans of those two types, the "nervous" and the "sentimental" respectively, and leave it to the reader to decide whether this identification is justified.

"The person of the nervous type is characterized by marked emotional instability, a small degree of activity, and an overwhelming strength of primary function, and is accordingly little inclined to regular work, has little persistence, and no tendency to get absorbed in his work. He is characterized by a high degree of sensitivity, emotional reactivity, and rapid change of mood. Such a person is characterized by inner contradictions and conflict between thought and action. He lacks self-sufficiency and fails to take a definite stand on matters of attitude. He is shy and there is a marked lack of inhibition. Among his primary interests, the most obvious is the erotic. Abstract virtues like punctuality, abstemiousness, honesty, reliability, and love of truth are largely absent in a person of this type. He shows a tendency to play a rôle; to pretend to be other than he is. The nervous person is lacking in judgment, practical sense, and suffers from an undevelopment of mathematical and systematic tendencies. Other characteristics are a tendency towards symbolism and a tendency to frequent change of address. The relatives of a nervous person frequently show neurasthenic or hysterical symptoms or are led by their uninhibited proclivities to commit crimes of one kind or another.

"Quite a different picture is presented by the 'sentimental' person. Of course, we find here again primarily those qualities which we have already found in the nervous person as characteristic of emotionality and lack of activity. Nevertheless, there are also considerable differences which throughout point to the inhibiting and regulating influence of the secondary function, which robs the passing moment of its omnipotence. Instead, we find those emotions which depend not so much on the passing emotion of the moment but on the after-effects of previous experiences, such as shyness, depression, and con-

9

stant irritation. As in the field of emotion, so in the field of action: mobility as well as the tendency to regular work are at a minimum, but persistence, the tendency to get absorbed in one's work, may be above average. Instead of the frivolity and exaggerated openness of the 'nervous' person, we find in the sentimental person seriousness and reticence. The seriousness can also be found in many other manifestations: in the frequency with which abstract virtues, like conscientiousness, honesty, and reliability are found; in the strength of his tendency towards idealism, in the frequent appearance of specific religious or ethical ideals, in his lack of tolerance, in the rareness of his laughter, and the lack of attention he pays to social intercourse. The sentimental person is given to self-analysis and speculation; he likes music, while his interest for the real world is far below the average. When translated into abnormal behaviour, this person is characterized in the main by melancholy or paranoia."

Little need be said in criticism of the work of Heymans and Wiersma. Such faults as are implicit in their methodology have characterized most of the work of their successors; we will return to them at the end of the chapter. The particular concepts advocated by them have been relatively neglected by later investigators; occasional echoes can be found in the studies carried out by Biesheuvel in South Africa, and one or two papers directly relevant to this system will be reviewed later. In the main, however, their influence has been indirect rather than direct, and we would agree with Webb's (1915) judgment of their contribution. "The work of these investigators has broken new ground in some important particulars. Their large range of questions aimed at a fairly complete diagnosis of each individual personality, and it was an advance in method to collect large masses of data, from judges working independently, in such a way as to afford conclusions by means of statistical methods. They modestly conclude a report of their work with the remark: 'Mais ces recherches ne sont qu'une première ébauche, pour laquelle la postérité n'aura certes qu'un sourire compatissant'; but we may hope that posterity, having smiled, will be able to build much useful work upon the foundations they have laid."

Far more influential than any other single piece of research on the organization of personality has been the work of Edward Webb (1915), who was the first to use the method of factor analysis in the non-intellectual field, and while the statistics which he used are far from adequate by modern standards, they are definitely superior to those used by Heymans and Wiersma. From several points of view,

Webb's research, which was carried on under the guidance of Spearman himself, is methodologically superior to many that have followed in later years. This judgment is supported by the fact that his table of intercorrelations has been subjected to analysis by more powerful modern methods by a variety of later students. Some of these re-analyses will be described in detail later, as they are essential to a complete understanding of Webb's contribution.

The subjects of his enquiry were two groups of 98 and 96 students respectively, and four groups of schoolboys of an average age of 12, numbering 140 in all. Assessments were made by at least two judges, working as independently of each other as possible. These judges were in a position to make observations of their subjects under conditions relatively free from restraint. The subjects were made available for observation under a wide range of environmental conditions —in the lecture-room, common-room, the social gathering, the playing-field, at home, during holidays, etc. Subjects throughout were unaware that assessments were being made concerning them. Ratings were carried out by fellow students of the subjects in the two experimental student groups, and by two class masters in the case of the children. Thirty-nine traits were rated in the case of the students and 25 in the case of the schoolboys, grouped under the headings of "Emotions", "Self-qualities", "Sociability", "Activity", and "Intellect". Tests of intelligence were also administered and estimates of physique and records of examination ability obtained.

Reliability of the ratings varied between ·5 and ·7 on the average, with one or two occasional values dropping below the former or rising above the latter. Average reliability of ratings retained for the calculations was ·55, and product moment correlations were calculated between the averaged ratings. In addition to the raw correlations between all the traits, tables in which the correlations were corrected for attenuation are also presented.

Using Spearman's well-known method of inter-columnar correlations and tetrad differences, Webb proceeded to extract a general factor of intelligence, based primarily on the tests administered to the subjects, but which correlated quite highly also with ratings on such items as quickness of apprehension, profoundness of apprehension, originality of ideas, and power of getting through mental work rapidly. These correlations range from ·5 to ·6; there is also a correlation of ·67 between intelligence tests and examination ability. These data which Webb considers as supporting Spearman's theory of "g" are of no great interest, although the correlation between ratings and test results may perhaps be considered evidence of validity of the ratings. Webb goes on, however, to show that the correlations cannot be accounted for entirely in terms of this general factor, and shows that a second factor, independent of intelligence, can be extracted from the intercorrelations of the data. He is therefore led to put forward the hypothesis "that a second factor, of wide generality, exists; and that this factor is prominent on the 'character' side of mental activity (as distinguished from the purely intellective side)". This factor he considers to be in some close relation to "persistence of motives". He goes on to say "this conception may be understood to mean *consistency of action resulting from deliberate volition or will.* For convenience, we will in future represent the general factor by the symbol '*w*' ".

The traits which characterize the person possessing a high degree of "*w*" are: tendency not to abandon tasks from mere changeability; tendency not to abandon task in face of obstacles; kindness on principle; trustworthiness; conscientiousness, and perseverance in face of obstacles.

This "*w*", or will factor, appears in many ways to be the opposite of Heymans and Wiersma's *emotionality*. In part it may perhaps represent a halo effect in the sense that it has often been shown that judges tend to group favourable qualities together because of their general like or dislike of the subject under investigation (Flemming, 1942). We will find ample evidence later, however, that this factor cannot be explained away entirely in terms of errors of rating, and there is no doubt that Webb in this study has made a significant contribution to the development of psychology. In many ways, his study is typical of what has become known at the London school; as P. Mabille (1951) puts it: "La caractéristique de l'école anglaise moderne semble bien être d'équilibrer harmonieusement les conceptions théoriques et les points de vue experimentaux, les nécessités cliniques et les exigences scientifiques de la statistique".

The first re-analysis of Webb's material, and the only one to make a genuine contribution to its understanding, was carried out by Garnett in 1918. His paper, which in its statistical development anticipates much of what was to become important later, such as the geometrical representation of patterns of correlations in terms of scalar products and the rotation of factor axes, used these methods to show that in addition to "*g*" and "*w*" another factor was contained in Webb's table of intercorrelations. This he called "*c*", because he conceived of this factor as being characterized by the trait of *clever-*

ness; seldom can brilliant mathematical treatment have resulted in a less appropriate naming of the factor discovered!

This will become apparent when we study the traits characteristic of "*c*" in both its positive and its negative aspects. On the positive side we have traits like cheerfulness, æsthetic feeling, sense of humour, desire to excel, desire to impose one's will, desire to be liked by one's associates, impulsive kindness, wideness of influence, and quickness of apprehension; on the negative side we have liability to extreme depression, unsociableness, lack of corporate spirit, tactlessness, little bodily activity, and pure-mindedness. This factor in many ways resembles the *primary* and *secondary function* of Heymans and Wiersma, or Jung's extraversion-introversion, and thus brings into fair agreement the results obtained by all the investigators mentioned so far.

Another re-analysis of Webb's data has been carried out by McCloy (1936), using the multiple-factor technique. He also carried out an independent factorial study of 43 traits on 31 students. The reliability of his ratings is claimed to be high. The first factor found in his own work is very similar to the first factor found in his re-analysis of Webb's data, and is closely related to "*w*". In his study, it is made up of the following traits: trustworthiness, vitality, thoroughness, sociability, respectful of rights of others, resourcefulness, courage, personality, perseverance, loyalty, leadership, integrity, and character. (The influence of the halo effect seems to be much more strongly in evidence here than in Webb's study.) The second factor in McCloy's study vaguely resembles the *c+* traits of Garnett's analysis, being characterized by aggressiveness, initiative, self-confidence, adaptiveness, conviction, enthusiasm, energy, and lack of modesty.

Reyburn and Taylor (1939) also re-analysed Webb's data, using only 19 traits from Webb's student sample. They extracted four factors, of which, however, only the first two ("*w*" and "*c*") are very meaningful. "*w*" in their analysis is characterized on its positive side by a tendency not to abandon a task in the face of obstacles, or for mere changeability, trustworthiness, conscientiousness, and tendency to do kindness on principle. Absence of "*w*" is characterized by the absence of these traits as well as by a readiness to become angry, an occasional liability to extreme anger, and the lack of permanence of mood, i.e. by qualities to which Heymans and Wiersma would apply the term "emotionality". In its positive aspects, "*c*" is characterized by sense of humour, fondness for large social gatherings, a general tendency to be cheerful, a high degree of corporate spirit, and a high degree of bodily activity and pursuit of pleasure.

In its negative aspects, "*c*" is characterized by occasional liability to extreme depression and conscientiousness. This analysis is probably the best that has been carried out on Webb's data and, interestingly enough, it shows the closest similarity to the Heymans and Wiersma data, as well as to a great deal of work reported elsewhere in this book.

Another research must be mentioned here, as it was carried out at about the same time as Webb's. Unfortunately, the report of this study, which was carried out by Burt (1915), is far too short and incomplete to make any judgment of its value possible. It appears that 172 children from 9–12, as well as another group of 329 adults and children (which may or may not have included the original group), formed part of this investigation. They were rated on 11 traits, which were adapted from McDougall's list of primary emotions. The author claims that the data give rise to a factor of general emotionality, which presumably would be similar to Heyman's and Wiersma's factor of the same name, but it is impossible to place much reliance on this interpretation, as it is not clear whether age was held constant in the children's group, whether I.Q. was properly taken into account, and as the method of carrying out the ratings is not described in sufficient detail.

Burt has returned to a discussion of his system in a recent popular account (1939) in which he deals with the relation between this factor of emotionality, which he labels "*e*", and Webb's "*w*". He says : "So far as they overlap, my factor is the negative of his. Anything making for emotional instability must, *ipso facto*, hinder the steadiness or persistence of moral motives." Similarly, Gibb (1942) concludes from an examination of the evidence that "the major difference between '*w*' and '*e*' may be summed up by saying that '*e*' is the inverse of '*w*'. The former is emotional instability, the latter is stability or persistence."

Another study by the same writer (Burt, 1937) is of great statistical interest as it reports a comparison of the results of factor analysis by correlating persons and correlating traits. Eleven problem children were rated on 11 traits, again derived from McDougall's list of instincts : anger, assertiveness, sociability, curiosity, joy, sex, disgust, tenderness, sorrow, fear, and submissiveness, and correlations run between traits and also between persons. Three factors were extracted, the first of which was called *general emotionality*, the second appeared to be a bipolar factor opposing the aggressive to the inhibited emotions, and the third another bipolar factor opposing the pleasurable to the unpleasurable emotions. While these results would fit in quite well with the data we have analysed so far, it is difficult to accept them as they stand. The children were extremely highly selected from a larger group of 124 children, who themselves were selected from a still larger one of 500. We do not know what influence this high degree of selectivity may have had, nor do we know anything about the adequacy of the ratings which, in view of the somewhat outmoded list of traits presented to the raters, cannot be accepted without a certain degree of doubt. But one's major reservation must be with respect to the statistical treatment. It is clearly impossible, in view of the very high standard of errors of correlations based on 11 cases, to extract more than one statistically significant factor. Burt has tried to avoid this difficulty by taking his estimate of the probable error from the total group of 124 cases of which the 11 children analysed were claimed to be a representative sample. It is also claimed that inter-correlations for the total group of 124 children were similar to those of the 11. However, correlations for the larger group are not given, and it is impossible to evaluate this claim. Even if it were justified, however, it would clearly be inadmissible to base standard errors for the group analysed on the number of cases in a group not being analysed. It would clearly have been much more satisfactory to have given the straightforward analysis of the total group of 124 children, and the results given in this article must be regarded in the main as an illustration of a statistical method rather than as a contribution to the analysis of temperament.

Much the same must be said of Burt's report on "A Distribution of Temperamental Types" in his book *The Factors of the Mind* (1940). Here, again, the actual figures given refer to a group of 12 persons only. He extracts two factors, the first one identified as "general emotionality" or "emotional instability", the second marking the difference between the sthenic, aggressive, unrepressed, or extra-verted type, and the asthenic, inhibited, repressed, or introverted type. Burt, after giving the detailed figures, goes on to say: "It is interesting to note that in their concrete nature, the several factors obtained from the small group of adults tally with those of the larger group of children", and gives as a reference the article we have discussed above.[1]

[1] It is not quite clear how we can reconcile this reference to a *larger* group of children with the fact that the analysis was carried out only on a small sample of 11 children, i.e. one less than the small sample of 12 adults; presumably, Burt is referring here to the total group of 124 children, of whom the 11 are only a sample, but of course this larger group was only referred to in his paper and no actual figures regarding it are given.

Quite recently, Burt (1948) has published two tables of correlations dealing respectively with 328 neurotic or unstable children, and with 483 normal children. These children, the majority of whom were between 9 and 13 years of age, were rated again for a number of McDougall's "primary emotions", that of "comfort" apparently being added to the 11 mentioned above. These ratings were carried out in the main by teachers, although the exact procedure is not described. The results from this study appear to be in agreement with Burt's earlier conclusions; a first factor of general emotionality, or instability, is followed by a bipolar factor dividing the emotions into a "sthenic" (or demonstrative) group and an "asthenic" (or inhibited) group. A third factor, also adumbrated in previous researches, divides the emotions into those accompanied by pleasurable and unpleasurable feeling tone respectively. These are the results from the normal group; those from the neurotic group are claimed to be roughly similar but certain interesting differences appear. The instability factor only accounts for just over half as much of the total variance in the neurotic group, compared with the normal, and the relative size of the factor saturations shows a different order altogether. Burt suggests that: "These features could readily be accounted for as the effects of selection. Elsewhere I have shown that the most conspicuous feature distinguishing the psycho-neurotic child from the normal is his increased emotional instability. Evidently, therefore, in selecting psycho-neurotic cases we have been taking cases from the upper end of the scale of general emotionality. The effect of this must be to curtail the range of variation for the general factor; hence the factor coefficients are automatically diminished." This argument possesses a certain superficial plausibility as far as the change in percentage of variance accounted for is concerned, although it has usually been found that correlations increase rather than decrease when taken on neurotic as compared with normal samples. However, no recourse can be had to selection in explaining the failure of the factor saturations for the two samples to correlate significantly with each other, and it is difficult to see how Burt can identify two factors with each other when the correlation between these two factors is not significantly different from zero.[1]

His previous third factor, which distinguished pleasurable from

---

[1] One's faith in Burt's correct identification of his factors must be considerably diminished by his failure to take into account such obvious discrepancies. The trait having the highest saturation for one group actually has the lowest saturation for the other; yet Burt considers the two factors identical!

unpleasurable emotions, does not appear at all in this table in a statistically significant form. The extravert-introvert factor does appear again rather more strongly than before. Also, a new factor appears amongst neurotic children, to which Burt, however, does not give a name. These differences in analyses carried out on normal and neurotic children are interesting but difficult to interpret in view of lack of information regarding the methods used for obtaining the ratings. The failure of the two analyses to agree at all closely, except with reference to the introvert-extravert factor, must make one rather doubtful about the adequacy of the research design.

The next author whose work has important bearings on our general problem is Cattell (1933, 1934). We will discuss first his early contribution; his later work forms a separate section. Having made a thorough search of the literature, he put together 28 pairs of opposites denoting traits supposedly characteristic of introverts, schizothymes, anal neurotics, and persons suffering from inferiority complexes. He also added others from studies of "w" and "c", as well as an I.Q. test, ending up with 48 items in all. Four judges were used to rate subjects on these traits; reliabilities (2 vs. 2 judges) ranged from ·12 to ·72. His statistical analysis is a complex mixture of cluster analysis and Spearman's method of tetrads, and it may be said to have resulted in a confirmation of the "c" and "w" factors, as well as in his finding of a third factor which he calls "a" and which in his view resembles schizothymia. The traits characteristic of "a" are secretiveness, pessimism, stinginess, subjectiveness, effectlessness, lack of trust, formality, lack of emotionality, and extremism.[1] The "c" factor was renamed by him as a factor of "surgency", and its two aspects therefore received the designation of "surgent" and "desurgent".

Cattell tried to go beyond the field of ratings and link up scores on objective tests of perseveration with "w". We have been concerned in more detail with the measurement of perseveration in a previous chapter, so we may just note here that his work confirmed Pinard's (1932) demonstration of a curvilinear relation between "p" and "w", somewhat as shown in Fig. 14. Other objective tests used by him include tests of fluency; speed of writing, of decision, of walking, and of reading comprehension; oscillation (reversal of perspective); and the psycho-galvanic reflex. Correlations between personality factors and these tests tended to be low, with possible indications that the

[1] These traits resemble the "prepsychotic" factor discussed by Moore and his students; their work is reviewed below.

surgent type tended to be more fluent and to have higher speeds in the speed tests as well as quicker oscillation.

Much later than these early studies of Cattell's, but essentially in the same tradition, is a recent analysis by Howie (1945). This study of ratings of personal qualities on a group of 295 12–14-year-old schoolboys required teachers to make ratings on 10 traits: bodily activity, perseverance, excitability, quickness of intelligence, cheerfulness, mental activity, common sense, continuity of interest, initiative, and self-consciousness. Four factors were extracted by the author from the table of intercorrelations, of which the first one in his view is strongly coloured by the scholastic background in which the ratings took place. The second and third factors he identifies respectively with "w" and "c". The fourth factor, which is perhaps

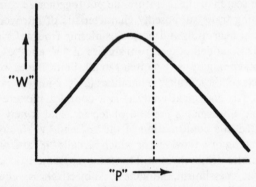

Fig. 14.—Curvilinear Relationship between "p" and "w".

of doubtful significance, contrasts, in Howie's view, excitability and placidity, and may remind the reader of Heyman's and Wiersma's "activity" factor.

Another study of children (50 children, 156 months of age on the average) was carried out in 1929 by Sister McDonough. The children were rated on 34 traits by three teachers with a mean average inter-correlation of ·72. They were also given the Woodworth-Cady questionnaire, which was found to correlate — ·38 with the ratings on stability. This study is noteworthy for its unusual carefulness in the organization of the ratings, although some of the traits rated, such as religiousness, are somewhat unusual and reflect the institutional background of the author. Using Kelley's method of analysis, Sister McDonough extracted four main factors, which were considered to represent *will*, *cheerfulness*, *sociability*, and *sthenic emotionality.* Brogden (1944) re-analysed her data and emerged with four factors, the first two of which were highly correlated however ($r_{12} = \cdot766$). In so far as these two correlated factors do not measure halo effect, they may be considered analogous to Webb's *"w"* factor, being characterized by such traits as reliability, will, self-control, stability, lack of emotionality, and lack of the following qualities: forwardness, quarrelsomeness, conceit, irritability, impulsiveness, expressiveness, and tendency to look for sympathy. The third factor was most highly loaded on intelligence and lack of credulity, and is obviously an intellectual one. The last factor is remarkably similar to Garnett's *"c"*, surgency, or extraversion, being characterized by a tendency to be affectionate, sympathetic, sociable, cheerful, contented, humorous, and lacking in self-consciousness.

One further rating study from the London school ought to be mentioned here, as it forms a transition from the field of normal personality to the abnormal. In this study Sahai (1931) was interested in following up some of the hypotheses originated by Kretschmer, and accordingly had 200 mentally defective boys and 50 students rated on a number of traits which from Kretschmer's writings he considered to be typical of the cycloid character. The traits chosen were: "frank, humorous, grateful, trustful, cyclic emotion, warm-hearted, sociable, and enjoys gifts of life". Coefficients of association were calculated, and were found to be positive as demanded by the hypothesis. The tetrad criterion was satisfied but indifferently; however, the author concludes that the results have established the reality of a trait of "circular mentality" or extraversion. It would probably not be too fanciful to see a good deal of similarity between this pattern of traits and the uninhibited, sthenic, extraverted, *primary function* type. It should be noted that four other traits (suggestible, little tenacity of purpose, takes life easily, self-possessed), which had been hypothesized to form part of this syndrome, were found to give such low intercorrelations that they had to be excluded.

While Sahai's study is interesting in its use of psychiatric concepts, it fell to T. V. Moore (1930, 1933) to carry out for the first time "the empirical determination of certain syndromes underlying præcox and manic-depressive psychoses". Three hundred and sixty-seven patients were rated for the presence or absence of 41 symptoms. Tetrachorics were calculated between these 41 items, and the table analysed by a rather complex and cumbersome procedure. Eight factors in all were isolated; the names given to these, together with the main symptoms identifying them, are given below:

(1) Cognitive defect: reasoning, perception, memory, shut-in personality.
(2) Catatonic: mutism, negativistic, refusal of food, stereotypism of attitudes.
(3) Uninhibited: stereotypism of action; destructive, giggling, talking to voices.
(4) and (5) Manic: irritable, tantrums, destructive, euphoria. (This factor was divided in two by Moore, according to the presence or absence of euphoria.)
(6) Deluded-hallucinations: auditory hallucinations, bizarre delusions, disorientation, stereotypism of words.
(7) Constitutional-hereditary: lack of intelligence, depressed, tearful, previous attacks, insane relatives.
(8) Retarded-depressed: depressed, retarded, neurasthenic, suicidal.

These factors were themselves found to be intercorrelated, giving rise to two "second-order factors", as they would be called nowadays. One of these factors is made up of the catatonic, cognitive defect, uninhibited and deluded-hallucinated syndromes; the other of the retarded-depressed, constitutional-hereditary, and manic components. Presumably, the former second-order factor may be identified with schizophrenia, the latter with circular insanity. However, statistical methods of multiple-factor analysis were not sufficiently advanced in Moore's time to enable one to give much credence to all the details of his results.[1]

Thurstone (1934) re-analysed Moore's data and arrived at a more satisfactory classification. He demonstrated the existence of five factors as follows:

(1) Catatonic: mutism, negativism, shut-in personality, stereotypism of actions, attitudes and words, giggling.
(2) Cognitive: logical fallacies, memory defect, perceptual defect, reasoning, disorientation.
(3) Manic: destructive, excited, irritable, tantrums.
(4) Hallucinatory: bizarre delusions, auditory and other hallucinations, speaking to voices.
(5) Depression: anxiety, depression, tearful, retardation of movement.

These factors are clearly more satisfactory than those advocated by Moore, and show that improvements in statistical technique can bring about clarification of personality description.

[1] A student of Moore's, J. T. Gannon (1939), has reported a rating study along similar lines on 123 normal students. His conclusions are difficult to interpret, however.

A further re-analysis has been made by Degan (1952), and in recent years there has been a veritable spate of analyses of rating data of psychotic behaviour by Wittenborn, Guertin, Lorr, Jenkins, Monro, Bryant, O'Connor, Venables, Blewett and others; the reader will find them listed in the bibliography, but no exhaustive discussion will be given here as the topic is rather specialized. In any case the writer has published a detailed comparison of all these studies elsewhere (Eysenck, 1960) to which the interested reader may be referred.

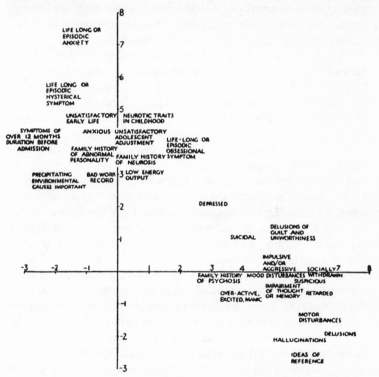

Fig. 15.—Items defining neuroticism and psychoticism factors.

Most of the thirty or so papers published in this field deal with behaviour conformities within psychotic groups; they do not, by and large, attack the question of the relationship between neurotic and psychotic disposition. An interesting analysis by Trouton and Maxwell (1956) has been published in which the absence or presence of 45 symptoms was rated in 819 male patients in a mental hospital. Their factor analysis disclosed two fairly clearcut factors which are shown in diagrammatic form in Fig. 15. One of these factors is made up of items like "lifelong or episodic anxiety", "neurotic traits in childhood", "unsatisfactory early life", "lifelong or episodic hysterical symptoms", "anxious", "symptoms of over twelve months' duration before admission", "unsatisfactory adolescent adjustment", "family history of neurosis", "lifelong or episodic obsessional symptoms", "low energy output", "bad work record", and "precipitating environmental causes important". These items are strongly reminiscent of the usual descriptions of neurotic illness and suggest that we are dealing with the factor of neuroticism.

Items on the other factor, which is quite independent of the first, are as follows: "delusions", "hallucinations", "ideas of reference", "motor disturbances", "mood disturbances", "impairment of thought or memory", "retardation", "suicidal", "socially withdrawn", "suspicious", "family history of psychosis". There is a marked clustering here of items traditionally regarded as characteristic of psychosis and we would appear to be dealing here with a general factor of psychoticism.

It will be seen that the item "depression" has equal loadings on both factors. This suggests that there may be two types of depression—neurotic depression, sometimes called *reactive depression*, and the psychotic type of depression, sometimes called *endogenous depression*. If this were true, it should be possible to discover objective tests to discriminate between these two types. Fig. 16 shows the "sleep" threshold and the sedation threshold of patients suffering from psychotic and neurotic depression respectively (Shagass, 1958). These thresholds define the reactions of the patients to the injection of certain doses of amylobarbital sodium, in terms of non-responsiveness (sleep) and certain quantitative EEG changes. It will be seen that the differentiation is almost perfect and therefore strongly supports the results of the factor analysis. Further support comes from certain analyses of objective test data which will be discussed in a later chapter. It should be noted that the method of analysis used by Trouton and Maxwell has been criticized by Lorr *et al.* (1957), but the criticisms advanced and the alternative analyses suggested cannot be regarded as constituting an improvement on the Trouton-Maxwell solution.

Also dealing with abnormal subjects is a study by Eysenck (1944), which is based on a definite hypothesis derived from the studies reviewed so far and from the theories of Jung and McDougall. According to these writers, hysteria is a mental disorder to which extraverts are constitutionally predisposed; anxiety, reactive depression, psychasthenia, and other dysthymic traits are parts of a

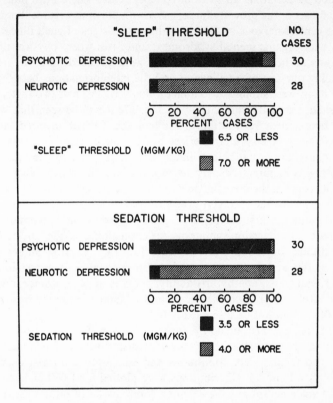

Fig. 16.—Comparisons of differentiations between neurotic and psychotic depression by the "sleep" and sedation thresholds.

disorder to which introverts are constitutionally predisposed. Logically, this view may be broken down into two hypotheses: (1) people differ with respect to their position on a factor of extraversion-introversion, and (2) people differ with respect to their position on a factor of emotional instability or neuroticism. The hysterics, according to this view, would be the persons having a high score on neuroticism and a high score on extraversion; the dysthymics would be the persons having a high score on neuroticism and a high score on introversion. Given a suitable set of ratings and subjects, it should be possible to verify the grouping of traits called for by this hypothesis.

Seven-hundred neurotic soldiers were selected from a total group of 1,000 by excluding all cases of epilepsy; cases where head injury formed part of the present illness; cases with previous organic illness of the central nervous system or with present signs of such illness; cases with organic mental syndromes; and cases where physical illness was an important factor. Ratings were obtained on 39 items, including one test of intelligence, and the intercorrelations between these items were submitted to a factor analysis. The first two factors extracted are plotted graphically in Fig. 17; it will be seen that we have here a clear verification of the hypothesis which inspired this study. The first factor, characterized by items such as badly organized personality, abnormal before illness, little energy, narrow interests, abnormality in parents, etc., is clearly one of emotional instability, or neuroticism, i.e. the opposite pole to "w"; the second factor opposes the introvert to the extravert group of traits, thus giving, in combination with the first factor, the typical picture on the one hand of the hysteric (conversion symptoms, sex anomalies, unskilled, hysterical attitude, degraded work history, low I.Q., narrow interests, little energy) and on the other of the dysthymic (anxiety, depression, obsessional traits, apathy, irritability, somatic anxiety, tremor, and effort intolerance). Two further factors of minor interest were obtained, but will not be discussed here.

An effort was also made by the same author (Eysenck, 1947) to verify another hypothesis, namely that distributions of people on these two factors were continuous and similar to a normal curve rather than bimodal. Distributions were plotted for 1,000 male and 1,000 female neurotics by a weighted combination of ratings for the various traits which go to make up these two factors. Distributions for both factors are closely similar to the normal curve of distribution, a result which is in good agreement with a similar demonstration by Burt on normal subjects (1940).

An independent confirmation of the existence of a neuroticism factor came in a study by Slater (1943), in which he intercorrelated, by means of tetrachoric correlations, notations on positive family history, childhood neurosis, poor work record, previous nervous breakdown, abnormal personality, and poor intelligence on 1,600 neurotic soldiers. Two factors were extracted, the first of which he labelled "neurotic constitution"; this factor had loadings of ·82 on

abnormal personality, ·66 on childhood neurosis, and ·59 on positive
family history. The second factor was one of "inadequate intelligence"
with loadings of ·49 on poor intelligence and ·59 on poor work
record. (The hypothesis of neurotic constitution was further developed in another study by Slater and Slater (1944).)

The work of the Slater brothers was taken further in a large-scale
study reported in three papers by Meyer Gross *et al.* (1949), Slater
(1947), and Rao *et al.* (1949). Two hundred and one neurotic and
55 non-neurotic army officers were rated by a psychiatrist on 13 main
behaviour "pointers"; ratings were confined to noting either the

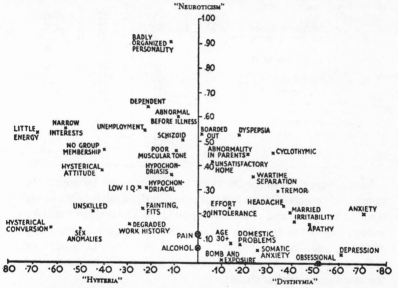

Fig. 17.—Two-factor Description derived from Psychiatric Ratings.

presence or the absence of the particular trait to be rated. A brief
statement of the traits used is given in Table 6, together with the proportion of cases showing any of the traits in either the normal or the
neurotic group. All the differences observed were found to be significant by means of a chi-squared analysis. Column D shows the observed differences in endorsements of each trait between the normal
and the neurotic groups. A factor analysis was carried out on a table
showing the frequency of concomitance of pairs of items, using a new
method which does not require the conversion of these frequencies into
correlation coefficients. Three factors were found, one of neuroticism
or "constitutional adequacy", the other two of "shyness" and "epi-

sodic instability" respectively. Factor loadings for the first factor are
also given in Table 13. It will be noted that these factor saturations
correlate ·88 with column D, thus proving the essential correctness
of the identification of this factor.

TABLE 13

Personality "Pointer" Rated:	Per cent Incidence:		D:	Factor Loadings[1]:
	Neurotics	Normals		
1. Heredity	·41	·13	76	2·13
2. Physical ill-health	·27	·00	54	2·11
3. Neurotic traits in childhood	·45	·16	82	4·62
4. Former psychiatric illness	·37	·05	71	3·45
5. Shy, solitary, etc., in childhood	·40	·11	74	3·96
6. Difficulty in making social contacts	·33	·07	62	3·28
7. Emotional instability	·73	·09	141	4·42
8. Obsessional features	·37	·13	67	1·74
9. Apprehensiveness	·59	·02	117	5·25
10. Dependence	·53	·04	105	4·61
11. Unstable work record	·23	·07	43	2·00
12. Marriage or sexual difficulties	·34	·05	65	2·81
13. Alcoholism	·21	·00	42	·57

Scores were derived for the three factors extracted by noting the
number of "pointers" of each class for each individual, thus obtaining
three scores (a, b, and c) for each individual. These three variables
were considered as defining a space of three dimensions in which any
particular individual could be presented by a point. Groups of
individuals could then be represented by a cluster of points around
the mean value of that cluster.

As the neurotic members of the sample used in this investigation
had been diagnosed into one of five syndromes (psychopathy, ob-
session, hysteria, anxiety state, post-traumatic personality change),
it was possible to use these psychiatric groupings in order to test the
hypothesis that differences between these syndromes were due entirely
to differences in severity of neurosis without any other principle of
differentiation. The appropriate test for this hypothesis consisted in
showing that the mean values of the groups in question were collinear
in the three-dimensional test space, and tests of significance showed
that this was indeed the case. Reasons for this failure to find any other

[1] Values of $p'i\sqrt{n}$ obtained directly from a matrix of 2×2 tables on the
assumption of a general factor and two group factors.

factors may lie in the original choice of variables and the unreliability of the ratings, or in the condensation of 13 variables into only three factors. We do not consider that the failure of the writers to disprove the null hypothesis should necessarily be taken to mean that no differences exist between various psychiatric syndromes, except in severity of disorder. This view seems to be shared by the writers, because they went on to calculate from their material the first two canonical variates and to plot the position of the various groups in the two-dimensional space thus generated. The first component (severity of neurosis) ranks the groups in order from normal to obsessional and psychopathic. The second component, although not significant statistically, produces a grouping closely in conformity with the one suggested by preceding work. The main division indicated by the second component is between the hysteric, psychopathic group on the one hand and the anxious, obsessional (dysthymic) group on the other.

A repetition of this study on larger numbers of cases (there are only 17 cases in the obsessional group for instance and only 5 in the "personality change" group) would be of great interest, particularly as the method of canonical variates used by these writers differs in many ways from the factorial methods used by other authors, and has possibilities which ought not to be neglected. In its main outcome, this experiment supports the conclusions of Eysenck's study.

Up to this point we have been concerned almost exclusively with studies carried out by members of the London school. We must now turn to a variety of experiments reported mostly by adherents of the Thurstone school. In dealing with the exponents of multiple-factor analysis, we must, of course, expect a certain change in tone and emphasis. We would expect, for instance, to find a much larger number of factors extracted from each matrix; we must expect to find that the more general factors dealt with by the London school (neuroticism and introversion-extraversion) will emerge, if at all, only as second-order factors; we may expect, finally, that these studies will throw more light on the combinations of behaviour units at the trait level (i.e. the "group factors" as opposed to the "general factors") than has been the case in the studies already reviewed. However, it would not be correct to say that all the work to be discussed in the following pages has made use of Thurstone's methods of analysis; some of the most interesting contributions have been made by writers who used factorial techniques of a much less systematic type, mainly some variety of cluster analysis, and these writers have, on the whole, come closer in their emphasis to the work already described.

Historically, pride of place goes to Kelley (1934), who used tests and ratings for such traits as courtesy, anxiety, loyalty, mastery, poise, and fair-play with groups of children. Using his own method of analysis, he isolated two traits, one of social conformity, the other of individualism or assertiveness, which may or may not be identifiable with "w" and "c". The traits used are too unlike those of other investigations to arrive at any reasonable conclusion.

Simultaneously with Kelley's work was published an important paper by Thurstone (1934), in which 1,300 raters each rated one subject on 60 traits. Multiple-factor analysis disclosed five main factors: (1) friendly, congenial, broad-minded, generous, cheerful; (2) patient, calm, faithful, earnest; (3) persevering, hard-working, systematic; (4) capable, frank, self-reliant, courageous; (5) self-important, sarcastic, haughty, grasping, cynical, quick-tempered. This study, like Kelley's, appears to be mainly of historical interest. Its results are difficult to interpret, and might be more intelligible if the analysis were repeated using oblique and second-order factors.

Equally difficult to interpret are the results from another pioneer study. In the monograph which introduces his method of "orthometric analysis", Tryon (1939) has analysed a table giving the intercorrelations between 20 personality ratings on 170 12-year-old boys in which each child's score in a given trait is a pooled rating by his companions. Five clusters were isolated which he labels respectively "disordered aggressiveness, hyperactivity, buoyancy, ascendancy, and likeableness". These clusters leave over several *residual variables* which do not fit in well with any of the groups. A correlation table containing these clusters and residual variables was formed and analysed, showing that disordered aggressiveness and hyperactivity correlate highly together, while the other three traits also form a definite group. These two "second-order clusters" Tryon called "social tenseness" and "approved sociability". Tryon's method of analysis is not such as to make interpretation easy, and no attempt will be made here to assimilate his findings to those of other writers. It is hoped that his table of intercorrelations will be re-analysed by one of the more orthodox procedures, as it is one of the few examples of peer ratings among children.[1]

Another early study should be mentioned in this connection, although neither its design nor its results appear to shed very much light on the organization of personality (Tschechtelin, 1944). The

Tschechtelin 22-trait Personality Rating Scale was administered to 300 children, and the average ratings of each trait for these 300 children by 8 classmates were used as a basis for tetrachoric correlations. Four factors were extracted from the table of intercorrelations and rotated. Factor I had relatively heavy loadings on good sportsmanship, entertaining, courtesy, dependability, boisterousness, punctuality, and intelligence. Factor II had loadings of six traits—sociability, pep, nervousness, intelligence, popularity, and disposition. Factor III seemed restricted to co-operativeness, with small loadings of sociability and punctuality: while Factor IV had one high loading only, namely for persistence. It had small loadings also for neatness, disposition, sense of humour, honesty, interest, and thoughtfulness. It is doubtful if these factors are very meaningful. No attempt will here be made to interpret them. The methodology of this study does not seem to make any crucial results appear very likely to emerge from the hodge-podge of traits rated or from the particular type of rating used.

A useful study by Rexroad (1937) is more strictly comparable with those analysed in the first part of this chapter. Ten traits were rated in 100 women students by faculty members, and the intercorrelations gave rise to three factors, of which the first one appeared to be one of general adjustment, corresponding to the "w" factor, whereas the second contrasted classroom interests with out-of-class situations, apparently an introvert versus extravert dichotomy. The actual traits involved in this dichotomy were, on the one hand, mastery of subject-matter, original ideas, independent working, seeing broader relations, of course material, as opposed, on the other hand, to social life, favourable impression socially, original ideas, and initiative out of class. The third factor, contrasting the "plodder" and the "gifted" scholar, is of doubtful significance and of little interest.

Of particular interest is a paper by Maurer (1941), using Thurstone's method to discover the patterns of behaviour of young children. Fifty women raters each rated one child (aged between 4 and 6) on a list of 50 adjectives. Tetrachoric correlations were run on 26 of these and three factors extracted. Thurstone's correction for uniqueness was applied and the clusters resulting from the analysis plotted. Fig. 18 shows the resulting diagrammatic picture of Maurer's result. Superimposed on her factor pattern, we have drawn two axes rotated through an angle of about 45°. When this is done, it will be seen that

---

[1] A more accessible account of this study is given by Tryon (1943).

her results agree very closely with the general scheme found in so many other studies. The second quadrant contains qualities characteristic of "*w*", thus leaving the fourth quadrant as being characteristic of neuroticism. Qualities in the first quadrant (talkative, active, forward, independent, noisy, plucky) are typical of the extraverted,

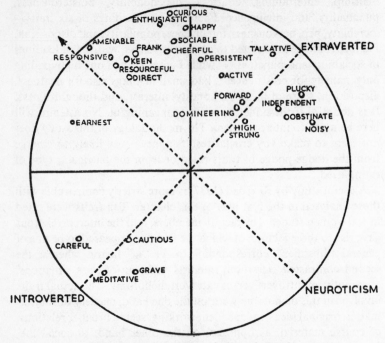

Fig. 18.—Representation of Maurer's Results.

surgent, $c+$ personality, whereas those in the third quadrant (careful, cautious, grave, meditative) are characteristic of the desurgent, $c-$, introverted personality. It is of particular importance to find that these general dimensions of personality can be recognized and rated already at such an early age.

A quite recent study by Reyburn and Raath (1950) illustrates the possibility of arriving at factors similar to those discussed in the preceding pages by means of oblique and second-order factors. The total experimental population consisted of 160 ratees, evenly balanced with respect to sex and university education. Eighty-three observers were used to rate two subjects each on a five-point scale, covering altogether 45 well-defined personality traits. The actual ratings were gone over in each case with the rater by one of the experimenters to ensure proper understanding of the categories used. Oblique factors were extracted from the table of intercorrelations; these six factors show considerable intercorrelations. These intercorrelations clearly give rise to higher order factors, which have been extracted by Eysenck (1952). The results are set out in Fig. 19 and Table 14. The first factor has a saturation of ·972 for stability. This identifies it clearly with "w" and as the opposite end of neuroticism. Persistence is found closely associated with stability, and assertiveness also has

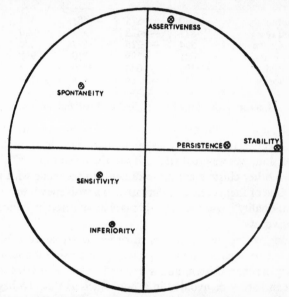

Fig. 19.—Representation of Reyburn and Raath Factorial Pattern.

a slight positive projection on this factor. Inferiority feeling and sensitivity are understandably loaded negatively on this factor. The second factor opposes assertiveness and spontaneity to inferiority and sensitivity. This agrees well with the hypothesis that the second factor is extraversion-introversion. We thus get a very interesting confirmation here for our view of "neuroticism" and "introversion-extraversion" as second-order factors in the orectic sphere, corresponding to Thurstone's second-order factor in the cognitive sphere.

One further study must at least be mentioned before we turn to the recent studies by Cattell, namely a paper by Horn (1944) in which he made use of ratings on 11 traits based on H. A. Murray's (1938) scheme of classification. Two groups of subjects were used, namely 28 male students and 41 schoolchildren, and a modified form of cluster analysis was performed on the intercorrelations between the 11 traits. Four clusters were found, of which two clearly resembled the main factors with which we are so familiar by now. One of these factors, "disorganized emotionality" as opposed to "organized

TABLE 14

	I	II	I′	II″	h^2
1. Spontaneity	− ·230	·575	− ·461	·414	·387
2. Stability	·872	− ·428	·972	·000	·945
3. Persistence	·554	− ·215	·592	·050	·353
4. Assertiveness	·621	·789	·210	·978	1·001
5. Sensitivity	− ·401	− ·044	− ·340	− ·218	·163
6. Inferiority	− ·472	− ·384	− · 256	− ·554	·372

Factor saturations for original and rotated solutions.

control", is clearly the neuroticism or "w" factor; the factor "imaginative, creative, introversion" as opposed to "practical, conventional, extraversion" shows great similarity to the usual bipolar "c" factor. The two other clusters are more difficult to reconcile with previous work. One of them contrasts "creative expressiveness" to "apathetic conventionality", whereas the other is characterized by "unorganized expressiveness".

Among writers using ratings in order to arrive at a descriptive scheme of personality, none has been more persistent and ingenious in his quest than Cattell, and a detailed review and criticism of his work can hardly be avoided in a book such as this. To begin with, Cattell recognizes the difficulty which many other writers have glossed over in their attempts to discover the principal factors in terms of which human behaviour can best be described. "The first and greatest theoretical difficulty in the path of this enterprise consists in finding a basis for testing when the chosen population of traits is truly comprehensive. In what way can one ensure that all aspects of personality are taken into account in the trait-element list?" This question of sampling within the field of traits is probably as crucial as the problem of sampling within the field of subjects tested, yet it has received very little in the way of attempts at a proper solution. Cattell introduces the concept of the personality sphere which "may be considered to present a complete surface constituted by many small 'trait areas', each trait area defined by a trait term and abutting on traits most closely resembling it, the whole constituting an endless but finite continuum of behaviour meaning. If trait character is represented by direction as in factor-analytic representation, the sphere must be considered as one in n-dimensional space. There is no guarantee, in the axioms of this formal system, that the trait terms in languages will be absolutely evenly distributed over the spherical surface. Intercorrelation must decide the actual closeness of different trait-term areas. However, it is part of our assumption from the study of language that no large area is completely neglected by vocabulary, and that all dimensions of personality receive some representation."

Taking his departure from Allport and Odbert's (1936) list of some 4,500 trait terms in the English language, Cattell (1943), by throwing together "terms which any average user of the language would consider synonymous", reduced the list to about 160 terms. Various additions raised this total number to 171 traits, most of which were listed in the form of pairs of polar opposites. This list was further reduced to 50 nuclear clusters by a review of previous researches; Cattell is quite conscious of the fact that a good deal of subjectivity must enter into each of these steps, and particularly the last one. For his actual empirical study, Cattell further reduced the number of clusters to 35, which were then rated on a male population with a mean age of 30 years. The number of subjects included was 208; this large group was divided into 13 small groups of 16 men each. Ratings and correlations were carried out independently for each of these groups, and the coefficients then averaged to obtain the correlation matrix for the factor analysis. This factor analysis resulted in what Cattell calls "the 12 primary source traits of personality".

Since then Cattell has carried out many further analyses, not only on what he calls "L-data" which he defines as "Life-record data covering behaviour *in situ* instead of in a test, and therefore including the specifically important behaviours of criteria. Often evaluated by behaviour rating", but also on "T-data", i.e. "Data from observed personality responses in standard objective-test situations, i.e. not questionnaires", and "Q-data", i.e. "Responses and response factors based on questionnaire behaviour, taken only as behaviour" (Cattell, 1957). In this chapter we shall only be concerned with a very brief summary of the main conclusions he draws from his study of L-data; later chapters will deal with T-data and Q-data.

The factors isolated by Cattell in his rating studies can best be presented by listing them in terms of the items having the highest positive and negative loadings. Each factor is given an identifying letter as well as a descriptive name; some of these names have been specially coined by Cattell for the purpose.

FACTOR A: *Cyclothymia vs. Schizothymia*

A+	A−
Easygoing	Obstructive, cantankerous
Adaptable (in habits)	Inflexible, "rigid"
Warmhearted, attentive to people	Cool, indifferent
Frank, placid	Close-mouthed, secretive, anxious
Emotional, expressive	Reserved
Trustful, credulous	Suspicious, "canny"
Impulsive, generous	Close, cautious
Co-operative, self-effacing	Hostile, egotistical
Subject to personal emotional appeals	Impersonal
Humorous	Dry, impassive

FACTOR B: *Intelligence*

B+	B−
Intelligent	Unintelligent
Thoughtful, cultured	Unreflective, boorish
Persevering, conscientious	Quitting, conscienceless
Smart, assertive	Dull, submissive

FACTOR C: *Ego strength vs. Neuroticism*

C+	C−
Emotionally stable	Emotional, dissatisfied
Free of neurotic symptoms	Showing a variety of neurotic symptoms
Not hypochondriacal	Hypochondriacal, plaintive
Realistic about life	Evasive, immature, autistic
Unworried	Worrying, anxious
Steadfast, self-controlled	Changeable
Calm, patient	Excitable, impatient
Persevering and thorough	Quitting, careless
Loyal, dependable	Undependable morally

FACTOR D: *Excitability vs. Insecurity*

D+	D−
Demanding, impatient	Emotionally mature
Attention-getting, exhibitionistic	Self-sufficient
Excitable, overactive	Deliberate
Prone to jealousy	Not easily jealous
Self-assertive, egotistical	Self-effacing
Nervous symptoms	Absence of nervous symptoms
Changeable, lacks persistence	Self-controlled
Untrustworthy	Conscientious

Factor E: *Dominance vs. Submissiveness*

E+	E−
Self-assertive, confident	Submissive, unsure
Boastful, conceited	Modest, retiring
Aggressive, pugnacious	Complaisant
Extrapunitive*	Impunitive, intropunitive
Vigorous, forceful	Meek, quiet
Wilful, egotistical	Obedient
Rather solemn or unhappy	Lighthearted, cheerful
Adventurous	Timid, retiring
Insensitive to social disapproval, unconventional	Tactful, conventional
Reserved	Frank, expressive

* In the sense introduced by Rosenzweig

Factor F: *Surgency vs. Desurgency*

F+	F−
Cheerful, joyous	Depressed, pessimistic
Sociable, responsive	Seclusive retiring
Energetic, rapid in movement	Subdued, languid
Humorous, witty	Dull, phlegmatic
Talkative	Taciturn, introspective
Placid, content	Worrying, anxious, unable to relax, obsessional
Resourceful, original	Slow to accept a situation
Adaptable	Bound by habit, rigid
Showing equanimity	Unstable mood level
Trustful, sympathetic, open	Suspicious, brooding, narrow

Factor G: *Superego strength*

G+	G−
Persevering, determined	Quitting, fickle
Responsible	Frivolous, immature
Insistently ordered	Relaxed, indolent
Conscientious	Unscrupulous
Attentive to people	Neglectful of social chores
Emotionally stable	Changeable

Factor H: *Parmia (Parasympathetic immunity) vs. Threctia (Threat reactivity)*

H+	H−
Adventurous, likes meeting people	Shy, timid, withdrawn
Shows strong interest in opposite sex	Little interest in opposite sex
Gregarious, genial, responsive	Aloof, cold, self-contained
Kindly, friendly	Hard, hostile
Frank	Secretive
Impulsive (but no inner tension)	Inhibited, conscientious
Likes to "get into the swim"	Recoils from life
Self-confident	Lacking confidence
Carefree	Careful, considerate

FACTOR I: *Premsia vs. Harria*

I+	I−
Demanding, impatient	Emotionally mature
Dependent, immature	Independent-minded
Kindly, gentle	Hard
Aesthetically fastidious	Lacking artistic feeling
Introspective, imaginative	Unaffected by "fancies"
Intuitive, sensitively imaginative	Practical, logical
Gregarious, attention-seeking	Self-sufficient
Frivolous	Responsible
Hypochondriacal	Free from hypochondria

FACTOR J: *Coasthenia (Thinking Neurasthenia) vs. Zeppia*

J+	J−
Acts individualistically	Goes with group
Passively, pedantically obstructs	Co-operatives in enterprises
Slow to make up his mind	Decisive in thinking
Inactive, meek, quiet	Active, assertive
Neurasthenically, neurotically fatigued	Vigorous
Self-sufficient	Attention-getting
Evaluates intellectually	Evaluates by common standards
Personal, peculiar interests	Common "wide" interests

FACTOR K: *Comention vs. Abcultion*

K+	K−
Intellectual interests, analytical	Unreflective, narrow
Polished, poised, composed	Awkward, socially clumsy
Unshakable	Easily socially embarrassed
Independent-minded	Going with the crowd
Conscientious, idealistic	Lacking sense of any social duty
Aesthetic and musical tastes	Lacking aesthetic interests
Introspective, sensitive	Crude

FACTOR L: *Protension (Paranoid trend) vs. Inner relaxation*

L+	L−
Suspicious	Trustful
Jealous	Understanding
Self-sufficient, withdrawn	Composed, socially at home

FACTOR M: *Autia vs. Praxernia*

M+	M−
Unconventional, eccentric	Conventional
Aesthetically fastidious	Uninterested in art
Sensitively imaginative	Practical and logical
"A law unto himself", undependable	Conscientious
Placid, complacent, absorbed	Worrying, anxious, alert
Occasional hysterical emotional upsets	Poised, tough control
Intellectual, cultured interests	Narrower interests

FACTOR N: *Shrewdness vs. Naivety*

N+	N−
Polished, socially skilful	Socially clumsy, awkward
Exact mind	Vague and sentimental mind
Cool, aloof	Company-seeking
Aesthetically fastidious	Lacking independence of taste
Insightful regarding self	Lacking self insight
Insightful regarding others	Naive

FACTOR O: *Guilt proneness vs. Confidence*

O+	O−
Worrying	Self-confident
Lonely	Self-sufficient
Suspicious	Accepting
Sensitive	Tough
Discouraged	Spirited

Cattell warns that "Although no more than fifteen L-data factors can be announced after several years of systematic research, based on the broad 'personality sphere' of common, real life, criterion behaviour, the student should not assume that this list is practically exhaustive. Doubtless some areas of behaviour are yet to be found not previously included in the personality sphere. . . . An estimate allowing for attenuation suggests that the present fifteen factors account for about two-thirds of the total personality sphere variance."

Cattell's fifteen factors are not independent, and the inter-correlations in turn require to be submitted to factor analytic studies. These have recently been undertaken by Cattell (1957) and their publication, as he points out, "yields two very striking findings—the general integration factor, and the introversion/extraversion factor". It would appear, therefore, that Cattell's studies line up with the others reviewed in this chapter to define the same two fundamental dimensions of personality we have encountered so often. Extraversion is defined in terms of the following primary factors given here together with their factor loadings on extraversion: F(Surgency): $+ \cdot 70$; M(Autia): $+ \cdot 54$; E(Dominance): $+ \cdot 54$; A(Cyclothymia): $+ \cdot 38$; H(Parmia): $+ \cdot 17$.

The main primary factors defining Neuroticism are: C(Ego strength): $- \cdot 50$; L(Protension): $- \cdot 47$; E(Dominance): $- \cdot 32$; H(Parmia): $- \cdot 20$. (It should be noted that Cattell prefers to call this factor "anxiety vs. integration or adjustment"; to preserve uniformity we shall continue to call it neuroticism.) Cattell derives some further second-order factors which he labels: sensitivity, constitutional adaptability, catatonic disposition (which may be similar to Eysenck's psychotism factor) and "unbroken success vs. maturity by frustration". The reader must be referred to the original writings of Cattell for a discussion of these further concepts.

We must turn now to a number of studies using various types of "cluster" analysis. One of the most systematic studies in this field has been that of Sheldon (1942). He began by collecting a list of 650 alleged traits of temperament, most of which were supposedly related to introversion or extraversion. After several revisions and a thorough study of some 30 students by means of a series of analytic interviews, the number of traits used was considerably reduced to 22, which appeared to fall into three main clusters. Traits in each of these clusters showed consistently positive intercorrelations among themselves and consistently negative correlations with the traits of each of the other clusters. Further traits were added to these clusters, until finally each cluster was made up of 20 traits altogether. These clusters were labelled "viscerotonia", "somatotonia", and "cerebrotonia" respectively, as they seemed to deal respectively with the functional predominance of the digestive viscera, the functional and anatomical predominance of the somatic structures, and the prepotency of the higher centres of the nervous system. (The linking up of the clusters of traits with bodily functions is apparent, and will be discussed in a later chapter.) The actual traits making up each cluster are given in Table 15.

TABLE 15

The Scale for Temperament

I VISCEROTONIA	II SOMATOTONIA	III CEREBROTONIA
( ) 1. Relaxation in posture and movement	( ) 1. Assertiveness of posture and movement	( ) 1. Restraint in posture and movement, tightness
( ) 2. Love of physical comfort	( ) 2. Love of physical adventure	— 2. Physiological over-response
( ) 3. Slow reaction	( ) 3. The energetic characteristic	( ) 3. Overly fast reactions
— 4. Love of eating	( ) 4. Need of enjoyment and exercise	( ) 4. Love of privacy
— 5. Socialization of eating	— 5. Love of dominating, lust for power	( ) 5. Mental overintensity, hyper-attentionality, apprehensiveness

TABLE 15—*continued*

I VISCEROTONIA	II SOMATOTONIA	III CEREBROTONIA
— 6. Pleasure in digestion	( ) 6. Love of risk and chance	( ) 6. Secretiveness of feeling, emotional restraint
( ) 7. Love of polite ceremony	( ) 7. Bold directness of manner	( ) 7. Self-conscious motility of the eyes and face
( ) 8. Sociophilia	( ) 8. Physical courage for combat	( ) 8. Sociophobia
— 9. Indiscriminate amiability	( ) 9. Competitive aggressiveness	( ) 9. Inhibited social address
— 10. Greed for affection and approval	— 10. Psychological callousness	— 10. Resistance to habit, and poor routinizing
— 11. Orientation to people	— 11. Claustrophobia	— 11. Agoraphobia
( ) 12. Evenness of emotional flow	— 12. Ruthlessness, freedom from squeamishness	— 12. Unpredictability of attitude
( ) 13. Tolerance	( ) 13. The unrestrained voice	( ) 13. Vocal restraint, and general restraint of noise
( ) 14. Complacency	— 14. Spartan indifference to pain	— 14. Hypersensitivity to pain
— 15. Deep sleep	— 15. General noisiness	— 15. Poor sleep habits, chronic fatigue
( ) 16. The untempered characteristic	( ) 16. Overmaturity of appearance	( ) 16. Youthful intentness of manner
( ) 17. Smooth, easy communication of feeling, extraversion of viscerotonia	— 17. Horizontal mental cleavage, extraversion of somatotonia	— 17. Vertical mental cleavage, introversion
— 18. Relaxation and sociophilia under alcohol	— 18. Assertiveness and aggression under alcohol	— 18. Resistance to alcohol, and to other depressant drugs
— 19. Need of people when troubled	— 19. Need of action when troubled	— 19. Need of solitude when troubled
— 20. Orientation toward childhood and family relationships	— 20. Orientation toward goals and activities of youth	— 20. Orientation toward the later periods of life

Note: The 30 traits with parentheses constitute collectively the short form of the scale.

Sheldon's prescription for the use of his scale is somewhat unusual. "The procedure recommended for using the scale for temperament is as follows: Observe the subject closely for at least a year in as many different situations as possible. Conduct a series of not less than twenty analytic interviews with him in a manner best suited to the situation and to the temperaments and interests of the two principals." Each trait is to be rated on a 7-point scale and the predominance of the three components—viscerotonia, somatotonia, cerebrotonia—is also indicated on a 7-point scale in such a way that for each person a formula is given containing three numbers, each measuring the strength of one of the three components. Thus, 1-1-7 would be a person almost entirely lacking in viscerotonia and somatotonia, with cerebrotonia completely dominant.

The final list of 60 traits is claimed by Sheldon to have been selected on the basis of intercorrelations among the ratings on 78 traits for a series of 100 male subjects. These correlations are given in his book; they are considerably higher than correlations between trait ratings usually are. Apart from his inspectional cluster analysis, Sheldon has not carried out any factorial study. Adcock (1948) has attempted such a study of Sheldon's figures, but in spite of several attempts found that he was faced each time with the problem of finding the root of a negative number. He remarks: "Obviously there is something peculiar about these intercorrelations", and goes on to attempt a rather complex interpretation.

Lubin (1950), who has made a statistical investigation of these intercorrelations, remarks that "the peculiarity is so great that one is forced to ask whether it may not be outside the bounds of mathematical possibility". He goes on to show that several of Sheldon's product moment correlations could not be simultaneously obtained from any actual set of measurements because they violate the well-known conditions for consistency. He concludes: "It follows that some at least of his figures must contain errors of arithmetical calculation." We may deduce from these observations that Sheldon's edifice is based on a somewhat insecure foundation, and any conclusions drawn from these figures should be regarded with great caution.

The three components isolated by Sheldon are not independent: viscerotonia correlates $-.34$ with somatotonia and $-.37$ with cerebrotonia; somatotonia and cerebrotonia intercorrelate $-.62$. It is clear that a much more parsimonious description of the 60 traits rated would be possible in terms of two orthogonal factors rather than three correlated components[1]; in any case, it is clear that the intercorrelations among the components themselves must be accounted for in terms of some kind of Thurstonian second-order factor. This point is completely neglected by Sheldon.

One difficulty in the way of a ready acceptance of Sheldon's work must be the difficulty of repetition. Few psychologists can observe their subjects for a whole year and give each one 20 or more analytic sessions before making a rating. In several studies Sheldon has shown that moderately satisfactory correlations can be obtained between his own ratings and those of relatively inexperienced judges, making use of the short form of his scale. He has also developed a 20-minute interview technique which shows correlations of between ·8 and ·9 with his final ratings. The figures given by him are interesting, but like so much else in his work, they are given *en passant*, without very much information being vouchsafed regarding conditions of the experiment, the controls adopted, or any of the other attendant circumstances which must be known before a judgment can be made. Consequently, it is difficult to arrive at a proper conclusion regarding these devices.

More recently, Sheldon (1949), with the help of Wittman, has extended his work to abnormal mental states. Considering the psychotic syndrome in each case to be merely an exaggeration of the neurotic, he posits three main components of abnormality, which are again rated on a 7-point scale where the numbers are prefaced by the Greek letter ψ. The three psychiatric components in each case signify the *absence* or *lack* of one of the three normal components. Thus, cerebropenia (the suffix penic denotes lack of, or an abnormally low degree of, the component named) signifies the absence of cerebrotonia; visceropenia signifies the absence of viscerotonia; and somatopenia signifies the absence of somatotonia. Corresponding to these three "penias" we have three great neurotic and psychotic syndromes. Cerebropenia at the neurotic level leads to hysteria; at the psychotic level to manic-depressive psychosis. Visceropenia at the neurotic level leads to psychasthenia; at the psychotic level to paranoid schizophrenia. Somatopenia at the neurotic level leads to neurasthenia, and at the psychotic level to hebephrenic schizophrenia.

These various relations are illustrated in Fig. 20. The three corners of the triangle denote respectively the personality components viscerotonia, somatotonia, and cerebrotonia. The central part of the side of the triangle opposite each corner denotes visceropenia, soma-

[1] This has been demonstrated on Sheldon's own material by Ekman (1951).

topenia, and cerebropenia respectively. Distance from the centre of the triangle denotes degree of abnormality. The terms endomorphy, mesomorphy, and ectomorphy written in brackets at the corners of the triangle relate to body types, which in Sheldon's hypothesis are usually found with the temperamental types in question. A discussion of these types is given in a later chapter.

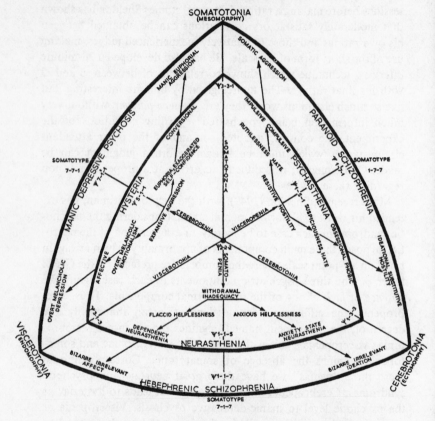

Fig. 20.—Diagrammatic Representation of Sheldon's Typology.

Most of the pioneering work in connection with this scheme has been carried on by Wittman (1948), who has constructed a check list of fundamental psychiatric behaviour reactions following the general scheme outlined. Interesting and suggestive as this instrument appears, the absence of correlational analysis of actual ratings makes it impossible to judge its value. Some supporting evidence is given by Sheldon and Wittman in their studies of body type, to be dealt with later.

In general, we may sum up Sheldon's contribution by emphasizing the novelty and comprehensiveness of his approach, the persistence of his endeavours, and the quantitative form in which his estimates are given. What militates against acceptance of his scheme is the extremely subjective character of the ratings, the obvious statistical errors in his computations, and the failure to use appropriate methods of analysis for the correlations he reports. A more thorough discussion of his contribution will be postponed until in a later chapter we can see his contribution in connection with his work on body types.

A rather different approach to the problem of personality organization, also by Wittman [1] is employed in a factorial study of the Elgin Prognostic Scale, in which correlations were calculated between 17 and 20 variables which enter into that scale. Two hundred successive admissions formed the sample, and three factors altogether were extracted from the intercorrelations. The first factor is characterized by the following items: defects of interest, insidious onset, shut-in personality, schizothyme personality, limited range of interests, constitutional bias, low energy tone, and asthenic build. This factor is labelled "schizoid withdrawal" by the authors. The second factor is one of schizophrenic delusions, and has loadings on the following items: ideas of influence, bizarre delusions, absence of atypical symptoms, hebephrenic symptoms, and long duration of psychosis. The third factor has loadings on: stubborn traits, careless indifference, and inadequate affect. "These scales suggest a factor of inadaptability or rigidity." This study is probably less inclusive than those of Moore and Wittenborn, and consequently its factors cover a much narrower field. The present writer is doubtful whether the scale used by Lorr, Wittman, and Schanberger is of a kind which lends itself readily to factorial analysis, at least in so far as broad factors of personality organization are concerned. From the point of view of prognostic indication, which determined the make-up of the scale, the usefulness of factor analysis is clearly doubtful, as a simple regression equation would presumably give at least equally good or probably better prediction than a combination of the three factors isolated.

The four studies next to be discussed all take their inspiration

[1] Lorr, Wittman, and Schanberger (1951).

from Harvard; although they are quite independent of each other in many ways, they share certain characteristics, such as excellence of psychiatric insight and wideness of scope, as well as a startling inadequacy of statistical treatment. The first of these studies is Murray's *Explorations in Personality* (1938), in which a large number of psychologists and psychiatrists used a great variety of procedures, many of them quite novel, on 50 Harvard undergraduates over a long period of time. As this book has become something of a classic in the literature of "personology", as Murray terms it, it will hardly be necessary to describe the many ingenious methods and techniques employed. From the point of view of the organization of personality, however, the yield is extraordinarily meagre. According to Murray, "the statistical analysis of the variables finally retained demonstrated that certain of them intercorrelated repeatedly to a significant degree. Most of these clusters seemed to correspond to our observations of people in everyday life. Hence, we concluded that they might be regarded as syndromes of functionally related factors which, for economy, could be used instead of the separate variables to portray character." To the reader whose appetite might be whetted by this announcement, it may come as a shock to find a footnote on the same page saying, "The chapter on the intercorrelations of variables and syndromes had to be omitted from this volume". He will instead have to make do with 100 pages of case-notes dealing with one subject ("The case of Earnst"), and a large amount of theorizing on the organization of personality by Murray and the other authors of this volume. It is fortunate that few other books eschew their duty to the conscientious reader who wishes to study the evidence for himself in so cavalier a fashion.

A very comprehensive rating study also is that of Sanford *et al.* (1943), which was clearly inspired by *Explorations in Personality*. 48 children altogether were followed up over a period of several years by a team of investigators who, in addition to ratings, used a number of techniques ranging from physical measurements and physiological determinations to projective techniques and studies of family background. In this chapter we will be concerned only with the personality ratings. Other results will be discussed in later chapters.

Sanford and his colleagues took over the general scheme outlined by Murray (1937). Ratings by three staff members on a large number of "needs" formed the basic data of the study; these ratings were "based on observations of the subjects in both free and controlled situations, ratings by teachers and parents, reports by teachers and by parents, and the results from a number of personality tests". 43 needs and traits were correlated with each other and syndromes constructed on the basis of a rather subjective form of cluster analysis. 20 such clusters were identified and intercorrelated with each other, but unfortunately no factor analysis was carried out on the resulting intercorrelations. The most clear-cut of the clusters is given the name "conscientious effort". "There is organized and persistent exertion to accomplish what is socially favored, and when obstacles are encountered there is renewed effort. There is the feeling that it is right to do these things and to some extent at least the subject takes pride in doing them. The syndrome denotes firmness, organization and persistence of action, and the capacity for living and working in accordance with standards. Underlying this factor, it may be supposed, there is considerable inner structure of personality." This cluster seems to represent most nearly the "w" factor, and, indeed, the similarity is quite striking. This syndrome correlates negatively with anxious emotional expressiveness and timid dependence, as well as with the syndrome called "sensation", "which seems to have a general tendency to seek for sensation or excitement".

Two opposed groups of traits resemble the extravert-introvert pattern, one made up of the items "good fellowship" and "social feeling"; the other made up of the items "self-sufficiency" and "counteractive endocathection".[1] Needless to say, these two groups of items intercorrelate negatively with each other.

An assessment of this study will be postponed until the other component parts of it are discussed in a later chapter. It would appear, however, that the excellence of the observational techniques and the rating methods are not matched by the quality of the statistical analysis, which appears subjective and almost perfunctory. It was considered at one stage that a factorial analysis of Sanford's table of intercorrelations of manifest personality syndromes might give interesting results, but it was found that out of 190 correlations, 10 were incorrect, by the simple check of comparing the two symmetrical halves of the table. Thus, the intercorrelations between "aggressive self-defense" and "good fellowship" are given variously as $- \cdot 48$ and $- \cdot 28$, and those between "aggressive self-defense" and "social feeling" as $- \cdot 59$ and $- \cdot 39$. "Counteractive endocathection" and "sensation" are correlated to the extent of either $- \cdot 52$ or $+ \cdot 52$, different signs appearing in different parts of the table. Such errors

---

[1] "The liking for thought or emotion for its own sake. Preoccupation with inner activity."

must seriously disturb one's faith in the results given in any part of the book.

Another Harvard production—*What People Are*—by Heath (1945) proclaims itself to be "a study of normal young men". It is a report on the first few years' work by investigators working on the Grant study. The subjects were some 250 young men "who had general all-round normal reactions". Their academic work had to be at least satisfactory, and their health and college records had to indicate lack of physical or psychological abnormalities. Participants were around 20 years of age, ranging from 17 to 24. Each boy was studied for about 20 hours by means of interviews, physiological observations, anthropological examination of body structure and development, and psychological testing for the measurement of various mental functions. Details regarding his socio-economic status were obtained and further psychiatric interviews held. A great deal of information was thus elicited from the participants, but not a single correlation coefficient is given throughout the book. The statistical treatment given to the data is of a purely actuarial kind, and in view of the non-representative nature of the sample can be of very little interest.

The only exception to this general criticism is the attempt made by the authors to rate their subjects on the basis of "soundness" into three groups : "Group A contained young men who were 'thoroughly sound' in Webster's meaning of 'free from flaws', 'on a firm foundation'. . . . Group B contained boys in whom there was a question of a minor flaw. For instance, if a boy was lacking in warmth in his touch with people, or if he was erratic or showed degrees of sensitiveness, leading to minor frustrations, he would be placed in this group. . . . Group C contained boys whose history revealed a definite handicap. A good illustration would be swings of mood which interfered noticeably with function." Of the 252 men so classified, the "A Group" included 37 per cent., the "B Group" 45 per cent., and the "C Group" 18 per cent.

"After several years sufficient information had accumulated to set up a tentative and descriptive classification by certain outstanding and significant traits and activities. All descriptive terms contained in the histories were listed, and close study of these disclosed the existence of trait clusters, combinations that occurred with special frequency." A list of these trait groups, together with the occurrence of each in the total number of cases, and their occurrence respectively in groups rated A, B, and C on "soundness" are given in Table 16, together with the correlation of each trait with the "soundness" classification.[1]

It will be seen that some items, such as "vital affect", "friendly", "well integrated", "practical organizer", showed high correlations with "soundness", whereas others like "incompletely integrated", "asocial", "unstable autonomic functions", "lack of purpose and

TABLE 16

Distribution of Various Traits according to "Soundness"
(A, B, and C) Classification

Trait Groups	Per cent. "Soundness" Classification in				Co-efficient of Con-tingency $C =$
	Total group	A	B	C	
	Per cent. in 251 cases	Per cent. in 93 cases	Per cent. in 112 cases	Per cent. in 46 cases	
1. Vital affect	20	40	11	2	·36*
2. Friendly	22	39	14	7	·30*
3. Well integrated	60	83	56	22	·40*
4. Practical organizing	37	47	37	15	·23*
5. Humanistic	16	20	16	7	·13
6. Pragmatic	38	48	38	17	·22*
7. Political	17	19	20	7	·13
8. Just-so	13	11	18	7	·13
9. Bland affect	18	15	21	15	·08
10. Self-driving	14	10	19	11	·12
11. Cultural	22	18	25	20	·08
12. Verbalistic	18	19	15	24	·08
13. Inarticulate	14	11	17	15	·08
14. Shy	18	8	30	11	·27*
15. Physical science	12	11	12	17	·07
16. Sensitive affect	17	10	22	22	·16*
17. Creative and intuitive	6	3	9	7	—
18. Mood fluctuations	14	9	15	22	·13
19. Inhibited	19	6	30	15	·27*
20. Ideational	21	13	23	33	·17*
21. Self-conscious and in-trospective	25	12	32	37	·24*
22. Lack of purpose and values	20	8	19	50	·35*
23. Unstable autonomic functions	14	3	17	28	·26*
24. Asocial	10	0	11	26	·30*
25. Incompletely integra-ted	15	0	12	52	·46*

* Statistically significant.

[1] These correlations were calculated by the writer: the book itself is content to give instead a ratio between the percentage occurrences of each trait for groups A and C, a measure which is statistically meaningless and psychologically misleading.

values", "self-conscious", and "introspective" showed negative correlations. There is little doubt that this "soundness" rating corresponds to the factor of neuroticism, or rather its opposite pole, "w".

Another table is given by the authors, again in terms of percentages, showing the frequency of occurrence of various pairs of traits. This is summarized by Heath as follows: "Among individuals with *sensitive affect* there is an association with *creative* and *intuitive, cultural, verbalistic, unstable autonomic functions, self-conscious and introspective,* and *incompletely integrated.*" It seems probable that if the general factor of "soundness" were partialled out from the intercorrelations of the traits, we would have here a description of the introvert as opposed to the extravert type. As it is, the description is a mixture of neuroticism and introversion and would appear similar to that given of the dysthymic type by Eysenck (1947). Nothing can show more clearly the need for a proper system of statistical analysis than this amateurish effort to sort out "how the traits group themselves together" by means of an inspection of percentage frequencies.

Some incidental findings are of interest. Some of the young men apparently had an almost perfect health record. "Their excellent health record often had its counterpart in good reports from the other examiners so that there seemed to be a link between good physical health and sound personality and adjustment, good balance of mental functions, freedom from structural defect, and normal physiology. The suggestion is sufficiently pronounced to warrant pursuit by further study."

In another publication, also by the Grant study (Woods, Brouha, and Seltzer, 1943), a figure is given showing the relationship between short interview ratings of mental health and a physical fitness index. This is reproduced below (Fig. 21), and shows a remarkable correlation between the two indices, taken on almost 2,500 officer candidates. At the opposite end of the scale we may note some figures given by Lovet Doust (1952), who showed that the incidence of various diseases was much higher in patients suffering from psychoses or neuroses than in normals; his figures are given in Table 17.[1] The old adage "mens sana in corpora sano" appears to derive considerable justification from these figures.

Follow-up data were available on over 200 of the young men studied by Heath, who went into the army, and a threefold classifi-

[1] 354 normals and 272 psychiatric patients with no gross physical disability filled in a questionnaire dealing with 110 disorders (38 symptoms and complaints, 72 actual diseases) from which they might have suffered in the past.

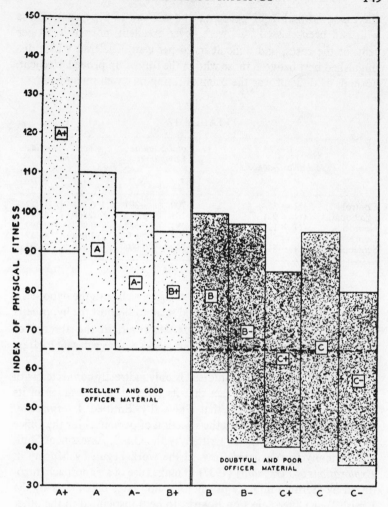

Fig. 21.—Relationship between Short Interview Rating and Physical Fitness Index.

cation of their adjustment was made into *excellent, normal,* or *difficult.* Of those in "soundness" classification "A", 31 per cent. were classed as excellent, 66 per cent. as normal, and 3 per cent. as difficult. Those who had been classified "B" were excellent in 10 per cent. of the cases, normal in 82 per cent., and difficult in 8 per cent. Those who had been classed "C" were never excellent, normal in 74 per cent. of the cases, and difficult in 26 per cent. The trait which distinguished best between those who in the follow-up proved excellent, normal, or difficult was the original rating on "well integrated".

TABLE 17

Psychiatric Diagnosis		Total Somatic Complaints		Total Somatic Diseases	
		M.	S.D.	M.	S.D.
Controls (N = 354)	. .	1·700	1·391	6·291	1·722
Psychopaths (N = 92)	. .	2·201	3·674	6·800	4·845
Neurotics (N = 120)	. .	3·491	6·552	8·907	2·799
Depressives (N = 59)	. .	8·334	2·176	13·654	4·447
Schizophrenics (N = 51)	. .	10·320	3·005	13·820	5·402

In so far as they go, then, these data agree well with the hypothesis of a general factor of neuroticism and seem to support the hypothesis of an introverted-extraverted factor. However, in the absence of proper statistical treatment of the data, it does not seem safe to draw any definite conclusion from them.

The last of the "Harvard studies" is only indirectly connected with Cambridge, Mass., by the fact that its orientation and much of its senior personnel came from that University. Entitled *Assessment of Men* (1948) and dealing with the selection of personnel for the Office of Strategic Services, it was written by the O.S.S. Assessment Staff, and in many ways carried forward the work begun by Murray in *Explorations of Personality* (1937). It makes use of an approach introduced by German military psychology, and later taken over by the British War Office Selection Boards, to be transplanted to the other side of the ocean in the selection procedures here outlined. The similarities of the approach to *Explorations of Personality* are obvious; we have again stress on psychiatric and semi-analytical interviews, on all sorts of projective devices, and quite generally on what is called "depth" or "dynamic" psychology.

Several hundred men went through this assessment process, each of them being observed by a large number of observers over quite a lengthy period; all of them were subjected to a great variety of tests, interviews, and other techniques, many of which showed again the

typical ingenuity and skilled insight of the authors. The validity of
the final ratings and the final recommendations made were assessed
by correlating them with four types of appraisal: overseas staff
appraisal, returnee appraisal, theatre commander's comments, and
reassignment area appraisal. For the main camp (Camp "S"), where
the men were investigated for three days in a very thorough-going
fashion, these correlations were respectively ·37, ·19, ·23, and ·08,
giving an average of about ·2 as an estimate of the validity of the
procedures. In another camp (Camp "W"), where a very much
shorter period of time was spent on each man, namely one day in
all, the figures were ·53, ·21, ·15, and ·30 respectively, giving an
average of almost ·3. It is interesting to note that the more information was obtained on the subjects of the rating technique, the less
valid did the final rating seem to become. The O.S.S. staff do not
consider that this result could have arisen because of differences in
quality of subjects in the two camps or because of differences in the
quality of the raters. They conclude a discussion of the problem by
saying: "It would be profitable in the long run for us to assume that
the additional information obtained by stretching the screening process from one to three days had diminished the validity of the final
decisions and that this much more knowledge was a dangerous
thing." (A similar point has been made by the authors of the Michigan Clinical Student Selection Programme (Kelly and Fiske, 1952),
which is mentioned elsewhere in this book.)

Unfortunately, in spite of its great interest, *The Assessment of Men*
does not throw very much light on the question of the organization
of personality. The writers are so convinced of the truth of their
"organismic hypothesis" that they have made certain that no data
should be published in their book, or should be obtainable from the
general set-up of their experiment, which could possibly throw any
light on the relative virtues of this organismic approach, as compared
with what they call the "elementalistic" method. They say: "The
scheme employed by us may be called the multiform organismic
system of assessment: 'multiform' because it consists of a rather large
number of procedures based on different principles and 'organismic'
(or 'Gestalt' or 'holistic') because it utilizes the data obtained through
these procedures for attempting to arrive at a picture of personality
as a whole; i.e. at the organization of the essential dynamic features
of the individual. The knowledge of this organization serves as a
base, both for understanding and for predicting the subject's specific

behaviour."[1] This of course is a reasonable hypothesis; it could easily be tested by comparing a prediction of final successes made on the basis of a statistical weighting of all the separate test results, ratings, etc., with the final rating based on such an organismic point of view. Such a procedure would have thrown a great deal of light on the process of organismic judgment formation itself, and would also have been something of a crucial experiment to test the organismic hypothesis. By assuming this hypothesis to be true, and by completely ostracizing any kind of statistical treatment which would have enabled them to test its validity, the authors have thrown overboard the possibility of convincing their theoretical opponents by proper scientific proof, and have, instead, relied on semantic argument. It has fallen to Kelly and Fiske (1950) in their recent study to show that when a study of this type is carried out in such a way as to enable a comparison to be made between the two methods of approach, then the organismic is decisively inferior to the elementalistic. The scientific reader will hardly need this additional evidence to show the superiority of actual proof over mere argument.

In view of this organismic bias of the authors, it is difficult to assess such intercorrelations as they have provided between ratings, as their method of arriving at these seems to make a halo effect even more certain than is usual in rating studies. They report intercorrelations for 133 men on such variables as motivation, energy, and intiative, effective intelligence, emotional stability, social relations, leadership, physical ability, security, observing and reporting, propaganda skills and overall ratings; they also report on a factorial study of this matrix of intercorrelation which gives rise to four non-orthogonal factors. The first of these is called adjustment, and is

---

[1] The view here put forward is similar to a general philosophical belief often labelled "idiographic", as opposed to the more atomistic "nomothetic" approach. These terms originated with the German philosopher Windelband, and were popularized in the English literature by Allport. Other labels under which this particular discussion has been carried on are: "understanding" versus "explanatory" approach, and "clinical" versus "statistical" methods (Meehl, 1954). The idiographic, understanding, clinical approach emphasizes the uniqueness of the individual, stresses the investigation of the "total personality", and rejects as "atomistic" the analysis of personality into traits, abilities, attitudes and so forth. The nomothetic, explanatory, statistical approach retains faith in the traditional scientific method, and believes in its applicability to human behaviour. The strongest arguments for the idiographic point of view have been put forward by members of the Harvard School, in particular Allport and Murray. For a detailed presentation of the nomothetic point of view, and a review of the relevant experimental literature, cf. Eysenck, 1952.

clearly again the "*w*" factor emerging in these rather novel surroundings. The second factor is called effective intelligence, and has high loadings on the ratings of effective intelligence, on observing and reporting, propaganda scales, and over-all ratings. The third factor, physical energy, is loaded on energy and initiative, leadership and physical ability. The last factor has only two loadings of any size ("energy and initiative" and "leadership") and is labelled "authoratative assertion". (The absence of an extravert-introvert factor is presumably due to the fact that none of the traits rated is relevant to such a factor.)

The four factors are highly intercorrelated. Thus, adjustment correlates ·58 with affective intelligence, ·70 with physical energy, and ·06 with authoritative assertion. Effective intelligence correlates ·37 with physical energy and ·48 with authoritative assertion. Physical energy and authoritative assertion are almost uncorrelated (R = ·09). No higher-order factor is derived, so that the study is manifestly incomplete.

It is interesting, however, to note that even in this organismic setting, a factor of adjustment or neuroticism emerges so clearly, particularly as it appears to give rise to what the writers seem to consider their main theoretical finding, namely that the "conception of the 'personality as a whole' points to goal-directed forces or conation as the chief unifying and integrating factor in personality". In this conclusion, of course, they are at one with Webb and many other members of the English school, although they make no reference to these earlier workers.

A detailed analysis of the interrelationships between the O.S.S. situational tests is given by Sakoda (1952). He made use of some 60 ratings which were considered in assessing the candidates' qualifications. "The trait names and the number of situations in which they were rated were as follows:

1. Energy and initiative, 7
2. Effective intelligence, 12
3. Emotional stability, 4
4. Social relations, 8
5. Leadership, 7
6. Physical ability, 4
7. Security, 4
8. Observing and reporting, 7
9. Propaganda skills, 5
10. Motivation for assignment, 2

Candidates were assigned to subgroups of five to seven members and were rated by a team of three staff members. Ratings of the staff members on a six point scale were pooled by a discussion procedure to arrive at a unanimous final overall rating." Fig. 22 shows

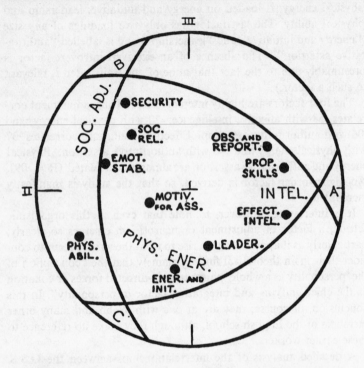

Fig. 22.—Spherical graph of the interrelationships among ten traits.

the three factors emerging from an analysis of the interrelations between the ten traits. In addition Sakoda also carried out an analysis of the intercorrelations between the individual tests within four of the traits used. The results are shown in Fig. 23. "Each situation is represented as a point on the surface of a sphere in order to portray at least three dimensions. The arcs drawn into the curve form a spherical right triangle and represent points of zero correlation with an X point opposite it. The Arc B-C for instance, represents points on zero correlation with crosspoint A. The distance between any two points indicates degrees of correlation, zero correlation being represented by exact coincidence of two points."

The results support Sakoda's contention that "One of the conclusions to be drawn from this series of factor analyses is that in assessing the qualifications of individuals it is necessary to consider the kind of situation as well as the kinds of traits. In other words, a trait is not meaningful unless it is considered in the context of a kind

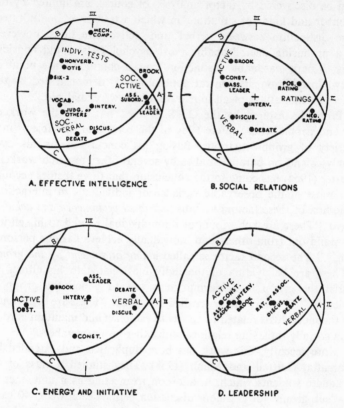

Fig. 23.—Sperical graphs of interrelationships of situational tests for four traits.

Situations: Assigned Leader, Assigned Subordinate, Brook, Construction, Debate, Discussion, Interview, Judgment of Others, Mechanical Comprehension, Negative Rating by Associates, Nonverbal, Obstacle, Otis, Positive Rating by Associates, Rating by Associates, SIX-2, Vocabulary.

of situation. Roughly, the O.S.S. study indicates that the ratings of different traits in different situations calls for the consideration of at least two general kinds of situation: the 'active' situation of the Brook and Assigned Leader sort, and the 'verbal situation' of the Debate and Discussion sort. In addition, it is necessary to consider some situations for some traits but not for others. For Effective

Intelligence, for instance, in addition to the 'active' and 'verbal' situations, it is necessary to consider the 'individual test' situations. For Social Relations, the Rating of Associates situation must also be considered. The number and kinds of general situations which can be discovered by factor analysis, of course, are limited by the number and kinds of situations in which a trait is originally rated. The distinction between 'verbal' and 'active' situations, however, is a promising one. Probably most psychologists would consider this to be a reasonable distinction from a common-sense point of view. In addition, its general applicability is demonstrated by the effect on the ratings of all four traits which were analysed."

Probably inspired by the O.S.S. studies, has been the work of several people whose interest lay in the behaviour of subjects in a variety of group situations. Basing his conclusions on his own analyses and on parallel studies by several other research workers, Carter (1954) has come to the conclusion that three factors account for most of the observable variance of individuals in interaction. The first of these factors he calls *individual prominence and achievement*. "These are behaviours of the individual related to his efforts to stand out from others and individually achieve various personal goals." The second factor is called *aiding attainment by the group*. "These are behaviours of the individual related to his efforts to assist the group in achieving goals toward which the group is oriented." The third factor is called *sociability*. "These are behaviours of the individuals related to efforts to establish and maintain cordial and socially satisfying relations with other group members."

More recently, this work has been duplicated and extended by Borgatta, Cottrell and Mann (1958). They studied a class of 47 graduate students which, in addition to meeting as a unit, met in five sub-groups for two-hour discussion periods each week. 40 variables in all were used, as shown in Table 18 and the data rankings were collected by the instructor as part of an ongoing student evaluation procedure, thus motivating the class members to give attention to the task of completing the forms. "*Rankings* of members by members within each of the five groups constituted the principal data of this study. These rankings were used both for 16 personality trait names and for 24 behavioral descriptive categories, and the variables were selected on the basis of their assumed relevance to the three factors described by Carter."

Intercorrelations were calculated and factor analysed and two major factors emerged called *individual assertiveness* and *sociability*;

these correspond directly to Carter's conclusions. "However, the third factor 'aiding attainment by the group' can be confused with either of two found in the current study, *manifest intelligence* or *task*

TABLE 18
Variables used in the factor analysis

Trait names

1. Social sensitivity	9. Conventionality
2. Friendliness	10. Assertiveness
3. Intelligence	11. Unreasonableness
4. Emotionality	12. Inquisitiveness
5. Likeability	13. Responsibility
6. Initiative	14. Suggestibility
7. Authoritarianism	15. Self-reliance
8. Agreeableness	16. Clearmindedness

Behavioural descriptive phrases

17. Makes others feel he understands them	30. Tends to direct when necessary
18. Pays most attention to task at hand	31. Discusses things in personal terms
19. Provides best ideas	32. Does most to determine discussion
20. Does most of the talking	33. Tends to be most nervous
21. Makes the most suggestions	34. Facilitates the group operation
22. Is most co-operative	35. Withdraws from active participation
23. Supports others' suggestions	36. Interrupts others
24. Shows solidarity and friendliness	37. Is most spontaneous in response
25. Tends to be antagonistic	38. Dismisses opinion of others
26. Disagrees most	39. Is most responsive to humour
27. Is most tense	40. Attempts to dominate others
28. Is most active	
29. Makes most emotional responses	

interest. The fifth factor found, *manifest emotionality* might be included in Carter's scheme because of the possibility of confusing such a factor (negatively stated) with sociability."

It is interesting that even in this somewhat unusual situation, extraversion (sociability) and neuroticism (manifest emotionality) emerge relatively clearly. It would seem to be an important task for future research to investigate the behaviour and success in different types of tasks of groups made up in varying but known proportions of strongly extraverted, strongly introverted, highly stable and highly unstable members. This method of experimental manipulating personality factors as the independent variable, and studying its influence on performance, as a dependent variable, should give us considerable insight into group functioning.

We must now turn to the more pedestrian but equally interesting work reported by a group of psychologists connected with the Fels study. 30 rating scales of unusually high inter-rater relia-bility were constructed by the psychologists, and 40 nursery children rated on 29 of these scales. The intercorrelations between the scales are relatively high; when submitted to a factorial analysis by Richards and Simons (1941), they gave rise to three factors. Table 19 sets out the names of the scales used, the saturations for the

TABLE 19

Scale	Factor Loadings				Chron. Age	Binet I.Q.	Merrill-Palmer S.D. Score	Vineland Social Quotient	Joël Behav. Quotient
	I	II	III	h²					
Affectionateness . .				·07	− ·16	·00	·06	·28	·23
Aggressiveness . .	·64	·60		·82	·25	·18	·02	·21	·49
Cheerfulness . .	·35	−·26	·70	·69	·07	·11	·07	·09	·32
Competitiveness . .	·80	·31		·73	·61	·36	·27	·12	·58
Conformity (non.) .		·74	−·32	·69	− ·22	−·00	− ·34	·27	− ·28
Cruelty . . .	·23	·81		·71	·00	−·08	− ·08	·06	·08
Curiosity . . .	·23	·29	·57	·46	·10	·08	− ·29	·18	·26
Emotional control (non.) . .		·79		·70	− ·14	−·10	− ·24	·23	− ·11
Emotional excitability .		·83		·71	− ·32	−·02	− ·21	·23	·17
Fancifulness . .	·62			·43	·51	·50	·53	·15	·49
Frequency of gross activity . . .	·68	·52		·77	− ·08	−·09	− ·15	·33	·31
Friendliness . . .	·71		·47	·74	·40	·15	·08	·18	·51
Gregariousness . .	·70	·36	·29	·70	·51	·02	·00	·04	·48
Intensity of emotional response . . .		·71		·56	− ·02	−·02	− ·16	·22	·17
Jealousy . . .		·69	·55	·79	·51	·16	·14	·08	·26
Kindness . . .	·52	−·61		·69	·43	·10	·05	− ·04	·30
Leadership . . .	·88			·84	·62	·41	·34	·20	·63
Obedience (non.) . .		·85		·74	·05	·01	·07	·28	·08
Originality . . .	·72			·57	·33	·22	·02	·07	·31
Physical apprehensive-ness (non.) . .	·27	·37	·62	·59	− ·09	·04	− ·00	·30	·27
Planfulness . . .	·71	−·28		·58	·55	·26	·38	− ·07	·41
Quarrelsomeness . .	·25	·89		·85	·09	−·07	− ·11	·15	·11
Resistance . . .		·86		·80	·26	·11	·05	·31	·05
Sense of humour .	·44		·66	·63	·34	·14	− ·02	·18	·24
Sensitiveness . .	·54		−·47	·51	·44	·15	·24	·07	·31
Social apprehensiveness (non.) . . .	·35	·37	·72	·78	·13	·11	− ·19	·23	·24
Suggestibility (non.) .		·73	·44	·75	− ·09	·11	·21	·16	·05
Tenacity . . .	·40	−·42		·33	·30	·20	·15	·03	·19
Vigour of activity .	·66	·53		·76	·18	−·17	− ·08	·35	·27

three factors, and the correlations of the scales with chronological age, with Binet I.Q., Merrill-Palmer sigma score, Vineland Social quotient, and the Joël behaviour quotient.

The interpretation of the factors is less certain than might be wished. "Inspection of these factor loadings suggests that Factor I has to do with desirability of behavior, in that desirable behavior at the nursery-school level is mature behavior. The pattern of coefficients is quite similar to that for the correlation of the scales with chrono-logical age. But the pattern is also similar to that for the correlation of the scales with the Joël scale, where age was partialled out by using the Behavior Quotient. A name for this factor might be 'desirability of behavior' or 'maturity of behavior'." This factor is considered similar by the authors also to Richards' (1940) factor of "desirability" derived from the Merrill-Palmer Personality Rating Scales, and to Van Alstyne's (1936) factor of the same name established on young elementary schoolchildren. It is not believed that this factor resembles those extracted from correlations of ratings for adults.

"Factor II . . . seems to be one of independence or non-conformity, or even antagonism. It is in most saturation in *quarrelsomeness, resistance, disobedience, emotional excitability, cruelty, lack of emotional control, non-conformity*, etc. Its pattern is similar to that for the Vineland Social Maturity Scale. . . . The guess may be hazarded that this factor corresponds in part at least to neuroticism; in the absence of other nursery-school studies, and lacking follow-up investigations of the future adjustment of the children prominently saturated with this factor, such identification must remain extremely speculative. Yet it fits in well enough with general psychiatric theories of child development."

"Factor III is of greatest amount in *lack of social apprehensiveness* ('poise'), *cheerfulness, sense of humor, lack of physical apprehensiveness*, etc. It might be called a mood factor, or an extroverted factor, with sensitiveness and independence at the negative end. It may be similar to the 'surgency' factor. . . ." This interpretation in terms of extraversion appears reasonable to the present writer, although again the lack of comparative data from other studies, and the absence of longitudinal investigations, makes correct identification difficult.

Brief mention should perhaps be made in connection with this discussion of the Fels Child Behavior Scales of the Fels Parent Behavior Rating Scales. These 30 scales, discussed in detail by Champneys (1941) and Baldwin, Kalhorn, and Breese (1945, 1949), were constructed with great care, and have been submitted to correlational analysis in four separate publications. In the first of these, Baldwin (1946) compared a sample of 74 sets of behaviour ratings of the parents of 3-year-old children with a sample of 79 sets of ratings of parents of 9-year-old children. (The ratings in each case were made by experienced home visitors.) Complete sets of intercorrelations were calculated, for the two age-groups separately; also calculated was a set of correlations between composite variables representing an average of the individual variables making up the composites. The correlations between these 13 composite variables are presented by the authors; unfortunately no factorial analysis was carried out to clarify the pattern of relationships disclosed.

This defect was made good by Roff (1949), who factor analysed correlations between all the 30 scales as given by Baldwin, Kalhorn, and Breese (1945). A summary of his results is given in Table 20. Roff labels the factors as follows: I. Concern for the child. II. Democratic guidance. III. Permissiveness. IV. Parent-child harmony. V. Solicitousness. VI. Activeness of the home. VII. Non-readiness of suggestion. (?) These factors themselves are intercorrelated, sometimes to a considerable extent ($r_{24} = \cdot 64$; $r_{13} = \cdot 36$; $r_{12} = \cdot 37$), and it seems unfortunate that Roff has neglected to calculate second-order factors. If he had done so, his analysis might have approximated somewhat more closely to Baldwin, Kalhorn, and Breese's original work (1945), where they isolated three main factors by means of cluster analysis, called by them "Warmth", "Objectivity", and "Parental control".

Another failure which runs through the whole of the Fels work tends to make the scientific value of these excellent studies somewhat less than it might be. As we have seen, factorial studies of child behaviour give rise to factors descriptive of child behaviour; factorial studies of parental behaviour give rise to factors descriptive of parental behaviour. It seems strange that no attempt has been made to bring together these two sets of data, and to show to what extent parental and child behaviour are themselves related. Only in such an imbrication of the two separate types of study can the whole work find its proper fruition; in its absence we can only hope that in time this lack will be made good.

An excellent example of the enrichment of knowledge which may follow upon such a step is fortunately already available in the work of Hewitt and Jenkins (1946), to which we must turn next. This research is the only one to apply factorial method *both* to behaviour *and* to environment, and to link the factors derived from the one with the factors derived from the other. Taking their material from routine case histories, these authors studied 500 problem children, 78 per cent. of whom were boys and 22 per cent. of whom were girls. The average age of this group was between 11 and 12 and the mean I.Q. was 94. 45 traits were taken from the case histories, and intercorrelations calculated by means of tetrachorics. A modified form of cluster analysis was then performed in which traits were grouped to-

TABLE 20

Summary of Factor Loadings

	I	II	III	IV	V	VI	VII
Factor I: Concern for Child							
7 Contact duration	69						
21 Protectiveness	69						
20 Babying	63						
6 Child-centred	57						
25 Solicitous	53				− 36		
26 Acceptance	39			31			
4 Family sociable	− 37				70		− 41
9 Non-restrictive	− 37	32	35		32		
Factor II: Democratic Guidance							
12 Justification		64					
13 Democracy		62					
24 Explanation		62					
18 Non-coercive		61					
27 Understanding		43			33		
14 Clarity policy		38					
19 Accelerational		36				36	
23 Favourable criticism		34					
28 Non-emotional		33		33	− 35		
9 Non-restrictive	− 37	32	35		32		
Factor III: Permissiveness							
11 Non-severity			61				
10 Non-enforcement			51				
9 Non-restrictive	− 37	32	35		32		
Factor IV: Parent-child Harmony							
16 Non-friction				63			
15 Effectiveness				61			
3 Home non-discord				42	31		
22 Non-criticism				41			33
30 Rapport				40			
28 Non-emotional		33		33	− 35		
26 Acceptance	39			31			
Factor V: Sociability-adjustment of Parents							
4 Family sociable	− 37				70		− 41
1 Home adjustment					55		
25 Solicitous	53				− 36		
28 Non-emotional		33		33	− 35		
27 Understanding		43			33		
29 Affectionate					32		
9 Non-restrictive	− 37	32	35		32		
3 Home non-discord				42	31		
Factor VI: Activeness of Home							
2 Home active						76	
5 Co-ordination						53	
19 Accelerational		36				36	
Factor VII: Non-readiness of Suggestion							
17 Non-suggestion							58
4 Family sociable	− 37				70		− 41
8 Intense contact							− 34
22 Non-criticism				41			33

gether in such a way that all the group correlations were higher than ·30, while the correlations of one cluster with another were a good deal lower than this value. Three clusters were found in this way. The first one was called "unsocialized aggressive behaviour" and is made up of the following traits: assaultive tendencies, initiatory fighting, cruelty, defiance of authority, malicious mischief, and inadequate guilt feelings. The second cluster is called "socialized delinquency behaviour" and is made up of the following traits: bad companions, gang activities, co-operative stealing, furtive stealing, school truancy, truancy from home, and staying out late nights. The third cluster, "over-inhibited behaviour", is made up of the following traits: seclusiveness, shyness, apathy, worrying, sensitiveness, and submissiveness.

Corresponding to these three behaviour patterns there are three situational patterns built up in the same way by means of cluster analysis. The first of the situational patterns is called "parental rejection". It is made up of the following items: illegitimate pregnancy, pregnancy unwanted by father or mother, post-delivery rejection by father or mother, mother unwilling to accept parent rôle, mother sexually unconventional, mother-person openly hostile to child, loss of contact with both natural parents. The second cluster, called "parental negligence", is made up of the following items: interior of home unkempt, irregular home routine, lack of supervision, discipline lax, mother mentally inadequate, discipline harsh, mother shielding, sibling delinquency, deteriorated area. The third cluster is called "family repression" and is made up of the following items: father's discipline inconsistent, father hypercritical, father or mother unsociable, mother demanding, sibling rivalry, and mother-compensated rejection. A fourth cluster of "physical deficiency" was also established, but is probably of less psychological interest than the others: it is made up of items like central nervous system disorder, abnormal growths pattern, convulsions, auditory or speech defect, diseased tonsils or adenoids, chronic physical complaints. The intercorrelations between these four patterns are not high. Negligence correlates negatively with repression ($-·21$) and with physical deficiency ($-·32$), repression and physical deficiency correlate ($·21$), and parental rejection and repression correlate ($·18$).

We must now turn to the fundamental hypothesis underlying the work of Hewitt and Jenkins. This hypothesis they state in the following way: "Children who differ from each other in expressing fundamentally different patterns of behaviour of maladjustment . . .

must have experienced fundamentally different patterns of environmental states; and conversely, children who are exposed to such fundamentally different patterns of situations will exhibit fundamentally different patterns of maladjustments." Proof for this hypothesis is sought in the table of correlations between the three clusters representing child behaviour and the four clusters representing situational patterns. This table is given below (Table 21), and it is certainly striking to observe the degree to which parental rejection is accompanied by unsocialized aggressive behaviour, negligence by socialized

TABLE 21

	Unsocialized Aggression	Socialized Delinquency	Over-inhibited Behaviour	Number of Cases
Parental rejection .	·48 ± ·07	·02	− ·20	101
Parental negligence	·12	·63 ± ·07	− ·17	78
Parental repression	·10	− ·12	·52 ± ·06	106
Physical deficiency .	− ·23	− ·31	·46 ± ·06	95

deliquency behaviour, and repression by over-inhibited behaviour (it is less surprising to find physical deficiency correlated positively with over-inhibited behaviour and negatively with unsocialized aggressive and socialized delinquent behaviour). Striking as these figures are, they cannot be taken as necessarily providing proof of the hypothesis advanced by Hewitt and Jenkins. Similar correlations might have been caused by the action of inheritance, which might be responsible both for the repressive behaviour of the parent and the over-inhibited behaviour of the child, or the negligent behaviour of the parent and the delinquent behaviour of the child, or even the rejective behaviour of the parent and the aggressive behaviour of the child, without assuming any direct causal relation between the behaviour of the parent and that of the child. The data given support the environmental view no more than they support the hereditary view; it is illusory to believe that the proof of the existence of a correlation between two variables can ever throw any light on the cause responsible for that correlation. Quite a different type of experimental design would be required to prove the hypothesis in question. In saying this we do not wish to detract from the interest and the importance of a piece of research which must be regarded as one of the most outstanding in the whole field of personality organization; the factorial findings remain quite unaffected by the criticism of the hypothesis regarding the origin of the observed interconnections.

Support for some of Jenkins' and Hewitt's findings comes from another study of *Children's Behavior Problems* by Ackerson (1942).[1] Taking a sample of 2,113 white boys and 1,181 white girls from the files of the Illinois Institute for Juvenile Research, this author selected a number of traits whose incidence seemed large enough to justify such procedures, and calculated tetrachoric intercorrelations between them. The number of traits used is quite large, amounting to 162. Two of the traits used are compound traits called "personality total" and "conduct total"; these terms refer to disorder manifestations either in the field of personality or conduct, and are, as it were, summed scores on a variety of sub-items.

Ackerson himself merely reports several thousand intercorrelations which result from his labour; he does not attempt to carry out a factorial study. This deficiency has been remedied by Himmelweit (1952), who selected 50 traits or notations from the total number given by Ackerson and carried out a centroid analysis. Fig. 24 gives a diagrammatic picture of the first two factors obtained from her analysis of the data for the boys in Ackerson's sample. The existence of a general factor of abnormality is quite marked, as is the division in the second factor between introverted items (sensitive, absent-minded, seclusive, depressed, day-dreams, inefficient, queer, inferiority feelings, nervous, and changeable moods, to which must be added psychoneurotic, which notation in Ackerson's work appears to refer to dysthymic disorders only), and extraverted items (stealing, truancy from home and school, destructive, lying, swearing, disobedient, disturbing influence, violent, rude, and egocentric). As these two groups of items were used to establish personality total and conduct total respectively, it is not surprising to find that these two notations have clear projections on the positive and negative end of the second factor respectively.

These data support an explanation of extraversion-introversion, which has sometimes been made by followers of Freud, namely that introversion appears to reflect a predominance of super-ego over id activities, whereas extraversion reflects a predominance of id over super-ego activities. It should be possible to test a hypothesis of this kind experimentally; in the absence of such experimental proof it constitutes merely an alternative way of describing the same set of data. Altogether, identification of these two factors must be regarded as rather speculative in view of the fact that not much work has been

[1] In England the work of H. Lewis (1954) has also given some support to the dimensional analysis carried out by Jenkins and Hewitt.

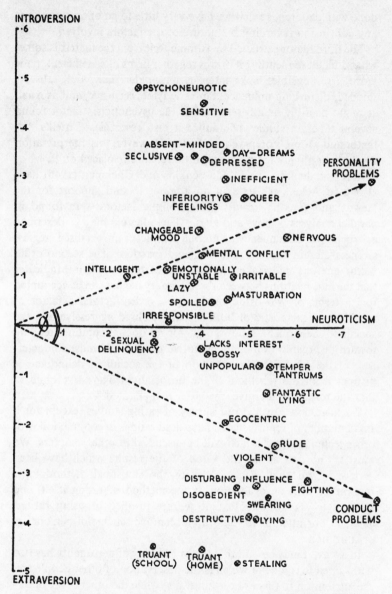

Fig. 24.—Two-factor Representation of Ackerson's Correlational Study.

done with children, so that we have very little to go on in arriving at any conclusion regarding the nature of the factors involved.

The third factor extracted by Himmelweit from the matrix is somewhat difficult to identify; it brings together items like inefficient, poor work, irresponsible, lacks interest, unpopular, lazy, dull, absentminded, disturbing influence, fantastic lying, seclusive, and asexual. It might possibly be a forerunner of the psychoticism factor found several times in studies of adults; it also resembles Cattell's "a" factor and Moore's prepsychotic factor. However, this interpretation also is exceedingly tentative and little reliance is placed on it.

Lorr and Jenkins (1953) and Jenkins and Glickman (1946) have also used Ackerson's data in an attempt to find support for the Hewitt and Jenkins' results. Five oblique factors were found in parallel analyses of boys and girls. "These factors may be described as 'socialised delinquency', 'internal conflict', 'unsocialised aggressiveness', 'brain damage' and 'schizoid reaction'. The second order factor analysis undertaken in the case of the boys only, indicates that the interrelations between these primary factors can be accounted for in terms of two orthogonal second order factors, a factor of rebellion characteristic of both the unsocialised aggressive and the socialised delinquent, and the factor of mal-adaptation tending toward disorganisation of the adaptive process and most characteristic of the schizoid. The rebellion of the socialised delinquent is distinct from the rebellion of the unsocialised aggressive child in that the former is adaptive, the latter mal-adapted."

We have now finished our survey of rating studies, except for a small number of reports which have used ratings in conjunction with other techniques and which will be discussed in other chapters. We must try now to assess the value of the results which have been reviewed. We shall deal, not with the statistical methodology, but rather with an evaluation of the method of rating itself, and attempt to see to what extent we are justified in using ratings at all in our attempt to build up a scientific scheme of personality organization.

In a way, it may be said that the psychology of personality has two paths open to it, one of which is the observation of other people and the attribution to them of certain traits, while the other is the observation of one's own self and one's own motives and thought processes. While these two methods are primary, they are clearly subject to many dangers. The vast volume of work which has been carried out in the field of ratings shows what some of these dangers are.

(1) *Differential Understanding of Trait Names*

It is only too obvious when talking to two persons who undertake to rate others that their conception of terms, such as suggestibility, sense of humour, persistence, and so forth, varies widely and that on occasions quite contradictory meanings are associated with the same trait name. It is possible to reduce the influence of this factor by very careful discussions with each judge of the exact meaning of the term used; in the absence of such clarification of terms, it is almost impossible to attribute any meaning to the results of rating studies.

(2) *The Halo Effect*

It was observed quite early in the history of psychology that sets of ratings on different traits tend to show unduly high intercorrelations which, as Thorndike maintained in 1920, might be due to the general impression of the ratee possessed by the rater. This general stereotyped attitude would then colour all the judgments made of particular traits. As Vernon (1938) points out: "Most commonly, halo consists largely of our general liking for, or our dislike of the ratees, for it is usually found that the desirable or admirable traits give high positive intercorrelations and negative correlations with undesirable traits. Doubtless, this has some basis in actual fact; persons of fine character do tend to be high on all good qualities. Others do tend to be weak all round, but one is very liable to exaggerate this and to attribute unwittingly all the virtues to our friends, and the vices to our enemies."

(3) *Differences in Rating Ability*

Persons who rate others on personality traits may be presumed to differ with respect to their ability to carry out this task. Thus, for instance, Sheldon (1942) reports correlations between his own ratings and those of a class of graduate students, ranging from ·17 to ·94. Even if we refuse to accept Sheldon's own ratings as providing an objective standard of validity, and even if we consider that defective ratings may be due not only to lack of ability but also to other factors, such as lack of interest, lack of time, or lack of inclination, the fact remains that very marked differences are usually observed between raters, and that as long as no objective standard of validity can be applied, selection of raters must be relatively haphazard and may include the good and the bad indifferently.

(4) *Influence of Unconscious Bias*

The halo effect in a way is unconscious, but it may be reduced by acquainting judges with the existence of such a factor. Some bias, however, is very much more deeply rooted in the personality organization of the rater. Thus Sears (1936), in an elaborate study of raters and ratings, came to the following conclusions:

(i) "Those subjects who lacked insight into the amount of a given trait they themselves possessed tended, on the average, to attribute a greater amount of that trait to other people than did those subjects who possessed an equal amount of the trait but had insight."

(ii) "Projection [of this type] was not operative in influencing the judgments of all subjects on any given trait; its occurrence was apparently confined to those who lacked insight."

(iii) "In the group of subjects who possessed insight a negative correlation was found between amount of trait possessed and amount attributed to others. This suggests the operation of a dynamic process, tentatively entitled *contrast-formation*, which has an effect opposite to that of projection on judgments about others' personalities."

(iv) "Judgments about other people with respect to both acceptable and unacceptable [reprehensible] traits showed the influence of projection and contrast-formation."

These tendencies towards projection and contrast-formation in rating others were also found by Frenkel-Brunswik (1942) in her very important monograph on motivation and behaviour.

(5) *Influence of Acquaintanceship*

Vernon (1938) has summarized the literature to date to show that prolonged observation and close acquaintanceship do not necessarily improve ratings. Additional information on this point has since come to hand in very large-scale rating studies carried out by the O.S.S. (1948) and by the participants in the Michigan selection study (Kelly and Fiske, 1950). Contrary to the expectation of the psychologists and psychiatrists concerned in these studies, it was found again that relatively superficial knowledge gave better predictive accuracy than more thorough and detailed knowledge of subjects. These findings would seem to rule out what might appear to be one of the most promising methods for improving ratings, namely the use as raters of people having an intimate acquaintanceship with the ratees.

(6) *Rating of Observed and Inferred Behaviour*

It is often believed that more reliable and valid ratings can be obtained by restricting ratings to actually observed behaviour rather than to rate traits inferred from behaviour thought to be relevant to the trait. However, Newcomb (1931) has shown that ratings on observed items of behaviour are not significantly superior to ratings on behaviour which has only been inferred, and Frenkel-Brunswik (1942) has brought forward impressive evidence to show the superiority, under certain circumstances, of rating hypothetical variables far removed from behaviour rather than traits closer to overt observed behaviour.

(7) *Alternative Manifestations*

Frenkel-Brunswik (1942) has shown that "different classes of behavioral expressions were often related to one drive as alternative manifestations of that drive". She found that "one drive variable may circumscribe a family of alternative manifestations unrelated to each other: the meaning of the drive concept emerges in terms of families of divergent manifestations held together dynamically or genotypically, though often not phenotypically. And, on the other

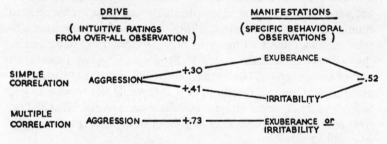

Fig. 25.—Alternative Manifestations of the same Drive.

hand, one overt expression may be related to several underlying tendencies." Her findings are illustrated in Fig. 25, where exuberance or irritability are taken to be alternative manifestations of the same drive of aggression.

(8) *Reliability and Validity*

When all the above-mentioned factors are taken into account, it will not surprise the reader to find the literature replete with indications of the low reliability of ratings, or to find that when reliabilities are high the explanation may be in terms of common bias or halo rather than in terms of validity. However, the picture is not altogether dark. Hartshorne and May (1928, 1929, 1930) found fairly high correlations between ratings and batteries of objective tests of honesty, self-control, and so forth, and many later writers have shown agreement between ratings on traits, such as neuroticism, and objective tests. Thus, it would be too radical a conclusion to say that ratings are entirely valueless, just as a too easy acceptance of the ratings must be deprecated as unlikely to lead to scientifically worth-while conclusions.

It will be clear from what has been said that a rating cannot be taken strictly as a description of the person rated; it is always quite inevitably an interaction between rater and ratee, and as such may, by appropriate methods of analysis, be used to throw light either on the ratee or on the rater, or on the interaction between the two, i.e. the process of rating itself. Most of the studies reviewed have failed to give due regard to the complexities of the subject, and if in spite of this there is such remarkable agreement at least on two main factors, namely emotional instability or neuroticism and introversion-extraversion, we must take this to indicate the great prominence of these factors which successfully penetrate the obscuring fog of the various influences outlined above. Just as ratings of intelligence are inaccurate, unreliable, and subject to many extraneous influences, so ratings of non-intellectual qualities are equally inaccurate, unreliable, and subject to many extraneous influences; nevertheless, the existence of something akin to Spearman's "g" or Thurstone's second-order factor of intellectual ability can be gleaned from ratings and personal observation. Beyond that it would not be wise to go; to lay too much stress on minute differences and refined statistical treatment in dealing with data so subject to disturbing influences is of doubtful value.

We may perhaps make two suggestions. In the first place, future studies using ratings should take into consideration all the difficulties involved and should attempt to set up the whole experiment in such a fashion as to obtain information, not only on the ratee but also on the raters and on the rating process. There is no justification any more for rating studies to neglect the contributions made by Sears, Frenkel-Brunswik, and others. If these more complex methods are adopted, we may hope to gain further insight into the organization of personality.

The second suggestion also relates to the design of experiments. Factor analysis has two main functions: (1) to explore a completely unknown territory and suggests principles of classification; (2) the setting up of explicit experiments on the basis of a clearly defined hypothesis which can be supported or refuted by the outcome of the experiment. The majority of the studies reviewed in this chapter are of the first type; surely the time has come when we can abandon an approach which can have merely suggestive results and take up instead an approach which follows more closely the hypothetico-deductive method so characteristic of the more developed sciences.

REFERENCES

Chapter IV

ACKERSON, L. *Children's Behavior Problems*. Chicago: Univ. Chicago Press, 1942.

ADCOCK, C. J. A factorial examination of Sheldon's Types. *J. Pers.*, 1948, **16**, 312–319.

ALLPORT, G. W., and ODBERT, H. S. Trait-names: A psycho-lexical Study. *Psychol. Monogr.*, 1936, **47**, 171.

BALDWIN, A. L. Differences in parent behavior toward three- and nine-year-old children. *J. Pers.*, 1946, **15**, 143–165.

BALDWIN, A. L., KALHORN, J., and BREESE, T. H. Patterns of parent behavior. *Psychol. Monogr.*, 1945, **58**, 1–75.

The appraisal of parent behavior. *Psychol. Monogr.*, 1949, **63**, 1–85.

BANKS, C. Primary personality factors in women: a reanalysis. *Brit. J. Psychol.*, *Stat. Sect.*, 1948, **1**, 204–218.

BLEWETT, D. B., and STEFANINK, W. B. Weyburn assessment scale. *J. ment. Sci.*, 1958, **104**, 359–371.

BORGATTA, E. F., COTTRELL, L. S., and MANN, J. H. The spectrum of individual interaction characteristics: an inter-dimensional analysis. *Psychol. Rep.*, 1958, **4**, 239–319.

BROGDEN, H. E. A multiple factor analysis of the character trait inter-correlations published by Sister Mary McDonough. *J. educ. Psychol.*, 1944, **35**, 397–410.

BRYANT, J. H., WUNTER, C. R., HINE, F. R., and DAWSON, J. G. A factorial analysis of behaviour ratings of hospitalised mental patients. *J. Psychol.*, 1958, **46**, 167–174.

BURT, C. *The Factors of the Mind*. London: Univ. London Press, 1940.

The general and specific factors underlying the primary emotions. *Brit. Ass. Ann. Rep.*, 1915, **84**, 694–696.

The analysis of temperament. *Brit. J. med. Psychol.*, 1937, **17**, 158–188.

The factorial analysis of emotional traits. *Charact. Pers.*, 1939, **7**, 238–254, 285–299.

The factorial study of temperament traits. *Brit. J. Psychol.*, *Stat. Sect.*, 1948, **1**, 178–203.

CARTER, L. F. Recording and evaluating the performance of individuals as members of small groups. *Personnel Psychol.*, 1954, **7**, 477–484.

CATTELL, R. B. Temperament Tests: I. Temperament. *Brit. J. Psychol.*, 1933, **23**, 308–329.

Temperament Tests: II. Tests. *Brit. J. Psychol.*, 1934, **24**, 20–49.

The description of personality. *Psychol. Rev.*, 1943, **50**, 539–594.

Oblique, second-order, and co-operative factors in personality analysis. *J. genet. Psychol.*, 1947, **36**, 3–22.

The primary personality factors in women compared with those of men. *Brit. J. Psychol., Stat. Sect.*, 1948, **1**, 114–130.

Personality and Motivation Structure and Measurement. London: Harrap & Co. Ltd., 1957.

CHAMPNEYS, H. The variables of parent behavior. *J. abnorm. soc. Psychol.*, 1941, **36**, 525–542.

DEGAN, J. W. Dimensions of functional psychosis. *Psychometr. Monogr.*, **6**, 1952.

DOUST, J. W. L. The psychiatric aspects of somatic immunity; the differential incidence of physical disease in the histories of psychiatric patients. *Brit. J. soc. Med.*, 1952, **6**, 49–67.

EKMAN, G. On typological and dimensional systems of reference in describing personality. *Acta Psychol.*, 1951, **8**, 1–24.

EYSENCK, H. J. Types of personality—a factorial study of 700 neurotics. *J. ment. Sci.*, 1944, **90**, 851–861.

Dimensions of Personality. London: Kegan Paul, 1947.

The Scientific Study of Personality. London: Routledge & Kegan Paul, 1952.

Classification and the problem of diagnosis. In: *Handbook of Abnormal Psychology* (Ed.: H. J. Eysenck), London: Pitman, 1959.

FLEMMING, E. G. The "halo" around "personality". *Teach Coll. Rec.*, 1942, **43**, 564–569.

FRENKEL-BRUNSWIK, E. Motivation and behavior. *Genet. psychol. Mon.*, 1942, **26**, 121–265.

Mechanisms of self-deception. *J. Psychol.*, 1939, **10**, 409–420.

GANNON, J. T. A statistical study of certain diagnostic personality traits of College men. *Stud. Psychol. Psychiat. Cathol. Univ. America*, 1939, No. 4, 45.

GARNETT, J. C. M. General ability, cleverness and purpose. *Brit. J. Psychol.*, 1918, **9**, 345–366.

GIBB, C. Personality traits by factorial analysis. *Austral. J. Psychol. Phil.*, 1942, **20**, 1–15, 86–110, 203–227.

GUERTIN, W. H. A factor analysis of the Bender-Gestalt test of mental patients. *J. clin. Psychol.*, 1952, **8**, 363–367.

A factor analytic study of schizophrenic symptoms. *J. consult. Psychol.*, 1952, **16**, 308–312.

An inverted factor-analytic study of schizophrenics. *J. consult. Psychol.*, 1952, **16**, 371–375.

A factor analysis of curvilinear distortions on the Bender-Gestalt. *J. clin. Psychol.*, 1954, **10**, 12–17.

A factor analytic study of the adjustment of chronic schizophrenics. *J. clin. Psychol.*, 1955, **11**, 174–177.

A factor analysis of schizophrenic ratings on the Hospital Adjustment Scale. *J. clin. Psychol.*, 1955, **11**, 70–73.

HARTSHORNE, H., and MAY, M. A. *Studies in Deceit.* New York: Macmillan, 1928.

Studies in Service and Self Control. New York: Macmillan, 1929.

HARTSHORNE, H., and SHUTTLEWORTH, F. K. *Studies in the Organisation of Character.* New York: Macmillan, 1930.

HEATH, C. W. *What People Are. A study of Normal Young Men.* Cambridge: Harvard Univ. Press, 1945.

HEWITT, L. E., and JENKINS, R. L. *Fundamental Patterns of Maladjustment. The Dynamics of their Origin.* Illinois: D. H. Green, 1946.

HEYMANS, G. Über einige psychische Korrelationen. *Ztschr. f. angew. Psychol.*, 1908, **1**, 313–381.

HEYMANS, G., and WIERSMA, E. Beiträge zur speziellen Psychologie auf Grund einer Massenuntersuchung. *Ztschr. f. Psychol.*, 1906, **42**, 81–127; 1906, **43**, 321–373; 1907, **45**, 1–42; 1908, **46**, 321–333; 1908, **49**, 414–439; 1909, **51**, 1–72.

HIMMELWEIT, H. T. *A factorial study of "children's behaviour problems".* Unpublished MS., 1952.

HORN, D. A study of personality syndromes. *Charact. and Pers.*, 1944, **12**, 257–274.

HOWIE, D. Aspects of personality in the classroom: a study of ratings on personal qualities for a group of schoolboys. *Brit. J. Psychol.*, 1945, **36**, 15–28.

JENKINS, R. L. The schizophrenic sequence, withdrawal, disorganisation, psychotic reorganisation. *Amer. J. Orthopsychiat.*, 1952, **22**, 738–748.

JENKINS, R. L., and GLICKMAN, S. Common syndromes in child psychiatry: I. Deviant behavior traits. II. The schizoid child. *Amer. J. Orthopsychiat.*, 1946, **16**, 244–261.

JENKINS, R. L., and LORR, M. Type-tracking among psychotic patients. *J. clin. Psychol.*, 1954, **10**, 114–119.

KELLEY, T., and KREY, A. C. *Tests and Measurements in the Social Sciences.* New York: Scribner, 1934.

KELLY, E. L., and FISKE, D. W. The prediction of success in the V.A. training programme in clinical psychology. *Amer. Psychol.*, 1950, **5**, 395–406.

The Prediction of Performance in Clinical Psychology. Ann Arbor: Univ. Michigan, 1952.

LEWIS, H. *Deprived Children.* London: Oxford Univ. Press, 1954.

LORR, M., and JENKINS, R. L. Patterns of maladjustment in children. *J. clin. Psychol.*, 1953, **9**, 16–19.

LORR, M., and O'CONNOR, J. O. The relation between neurosis and psychosis: a re-analysis. *J. ment. Sci.*, 1957, **103**, 376–380.

LORR, M., and RUBINSTEIN, E. A. Factors descriptive of psychiatric outpatients. *J. abnorm. soc. Psychol.*, 1955, **51**, 514–522.

LORR, M., JENKINS, R. L., and O'CONNOR, J. P. Factors descriptive of psychopathology and behavior of hospitalized psychotics. *J. abnorm. soc. Psychol.*, 1955, **50**, 78–86.

LORR, M., O'CONNOR, J. P., and STAFFORD, J. W. Confirmation on nine psychotic symptom patterns. *J. clin. Psychol.*, 1957, **13**, 752–.

LORR, M., RUBINSTEIN, E., and JENKINS, R. L. A factor analysis of personality ratings of out-patients in psychotherapy. *J. abnorm. soc. Psychol.*, 1953, **48**, 511–514.

LORR, M., WITTMAN, P., and SCHANBERGER, W. An analysis of the Elgin Prognostic Scale. *J. clin. Psychol.*, 1951, **7**, 260–263.

LUBIN, A. A note on Sheldon's Table of Correlations between Temperamental Traits. *Brit. J. Psychol., Stat. Sect.*, 1950, **3**, 186–189.

MABILLE, O. Revue de morpho. *Psychologie Humaine*, 1951, **4**, No. 9, 29.

McCLOY C. H. A factor analysis of personality traits to underlie character education. *J. educ. Psychol.*, 1936, **27**, 375–387.

McDONOUGH, M. R. The empirical study of character. *Cath. Univ. Amer. Stud. Psychol. Psychiat.*, 1929, **2**, 3.

MALAPERT, G. *Les eléménts du Charactère et leurs lois de Combinaisons*. Paris, 1897.

MARTINY, M. *Essai de Biotypologie Humaine*. Paris: Peyronnet, 1948.

MAURER, K. U. Patterns of behaviour of young children as revealed by a factor analysis of trait clusters. *J. genet. Psychol.*, 1941, **59**, 177–188.

MEYER-GROSS, W., MOORE, J. N. R., and SLATER, P. Forecasting the incidence of neurosis in officers of the Army and Navy. *J. ment. Sci.*, 1949, **95**, 80–100.

MONRO, A. B. A rating scale developed for use in clinical psychiatric investigations. *J. ment. Sci.*, 1954, **100**, 657–669.

Behaviour patterns in mental disorder. *J. ment. Sci.*, 1956, **102**, 742–752.

MOORE, T. V. The empirical determination of certain syndromes underlying praecox and manic-depressive psychoses. *Amer. J. Psychiat.*, 1930, **9**, 719–738.

MURRAY, H. A. Techniques for a systematic investigation of fantasy. *J. Psychol.*, 1937, **3**, 115–143.

Explorations in Personality. New York: Oxford Univ. Press, 1938.

NEWCOMB, F. M. An experiment designed to test the validity of a rating technique. *J. educ. Psychol.*, 1931, **22**, 279–289.

O'CONNOR, J. A statistical test of psychoneurotic syndromes. *J. abnorm. soc. Psychol.*, 1953, **48**, 581–584.

O. S. S. ASSESSMENT STAFF. *Assessment of Men. Selection of Personnel for the Office of Strategic Services*. New York: Rhinehart & Co., 1948.

PINARD, J. W. Tests of perseveration: I. Their relation to character. *Brit. J. Psychol.*, 1932, **23**, 5–19.

Tests of perseveration: II. Their relation to certain psychopathic conditions and to introversion. *Brit. J. Psychol.*, 1932, **23**, 114–128.

QUEYRAT, P. *Les Charactères et l'Education Morale*, 1896.

RAO, C. R., and Slater, P. Multivariate Analysis applied to differences between neurotic groups. *Brit. J. stat. Psychol.*, 1949, **2**, 17–29.

REXROAD, C. U. A factor analysis of student traits. *J. educ. Psychol.*, 1937, **28**, 153–156.

REYBURN, M. A., and RAATH, M. J. Primary factors of personality. *Brit. J. Psychol.*, *Stat. Sect.*, 1950, **3**, 150–158.

REYBURN, M. A., and TAYLOR, J. G. Some aspects of personality. *Brit. J. Psychol.*, 1939, **30**, 151–165.

RIBOT, T. *La Psychologie des Sentiments*. Paris: Alcan, 1892.

RICHARDS, T. W. Factors in the personality of nursery school-children. *J. exp. Educ.*, 1940, **9**, 152–153.

RICHARDS, T. W., and Simons, M. P. The Fels Child Behavior Scales. *Genet. Psychol. Mon.*, 1941, **24**, 259–309.

ROFF, M. A factorial study of the Fels Parent Behavior Scales. *Child Development*, 1949, **20**, 29–45.

SAHAI, M. *Circular mentality and the pyknic body build*. Ph.D. Thesis. London: Univ. London Lib., 1931.

SAKODA, J. N. Factor analysis of O. S. S. situational tests. *J. abnorm. soc. Psychol.*, 1952, **47**, 843–852.

SANFORD, R. N., ADKINS, M. M., MILLER, R. B., and COBB, E. Physique, personality and scholarship. *Mon. Soc. Res. Child Dev.*, **7**, Ser. No. 34.

SEARS, R. R. Experimental studies on projection. I. *J. soc. Psychol.*, 1936, **7**, 151–165.

SHAGASS, C., and KERENYI, A. The "sleep" threshold. A simple form of the sedation threshold for clinical use. *Canad. Psychiat. J.*, 1958, **1**, 101–109.

SHELDON, W. H. *The Varieties of Temperament.* New York: Harper, 1942. *The Varieties of Delinquent Youth. An Introduction to Constitutional Psychiatry.* New York: Harper, 1949.

SLATER, E. The neurotic constitution. A statistical study of 2,000 neurotic soldiers. *J. Neurol. and Psychiat.*, 1943, **6**, 1–16.

SLATER, E., and SLATER, P. A heuristic theory of neurosis. *J. Neurol., Neurosurg., Psychiat.*, 1944, **7**, 49–55.

SLATER, P. The factorial analysis of a matrix of 2 × 2 tables. *J. Roy. Stat. Soc.*, 1947, **10**, 112 (Supplement).

THURSTONE, L. L. The vectors of mind. *Psychol. Rev.*, 1934, **41**, 1–32.

TROUTON, D. S., and MAXWELL, A. E. The relation between neurosis and psychosis. *J. ment. Sci.*, 1956, **102**, 1–21.

TRYON, C. McC. Evaluations of adolescent personality by adolescents. In: *Child Behavior and Development.* (Barker, R. G., Kounin, J. S., and Wright, H. F.) London: McGraw-Hill, 1943.

TRYON, R. C. *Cluster Analysis.* Michigan: Edward, 1939.

TSCHECHTELIN, S. M. A. Factor analysis of children's personality rating scales. *J. Psychol.*, 1944, **18**, 197–200.

VAN ALSTYNE, D. A new scale for rating behavior and attitudes in the elementary school. *J. educ. Psychol.*, 1936, **27**, 677–693.

VENABLES, P. H. A short scale for rating "activity-withdrawal" in schizophrenics. *J. ment. Sci.*, 1957, **103**, 197–199.

VERNON, P. E. The assessment of psychological qualities by verbal methods. London: H.M.S.O., 1938.

WEBB, E. Character and intelligence. *Brit. J. Psychol., Monogr. Supp.*, 1915, **1**, 3.

WITTENBORN, J. R. Symptom patterns in a group of mental hospital patients. *J. consult. Psychol.*, 1951, **15**, 290–302.

Patients diagnosed manic depressive psychosis–manic state. *J. consult. Psychol.*, 1952, **16**, 193–198.

WITTENBORN, J. R., and BAILEY, C. The symptoms of involutional psychosis. *J. consult. Psychol.*, 1952, **16**, 13–17.

WITTENBORN, J. R., and HOLŻBERG, J. D. The generality of psychiatric syndromes. *J. consult. Psychol.*, 1951, **15**, 372–380.

The Rorschach and descriptive diagnosis. *J. consult. Psychol.*, 1951, **15**, 460–463.

The Wechsler-Bellevue and descriptive diagnosis. *J. consult. Psychol.*, 1951, **15**, 325–329.

WITTENBORN, J. R., and LESSER G. S. Biographical factors and psychiatric symptoms. *J. clin. Psychol.*, 1951, **7**, 317–322.

WITTENBORN, J. R., and METTLER, F. A. Practical correlates of psychiatric symptoms. *J. consult. Psychol.*, 1951, **15**, 505–510.

WITTENBORN, J. R., BELL, E. G., and LESSER, G. S. Symptom patterns among organic patients of advanced age. *J. clin. Psychol.*, 1951, **7**, 328–331.

WITTENBORN, J. R., HESS, M. I., KRANTZ, K. H., MANDELL, W., and TATZ, S. The effect of rater differences on symptom rating scale clusters. *J. consult. Psychol.*, 1952, **16**, 107–109.

WITTENBORN, J. R., HOLZBERG, J. D., and SIMON, B. Symptom correlates for descriptive diagnosis. *Genet. Psychol. Monogr.*, 1953, **47**, 237–301.

WITTENBORN, J. R., MANDLER, G., and WATERHOUSE, I. K. Symptom patterns in youthful mental hospital patients. *J. clin. Psychol.*, 1951, **7**, 323–327.

Wittman, P. M. A proposed classification of fundamental psychotic behavior reactions. *Amer. Psychol.*, 1947, **2**, 420.

The Elgin Check List of fundamental psychotic behavior reactions. *Amer. Psychol.*, 1948, **3**, 280.

Woods, W. L., Brouha, L., Seltzer, C. C., *et al. Selection of Officer Candidates.* Cambridge: Harvard Univ. Press, 1943.

THE ANALYSIS OF QUESTIONNAIRES AND INVENTORIES

IF THE MAJORITY OF factorial studies making use of ratings have come from England, nearly all the questionnaire, inventory, and other self-rating studies have come from America. This fact has given rise to differences in the treatment of data which may at first appear confusing to the reader. As pointed out before, the London school, in their analysis of ratings, have followed, by and large, the principle of extracting the most comprehensive factors first and of keeping factors orthogonal; the Americans have rather followed the principle of extracting smaller "group" or "primary" factors first and letting these factors be intercorrelated. It is from the inter-correlations of these primary factors that they then proceed to extract the broader, more general factors which the English school would have extracted right at the beginning. As has been mentioned before the two procedures do not involve any fundamental difference in the final outcome of the analysis provided they are both carried out competently by workers who are clearly aware of the difficulties and fallacies involved. However, sometimes the analysis is not carried to a proper conclusion—a member of the London school may only extract the most important one or two factors; the follower of Thurstone may not complete his analysis by extracting second-order factors—and in that case there may be a superficial contrast between the two methods of analysis which may appear to give substance to the view held by some psychologists, namely that factor analysts agree with each other as little as do psychoanalysts.

The group of studies to be reviewed falls mainly into two periods, linked by a few researches which mark the transition. In the first period, attempts were made to use correlations between existing scales which were assumed to be separate measures of neuroticism, extraversion, ascendance, self-sufficiency, depression, etc., in order to discover either more parsimonious ways of arranging and scoring the tests, or of discovering more fundamentally meaningful psychological variables. In the second period, analysis became more detailed and correlations were run between individual questions, no

assumption being made about the factors which might be defined
by these questions.

It may be said without fear of contradiction that the efforts of the
first period ended in almost complete failure. As Vernon (1938)
points out: "The attempts to classify test items or symptoms logically
into distinct groups has not, we must admit, been successful. On the
one hand, it is found that tests of presumably different traits intercorrelate very highly; on the other hand, different tests of nominally
the same trait . . . tend to give very poor correlations with one another. It is doubtful, then, whether most of the traits at which the
tests have been directed are unitary and discrete."

This overlap between hypothetically different traits is most
apparent in attempts to measure neuroticism and introversion-
extraversion. Vernon (1938) quotes the results of 40 experiments
showing that the average correlation between different introversion
tests, and the average correlation between introversion and psychoneurotic tendency tests are practically identical, namely $+ \cdot36 \pm \cdot10$.
A further 18 experiments with the Ascendance-Submission test
showed an average correlation of $+ \cdot30$ between submissiveness and
introversion, or psychoneurotic tendency. Tests of inferiority feelings
also agree quite closely with tests of introversion.[1]

At first sight, such findings may appear to contradict explicitly the
results arrived at in the last chapter. There, introversion and neuroticism were considered quite unrelated orthogonal dimensions of
personality; now we seem to find evidence that they are not only
related but identical. The answer to this problem is provided in an
excellent paper by Collier and Emch (1938), who show that most
questionnaire constructors have used Freud's conception of introversion rather than Jung's. Freud tends to identify introversion with
incipient neuroticism. According to him: "An introvert is not yet a
neurotic but he finds himself in a labile condition; he must develop
symptoms at the next dislocation of forces if he does not find other
outlets for his pent-up libido" (1920). Jung's position, already

[1] Failure to obtain interrelations among measures hypothetically indices of the
same trait is not confined to this early work. Fiedler *et al.* (1958) reports that
"This paper has presented intercorrelations among a variety of indices which
have been used as measures of personality adjustment. The most important
factor which emerges is a general lack of correlation among different indices—
even among those which are reliably measurable and which could be expected to
correlate with each other. Thus our data yield no evidence justifying the assumption that adjustment in its present state of definition, should be considered a
unitary trait in clinically unselected populations."

quoted, is quite different. He considers that: "It is a mistake to believe that introversion is more or less the same as neurosis. As concepts the two have not the slightest connection with each other" (1921). This conceptual identification of introversion and neuroticism, so common in much recent work, rests on the misapprehension of Jung's theory and does not invalidate our findings from the preceding chapter.

Two further difficulties were pointed out by Eysenck (1947). The first of these relates to the trait of "sociability", which is considered by many American writers to be the main characteristic of the extravert. Thus, Freyd (1924) considers the extravert to be "an individual in whom exists a diminution of the thought processes in relation to directly observable social behaviour with an accompanied tendency to make social contacts". Equally, there is much evidence that lack of sociability characterizes the neurotic; indeed, difficulty in making good social contacts is one of the outstanding traits of the neurotic (Russell Fraser, 1949). The implication of this statement of course is that "sociability" is not a univocal trait; in other words, in the two-dimensional space generated by the two orthogonal axes, neuroticism and introversion, the trait sociability does not lie on either axis but has projections on both. In this it is probably similar to other traits, such as persistence, and autonomic imbalance, which have been found to be correlated with both neuroticism and introversion. It follows that we cannot derive from ratings on sociability alone a score for either neuroticism or introversion. Yet this is precisely what many writers seem to have done. Their argument runs something like this: Introversion correlates with lack of sociability; neuroticism correlates with lack of sociability. Consequently, neuroticism = introversion. The arguments need only be stated to be seen to be erroneous.

The other difficulty in questionnaire studies of this type is brought out most clearly when we take the Jungian prototypes of the introvert and extravert respectively, namely the hysteric and the dysthymic patient. "The majority of symptoms listed in questionnaires are *affective* symptoms; indeed, it is almost insuperably difficult to design a questionnaire containing many hysterical symptoms. The dysthymic patient is troubled by the consciousness of emotional disturbances; it is easy to list a number of the more common of these disturbances, and a list of this nature is likely to cover most of the symptoms of which the patient complains. The symptomatology of the hysteric, on the other hand, is more *protean*; it relates to his attitude to associates rather than to individual symptoms, and is therefore much more difficult to put into the form of simple 'Yes' –'No' questions. Also, the hysteric has little insight into the pathological character of these attitudes, and is therefore unlikely to give very meaningful answers to a simple questionnaire" (Eysenck, 1947).

With a full appreciation of these difficulties we now turn to a detailed examination of the actual results obtained in the first period of the factorial analysis of questionnaire data.

The best starting-off point is a study by Willoughby (1932), in which 152 married couples and 144 female students filled in the Thurstone Personality Schedule. Willoughby on *a priori* grounds grouped the items in 6 sub-scales dealing with the following topics: (1) social; (2) extravert; (3) fantasy; (4) physical; (5) parental; (6) sex. Table 22 gives the intercorrelations between these six scales for husbands (top half) and wives (bottom half) respectively, as well as the results of two factor analyses carried out by the use of Thurstone's and Spearman's methods respectively. One factor was sufficient to account for all the intercorrelations, and it is interesting to note that this factor satisfied Spearman's tetrad criterion. Its identification as neuroticism is fairly obvious from the nature of the data used.

TABLE 22

	1	2	3	4	5	6	*Thurstone Analysis* *Husbands:*	*Wives:*	*Spearman Analysis* *Husbands:*	*Wives:*
1. Social .	—	·34	·59	·36	·46	·46	·77	·65	·69	·52
2. Extravert	·38	—	·57	·23	·40	·47	·70	·74	·60	·72
3. Fantasy .	·59	·55	—	·43	·60	·44	·84	·77	·86	·76
4. Physical .	·08	·22	·22	—	·34	·25	·63	·49	·46	·29
5. Parental .	·37	·39	·40	·19	—	·33	·72	·68	·65	·61
6. Sex .	·08	·32	·20	·17	·29	—	·68	·53	·59	·33

Perry (1934) gave three intelligence tests and nine personality questionnaires to 178 boys and 144 girls. These personality questionnaires, which included the Bernreuter, the Laird, and the Allport Ascendance-Submission Scales, gave rise to two main factors, one of neuroticism, the other of sufficiency, dominance, or ascendance. Two further factors were isolated—one of intelligence, the other seemingly very similar to the second factor. Identification of the first two factors with neuroticism and extraversion does not appear too far-fetched.

Not quite so clear is the interpretation of Flanagan's (1935) study of the intercorrelations between the four Bernreuter scales by means of Hotelling's technique. He finds two factors or components: the first of which he describes as "lack of self-confidence", whereas the second one is labelled "sociability". While it would be tempting again to identify these two factors in the same way as before, it is not really possible to do so in view of the fact that only four scales were included in the factor analysis.

Vernon (1938) analysed the replies to the Boyd Personality Questionnaire given by 50 men and 50 women. This test contains 120 items classified under 20 headings or general tendencies which, however, are not disclosed to the subject. The sets of scores on these "general tendencies" were intercorrelated and a factor analysis with rotation of axes performed. Three factors resulted, the first of which Vernon identified as "psychoneurotic tendency"; it contained such items as depression or melancholia; instability or temperamentalness; worry or anxiety; lack of self-control; shirking of responsibility; lack of self-sufficiency or confidence. The second and third factors, named respectively "carefreeness" and "scrupulousness", closely resemble the extravert and introvert types. The carefree person apparently shirks responsibility, is free from worry and emotional thinking, is not self-conscious, is free from tenseness, lacks definite interests, and is unable to concentrate. The "scrupulous" person is characterized by obsessional carefulness, suspiciousness, strong self-control of feelings, freedom from instability, from emotional thinking, and from inability to concentrate.

One of the latest studies using this type of approach is reported by Gibb (1942), who gave various personality inventories as well as tests of fluency, perseveration, and intelligence to 200 subjects. He arrived at four factors, the first of which he identified with Flanagan's lack of self-confidence or neuroticism; the others he labelled "fluency", "solitariness", and "concentration". Possibly a clearer picture is presented by his re-analysis of the data after the elimination of the Bernreuter scales. The first factor is very clearly one of emotional instability, which was found to correlate with low intelligence. The other factors are rather more complex, and too narrowly specific to be of great interest here.

We must now turn to the studies which form our second group, i.e. those in which correlations are run not between scores on clusters of items selected on *a priori* grounds, but between individual items themselves. Pride of place here must go to J. P. and R. B. Guilford (1934, 1936, 1939), whose work has opened up an entirely new and important field of investigation. In their first study (1934), 36 typically introvert-extravert questions were administered to 930 students and intercorrelated. Four factors were extracted as the Spearman-Dodd test showed that a two-factor pattern would not apply to the data. These four factors were tentatively identified as (a) social introversion-extraversion, (b) emotional sensitiveness, (c) impulsiveness, and (d) interest in self. In 1936 the analysis was repeated, using more up-to-date methods of analysis, and three main factors were found and identified. Factor I is defined by the following items: inclined to keep in the background on social occasions; does not enjoy getting acquainted with most people; generally prefers not to take the lead in group activities; inclined to limit acquaintances to a select few. As the Guilfords point out, "the first factor is undoubtedly of a social character. . . . One might name this dimension social introversion-extraversion, sociability, shyness, or other similar designations." They label this factor S.

The second factor is characterized by the following items: has frequent ups and downs in mood; his feelings are rather easily hurt; inclines to worry over possible misfortunes; expresses his emotions readily; day-dreams frequently. "The second factor gives a rather neat picture. It is undoubtedly an emotional factor . . . running throughout the list of characteristics is a thread of emotional immaturity or emotional dependency. . . . We shall call this dimension factor E." The third factor is characterized by the following items: is a male; is not frequently absent-minded; likes to sell things; has not kept a personal diary of his own accord; is more interested in athletics than in intellectual things. "This suggests . . . the dimension of masculinity-femininity. . . . There is an element of aggressiveness in some of the items; this might be the oft-mentioned trait of dominance or of ascendance-submission. . . . One might name the factor the 'masculine-ideal'. However, for the present we shall name it with the more noncommittal letter M."

Two further factors were extracted, but were found rather difficult to define. The fourth one was tentatively labelled factor R, "the letter R standing for a word coined from the Greek, 'rhathymia', which means freedom from·care". The fifth factor also was difficult to interpret. "The aspect emphasized is the liking for thinking and tackling problems requiring thought, versus a liking for prompt, overt action. We shall refer to this factor temporarily as factor T."

Scales were developed by the writers for the measurement of the first three factors and were applied to 200 new subjects. Instead of the hoped-for zero intercorrelations, S and E were found to be intercorrelated to the extent of ·463 and S and M to the extent of ·402. E and M intercorrelated to a negligible extent.

Two further factors were isolated, and the provisionally identified factors R and T were investigated more fully in a later paper by the same authors (1939). Thirty items were administered to 1,000 students and factor analysed. Nine factors were extracted. The first of these was one of depression (D); the second a factor of rathymia (R) previously noted; the fourth factor was the shyness or seclusiveness factor (S) isolated before; the sixth factor was labelled thinking introversion, and appears similar to the suggestive factor T isolated before; factor eight was called an alertness factor (A); factor nine was not found to be meaningful, and interpretations of factors three, five, and seven were not made with any degree of confidence.

Two further factors were isolated in another paper (1939), in which 600 subjects were given a questionnaire of 24 items. One of these was factor N (nervousness or jumpiness), the other factor GD (general drive, characterized chiefly by pleasure in action). This last factor may be compared with Heymans' and Wiersma's "activity" factor.

The Guilfords' factors are oblique, and unfortunately they have not carried out a second-order factor in order to clarify the relationship between their factors. In their 1939 paper they show that there are considerable correlations between factors D, S, and T, ranging from ·5 to ·7. "These relationships have distinct bearing on the question as to just what is introversion-extraversion . . . it would seem that there is some basis for lumping together some characteristics bordering on seclusiveness with some implying a thinking person, and still others that indicate depressed emotional tendencies and for calling the resultant picture the introvert. Because of the relationship between these three primary traits, it is easy to see how a more cursory inspection of personalities would lead to the conviction of a composite trait like introversion. The opposite composite of sociability, cheerfulness, and lack of meditative thinking would, of course, be the extravert picture. . . . The use of the term 'introvert', as we have indicated, to represent the person who is simultaneously on the side of the shy, depressed, and thinker, for the dimensions S, D, and T, would then seem to be justified by this statistical analysis."

This passage is very important. Guilford is frequently misquoted as having shown in his study that such type concepts as introversion are meaningless and conclusively disproved by his analysis into a number of independent traits. This is not at all a true picture of

Guilford's contribution. What he has done rather has been to verify some of Jung's hypotheses relating to the correlation between certain traits (sociability, lack of depression, lack of desire to think), and to disprove others; if anything, it is the correlations between these "primary traits" which are impressive, not their independence.[1]

In more recent publications, Guilford has isolated further factors which again are not independent of each other or of those isolated before; those added to his previous list are: C (for cycloid disposition or stability of emotional reactions as opposed to "instability"); A (ascendance-submission); I (inferiority feelings as opposed to self-confidence); O (for objectivity as opposed to hypersensitiveness; Co (for co-operativeness); and Ag (for agreeableness as opposed to quarrelsomeness).

TABLE 23

Intercorrelations of Factor Scores

	S	T	D	C	R	G	A	M	I	N	O	Ag	Co
S	—	·423	·638	·439	·655	·379	·733	·101	·591	·384	·465	·140	·222
T	—	—	·645	·588	·300	−·070	·197	·212	·335	·391	·405	·169	·237
D	—	—	—	·901	·228	−·040	·481	·315	·740	·710	·746	·337	·442
C	—	—	—	—	−·021	−·188	·308	·330	·675	·701	·722	·351	·416
R	—	—	—	—	—	·559	·525	·039	·270	·079	·207	−·084	−·019
G	—	—	—	—	—	—	·438	−·067	·088	−·231	−·059	−·314	−·169
A	—	—	—	—	—	—	—	·256	·570	·325	·460	·001	·200
M	—	—	—	—	—	—	—	—	·326	·348	·365	·006	·210
I	—	—	—	—	—	—	—	—	—	·674	·746	·350	·448
N	—	—	—	—	—	—	—	—	—	—	·720	·470	·529
O	—	—	—	—	—	—	—	—	—	—	—	·495	·616
Ag	—	—	—	—	—	—	—	—	—	—	—	—	·631
Co	—	—	—	—	—	—	—	—	—	—	—	—	—

Intercorrelations for these 13 factors were calculated on 122 men and 78 women by Lovell (1945); these correlations are given in Table 23. A factor analysis of this table of correlations between primary factors resulted in the extraction of a number of second-order or super-factors. Six of these were extracted, although Lovell admits that a comparison of the standard deviations of the residuals with the standard error of the average correlation indicated that not more than three factors should be extracted. To the writer it is

[1] Emphasis on this correlation between primary factors may seem to many to be labouring the obvious, but misunderstanding has been frequent. Thus, Allport (1937) maintains "that the Guilfords' factor analysis of items included in many tests for extraversion-introversion shows that quite independent clusters of responses may be involved", but, as we have seen, these clusters of responses are really far from independent, and it is precisely on their intercorrelations that such higher order concepts as introversion-extraversion are built up.

doubtful if any but the first two factors can be considered significant when proper extimates are made of the communalities in such a way as to reduce the number of factors extracted to a minimum, and

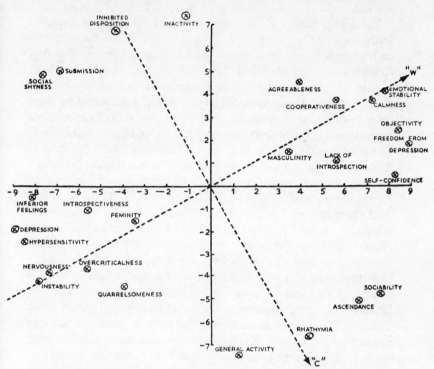

Fig. 26.—Two Second-order Factors derived from Guilfords' Primary Factors.

accordingly a plot has been prepared of the saturations of the 13 primary factors on the first 2 centroid super-factors (Fig. 26). When a rotation is carried out as indicated in the diagram, the resulting factors appear quite clear-cut and meaningful. The first factor is characterized by emotional stability, calmness, objectivity, freedom from depression, self-confidence, co-operativeness, lack of intro-spection, agreeableness, and sociability, as opposed to instability, depression, nervousness, hypersensitivity, inferiority feeling, over-criticalness, quarrelsomeness, introspectiveness, and social shyness. The resemblance of this factor to "w" in its positive and to neuro-ticism in its negative aspect is striking.

The second factor is equally clear. It contrasts inhibited disposition, inactivity, submission, social shyness, inferiority feelings, and depression to sociability, ascendance, rhathymia, self-confidence, freedom from depression, and general activity. The similarity of this factor to "c", surgency or extraversion-introversion is again very marked.

These two factors also emerge from the rather more complex analysis carried out by Lovell (1945), and are indeed the only two clearly marked and meaningful factors among her six. Her first factor is tentatively identified "as a drive restraint variable". "Those factors with sizable loadings on it appear to have in common an active approach to experience. The person with high scores on them tends to engage in *vigorous overt action*, to give relatively *uninhibited expression* to impulse, to seek social contacts, and be a social *leader*." The items having high loadings on this factor are clearly the same as those which characterize the introvert-extravert factor in the writer's solution. Lovell's factor III "has been defined tentatively as an emotionality variable. At the low extreme on it would be the individual characterized by hampering emotional excess. At the other extreme . . . would be found the individual who is dependably cheerful and optimistic, free from constant analysis of himself and others, with some tendency to be (1) free of nervous habits, (2) lacking in hypersensitivity, (3) self-confident, sociable, and tolerant, and (4) lacking in domineering qualities." This factor is clearly the one labelled "w" or neuroticism in the writer's analysis. Lovell's super factors two and four appear very similar to each other, and seem to present no underlying principle which would make psychological sense. Both have high loadings on objectivity, tolerance, and lack of nervousness. Super factors five and six Lovell herself admits to be "too weak to be of any importance".

Similar to Lovell's work is that of North (1949), who administered the Guilford inventories for factors STDCR to 170 students, together with the Kuder Preference Record and an intelligence test. A factor analysis of the intercorrelations between the Guilford factors resulted in a two-factor pattern, which is reproduced in Fig. 27; the rotation indicated in this figure was carried out by North. It will be seen that the two factors I' and II' bear a striking resemblance to Neuroticism and Extraversion-Introversion. The former is characterized by C (emotional instability), D (depression), T (introspectiveness), and to some extent S (social shyness). The latter is characterized by R (happy-go-lucky carefreeness) on the extraverted side, and by S (social shyness) on the introverted side.

Of some interest are the correlations between neuroticism and extraversion on the one hand, and the remaining variables measured by North on the other. Neuroticism shows a significantly negative correlation of − ·25 with intelligence (we will have occasion again and again to note such correlations of the order ·2 to ·3 between

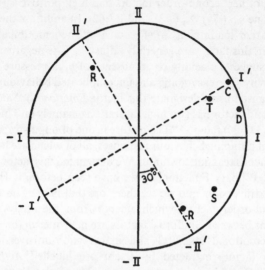

Fig. 27.— Plot of the STDCR Vectors with reference to the Centroid Axes I and II, and to the Orthogonally Rotated Axes I' and II'.

"w" and "g"); it also shows negative correlations with Kuder Preferences for mechanical (− ·30), computational (− ·31), and scientific (− ·20) activities, as well as a positive correlation of ·23 with literary interests. Extraversion correlates positively with the weight-height ratio (·17); in a later chapter we will find a summary of the extensive evidence linking extraversion with the type of body-build indicated by this ratio. Extraversion also correlates negatively with computational (− ·16) and positively with persuasive (· 35) Kuder Preferences. These results are hardly surprising, and fit in well with the stereotyped picture of the extravert.

A somewhat different approach from that used by Lovell and North is that of Thurstone (1951). Basing himself on the intercorrelations between 13 sets of scores for the various Guilford factors, he showed that nine linearly independent factors could account for all the intercorrelations. These factors he named R (reflective), S (sociable), E (emotionally stable), V (vigorous), D (dominant), A (active), I (impulsive), X_1 (tentatively designated as confident), X_2

188 THE STRUCTURE OF HUMAN PERSONALITY

(left without interpretation). The correlations between these factors were quite considerable, the highest being ·52 (E and S) and ·71 (I and D), and a second-order analysis of this matrix was accordingly undertaken by Baehr (1952).

The first of her second-order factors had high positive saturations on Thurstone's S (·79), X_1 (·73), and E (·62). In addition, there was a small negative loading of − ·46 on A. "The emotionally-toned responses in this factor are generally adjustive. The negative loading on Active suggests placidity or an absence of high-pressure or high-strung activity. The easy-going and uncomplicated behaviour evident here has caused us to designate this factor *Emotionally Stable.*"

The second factor has two high saturations, namely on Thurstone's I (·85) and D (·80) factors. "The picture is one of impulsive, carefree, and general outgoing behaviour responses, all of which are facilitated by spontaneous reaction to stimuli. We designated this factor *Primary Function.*" Primary Function, as we have seen before, is Heymans' term for extraversion, and we see therefore that here again the main two second-order factors which emerge from the analysis of the correlations between Guilfords' factors are neuroticism (or rather its obverse, emotional stability) and extraversion-introversion. The other two factors extracted by Baehr are labelled *Activity* and *Emotionally Unstable*; the latter, presumably, is the obverse aspect of her second factor, whereas the former is related by her to Heymans' postulated factor of the same name.

As a follow-up of this investigation, Baehr used a list of 22 behaviour items, employing a modified form of paired-comparison technique on 200 subjects. A factor analysis of the correlations between the 22 items resulted in four factors which she considered to allow of a clear interpretation, as well as two additional relatively meaningless factors. One of the interpretable factors she labelled emotional stability; it has positive saturations on cheerful (·56), even-tempered (·46), emotionally stable (·42), and negative correlations on high-strung (− ·60), impulsive (− ·56), and demonstrative (− ·41). Another factor which she labelled primary function, and which we may agree represents the extraversion-introversion dichotomy, is characterized by items "impulsive" (− ·56), demonstrative (− ·42), happy-go-lucky (− ·32), steady worker (·47), and persevering (·45).

Her third factor is again one of activity, while her fourth factor is called hypomania, and is considered to be "the resultant of a combination of some of the elements of primary function and emotional stability". Baehr's solution is not wholly acceptable; there are high correlations between these various factors (activity and primary function, for instance, intercorrelate — ·504), and no second-order analysis has been carried out. Nevertheless, in so far as it goes, this study fits in reasonably well in its main conclusions with those reviewed earlier.

Somewhat unhappy with the Thurstone and Baehr analyses, Guilford and Zimmerman (1956) returned to the fray and carried out a very large factor analysis embracing grouped items representative of the thirteen factors originally hypothesized by Guilford. Intercorrelations were calculated for altogether 70 such small groups of items, and the factor analysis revealed thirteen factors either identical with those previously discovered, or at least similar to them. Guilford and Zimmerman gave a brief description of these factors, together with the letters by which they are to be known and as these descriptions may make an understanding of our discussion easier, it is here quoted in full.

G. *General activity:* Energetic, rapid-moving, rapid-working person, who likes action and may sometimes be impulsive.

A. *Ascendance:* The person who upholds his rights and defends himself in face-to-face contacts; who does not mind being conspicuous, in fact may enjoy it; who through social initiative gravitates to positions of leadership; who is not fearful of social contacts; who is not inclined to keep his thoughts to himself. There is little to indicate that "submission" accurately describes the negative pole, as was formerly believed.

M. *Masculinity vs. femininity:* Has masculine interests, vocational and avocational; not emotionally excitable or expressive; not easily aroused to fear or disgust; somewhat lacking in sympathy.

I. *Confidence vs. inferiority feelings:* Feels accepted by others, confident, and adequate; socially poised; satisfied with his lot; not self-centered.

N. *Calmness, composure vs. nervousness:* Calm and relaxed rather than nervous and jumpy; not restless, easily fatigued, or irritated; can concentrate on the matter at hand.

S. *Sociability:* Likes social activity and contacts, formal or informal; likes positions of social leadership; has social poise; not shy, bashful, or seclusive.

T. *Reflectiveness:* Given to meditative and reflective thinking; dreamer; philosophically inclined; has curiosity about and questioning attitude towards behaviour of self and others.

D. *Depression:* Emotionally and physically depressed rather than cheerful; given to worry and anxiety and to perseverating emotions and changeable moods.

C_1. *Emotionality:* Emotions easily aroused and perseverating, yet shallow and childish; daydreamer. (Not identical with Factor C.)

R. *Restraint vs. rhathymia:* Self restrained and self controlled; serious minded rather than happy-go-lucky; not cheerfully irresponsible.

O. *Objectivity:* Takes an objective, realistic view of things; alert to his environment and can forget himself; not beset with suspicions.

Ag. *Agreeableness:* Low-scoring individual is easily aroused to hostility; resists control by others; has contempt for others; and may be aroused to aggressive action. High-scoring person is friendly and compliant.

Co. *Co-operativeness, tolerance:* Low-scoring person is given to critical fault-finding generally; has little confidence or trust in others; self-centered and self pitying.

It would seem to follow from Jung's hypothesis that hysterics and psychopaths should be differentiated from the more dysthymic type of neurotic suffering from anxiety, reactive depression and obsessional illness, in terms of the "R" scale and also to a somewhat lesser extent in terms of the "S" scale. Hildebrand (1957) has presented evidence that this is in fact so. Using these scales in addition to a battery of objective and questionnaire tests, on groups of normal and neurotic subjects, he showed (*a*) that two main factors of neuroticism and extraversion/introversion emerged from the analysis; (*b*) that the neurotic groups were high on the neuroticism factor as compared with the normal group; (*c*) that hysterics and psychopaths were placed towards the extraverted end, and the dysthymic groups towards the introverted end of the extraversion/introversion factor. He also showed that the "R" and "S" scale had loadings on the extraversion/introversion factor in line with prediction.

His study was followed up by Eysenck (1956) who carried out extensive item analyses and factor analyses of Guilford's scales in an effort to improve the validity and reliability of these scales for the measurement of neuroticism and extraversion. The two new scales constructed consist of 24 items each (Eysenck, 1959); for certain purposes even shorter scales are desirable and two short scales, including six items from each of the long scales, have been constructed (Eysenck, 1958). (These scales have been given in full in Chapter 2 in order to illustrate the meaning of orthogonal factor structure.) The final scales resulting from this work (Eysenck, 1959) have been published under the title of the Maudsley Personality

Inventory and their success in differentiating various normal and neurotic groups can be seen below in Table 24.

TABLE 24

Standardization Groups

Description of Group	Size	N, mean	N, σ	E, mean	E, σ
Normals (English): Quota sample	1,800	19·89	11·02	24·91	9·71
Normals (American students)	1,500	20·91	10·69	28·53	8·28
Dysthymics (Hospital patients)	84	38·18	10·84	17·86	10·02
Prisoners (Recidivists)	146	30·35	10·73	24·09	9·11
Hysterics (Hospital patients)	58	30·82	11·84	24·91	9·26
Psychosomatics (Hospital patients)	108	35·69	10·89	25·38	9·33
Psychopaths (Hospital patients)	36	35·58	10·91	30·77	9·51

On the whole, we may conclude our discussion of Guilford's contribution by saying that in so far as questionnaire responses can be admitted as evidence in our analysis of the organization of personality, a flood of light has been thrown on the principles of organization at the trait level, and that the higher-order constructs emerging from the intercorrelations of these traits confirm to a remarkable extent the results obtained previously by rating studies. Both these contributions are of outstanding importance; the first because analysis in terms of such very general factors as neuroticism and introversion lack the requisite applicability to many practical and theoretical problems, and the second because objections which may legitimately be made to questionnaire studies are entirely different from the objections which may legitimately be made to rating studies, and if it can be shown that to a considerable extent the main results from these two types of study agree, then the evidential value of the proof is very much increased.

Compared to Guilford's patient, long-continued, and fruitful work, most of the other researches in this field must be regarded as being of comparatively little interest, except in so far as they confirm or fail to confirm Guilford's findings. An exception to this appraisal may be made in the case of Cattell, who has tried to develop a system along somewhat independent lines, and who has also tried to link up factors found in questionnaire responses with factors at the level of ratings.

One of the most important studies confirming many of Guilford's findings is one carried out by Mosier (1937), who intercorrelated responses made by 500 male students on 39 items from the Thurstone neurotic inventory, and on the A.C.E. psychological examination. He found 8 factors, of which 3 were doubtful and not readily interpretable. The 5 factors readily identified were:

(1) Cycloid: ups and downs in mood, happiness to sadness, frequently in low spirits, often just miserable, worried over possible misfortunes, frequently grouchy.

(2) Depression: periods of loneliness, lonesome even with others, frequently in low spirits, often just miserable, difficulty in making friends.

(3) Hypersensitive: feelings easily hurt, cannot stand criticism, nervous, often in state of excitement.

(4) Inferiority: lack of self-confidence, easily discouraged, feelings of inferiority.

(5) Shyness: troubled with shyness, keeps in background on social occasions, feelings of inferiority, difficulty in starting conversations, not confident about abilities.

Mosier comes to the conclusion that "there is no single trait of neurotic tendency which can be postulated in a parsimonious description of behaviour", but this statement seems to reflect more the undeveloped state of multiple-factor analysis, which at that time had not advanced to the concept of second-order factors and oblique first-order factors, than the actual data analysed by Mosier. A reanalysis of his work by more modern methods would be of interest; it may be predicted with considerable confidence that such an analysis would, to a large extent, duplicate the results found by Lovell in her analysis of the intercorrelations between Guilford's primary factors.

Much in line with the results obtained by Lovell, North, and Thurstone is a research by Jenkins (1950). He posits two theorems. According to the first, "personality trait factors contain variances which comprise two independent basic factors or superfactors . . . these superfactors are neither antagonistic, oppositional, reciprocal, nor bipolar. In fact our evidence indicates that they are statistically independent behaviour tendencies, and hence neutral to each other".

The second theorem asserts that "*personality factors are unipolar*, and, by implication, constitutes a general denial of bipolar factors of personality. This theorem is not necessary for the truth of the first one, but it is important for its rationale as a part of a general theory of personality".

We will not here deal with the second theorem which, as far as the writer can see, is almost completely meaningless, but will instead examine the evidence given for the first. Unfortunately, this evidence is rather sketchy and depends essentially on correlations between nine traits which appear to fall into two groups. The traits within each group correlate positively with each other, but the groups do not correlate one with the other. Thus, we obtain two superfactors, referred to by Jenkins as factors C and A. (These letters stand for cholinergic and adrenergic respectively, although no evidence is given for this identification.)

The "C" factor is characterized by the traits of buoyancy, dynamism, emotional spontaneity, and carefreeness, i.e. a group of typically extravertive traits. Factor A is characterized by depression, lethargy, hypersensitiveness, anxiety, and feeling of social insecurity. The picture here presented is typical of the neurotic syndrome, or the obverse of factor "w". Also associated with these factors respectively, and well in agreement with our provisional interpretation of them as extraversion and neuroticism, are the following traits: for the "C" factor—feeling of strength, high activity level, feeling of well-being, spontaneity, and carefreeness; for the "A" factor—feeling of weakness, low activity level, hypersensitiveness, general inferiority, feelings of social insecurity, indecision, and procrastination.

It is to be hoped that Jenkins will publish his data in somewhat more extended form, indicating, among other things, the number of subjects used, and their selection, and that he will clarify the meaning of his second theorem. In so far as his research goes, however, it

TABLE 25

Factor Loadings according to the Centroid Method (1945 *Group; Rotated Factors*)

Variable	I	II	III	IV
1. Theoretical intelligence . . .	48	13	− 09	24
2. Practical intelligence . . .	00	70	19	16
3. Mechanical comprehension . .	30	66	− 11	25
4. Manual dexterity	− 15	78	39	− 06
5. Rote memory	64	− 28	28	05
6. Memory for contexts . . .	63	− 11	07	35
7. Perseverance, energy . . .	− 12	13	67	37
8. Readiness to assume responsibility .	− 28	21	27	70
9. Carefulness	33	07	51	12
10. Ability to take the initiative . .	− 11	01	30	79
11. Co-operativeness	11	21	57	37
12. Capacity for leadership . . .	26	15	18	75

is not in contradiction to the general picture given by those previously cited.

The same may be said of a research somewhat more fully reported (Husen, 1951). Using self-ratings on 12 traits of 100 matriculants called up for the Swedish army, this author calculated intercorrelations and carried out a factor analysis the outcome of which is shown in Table 25. The four factors emerging from this analysis are fairly clear in their interpretation; two are cognitive, two orectic. The two cognitive factors correspond to Vernon's (1950) *v-ed* and *k-m* factors, i.e. the verbal-educational and the practical-mechanical; the former here is characterized by high loadings on "theoretical

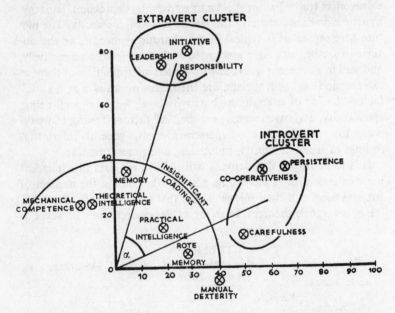

Fig. 28.—Two-factor Diagram showing results of Husen's Self-rating Scale.

intelligence", "rote memory", and "memory for contexts", the latter by "practical intelligence", "technical comprehension", and "manual dexterity".

The two orectic factors bear a marked similarity to extraversion and introversion respectively. The extraverted cluster is characterized by leadership, initiative, and readiness to assume responsibility, the introverted cluster by persistence, co-operativeness, and carefulness. All six qualities are "*w*" traits, and we might expect factors III and

IV to be non-independent and to give rise to a "w" superfactor. That this is so can be seen from Fig. 28, which represents in diagrammatic form these two factors; the angle alpha between the two centroid vectors drawn through the two clusters is clearly less than 90°, and the two clusters can therefore be seen to be correlated. Husen himself agrees that we are here dealing with a "general character factor", which is a "second-order factor . . . situated behind factors III and IV".[1]

Reyburn and Taylor (1940) carried out a self-rating study in which 115 subjects responded to 10 items on a 5-point scale: also given was a perseveration test made up of three tests of the type used by Cattell. Three main factors were extracted of which the first is identified by them as "w", the second as "c", and the third as perseveration. A possible fourth factor of sociability appears also suggested by the results. Table 26 opposite shows the items included in this study as well as the factor saturations obtained by Reyburn and Taylor.

Reyburn and Taylor (1943) also contribute a re-analysis of Guilford's studies on factors D, R, T, A, N, and GD. The most prominent factors to appear in their re-analysis are "c" and "w", a result which must be attributed in part to their particular method of analysis, but which is in good agreement with Lovell's work quoted above. Several other factors are suggested, one of which they name "flexibility", while another is named "tension"; some of these factors duplicate the primary factors of Guilford's.

While this analysis is of interest, it is not methodologically satisfactory, as it does not separate out clearly primary and second-order factors, and also because up to a point the method of analysis used tends to beg the question.[2] The former objection in the writer's view is more formidable than the latter; if the data are clearly contradictory to the hypothesis in accordance with which Reyburn and Taylor rotate their axes, results will be negative, whereas if the data can be made to appear congruent with the hypothesis which determines their rotation, this in itself is of some interest. However, this is a debatable point, and the author would not like to argue it with any conviction.

Layman (1940) has presented an analysis of intercorrelations of 67

[1] Another paper which essentially supports the general outline emerging from the studies mentioned, is one by Banks and Keir (1952).

[2] Reyburn and Taylor rotate axes in accordance with an hypothesis regarding the most likely factors to be found.

TABLE 26

	2	3	4	5	6	7	8	9	10	p	"w"	"c"	"p"
1. Makes friends easily	·07	·01	−·14	−·05	·03	·40	·08	·29	·02	−·04	·00	−·08	—
2. Easily hurt by remarks and actions of others		·02	·28	−·22	−·05	·00	·18	·06	·25	·05	−·25	·31	·29
3. Not suspicious of motives of others			−·03	−·05	−·08	·06	−·13	−·16	−·25	−·09	·30	·12	—
4. Worries about possible misfortunes				·30	·16	−·17	−·08	−·09	−·10	−·15	−·30	·35	—
5. Indulges in self-pity when things go wrong					·33	−·15	−·18	·03	·28	−·05	−·33	·62	—
6. Is easily rattled						−·04	−·01	·11	−·16	−·10	−·09	·42	—
7. Takes prominent part in social affairs							−·09	·53	−·13	·19	·06	−·28	—
8. Does not criticize others and is careful of their feelings								·09	−·07	·24	·07	·18	·37
9. Prefers working with others									−·17	−·18	·35	·29	—
10. Subject to change of mood without apparent cause										·19	−·74	·00	—
11. p											−·03	−·06	·48

Factor Loadings: "w", "c", "p"

items, which were subdivided into nine partially overlapping groups under hypothetical traits. Each table was factor analysed, and 51 items having factor loadings of ·5 or more on one or more factors were combined into one matrix and re-factored. Twelve factors altogether were extracted from this latter analysis; social inadequacy; social gregariousness; social initiative; social aggressiveness; self-sufficiency; impulsive action; changeability of interest; emotionality-moodiness; inferiority; emotionality-easily aroused; emotionality-introverted; inability to face reality. Some of these factors will be seen to be similar to Guilford's primary factors, but on the whole the work is clearly left in an unsatisfactory state as no second-order factors are extracted, thus making any detailed interpretation impossible. The study has one interesting feature, however, in that it appears to sub-divide a primary factor of sociability or social shyness into a number of components.

This possibility has been further explored by Brogden and Thomas (1943), who gave a questionnaire made up of 25 Bernreuter items relating to sociability to 365 students in order to discover "the primary traits in personality items purporting to measure sociability". Some of the five factors they extract are difficult or impossible to interpret, but others are relatively clear and intelligible. Factor I appears to be a factor of intellectual independence, and of liking for ideational activities, such as reading; factor two, which also occurred in Layman's analysis, is one of gregariousness; a third factor is interpreted as indicative of the need for primary emotional relationships. These results are very intriguing and of great potential importance. If the hierarchical scheme of personality organization outlined in the first chapter is correct, it follows not only that the most general traits like neuroticism and introversion-extraversion are made up of primary traits; it also follows that these primary traits themselves are made up of different clusters of reaction tendencies. Sociability lends itself particularly easily to further analysis in view of the fact that items supposedly characterizing it clearly relate to several different underlying tendencies, such as the three isolated by Brogden and Thomas. It is to be hoped that similar analyses will be carried out of all the other primary factors reported by Guilford, as in this way our knowledge will become more and more detailed.

In contrast to the Brogden-Thomas study of sociability, we have Pallister's (1933) work on the negative or withdrawal attitude. 209 women students were given a number of inventories, including the Leckey individuality record, broken up into eight categories (social confidence, co-operation, attitude toward family, nervous symptoms, optimism, physical symptoms, attitude towards sex, and work habits), a personal data-sheet, a vocabulary test, a set of ratings, and a number of physical measures. Correlations are given between the various Leckey categories, and by means of a tetrad analysis a generalized attitude of "withdrawal" established. Women having high withdrawal scores were, on the average, rated to be below the average for any of the characteristics rated (beauty, health, popularity, optimism, nervousness, temperament, attitude towards sex and family, work habits, and social confidence). Withdrawal attitude was related to verbal ability to the extent of ·28. This study, while it does not add much to our knowledge of sociability, does represent an interesting early application of factor analysis to personality study.

More recently there have been several attempts to qualify the nature of sociability. Storm *et al.* (1958) used a self-rating questionnaire to measure ten forms of social behaviour and anxiety about each one. "A factor analysis of the correlations among these twenty variables, plus its anxiety, indicated that the pattern of correlations could be interpreted in terms of six general tendencies, which have been labelled independence, conscientiousness, conformity, friendliness, fear of failure, power striving and (tentatively) mistrustfulness."

Most of these studies were concerned with an analysis of intercorrelations without benefit of an *a priori* hypothesis. A recent paper by Eysenck (1956) investigated the specific hypothesis that "*introverted* social shyness is different in many ways from *neurotic* social shyness. To put the hypothesis suggested here in a nutshell, we might say that the introvert does not care for people, would rather be alone, but if need be can effectively take part in social situations, whereas the neurotic is anxious and afraid when confronted with social situations, seeks to avoid them in order to escape from this negative feeling, but frequently wishes that he could be more sociable. In other words, the introvert does not *care* to be with other people; the neurotic is *afraid* of being with other people. If this hypothesis were true it seems likely that different items in the (Guilford) S Scale would be chosen by introverts and neurotics respectively to express their unsociable attitude."

Using a population of 200 men and 200 women and employing the R Scale as a measure of extraversion and the C Scale as a measure of neuroticism, Eysenck tabulated all items of the S Scale on which members of either sex produced significant Chi-square with either the R or C Scale. The table below lists all these items and their associated Chi-squares.

TABLE 27A

Items from the S Scale Significantly Related to the R Scale

Question	Chi-Squared			
	R		C	
	M	F	M	F
Are you inclined to be quick and sure in your actions?	45	24	1	0
Can you usually let yourself go and have a hilariously good time at a gay party?	44	43	1	5
Do you like to mix socially with people?	40	22	0	0
Are you inclined to take life too seriously?	40	12	10	0
Would you rate yourself as a lively individual?	54	35	0	0
Are you usually a "good mixer"	32	31	4	0
Are you inclined to keep in the background on social occasions?	52	30	0	0
Do you usually take the initiative in making new friends?	26	28	1	0
Would you rather spend an evening reading at home than attend a large party?	8	26	0	0
Do you like to have social engagements?	25	52	9	0
Does it embarrass you a great deal to say or do the wrong thing in a social group?	23	8	6	6
Do you adapt yourself easily to new conditions, that is, new places, situations, surroundings, etc.?	24	13	0	4
Is it easy for you to act naturally at a party?	22	22	7	2
Are you inclined to keep quiet when out in a social group?	22	18	0	0
Do you often "have the time of your life" at social affairs?	52	52	2	9
Are you inclined to limit your acquaintances to a select few?	18	17	5	0
Do you generally prefer to take the lead in group activities?	19	8	1	2
In social conversations, are you usually a listener rather than a talker?	7	19	1	0
Do you find it easy, as a rule, to make new acquaintances?	17	17	1	0
Do you have difficulty in making new friends?	17	17	4	0
Do you shrink from speaking in public?	4	17	3	0
Were you ever the "life of the party"?	5	16	5	8
Do you generally feel uncomfortable when you are the centre of attention on a social occasion?	12	15	6	0
Would you be very unhappy if you were prevented from making numerous social contacts?	14	15	1	2
Do you nearly always have a "ready answer" for remarks directed at you?	14	9	1	0
Do you usually prefer to let someone else take the lead on social occasions?	13	8	0	1
Do you enjoy getting acquainted with most people?	14	7	2	2
Are you often hesitant about meeting important people?	13	9	6	7
Do you enjoy entertaining people?	13	7	0	4
Are you inclined to be shy in the presence of the opposite sex?	12	10	0	0
Is it usually difficult for you to make decisions?	10	5	7	6
Do you like to speak in public?	6	10	6	1
Are you troubled with feelings of inferiority?	2	17	14	28

'For the men it is found that *none* of the items showing a significant relation with R shows a significant relation with C. Similarly, not one of the items showing a significant relation with C shows a significant relation with R, with the exception of one item the same is true for the women. . . . A glance at Tables 27A and 27B will

TABLE 27B

Items from the S Scale Significantly Related to the C Scale

Question	Chi-Squared			
	R		C	
	M	F	M	F
Do you often experience periods of loneliness?	2	6	10	38
Do you "get rattled" easily at critical moments?	3	0	32	16
Are you troubled about being self-conscious?	7	7	32	23
Are you troubled with feelings of inferiority?	2	17	14	28
Are you self-conscious in the presence of your superiors?	5	5	23	10
After a critical moment is over, do you usually think of something you should have done but failed to do?	0	3	14	23
Are there times when your mind seems to work very slowly and other times when it works very rapidly?	0	0	23	16
Do you feel that the world is distant and unreal to you?	0	0	16	24
Do you worry over humiliating experiences longer than the average person?	17	9	4	19
Do you think there is a great deal more happiness in the world than misery?	3	0	15	10
Are you usually well-poised in your social contacts?	3	5	12	2
Are you worried about being shy?	3	2	7	12
Do you often feel ill at ease with other people?	2	7	19	12

indicate to what extent our hypothesis regarding the precise nature of the difference between introvertive and neurotic sociability is borne out. The sociable extravert lets himself go and has a hilarious time, likes to mix socially, is a lively individual who does not take life seriously, is a good mixer who does not stay in the background on social occasions, who takes the initiative in making friends, has many social engagements, acts naturally at parties, adapts easily and so forth. In other words, he is a person who enjoys social intercourse with people as opposed to the introvert who does not enjoy social intercourse with people. When we turn to the items indicative of neurotic social shyness, we find the shy person troubled about being self-conscious, experiencing periods of loneliness, troubled with feelings of inferiority and self-consciousness with superiors, worrying over humiliating experiences and about being shy, ill at ease with other people, not well poised in social contacts. In other words, we meet a kind of person who is troubled and worried over his social contacts, and would like to be more adequate in his dealings with other people, but whose emotional reactions seem to interfere with his social adjustment."

Most of the studies mentioned so far fail to make reference to psychiatric concepts. An outstanding exception to this rule is the work of Hsü (1943), who adapted Moore's approach to normal subjects. A 57-item questionnaire was given to 121 juniors and seniors from a Catholic women's college. Each item included examples of behaviour varying in number from 5 to 39. Certain groupings were arrived at on the basis of Yule's coefficient of association, and the method of tetrad differences used in connection with clusters forming a hierarchy. In this way a number of "fundamental character traits" were isolated. The nature of these is indicated by the descriptive titles given them: violent actions in anger, restricted sociability, staying by oneself in trouble, timidity, impracticability in using money, lack of interest in study, suspiciousness, tendency to depression, lack of self-confidence, timidity in social affairs, sulk and pout, sedentary recreations, active recreations, tendency to inactivity, and tendency to control temper. These primary factors were themselves intercorrelated, and what Hsü calls "super-factors" taken out. Eight such super-factors were extracted, which were labelled in psychiatric terms: "suspicion-depression", schizoid, præcox, laziness, paranoid, catatonic, manic-depressive, and social shyness. "Since several super-factors can be isolated in the present study, it may be interesting to see whether some supra-super-factor exists." Four super-factors were selected and intercorrelated and were shown to form a hierarchy which satisfied the tetrad criterion. Super-factor "manic-depressive configuration" is negatively correlated with the rest of the super-factors: "simple schizophrenic configuration", "paranoid configuration", and "catatonic configuration". "The fact that these three are . . . positively intercorrelated with each other seems to agree with the customary grouping of these three syndromes in psychiatry. Since these four super-factors resemble so closely the schizophrenic and manic-depressive syndromes, the nature of this supra-super factor can only be inferred as a factor of potency to psychosis."

While the statistical method used with its combination of features from Spearman and Thurstone is so clumsy as to make it almost impossible for the reader to reconstruct the various steps of the argument, and while terms such as "supra-super factors" call to mind Hollywood film advertisements rather than scientific concepts, some of the conclusions of this work do seem to point to a rather interesting similarity between psychiatric syndromes and trait clusters in normal people. Nor can the factor of "potency to psychosis" be dismissed too lightly, because we shall find ample evidence later to support the existence of such a factor.

We must now turn to another example of large scale long continued work which deserves to take its place alongside that of Guilford already referred to. In the preceding chapter, we have dealt with Cattell's analysis of L data; we must now discuss his study of Q data which has resulted in a group of 16 main factors derived from a long series of different analyses. As most of the factors have already been introduced in the last chapter, we shall simply list the names of factors derived from questionnaires. They are:

(a) Cyclothymia vs. psychothymia
(b) Intelligence
(c) Ego strength vs. general emotionality
(d) Excitability
(e) Dominance
(f) Surgency
(g) Superego strength
(h) Parmia
(i) Premsia
(j) Coasthenia
(k) Comention
(l) Protension
(m) Autia
(n) Shrewdness
(o) Guilt proneness

In addition to these there are a number of factors which emerge only in questionnaires and not in L data; a discussion of these is omitted here. Cattell (1949) has published questionnaires for the measurement of his main factors under the title of "The 16 P-F Test"; this will be useful for anyone attempting to relate Cattell's factors to other variables in research.

Cattell has done a considerable amount of work trying to match factors and has given a table on page 326 of his *Personality and Motivation Structure and Measurement* showing such matching as reasonably successful as far as L data and Q data are concerned. He concludes his discussion on matching by saying "That, among 18 or more factors only 6 fail to cross match in L and Q data, indicates that we are essentially covering the same realms in these media. For almost certainly there are more nearly two or three dozen personality factors of general importance rather than the 12 to 18 we now have, and which of these shall appear eventually at the tail end of the variance distribution in each medium depends partly on accidental sampling circumstances."

We noted in our discussion of Cattell's L data that the two main second order factors emerging from his work were neuroticism and extraversion. The same is true in his second order factor analyses of Q data; here also neuroticism and extraversion are the two main factors and they are suitably matched with those emerging from L data. It is interesting to note that Cattell has made it possible to measure neuroticism and extraversion in terms of his second order factor, and that these measures correlate reasonably highly with the neuroticism and extraversion measures of the M.P.I. (Eysenck, 1959), derived from Guilford's work. This is particularly interesting because the primary factors derived by these two authors are quite unlike each other; nevertheless, the second order factors are closely similar. This suggests to the present writer that the so-called primary factors depend very much more than either Guilford or Cattell would seem to realize on chance selection of items and consequent refinement of relatively arbitrary vectors. Regardless of the particular vectors chosen, however, the same second order factors emerge. Thus it would seem reasonable in research to place more emphasis on these more stable higher order factors rather than on the more accidental lower order ones.[1]

Cattell's belief in the similarity of factors derived from rating studies and questionnaire studies appears strengthened considerably by a study of outstanding interest published by Fiske (1949). This writer made use of the data accumulated by the well-known

[1] The possibility here envisaged is that in the two factor space generated by extraversion and neuroticism, the items used by Cattell, Guilford and others cluster more or less randomly around the two factor axes, very much as if iron filings on a sheet of paper had been held over two magnets arranged at right angles to each other, and slightly shaken. Within each of the two groups of questions, there are no objective principles for marking out one "grouping" from another, and chance will decide around which items the analyst will construct his factors. This hypothesis will account for the curious fact that Guilford and Cattell, both starting with not dissimilar pools of questions, arrived at quite dissimilar primary factors; it will also account for the fact that both arrived at similar second order factors, namely extraversion and neuroticism. This hypothesis is suggested very tentatively, but it may repay experimental analysis.

research project on the Selection of Clinical Psychologists, which was sponsored by the Veterans' Administration and carried out at the University of Michigan (Kelly and Fiske, 1952). In this project, an extensive assessment programme was undertaken to evaluate students selected by Universities for first year positions in the V.A. Clinical Psychology Training Programme. 128 men constitute the sample of subjects. Three different modes of assessment were employed.

(1) A staff team of three experienced psychologists pooled their judgments, which were based on a mass of extensive and intensive material on each subject.
(2) Three team-mates, who had spent seven days with a subject, living and working together, rated him.
(3) The subjects rated themselves.

A rating scale of 22 items adapted from Cattell was used throughout.

Correlations were run between these 22 items for the three groups of data (A, B, and C) separately, and the three matrices factor analyzed independently. Five primary factors were extracted from each of the three matrices of intercorrelations, and thus it becomes possible to study the similarity of factors derived from questionnaires, ratings by peers, and ratings by clinicians.

Similarity of the factor patterns for the three groups can best be shown in the form of a diagram, and Fig. 29 is quoted from the original paper. Except for the fifth factor, agreement is surprisingly close, as is evident, too, from the average intercorrelations between the loadings on the primary factors, also published by Fiske. It is apparent that the three methods of evaluation give consistent results, a finding which may appear surprising to those who have tended in the past to condemn out of hand either or both of the methods of rating or self-appraisal.

Of most interest for our purpose are probably factor two, called by Fiske "*emotional control*", and factor three, "*conformity*". "Emotional control" apparently corresponds to the obverse of neuroticism; from his inspection of the most highly loaded item, Fiske concludes that "we can designate this ... factor as *emotional control* or *emotional self-possession*, keeping clearly in mind that this is probably a mature guidance of emotional expression in an inhibitive constricted pattern. Further explorations might well identify it more definitely as emotional maturity". Factor three is identifiable, though perhaps less clearly, with introversion. Items having high loadings in the various analyses are: serious, conscientious, submissive, silent, predictable, cautious,

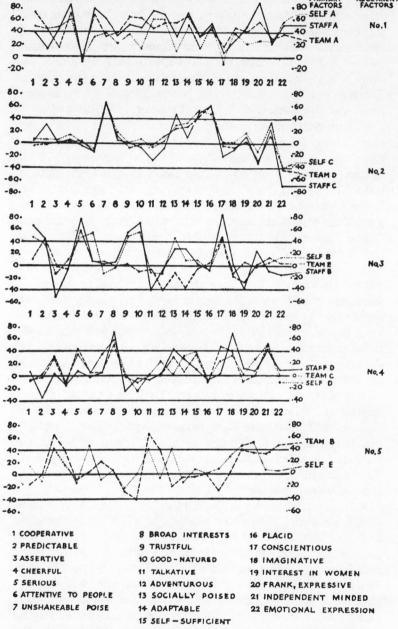

1 COOPERATIVE	8 BROAD INTERESTS	16 PLACID
2 PREDICTABLE	9 TRUSTFUL	17 CONSCIENTIOUS
3 ASSERTIVE	10 GOOD - NATURED	18 IMAGINATIVE
4 CHEERFUL	11 TALKATIVE	19 INTEREST IN WOMEN
5 SERIOUS	12 ADVENTUROUS	20 FRANK, EXPRESSIVE
6 ATTENTIVE TO PEOPLE	13 SOCIALLY POISED	21 INDEPENDENT MINDED
7 UNSHAKEABLE POISE	14 ADAPTABLE	22 EMOTIONAL EXPRESSION
	15 SELF – SUFFICIENT	

Fig. 29.—Diagram showing similarity of three Independent Factorial Studies.

15

ready to co-operate, and slight overt interest in women. The picture is not quite consistent, as might be expected from the fact that these are primary factors which themselves are intercorrelated, although these intercorrelations appear to be relatively low. Nevertheless, without a second-order factor analysis we should not expect unambiguous identification of factors with those of our last chapter. Keeping this in mind, however, the general fit of this study, as compared with those described in the last chapter, is not too bad.

We may briefly mention the interpretation given by Fiske to the other factors. The first he terms "*social adaptability*", the fourth the "*inquiring intellect*", and the fifth "*confident self-expression*". It will be seen from Fig. 29 just which items have high saturations on these factors. It might be thought that as the traits rated were taken from Cattell's list, the resulting factor should also be similar to his. Up to a point this expectation seems to be borne out. As Fiske points out, "These findings bear certain marked resemblances to those from Cattell's studies, although many discrepancies are also present. . . . A thorough study of these two sets of factors, one from Cattell and one from our ratings, leaves one with feelings of both optimism and discouragement. Even in the face of no complete congruence, the similarities support a belief in the possibility of eventual agreement upon the basic variables in personality. Yet, with such comparable rating scales and subjects, why are the results not more similar?" To the present writer the obvious answer to this question would lie in the absence of second-order analyses by the two writers, as well as in certain statistical differences between Fiske and Cattell in their method of rotation. Fiske attempted to maximize the number of "pure" loadings, whereas Cattell did not. Again, "Cattell uses unusually low loadings to help him identify his rotated factors"; Fiske "does not share this confidence in the significance of low loadings". The agreement found in spite of such differences in methodology is distinctly encouraging.

Rather less favourable is the outcome of a research by Carroll (1952). He used 110 men who filled in the STDCR questionnaires and rated themselves and five others on these traits. We thus have three scores: S for self-rating, P for peer-rating and T for test or questionnaire. Correlations are given in the table below. They will be seen to be relatively low. Furthermore, "Self-rating trait D correlates more highly with peer-rating trait C than it does with peer-rating trait D. If we proceed with this type of analysis, we gain an overall impression that the highest correlations are found between corresponding measures of the same trait but that there are a considerable number of exceptions." A multiple regression analysis was carried out, and it was found that "Confusions are most often found between traits S and R and between traits D and C."

TABLE 28

Trait	S vs. P	S vs. T	P vs. T
S	·42	·57	·37
T	·39	·65	·32
D	·29	·53	·27
C	·30	·52	·26
R	·56	·34	·45

(S = self-rating, P = peer, T = test)

These results are not perhaps as difficult to explain as one might at first suppose. As we have seen before, traits S and R are both measures of extraversion/introversion and traits D and C are both measures of neuroticism. Indeed, questionnaire measures D and C correlate together about as highly as their reliabilities permit. The "confusions" are, therefore, in large measure due to the selection of highly similar or identical traits which have been rather arbitrarily given different names. Carroll's results do not on the whole contradict those of Fiske to any significant extent.

In all the studies mentioned in this chapter, it will have been noticed that factors identical with, or similar to, the concept of neuroticism have been invoked time and again; it would seem reasonable to enquire whether none of the investigators has taken the trouble to verify a hypothesis of this nature by testing both normal and neurotic groups and comparing their responses. By this we do not mean the kind of validation studies summarized by Ellis (1946) and Ellis and Conrad (1948), in which a particular personality inventory is considered valid if it discriminates between normals and neurotics at a reasonably satisfactory level. What we have in mind rather is the setting up of a definite hypothesis regarding the nature of the factor to be investigated, and a deduction from this hypothesis which can be verified by data collected from normal and abnormal groups. A fuller discussion of the type of analysis required and the type of reasoning underlying it will be given in a later chapter (cf. p. 148). Here we will only note two researches which have made use of questionnaire and self-rating material in a study of normal and neurotic groups.

The first of these studies was carried out by Bennett and Slater (1945) on 80 normal and 80 neurotic soldiers. The tests used by them were:

(1) A neurotic inventory divided into three sections dealing with questions related to the clinical syndromes of anxiety, hysteria, and depression.

(2) An annoyance test listing 60 possible annoying stimuli for situations of four kinds, 15 for each, the whole in random order. These four types of stimuli are: (*a*) frustration of self-assertion; (*b*) personal inadequacy; (*c*) dirt or untidiness; (*d*) noise.

(3) Three sections of the Pressey X-O Test, modified from the original, and dealing with (*a*) activities for which an individual should be blamed; (*b*) things about which he has ever felt worried, nervous, or anxious; (*c*) items which he likes or in which he is interested.

Scores on these 10 sub-tests were obtained and intercorrelations established for the two groups separately, as well as for the combined group of normals and neurotics. Biserial correlations were calculated between the normal-neurotic dichotomy for each of the 10 tests. These are reproduced under "D" in Table 18. Also given are first-factor saturations for the normal, the neurotic, and the combined groups.

TABLE 29

First Factor

		Neurotics	Normals	Combined	"D"
Inventory:	Anxiety	·77	·70	·77	·72
	Hysteria	·49	·55	·53	·43
	Depression	·78	·75	·70	·72
Annoyances:	*a*	·18	·03	·13	·25
	b	·46	·50	·47	·49
	c	·12	·21	·13	·10
	d	·63	·48	·54	·72
Pressey X-O:	*a*	·06	·02	·08	·19
	b	·43	·55	·49	·65
	c	·29	— ·23	— ·18	·56

It will be seen from Table 29 that there is a high correlation between column D and the first-factor saturation of the groups, whether separate or combined. This indicates quite clearly that a test which has a high power of discrimination between normals and neurotics also has a high saturation on the first factor extracted from a matrix of intercorrelations *of the normal, the neurotic, or the combined groups*. Similarly, a test having a low power of discrimination between normals and neurotics also has low saturations on the factor. Quite clearly, then, this correspondence between discriminant capacity of a test and factor saturation gives us considerable justification in labelling the factor one of neuroticism. We appear to get away in this fashion from the usual method of arbitrary and semantic labelling, which has been so severely criticized by many psychologists, and to go some way towards an objective method of defining and labelling factors.

Of equal interest is a second study to be mentioned in this connection (Stouffer, 1949). 15 scales were constructed according to the method of Guttman's scale analysis, dealing with a variety of topics which were thought to be relevant to neurotic disorder. These 15 scales were then applied to large numbers of normal and neurotic soldiers and intercorrelations calculated for normals separately, neurotics separately, and the combined groups. Also available was an estimate of the degrees to which each of the 15 scales discriminated between the normals and the neurotics, given in the form of a biserial correlation between scales and the dichotomy: normal versus neurotic. These correlations are given under the heading Criterion Column in Table 30, together with the factor saturations for the

TABLE 30

Title of Scale	Criterion Column	Factor Saturations, Normal Group		Factor Saturations, Neurotic Group	
		I	II	I	II
1. Psychosomatic complaints .	·66	·69	·15	·56	·16
2. Childhood neurotic symptoms	·38	·49	·09	·58	− ·01
3. Personal adjustment (−) .	·42	·67	·09	·68	·05
4. Over-sensitivity . . .	·33	·48	·45	·56	·50
5. Childhood fears . . .	·33	·42	·16	·52	·02
6. Acceptance of soldier role (−)	·35	·58	− ·15	·48	− ·29
7. Worrying	·27	·59	·02	·56	·09
8. Sociability (−) . . .	·33	·33	·03	·56	·08
9. Participation in sports (−) .	·28	·28	− ·14	·34	− ·26
10. Identification with war (−) .	·12	·40	− ·02	·31	− ·00
11. Childhood fighting behaviour (−)	·18	·30	− ·32	·17	− ·59
12. Childhood school adjustment (−)	·11	·15	·09	·19	·06
13. Relations with parents . .	·12	·10	·06	·20	·20
14. Emancipation from parents (−)	·08	·20	− ·34	·18	− ·24
15. Mobility	.09	− ·04	·31	·05	·24

normal and neurotic groups respectively as calculated by Eysenck (1952). We find again the same phenomenon already described in connection with the work of Bennett and Slater: there is a close correspondence between the values in the criterion column and the first factor saturations both for the normal and for the neurotic group. Again, therefore, we have external validation for our identification of this factor as one of neuroticism. (The second factor appears almost identical for the two groups, and may be identified with extraversion-introversion, although there is the obvious disadvantage that without an external method of validation this identification is subjective and insecure. However, the items characterising this factor are sufficiently similar to those which in a previous study were used to identify the "c" factor to make this interpretation reasonable.)

There have been alternative methods of constructing multifactorial questionnaires, making use of clinical psychiatric diagnoses, rather than relying on correlational methods. The best known questionnaires of this type are the Humm-Wadsworth Inventory and the Minnesota Multiphasic Personality Inventory (Hathaway and McKinley, 1943). In principle these scales are constructed by taking a number of clinical diagnoses and selecting questions either in terms of text book descriptions or in terms of actual reply patterns produced by samples of patients suitably diagnosed. The Humm-Wadsworth scale attempts to measure seven components; these and the behaviour tendencies associated with them are given below:

Normal—integration, adjustment, and well-rounded development of the subject; *Hysteroid*—evidence of self-concern, self-interest, and possessiveness; *Manic*—evidence of cheerfulness, drive towards activity, alertness, and excitability; *Depressive*—evidence of depression, retardation, and indecision; *Autistic*—evidence of imaginativeness, retiring disposition, and tendency to flinch from social situations; *Paranoid*—evidence of tenacity of opinion and defence of systematized ideas; and *Epileptoid*—tendencies towards projects and inspiration towards achievement. The M.M.P.I. consists of some 500 questions which have been grouped in a great variety of ways to produce a large number of scales; the following set of 15 is by no means all inclusive:

TABLE 31

Hs Hypochondriasis	Concern over bodily functions, concern about health, tendency toward physical complaint.
D Depression	Depression, dejection, discouragement, despondency.

QUESTIONNAIRES AND INVENTORIES 211

Hy Hysteria	Immature, unrealistic, amenable to group ideas, kindly, courteous, naive, needs social acceptance.
Pd Psychopathic Deviate	Irresponsible, undependable, impulsive, egocentric, defiant, asocial, individualistic.
Pa Paranoia	Aggressive, critical, irritable, moody, sensitive, sensitive to criticism.
Pt Psychasthenia	Apprehensive, tense, hesitant, insecure, self-conscious, feelings of inadequacy.
Sc Schizophrenia	Bashful, withdrawn, oversensitive, secretive, cautious.
Ma Hypomania	Confident, hypersensitive, not persistent, aggressive, charming, expansive.
Mf Masculinity-Feminity	Masculinity or feminity of interests.
Pr Prejudice	Cynicism, poor morale, suspiciousness, feelings of ill will, lack of faith in others.
Si Social Introversion	Tendency to avoid social contacts, little dependency upon people.
Ac Academic Achievement	Tenseness, docility, insecurity (producing greater academic output).
St Status	Self-confidence, poise, resourcefulness.
Re Responsibility	Dependability, integrity, seriousness, steadiness, tenacity.
Do Dominance	Optimism, persuasiveness, self-discipline, resoluteness.

The literature about these tests is legion, and the M.M.P.I. in particular has been used very widely indeed. Several authors have contributed factor analyses of different selections of scales, among them Cottle (1950), Cook and Wherry (1950), Tyler (1951), Wheeler *et al.* (1951), and Karson (1958). Results are difficult to evaluate and appear to depend on the particular scales included in the analysis, and the particular population studied. There is some evidence of a neuroticism factor and of an independent psychoticism factor; thus Wheeler *et al.* concluded that "The results from the present factor analysis of the M.M.P.I. seem to indicate that the ambitious goal of measuring specific clinical syndromes has not been completely achieved. The test permits diagnosis mainly in terms of 'neurotic' or 'psychotic', but not in terms of *type* of neurosis or psychosis or other more specific category."

The rather disappointing results from all this work appear to be due to three main reasons. In the first place, different scales often show overlapping item content, and this, as Guilford (1956) has pointed out, automatically makes factor analyses suspect. (Welsh (1952) has contributed a factor study of the M.M.P.I. using scales with item overlap eliminated, but his report is too short to make interpretation feasible.)

The second difficulty is the *a priori* method of scale construction and the heavy dependence on psychiatric theory and classification. Gilliland (1951) has contributed an interesting study comparing the

Humm-Wadsworth and the M.M.P.I. with respect to the scores obtained by various groups of subjects on five scales which they have in common. This table is given below, and as Gilliland points out "A study of the table of correlations shows almost exactly a chance distribution from zero as the mean. No general agreement between scores on the two tests can be found."

TABLE 32

No. of cases	Hysteroid-Psych. Deviate	Mania-Hypomania	Depression	Autistic-Schizoid	Paranoia
45*	·08	— ·15	·16	·00	— ·19
127*	·10	·20	·07	— ·02	— ·05
23*	·00	·11	·25	·21	·00
34*	·08	— ·03	·16	·15	·13
50†	·12	·03	—	—	— ·24
50†	·00	— ·21	·30	·10	— ·06

* Group was administered the M.M.P.I. Group Form
† Group was administered the M.M.P.I. Individual Form.

(A similar study by Nelson and Shea (1956) unearthed a similar lack of relationship between the M.M.P.I. and the Guilford set of factors STDCR.)

The third difficulty which arises has been pointed out by Barnes (1956), who investigated the hypothesis that psychoticism and neuroticism factors on the M.M.P.I. were due to certain types of response bias. "It was concluded that the number of atypical true answers is a 'pure factor test' of the psychotic factor and that a number of atypical false answers have a heavy loading on the 'neurotic factor'. It was also concluded that some allowance should be made in the interpretation of the M.M.P.I. to allow for the influence of response set."

Particular point is given to these criticisms by the very important recent analyses contributed by A. L. Comrey (1957, 1958). This writer took each of the M.M.P.I. scales in turn, intercorrelated items within it and carried out a factor analysis of the resulting correlations. To be of any great practical use the items within a scale should obviously have a certain uniformity, while different scales should be as independent from each other as possible. Neither of these desirable states of affairs was in fact found. The psychopathic deviate scale, to take but one example, could be analysed into as many as seven main independent factors which were named by

Comrey—neuroticism, paranoia, psychopathic personality, shyness, delinquency, euphoria and anti-social behaviour. The hysteria scale contained five main factors labelled neuroticism, cynicism, shyness, poor physical health and headaches. Quite generally Comrey found great diversity of content within any one scale; but also found considerable overlap in factorial content between scales. His work leaves little doubt that the reliance of the men who constructed the M.M.P.I. on the meaningfulness of clinical diagnosis was misplaced and that much of the work done with these scales has in fact been wasted.

We have noted in the first chapter that psychoanalytic theories, like the Jungian one, give rise to certain typology concepts, and in recent years factor analysis has been used quite extensively in an attempt to find evidence for or against these hypotheses, in particular those associated with Freud. Among the earliest experiments in this field is the work of Goldman-Eisler (1948, 1950, 1951). This writer makes use of the concepts of oral pessimism and oral optimism advanced by Abraham (1916, 1924, 1942), Freud (1938), and Glover (1924, 1925). "Oral character traits are assumed to originate from repressed or deflected oral impulses which are dominant during the nursing period, and which have undergone transformation into certain permanent behaviour patterns by the processes of reaction-formation, displacement, or sublimation. Two main syndromes of bipolar significance seem to emerge from Abraham's and Glover's studies. . . . The basic conditions for the development and fixation in character of the one or the other syndrome are assumed to be the experiences of gratification or frustration attached to the oral stage of libido development." On the one hand, we have the orally gratified type, which is described by analytic writers as being distinguished by imperturbable optimism, generosity, bright and sociable social conduct, accessibility to new ideas and ambition accompanied by sanguine expectation. On the other hand, the orally ungratified type is characterized by a profoundly pessimistic outlook on life, sometimes accompanied by moods of depression and attitudes of withdrawal, a passive, receptive attitude, a feeling of insecurity, an ambition which combines an intense desire to climb with a feeling of unattainability, a grudging feeling of injustice, sensitiveness to competition, and dislike of sharing.

Clearly, two hypotheses are involved here; first, the existence of a syndrome of personality traits corresponding to that described above, and second, the correlation between this syndrome and early weaning. To investigate the first of these hypotheses, Goldman administered verbal self-rating scales for 19 traits, mentioned by psycho-analytic writers as having an oral connotation, to 115 adult subjects. Each scale contained between 6 and 10 items, and the reliability coefficients for the various scales were satisfactory. Inter-

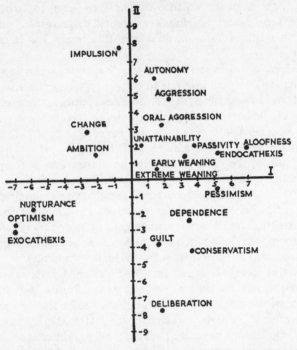

Fig. 30.—Plot of the Factor Loadings of nineteen tests as related to Variable "Early Weaning".

correlations between the scales were run, and two factors extracted from the matrix of intercorrelations. The resulting configuration of traits is shown in Fig. 30, which indicates quite clearly that the first factor to appear is one very similar to the hypothetical trait of oral optimism and oral pessimism. The trait "early weaning", which was defined as "having been weaned not later than at the age of 4 months", as contrasted with "having been weaned later", can be seen to have a saturation of ·337 on the "oral pessimism" side of this factor, thus confirming the hypothesis linking syndrome and orality. (This connection between syndrome and early weaning was also confirmed independently by means of analysis of variance procedures.)

The second factor is "characterized by extreme impulsiveness and a disinclination to wait or refrain from action (impulsion, ·761; deliberation, — ·766), by independence or a disinclination to conform (autonomy, ·560), by aggression, general and oral (aggression, ·479; oral-aggression ·303), and by a tendency to change, to seek the new, rather than to stick to the well-known and familiar (change, ·267; conservation, — ·436)". This factor appears to go counter to the firmly established psycho-analytic view that "oral frustration, oral impatience, oral sadism are inseparable"; factor II is highly loaded with impatience (impulsion) and aggression (sadism), but has no significant relationship to weaning (if early weaning be taken as a measure of oral frustration).

This study raises many problems which can only be hinted at here. There are certain obvious resemblances between the constituent traits of "oral optimism" and Guilford's "rathymia", which in turn was shown to be a good measure of extraversion. Indeed, Goldman's first factor is remarkably similar to the description of introversion-extraversion, as found in both the previous chapter and this one. This need cause no surprise because different clinical observers might be expected to observe the same fundamental relationships in the material at their disposal, although giving them different names and accounting for their emergence in terms of different hypotheses.

The hypothesis tested by Goldman is, of course, an environmental one; early oral deprivation (early weaning) causes the child to become pessimistic, aloof, passive, and so forth. Her results would seem to be in accordance with this hypothesis, but an equally likely alternative explanation should not be passed over too lightly. If we assume that introversion is an inherited quality, we might account for the observed correlation between early weaning and introversion by referring both the observed introverted behaviour of the child and his early weaning to the introverted tendency of the mother which leads her to an early interruption of weaning. The environmental explanation, of course, is the one preferred by Goldman, but her data do not offer any possibility of deciding in favour of one hypothesis as opposed to the other, and it would be quite unscientific to let one's choice be determined by personal preference. It should be possible, of course, to make deductions from these two alternative hypotheses which could be capable of disproof, but until such proof is forthcoming we must leave the decision between the environmentalistic and the hereditary view indeterminate.[1]

Similar in many ways to the Goldman-Eisler Study is one by Halla Beloff on the structure and origin of the anal character (1957). It is supposed by Freud that certain people are exceptionally *orderly*, *parsimonious*, and *obstinate*, and it is supposed that severe toilet training, either in terms of cleanliness enforced too early or too harshly, or both, will result in the development of the above mentioned traits; permissive training, accomplished relatively late and gently, will tend to encourage the development of traits opposite to those mentioned.

Twenty-eight items supposedly characteristic of anal traits were embodied in a questionnaire and administered to 75 undergraduate students; the questions were intercorrelated and a factor analysis performed. One general factor appeared with 22 out of 28 loadings above the ·30 level. These questions, together with their loadings are given below in Table 33. Ratings were also obtained and factor analysed, and here also only one significant factor was obtained. These results strongly argued in support of the hypothesis of the existence of a trait similar to that postulated by Freud.

In order to test the aetiological hypothesis the bowel training histories of 43 postgraduate students were investigated by means of interviews with the mothers. For the purpose of the analysis relatively early completion of training was equated with relatively coercive training. These mothers also completed the above mentioned questionnaire. "The relative predictive powers of the anal score of the mother and the age of completed toilet training for the score of the student subject, were compared by means of a 2×2 analysis of variance. Only one turn proved significant (and that beyond 1 per cent.)—the questionnaire score of the mother. From our data then we may conclude that although the anal character is a meaningful dimension of variation for the description of our subjects' attitudes and behaviour, it is not related to toilet training experiences, but strongly to the degree of anal character exhibited by the mother."

Another writer to undertake "A statistical study of the Freudian theory of levels of psychosexual development" is C. A. Barnes (1952). "The hypothesis under consideration was that the conscious attitudes and feelings which were related to the three levels of development,

[1] Those interested in the problem presented by the "oral character" in relation to correlational analysis may wish to consult the more recent paper by Blum and Miller (1952).

TABLE 33

Self-Ratings on Anal Character Traits

Item No.	Loading	
16	·677	Often in the position to say, "I told you so." (·681)*
10	·505	Takes an active part in family affairs, even to the extent of being considered "bossy". (·465)
24	·483	Enjoys the sense of power which comes from a victory of his will over other people's. (·645)
13	·483	Annoyed to hear people express strong opinions, because they seldom know enough about the subject being discussed. (·613)
1	·483	Feels that unpunctuality is one of *the* most annoying social vices. (·490)
11	·468	Would often get real pleasure telling people what he thought of them. (·488)
20	·463	Has "off days", when friends say he must have got out of the wrong side of the bed. (·597)
4	·436	Agrees that it is necessary for a houswife to have everything "just so". (·309)
27	·425	Blames newspapers very much for distorting the news in order to make a better story. (·298)
12	·420	Does not find it difficult to see a job through to the end. (·238)
25	·419	Admits that sometimes revenge is sweet. (·369)
21	·414	Dislikes lending books and other possessions. (·596)
22	·411	Is often the last to give up trying to do a thing. (·286)
14	·394	Becomes stubborn when others interfere with his way of doing things, even when there is something in what they say. (·525)
3	·373	Agrees that in modern life there is an awful lot of waste of time, of energy, of money. (·340)
19	·372	Often spends so long working out the best way to do things, the actual doing gets delayed. (·379)
9	·366	Would not eat a biscuit which had fallen on the floor. (·570)
18	·330	Feels uncomfortable when looking at a crooked picture on the wall. (·689)
26	·329	Sets himself standards, compared with acquaintances. (·758)
5	·326	Has often lost out on things because he did not make up his mind soon enough. (− ·039)
6	·324	Although he tries to remain calm and even-tempered, things do often occur which upset him. (·515)
8	·305	When he needs to buy something, goes on looking and looking until he finds just the right thing. (·416)
28	·284	Prefers to work alone rather than with a group. (·127)
23	·271	Agrees that "cleanliness is next to godliness". (·465)
17	·266	Agrees that a man's first duty is to make enough money to look after his family really well, personal work preferences come after this. (·323)
2	·256	Is often amazed at the muddles other people get into. (·411)
7	·220	Would rather buy a record than a ticket for a concert. (·163)
15	·066	Does not agree that there is usually a good reason for people being late for an appointment. (·206)

* Figures in parentheses are the loadings on the Ratings.

the oral, the anal and the phallic, would be found to be empirically grouped as the Freudian theory predicted." "Questionnaire type" tests were designed and administered to 266 male students and their responses were correlated and factor analysed. 11 factors were extracted and the author concludes that "The Freudian theory of levels of psychosexual development has not been supported as a whole." He did, however, find support for an anal factor similar to that of Beloff, and in one or two other points his results were not necessarily opposed to Freudian teaching. We may perhaps agree with his final summary that "The theory of levels of psychosexual development is difficult to test because the characteristics used by analysts are not classified consistently."

The last study we shall be concerned with in this section on Freudian concepts is the work of Stagner *et al.* (1955, 1956). In his work Stagner used a scale developed by Krout and Krout (1953) which "extends orthodox Freudian theory somewhat in that it specifies ten sets or patterns of psychosexual development". These ten patterns are described in the manual as follows:

I. *Prenatal.* Items symbolic of prenatal comforts. "It is assumed that an individual who rates low on these items feels secure and thus tends to be active, outgoing, and inclined to seek new experiences; while one who scores high is insecure and tends to be regressive and inclined to cling to the past."

II. *Early Oral.* "One who is low here may be considered taciturn, pessimistic, inclined to withdrawal from contact; while one who is high tends to be communicative, optimistic, inclined to seek close object relations."

III. *Late Oral.* "A low score here should represent adequate control of verbal hostility—hence, altruistic, tolerant social behaviour; a high score, on the other hand, should point to an oral-sadistic type of person who drains his hostility via oral channels—hence, tends to be subtly punitive (sarcastic) in his social attitudes."

IV. *Early Anal.* "A high score should represent an emotionally labile, 'easy going' sort of attitude, while a low score, on the other hand, should spell a tendency to emotional rigidity."

V. *Late Anal.* "Here a low score indicates irregular, rather inconsistent behaviour trends. A high score points to a methodical, punctilious, stubborn, parsimonious type of individual."

VI. *Narcissistic.* "Here a low score should imply a self-effacing type of attitude, and should point to a relatively low aspiration level. A high score, on the other hand, should imply ambition. However, as ambition is used here, it refers to aspiration rather than drive."

VII. *Feminine.* "A high score on this section should point to a submissive—'co-operative' attitude (in a male or female), because the traits are all of a passive-receptive nature."

VIII. *Masculine.* "Here a low score should indicate a generally unaggressive, apprehensive type of personality, in a male, and perhaps a normal attitude in a female; whereas a high score should point to a masculinoid-aggressive make-up, in a male, and perhaps an over-compensated masculinity in a female."

IX. *Intra-familial sublimation.* "A low score here denotes an insensitive, unsentimental, unsublimated type of attitude and relatively loose personal ties. A high score points to sublimated, sensitive, emotionally mature attitudes, high personal loyalty, acceptance of authority, and enjoyment of personal services."

X. *Social sublimation.* "A low score stamps the testee as a socially immature individual, unconcerned about impersonal situations, unable to conceptualize his relationships; whereas a high score should stamp him as a socially mature personality with strong feelings about the larger world and a tendency to leadership."

There are ten items in the subtest, 100 in the total test. The items in the subtest were intercorrelated and factor analysed, and the three items with the highest weightings chosen to represent the subtest in a larger matrix, made up of 30 items altogether. "The evidence favours the view that there are ten factors necessary to account for most of the variance. However, they do not fit theoretical expectations in a completely satisfactory way. The assumed post-genital stages give rather good fits; the pre-genital stages were cluttered and did not separate clearly. On the whole, the evidence is interpreted as confirming the Freudian hypothesis."

In the second study Stagner proceeded to test a further deduction which he calls the "type hypothesis". He argues that "trait theorists have generally held that organization can be conceived in terms of generalized ways of perceiving and responding to a class of situations. . . . Different traits are relatively independent of one another. Type theorists, on the other hand, have argued for an overall unity of personality, a Gestalt quality, such that all the parts have a certain necessary relationship to one another. The organization principle . . . is assumed to cover a much more inclusive personality configuration than a specific trait." Using the results from the previous study, Stagner argues that "Since the 100 items utilized by Krout and Tabin (1954) relate to the different 'developmental stages' of Freudian theory, they should afford a suitable medium for testing the typology conception. Our statistical test is thus: persons selected as representatives of one type should correlate more highly among themselves than with persons selected as representatives of other types." Three men were chosen to exemplify each of the ten "types", and intercorrelations were obtained among all cases "by an analysis of variance technique, a test was made of the hypothesis that the mean within-type correlation did not differ significantly from the mean between-type correlations. The statistical tests indicated no significant differences for any of these comparisons. The data are interpreted as casting doubt on the appropriateness of using typological formulations as proposed by Freud and some of his followers."

These various studies of Freudian conceptions are difficult to evaluate. They suggest, as might have been expected, that the implicit observation of congruent behaviour patterns of such an able observer as Freud undoubtedly was, resulted in the delineation of certain trait constellations which can be shown by more objective methods to have a certain amount of functional unity. His much more speculative aetiological theories would not, on the whole, appear to have received much support. Indeed, as was argued earlier, it is doubtful whether the logic of experimental analysis would permit one to draw any conclusions from what are in fact purely correlational experiments; aetiological arguments require an entirely different type of experiment to that reported hitherto. These conclusions must be qualified in one way. A positive correlation between a putative causal factor and a personality trait cannot be regarded as proving the causal hypothesis. However, a zero correlation between a putative causal influence and a given trait, may be interpreted as casting grave doubts on the truth of the aetiological hypothesis. It is to be hoped that further and perhaps more sophisticated experiments will be carried out in this field to clarify the rather obscure position which obtains at the moment.

In assessing the evidential value of the studies reviewed in this chapter, we must of course also have recourse to such work as has been done on their validation. A very thorough review of some 350 studies by Ellis (1946) concludes "that group administered pencil and paper personality questionnaires are of dubious value in distinguishing between groups of adjusted and maladjusted individuals and that they are of much less value in the diagnosis of individual adjustment or personality traits". In a review of the validity of personality inventories in military practice, Ellis and Conrad (1948) come to a slightly different conclusion: "Military applications of personality inventories have yielded enough favourable results to command attention. In contrast, personality inventories in civilian practice have generally proved disappointing." In these evaluations Ellis has taken an unusually severe criterion of validity. He claims that he will in his review "usually evaluate the reported coefficients of correlation in terms of the conventional estimations given them in the consideration of psychological and educational tests. Thus, we shall say that r's from zero to ·19 indicate negative validity; from ·20–·39 mainly negative validity; from ·40–·69 questionably positive validity; from ·70–·79 mainly positive validity; and from ·80–1·00 positive validity". These standards can hardly be considered usual, and are very much more severe than those applied by most authors. Even so, the studies quoted by Ellis in his Table 2 indicate that some 35 per cent. give validation coefficients in excess of ·7, while only about 40 per cent. give validation coefficients lower than ·4.

These results to most psychologists would seem rather promising, particularly in view of the fact that they were obtained in civilian work, and that according to Ellis and Conrad military application of questionnaire results have even higher validation coefficients. In any case, it would seem inadmissible to take these coefficients at their face value. They validate questionnaires against criteria which are themselves imperfect, and consequently even a perfect measuring instrument could not be expected to give very high correlations with such imperfect criteria. All we can deduce from figures such as those given by Ellis is that there are high agreements between some questionnaires and some external criteria; to estimate the exact validity of questionnaires would require the presence of a perfect criterion and in the absence of such a criterion must be impossible.

A different way of attacking the problem of evaluation has already been indicated elsewhere in this chapter. As has been pointed out there, the criticisms made justifiably of questionnaire studies are essentially different from those made equally justifiably of rating studies. If, therefore, the two methods of assessment give results which are identical, or at least essentially similar, we may have more confidence in the general picture provided by them. It has been shown throughout the chapter that in the main there is remarkable congruence between findings, and in at least one individual research (Fiske, 1949) this congruence has been demonstrated along strictly experimental lines independent of subjective estimation.

It is rather curious that such conformities should be so readily observable. In recent years there has grown up a body of experimental research related to the problem of response set in questionnaire studies (Cronbach 1946, 1950; Jackson and Merrick, 1958) which suggests strongly that subjects may tend to reply to questionnaire items not entirely or only in terms of the content of the item but also in terms of their individual set to reply "Yes" rather than "No", or to give many "question mark" answers, or to answer five or seven point questions in the most definite *pro* or *con* manner. Jackson and Merrick (1958), in summarizing much of this literature, distinguish between "content and style in personality assessment", and they conclude that "stylistic determinants such as acquiescence, over-generalization and tendency to respond in an asocial, undesirable manner, as distinct from specific content, account for a large proportion of response variance on some personality scales." When we add to this well authenticated observation the fact that high anxiety groups may tend to give more extreme answers (Berg and Collier, 1953; Lewis and Taylor, 1953), we can see that there are considerable opportunities here for distortion, even apart from those quite naturally given by the fact that individuals in many situations will be unwilling to bear witness against themselves (Heron, 1956). Much of the work which has been done with existing questionnaires may well require revision, and further information on the relationships between response set and personality are urgently required. In spite of these facts the validity coefficients empirically discovered, and the relationships between ratings and questionnaires discussed above, do indicate that questionnaires can contribute a certain proportion of true variance.

That is not to say that the position is a very satisfactory one. Quite clearly, the conditions under which questionnaires are filled in, the intelligence and co-operativeness of the subjects, their suggestibility and insight, as well as their mood and various unconscious factors of the type mentioned in connection with ratings, will powerfully affect and distort the results which may be expected in the use of questionnaires. Some of these difficulties can be overcome by the use of modern developments (the Humm-Wadsworth no-count, the Minnesota Multiphasic Personality Inventory lie and K scales, and similar empirical methods of improving forecasting efficiency), but on the whole it must be clear that questionnaire answers can never be taken at their face value. Only when their empirical relationships with other variables have been definitely established, under a reproducible set of conditions, will they take their place among other methods of investigation and throw important light on certain facets of the subject's personality (his own picture of himself, his degree of insight, his desire to give a good account of himself, etc.) which would be difficult to obtain by any other method. As in the case of ratings, questionnaires are a necessary but not sufficient means for arriving at a complete and adequate picture of a person's major traits and personality variables. Neither uncritical praise nor exaggerated blame would help in a proper evaluation of the usefulness of questionnaires in personality study.

REFERENCES

Chapter V

ABRAHAM, K. The first pregenital stage of the libido. In: *Selected Papers*. London: Hogarth Press, 1916.

A short study of the development of the libido, viewed in the light of mental disorders. In: *Selected Papers*. London: Hogarth Press, 1924.

The influence of oral eroticism on character-formation. In: *Selected Papers*. London: Hogarth Press, 1942.

ALLPORT, G. W. *Personality. A Psychological Interpretation*. London: Constable & Co. Ltd., 1937.

BAEHR, M. A Factorial Study of Temperament. *Psychomet. Lab.*, Univ. Chicago, 1951.

BANKS, C., and KEIR, G. A factorial analysis of items in the Bernreuter Personality Inventory. *Brit. J. Psychol., Stat. Sect.*, 1952, 5, 19–30.

BARNES, C. A. A statistical study of the Freudian theory of levels of psychosexual development. *Genet. Psychol. Monogr.*, 1952, 45, 105–124.

BARNES, E. H. Factors, response bias, and the MMPI. *J. consult. Psychol.*, 1956, 20, 419–421.

Response bias and the MMPI. *J. consult. Psychol.*, 1956, 20, 371–374.

BELOFF, H. The structure and origin of the anal character. *Genet. Psychol. Monogr.*, 1957, 55, 141–172.

BENNETT, E., and SLATER, P. Some tests for the discrimination of neurotic from normal subjects and the psychometric differentiation of neurotic from normal subjects. *Brit. J. med. Psychol.*, 1945, 20, 271–282.

BERG, I. J., and COLLIER, J. S. Personality and group differences in extreme response sets. *Educ. Psychol. Measmt.*, 1953, 13, 164–169.

BLUM, G. S., and MILLER, D. R. Exploring the psychoanalytic theory of the "oral character". *J. Pers.*, 1952, 20, 287–307.

BROGDEN, H. E., and THOMAS, W. F. The primary traits in personality items purporting to measure sociability. *J. Psychol.*, 1943, 16, 85–97.

CARROLL, J. B. Ratings on traits measured by a factorial personality inventory. *J. abnorm. soc. Psychol.*, 1952, 47, 626–632.

CATTELL, R. B. *The 16 P.F. Test*. Champaign: Institute for Personality and Ability testing, 1949.

The main personality factors in questionnaire, self-estimate material. *J. soc. Psychol.*, 1950, 31, 3–38.

COLLIER, R., and EMCH, M. Introversion-extraversion: the concepts and their clinical use. *Amer. J. Psychiat.*, 1938, **94**, 1,045–1,075.

COMREY, A. L. A factor analysis of items on the MMPI depression scale. *Educ. Psychol. Measmt.*, 1957, **17**, 578–585.

A factor analysis of items on the MMPI hypochondriasis scale. *Educ. Psychol. Measmt.*, 1957, **17**, 568–577.

A factor analysis of items on the MMPI hysteria scale. *Educ. Psychol. Measmt.*, 1957, **17**, 586–592.

A factor analysis of items on the MMPI paranoia scale. *Educ. Psychol. Measmt.*, 1958, **18**, 99–108.

A factor analysis of items on the MMPI psychopathic deviate scale. *Educ. Psychol. Measmt.*, 1958, **18**, 91–98.

A factor analysis of items on the MMPI F scale. *Educ. Psychol. Measmt.*, 1958, **18**, 621–632.

A factor analysis of items on the MMPI K scale. *Educ. Psychol. Measmt.*, 1958, **18**, 633–640.

COOK, E. B., and WHERRY, R. J. A factor analysis of the MMPI and aptitude test data. *J. appl. Psychol.*, 1950, **34**, 260–266.

COTTLE, W. C. A factorial study of the Multiphasic, Strong, Kuder and Bell inventories using a population of adult males. *Psychometrika*, 1950, **15**, 25–47.

CRONBACH, L. J. Response sets and test validity. *Educ. Psychol. Measmt.* 1946, **6**, 475–494.

Further evidence on response sets and test designs. *Educ. Psychol. Measmt.*, 1950, **10**, 3–31.

ELLIS, A. The validity of personality questionnaires. *Psychol. Bull.*, 1946, **43**, 385–440.

ELLIS, A., and CONRAD, H. S. The validity of personality inventories in military practice. *Psychol. Bull.*, 1948, **45**, 385–426.

EYSENCK, H. J. *Dimensions of Personality*. London: Kegan Paul, 1947.

The Scientific Study of Personality. London: Routledge & Kegan Paul, 1952.

The questionnaire measurement of neuroticism and extraversion. *Rivista di Psicologia*, 1956, **50**, 113–140.

A short questionnaire for the measurement of the dimensions of personality. *J. appl. Psychol.*, 1958, **42**, 14–17.

Manual, the Maudsley Personality Inventory. London: Univ. Lond. Press, 1959.

FIEDLER, F. E., LODGE, J. A., JONES, R. E., and HUTCHINS, E. B. Interrelations among measures of personality adjustment in nonclinical populations. *J. abnorm. soc. Psychol.*, 1958, **56**, 345–351.

FISKE, D. W. Consistency of the factorial structures of personality ratings from different sources. *J. abnorm., soc. Psychol.*, 1949, **44**, 329–344.

FLANAGAN, J. C. *Factor Analysis in the Study of Personality*. Stanford: Univ. Press, 1935.

FRASER, R. *The Incidence of Neurosis among Factory Workers*. London: H.M.S.O., 1947.

FREUD, S. *General Introduction to Psychoanalysis*. New York: Liveright, 1920.

Three Contributions to a Theory of Sex. In: *The Basic Writings of Sigmund Freud*. New York: Modern Library, 1938.

FREYD, M. Introverts and extraverts. *Psychol. Rev.*, 1924, **5**, 74–87.

GIBB, C. Personality traits by factorial analysis. *Australian J. Psychol. and Phil.*, 1942, **20**, 1–15, 86–110, 203–227.

GILLILAND, A. R. The Humm-Wadsworth and the Minnesota Multi-phasic. *J. consult. Psychol.*, 1951, **15**, 452–459.

GLOVER, E. The significance of the mouth in psychoanalysis. *Brit. J. med. Psychol.*, 1924, **4**, 134–155.

Notes on oral character-formation. *Int. J. Psychoanal.*, 1925, **6**, 131–153.

GOLDMAN-EISLER, F. Breast-feeding and character-formation. *J. Pers.*, 1948, **17**, 83–103.

Breast feeding and character-formation: the etiology of the oral character in psychoanalytic theory. *J. Pers.*, 1950, **19**, 189–196.

The problem of orality and of its origin in early childhood. *J. ment. Sci.*, 1951, **97**, 765–781.

GUILFORD, J. P. When not to factor analyse. *Psychol. Bull.*, 1952, **49**, 26–37.

GUILFORD, J. P., and GUILFORD, R. B. An analysis of the factors in a typical test of introversion-extraversion. *J. abnorm. soc. Psychol.*, 1934, **28**, 377–399.

Personality factors, S, E, and M, and their measurement. *J. Psychol.*, 1936, **2**, 109–127.

Personality factors, D, R, T, and A. *J. abnorm. soc. Psychol.*, 1939, **34**, 21–26.

GUILFORD, J. P., and MARTIN, H. G. *An inventory of factors GAMIN.* Beverley Hills, Cal.: Sheridan Supply Co., 1943.

Personnel inventory. Beverley Hills, Cal.: Sheridan Supply Co., 1943.

GUILFORD, J. P., and ZIMMERMAN, W. S. Fourteen dimensional temperament. *Psychol. Monogr.*, 1956, **70**, No. 10, 1–26.

HATHAWAY, S. R., and MCKINLEY, J. C. *The Minnesota Multiphasic Personality Inventory.* New York: The Psychological Corporation, 1943.

HERON, A. The effects of real life motivation on questionnaire response. *J. appl. Psychol.*, 1956, **40**, 2.

A two-part personality measure for use as a research criterion. *Brit. J. Psychol.*, 1956, **47**, 243–251.

HILDEBRAND, H. P. A factorial study of introversion-extraversion. *Brit. J. Psychol.*, 1958, **49**, 1–11.

HSÜ, E. H. The construction of a test for measuring character traits. *Stud. Psychol. and Psychiat.*, 1943, **6**, 3–55.

HUMM, D. G., and WADSWORTH, G. W. *Humm-Wadsworth Temperament Scale.* Los Angeles: Humm Personnel Service, 1940.

HUSEN, T. The popular conception of personality as revealed in self-ratings. Paper read at *13th Internat. Cong. Psychol.*, Stockholm, July 1951.

JACKSON, D. N., and MERRICK, S. Content and style in personality assessment. *Psychol. Bull.*, 1958, **55**, 243–252.

JENKINS, T. N. Some contributions in support of a neutral theory of personality. *Trans. N.Y. Acad. Sci.*, 1950, **13**, 9–12.

JUNG, C. G. *Psychologische Typen.* Zürich: Rascher & Cie., 1921.

KARSON, S. Second-order personality factors and the MMPI. *J. clin. Psychol.*, 1958, **14**, 313–315.

KELLY, E. L., and FISKE, D. W. *The Prediction of Performance in Clinical Psychology.* Ann Arbor: Univ. Michigan, 1952.

KROUT, M. H., and KROUT, J. *A Guide to Personal Preference Scale.* Chicago: Psychol. Inst., 1953.

KROUT, M. H., and TABIN, J. K. Measuring personality in developmental terms: the P.P.S. *Genetic Psychol. Mon.*, 1954, **50**, 289–335.

LAYMAN, G. M. An item analysis of the adjustment questionnaire. *J. Psychol.*, 1940, **10**, 87–106.

LEWIS, N. A., and TAYLOR, J. A. Anxiety and extreme response set preferences. *Educ. Psychol. Measmt.*, 1955, **15**, 115–116.

LOVELL, C. A study of the factor structure of thirteen personality variables. *Educ. Psychol. Measmt.*, 1945, **5**, 335–350.

MEEHL, P. E. *Clinical versus Statistical Prediction.* Minnesota: Univ. Press, 1954.

MOSIER, C. I. The factor analysis of certain neurotic symptoms. *Psychomet.*, 1937, **2**, 263–286.

NELSON, M. O., and SHEA, S. MMPI correlates of the inventory of factors STDCR. *Psychol. Rep.*, 1956, **2**, 433–435.

NORTH, R. D. An analysis of the personality dimensions of introversion-extraversion. *J. Pers.*, 1949, **17**, 352–367.

PALLISTER, H. The negative or withdrawal attitude. A study in personality organization. *Arch. Psychol.*, 1933, **23**, 5–56.

PERRY, R. C. A group factor analysis of the adjustment questionnaire. *Univ. S. Calif. Educ. Mon.*, 1934, **5**.

REYBURN, M. A., and TAYLOR, J. G. Some factors of temperament—a re-examination. *Psychomet.*, 1934, **8**, 91–104.

Factors in introversion and extraversion. *Brit. J. Psychol.*, 1940, **31**, 335–340.

STAGNER, R., LARSON, E. D., and MOFFITT, J. W. The Krout personal preference scale: a factor-analytic study. *J. clin. Psychol.*, 1955, **11**, 101–113.

STAGNER, R., and MOFFITT, J. W. A statistical study of Freud's theory of personality types. *J. clin. Psychol.*, 1956, **12**, 22–74.

STORM, T., ROSENWALD, G. C., and CHILD, I. J. A factor analysis of self-ratings on social behaviour. *J. soc. Psychol.*, 1958, **118**, 45–49.

STOUFFER, S. A. *The American Soldier, IV. Measurement and Prediction.* Princeton: Princeton Univ. Press, 1949.

THURSTONE, L. L. The dimensions of temperament. *Psychomet.*, 1951, **16**, 11–20.

TYLER, F. I. A factorial analysis of fifteen MMPI scales. *J. consult. Psychol.*, 1951, **15**, 451–456.

VERNON, P. E. *The Assessment of Psychological Qualities by Verbal Methods.* London: H.M.S.O., 1938.

The Structure of Human Abilities. London: Methuen, 1950.

WELSH, G. S. A factor study of the MMPI using scales with item overlap eliminated. *Amer. Psychologist*, 1952, **7**, 34–342.

WHEELER, W. M., LITTLE, K. B., and LEHNER, P. F. J. The internal structure of the MMPI. *J. consult. Psychol.*, 1951, **15**, 134–142.

WILLOUGHBY, R. R. Some properties of the Thurstone Personality Schedule. *J. soc. Psychol.*, 1932, **3**, 401–424.

CHAPTER VI

THE ANALYSIS OF OBJECTIVE BEHAVIOUR
TESTS

As in each of the previous chapters we found one particular group of studies outstanding in their psychological importance, their technical competence, and the excellence of statistical treatment, so here also we find one unified body of work which has rightly gained credit for its brilliance. We are referring to the three volumes in which Hartshorne and May (1929, 1930) have published the results of the famous Character Education Enquiry: *Studies in Deceit, Studies in Service and Self-Control*, and *Studies in the Organization of Character*. These three books may still be regarded as a landmark which has not been surpassed by later work. If in some ways we are forced to be critical of the theoretical interpretation of the results offered by the authors, we nevertheless wish to pay tribute to the scientific integrity which makes available all the data on which such criticism can be based.

The Character Education Enquiry was undertaken in the autumn of 1924 at the request of the Institute of Social and Religious Research "in order to carry out investigations which would relate to those experiences of children having moral and religious significance, and to apply the objective methods of the laboratory to the measurement of conduct under controlled conditions". After a detailed consideration of the literature, Hartshorne and May constructed a large battery of tests, which must be described in brief outline now to make intelligible the discussion of their results. They laid down certain general rules to which all tests should, as far as possible, conform. Thus, a test situation should be as far as possible a natural situation as well as a controlled situation; the test situation and the method of response should be such as to allow all subjects equal opportunity to exhibit the behaviour under investigation; the child should not be subjected to any moral strain beyond the usual, and the tests should not be allowed to put the subject and the examiner in a false social relation to each other; the tests should have "low visibility", i.e. they should not arouse the suspicions of the subject.

Various techniques were found to conform with these rules, such

227

as, for instance, the "Duplicating Technique". The child is given any pencil-and-paper type of test; the papers are collected and a duplicate of the answers made in the office. At a later session of the class, the original papers are returned, and each child told to score his own paper according to a key supplied. Deception consists in illegitimately increasing one's score by copying answers from the key. Other tests made use of the "Improbable Achievement Technique". This consists in giving a test under conditions such that achievement above a given level is an almost certain indication of deception. Thus, a child who, when asked to put dots into the centre of a number of irregularly spaced circles on the blackboard with his eyes closed, succeeds in doing so well beyond what is known to be within the capacity of children may be presumed to have peeped.

Another type still is the "Double-testing Technique". In this method the children are tested twice on alternate versions of a given test; on one occasion conditions are such as to permit deception, on the other there is strict supervision and no opportunity to deceive. The difference between scores made on the two occasions is a rough measure of the tendency to deceive, i.e. either to copy answers from the key or to change answers to match the key. It is, of course, essential in this procedure that material be available in two equivalent forms having the same degree of difficulty at all levels. It may also be noted that, unlike the previous techniques, this one lends itself to showing deception in work done at home as well as in the classroom situations. It also lends itself to testing in another and different context, namely that of athletic contests, when the achievement of the child on such activities as "pull-up" or "chinning", the "standing broad jump", or dynamometer and spirometer tests can be measured when the test is given by the examiner and when it is self-administered, and the differences noted as evidence of cheating through inflated claims.

All these techniques for measuring cheating permit, of course, a large number of variations, and some of them may be applied in situations quite different from those originally envisaged. Thus, the authors found it possible to use tests of this kind in connection with parlour games, and on other occasions when motivation is high and when conditions are markedly different from those obtaining at school or in the home.

In contrast to these tests, all of which deal with cheating of one kind or another, there are others dealing with stealing and lying. In each case an opportunity was given for the child to steal or lie under conditions which made it seem unlikely to the child that he could be caught out, but which were so much under the control of the experimenters that a complete check was possible. Thus, for instance, in connection with the administration of one test, a little box was given to each pupil containing several puzzles not all of which were used. In each box was a coin ostensibly belonging to another puzzle which the examiner showed to the children but did not ask them to do. Each child returned his own box to a large receptacle at the front of the room. It was possible to check which children took the coin before returning the box by a system of numbering and distributing the boxes according to the seating plan of the class. Lying could be detected, for instance, by asking the children whether they had cheated on any of the tests; it was known, of course, whether they had cheated or not, and if they denied having done so the lie was apparent.

A large number of different populations were studied coming from different types of schools, institutions, urban and rural areas, and from variegated racial backgrounds. Altogether, some 170,000 tests were administered to over 8,000 public-school children and almost 3,000 children in private and standardized schools.

Attempts were made to find data outside the experimental situation which would throw light on the validity of the techniques employed. In the first place, ratings were used which showed a reasonable reliability of almost ·70 (first versus second ratings) and ·55 (one rater versus another). Correlations between behaviour tests and ratings were between ·35 and ·40, and increased to almost ·5 when corrected for attenuation. In view of the unknown validity of the ratings themselves, this correlation is encouraging.

We may now turn to the organization of personality as revealed in the intercorrelations of the different tests. Hartshorne and May give the intercorrelations of nine types of deceitful behaviour; the average intercorrelation of the nine tests is ·227. This would give a predictive reliability of ·725 and a predictive validity of ·851. In other words, the correlation between the nine tests in the battery and another nine tests of a similar character would be ·725; that of the battery with an infinite number of similar tests, i.e. with what we might call the theoretically "true" measure of dishonesty, would be ·851. Hartshorne and May calculate that it would take 31 tests of this type to give an internal validity of ·948.

The same techniques applied to the study of deceitful behaviour were also used in a study of socially approved behaviour. Hartshorne and May consider as socially desirable the tendency to do things for others rather than for oneself, and the tendency to work with others rather than to stand alone, a tendency which they believe "passes into and through a stage of *co-operation for the sake of organized competition* to a higher level of *co-operation for a non-competitive object*, the significance of which lies in the relation of the co-operating individuals to one another". In their attempts to devise test situations they have these two modes of response in mind.

Five tests were given to make up what are called the "service" tests.

(1) *The Self-or-class Test.*—A spelling contest was set up in which each pupil could compete for one of two sets of prizes, one for the winning classes and one for the winning individuals. No one could enter both contests. Each had to choose whether his score was to count for himself and help himself towards getting a prize or count for the class and help the class get a prize.

(2) *The Money Voting Test.*—In this test the class had to decide what to do with the money that might be, or had actually been, won in the previous contest. Scoring was in terms of the altruistic nature of the choice, ranging from (i) "Buy something for some hospital child or some family needing help or for some other philanthropy" to (ii) "Divide the money equally among the members of the class".

(3) *The Learning Exercises.*—This test attempts to measure the amount of drive induced by opportunities to work for the Red Cross, for the class, or for oneself, on a digit symbol matching test, using as scores gains from the basic unmotivated score of the first day.

(4) *The School Kit Test.*—Each child was provided with a pencil case containing 10 articles which came "as a present from a friend of the school". It was then suggested to them that they might give away any part or all of the kit in an inconspicuous way in order to help make up some kits for children who had no useful pretty things of this kind.

(5) *The Envelopes Test.*—The children were asked to find jokes, pictures, interesting stories, and the like for sick children in hospital, and were issued with envelopes in which to collect them. The number of articles collected was scored according to a complex scoring system.

Various other tests were also tried out, such as the Efficiency Co-operation test, in which work for self in a contest with other individuals was compared with work for one's class in an inter-class contest. In the Free Choice test carried out after the previous one, the choice was given as to whether the child wants to go on working for himself or for the class.

An effort was made again to test the validity of these tests by means of ratings, using a portrait-matching device, the guess-who technique, a check list, a conduct record, and a record of social service in school projects. The various validation scores had medium to low correlations ranging in the neighbourhood of ·3 to ·5. It was possible to make up a "total reputation for service" score which had a correlation with the theoretical "true" total reputation of ·77. Individual tests correlated with this total reputation score about ·2 to ·3. In combinations of two the tests correlated ·3 to ·5 with total reputation scores. Correlation between the total service score and the total reputation score was ·61. This is a very encouraging result in view of the well-known fact that correlations between ratings for intelligence test scores are seldom higher than this.

Turning now to the intercorrelations of the tests, we find an average correlation of ·201. The detailed figures are given in Table 34. The correlation of this battery with the "true score" would be about ·745. It would require 17 tests in all to give a high enough validity for individual prediction.

TABLE 34

Intercorrelations of Final Service Tests—Populations X, Y, and Z

	2	3	4	5
1. Free choice . . .	·20 ± ·02	·17 ± ·02	·13 ± ·03	·20 ± ·02
2. Efficiency co-operation .	—	·27 ± ·02	·32 ± ·02	·21 ± ·02
3. Money vote . . .	—	—	·27 ± ·02	·12 ± ·03
4. Kits	—	—	—	·12 ± ·03
5. Envelopes . . .	—	—	—	—

In addition to the battery of service tests described above a number of tests of self-control were also developed. In particular an attempt was made to measure persistence and inhibition. Persistence tests will be described in some detail in a later chapter, and therefore we will not give any detailed account of those used by Hartshorne and May. Inhibition tests, however, are not discussed elsewhere. Six techniques altogether were tried out:

(1) The Story Inhibition Test.
(2) The Safe Manipulation Test.
(3) The Puzzle Manipulation Test.

(4) The Ruggles Distraction Test.
(5) The Picture Inhibition Test.
(6) The Candy Inhibition Test.

In the first of these, each child has a copy of a story which is read aloud by the examiner up to the climax. The child is then asked to turn the sheets over and write on the back of the last page how he thinks the story will end. The child is thus expected to inhibit the drive to know how the story ends and instead has a guess at it. If he chooses to guess, he is not told how the story comes out.

In the second test a small toy safe with a combination lock is put on each pupil's desk. He is instructed not to touch it for a lengthy period, during which a paper and pencil test is given; self-control consists in inhibiting the tendency to touch and play with the safe.

In the third test a box is passed to the children containing a peg test, as well as five small puzzles, definitely attractive to children, with which they are asked not to play. Inhibition consists in leaving these puzzles alone and concentrating on the major task.

In the Distraction test an arithmetic test is set out on a page covered with distracting and interesting drawings. Self-control consists in not giving way to the temptation of looking at these.

The Picture Inhibition test is similar to the Distraction test, and the Candy Inhibition test resembles the Safe Manipulation test.

Reputation for self-control was canvassed in a similar way to that used for service. This has a theoretical validity of ·86 for persistence and ·76 for inhibition. The correlations of reputation with the persistence test are not very large; neither are those between inhibition tests and reputation. The theoretical validity of the persistence tests is ·78 (obtained from their average intercorrelation of ·239). That of the inhibition tests is ·65, based on an average intercorrelation of ·16. These low and somewhat unsatisfactory correlations may be due to the fact that group tests were used; it is doubtful if group testing is well suited to this type of problem. A number of individual tests of persistence and inhibition were applied and gave somewhat higher intercorrelations, particularly as far as the tests of inhibition were concerned (average intercorrelation of 6 tests = ·225). Hartshorne and May conclude their brief discussion of these measures, which were unfortunately confined to a very small group of children, by saying that they "are very suggestive of the possibilities of individual testing in this field and offer a most promising research problem".

The entire battery of tests of honesty, service, and self-control was given to three groups of children, populations X, Y, and Z, totalling about 850 children. To these children were given 64 tests of behaviour and opinion, 37 performance tests of the type described, 20 paper-and-pencil tests, and various schedules and data sheets of one kind or another. Correlations between different types of test are given in Table 35; the raw intercorrelations are in the upper right section, correlations corrected for attenuation in the lower left section. Reliabilities are given in brackets.

TABLE 35

Intercorrelation of Total Conduct Scores—Populations X, Y, and Z Combined

Test	Honesty	Service	Inhibition*	Persistence
Honesty	(·86)	·303	·361	·129
Service	·439	(·56)	·276	·049
Inhibition	·487	·472	(·61)	·123
Persistence	·166	·083	·202	(·61)

*Omitting the Picture Inhibition test.

Moral knowledge tests of various kinds were also given to these children and correlated with conduct scores. Corrected for attenuation, these correlations turned out to be ·464 with honesty, ·300 with co-operation, ·373 with inhibition, and ·336 with persistence. Moral knowledge, therefore, seems to be to a moderate extent related to moral conduct.

Reputation scores of the type discussed above were also available for the children in this study; correlations found between objective test scores and reputation scores, corrected for attenuation, were ·48 with honesty, ·63 with service, ·62 with inhibition, and ·50 with persistence, giving a grand average of ·558. Reputation and conduct may therefore be considered to be related to quite a considerable extent.

We must now turn to what is perhaps the most important analysis carried out by Hartshorne and May, namely their study of integration. Most definitions of personality use this term, although they seldom attempt any adequate operational definition of it. Interpreting the term "integration" as "consistency of performance", they maintain that the integrated or consistent person gives responses that are organized in such a way that the person's conduct can be predicted. "On an altitude scale they may have excellent or bad characters, but . . . they may be depended upon to function consistently on their own level. . . . Heretofore we have been placing children on a vertical scale and ranking them high or low. We shall now attempt to place them on what may be called, for convenience, a horizontal scale, and shall arrange them according to the consistency with which they function on their given level ... Our definition of integration as consistency of performance holds fairly close to a widely used meaning of the term. By *integration* is often intended a certain dependability or stability of moral conduct. Conversely, the individual lacking in integration is at the mercy of the varying temptations of every situation. His conduct is inconsistent, undependable, unpredictable, or even contradictory."

Taking as their point of reference the mean of the population to which the child belonged, Hartshorne and May calculated a modified form of standard score to make deviations from the mean comparable from test to test. Using such scores for 21 tests, they then calculated for each child separately the amount of variability (standard deviation) for his 21 scores. This means that the more consistent the child the more closely would his 21 scores be grouped together round the mean and the smaller would the standard deviation be. Similarly, the more inconsistent the child the more variable his scores about the mean and the larger his standard deviation. The distribution of these "integration indices" were not very different from the normal curve of distribution. The reliability of this integration score was found to be only ·4.

Integration, as defined, shows a considerable correlation with honesty. In the Y population, the correlation between honesty and integration is ·522, which rises to ·882 when corrected for attenuation. The correlation for the Z population, for various reasons discussed by the authors, is rather lower, but the two populations combined still give a corrected coefficient of correlation of ·776. These correlations cannot be taken too seriously in view of the heteroscedastic nature of the scatter diagram, but we must agree with Hartshorne and May that the observed correlation "indicates the presence of a genuine association between level and consistency of achievement". Among the variables correlated with integration, perhaps the most interesting is intelligence. For the various groups, these correlations are ·314, ·219, and ·266. These correlations are almost identical with the best estimates available of the correlation between "*w*", or lack of neuroticism, and intelligence, suggesting the possibility that this quality of integration isolated by Hartshorne and May may be closely linked to integration as understood by the psychiatrist, i.e. as the opposite of neuroticism. This interpretation is strengthened by the fact that Hartshorne and May found ratings of emotional stability (admittedly of doubtful validity) to show a highly significant correlation of ·28 with integration. Also, persistence and resistance to suggestion showed correlations with integration of ·435 and ·367; it will be noted in later researches that both lack of persistence and suggestibility appear again and again as defining "neuroticism".

Nowhere do Hartshorne and May carry out factorial analyses of their data. One of the associates working with them for part of the time, J. Maller (1934), has used some of the intercorrelations reported by them between the four types of test used (honesty, co-operation, inhibition, persistence) to carry out a Spearman-type analysis. He found tetrad differences not significantly different from zero and concluded therefore that all the intercorrelations could be accounted for in terms of one general factor which, it is quite clear from the correlations presented by Hartshorne and May, cannot be identified with intelligence. He concludes that "the factor common to the various character tests, which may be referred to as factor C, is a readiness to forgo an immediate gain for the sake of a remote but greater gain". Unfortunately, the tests used in these studies are too different from those used by other authors to make identification of this factor very easy, but in view of the high correlations of these tests with "integration" the present writer feels that the possibility of identifying Maller's "C" with Webb's "w" cannot be gainsaid. An experimental proof of this hypothesis should not be too difficult to arrange.

While the Hartshorne and May studies are included in this volume because of their great general importance and theoretical interest, and in spite of the fact that the data were not in any consistent way treated factorially, the pioneering work of Oates (1929) deserves its place as effectively the first factorial study of objective behaviour tests. This work is of interest in many directions. It may be noted here particularly because, unlike so many more recent studies, it sets out with a clear-cut hypothesis which is testable by means of factorial analysis, and which is decisively disproved. Instead of resting content, however, with such a negative conclusion, Oates goes on to show that his data are compatible with an alternative hypothesis, which is in fact identical with that discussed in the previous two chapters.

The tests used by Oates, as well as the original hypothesis tested, are those put forward by June Downey (1919). Her "will-temperament" tests, which had a great vogue in the years immediately after the First World War, had the misfortune of being both incontinently praised and equally incontinently criticized. Their history is amusingly told by Symonds (1931), whose very full account, unfortunately, leaves out Oate's research, which is the only direct attack on the problem posed by June Downey.

Briefly, Downey presents twelve tests divided into three groups. Each of these is composed of four tests designed to measure (a) "fluidity" or speed of response; (b) "forcefulness" or decisiveness of action; and (c) "carefulness" and persistence of reaction. The tests used to measure these three variables were largely drawn from graphology, and there is no doubt about the ingenuity with which Downey has adapted graphological principles to test construction.

The four tests designed to measure "fluidity" are:

(1) *Speed of Movement.*—This is simply the speed at which the subject writes the words "United States of America".

(2) *Freedom from Load.*—On the hypothesis that some people habitually write near their maximum speed while others are subject to "load", or inhibition, and therefore write considerably below their maximum, the subject is instructed to write "United States of America" as rapidly as possible; the ratio between speeded and normal writing constitutes the score.

(3) *Flexibility.*—The subject is instructed to write "United States of America", changing the style of writing as much as possible.

(4) *Speed of Decision.*—This is the speed with which judgments are made on 22 pairs of opposite traits which the subject has to check as characterizing himself.

The four tests to measure "forcefulness" are:

(1) *Motor Impulsion.*—The subject writes his name in his usual manner, and then under distraction. The assumption is that persons high on motor impulsion, or muscular tension, tend to speed up and enlarge their handwriting when working under distraction.

(2) *Reaction to Contradiction.*—This measures the subject's reaction to being contradicted by the examiner on a point on which the subject is right.

(3) *Resistance to Opposition.*—The subject's behaviour when a small obstruction is placed in front of his pen point whilst the subject is writing his name with his eyes closed.

(4) *Finality of Judgment.*—The subject rechecks the list of traits on which he earlier rated himself, and the time consumed in rechecking constitutes the score.

The four tests to measure "carefulness" are:

(1) *Motor Inhibition.*—The subject is told to write "United States of America" as slowly as possible.

(2) *Interest in Detail.*—The subject copies some handwriting from the test booklet. This is done twice, once as rapidly as possible, then as exactly as possible. The score is a combination of the difference in speeds and the degree to which the model is approximated.

(3) *Co-ordination of Impulses.*—The subject has to write the words "United States of America" on a line just over an inch in length, taking care to write very rapidly but not to run over the line. The score is the number of letters omitted or which run over the line, as well as the degree to which the time approximates the time for normal writing.

(4) *Volitional Preservation.*—In the "disguised handwriting" test the subject is given a certain amount of time for practice. The present test gives him a score according to the length of time spent on practising.

Here we have a very clear-cut hypothesis, according to which the tests when intercorrelated should group themselves in three groups of four, such that within each group the correlations should be high, and between one group and the others, low or zero. Downey explicitly denies the existence of a general factor, so the "between-group" intercorrelations should not be significantly different from zero, whereas all the "within-group" correlations should be significant. Oates gave the 12 tests in this scale to 50 secondary schoolboys, to whom he also administered 10 intelligence tests; examination results, too, were available to him. The pattern of correlations which he found is entirely different from that called for by the hypothesis. In factorial terms it can be represented not by three independent group factors but rather by one general and one bi-polar factor. The general factor has high loadings on freedom from load or inhibition, speed of decision, co-ordination of impulses, interest in detail, speed of movement, and finality of judgment. This general factor is identified by Oates as one of temperament, and in his view appears very similar to Webb's "w". He tries to point this analogy in a very interesting manner by comparing the intercorrelations of total score on the Downey tests (which of course would be a rough measure of the general factor) with intelligence and scholastic ability, with similar correlations obtained by Stead (1925) on character ratings (persistence, trustworthiness, conscientiousness, general excellence, etc.), with intelligence and scholastic ability. These various combinations of three traits (character or temperament, scholastic ability, intelligence) taken two at a time, are given in Table 36, as well as the partial correlations, with the third trait in each case partialled out. It will be seen that the correlations are remarkably similar, showing that total score on the June Downey test is related to scholastic ability and intelligence in very much the same way that the character ratings of "*w*" qualities used by Stead are correlated with the same variables.

TABLE 36

	Oates		Stead	
	r	partial r	r	partial r
Scholastic ability and intelligence: .	·573	·548	·573	·568
Scholastic ability and temperament .	·357	·298	·335	·243
Intelligence and temperament . .	·205	·001	·250	·067

The second factor is identified by Oates as opposing speed to inhibition. The former he considers diagnostic of unrepressed or extraverted personality, the latter of introverted personality. Thus, this first factorial study of objective behaviour tests from the London school supports in remarkable fashion the conclusions derived from ratings and questionnaire studies.

The same may be said of another study directed by a former student of Spearman's and carried out in Canada, in which, for the first time, we find factorial analyses carried out on objective test scores obtained from both normal and abnormal subjects. In the first of these studies Line and Griffin (1935) gave a battery of 10 tests, of which, however, 4 were questionnaires, to "a group of some 50 individuals chosen to show in a very marked and obvious way the functional gradient in which we were interested. About one-third of the group were graduate students at the University of Toronto, and were selected as carefully as possible on the basis of obviously sound mental health . . . individuals whose mental health, while not obviously bad, seemed at least to be in a slightly precarious state, comprised the middle third of our group . . . the rest of our subjects were in-patients at the psychiatric hospital. Many of them were certified insane, and all of them required full-time supervision". (It is not quite clear to the writer just how many subjects were included altogether, or how they were distributed among these three groups, because the figures given in various tables by the authors do not agree.)

The tests included in this battery were:

(a) Kent-Rosanoff Word Association test; average reaction time.
(b) Variation in reaction time.
(c) Total number of responses on 10 Rorschach ink-blots.
(d) Oscillation or variation in output in such tasks as addition of pairs of digits.
(e) Speed test: the score here is the total number of responses made in the oscillation test.
(f) Speed of response: total number of symbols written during test (g).
(g) Perseveration: 6 tests averaged.
(h), (i), (j), (k) are the neurotic, introvert, self-sufficiency, and dominance scales respectively of the Bernreuter Personality Inventory.

The intercorrelations of the tests for the total group, as well as factor saturations for two factors, are given in Table 37. The first factor is called "objectivity" by Line and Griffin; they believe that "it may be closely related . . . to the 'w' factor investigated by Webb with normal subjects". Nearly all the tests have high scores on this factor, which characterizes a person who makes neurotic, introverted, submissive answers on the Bernreuter scales and is not self-sufficient; who has a long word reaction time and shows considerable variation in his speed of reaction; who oscillates markedly in his work, perseverates, is slow in speed tasks and gives few responses on the Rorschach. The second factor is characterized according to them by fluency. Its highest loadings are a number of words given in response to the Rorschach cards, the speed tests, self-sufficiency, and dominance. In view of data already mentioned or to be summarized in later chapters, it seems likely that this factor bears some relation to extraversion.

TABLE 37

	B	C	D	E	F	G	H	I	J	K	"Objectivity" I	"Fluency" II
A	·92	−·44	·29	−·39	−·64	·27	·29	·35	−·39	−·30	·76	−·01
B	—	−·51	·33	−·40	−·68	·32	·50	·38	−·51	−·34	·84	−·04
C	—	—	−·27	·34	·24	−·26	−·33	−·35	·39	·38	−·52	·50
D	—	—	—	−·77	−·56	·49	·14	·16	−·09	−·06	·58	−·06
E	—	—	—	—	·61	−·30	−·17	−·23	·16	·19	−·55	·42
F	—	—	—	—	—	−·38	−·07	−·07	·10	·02	−·58	·19
G	—	—	—	—	—	—	·04	·12	−·19	−·27	·54	·07
H	—	—	—	—	—	—	—	·94	−·61	−·73	·70	·04
I	—	—	—	—	—	—	—	—	·60	−·78	·71	−·01
J	—	—	—	—	—	—	—	—	—	·65	−·58	·37
K	—	—	—	—	—	—	—	—	—	—	−·60	·31

This pioneering research is obviously open to several criticisms. The groups investigated are not characterized sufficiently to make a repetition of the research possible; neurotics and psychotics are indiscriminately thrown together into the abnormal group; the influence of age and intelligence has not been held constant, thus leaving a spurious factor to disturb the pattern of intercorrelations. Some of these criticisms are obviated in a paper by Line, Griffin and Anderson (1935), in which four homogeneous groups were given tests similar to or identical with those already used. These groups were:

(1) 42 men in the Ontario Reformatory at Mimico.
(2) 120 University students.
(3) 70 teachers in the Ontario public schools.
(4) 40 women engaged in social service work.

Some of the additional tests used consisted of the Thurstone Neurotic Inventory, the Army Alpha, and the Chant Optimism-Pessimism Scale. It is difficult to summarize all this work; on the whole, it would appear that in each group a factor of "objectivity", or, as the authors are now inclined to call it, "stability", can be found, although the average loadings tend to reflect a curtailment in range of stability such as might be expected on theoretical grounds.[1] Thus, for the original mixed group, the average loading on this factor is ·62, for the Ontario Reformatory Group Test ·52; at the other end for teachers and University students it is ·47 and ·42 respectively. It is noteworthy that in the only group in which an intelligence test was included, it has a relatively high saturation (·46) for this factor of stability, suggesting that there is a certain degree of contamination with intelligence. As will be shown later, "stability" and intelligence, while not completely unrelated, tend to show considerably smaller correlations than that.

In putting forward these criticisms, we do not wish to detract from the importance of the work described. Perfection is not to be expected in pioneering efforts, and the lack of adequate methods of analysis at the disposal of the investigators is a handicap not often appreciated by later writers who have available more powerful methods. It is unfortunate that until quite recently the field of investigation opened up by Line has not been followed up by others; of those discussed in this book it is perhaps one of the most promising.

Quite a different type of research, which, nevertheless, also comes under the heading of "objective behaviour", is the work of Koch (1934, 1942) on "certain measures of activeness in nursery-school children". In her first article Koch carried out a multiple-factor

[1] Justification for the use of the term "stability" can be found in the writers' demonstration that the factor score differentiates at a high level of significance between the normal and abnormal groups from which the intercorrelations were derived.

analysis of correlations between 9 different measures of activeness, resulting in three factors:

(1) Strength or maturity.
(2) Nervousness or emotionality.
(3) Spontaneous activeness or aggression.

The second factor from her description is clearly identifiable with neuroticism, and the third, not quite so clearly, is similar to extraversion.

In her later paper an improvement in methodology makes these factors come out much more clearly. Two observers carried out a time-sampling study of pre-school children, using 400 half-minute units of observation. Thirty-eight variables were intercorrelated, ranging from laboratory tests, such as the psycho-galvanic reflex, to nervous habits (genital, pedal, ocular, scalp, hair, aural, nasal, respiratory, digital, and corporal) and behaviour items (crying, daydreaming, bossing others, etc.). Three main factors were found from the intercorrelations of the 38 items used. One of these is a "tension" factor, which is loaded positively with the nervous habit items and constipation, as opposed to "persistence of speed"; this bears a marked resemblance to "w" as opposed to neuroticism. Another factor is called "social introversion", contrasting the individual who "mobilizes his energy well, is relatively uninhibited and socially outgoing" to the individual who fails to show these traits. A third factor is called "lack of vigour", and may correspond to the "strength or maturity factor" in Koch's earlier work. (It may be the opposite of Heymans' and Wiersma's "activity factor".) The other factors isolated by her are difficult to interpret. However, those already mentioned will suffice to show that the most marked factors in the behaviour of nursery and pre-school children are similar to those which we found so clearly marked in the behaviour of normal and abnormal adults.

More recently, Brogden (1940) has reported a "factor analysis of 40 character tests" administered to 100 white boys. Many of these tests were questionnaires and opinionnaires; 10 tests were sub-tests of the Otis measure of intelligence. Most of the character tests were similar to those used by Hartshorne and May. In spite of the rather homogeneous and biased sample of tests used, it is noteworthy that the first of the eight centroid factors extracted is clearly identifiable with Webb's "w", being highly loaded on resistance to suggestion, conscientiousness, and lack of perseverance. The other factors are labelled respectively "honesty", "persistence", "general intelligence", "self-control" or "inhibition", "achievement", and "compliance to moral code". Of these, the self-control or inhibition factor bears some similarity to introversion, but it is impossible to be certain of this identification in view of the unusual nature of the tests employed in this case, and the failure to extract second-order factors.

It will be clear to those who have made an attempt to identify factors derived from intercorrelations between objective behaviour tests that such interpretation is markedly subjective, and has certain dangers and difficulties different from, but no less marked than, those encountered in connection with ratings and self-ratings. It appears certain that the most meaningful results will be obtained when we get away from the habit of including only one type of material in a given study, but try instead to cross-validate factors over all the different fields of material available. The need for such cross-validation has been seen most clearly perhaps by R. B. Cattell (1946), whose attempt to match factors derived from ratings and self-ratings has already been mentioned. In his first study in the field of objective behaviour tests, Cattell (1948) used 50 test scores obtained from 130 men and 240 women. Testing was partly group and partly individual, and the tests used covered a great variety of different techniques. Included were tests of intelligence, perseveration, fluency, reaction-time, speed of judgment, psychomotor speed, perceptual speed, dark adaptation, oscillation, fluctuation of attitudes, honesty, suggestibility, endurance, persistence, sense of humour, colour-form tendency, repression, mirror drawing, criticalness, self-confidence, mysticism, level of aspiration, psycho-galvanic reflex, work curves, and various others.

Correlations between these tests present rather an arid picture of near-zero coefficients. This is partly explained by Cattell on the grounds "(1) that the tests are deliberately chosen to represent the whole range of the *personality sphere* and are thus mostly remote from one another, and (2) that the tests, being intended to be exploratory, are uniformly brief and of proportionally low reliability". The correlation matrix was factored by Thurstone's grouping method, 10 factors being found significant by Tucker's rather lenient criterion.

Identification of these factors is extremely difficult. Most of the saturations which are used to define factors are very low, and only one of Cattell's final 11 factors is identified by more than two tests having factor saturations of above ·3; 4 factors have no saturations at all above this level. Nor does it seem easy to identify the factors isolated with those emerging from Cattell's previous studies. A determined attempt to do so is made by Cattell, but to the present writer these tentative identifications, while suggestive, certainly do not appear conclusive. While we may agree with Cattell that "this research can claim to have achieved only a low degree of definition of the factors" we rather doubt whether he is right in claiming that "the catholicity of the tests, their deliberate spacing with regard to primary personality factors, and their representation of previously found objective test factors perhaps justifies the conclusion that the factors found here cover the main structure of personality—at least in groups of this age".

A similar, essentially negative conclusion must follow a perusal of Cattell and Saunders' paper (1950). In this study, 370 students were rated, 405 completed the questionnaire used, 358 took part in the group sessions in objective testing, 140 completed the individual objective testing, and 35 the assessment by special physiological measures. All subjects were undergraduates in the proportion of about two women to one man. Thirty-seven variables altogether were included. It would be difficult to discuss the results in any great detail because of the large number of variables involved and of the necessity of discussing Cattell's terminology and use of concepts. His own conclusion seems quite acceptable to the present writer. He says that if this factorization "is doing what we intended it to do, only one conclusion is possible, i.e. except for two or three instances, the known personality factors, contrary to our hypothesis, are not out-crops of the same factors in different media. This does not mean that every factor may not have a manifestation in all three regions; it only means that the examples we have taken from each region do not coincide. If we accept tentatively the matches that are made above, we have left over, unmatched and unrepresented, three rating factors, nine questionnaire factors, and three objective test factors.... Where factors are unmatched we should expect to obtain factors among them that are second-order factors. Thereby we are delivered into the nightmare statistical situation of having first- and second-order factors intermixed in the same study, with all the difficulties of interpretation which that involves." These negative results should not be taken to mean that the goal which Cattell has set himself is impossible to reach or that his failure to cross-identify factors is inherent in the material. On the other hand, it would be idle to pretend that these results do not present a powerful barrier to easy acceptance of Cattell's set of factors.

As Thorndike (1950) has pointed out, "the reader may be somewhat hesitant to accept Cattell's characterization of the different factor dimensions and may be somewhat disturbed at the complexity of the correlated and descriptively quite complex factors, and may be rather less prepared than the author to accept the factors in different studies as identical". Admittedly, the analyses of objective tests published by Cattell are exploratory, but, as Thorndike goes on to say, they do "raise the question of how low reliabilities and communalities may be and still permit a factor analysis which can yield clear and interpretable results. The writer has a feeling that with communalities as low as those found in this study, the small amount of variance which is represented by common factors is almost sure to be obscure and unclear. In these studies, Cattell has ambitiously undertaken to plot out the whole sphere of personality variables, and the representation of any sector of this sphere has necessarily been limited. It is to be hoped that more intensive exploration of more limited segments will serve to refine and, if necessary, to revise the picture which has been sketched for us".

Cattell has been engaged in doing precisely this (Cattell, 1957) and certainly the picture has become somewhat more clarified in this most recent work. However, correlations are still low, and matchings with questionnaire and rating data somewhat questionable. Cattell points out that "the reader should keep in mind that the strategy of using many tests implies short tests and often low reliabilities in the exploratory stage. This needs to be considered, for in the tables below a matching of factors will occasionally be claimed when the absolute size of the loadings for the same variable are fairly discrepant, or even when loadings on one or two variables, essentially in the hyperplane, differ in sign. As to the first, experience shows that the very same factor may alter in its *absolute* loadings fairly markedly from sample to sample, but that the same variables tend to remain significantly loaded, i.e. to be classed as salients, lying out of the hyperplane. As to the second, one should note that agreement, even on sign pattern alone, when existing over about a dozen salients is an event of exceedingly high improbability when no systematic cause exists. Also the casual examiner of such lists should bear in mind that the matched factors agree not only on the published salient loadings listed in our tables *but also on three or four times as many variables which have insignificant (hyperplane) loadings on the factors matched*. The psychologist who cares to make an extensive scrutiny and cataloguing of the factor literature will find that our placing of these seven or eight core studies centrally in the argument, and any comparative discounting of certain other experiments, e.g. Eysenck's theory of a factor of hysteria-dysthymia as the second most important factor, is justified by regard for proper technical attention to the four basic requirements listed above." Some of this is undoubtedly true, particularly Cattell's insistence that the use of many tests implies short tests and consequently low reliabilities in the exploratory stage. The questions that will worry the reader will be just when this exploratory stage is over and gives way to a stage of detailed consideration of the many independent variables determining performances on any given test. While many of the tests used by Cattell carry time-honoured names like conditioning, dark-adaptation and so forth, it is very doubtful whether his actual testing practice pays attention to the best available experimental techniques and implies all the controls considered essential by experimentalists. The problem raised by Cattell is a very real one and it is impossible to condemn his research strategy as being in any sense unscientific; perhaps this type of approach will produce the results Cattell promises. To the present writer, however, it seems that, as pointed out below, a more hypothetico-deductive type of approach would be less time consuming and more in line with the usual scientific methodology.

The reader may like to see just precisely the kind of test used by Cattell to define a factor and the kind of loading contributed by each test. Table 38 gives twelve objective tests, identified simply in terms of their titles, together with their loadings on neuroticism in seven different experiments. It will be seen that even these specially selected tests tend to have very low loadings throughout; out of some fifty coefficients, eleven are ·1 or below and another fourteen are ·2 or below, so that even in this specially selected group of tests only one half have loadings higher than ·2.

A further point which should be borne in mind is the relatively small number of cases which is often used in studies giving rise to a large number of factors. In a recent paper by Scheier and Cattell (1958), "a total of 113 measurements were made on each of 87 male University of Illinois undergraduates"; 15 factors were extracted from this matrix, i.e. roughly one for every six subjects! When the very low level of correlations throughout is borne in mind, most statisticians would probably agree that the criterion of significance used by Cattell in this work is far too lenient.

It should not be thought that Cattell's failure to obtain high correlation between tests is in any sense an isolated phenomenon or

TABLE 38

Neuroticism (reversed)

Title	1	2	3	4	5	6	7
Low motor rigidity (classical perseveration) . . .	−15	−29	−58	−20	−37	−42	
Good two-hand co-ordination .	02	20	(−15)	37	36		42
Low body sway suggestibility .	−20	−13	−26	−12	−10	−64	−12
Low ratio of inaccuracy to speed			−20	−29	−36	−40	
Slower decision on principles than particulars			31	27			
High "dynamic momentum" (endurance)	−01		12	36		50	16
Smaller PGR to mental than physical stimuli (threat) . .		−07	−31				
Little excess of aspiration over achievement . . .			−29	−02	−56	−17	
High ratio of normal to shock performance . . .			26	46	26		
High fluency	00	09			10	40	
Good immediate memory . .			14	(−01)	01	00	33
Low suggestibility to shock .					−17		−15

due to poor selection of tests. Much the same phenomenon is reported by other writers. Holtzman and Bitterman (1956), using 135 students, correlated a battery of measures derived from ratings of personality, objective and projective personality tests, measurements of performance in stressful situations, the conditioning of the galvanic skin response, perceptual tests, and the analysis of urinary components. "In general, the degree of relationship among the measures derived from different types of tests was very low, although in some cases there were statistically significant and meaningful correlations between the ratings, the personality tests, and the laboratory variables." The factor analysis performed by them tended to group the correlations into clusters derived from different types of procedures; thus, "Factor I was defined chiefly by measures derived from the ratings, II by perceptual measures, III by variables derived from one of the stress tests, IV by conditioning measures, and V by M.M.P.I. measures; the meaning of VI was in doubt and VII appeared to be mainly a residual factor." Similarly, Martin (1958) carried out a research "to investigate the existence and generality of an individual differences dimension that could properly be called anxiety." On the basis of previously published research a number of measures were selected which were reported to be affected by level of anxiety of the subjects being measured. These measures were obtained on a sample of 89 female students, and a factor analysis was performed on the correlation matrix. Eight factors were extracted, one being interpreted as an anxiety dimension. "In general, the results obtained under the conditions of the present study indicated that individual differences in anxiety level accounted for a relatively small percentage oi the variance of the obtained scores."

It may be interesting to discover the tests having loadings on this anxiety factor. "*Factor* 4. The Taylor MAS and its subscales have loadings ranging from ·20 to ·39 on this factor. The hard paired associated list, which was designed to enhance competing responses, and the difference score between the hard and easy paired associate lists have loadings of ·51 and ·53 respectively. The two-choice and five-choice verbal mazes have loadings of ·30 and ·35 respectively. Body sway has a loading of ·39 and the three error scores on the cancellation task have loadings ranging between −·48 and −·58." (The results of this study as well as of the one to be described presently may be compared with the attempts of Cattell and Scheier (1958) to define the nature of anxiety in thirteen multivariate analyses comprising 814 variables.)

Kamin *et al.* (1955) also attempted to define anxiety in factorial terms, using three tests of anxiety and performances on a stressful conditioned discrimination task. Intercorrelations were again low, but the authors were able to interpret the intercorrelations "In terms of two independent factors: avoidance tendency and general upset or arousal. These factors can be regarded as representing two of the many dimensions that are involved in "anxiety".

We may now return to our discussion of Cattell's research strategy. In his discussion of the problems of factor analysis, Cattell (1946) deals with the choice which has to be made among the unlimited number of factorial solutions possible for any given matrix. Quite rightly, he points out that the scientist "will want to find the set of factors which corresponds to a set of psychologically real influences because he is interested in understanding the psychological meaning of his predictions and because he is curious to gain truth for its own sake. In that case, he may (1) devise possible ways of over-determining the analysis of the given correlation matrix, so that only the one set of true factors will emerge, or (2) start from the opposite shore and propound, on psychological grounds alone, a hypothesis about what source traits are operative in the variables. Then he will see if these factors correspond to any of the possible mathematical factors found in the matrix". Cattell goes on to endorse the former and reject the latter possibility. "This latter procedure is a very common and respected one in science. Typically the researcher invents a hypothesis and tests it against measurements, but unfortunately, in the present situation, this scientific habit of working is far from being a happy one. For, in the first place, personality study has so few other reliable avenues for arriving at or even suspecting the basic source traits, that hypotheses are likely to be erratic. In the second place, the mathematical solutions to any set of correlations are so numerous and varied that unless the hypothesis can be studied in very precise quantitative terms, the proof of it is easy—so easy as to be worthless."

In thus rejecting the hypothetico-deductive method and leaning exclusively on the concept of statistical over-determination as expressed in simple structure, Cattell has gone to one extreme of a continuum, the other end of which is represented by those who maintain what might be called the "engineering" approach. If we want to discover the validity of a test which has been constructed to measure a given trait, we have traditionally two methods of doing this. We can find an estimate of validity by correlating the test with an outside criterion; this may be called a test of "practical validity". Or we can correlate it with other tests, presumably measuring the same trait, intercorrelate these tests, and carry out a factor analysis; the factor saturation of the test in question with that factor will then be a measure of its theoretical validity. Both methods have obvious disadvantages. We seldom have a tested criterion available for truly significant psychological variables, such as neuroticism, introversion, persistence, suggestibility, intelligence, etc. (Sometimes, of course, we have a large number of different criteria available, which correlate only slightly or not at all with each other. Our problem then is to find a criterion for selecting a criterion, and we are thus being confronted with an infinite regress.) The difficulties of the other approach are possibly most apparent to those who have a healthy scepticism of an exaggeratedly mechanical and statistical approach to psychological problems; while these objections in the writer's view are less fundamental than those to the first approach, relating as they do largely to imperfections of present-day methods, they are, nevertheless, at the moment very real and make exclusive reliance on theoretical validity a very dangerous precept.[1]

[1] The dilemma presented by the apparent "forced choice" between these two courses of "practical" and "theoretical" validity, and the solution to the problem here presented, recall Bacon's words in the *Novum Organum:* "They who have handled the sciences have been either empirics or dogmatists. The empirics, like the ant, amass only and use; the dogmatists, like spiders, spin

Under these conditions, an attempt has been made by Eysenck (1947, 1952) and his colleagues to combine these two methods of validation into one approach which, as far as possible, should follow the dictates of the hypothetico-deductive method. This approach and some of the results obtained from it will be described in the succeeding paragraphs.

From the literature so far surveyed, it appears that the one factor in the non-cognitive personality field on which there is almost universal agreement is the factor of "w", or stability, as opposed to instability or neuroticism. We may set up a hypothesis regarding this factor, namely that human beings can be ranged along a continuum from one extreme (the very stable, mature, well-adjusted type of person) through the average, normal sort of person—to the other extreme (the highly neurotic, unstable, poorly adjusted sort of person). We may further add the hypothesis that a person whose position on the continuum is close to the unstable extreme will be quite likely to be brought to the attention of a psychiatrist, or himself seek psychiatric aid. Thus we might obtain two groups, those seeking psychiatric aid for reasons fundamentally related to emotional instability, and those not seeking such aid. We would not need to hypothesize that degree of instability was the only variable determining the position of a person in either group, nor would we need to make the assumption that the psychiatrist's decision as to whether a given person was suffering from instability or from other causes had a very high reliability. It is sufficient, from our point of view, that a group, the members of which had never been to see a psychiatrist, would, on the average, have a different position on the neuroticism continuum from a group, the members of which had visited a psychiatrist. We may call members of the first group "normal" and members of the second group "neurotic", realizing full well, of course, that there is likely to be a great deal of overlap on the basis of such a very rough-and-ready criterion as the one we have employed.

The degree of overlap existing between "normals" and "neurotics" is not always realized. It is very likely considerably greater than the overlap which can be found along a different dimension of personality, namely that of intelligence, between the mental defectives and

webs out of themselves. But the course of the bee lies midway—she gathers materials from the flowers of the garden and the field, and then by her own powers changes and digests them. Nor is the true labour of philosophy unlike hers. It does not depend entirely, or even chiefly, on the strength of the mind, nor does it store up in the memory unaltered the materials provided by natural history and mechanical experiments—but changes and digests them by the intellect."

the normals. As Tizard and O'Connor (1950) have shown, in a typical high-grade mental defective population several individuals can be found to have I.Q.s above 100 and the average I.Q. of such a population is in the neighbourhood of 75. On the other hand, in the "normal" population will be found many individuals with I.Q.s as low as 65, or even 50 and below. Nevertheless, when we compare the average institutionalized population with the average non-institutionalized population, we will undoubtedly find a marked difference in the position of the two means on the hypothetical continuum of intelligence; we will also, of course, find a great deal of overlap. Thus in the intellectual field the position is precisely analogous to the hypothetical position outlined above with respect to the "w" factor. Russell Fraser (1946) has, for instance, shown that a "normal" group of this kind contains a fair percentage of severely neurotic and an even higher percentage of slightly neurotic people who would benefit from a visit to a psychiatrist, and conversely, everyone working in a mental hospital is well aware of the fact that many people who come to seek the help and advice of a psychiatrist are suffering from disabilities not closely related to lack of emotional stability.

Let us next assume the existence of a set of tests $T_1, T_2, T_3, \ldots T_n$, all of which have a linear regression on the hypothetical neuroticism factor. It will be immediately obvious that each of these tests will differentiate between groups of normals and neurotics. It will also be obvious that the degree of success with which the test differentiates between normals and neurotics is a function of its correlation with the hypothetical factor of neuroticism. We may calculate an index for the purpose of showing the degree of differentiation achieved by each test by correlating (biserial or tetrachorics) the test with the normal—neurotic dichotomy. Let us call these correlations "criterion correlations" and the set of correlations obtained in this way the "criterion column". If our hypothesis is correct, then the criterion correlation should be exactly proportional to the correlations of the tests with the hypothetical neuroticism continuum.

The only method of verifying this deduction consists in intercorrelating our n tests, factor analysing the matrix of intercorrelations and using the resulting factor coefficients as approximations to the correlations of our tests with the hypothetical neuroticism factor. If these saturations are proportional to the criterion correlation, then we may consider the various hypotheses outlined above verified, and we may safely and without sematic argument identify the factor thus isolated as one of emotional instability, or neuroticism. The crucial test of the original hypothesis then lies in the correlation between the

factor saturations and the criterion correlations; we would not expect this correlation to be unity because some of the assumptions of
linearity of regression, and so forth, are not likely to be fulfilled
exactly by most existing test data; proper refinement of these tests,
however, should lead us closer and closer to a perfect correlation.

If we are willing to follow the argument outlined above, it will be
clear that we have an excellent method for selecting tests for defining
our factor of neuroticism. According to the hypothesis, tests which
fit into the general pattern would all significantly differentiate between normal and neurotic groups, and consequently a large number
of experiments have been carried out in an attempt to select tests
differentiating at an acceptable level of significance between normals
and neurotics (Eysenck, 1947). Thus, it was found, for instance, that
normals have better dark vision, are less suggestible on the body-
sway test, have better motor control, have smaller goal and judgment
discrepancy scores on the level of aspiration test, show greater
flexibility on the aspiration tests, have better manual dexterity,
quicker personal tempo and greater fluency, are more persistent,
tend to be less extreme on perseveration tests, and recover more
rapidly on stress tests. They also give fewer neurotic answers on an
inventory of neuroticism.

If these tests were given to groups of normals and neurotics, we
should be able to make three perfectly definite predictions on the
basis of our hypothesis. In the first place, we can predict the direction
of the difference between the two groups on each test. In the second
place, we can predict that if all the tests are scored in such a manner
that the normal response obtained the plus score and the neurotic
response the minus score, then all the intercorrelations of the tests
within the normal group, or within the neurotic group, should be
positive. Thirdly, we can predict that if a factor analysis is carried out
on this table of intercorrelations, a general factor of neuroticism
with positive saturations throughout should make its appearance,
and the saturations of each test with this factor should be proportional to the criterion correlations, i.e. the correlations of each test
with the normal-neurotic dichotomy.[2]

[1] The method of analysis outlined above, which has been called "criterion
analysis" (Eysenck, 1950), is rather more complex than this, and involves rotation of factors into maximum conformity with the criterion column. It also, at
a later stage, calls for a readjustment of the criterion itself in accordance with a
double maximization principle. These refinements are not necessary, however,
for the understanding of the underlying logic of this method, and as they are
somewhat technical they have not been included in this brief account.

[2] Formal development of these deductions will be found in Eysenck's (1950)
paper on Criterion Analysis.

An experiment to test this hypothesis was carried out by Himmel-weit, Desai, and Petrie (1946). 105 male Service patients constituted the experimental group; they were returned prisoners-of-war from Germany who had shown difficulties in adjustment and had been sent to the special psychiatric section of the hospital for treatment. In order to make the demonstration more convincing, relatively mild cases of neurosis were chosen to make up this group. The control group was made up of 93 surgical cases who were chosen from the same environment in order to equalize the effect of hospitalization. The two groups were matched with respect to age and educational background. A detailed analysis of the data was carried out by Eysenck (1950), who calculated product-moment correlations between 16 tests individually administered to the group. The number of subjects was only 64, as not all had taken each test. All these 64 were normal in the sense that they were not under psychiatric treatment at the moment. (It is important to realize that by restricting the analysis to the normal group only we make the test of our hypothesis much more stringent. If each test included in the battery discriminates between the normal and the abnormal group, it follows automatically that if we calculate intercorrelations over both the normal and the abnormal group, then a general factor of neuroticism must emerge which would almost inevitably be proportional to the criterion correlation. There is no reason to expect such an outcome when we restrict ourselves to one of the groups only, either the normal or the neurotic, unless we accept the hypothesis which the experiment was designed to test.)

The outcome of the experiment was quite clear. There were no significant negative correlations in the table of intercorrelations. All the tests differentiated in the expected direction, although not always at an acceptable level of significance, and all the factor saturations for the first factor were positive. In addition, there was a correlation of ·574 between the criterion column and the general factor.

The list of tests employed is given below.

A. Maudsley Medical Inventory—40-item neuroticism questionnaire. Score = number of questions answered "No" (non-neurotic).
B. Dark Adaptation—U.S. Navy Radium Plaque Adaptometer. Score = goodness of dark vision.
C. Non-suggestibility—body-sway test. Ability to resist suggestion to sway forward.
D. Motor Control—absence of static ataxia; given as preliminary test to C.

E. Goal Discrepancy Score—*smallness* of level of aspiration scores on O'Connor Tweezers test.

F. Judgment Discrepancy Score—*smallness* of judgment discrepancies on O'Connor Tweezers test.

G. Index of Flexibility—number of shifts in aspiration scores on O'Connor Tweezers test, irrespective of size or direction.

H. Manual Dexterity—best score of nine trials on tweezers test.

I. Personal Tempo—speed of writing 2, 3, 4 repeatedly for two trials of 15 seconds each.

J. Fluency—number of *round things* and of *things to eat* mentioned during 30-second periods.

K. Speed Test (1)—speed of tracing when instructed to be both quick and accurate. (Choice conditions.)

L. Speed Test (2)—speed of tracing prescribed path on track tracer under instruction to be quick.

M. Persistence Test I—length of time during which leg is held in uncomfortable and fatiguing position.

N. Persistence Test B—holding breath as long as possible, without inhaling or exhaling.

O. Stress Test—ability of S to recover previous scoring rate on pursuit-meter type of test after special stress period.

P. Non-perseveration—extremes of perseveration (SZ test), either very high or very low, are scored low, while scores nearer the average are scored high.

Also given is a diagram (Fig 31), showing the relative position of the various tests in a two-factor space. Number 1 represents the first centroid factor extracted from the intercorrelations; Ď represents the same factor rotated into maximum agreement with the criterion column. I', and II', indicate the best possible "simple structure" rotations, which will be seen to give no very intelligible or meaningful results.

The second factor which emerged from this analysis gave rise to a grouping of tests which "is in conformity with what in previous investigations had been shown to be characteristic of the introvert-extravert (dysthymic-hysteric) dichotomy. Thus, introverts (dysthymics) have been shown to be more persistent, extraverts (hysterics) to show less judgment discrepancy, and somewhat less suggestibility, as well as better dark adaptation. However, not all the tests are in agreement with this hypothesis, and little emphasis is laid on the possible identification of this second factor."

It is interesting to note that out of 16 tests, only three failed to have saturations of ·30 or above with the factor of neuroticism, one of these three being the questionnaire. Two tests, Body-sway Suggestibility and Static Ataxia, have loadings above ·65; another five tests have loadings of ·5 or above. When it is realized that the tests with the higher saturations are precisely those which in previous work, as well as in this particular research, gave the best discrimination between normals and neurotics, there remains very little doubt about the identification of this factor.

In a more recent experiment, Eysenck (1952) has duplicated many features of the original one. Two groups of male soldiers, one neurotic and the other normal, again formed the experimental and control groups respectively. The total group was made up of 200 men in the normal and of 120 in the neurotic group. These were submitted to a battery of individual and group tests, including examples of all types of personality tests, although, unfortunately, it was impossible for every test to be given to every subject. The tests used included tests

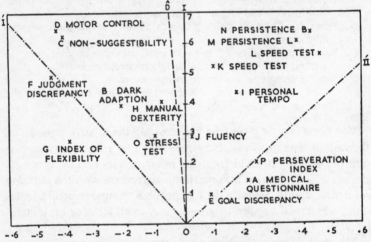

Fig. 31.—Two-factor Representation of Objective Test Results.

of intelligence and vocabulary, various questionnaires, such as scales from the M.M.P.I., the Maudsley Medical Questionnaire, the Word Connection List, and Annoyances, Worries, Likes, and Dislikes tests. Also given were Manual Dexterity tests, Persistence, Tapping, Speed of Decision, Level of Aspiration, Oscillation, Writing Pressure, Suggestibility, Word-association, Motor Disorganization, Abstraction, Concentration, Dark Vision, Flicker Fusion, Perseveration, Speed, Expressive Movement, and Group Rorschach tests. Results are far too numerous to be discussed at any length, but it was again found that the tests differentiated in almost every case in the expected direction between normal and neurotic groups.

Twenty-eight tests were intercorrelated for the normal group and a factor analysis carried out. A very clear factor of neuroticism emerged again, and an attempt was made to estimate the accuracy with which this factor could be measured by the various tests used. The method of multiple R, although it gave a satisfyingly high value in the neighbourhood of ·9, was rejected, as it is well known that this method capitalizes on chance differences. Instead, a score was derived from 16 tests which had been designated before the experiment was carried out, giving equal weight to all the tests and thus making no use whatsoever of the statistical finding of the analysis itself. Using this combination of scores, a validity estimate for the sum of these tests of approximately ·80 was established.

O'Connor (1952) has used the same methodology in a study of 159 normal and 53 neurotic children, using many of the tests from Eysenck's battery, such as body-sway suggestibility, manual dexterity, persistence (both ideational and physical), as well as several questionnaires from the Himmelweit and Petrie (1951) study (mentioned on the next page). All the tests mentioned gave a highly significant differentiation between the two groups of children; it should be noted that these had been reasonably well matched for age, intelligence and sex. A criterion analysis was carried out giving results very similar to those reported by Eysenck (1952).

One further investigation may be mentioned here because it throws some light not only on the organization of personality but also on the origin and development of such organization. Eysenck and Prell (1951) gave 17 objective tests of neuroticism to 50 monozygotic and 50 dizygotic twins, all of whom were normal "in the sense of never having been patients at a child guidance clinic, or in any other way suspected of mental disorder". The same tests were given to a group of 21 neurotic children, similar in age and intelligence to the normal twins. A factorial analysis of the intercorrelations of the tests for the normal children gave rise to a very clearly defined factor of neuroticism, and when factor scores were calculated on this factor for the "normal" and the "neurotic" children, the two distributions were found to be differentiated at a very high level of significance ($p <$ ·001). A diagrammatic representation of the distributions, equated for number of cases, is given in Fig. 32. It will be seen that none of the neurotic children had normality scores as high as the mean of the normal children, and that some of the normal children had scores as high as 14σ above the mean of the neurotic group. There can be little doubt, therefore, that the factor isolated can be correctly identified as a factor of neuroticism (Eysenck and Prell, 1952).

On the hypothesis that neuroticism is inherited, we would expect factor scores on neuroticism to be much more alike in monozygotic than in dizygotic twins, and this deduction is borne out by the data. The intra-class correlation between monozygotic twins is ·851; that between dizygotic twins is ·217. Calculation of Holzinger's h^2, which is presented by him as an estimate of the degree to which a given score is determined by hereditary factors, shows that $h^2 = ·81$ While Eysenck and Prell are somewhat critical of this statistic, in view of that fact that some of the assumptions involved in its derivation are clearly not fulfilled in actual practice, it should be borne in mind that some of these questionable assumptions will lead to an over-estimate, others to an underestimate, of the true value of h^2, so that on the whole the obtained figure of 81 per cent. represents the best available estimate of the contribution of heredity to neuroticism. This compares well with the figures obtained in the field of intelligence, and suggests that neuroticism is inherited to at least as marked an extent as are cognitive abilities.

One point should be noted here because it is of considerable importance in any estimate of the value of factor analysis in arriving

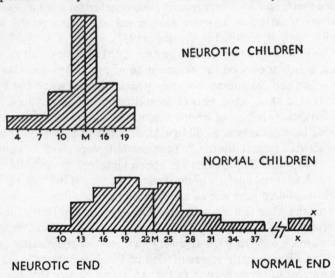

Fig. 32.—Objective Test Discrimination between Normal and Neurotic Children.
x 2 sets of normal twins are respectively 8 and 14 times the neurotic S.D. removed from the neurotic mean, so that their proper scale positions would fall outside the limits of this diagram.

at psychologically meaningful factors. Eysenck and Prell found that the factor score on neuroticism showed an hereditary determination to a greater extent than did scores on any of the individual tests, which contributed to the factor in proportion to their correlations with each other. It would appear to follow from this that the factor of neuroticism must have some degree of biological reality and be more than a mere statistical artefact, as otherwise it is difficult to see how the factor could be determined hereditarily to a greater extent than its constituent parts. This demonstration is important because it appears to be the first time that an experimental answer has been given to one of the most frequent criticisms made of factorial studies.

Yet another study, carried out by Himmelweit and Petrie (1951), uses the general method outlined above. 50 neurotic children and 50 normal children in the age range from 9–14 were tested by means of a large battery of objective, projective, and questionnaire tests, many of them specially designed for the investigation by the writers. The groups were matched for age and I.Q. By and large, the detailed findings agreed well with those found in earlier work; in the case of newly designed tests differences were usually in the expected direction. A factorial analysis was not carried out, but use was made instead of the Penrose (1947) method of discriminant function, which results in two orthogonal axes (the "size" and "shape" scores), and which resembles in some ways a two-factor solution. Using this method on the 14 most diagnostic tests, multiple correlations of ·73 were found. In view of the fact that such coefficients must be viewed with suspicion until they are applied to a new group, scores derived from these tests were calculated for the neurotic group and correlated with a psychiatric assessment of these children. This cross-validation test showed that even when applied to a new group, significant differentiation could still be obtained.

Somewhat less successful than these studies was one carried out by Thorpe and James (1957), again using many of the Eysenck and Himmelweit and Petrie tests. Thorpe and James demonstrated that the location where the test is carried out determines in part the results achieved; thus they found that neurotic children tested in the clinic gave more neurotic scores than neurotic children tested at school and selected in an apparently chance manner from the other children in their class. As they point out "the results indicate quite clearly that when the influence of the testing situation upon test scores is taken into account, the questionnaire type of test has no value whatsoever in the discrimination of normal and neurotic children though this sobering conclusion does not apply to the objective performance tests, most of them showing the sort of group differences that we have come to expect. It should be noted, however, that the obtained differences were smaller than has previously been the case." Thorpe and James pointed out that some of the difficulties associated with this work might be due to the fact that the reliability of syndrome assessment is even lower with children than it is with adults, thus making the criterion less valid than one might want it to be.

Most of the investigations described have been carried out on children, soldiers, and students. Quite different is the work of A. Heron (1951), who gave a battery of performance and questionnaire tests to 80 unskilled workers. Tests used included the Dominoes Intelligence test, the U.S.E.S. Paper Form Board, the Mill Hill Vocabulary test, a Letter Series test, and, on the non-cognitive side, Crown's Word Connection List, Persistence, Perseveration, Dexterity, Static Ataxia, and Aspiration tests, as well as Worries, Annoyances, Interests, and Food Dislikes inventories. Also included in the factor analysis was Work Adjustment as rated by a panel of six raters, and a psychiatric rating. A diagrammatic representation of the results is given in Fig. 33, showing the relation of the various tests to two factors extracted (rotated positions). The differentiation of the intelligence and the neuroticism factors will be seen very clearly.

Intelligence is defined by Dominoes, Letter Series, Vocabulary, Paper Form Board, and various writing tests. Neuroticism is defined by Static Ataxia, Annoyances, Worries, Interests, poor job adjustment, non-persistence, and so forth. It seems clear that in this population, too, a factor of neuroticism can be demonstrated which is defined by much the same tests as previously. A third factor also emerging from this study is possibly similar to extraversion-introversion, although not much reliance can be placed on this identification.

This work has been carried further by Heron in two papers (1954, 1955) in which objective measures of personality were applied to a group of male unskilled factory workers and a group of female unskilled workers in a light engineering factory. Twenty-two and 19 tests respectively were administered and intercorrelated. In the case of the women, the factor analysis "gave rise to four factors of which three were readily identified as general mental ability, neuroticism and extraversion/introversion". In the case of the men general mental ability and neuroticism were again encountered but the third dimension was not as clearly identified as one might have wished. Altogether these researches by Heron are of particular interest because unlike the vast majority of studies in this field they

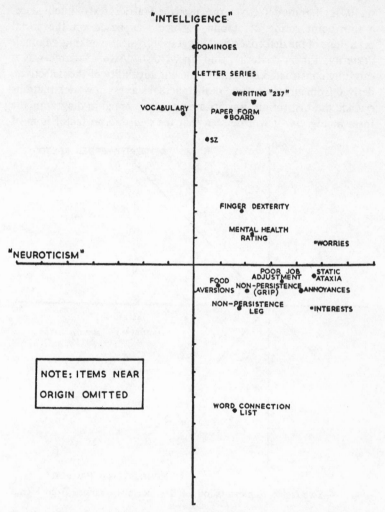

Fig. 33.—Two-factor Representation of Test Results obtained from Unskilled Workers.

concentrated on ordinary working class subjects rather than university students or mental patients. The agreement shown between results from these studies and those mentioned earlier is all the more valuable for this reason.

Quite a different population again was used in the work of Tizard and O'Connor (1951). Cf. also O'Connor (1952). Basing themselves on 104 high-grade defectives, they used the Matrices test of intelligence, a four-point rating of stability, which was based on the social behaviour of the defectives, and Suggestibility, Rail-walking, Manual-dexterity, Finger-dexterity, and Speed tests. Also available was a carefully constructed estimate of the employability of the defectives, derived from an observation of their actual success in work situations outside the Institution. Results are again presented in diagrammatic form in Fig. 34. It will be seen that the neuroticism factor is most

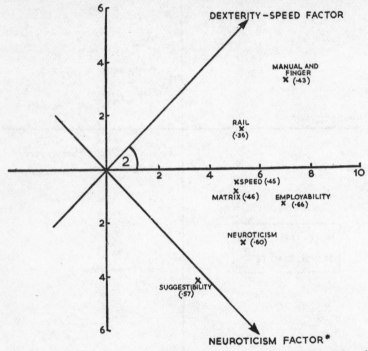

Fig. 34.—Two-factor Representation of Test Results obtained from Mental Defectives.

clearly defined by the neuroticism rating, the Suggestibility test, and the employability criterion, followed closely by the Manual- and Finger-dexterity tests, the Rail-walking test, and the Speed test. The intelligence test has a higher saturation on this factor than is usual (·46); there is of course no reason to expect the correlation between intelligence and neuroticism to be identical in samples which deviate so very markedly from the normal.

The last experiment to be discussed in this chapter goes somewhat beyond the pattern set by the two preceding chapters, and relates directly to a query raised by the two experiments of Line reported earlier. It will be remembered that he found a factor of "stability" by contrasting normal with neurotic and psychotic groups. This raises the question of whether it is justifiable to lump together different types of abnormality. Psychiatric opinion tends toward the belief that psychosis and neurosis are characterized by fundamentally different reaction tendencies, and if that were true, of course, no meaningful result could be expected from an experiment in which those two reaction types were thrown together. On the other hand, writers like Freud believe that psychosis is merely a more advanced state of regression than is neurosis, so that we could represent those two types of disorder as lying on one and the same dimension. Yet another possibility, of course, would be represented by the view that psychosis is a disorder qualitatively different from normal states of behaviour, and consequently not represented on any continuum, but either present or absent. An attempt to provide data to settle this controversy was made by Eysenck (1952).

The method of analysis used was again that of criterion analysis, which has been briefly explained above. The set-up of the experiment was very simple. Three groups of patients were tested—a normal group, a schizophrenic group, and a manic-depressive group. The normal group was made up of 100 subjects; the psychotic groups each contained 50 subjects. No chronic cases of psychosis were included and no one was tested during acute psychotic episodes. Manic-depressive patients were tested exclusively during their non-manic states. Altogether, 84 different sets of scores were obtained from a somewhat smaller number of tests, and an F test of significance was carried out on each score for the three groups. Of the scores, 27 were non-significant, 6 were significant at the 5 per cent. level, 12 at the 1 per cent. level, and 39 at the ·1 per cent. level. These values show fairly conclusively that on the basis of objective tests, the three populations tested were not chance samples from a single universe, but significantly differentiated from each other. Twenty tests were selected from the whole battery and product-moment correlations calculated between them for the normal and psychotic groups separately. Also calculated were biserial correlations of each test with the following dichotomies: normals versus depressives; normals versus schizophrenics; schizophrenics versus depressives; normals versus psychotics.

The two tables of correlations (one for the normal and one for the psychotic group) were factor analysed by means of Thurstone's centroid method, and two significant factors extracted. On the hypothesis of a normal-psychotic continuum, we would expect the factors for the two analyses to be proportional to each other, and this was indeed found to be the case. Correlations between factors from one group and those from the other came to ·868 and ·746. We would also expect, on the basis of this hypothesis, that the first factors should be proportional to the criterion correlations of the tests with the normal-psychotic dichotomy. These correlations were ·895 and ·954, so that again we may say that the deduction has been verified. Apparently, psychotic states do in fact form a continuum with normal mental states, and cannot be said to be qualitatively differentiated from the normal.

An attempt was also made in this study to find evidence for the hypothesis usually associated with Kretschmer, namely that there exists a fundamental personality variable of schizothymia-cyclothymia, which in its most extreme form is characterized by the distinction between schizophrenics and manic-depressives. The possibility that the second factor obtained in the analysis of the intercorrelations between the 20 tests might be identifiable with schizothymia-cyclothymia was canvassed, and correlations run between the saturations for this factor and the criterion column made up of the correlations between each test and the schizophrenic-manic-depressive dichotomy. These correlations turned out to be quite insignificant (·029 and ·085), so that we find no support for this hypothesis whatsoever. These data should not be taken to mean that Kretschmer's hypothesis is conclusively refuted; it is possible that with a better selection of tests a more positive result could be attained.

That such an outcome is not very likely is shown by a recent study in which Brengelmann (1952) gave a number of objective behaviour tests which, according to Kretschmer, were diagnostic of the schizothymia-cyclothymia dimension, to 100 normal subjects. The tests included one of Personal Tempo (Tapping), on which schizothymes should obtain higher scores; a Tremometer test, in which schizothymes should make fewer mistakes and take less time than cyclothymes; the Muller-Lyer Illusion, in which cyclothymes should evince higher degrees of illusion than schizothymes; a Colour-form test, in which schizothymes should be form reactive, cyclothymes colour reactive; and a Reading test in which the tachistoscopically presented stimulus words should be apprehended by the schizothyme by an analytic method, and by the cyclothyme by a Gestalt method.

TABLE 39

Tests	1	2	3	4	5	6	7	8
1. Personal tempo . . .	—	−·086	−·122	−·166	·183	−·056	·139	·093
2. Tremometer mistakes . .	—	—	−·522	·056	−·040	·157	·046	·121
3. Tremometer time . . .	—	—	—	−·106	·102	−·128	−·190	·045
4. Muller-Lyer Illusion Total .	—	—	—	—	−·063	·086	−·009	·084
5. Muller-Lyer Illusion Difference	—	—	—	—	—	·083	·054	·017
6. Colour form (spontaneous) .	—	—	—	—	—	—	(·455)	·203
7. Colour form (special instruction)	—	—	—	—	—	—	—	·072
8. Tachistoscopic Reading test .	—	—	—	—	—	—	—	·072

Values in parentheses derived from tests not experimentally independent.

Reliabilities of these tests were found to be satisfactory.

The intercorrelations between these tests are given in Table 39. Only one correlation is significant at the 1 per cent. level, and this is contrary to expectation. One further correlation is significant at the 5 per cent. level, namely that between the two colour-form tests; all the other correlations are insignificant, and so variable that they cannot be interpreted to support in any way the Kretschmerian hypothesis. We must conclude that tests, all of which are declared by Kretschmer to measure the dimension cyclothymia-schizothymia in normal people, do not, in fact, produce a pattern of intercorrelations which would support the hypothesis. Here, then, we have another example of definite disproof of a hypothesis by factorial methods. Taken together with the previously mentioned research, these data must throw considerable doubt on the existence of a schizothymia-cyclothymia dimension, although a good deal of further experimental work should be required to finalize such a conclusion.

It has been demonstrated above that a normal-psychotic dimension appears to be called for by the results of the experimental tests and the intercorrelations. The question has not yet been answered whether this dimension is identical with that of neuroticism, or whether it is in fact quite separate and different. A long discussion of this problem is given by Eysenck (1952), who quotes several original experiments to show that two dimensions at least are required to accommodate the three populations of normals, neurotics, and psychotics. We need not here go into the statistical basis of this argument beyond noting that it is essentially dependent on the fact that those tests which discriminate successfully between normals and psychotics do not on the whole discriminate between normals and neurotics. Thus, the Body-sway Test of Suggestibility, which has always given a very good discrimination between normals and neurotics, does not discriminate at all between normals and psychotics; neither do tests of persistence, perseveration, oscillation, or word association. It is difficult to reconcile data of this type with the Freudian hypothesis of one dimension of "regression" from the normal, through the neurotic, to the psychotic, and consequently it appears probable that in addition to a factor of neuroticism we must also recognize the existence of what ought perhaps to be called a factor of psychoticism, although the term has an unusual and unattractive sound, which may make it difficult of acceptance.

Several more recent studies by S. B. G. Eysenck (1956) and H. J. Eysenck (1955), have used the technique of canonical variate analysis to pursue this question further. Tests known to discriminate normal from neurotic and psychotic groups were given to normal subjects and to neurotic and psychotic patients; an analysis was then carried out to determine whether an optimal combination of scores from these tests chosen for the purpose of discriminating three groups would place them in one or two dimensions. It was shown that in both cases two dimensions were required rather than one, so that the hypothesis of a linear continuum from normal through neurotic to psychotic could not be maintained. Subsidiary hypotheses could, of course, be made to rescue the one-dimensional theory from this impasse, but these hypotheses would be entirely *ad hoc* and would in effect amount to an admission that two dimensions are required for a proper description of neurotic and psychotic disorders. This finding links up with the factor analytic study of Trouton and Maxwell referred to in an earlier chapter, which also resulted in a similar conclusion.

We may now summarize the results of work carried out with objective behaviour tests. As far as the "w" factor (neuroticism) is concerned, there can be little doubt that these tests have strongly supported the evidence available from ratings and self-ratings, and have added considerably to our understanding of the nature of this factor. They have also enabled us to measure it with considerable accuracy and to make predictions regarding it which can be tested and verified. These contributions are particularly important, in that they are made on an objective basis and are not dependent on subjective interpretation of mental states, either one's own or someone else's. Consequently, most of the objections to ratings and self-ratings are not applicable to objective behaviour tests, and for any thorough understanding or description of personality we consider it essential that tests of this type should be included. With respect to extraversion-introversion, there is no clear-cut evidence derived from objective tests along factorial lines. There are many indications, as is shown, for instance, in a review of the literature by Eysenck (1952), that quite a number of tests can be found which can discriminate at a high level of significance between hysterics and dysthymics, i.e. between the groups which, according to Jung, are the prototypes of extraversion and introversion respectively.

Table 40 taken from Eysenck (1957) suggests a number of variables which at various times have shown significant correlations with this dimension.

TABLE 40

	I	*E*	*Reference*
Neurotic syndrome	Dysthymia	Hysteria; Psychopathy	Eysenck, 1947
Body build	Leptomorph	Eurymorphy	Eysenck, 1947
Intellectual function	Low I.Q./ Vocabulary ratio	High I.Q./ Vocabulary ratio	Himmelweit, 1945; Foulds, 1956
Perceptual rigidity	High	Low	Canestrari, 1957
Persistence	High	Low	Eysenck, 1947
Speed	Low	High	Foulds, 1952
Speed/accuracy ratio	Low	High	Himmelweit, 1946
Level of aspiration	High	Low	Himmelweit, 1947; Miller, 1951
Intra-personal variability	Low	High	Eysenck, 1947
Sense of humour	Cognitive	Orectic	Eysenck, 1947, 1956
Sociability	Low	High	Eysenck, 1956, 1957
Repression	Weak	Strong	Eriksen, 1954
Social attitudes	Tender-minded	Tough-minded	Eysenck, 1954
Rorschach test	M % High	D High	Eysenck, 1956
T.A.T.	Low productivity	High productivity	Foulds, 1953
Conditioning	Quick	Slow	Franks, 1956, 1957
Reminiscence	Low	High	Eysenck, 1956
Figural after-effects	Small	Large	Eysenck, 1955
Stress reactions	Over-active	Inert	Davis, 1948; Venables, 1953
Sedation threshold	High	Low	Shagass, 1956
Perceptual constancy	Low	High	Ardis & Fraser, 1957

Why, it could be asked, have these variables not been used in a factor analytic study? The answer has already been implied in our discussion of Cattell's research methodology. It was indicated there that instead of using short and necessarily unreliable tests in a large factorial battery, it might be better to devote considerable time to single tests, their detailed study and their experimental improvement. If this were to be done, however, clearly the factor analytic paradigm would have to be altered. A single conditioning experiment may take several days, and clearly to multiply testing of this kind so as to include even fifty or sixty variables, would place a strain on both subject and experimenter which neither would be likely to be able to bear. The alternative method is that of studying each test in its own right and correlating it with a criterion measure having both a high theoretical probability of being closely related with the trait in question (extraversion/introversion in this case), and also having reasonably high empirical saturations on previous factor analytic studies. This line of reasoning has led to the use of specially developed questionnaires and of clinical diagnoses (hysteria/psychopathy vs. dysthymia), either singly or together, as criteria for the detailed study of conditioning, reminiscence, level of aspiration, figural after effects, sedation thresholds and perceptual constancy in relation to extraversion/introversion.

It must, of course, be realized that the correlations obtained, which tend to be between ·2 and ·5, are very much attenuated by the imperfections of the criterion used. Ideally one would correlate a given test which is theoretically related to extraversion/introversion with a factor score on extraversion/introversion derived from a whole battery of well established tests including questionnaires, ratings, objective, projective and automatic measures. By choosing only a questionnaire, or only a psychiatric rating, as one's criterion, one immediately lessens by more than 50 per cent. the probability of finding a significant relationship—both ratings and questionnaires having loadings on the extraversion/introversion factor of only between ·5 and ·6. Nevertheless, the fact that fairly significant positive relationships can be established in this way is encouraging and suggests that if the criterion were to be improved correlations would go up by a considerable amount. This method also has the advantage that it requires less expenditure of time on the part of the subject, it is more easily replicable by students in other departments, and lends itself more readily to detailed control of the experimental conditions.

Two factorial studies have recently been completed of tests such as those mentioned above, one on a neurotic, the other on a normal population (Eysenck, 1960). Both gave rise to clear-cut factors of neuroticism and introversion/extraversion, and in both studies the factor loading of the extraversion scales was in the neighbourhood of ·5. There is little doubt that factorial studies such as these are preferable to studies using diagnosis or questionnaire as a criterion, and are much more likely to reveal interesting and important relations.

In summing up the role and usefulness of objective tests in the measurement of personality, it would not perhaps be exaggerated to say that they represent the main hope of psychology as far as the scientific study of personality is concerned. The usefulness of ratings and questionnaires is not in doubt; nevertheless, they do not in their very nature seem to be susceptible to the objectification which is a first essential of true scientific experimentation. They give essential evidence on two aspects of personality—how a person strikes others, and what he thinks about himself. When we study a person's behaviour, however, it seems only reasonable to rely more on selected aspects of his actual behaviour in experimental situations than on what he or anyone else thinks or says about his behaviour.

Nevertheless, there is a certain subjectivity attending even the most objective test, a subjectivity which should be minimized even if it cannot be eliminated completely. Motivation enters into any test, however objective, and motivation may be intimately linked up with a personal relationship obtaining between tester and subject. We need only consider the probable change in performance on a persistence test by a group of impressionable young men tested respectively by Sabrina (Jayne Mansfield for American readers) on the one hand, and Tugboat Annie on the other! Far too little research has been devoted to the influence of attitudes on tests of conditioning, learning and perceptual behaviour to be certain that the proportion of the variance due to different testers was in fact large, but the possibility cannot be dismissed and precautions should always be taken to minimize such differences and standardize the social situation as far as possible.

Even so, it is, of course, true that from many points of view the objective test is expensive, lengthy, complex and difficult. It requires laboratories (preferably soundproof and air conditioned), it requires expensive equipment (and technicians to maintain it); and it requires competent psychologists trained in experimental research and learning theory. None of these are usually found in the typical clinical situation, or the employment selection office, or the students' advisory bureau; consequently it is unlikely that for a long time to come the objective test will be assigned the role which it deserves.

Chapter VI

ARDIS, J. A., and FRASER, E. Personality and perception: the constancy effect and introversion. *Brit. J. Psychol.*, 1957, **48**, 48–54.

BEECH, H. R., and MAXWELL, A. E. Differentiation of clinical groups using canonical variates. *J. consult. Psychol.*, 1958, **22**, 113–121.

BRENGELMANN, J. C. Kretschmer's zyklothymer und schizothymer Typus im Bereich der normalen Persönlichkeit. *Psychol. Rund.*, 1952, **3**, 31–38.

BROGDEN, H. E. A factor analysis of forty character tests. *Psychol. Mon.*, 1940, **234**, 35–55.

CANESTRARI, R. Sindromi psichiatriche e rigidita percettiva. *Riv. experimentale di Freniatria*, 1957, **81**, 1–10.

CATTELL, R. B. *The Description and Measurement of Personality*. London: Harrap & Co. Ltd., 1946.

Primary personality factors in the realm of objective tests. *J. Pers.*, 1948, **16**, 459–487.

The principal replicated factors discovered in objective personality tests. *J. abnorm. soc. Psychol.*, 1955, **50**, 291–314.

Personality, and Motivation Structure and Measurement. London: Harrap & Co. Ltd., 1957.

CATTELL, R. B., and SAUNDERS, D. R. Inter-relation and matching of personality factors from behaviour rating, questionnaire, and objective test data. *J. soc. Psychol.*, 1950, **31**, 243–260.

CATTELL, R. B., and SCHEIER, I. H. The nature of anxiety: a review of thirteen multivariate analyses comprising 814 variables. *Psychol., Rep.*, 1958, **4**, 351–388.

DAVIS, D. R. *Pilot Error—Some Laboratory Experiments*. London: H.M.S.O., 1948.

DOWNEY, JUNE E. *The Will-profile*. Dep. Psychol. Bull. No. 3. Wyoming: Univ. Wyoming, 1919.

ERIKSEN, C. W. Psychological defences and "ego-strength" in the recall of completed and incompleted tasks. *J. abnorm. soc. Psychol.*, 1954, **49**, 45–50.

EYSENCK, H. J. *Dimensions of Personality*. London: Kegan Paul, 1947.

Criterion Analysis: an application of the hypothetico-deductive method to factor analysis. *Psychol. Rev.*, 1950, **57**, 38–53.

Schizothymia-cyclothymia as a dimension of personality. II. Experimental. *J. Pers.*, 1952, **30**, 345–384.

The Scientific Study of Personality. London: Routledge & Kegan Paul, 1952.

The Psychology of Politics. London: Routledge & Kegan Paul, 1954.

Cortical inhibition, figural after-effect, and the theory of personality. *J. abnorm. soc. Psychol.*, 1955, **51**, 94–106.

Psychiatric diagnosis as a psychological and statistical problem. *Psychol. Rep.*, 1955, **1**, 3–17.

Reminiscence, drive and personality theory. *J. abnorm. soc. Psychol.*, 1956, **53**, 328–333.

Dynamics of Anxiety and Hysteria. London: Routledge & Kegan Paul, 1957.

Experiments in Personality. London: Routledge & Kegan Paul, 1960.

EYSENCK, H. J., and PRELL, D. B. The inheritance of neuroticism: an experimental study. *J. ment. Sci.*, 1951, **97**, 441–465.

A note on the differentiation of normal and neurotic children by means of objective tests. *J. clin. Psychol.*, 1952, **8**, 202–204.

EYSENCK, S. B. G. Neurosis and psychosis: an experimental study. *J. ment. Sci.*, 1956, **102**, 517–529.

FOULDS, G. A. Temperamental differences in maze performance. *Brit. J. Psychol.*, 1952, **43**, 33–41.

A method of scoring the T.A.T. applied to psychoneurotics. *J. ment. Sci.*, 1953, **99**, 235–246.

The ratio of general intellectual ability to vocabulary among psychoneurotics. *Internat. J. soc. Psychiat.*, 1956, **1**, 5–12.

FRANKS, C. M. Conditioning and personality: a study of normal and neurotic subjects. *J. abnorm. soc. Psychol.*, 1956, **52**, 143–150.

Personality factors and the rate of conditioning. *Brit. J. Psychol.*, 1957, **48**, 119–126.

HARTSHORNE, H., and MAY, M. A. *Studies in Deceit*. New York: Macmillan, 1928.

Studies in Service and Self Control. New York: Macmillan, 1929.

HARTSHORNE, H., and SHUTTLEWORTH, F. K. *Studies in the Organisation of Character*. New York: Macmillan, 1930.

HERON, A. *A Psychological Study of Occupational Adjustment*. Ph.D. Thesis. London: Univ. London Lib., 1951.

The objective assessment of personality among factory workers. *J. soc. Psychol.*, 1954, **39**, 161–185.

The objective assessment of personality among female unskilled workers. *Educ. Psychol. Measmt.*, 1955, **15**, 112–126.

HIMMELWEIT, HILDE T. The intelligence-vocabulary ratio as a measure of temperament. *J. Pers.*, 1945, **14**, 93–105.

Speed and accuracy of Work as related to Temperament. *Brit. J. Psychol.*, 1946, **36**, 132–144.

A comparative study of the level of aspiration of normal and neurotic persons. *Brit. J. Psychol.*, 1947, **37**, 41–59.

HIMMELWEIT, HILDE T., DESAI, M., and PETRIE, A. An experimental investigation of neuroticism. *J. Pers.*, 1946, **15**, 173–196.

HIMMELWEIT, HILDE T., and PETRIE, A. The measurement of personality in children. *Brit. J. educ. Psychol.*, 1951, **21**, 9–29.

HOLTZMAN, W. H., and BITTERMAN, N. G. A factorial study of adjustment to stress. *J. abnorm. soc. Psychol.*, 1956, **52**, 139–185.

KAMIN, L. J., BINDRA, D., CLARKE, J. W., and WAKSBERG, H. The interrelation among some behavioural measures of anxiety. *Canad. J. Psychol.*, 1955, **9**, 79–83.

KOCH, H. Z. A multi-factor analysis of certain measures of activeness in nursery school children. *J. genet. Psychol.*, 1934, **45**, 3, 482–487.

A factor analysis of some measures of the behaviour of pre-school children. *J. genet. Psychol.*, 1942, **27**, 257–287.

LINE, W., and GRIFFIN, J. D. M. The objective determination of factors underlying mental health. *Amer. J. Psychiat.*, 1935, **19**, 833–842.

LINE, W., GRIFFIN, J. D. M., and ANDERSON, G. V. The objective measurement of mental ability. *J. ment. Sci.*, 1935, **81**, 61–106.

MALLER, J. General and specific factors in character. *J. soc. Psychol.*, 1934, **5**, 97–102.

MARTIN, B. A factor analytic study of anxiety. *J. clin. Psychol.*, 1958, **14**, 133–138.

MILLER, D. R. Responses of psychiatric patients to threat of failure. *J. abnorm. soc. Psychol.*, 1951, **46**, 378–387.

OATES, D. V. An experimental study of temperament. *Brit. J. Psychol.*, 1929, **19**, 1–30.

O'CONNOR, N. The prediction of psychological stability and anxiety-aggressiveness from a battery of tests administered to a group of high grade male mental defectives. *J. genet. Psychol.*, 1952, **46**, 3–18.

PENROSE, L. S. Some notes on discrimination. *Ann. Eug.*, 1947, **13**, 228–237.

SCHEIER, I. H., and CATTELL, R. B. Confirmation of objective test factors and assessment of their relation to questionnaire factors: a factor analysis of 113 rating questionnaire and objective test measurements of personality. *J. ment. Sci.*, 1958, **104**, 608–624.

SHAGASS, C. Sedation threshold. *Psychosom. Med.*, 1956, **18**, 410–419.

STEAD, N. G. Factors in mental and scholastic ability. *Brit. J. Psychol.*, 1925, **16**, 199–221.

SYMONDS, P. M. *Diagnosing Personality and Conduct.* New York: Century Psychology Series, 1931.

THORNDIKE, R. L. Individual differences. *Ann. Rev. Psychol.*, 1950, **1**, 87–104.

THORPE, J. C., and JAMES, D. P. Neuroticism in children. I. An investigation of normal and neurotic group differences. *Brit. J. Psychol.*, 1957, **48**, 26–34.

TIZARD, J., and O'CONNOR, N. The abilities of adult and adolescent high grade male mental defectives. *J. ment. Sci.*, 1950, **96**, 889–907.

Predicting the occupational adequacy of certified mental defectives: an empirical investigation using a battery of psychological tests and ratings. *Occup. Psychol.*, 1951, **25**, 205–211.

VENABLES, P. H. A study of motor and autonomic responses to experimentally induced stress in an industrial setting. London: Ph.D. Thesis, 1953.

THE ANALYSIS OF PROJECTIVE TECHNIQUES

SO FAR IN THIS book we have dealt with traits, or hypothetical traits, defined in terms of objective test procedures. It may appear somewhat unusual to include the Rorschach and other projection tests in this book, because, in the opinion of most of its devotees, its main virtue lies in its being a global instrument (i.e. in not dealing with separate traits), and in being not an objective test but a technique essentially relying on interpretation. However, it is clear that scores may be derived from the Rorschach in terms of the usual categories (R, C, F, D, and so on), so that the tests may be used as an objective, or at least semi-objective, procedure, and the possibility that by means of factor analysis we would discover certain traits cannot be ruled out on *a priori* grounds. Indeed, Rorschach himself had hypothesized the existence of introvertive-extratensive tendencies, which could be diagnosed in terms of certain scoring categories. We may, therefore, with some justification, include the small number of factorial studies which have been done on the Rorschach test in this account, adding the proviso that this use of the Rorschach is different from the usual and probably objectionable to most Rorschach experts.

The first paper in this connection, that of Hsü (1947) would seem to justify these hypothetical feelings of Rorschach workers, as it appears to violate in every detail the rationale of the test. Using 76 children, Hsü made a recording of their responses to Plate I only, and finally decided to use 15 variables (number of words, number of nouns, number of adjectives, number of verbs, use of number, human, human detail, animal, animal detail, and five single, frequently occurring responses). Intercorrelating these items and factor analysing the resulting matrix, six factors, which he considered meaningful, were extracted. These were: (*a*) facility in use of words; (*b*) "appears to be the ability of using nouns alone and in non-human context. Time also has a high loading here"; (*c*) "probably suggests a 'face' factor, as this seems to centre chiefly on the human face"; (*d*) "appears to be indicative of the ability of using verbs and adjectives other than nouns"; (*e*) "apparently indicates a 'bat' factor... This is a most interesting part of this analysis" (!); (*f*) "is essentially a human factor". Having discussed the meaning of these factors in some detail, Hsü goes on to say: "If the factors for each plate could be discovered and used in a linear description of the traits of a sufficiently large population, the further quantification and standardization of the Rorschach tests would be highly plausible." To the present writer, this does not seem a reasonable expectation, nor does he feel that Hsü's use of factor analysis is likely to advance our knowledge either of the Rorschach or of personality structure. To throw away the accumulated experiments of hundreds of clinical workers and to start with a *tabula rasa* rather than attempting to verify hypotheses based on previous work with the Rorschach appears a misuse of the technique, and the barrenness of the results is ample confirmation of the correctness of this view.

In sharp contrast to the work of Hsü stands that of Cox (1951) and Sen (1950). Cox gave the Rorschach test, in its orthodox form, to two groups of normal and neurotic children equated for age and intelligence. The records were scored by the use of the ordinary Rorschach scoring categories, using both formal and content scores, and 26 of these categories were then intercorrelated for the whole group of 120 children. A twenty-seventh variable was introduced, namely the dichotomy: normal versus neurotic. Five factors were extracted of which the first appeared to be a general factor of productivity or number. This interpretation was based on the fact that it had the highest loading in the total number of responses (·90) and total number of responses involving the use of form (·94). It had high loadings also in total number of responses involving poor form, together with a high negative loading in "failure to respond". The second factor was interpreted as one of neuroticism. Its highest loading was in the normal-neurotic dichotomy (·73). "High loadings appear also in human and animal detail . . . pure good form also had a high saturation with this factor. At the opposite end of the pole it has high negative loadings in Fire, Water, the Miscellaneous group, CF—, C, D, and Y." The third factor was interpreted as one of intelligence, having high loadings on I.Q., and original and unusual responses. The fourth factor was not clearly identified, but in terms of customary Rorschach procedure appeared to bear some relationship to extraversion-introversion, while the fifth factor is of no interest in this connection. This paper, therefore, results in the objective identification of two factors (neuroticism by reference to the external criterion of clinical diagnosis, and intelligence by reference to I.Q. test), and contains at least suggestive evidence of the extraversion-introversion factor. It would appear, then, that the treatment of the Rorschach as an ordinary objective type of psychometric test gives results essentially similar to those obtained by other objective types of tests.

This conclusion is strengthened by the findings of Sen (1950), who used as subjects 100 Indian students—60 men and 40 women—who were given an individual Rorschach test, two intelligence tests, and Cattell's test of fluency, as well as two questionnaires intended to elicit relevant traits of personality. Each of the subjects tested was also rated independently by two judges on neurotic tendencies, extraversion-introversion, general emotionality, imagination, perception of relations, and intelligence. Three main factors were extracted, of which the first one was clearly a fluency of association factor, having a saturation of ·962 on "total number of responses". Factor measurements for this factor correlated ·485 with results of the fluency test and ·530 with the judges' assessment of imagination. Correlation with intelligence was zero. The second factor is clearly one of intelligence, having its highest saturations on Klopfer's form level score, and its highest negative saturation on Beck's low modified "z" score. Factor measurements correlate to the extent of ·5 with intelligence tests, and also the extent of ·5 with ratings of intelligence. It is interesting to see that this factor also shows slight negative correlation with neurotic tendencies (− ·212), which is in line with many of the researches mentioned previously.

The third factor is one of neuroticism, correlating ·685 with ratings for neurotic tendencies. This factor has high saturations on colour and various other well-known indicators of neurotic tendency. Taken together, the results of Cox and Sen throw a good deal of light on the factors which the Rorschach test measures, and indicate that when this test is used as an ordinary psychometric measuring device, results from it do not deviate from those obtained by means of other types of test.

One further attempt to carry out a factorial study on Rorschach scores should be noted. Sandler (1949) and Sandler and Ackner (1951) administered the Rorschach to 50 patients suffering from a variety of psychiatric disorders; in addition, two psychiatric rating scales were used, one referring to overt symptomatology and the other to previous personality. A form of analysis was used in which persons were intercorrelated rather than scores, and four factors were extracted of which the first was again a fluency or productivity factor. This factor accounts for 29 per cent. of the total variance.

The other three factors account, respectively, for 3 per cent., 2 per cent., and 2 per cent. of the variance, and may thus be considered to be of very slight interest indeed. Nor are they easily interpretable or meaningful psychologically. With some poetic licence, factor two is labelled "internal anatomical responses" versus "external objects", and factor three is defined as "*animated*" against "*inanimate percepts*". "It is more than a differentiation between human and non-human perceptions, but is rather a distinction between perceptions invested with animate expression on the one hand and perceptions devoid of such animation on the other." Factor four is defined as "defensive percepts as opposed to well-defined human parts".

Correlations were then run between Rorschach factors and items in the psychiatric inventories. Very few of these are significant, and altogether they do not seem to present any kind of clear-cut picture. On the whole, this study is of interest more as a statistical exercise in a somewhat novel form than for any light it may shed on the organization of personality.[1]

More recently Eysenck (1956) carried out a study on the inheritance of extraversion/introversion with the assistance of McLeod (1953) and Blewett (1953, 1954). In addition to certain Rorschach indices, various objective tests and sociometric and other ratings were used. The subjects of the investigation were thirteen pairs of male identical

---

[1] Three further factorial studies of the Rorschach ought to be mentioned at least in passing. Wittenborn (1950) has attempted to clear up the muddle of Rorschach scoring categories, with the result that his study "suggests that an incorrect emphasis may have influenced the development of current Rorschach scoring procedures and interpretive practices. . . . Many of the scoring categories which belong to the various broad classes of determinants, e.g. colour, texture, or diffusion, have a quite dissimilar factorial composition, and in general the manner in which the various determinant scoring categories cluster together could not be predicted by an employment of the usual beliefs concerning behavioural implications of determinants".

Adcock's (1951) study, while potentially of great interest because of his use of native Cook Islands children as well as of New Zealand white children, is difficult to interpret because of the small number of children involved. (Tetrachoric correlations on 30 Ss. have such large sampling errors as to be hardly worth calculating.) Three of the factors emerging from the two populations are interpreted as fluency, introversion, and intelligence and "suggest that these are basic dimensions which might be expected in any culture". Further evidence would be required before these interpretations could be accepted as more than possible guesses.

Hughes (1950) presents an extremely important paper involving the use of criterion groups. A detailed discussion of his results would be supererogatory, as his main success in differentiation lies in the field of brain-injury, which is of little direct relevance to our main theme; it is more with respect to method that his paper appears of importance in this context.

twins; thirteen pairs of female identical twins, thirteen pairs of male fraternal twins and thirteen pairs of female fraternal twins. A factorial analysis of the intercorrelations between the data give rise to a clearly marked two-factor pattern which is shown below in Fig. 35.

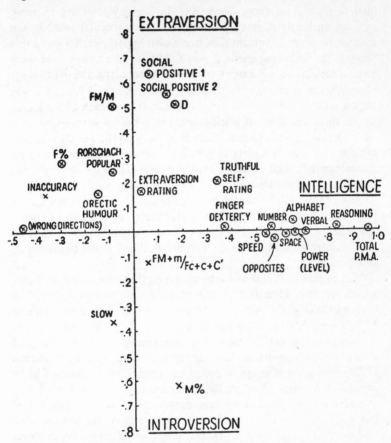

Fig. 35.—Tests defining two factors of extraversion and intelligence in two-dimensional factor space. (Eysenck, 1956.)

It will be seen that the intelligence factor is clearly defined in terms of the Thurstone Primary Mental Ability tests as well as the Nufferno Level Test; little interest attaches to this factor, other than the fact that none of the Rorschach indices used had any significant loading on this factor.

As regards the extraversion/introversion factor, it will be simplest to quote Eysenck's description of the methodology used to objectify interpretation. "While there is a good deal of agreement among Rorschach writers in the interpretation of certain scores, this agreement is far from perfect, and it would be possible in *a posteriori* fashion to explain away discordant findings by referring to some obscure authority as having interpreted this particular score in the manner required to substantiate one's own hypothesis. To avoid this danger, the following method was followed. The scores used were communicated to an expert who had been using the Rorschach clinically and teaching it to students for a number of years. He was requested to write down in detail the relevance of each of the scores to the three variables of intelligence, extraversion-introversion, and neuroticism. He was to base himself entirely on the agreed interpretations of the most widely accepted Rorschach authorities, and on independent factual research evidence. His decisions were written down and implicitly followed in our interpretation; wherever necessary they will be quoted in full. This, of course, does not ensure that other Rorschach experts will necessarily agree; it does ensure that our interpretation of the results is not falsified by an attempt to justify observed findings in the manner outlined at the beginning of this paragraph.

"Let us now look at the variables defining the two poles of the factor which we have identified as one of extraversion-introversion. The variable having the highest saturation on the introverted side is $M\%$ ($-\cdot626$). According to the expert 'a high M suggests introversion, a low M extraversion'. This interpretation has found a good deal of factual support, such as, for instance, a recent study by Barron (1955) who has attempted to devise a psychometric measure of M by means of a series of specially constructed blots, and who found considerable correlations between movement scores and introverted personality traits. The other introversion score is indicative of slow and accurate work on the track tracer ($-\cdot378$); this Himmelweit (1946) and Eysenck (1947) have found indicative of introversion.

"On the extraverted side, the two scores having the highest saturations are the two sociometric scores indicative of social popularity and general social liking ($\cdot632$ and $\cdot574$). This relationship between extraversion and positive social relationships is, of course, in line with our hypothesis. Only slightly less highly correlated with extraversion is the Rorschach D score ($\cdot510$). This is what our authority has to say about a high D score: 'A high D is said to indicate a "practical" man, a down to earth extravert; a low D is said to indicate a "theoretical" man, a "theoriser". A high D is associated with hysteria, a low D with dysthymia.' The interpretation is thus in accord with our hypothesis. Almost equally high as the D score is the FM:M score (·501). This score, of course, is not independent of the M score we have already considered, and can therefore not be used to add very much to our interpretation of the latter. However, for what it is worth, our authority summarizes the literature by saying that a high FM:M ratio 'may indicate extraversion', a low FM:M ratio 'may indicate normality, but also introversion and intelligence'.

"The F% score has a correlation with the extra version factor of ·286. The interpretation of this score appears excessively difficult. Our authority says that 'a high F% is found in the records of psychopaths'; a high F% is found in the records of many hysterics ('flat hysterics'). This would suggest that a high F% is indicative of extraversion. Against this hypothesis speaks the fact that 'a high F% indicates "over-control" which could characterize an introverted neurotic'. Altogether, 'experts seem in some disagreement' so that we cannot really interpret this particular score. The next Rorschach score, the number of popular replies, has a factor of ·242. According to our expert 'a large number of popular responses suggests a dull extraverted person or hysteric'. Apparently 'a small number of popular responses suggests a person out of contact with his environment, or may be due to a perfectionist attitude exhibited by obsessive, compulsive neurotics'. In all, he concludes that 'a high number of popular responses might, therefore, suggest extraversion, a low number introversion'.

"Three more scores are to be considered and lend weight to this interpretation. Inaccurate work on the track tracer has a loading of ·162 which, although low, is in the right direction. Orectic humour also has a loading of ·162 which is also low, but again in the right direction. Truthful self-ratings, with a loading of ·200 is slightly higher and also in line with previous work which has shown a slight tendency for extraverts to obtain more truthful scores on the lie scale. With the possible exception of the F% score, we can therefore say that all the scores considered support the interpretation of this factor as one of extraversion-introversion."

Factor scores were estimated for extraversion and introversion; the correlation was ·030 for fraternal twins and ·155 for identical twins; neither of these correlations, of course, approaches significance. The intraclass correlation for identical twins on extraversion was

·499; for fraternal twins it was —·331. The difference between these values is fully significant and suggests the presence of hereditary determinants for extraversion-introversion.[1]

Two studies by Williams and Lawrence (1953, 1954) have attempted to factor analyse Rorschach determinants and relate these to the M.M.P.I. Results, as far as the correlations between determinants are concerned, are rather similar to those of Wittenborn (1950) whose study was mentioned before. The five main factors discovered were (a) productivity, (b) movement, (c) lack of perceptual control, (d) shading, and (e) intelligence, as determined by the Wechsler Bellevue. Little relationship was found between the Rorschach data and the M.M.P.I. although such relationships as did appear were not contrary to those discussed previously.

One further Rorschach study must be mentioned here, although it does not make use of the factorial method. In their attempt to develop what they called a "basic Rorschach score", Bühler, Bühler and Lefever (1949) make use of a statistical technique which illustrates very vividly the need for factorial methods in this field. Beginning with five initial criterion groups (normal, neurotic, psychopathic, organic, and schizophrenic), they prepared a diagnostic sign list for each of the 207 cases included. Each group was compared with each of the others with respect to each of the many Rorschach signs scored, and scoring weights were determined for each sign in accordance with its ability to discriminate between any of the pairs of groups studied. Ten sets of scoring weights were thus obtained, all of which gave good discrimination between normal and abnormal groups. The basic Rorschach score was then derived from the "normal versus schizophrenic" comparison. This basic Rorschach score has a reliability of ·83 (Spearman-Brown, corrected). Its ability to discriminate between clinical groups is shown in Fig. 36, where main basic Rorschach scores and standard deviational ranges for larger clinical categories are shown.

It will be noticed that this figure is divided into four levels. These are described by the authors as follows. Level I: "In the *ideally integrated dynamic pattern* tendencies to execution are proportionate to an adequate aspiration focus, adequate reality-awareness and relative consideration of immediate and long-range goals. . . . We

---

[1] Eysenck failed to find any strong relationship between Rorschach indices and intelligence in this study. Similar failures have been reported by Lotsoff (1953) and Lotsoff *et al.* (1958); they conclude that "the Rorschach should not be used as a test of intelligence, if one wishes to predict intelligence".

assign a personality to Level I as long as the two basic problems, the conflict of deferment and the co-ordination of goal striving with reality, have not yet overthrown the ego-organisation. We call this the *Level of Adequacy*." On Level II "the personality is in conflict

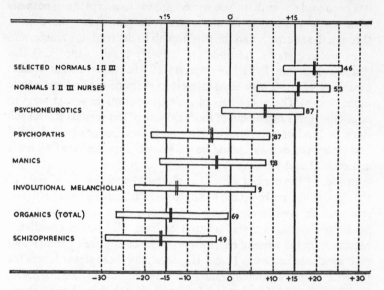

Fig. 36.—Basic Rorschach Scores of various Normal and Clinical Groups.

with reality but has not lost contact with it. However, the ego-organisation is overthrown because of the unresolved conflict between immediate and deferred goals. This conflict prevents unification of strivings. We call this the *Level of Conflict*." On Level III "unification of strivings is abandoned. The dynamics of this defect vary in the different clinical groups falling to this level. Outstanding in the statistical picture is a psychopathic pattern which shows conflict resolved by pursuing immediate satisfaction without regret as a result of a debilitated emotionality. . . . The term *Level of Defect* refers to the incomplete and disproportionate representation of personality factors and the scope of action for Level III. It may or may not refer to defective equipment." On Level IV "goals are too unco-ordinated to compete. They are in conflict with existing executive tendencies and reality is beyond reach. Level IV is called the *Level of Reality Loss*."

Bühler *et al.* recognized that this scheme does not altogether fit the clinical groups appearing on these various levels; "It must be emphasized that these are schematic characterizations which do not quite fit all clinical groups encompassed by a given level. The picture is blurred for a number of clinical groups, but not to the extent that level characterization loses all meaning." It will be clear from what has been said so far that these writers appear to accept the hypothesis of a single dimension of abnormality ranging from the normal through the neurotic, and the psychopath to depressive, organic, and schizophrenic states. As these are the only results supporting this single continuum hypothesis among all the experimental studies examined so far, it may be of interest to examine the findings a little more closely. The hypothesis of a single continuum would seem to imply the linear regression of the incidence of the various Rorschach signs on level of adjustment, i.e. signs shown frequently at Level I and rarely at Level IV should be shown with intermediate frequency at Levels II and III.

In Fig. 37 the present writer has plotted the regression of eight of the signs which make up the basic Rorschach score in terms of sigma scores for the four levels. It will be seen that these eight indices, very far from showing a linear relation to level, all show a curvilinear regression in the sense of having low incidence at Levels I and IV and high incidence at Levels II and III. Summing these sigma scores for the four levels, we obtain values of -3.0 at Level I, 3.8 for Level II, 0.1 for Level III and -7.2 for Level IV. On these scores, therefore, we find no evidence for the hypothetical continuum: normal, neurotic, organic, psychotic; rather we find the neurotics at one extreme and psychotics at the other, and normals and organics intermediate.

It is difficult to see how these results can be reconciled with the hypothesis underlying the basic Rorschach score. It is indeed admitted by Bühler *et al.* that not all signs follow the trend from high respectively low on Level I to low respectively high on Level IV, indicating that integration (or whatever the Rorschach measures) is not likely to be a one-dimensional function. "There are probably at least two factors involved. . . . A remarkable dichotomy is found. Beginning with Level II, we find here the peak of uncontrolled emotionality (CF + C), the peaks of anxiety (K + k), insecurity (c), and unsatisfied instinctual drive in proportion to deferred goals (FM : M); these signs with low F (disregard of reality) present the pattern we would expect in neurosis. *The pattern expresses the conflict between tendencies towards immediate satisfaction and tendencies towards deferred satisfaction, i.e. the characteristic of neurotic conflict.*

... On Level IV the problem no longer exists; all striving appears in regression below the conflict level. *The conflict between immediate and deferred satisfaction is repressed by a much more severe problem expressed in the W : M proportion and also in the antagonism between the very high W and the high F.*" This admission that the basic Rorschach score is not a one-dimensional function is in agreement

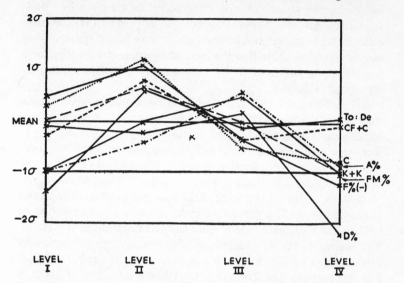

Fig. 37.—Diagram showing Curvilinear Regression of eight Constituents of Basic Rorschach Score on Level of Abnormality.

with our analysis and indicates that this score cannot properly be used to support the single continuum hypothesis. Quite on the contrary, if, as we have shown and as the authors admit, integration is not likely to be a one-dimensional function, and if a clear dichotomy appears between neurotic and psychotic lack of integration, then clearly these results may rather be taken to disprove the hypothesis of a single continuum and to support the view that we are dealing with two radically different dimensions, i.e. a neurotic and a psychotic one.

While the results appear to favour such a solution, they are really not of a kind to make a proper answer possible. The study itself was not designed along factorial lines, and consequently it is not to be expected that definite conclusions regarding either the number of dimensions required or the types of dimension indicated would be forthcoming. In the absence of such knowledge it is very difficult to attribute any theoretical or practical importance to the work of these investigators. On the theoretical level our criticisms have already been made and have by implication been accepted by Bühler *et al.*; on the practical level it is clear that some simple form of regression or discriminant function analysis would have given more discriminative results for the various groups concerned than are given by "Basic Rorschach Scores". These comments do not imply that the main contentions of Bühler, Bühler and Lefever have been disproved; they merely intend to show that the method of argument used by them cannot in the nature of the case answer the questions which they attempted to answer.

Rather different from the studies so far mentioned in this chapter is the work of Keehn (1953, 1954). He attempted to test the well-known hypothesis that so-called colour reactions on the Rorschach are in fact part of a general colour-factor reactivity tendency. He constructed a battery of colour from tests and applied these to a group of 200 subjects. Two factors were extracted. "The first, a colour-form factor, indicated that some of the tests in the battery did measure along one dimension depending upon reaction or non-reaction to colour. The Rorschach colour score had no saturation on this factor. The second factor was tentatively identified as one of whole-part reaction as it passed through a cluster of tests designed to measure just this attitude. The Rorschach score had a saturation of about ·6 on this factor. On this evidence the hypothesis was suggested that Rorschach colour responses depend not upon colour reaction *per se* but upon reaction to the stimulus as a whole rather than to any particular part of it." This study represents an interesting application of factor analytic methods to the more detailed study of complex tests such as the Rorschach, and the results will be seen to contradict many widely held assumptions which have never been put to a properly designed test before.

The work reported in this chapter has dealt almost exclusively with the Rorschach, not because the writer has any particular preference for this test, but because there has been little work on other tests. One study by Dörken (1953) concerned itself with an analysis of finger painting data in normal and psychotic subjects, relating the findings to results obtained from the Rorschach test. He found that "No significant *inter*test correlations could be obtained for the psychotic group, suggesting that projective tests of a different nature may yield results with no necessary relation. The consistency of the normal personality structure was thought to account for the substantial intertest correlations found in the normal group." This latter result appears hardly justified by the data, the majority of correlations being quite insignificant. Lorr (1953) *et al.* carried out a factor analysis of some handwriting characteristics which may improve future studies of this promising but hitherto useless method of personality analysis. Clark and McClelland (1956) attempted a factor analytic integration of imaginative and performance measures of the need for achievement, with results which are at best suggestive. Gordon (1953) carried out a factor analysis of the 48 Szondi pictures; he found that "An individual's liking or disliking of the Szondi picture is to a large extent related to such identifiable characteristics of the patient pictured as age, sex, mood, conventionality of appearance, etc. . . . In a standard administration the test probably cannot be scored to yield reliable measures of these attitudes since there is little similarity of factor content between sets and a wide range of popularity or preference value occurs with insets." Webster (1952) applied multiple discriminant techniques to three T.A.T. variables; his findings will be of interest to the statistician, but throw relatively little light on psychological processes.

It will be seen from what has been said in this chapter that the use of factor analytic methods has already given rise to interesting results in relation to the Rorschach test and has shown that the main personality factors of neuroticism, extraversion and psychoticism can be discovered in this projective field also. It seems unfortunate that so little work has been done on the T.A.T. and other projective techniques; the work of Gordon on the Szondi test, to mention only one example, suggests strongly that valuable results could be obtained in this fashion.

The writer has reviewed validity studies on the Rorschach administered in an orthodox form (Eysenck, 1959), and has come to the reluctant conclusion that no definite relationships have been established in technically competent experiments between Rorschach records and objective or psychiatric criteria. It is curious that when the test is used, as was the case with the writers quoted in this chapter, in a purely psychometric manner, results appear to be much more positive and favourable. This is not the place to draw a moral from this possibly unexpected finding; the facts as presented suggest that further work along the lines of Keehn, Barron and others on the design of separate tests of individual Rorschach hypotheses may lead us away from the promising but apparently not very fruitful holistic approach of the traditionalists, to the more scientific and apparently more valid altruistic type of approach.

REFERENCES

Chapter VII

ADCOCK, C. J. A factorial approach to Rorschach interpretation. *J. genet. Psychol.*, 1951, **44**, 261–272.

BARRON, F. Threshold for the perception of human movement in introverts. *J. consult. Psychol.*, 1955, **19**, 33–38.

BLEWETT, D. B. *An Experimental Study of the Inheritance of Neuroticism and Intelligence.* London: Ph.D. Thesis. 1953.

An experimental study of the inheritance of intelligence. *J. ment. Sci.*, 1954, **100**, 922–933.

BUHLER, C., BUHLER, K., and LEFEVER, D. W. *Development of the Basic Rorschach Score, with Manual of Directions.* California: Copyright, 1949.

CLARK, R. A., and MCCLELLAND, D. C. A factor analytic integration of imaginative and performance measures of the need for achievement. *J. genet. Psychol.*, 1956, **55**, 73–84.

COX, S. M. A factorial study of the Rorschach responses of normal and maladjusted boys. *J. genet. Psychol.*, 1951, **79**, 95–115.

DÖRKEN, H. Projective tests and the consistency of the personality structure: a pilot study. *J. abnorm. soc. Psychol.*, 1953, **48**, 525–531.

EYSENCK, H. J. *Dimensions of Personality.* London: Kegan Paul, 1947.

The inheritance of extraversion-introversion. *Acta Psychol.*, 1956, **12**, 95–110.

Personality tests: 1950–1955. In: *Recent progress in psychiatry.* (Ed. G. W. T. N. Fleming.) London: J. & A. Churchill, 1959.

GORDON, L. V. A factor analysis of the 48 Szondi pictures. *J. Psychol.*, 1953, **36**, 387–392.

HIMMELWEIT, HILDE T. Speed and accuracy of work as related to temperament. *Brit. J. Psychol.*, 1946, **36**, 132–144.

HSÜ, E. H. The Rorschach responses and factor analysis. *J. genet. Psychol.*, 1947, **37**, 129–138.

HUGHES, R. A factor analysis of Rorschach diagnostic signs. *J. genet. Psychol.*, 1950, **43**, 83–103.

KEEHN, J. P. Rorschach validation III. An examination of the role of colour as a determinant in the Rorschach test. *J. ment. Sci.*, 1953, **99**, 910–1138.

KEEHN, J. P. The color-form responses of normal, psychotic and neurotic subjects. *J. abnorm. soc. Psychol.*, 1954, **48**, 535–537.

LORR, M., LEGRINE, L. T., and GOLDER, T. V. A factor analysis of some handwriting characteristics. *J. Pers.*, 1953, **22**, 348–353.

LOTSOFF, E. J. Intelligence, verbal fluency and the Rorschach test. *J. consult. Psychol.*, 1953, **17**, 21–24.

LOTSOFF, E. J., COMREY, A., BORANTZ, V., and ARSFIELD, P. A factor analysis of the WISC and the Rorschach. *J. projective Techniques*, 1958, **22**, 297–301.

MCLEOD, H. *An Experimental Study of the Inheritance of Introversion-Extraversion.* London: Ph.D. Thesis, 1953.

SANDLER, J. *An Experimental Investigation into some Factors entering into the Rorschach Test.* Ph.D. Thesis. London: Univ. London Lib., 1949.

SANDLER, J., and ACKNER, B. Rorschach content analysis: an experimental investigation. *Brit. J. med. Psychol.*, 1951, **24**, 180–201.

SEN, A. A statistical study of the Rorschach test. *Brit. J. Psychol., Stat. Sect.*, 1950, **3**, 21–39.

WEBSTER, H. Rao's multiple discriminant technique applied to three T. A. T. variables. *J. abnorm. soc. Psychol.*, 1952, **47**, 641–648.

WILLIAMS, H. L., and LAWRENCE, J. F. Further investigation of Rorschach determinants subjected to factor analysis. *J. consult. Psychol.*, 1953, **17**, 261–264.

WILLIAMS, N. L., and LAWRENCE, G. F. Comparison of the Rorschach and M.M.P.I. by means of factor analysis. *J. consult. Psychol.*, 1954, **18**, 193–197.

WITTENBORN, J. R. A factor analysis of Rorschach scoring categories. *J. consult. Psychol.*, 1950, **14**, 261–267.

A new procedure for evaluating mental hospital patients. *J. consult. Psychol.*, 1950, **14**, 500–550.

THE ANALYSIS OF PHYSIOLOGICAL
MEASURES

COMPARED WITH THE number of studies using body build as a variable, there is a dearth of studies dealing with physiological differences. Nevertheless, the few investigations which have been carried out suffice to show that in this borderland between mind and body there is a rich harvest to be reaped, and few of the studies reviewed in this book are of greater fundamental importance than those which relate psychological traits to physiological functioning.

The pioneer study in this field is the work carried out by Darrow and Heath (1932) on "Reaction Tendencies Relating to Personality". Their work bears the mark of that early period both in the statistical method of analysis employed and the type of psychological test used; nevertheless, it would ill become us to smile at this early attempt, which in many ways still constitutes an example of objective procedure and insightful analysis.

On the psychological side, the Thurstone Neurotic Inventory and the Northwestern University Introversion-Extraversion test were used on the 80 or so students who constituted the experimental group. On the physiological side, Darrow and Heath say that the laboratory test used by them "was formulated for the purpose of eliciting behaviour of psychological significance, such as anticipation or anxiety, relief, adaptation to repeated stimuli, summation of responses to repeated stimuli, conditioning to indifferent stimuli, and rate of extinction of the conditioned responses. These terms are, of course, only general designations of the kinds of physiological activity on which information was sought". A polygraph recording was made of blood pressure, arm movement, respiration, and the P.G.R. "The stimuli employed in this study consisted of verbal warnings of the impending shocks, verbal information concerning periods of rest with no shocks, the clicks of the pendulum and pendulum release (part of the time mechanism governing the duration of the shocks), and a standardized electric shock acting on the flexor muscle of the thumb."

It would be impossible to describe here in any detail the actual procedures used, nor would it be possible to give the many tables relating physiological activity to individual questions on the question-naire. We must instead turn to the factorial analysis which was carried out along rather original lines. First of all, single questions were combined into composite scores, the groupings of personality items being empirical groupings, "depending on relationships in-trinsic to the material with which we have to deal. Empirical or intrinsically determined groupings of personality and physiological reaction tendencies have been arrived at by tabulating instances where our original list of histograms showed regressions between various physiological measures and specific personality items. Where several of the physiological measures appear related to two or more of a group of questions, each of which was, in turn, related to two or more of the related physiological measures, we have inferred that there was possibly a significant personality-physiological inter-relationship to be studied."

When these personality constellations had been determined, the subjects were given scores on each on the basis of the number of questions answered in a "neurotic" manner. Correlations were then determined between constellation scores and the standard scores on the physiological measures. These correlations were then arranged in such a way that there was the least possible scatter of the larger coefficients, both along the ordinate of Table 41, on which the physiological measures are listed, and along the abscissa, where the personality constellations are given. "The groupings and their order are, in other words, empirically determined by internal relationships and not by theoretical considerations. By this method of presentation it is possible to observe at a glance the amount of overlapping of the various personality-physiological relationships. It is also possible, where overlapping occurs, to find some logical unity relating neigh-bouring groups of personality constellations and to apply a more or less general term of designation to the adjacent measures." This table is of the greatest possible interest, and will repay considerable study in detail.

Darrow and Heath summarize their results by saying that the data of Table 41 "show a marked tendency for a group of personality constellations including (1) 'socially inactive tendencies', (2) 'neuras-thenic tendencies', (3) 'hyper-sensitivity', (4) 'depression', and (5) 'anxiety' to correlate highest with the following group of physio-logical measures: (1) the recovery-reaction quotient; (2) the resistance rise during two minutes of rest after stimulation; (3) the percentage of association of the conditioned with the conditioning stimuli, and (4) the conditioned blood-pressure rise. We have called this group of personality constellations, all relating more or less to the same physiological measures, the 'neurotic' constellation because it comprised the larger part of what we judged to be the truly 'neurotic' tendencies. We have tentatively designated the four physiological measures the 'neurotic syndrome' because of their relationship to this 'neurotic' constellation." This "neurotic syndrome" correlates ·304 with socially negative tendencies, ·330 with neurasthenic tendencies, ·303 with depression, ·338 with anxiety, ·346 with hypersensitivity, ·238 with excitability, ·299 with total score on the neurotic inventory, and ·066 with intelligence. The data leave little doubt that we are dealing here again with "w", or neuroticism, though in a somewhat unusual form.

Darrow and Heath also find in their table a tendency for the measures "which are correlated with anxiety to be correlated with neurotic scores on the inventory used". They also found that practically none of the measures which were in any degree functions of "neurotic" tendencies gave better than near zero correlations with extraversion-introversion. They conclude that "in a general way extraversion appears to correlate with large physiological reactivity in measures where this reactivity is not measurably affected by "neurotic trend." The writer does not feel entirely happy with this conclusion in view of the rather low correlations reported and in view of the doubtful validity of the measure of extraversion-introversion used. While physiological verification of this factor could be of very great interest indeed, this study requires repetition (perhaps on groups of hysterics and dysthymics) before the interpretation of Darrow and Heath can be accepted.

Like most pioneers, Darrow has failed to be appreciated properly by psychologists, who instead of following up his trail-blazing study stubbornly persisted in working with the meritritious questionnaire and the ambiguous rating. It is perhaps only right that we should quote Darrow's recommendations for further work which appear at the end of his paper: "There is evidence that the various measures we have used may become more valuable (1) as we improve on our classification of the various personality variables, (2) as we study individuals on whom we have other data than those available by the questionnaire method, (3) as information is accumulated governing extreme or limiting conditions, and (4) as data accumulate on pathological cases."

Another study which deals with physiological variables is the work of Sanford *et al.* (1943), described in the book on *Physique, Personality, and Scholarship*, which was referred to in a previous chapter. Intercorrelations are given for a large number of variables, such as creatinine excretion, osseous development, endrogenes and estrogenes, as well as B.M.R., calory output, and other variables. Most of the data are of interest more to the study of development, the subjects being children and adolescents, rather than to that of the inter-relationship between physiology and psychology. Also given by him is a table of intercorrelations of a number of autonomic variables. While few of these are significant, "a syndrome was defined for further study consisting of flushing, sweating, skin-stroking intensity, odour, acne, and palpable thyroid. This has been called the parasympathetic response syndrome.... On the other hand, pupillary size, pella, skin stroking, colour, sinus arrhythmia, blood-pressure variability, do not correlate highly with any of the variables in the above syndrome".

Correlations were run between the response systems thus defined and various personality and phantasy syndromes. The parasympathetic response appears to be positively correlated with conscientious work and counteractive endocathection, and negatively with passive timidity, good fellowship, and social feeling. Sympathetic response is positively correlated with willing obedience, timid withdrawal, and anxious emotional expressiveness. In view of the small number of cases, none of these correlations can be taken very seriously as none of them are as high as ·4 even. Of the correlations between physical syndromes and phantasy syndromes only two are suggestive. The phantasy syndrome "strong character" correlates ·44 with parasympathetic response and —·65 with sympathetic response. As both mental age (positively) and male sex (negatively) are correlated with parasympathetic response, and as these factors are not partialled out from the other correlations, it is difficult to interpret these findings in any consistent fashion. Altogether, this study is too unsystematic and too little guided by any kind of hypothesis to be of much value in linking up psychological and physiological variables.

The same comment applies to another pioneering study in this field, namely that of Darling (1940). Using 58 children over the age of eight from the Institute for Juvenile Research in Chicago as his subjects, this writer obtained six ratings and ten autonomic measures. The ratings had rather low inter-rater reliabilities in the neighbourhood of ·35; the traits rated can be found in Table 30. The autonomic measures taken were pulse-rate, systolic and diastolic blood pressure, the differences between these two pressures, blood-pressure change from first to second visit to the laboratory, P.G.R. resistance, conductance, change, and startle reaction, and continuous blood-pressure recording. The six ratings and five autonomic measures (some of them combinations of the simple recordings mentioned above) were intercorrelated, and a factor analysis performed. The resulting four factors are shown in Table 42, together with Darling's interpretation of these factors.

TABLE 42

Tests	Factor Loadings			
	I	II	III	IV
1. Attention	·047	·822	− ·107	·049
2. Co-operation	·051	·802	·010	− ·069
3. Alertness	− ·120	·844	·262	− ·084
4. Boldness	− ·104	·668	·297	·096
5. Excitement	·008	·626	·565	·058
6. Hyperactivity	·030	·497	·577	− ·055
7. Cholinergic activity (Cond. react. − S.B.P.) . .	·796	·149	− ·082	·013
8. Conductance reactivity . . .	·705	·048	·101	·696
9. Conductance level . . .	·298	− ·133	·286	·119
10. Sympathetic activity (Cond. react. − S.B.P.) . .	·021	·038	− ·094	·795
11. Systolic blood pressure . . .	− ·721	− ·083	·005	·544

Tentative interpretation of factors:	Cholinergic (parasympathetic?) activity	Attention-alertness	General motor activity	Sympathetic (adrenergic) reactivity

It will be seen that factors I and IV are named cholinergic (parasympathetic) and adrenergic (sympathetic) respectively; these two factors are quite orthogonal to each other, not opposite poles of one factor, as one might have anticipated. Factors II and III have loadings exclusively on the ratings, just as the other two factors have loadings of any size exclusively on the autonomic measures; they are labelled attention-alertness and general motor activity. The only bridge between ratings and autonomic activity is provided by the fact that factors I and II correlate to the extent of $r = ·310$. If this correlation, whose significance is of course extremely doubtful, can be taken seriously, it would seem to indicate a tendency for alert children to be cholinergic. But in view of the smallness of the correlation, the extreme unreliability of the ratings, and the lack of independence of the autonomic measures this work must be considered suggestive rather than conclusive. If we are willing to regard the qualities which go to make up factor II as "*w*" qualities, we might find in this study an adumbration of Wenger's finding that neuroticism was significantly correlated with adrenergic (sympathetic) reactivity.

Much more systematic is a whole series of studies by Wenger, which shows most clearly how valuable the factorial approach can be when guided by a definite hypothesis. Taking his lead from the well-known Eppinger and Hess (1917) theory of "vagotonia", Wenger (1942) set up the following two hypotheses: "(A) The differential chemical reactivity and the physiological antagonism of the adrenergic and cholinergic branches of the autonomic nervous system permit of a situation in which the action of one branch may predominate over that of the other. This predominance of autonomic imbalance may be phasic or chronic and may obtain for either the adrenergic or the cholinergic system. (B) Autonomic imbalance, when measured in an unselected population, will be distributed continuously about a central tendency which shall be defined as autonomic balance."

It will be noted that Wenger follows Dale rather than Eppinger and Hess in stressing the chemical rather than the anatomical differentiation of autonomic nerves. "For most practical purposes, the terms 'adrenergic' and 'sympathetic', or 'cholinergic' and 'parasympathetic' may be considered as synonyms."

In his first study, Wenger (1941) used 62 elementary schoolchildren, aged between 6 and 11, to whom was given a battery of autonomic tests, each of which was selected on definite hypotheses regarding its relation to autonomic innervation. These tests were intercorrelated, age was partialled out, and a factor analysis undertaken. Two main factors appeared, of which one was considered to be an autonomic factor, the second a muscular-tension factor. "The first factor is defined chiefly by sparcity of saliva, high percentage of solids in saliva, fast heart rate, little sinus arrhythmia, much palmar and volar sweating, high basal metabolic rate, and low blood pressure." Factor saturations are given in Table 43 below. It will be seen from the signs and the high factor loadings, as well as from the description just given, that the syndrome isolated is one of sympathetic or adrenergic predominance. (The second factor, labelled "muscular tension", while of great interest from the research point of view, is not strictly relevant to our main theme, and will here be disregarded. A brief discussion of it will be found in Chapter IX.)

TABLE 43

Measure	Autonomic Factor	Muscular Factor
Short dermographic latency . .	− ·06	·31
Short dermographic persistence .	·20	− ·28
Low salivary output . . .	·56	·05
Per cent. solids in saliva . . .	·52	·17
Short heart period	·42	·62
Little sinus arrhythmia . . .	·46	·51
Reaction time	·02	·31
Change in palmar log conductance .	− ·07	·74
Muscular relaxation . . .	·02	·18
Little restlessness (rating) . . .	·02	·21
Standing palmar conductance . .	·48	− ·03
Reclining palmar conductance . .	·50	− ·42
Non-palmar conductance . . .	·30	− ·08
B.M.R.	·36	·17
Small sigma respiration amplitude .	− ·07	·19
Respiration rate	·07	·30
Change in systolic blood pressure ,	− ·11	·06
Systolic blood pressure . . .	− ·29	·26
Diastolic blood pressure . . .	·19	·50
Low pulse pressure	·35	·23

A regression equation was derived from seven of the measures having reasonable saturations on this factor, and it has been found that, on repetition of the investigation over periods varying from six to twelve months, retest correlations for the factor scores would run between ·5 and ·7 for the various groups. The factorial solution itself seemed to be very stable. When the whole investigation was repeated and a new regression equation derived from the new factor saturations, this was found to be remarkably similar to the original one. Factor scores derived from the two equations correlated ·84 and ·85 for the two sets of data. "The relationship between the two equations approximates the reliability of measurement of either one. For both solutions, the autonomic factor may be regarded as relatively stable and therefore basically valid" (Wenger, 1942). This device of repeating the whole procedure of testing, intercorrelating of measures, and factor analysing the resulting table in order to test the stability of factors provides a much more impressive proof of the stability of factors than could be derived from any theoretical argument. Unfortunately, this is a technique that is relatively rare, and it may be hoped that in the future more workers will follow the example set by Wenger.

Before turning to his large-scale studies on adults, we may note just one further observation contributed by Wenger. He considered that children with scores indicating parasympathetic predominance were less emotional, showed more controlled behaviour, and were more shy than those with scores showing sympathetic predominance. This description would seem to link up the adrenergous-sympathetic type with extraversion, and the cholinergic-parasympathetic type with introversion, with deviation from the mean towards either extreme perhaps being considered as a measure of neuroticism.

This plausible hypothesis, however, is not supported by Wenger's later work. Essentially, in these later studies, Wenger (1948) contrasted samples of normal aviation students with other groups suffering from operational fatigue or neurosis, on the hypothesis that excessive sympathetic functioning is characteristic of neurotic malfunctioning. Almost 500 normal cadets and aviation students constituted the control group, and 298 patients suffering from operational fatigue constituted the experimental group. The results of the study in terms of the ability of various tests to discriminate between the two groups are given in Table 44, column 1 setting out the critical ratios for the various comparisons. For the second experiment an identical design was used comparing the same control group with an experimental group made up of 98 psychoneurotic patients coming from a similar Army aviation background. The critical ratios for the

TABLE 44

Item	I CR, Normal v. Operational Fatigue	II Factor Saturations, Normal Group	III Factor Saturations, Operational Fatigue Group	IV CR, Normal v. Neurotics
Salivary output	2·86	·25	—	8·13
Salivary pH	2·50	—	·48	4·23
Dermographic latency	1·00	·17	—	0·38
Dermographic persistence	0·93	·11	− ·01	0·61
Palmar conductance	4·84	·19	·45	0·47
Log conductance change	1·06	·31	·23	3·36
Volar conductance	1·43	·19	·14	—
Systolic blood pressure	6·52	—	·37	4·46
Diastolic blood pressure	8·60	·30	—	4·60
Heart period	7·82	·60	·36	6·65
Sublingual temperature	2·50	·47	·45	2·00
Finger temperature	3·08	·03	− ·02	3·81
Tidal air mean	5·92	—	—	2·47
Tidal air sigma	0·42	·15	—	1·58
Oxygen consumption	0·80	·13	·35	3·43
Pupillary diameter	—	—	—	—

same tests are given in Table 32, column 4, where it will be seen that most of them give satisfactory discrimination between normals and neurotics.

Factor analyses were also carried out on the intercorrelations of the tests for the normal group and for the operational fatigue group separately. Saturations for an autonomic factor extracted from both these studies are also given in Table 32, columns 2 and 3. These various columns of factor saturations show a distinct tendency to be proportional to each other, and it is apparent that those tests having the highest factor saturations are also the tests discriminating best between normals and neurotics, or between normals and operational fatigue cases. On the whole, it will also be seen that the factor saturations are similar to those obtained from the groups of children, thus lending additional support to Wenger's general hypothesis. "It may be concluded . . . that we are dealing here with a fairly stable physiological pattern. The important tests and relationships are Salivary Output (high), Palmar Conductance (low), Volar Conductance (low), Heart Period (long), and Oxygen Consumption (low); with Pulse Pressure (high) and Diastonic Pressure (low) significant for children, and probably both Systolic and Diastolic Pressure (low) significant for adults. Dermographic Persistence (long) seems to be significant at the child level, but not at the adult level; Sub-lingual Temperature (low) undoubtedly is important, at least at the adult level. . . . It is concluded, therefore, that the factor represents the functional status of the autonomic nervous system, and that it is valid at both the child and young-adult levels of physiological development."

The results quoted so far show a distinct tendency for Wenger's factor of autonomic imbalance to be significantly correlated with neuroticism, as judged psychiatrically. In another part of his study Wenger attempts an interesting correlation between personality factors and physiological factors. Having obtained a factor score for the autonomic factor on 264 normal Army Air Force cadets, he administered thirteen of the Guilford Personality Inventory Scales, discussed in a previous chapter, to these cadets and correlated scores on the questionnaires with the automatic factor scores. None of these correlations is very high, but they present a very clear picture.

"At the 1% level, parasympathetic predominance is positively associated with Factors D and C (depression and cycloiddisposition) and is negatively related to Factors O and Co (objectivity and co-operativeness); at the 5 to 7% level it is positively associated with Factors S and T (social and thinking introversion) and negatively related to Factors N and Ag (lack of nervousness and irritability and agreeableness)." Taken in conjunction with the factor studies of the Guilford Scales as shown in Fig. 26 on a previous page, these results suggest strongly a relationship between neuroticism and parasympathetic predominance. This relationship is the exact opposite to that found previously by Wenger in his studies concerned with psychologically abnormal groups, where it will be remembered that neuroticism and sympathetic predominance went together. Wenger himself does not comment on this contradiction nor does he offer any explanation. Until such an explanation is forthcoming, these contradictory results must inevitably weaken the case in favour of the postulated relationship between neuroticism and the autonomic factors.

Wenger's contribution is of considerable interest and importance, although it inevitably leaves several questions unanswered and raises doubts on certain points of interpretation. To take the latter first, the occasional inversions of prediction encountered in his work are very much more damaging than is usually the case in this type of work because of the definiteness of the hypothesis under investigation. Thus the prediction of an association between high sub-lingual temperature and sympathetic stimulation was not borne out in fact. Pupillary diameter, which theoretically should have high loadings on the factor, is practically unrelated to the other variables. There are several other inconsistencies, and although Wenger's arguments in defence of his position cannot be dismissed, they are not always convincing. However, when all is said and done, the number of inconsistencies is relatively small and the number of agreements very much larger than would have been expected on any alternative hypothesis.

Regarding the relation of this factor with personality, Wenger often speaks of autonomic imbalance as being related to neurotic disorder, but, in effect, what he has related to neuroticism is sympathetic predominance. It is not at all clear from his writings whether the opposite of the neurotic sympathetic-adrenergic person would be someone having no autonomic imbalance either way, or perhaps rather the person having parasympathetic-cholinergic predominance. This point is quite crucial to an adequate understanding of the relation between autonomic functioning and personality, yet nothing is said about it in Wenger's publications. Possibly, later work will throw some light on this point. Until it is cleared up, however, we cannot altogether dismiss the hypothesis advanced in connection with our discussion of Wenger's work on children, namely that neuroticism is correlated with deviation from autonomic balance in either direction, while extraversion and introversion are related to the direction of the deviation from autonomic balance.

A series of autonomic measures different from those in Wenger's battery was used by Theron (1948) and Van der Merwe (1948) in their attempts to use peripheral vasomotor reactions as indices of basic emotional tension and lability. In the first of these two studies, Theron carried out a factorial investigation of 50 normal students at the University of Stellenbosch. Plethysmographic records were taken according to a method described by Van der Merwe and Theron (1947), while the subject was relaxed, while his left hand was immersed in a cold-water bath, while the subject inhaled deeply and held his breath as long as possible, and while the subject was given mental arithmetic problems to solve. 12 scores entered into the final table of intercorrelations, namely (1) room temperature; (2) temperature of hot-water bath, in which the subject held both his hands before the beginning of the experiment; (3) pulse volume during relaxation; (4) pulse volume immediately before the cold-water test; (5) pulse volume immediately before deep-breathing test; (6) volume before the arithmetical tasks; (7) the rate of change in finger volume with the cold-water test; (8) rate of change in finger volume with the deep-breathing test; (9) the rate of change in finger volume during the arithmetical tasks; (10) the Bell Inventory emotional stability score; and (11) the Bell Inventory total score; (12) the rate of change in finger volume during tasks when the pulse volume before tasks was made statistically equal for all subjects.

Three rotated factors extracted from the matrix of intercorrelations are given in Table 45. Factor 1 is called "emotional stability" by Theron, and is clearly similar to "w" or the inverse of neuroticism. It is highly loaded on the two Bell Inventory variables and on the rates of change in finger volume (variables 9 and 12). Variables 3, 4, and 6, .e. the three pulse-volume measures, have negative loadings with this factor, indicating that the labile subjects with larger Bell and finger-volume scores tend to have smaller pulse volumes than the stable. Variable 7, the rate of change in finger volume with the cold-water test, also has a negative loading on this factor. A factor score was computed using variables 3, 4, 6, 7, and 9, which gave a multiple correlation with the factor of ·788. Factor measurements of the 50 individuals correlated ·653 with the Bell emotional scores.

TABLE 45

| Variable | Matrix of Multiple-factor Loadings | | | |
	K^1	K^2	K^3	h^2
1	·114	·116	·341	·142
2	·023	·234	− ·031	·057
3	− ·429	·778	·141	·809
4	− ·368	·883	− ·039	·917
5	− ·212	·879	·210	·860
6	− ·319	·848	·120	·835
7	− ·470	·437	·207	·455
8	− ·174	·442	− ·194	·263
9	·420	·413	·812	1·005
10	·882	·024	− ·112	·792
11	·904	·134	− ·113	·848
12	·584	·136	·649	780

The second factor was labelled "basic emotional tension" by Theron and was highly loaded in all the physiologic variables (3–9) and especially high in the different pulse volumes. Theron concludes his discussion by saying: "This factor could therefore be designated as basic emotional tension and is quite probably similar to the autonomic factor . . . found by Wenger." (It is difficult to accept this identification as Wenger's factor correlates highly with neuroticism; Theron's not at all.) Theron obtained factor measures by combining variables 3, 4, 5, and 6; the multiple correlation between these variables and the factor was found to be ·923.[1]

Van der Merwe (1948) applied the factor measures as determined by Theron to 8 patients with anxiety symptoms (dysthymics) and 12 hysterics. The results are presented in the form of two diagrams. Fig. 38 shows that the *emotional lability* scores of the hysterical and anxiety groups combined differ significantly from those of the normal group; the difference between the two clinical groups was not significant. Fig. 39 shows that on *basic emotional tension* hysterics deviate from the normal group in one direction (showing an imbalance or shift to parasympathetic predominance), while the anxiety group differs in the opposite direction from the normals, showing a shift in the direction of sympathetic predominance. The combined hysteric-anxiety group is not differentiated significantly from the normal group.

These results tend to support the hypothesis put forward in con-

[1] The third factor is of no importance or interest here.

nection with Wenger's data regarding the differential predominance of sympathetic and parasympathetic function in introverts and extraverts. They cannot, however, be admitted as in any sense definitive, as the number of measures used is not large enough to allow of any definite identification of the factors with the main autonomic systems. Repetition of this study with the inclusion of some of Wenger's variables would be of very great interest indeed.

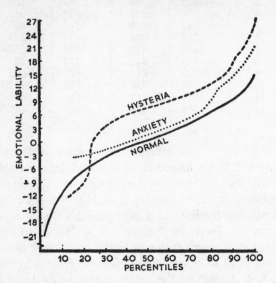

Fig. 38.—Percentile Curves showing the Emotional Lability Scores of Hysteria and Anxiety Patients as compared with Normal Subjects. (Curves slightly smoothed.)

Similar to Wenger's work, and in many ways complementary to it, is that of Jost and his various collaborators.[1] Where Wenger is concerned with the resting level of autonomic functions, Jost is interested in autonomic reactions to frustration, and his work gives a clear indication that the changes following upon frustration are closely related to personality factors of an important kind. Only one of the studies reported by him is factorial (Sherman and Jost, 1942), but the others are so closely relevant to the problem discussed there that they will also be mentioned. In this factorial study, two

[1] Jost succeeded Wenger as psychologist to the Fels Study. In a later chapter we shall encounter further examples of work done by this very active group of investigators.

groups of 18 children were tested. The control group consisted of children known to be extremely well adjusted. The experimental group included 15 neurotic and 3 psychotic children.

"The physiological reactions in 7 situations were measured in each of the subjects and remeasurements were taken in order to confirm the observations. These situations were used: attention to a learning situation, the process of learning in a frustration situation, the process

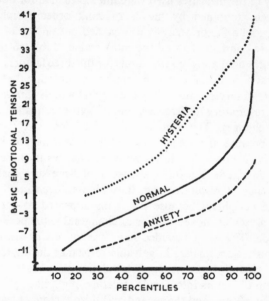

Fig. 39.—Percentile Curves showing the Basic Emotional Tension of Hysterical and Anxiety Patients as compared with Normal Subjects. (Curves slightly smoothed.)

of recall, sensory stimulation, and a final period of rest. The reactions during the rest period were employed to represent the basal physiological levels. The attention-to-learning periods were used in order to obtain measurements of the physiological changes of the subjects during mild tension situations. The sensory stimulation was produced in order to compare the physiological reactions during a sudden stimulation with the reactions during frustration; that is, the reactions during actual physical stimulation were compared with the reactions during ideational and emotional stimulation. The sensory stimuli were bright light, a loud noise, and a painful stimulus produced by pinching."

Frustration in these situations was produced by instructing subjects to learn a sequence of digits by the anticipation method; the first few series were easy, but later ones were so complex that failure followed inevitably. Physiological measures taken included the galvanic skin response, respiratory rate, and amplitude pulse rate, blood pressure, hand tremor, gross bodily measurements, and the electro-encephalogram.

Twenty of the measures used were intercorrelated for both groups of children combined by means of rank order correlation coefficients, and a factor analysis was carried out on the 14 measures which were considered to be the most stable. Table 46 reproduces the measures used and the saturations for the three factors extracted.[1]

The first factor "included the ratings of emotional stability as made by observers, the electro-encephalograph findings, hand tremors, respiratory differences, initial galvanic response, blood-pressure changes. The second factor was tentatively called the 'central' because the items included the measures of heart and respiratory function. The items were the changes in pulse rate, the per cent. change in galvanic response, blood-pressure changes, and the frequency of respiration per half-minute. The third factor was called the peripheral because the items appeared to be measures either of muscular movements or of changes due to specific sensory stimulation. The items included hand tremor, change in pulse rate during frustration, change in galvanic resistance during frustration, and hand tremor during sensory stimulation."

Rotation of factors into simple structure might have given a more meaningful picture, and the second and third factors at least are not at all clear as they stand. The first factor, however, is an approximation to emotional stability ("w") with comparatively high loadings on quite a number of physiological measures. It is doubtful if we can regard the results as proving the hypothesis that frustration induces differential reaction physiologically in normal and neurotic children, as the two measures of frustration reaction included in the factor analysis (numbers 2 and 13) have rather low saturations on

[1] Also given in the table are critical ratios for these measures taken from another paper by Jost (1941). Subjects in this experiment were 18 emotionally unstable and 20 very stable children. It is not quite clear whether these children are partly identical with those taking part in the Sherman-Jost research described above. Some of the measures in the factor analysis could not be identified in Jost's table of critical ratios. It will be seen that there is a clear tendency for the measures having high saturations on the factor of emotional stability to have high critical ratios, and vice versa.

TABLE 46

Factor Loadings

Measure	Contributions			
	F_1	F_2	F_3	C.R.
1. Rating of emotional stability . .	·92	− ·19	·34	—
2. Per cent. change resistance (frustration) .	·48	− ·66	·29	3·70
3. Initial resistance	·52	− ·13	·41	3·06
4. Equation of galvanic response . .	·44	·28	·55	—
5. Blood-pressure change (stimulation) .	·48	− ·42	− ·16	3·90
6. Electro-encephalogram . . .	·76	·19	− ·09	—
7. Sigma respiratory curve . . .	·54	·41	− ·05	2·86
8. Hand tremor (first rest period) . .	·74	·31	− ·54	3·34
9. Hand tremor (last rest period) . .	·65	·11	− ·28	5·45
10. Per cent. change pulse-rate (attention) .	·37	·63	·08	2·30
11. Vineland emotional stability schedule .	·35	− ·12	− ·12	—
12. Number of respirations per half minute .	·28	·39	− ·22	2·00
13. Per cent. change pulse rate. (frustration) (−)	·08	− ·78	− ·50	2·44
14. Per cent. change resistance (learning) .	·39	− ·20	·02	3·52
	4·11	2·27	1·40	
Total		7·78		

the "stability" factor. It would seem rather that the second factor can be regarded as somewhat specific to frustration reactions, as the two measures just mentioned have the highest saturations on this factor. The third factor appears in some ways similar to Wenger's factor of muscular tension, although the identification is by no means clear.

In spite of these criticisms, we may agree with the main conclusions of the authors. "The physiological measures showed that the neurotic individuals reacted more intensively to the frustration situation; the initial reactions, that is during rest and during the attention and learning periods, were also more intense in the neurotic children . . . frequency of the hand tremors was much greater in the neurotic children than in the normal, both before and after frustration . . . the pattern of physiological reactions was significantly different between the two groups. . . . The schizophrenic children presented a very stable physiological picture . . . [this] may mean . . . that their mental condition precludes their being disturbed by situations which ordinarily produce tensions in normal individuals and especially in neurotic persons."

The generalization suggested in this summary, namely that the neurotic child is much more unstable physiologically than the normal, while the psychotic child is more stable than the normal, was taken up in another paper by Sherman and Jost (1945). Using 25 well-adjusted boys, 16 neurotic, and 4 psychotic children, they again took a number of physiological measures (brain potentials, blood-pressure changes, respiration, galvanic skin resistance, heart rate, and hand tremor), using measures at resting levels, during a word-association task, and during the frustration task consisting of increasingly difficult arithmetical problems. Scores on all the measures were transformed into standard scores so that the normal children would be at the 50th percentile on the average on all measures. According to the hypothesis, the neurotic children should then have mean scores at a higher and the psychotic children mean scores on a lower percentile than the normals. This prediction was borne out at a high level of confidence. Out of nine scores the neurotics were at a much higher percentile on eight measures, while the psychotics were at a lower percentile than the normals on eight measures also.

These results, which are more systematic, but in essence similar, to those reported by Odegard (1930), Hoch *et al.* (1944), Whitehorn and Richter (1937), and others, clearly support the conclusion, quoted in an earlier chapter on the basis of objective behaviour tests, that the hypothesis of a single continuum going from the normal through the neurotic to the psychotic, cannot be maintained, but that instead we are dealing with a two-dimensional problem and must therefore posit two factors at least to account for the observed facts.

Where Wenger used physiological measures of the resting organism and Jost physiological reactions to frustration, G. L. Freeman (1948) lays special stress on physiological recovery after stress. This emphasis derives from his basic hypothesis, namely "that all behaviour is an attempt to preserve organismic integrity by homeostatic restoration of equilibrium". According to him: "Total behaviour dynamics is a study of an energy system undergoing change. . . . As a biological energy system, man has a remarkable facility for maintaining his identity and for organizing himself, and even the world about him to that end. . . . The basic construct for ordering the behaviour of an energy system is *homeostasis* or the maintenance of essential *constant states*. The latter term refers to a pattern or distribution of energies which the system is so constructed to restore when such states are disturbed."

This stress on the theoretical concept of homeostasis or restoration of the original state after disturbance, naturally leads to the investigation of physiological recovery from stress as the experimental model for investigating this hypothesis. "The typical homeostatic response curve can be treated somewhat in isolation. The human subject is brought into the laboratory and 'relaxed down' until a measure of basal tissue activities 'levels off' to indicate the more persistent background conditions of quiet rest. From this *basic energy level* the subject is 'displaced' by an external stimulus of controlled intensity and duration. The equilibratory sequence has three phases: (1) *mobilisation*, wherein bodily energies are internally aroused to meet the stimulus-induced displacement; (2) *discharge*, wherein the aroused energies are externally expressed by overt response; and (3) *recovery*, wherein the organismic system returns toward its pre-stimulus condition."

Freeman relates stimulus intensity to organismic arousal by quoting the work of Darrow (1937) and himself to show that "systematic studies of the skin-conductance measures have shown that as stimulus intensity is arithmetically increased, this index of energy mobilization varies as a logarithm of its base". From this Freeman derives his recovery quotient (RQ): $\frac{B - C}{B - A}$, in which B is arbitrarily defined as the level reached on the P.G.R. one-half minute after stimulation; point C as the level reached five minutes after peak mobilization (B); and A as the level at which the stimulus is applied. "With time relations of A, B, and C in this constant ratio, the degree of homeostatic recovery is reliably indicated by dividing the per cent. discharge decrement by the per cent. mobilization increment that occurred in the standardized periods of measurement. This fundamental integrative measure of neuromuscular homeostasis was given the name *physiological recovery quotient*."

We cannot go further into Freeman's hypothesis, but must turn to his experimental studies to discover how far they can aid us in our description of the organization of personality. In the one factorial analysis reported, Freeman and Katzoff (1942) used 24 college men as subjects. Measures were obtained under four conditions aside from rest. These conditions were: (1) Startle; a blank cartridge fired without warning; (2) Motor Conflict: wrong or delayed responses on pushing keys in accordance with a stimulus light were punished by electric shock delivered through reaction key; (3) Verbal Associations to critical and non-critical words; (4) Sensory Discrimination going from easy to difficult pitch discriminations and including distractions. In addition, questionnaires and ratings were used, and time samples of nervous movements obtained.

Thirty measures were intercorrelated and subjected to factor analysis. Of these, 10 were measures of covert physiological activity, 11 were measures of overt behaviour, and 9 were ratings and personality tests. Factor analysis carried out on these variables produced four factors. (Factor saturations are those obtained after rotation with orthogonal axes to simple structure.)

The interpretation of factor one is relatively clear. It is characterized by the psychiatric rating for emotional stability, three different recovery quotients (startle, verbal, and motor), variability in basal movements, motor-movement increment, main basal movement, and the voice level R.Q. Freeman called this factor a control factor, and it is reasonable to suppose that it is the physiological equivalent of Webb's "w". It presents conclusive evidence in favour of Freeman's view of the recovery quotient as a suitable physiological measure for this fundamental personality variable.

When we turn to factor two, interpretation is somewhat less certain. "The measures with significant loadings on the second factor are clearly concerned with 'per cent. conductance increment' or the extent to which any given individual is physiologically aroused by the experimental situations. . . . We may identify the second as an 'arousal factor'."

There is some question as to the identity of factor three in Freeman's opinion. "The major variables with high loadings are self-ratings on various aspects of emotionality ('general neuroticism', 'nervousness', 'visceral disturbance', etc.). The principal exceptions are 'time sampling of nervous movements' and (possibly) 'variability of basal movement'. We might therefore conclude that this as a factor represents S's stereotype of how he reacts—a kind of 'rated emotionality'. Certainly the factor is heavily weighted with pencil and paper tests." A similar factor was found by Eysenck (1952), and identified in an identical manner. The fourth factor in Freeman's study has only two significant loadings and we may agree with him in regarding it as a "specific".

This analysis has given rise to a general picture of personality organization which Freeman presents in the form of a personality sphere showing the three major axes of differentiation. This is reproduced in Fig. 40. (In this reproduction a number of dots will be found which make the personality sphere look as if it had measles. The dots represent the position of people in Freeman's three-dimensional representation, and are used by him to illustrate an argument irrelevant to our presentation.) "The uniqueness of the individual personality pattern is conceived . . . to depend upon the interaction of quantitative gradations in such factors as *discriminate capacity*, *drive arousal*, and *discharge control*. A visualization of such patterns should somehow relate these major axes of differentiation with each other and make it possible to show each individual's position with reference thereto." It is clear that Freeman's "discriminative capacity" is identical with Spearman's "*g*" or Thurstone's second-order factor of intellectual ability. Can we identify the factors of "discharge control" and "drive arousal" in a similar way? We must turn

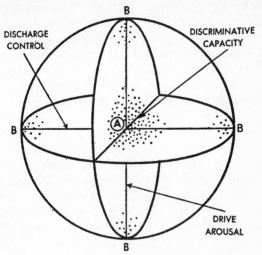

Fig. 40.—The Personality Sphere, showing three Major
Axes of Differentiation.

to Freeman's various experimental studies for our answer to the question.

In one study, for instance, Freeman (1939) used as *stress* the inhibition of micturition, and determined galvanic skin response, blood pressure, and muscle-action potentials under resting or *pre-load* conditions, under *load* conditions (when the subject following water intake reported that the urge could be delayed no longer), and under *post-load* conditions, i.e. after micturition had taken place. Other stress conditions used included the time that painful electric shock could be endured. Ratings and self-ratings on neuroticism were also available. "The result of the various approaches described above seem to be in the same direction. In meeting experimentally induced frustration, the human organism mobilizes bodily resources in varying amounts. When the tension load is removed . . . the speed with which the organism returns to its resting reactivity level correlates with objective indices of success, in withstanding the stress imposed, and with ratings of neurotic tendency. Assuming the experimental loading is standard for all, the extent that an individual returns to his pre-load reactivity within an arbitrary time limit probably constitutes the best single measure of inherent nervous stability."

In another paper, Freeman and Pathman (1942) showed that low-recovery quotients, i.e. failures of the measures of autonomically controlled activity to show rapid recovery, were related to inhibition of overt muscular discharge. Using four experimental situations (startle stimulus, motor conflict, verbal conflict, and sensory discrimination), a standard procedure was followed. The subject was allowed to relax in a cot until his basal activity at rest was established and one of the four emotionally displacing stimuli was introduced. It was then removed, and the rate of return in palmar-skin conductance and movement measures observed from the levels they had reached during the displacing situation. Test-retest reliabilities for both recovery quotients and movement increments were high (.8–.9), and it was found that recovery quotients in the four situations correlated between .5 and .6, while motor increment scores correlated .6–.8. Recovery quotients and motor increments over all the tests correlated to the extent of approximately .53. "The results provided tentative confirmation of the hypothesis that within the limits of these tests individuals tend to recover internal equilibrium most rapidly who readily discharge aroused excitation by overt muscular action, even though this is apparently unadaptive."

In yet another study, Freeman and Pathman (1943) investigated the reactions of 15 manic-depressives and 11 schizophrenics to experimentally induced displacement. No differences were found between psychotics and normal subjects in terms of basal physiological activity, and while manics showed a greater internal arousal and greater overt discharge than normal subjects, schizophrenics failed to show the hypothesized lack of internal arousal and lack of overt discharge. Schizophrenics and manics were found not to be defective with respect to neuromuscular homeostasis; they failed to show lower physiological recovery quotients when compared with normals. Altogether, it was found that physiological reactions to experimentally induced displacement were more diagnostic of the duration of the psychosis than of its classification.

It seems established, then, that quick recovery on the physiological side and an increase in motor movement over the resting level characterize the normal as opposed to the neurotic person; there is no differentiation by these measures as between the normal and the psychotic, a finding well in line with those mentioned previously in connection with the work of Jost. Can we, then, interpret Freeman's factor of discharge control and drive arousal with any of the factors isolated before? In principle this seems unlikely. Freeman's factors are derived almost entirely from physiological measures and within broad limits fulfil the demands of simple structure. They must, therefore, be regarded as primary factors whereas both neuroticism and extraversion-introversion are second-order factors. Discharge control and drive arousal may therefore correlate with, but cannot be identical with, these second-order factors.

The studies summarized above seem to show fairly conclusively that Freeman's discharge control factor is closely related to neuroticism and is likely to constitute an extremely good measure of it. The factor of drive arousal, however, appears to be much less definitely established and its relationship to our two second-order factors remains difficult to disentangle. It should be realized that the factorial analysis on which Freeman bases himself was carried out on only 24 subjects, and that it seems quite unwarranted to take out four factors from a correlation matrix having the extremely high standard errors associated with correlations based on such small numbers. This consideration must also influence, of course, the acceptability of the rotation. Freeman claims "that there are no significant negative loadings in the final factors". It should be realized, however, that for a correlation to be significant at the 1 per cent. level with an N of 24 cases, it would have to be ·515, or even higher since the S.E. of rho, the coefficient used, is greater than that of r. It will be remembered that Spearman was able to claim fulfilment of the tetrad criterion in his earlier work because he analysed tables derived from very small numbers of subjects so that the standard errors were sufficiently large to swamp any deviations from the hypothesis. Until Freeman's work is repeated on much larger numbers, we find it difficult to accept his factors, other than the first, as firmly established building stones, and must rather regard them as plausible hypotheses of great intrinsic interest and value.

It should be noted that Freeman in his own interpretation is somewhat more ambitious than this. In a table of his, Freeman (1948) identifies his arousal factor with Wenger's factor of emotional lability, or autonomic imbalance, and with Jost's emotionality factor; he also identifies his discharge control factor with Wenger's muscular tension and Jost's so-called central factor. This identification does not rest on a secure basis. Fortunately we have an objective test for its adequacy. The discharge control factor is based very largely on recovery quotient measures, and has high correlations with ratings on emotional instability or neuroticism. Similarly, the emotional lability-autonomic imbalance factor of Wenger and the emotional factor of Jost showed high correlations with neuroticism. In consequence, if there is to be any identification of factors for these various workers, surely it would be along the lines indicated by the above correlations, i.e. discharge control would be identified with emotional lability-autonomic imbalance, and with emotionality. Freeman's arousal factor has no significant correlation with neuroticism. It is difficult therefore to see how he can identify it with Wenger's and Jost's factors having high correlations with neuroticism.

We do not claim that this brief discussion of factor identification can have any finality. Until all the measures used by these various workers are included in one battery, it will be impossible to give an adequate appraisal of Freeman's hypothesis. However, in so far as the data have been presented, they seem to contra-indicate Freeman's identification and support the one suggested above. Here indeed is a most fruitful field of research, full of great possibilities, and it would be ungenerous to end this account of Freeman's outstanding work on a note of minor criticism. His contribution is one of the very few in the field of personality organization which follows the dictates of scientific method, beginning as it does with a clearly defined hypothesis and going on to verify deductions made from this. If at times the reader may find it difficult to agree with some of the assumptions made (the writer, for instance, finds it difficult to accept the proposition that as stimulus intensity is arithmetically increased the skin conductance index of energy mobilization varies as a logarithm of its base), he is always enabled to set his mind at rest by direct experimental proof. Hitherto, unfortunately, Freeman's contribution has been somewhat neglected by clinical psychologists, who appear to prefer the unverified and often unverifiable claims of "organismicists" and projective techniques experts to the demonstrated validity of at least some of Freeman's procedures. Future scientists may regard this phenomenon as an odd misplacement of energy, and it is to be hoped that the balance will soon be restored.

Supporting the work of Freeman in some respects is a study by Ellison (1953) who studied "Four groups of children composed of normals, behaviour problems, children with one schizophrenic parent and children with one epileptic parent . . . with respect to their physiological reactions to stress conditions induced by hyperventilation and the cold pressor test. Physiological measures consisted of electro-encephalogram, electromyogram, galvanic skin response, respiration and heart rate." It was found that resting or "basal" levels of activity did not differentiate the groups, but both testing procedures resulted in patterns of somatic and autonomic responses which were differential for normal and behaviour problem children. These have been interpreted as instabilities of physiological adjustment, possible predisposition to behavioural maladjustment. Children

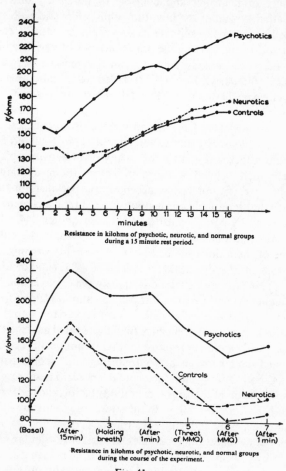

Resistance in kilohms of psychotic, neurotic, and normal groups
during a 15 minute rest period.

Resistance in kilohms of psychotic, neurotic, and normal groups
during the course of the experiment.

Fig. 41. —

of schizophrenics tended to react more like the behaviour problem children, whereas the children of epileptics were more like the normal group.

Significant differences both in resting level and in reaction to stress have also been found by S. B. G. Eysenck (1956) between psychotic, neurotic and normal control subjects. The stresses in this case were rather minor, consisting of such things as holding the breath, being told that some questions from the Maudsley Medical Questionnaire would be asked, and actually asking these questions. Some of the results are shown in Fig. 41.

The failure of neurotics and controls to be clearly differentiated here is rather typical of the literature; thus, Herr and Kobler (1953) concluded that "When suitable care is taken to satisfy reasonably the assumptions underlying the use of analysis of variance in PGSR data, it becomes unlikely that one can differentiate normals from neurotics." Similarly, Hsü (1952) failed to obtain any striking correspondence between PGR and word association data in students.

In recent years there has been an increase in the interest taken in electroencephalography and as long ago as 1946 Hsü and Sherman carried out a factorial analysis of twenty-two electroencephalogram variables which resulted in five main factors, the meaningfulness of which, however, is not widely accepted by specialists in this field. Since then the literature has grown considerably and has been reviewed most recently by Mundy-Castle (1958) who quotes 444 references. Most of these are not directly relevant to the topics here discussed but some of them do relate directly to personality organization.

The work of Mundy-Castle himself (1956, 1957) and of Biesheuvel and Pitt (1956) suggests a relationship between extraversion and high alpha frequency, and between introversion and low alpha frequency. "Subjects rated as relatively quick, impulsive, variable and stimulable ... possess higher alpha frequency than those rated as relatively slow, cautious, steady and hyporeactive ... Significant positive correlations were also found between alpha frequency and scores from tasks involving both motor and perceptual speed. These results were explained in terms of the central excitability factor, and it was proposed that the behavioural qualities in question are genetically influenced, forming a relatively enduring substrate of personality. As such they are believed to reflect a temperamental variable." Similar results are reported by Gastaut (1951, 1957; see also Delafresnaye, 1954). In addition, Gastaut also introduced an independent variable labelled lability or cortical instability, encompassing theta and beta rhythms on a background of 9–11 c/sec. alpha rhythms. As Mundy-Castle points out "The psychological correlates of this third class relate chiefly to instability and immaturity of personality and to affective lability, the underlying mechanism being considered as a lack of stability in the regulation of cortical excitability."

It seems likely that this second factor is an index of what we have called neuroticism. To quote Mundy-Castle again, "The occurrence of slow (theta and delta) and/or fast beta rhythms, have [sic!] often been reported as prominent in maladjusted and unstable personality"; twenty references are then given by Munday-Castle to these studies. The possible relationship between electroencephalographic records and basic temperamental traits may be as shown in Fig. 42.

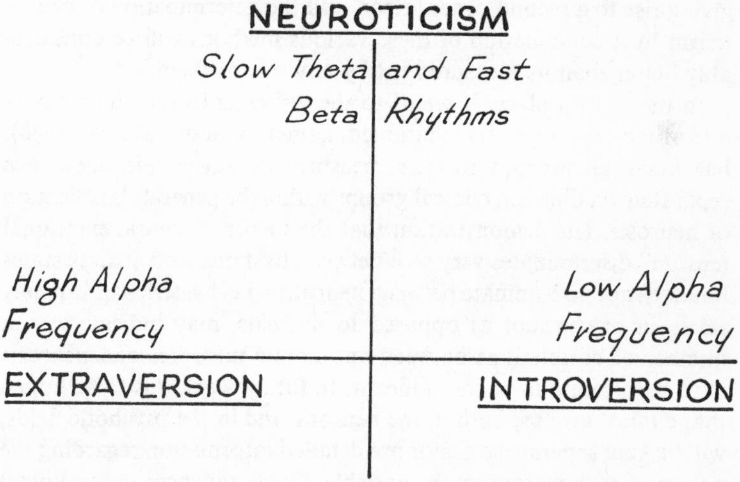

NEUROTICISM

Slow Theta and Fast Beta Rhythms

High Alpha Frequency

Low Alpha Frequency

EXTRAVERSION   INTROVERSION

Fig. 42.

It cannot be too strongly emphasized, however, that the evidence for this postulated relationship is very indirect and that until more psychologically orientated studies are carried out to test the hypothesis directly, it cannot be regarded as being more than suggestive.

In coming to a general conclusion regarding the value of the work presented in this chapter, several points should be emphasized. In the first place, it does not seem to the writer that the factors isolated by Wenger, Jost, Theron, Freeman, and so forth can be identified directly with each other, as several of these authors have tried to do. It is quite likely that there is a certain amount of communality between tests of autonomic function taken in the resting state, taken during frustration or under stress, and taken during the period of recovery, but as each of the authors mentioned has concentrated almost entirely on one of these different methods, the factors isolated cannot be generalized to cover all of them. In view of the fact that each author has demonstrated considerable correlation between neuroticism, as assessed either clinically, or by ratings, or inventories, and one of the factors isolated, it follows that either the multiple determination of neuroticism by all these methods combined will have very high validity indeed, or, of course, that all these methods would correlate highly together. The truth will probably be found to be intermediate between these extremes; the various factors isolated will probably be correlated to a fairly appreciable extent, giving rise to a second-order factor, and the determination of neuroticism by a combination of these various methods will be considerably better than its measurement by any one of them.

In the second place, it seems to the writer unfortunate that only one of the experimenters mentioned, namely Van der Merwe (1948), has made an attempt to take measures of autonomic imbalance separately on different clinical groups within the general classification of neurosis. His demonstration that the factor of "basic emotional tension" discriminates very well between hysterics and anxiety states but does not discriminate between neurotics (i.e. hysterics and anxiety states in one group) as opposed to normals, may indicate why a number of correlations between autonomic measures and neurosis have been found to be insignificant. In future work it is to be hoped that clinical groups, both in the neurotic and in the psychotic fields, will be kept separate so that more detailed information regarding the nature of each factor may be possible. Great advances in our knowledge are likely to accrue from such a procedure.

In the third place, it seems to the writer that the number of cases used in the factorial studies mentioned has usually been rather inadequate, the only exception to this rule being the work of Wenger. This writer has established his conclusions beyond cavil in two ways: (1) by repeated measurements, factor analysis, and determination of factor scores several times on small samples, showing that each time results were very similar; and (2) by using really large groups of between 400 and 500 people in his work. It is only by such long-continued experimentation and demonstration of repeatability of results that factor analysis can overcome its inherent difficulty of not possessing adequate tests of factorial significance.

In the fourth place attention should be drawn to the fact that in spite of the large volume of work that has been done in the field of autonomic reactivity, its quality has not usually been high. This is particularly obvious in studies using the PGR; over 90% of published work makes use of indices of change which are highly contaminated with resting level resistance. Many of the errors committed are no doubt avoidable, but in many cases sufficient knowledge is simply not available on the physiological basis of the phenomena in question to make meaningful measurement possible. Here, as in so many other parts of psychology, the desire to apply promising new methods has led to a tendency on the part of research workers to neglect fundamental problems and to rush instead into the applied field. This point is developed in great detail by Martin (1959) in her review of "Somatic Responses"; it will not be further documented here.

Altogether, it is the writer's opinion that while only a beginning has been made in this field of study, this beginning is so promising that a great deal of research endeavour should be devoted to clarifying some of the issues involved. The obvious promise of a method which would enable us to establish a person's degree of neuroticism or introversion-extraversion by means of quite objective physiological measures will not be gainsaid by anyone; we are clearly dealing with constitutional factors of the greatest importance.

One great difficulty, however, has been pointed out and experimentally demonstrated by Lacey (1950) and his collaborators (1952, 1953, 1958). This relates to what he has called "The principle of autonomic response—stereotypy" or, more simply, autonomic response specificity. Using a variety of response channels, he found that his subjects "respond with a hierarchy of activation, being relatively over-active in some physiological measures, under-active in others, while exhibiting average reactivity in still other measures. These patterns of response seem to be idiosyncratic, each S's pattern is different. For a single stressor, patterns of response have been shown to be reproducible, both upon immediate retest and over a period of nine months. Moreover, the pattern of response obtained with one stimulus condition tends to be reproduced in other, quite different, stimulus conditions." Lacey stated his findings in the form of a general principle which reads as follows: "For a given set of autonomic functions, S s tend to respond with an idiosyncratic pattern of autonomic activation in which maximal activation is shown by the same physiological function, whatever the stress." Lacey also postulated and found "That continuous quantitative variation among

314   THE STRUCTURE OF HUMAN PERSONALITY

S s exists in the degree to which they exhibit stereotypy (reproducibility) of their pattern of response." (Two examples of idiosyncratic response patterns may be quoted from a paper by Lacey and Lacey (1958); they are given below in Fig. 43.)

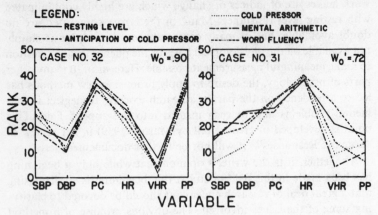

Fig. 43.—Two examples of idiosyncratic response-patterns (autonomic-tension scores) reproduced over five occasions of measurement.

Physiological variables are on the abscissae. The ordinates are ranks, showing the relative position of the S in the total group of 42 Ss. High ranks are given to high physiological levels of function. W_0' is the coefficient of pattern-concordance, corrected for continuity.

The variables at the base line are systolic and diastolic blood pressure, palmar conductance, heart rate, variability of heart rate and pulse pressure. The four stressors used in addition to the resting level are shown in the legend above the figure.

The reader may remember our discussion of the difficulties raised by the possibility of "alternative manifestations" in the case of ratings, where Frenkel-Brunswik (1942) had pointed out that "Different classes of behavioural expressions were often related to one drive as alternative manifestations of that drive." Apparently the same problem arises in the case of physiological response measures where neuroticism and other general behaviour patterns may be reflected not in the general elevation of autonomic activity, but rather in the specific elevation of one or two specific autonomic indices. If this were so and Lacey's work certainly lends strong support to this hypothesis, then we can understand at once the reason for the universally low correlations obtained even by the most successful experimenters such as Wenger, and we can also understand the reasons for the contradictory results so frequently reported in the literature.

It is important to realize that while Lacey's results leave no doubt about the existence of a considerable degree of response specificity, they do not rule out completely the existence of a certain amount of general reactivity, as shown in the work of Wenger. These two writers stress different aspects of a given situation, but the positive results achieved by either does not rule out or contradict those achieved by the other. As pointed out in an earlier chapter, the question is not one of specificity or generality, but rather a quantitative question of how much specificity and how much generality. Until both aspects are studied in one and the same investigation only a very hesitant answer can be given to this question. It is to be hoped that more detailed comparative studies of these two factors will be carried out in the near future to clarify this issue. The only study which has come to hand (Terry, 1953) certainly supports Lacey's point of view rather than Wenger's. (Indeed Wenger's most recent work (1957) suggests the modification of an earlier view although he still stresses patterns of reactivity.) Terry used a variety of physiological measures (skin conductance and potential, blood pressure and heart periods) with particular reference to autonomic change and to resting level; but also included a number of the Guilford questionnaires in his factor analysis. Two main findings from his work are relevant here. In the first place, "Far from supporting the assumption of generalized autonomic balance and imbalance, the present investigation has separated out the various measures of autonomic response into factors representing mainly single organs and systems. The data are in close accord with the findings of Lacey and his associates on autonomic response specificity and offer rather strong support to the concept of specialized autonomic balance." The other main finding is that "The relationships reported here between patterns of autonomic response and traits of temperament are so uncertain as to require little discussion. The correlations between autonomic activity and self-rated traits bear no similarity to the findings of Darling (1940) and of Wenger (1941), nor can the correlations be compared with the results of the study in which Wenger (1948) used the Guilford-Martin Scales . . . On the basis of the present study, then, one must conclude that there are no clearly demonstrable relationships between measures of traits of temperament and sets of scores in autonomic reactivity."

REFERENCES

Chapter VIII

BIESHEUVEL, S., and PITT, D. R. Some tests of speed and tempo of behavior as predictors of the primary-secondary function temperament variable. *J. Nat. Inst. Personnel Res.*, 1956, **6**, 87–94.

DARLING, R. P. Autonomic action in relation to personality traits of children. *J. abnorm. soc. Psychol.*, 1940, **35**, 246–260.

DARROW, C. W. The equation of the galvanic skin reflex curve. *J. genet. Psychol.*, 1937, **16**, 285–309.

DARROW, C. W., and HEATH, L. L. Reaction tendencies relating to personality. In: *Studies in the Dynamics of Behavior*. (Ed. Lashley, K. S.) Chicago: Univ. Chicago Press, 1932.

DELAFRESNAYE, J. F. *Brain Mechanisms and Consciousness*. Oxford: Blackwell, 1954 (Ed.).

ELLISON, A. J. Response to physiological stress in normal and behaviour problem children. *J. genet. Psychol.*, 1953, **83**, 19–29.

EPPINGER, H., and HESS, W. R. Vagotonia. *Nerv. Ment. Dis. Monogr.*, 1917, **20**.

EYSENCK, H. J. *The Scientific Study of Personality*. London: Routledge & Kegan Paul, 1952.

EYSENCK, S. B. G. An experimental study of psychogalvanic reflex responses of normal, neurotic, and psychotic subjects. *J. psychoanal. Res.*, 1956, **1**, 258–272.

FREEMAN, G. L. Towards a psychiatric Plimsoll mark: physiological recovery quotients in experimentally induced frustration. *J. Psychol.*, 1939, **8**, 247–252.

The Energetics of Human Behavior. Ithaca, N.Y.; Cornell Univ. Press, 1948.

FREEMAN, G. L., and PATHMAN, J. H. The relation of overt muscular discharge to physiological recovery from experimentally induced displacement. *J. exp. Psychol.*, 1942, **30**, 161–174.

Physiological reactions to experimentally induced displacement. *Amer. J. Psychiat.*, 1943, **100**, 406–412.

FREEMAN, G. L., and KATZOFF, E. T. Individual differences in physiological reactions to stimulation and their relation to other measures of emotionality. *J. exp. Psychol.*, 1942, **31**, 527–537.

FRENKEL-BRUNSWIK, E. Motivation and behavior. *Genet. Psychol. Monogr.*, 1942, **26**, 121–265.

GASTAUT, H. Confrontation entre les données de l'électroencéphalogramme et des examens psychologiques chez 522 sujets répartis en trois groupes différents. Conclusions d'ensemble. *EEG Clin. Neurophysiol. Supp.*, 1957, **6**, 321–338.

GASTAUT, H. & Y., ROGER, A., CARRIOL, J., and NAQUET, R. Etude électrographique du cycle d'excitabilité cortical. *EEG. Clin. Neurophysiol.*, 1951. **3**, 401–428.

HERR, V. V., and KOHLER, F. J. A psychogalvanometric test for neuroticism. *J. abnorm. soc. Psychol.*, 1953, **48**, 410–416.

HOCH, P., KUBIS, J. F., and ROUKE, F. L. Psychogalvanometric investigations in psychoses and other abnormal mental states. *Psychosom. Med.*, 1944, **6**, 237–243.

Hsü, E. H. Quantification of electroencephalography. *J. Psychol.*, 1946, **22**, 125–129.

Comparative study of factor patterns, physiologically and psychologically determined. *J. genet. Psychol.*, 1952, **47**, 105–128.

Hsü, E. H., and SHERMAN, M. The factorial analysis of the electroencephalogram. *J. Psychol.*, 1946, **21**, 189–196.

JOST, H. Some physiological changes during frustration. *Child Develpm.*, 1941, **12**, 9–15.

LACEY, J. I. Individual differences in somatic response patterns. *J. comp. physiol. Psychol.*, 1950, **43**, 338–350.

LACEY, J. I., and LEHN, R. V. Differential emphasis on somatic response to stress. *Psychosom. Med.*, 1952, **14**, 71–81.

LACEY, J. I., BATEMAN, D. E., and LEHN, R. V. Autonomic response specificity: an experimental study. *Psychosom. Med.*, 1953, **15**, 8–21.

LACEY, J. I., and LACEY, B. C. Verification and extension of the principle of autonomic response-stereotypy. *Amer. J. Psychol.*, 1958, **71**, 50–73.

MARTIN, IRENE. *Somatic Responses.* In: Eysenck, H. J. (Ed.), *Handbook of Abnormal Psychology.* London: Pitmans, 1960.

MUNDY-CASTLE, A. C. The relationship between primary-secondary function and the alpha rhythm of the electroencephalogram. *J. Nat. Inst. Personnel Res.*, 1956, **6**, 95–102.

L'électroencéphalogramme et sa rélation avec le tempérament. *EEG Clin. Neurophysiol.*, 1957, Suppl. **6**, 221–233.

An appraisal of electroencephalography in relation to psychology. *J. Nat. Inst. Personnel Res.*, *Monogr.*, Suppl. 2., 1958.

ÖDEGARD, O. The psychogalvanic reactivity in normals and various psychopathic conditions. *Acta psych. and Neur.*, 1930, **5**, 55–105.

SANFORD, R. N., ADKINS, M. M., MILLER, R. B., and COBB, E. Physique, personality and scholarship. *Mon. Soc. Res. Child Develpm.*, 1943, **7**, Ser. No. 34.

SHERMAN, M., and JOST, H. Quantification of psycho-physiological measures. *Psychosom. Med.*, 1945, **7**, 215–219.

Frustration reactions of normal and neurotic persons. *J. Psychol.*, 1942, **13**, 3–19.

TERRY, P. G. Autonomic balance and temperament. *J. comp. physiol. Psychol.*, 1953, **46**, 454–460.

THERON, P. A. Peripheral vasomotor reactions as indices of basic emotional tension and lability. *Psychosom. Med.*, 1948, **10**, 335–346.

VAN DER MERWE, A. B. The diagnostic value of peripheral vasomotor reactions in the psychoneuroses. *Psychosom. Med.*, 1948, **10**, 347–354.

VAN DER MERWE, A. B., and THERON, P. A. A new method of measuring emotional stability. *J. genet. Psychol.*, 1947, **37**, 109.

WENGER, M. A. The measurement of individual differences in autonomic balance. *Psychosom. Med.*, 1941, **3**, 427–434.

The stability of measurement of autonomic balance. *Psychosom. Med.*, 1942, **4**, 94–95.

Studies of autonomic balance in Army Air Forces personnel. *Comp. Psychol. Mon.*, 1948, **19**, 1–111.

Pattern analyses of autonomic variables during rest. *Psychosom. Med.*, 1957, **19**, 240–244.

WHITEHORN, J. C., and RICHTER, H. Unsteadiness of the heart rate in psychotic and neurotic states. *Ann. Rev. Neur. Psychiat.*, 1937, **38**, 62–70.

THE ANALYSIS OF PHYSIQUE (BODY BUILD)

THE BELIEF THAT constitutional factors play an important part in personality is held very widely. Unfortunately, there are few areas of psychology in which a greater superstructure has been built on so small a factual foundation. A salutary check to the endless speculation of psychologists, physiologists, phrenologists, psychiatrists, anthropometrists, endocrinologists, and others was provided in 1930 by the publication of Patterson's *Physique and Intellect*. In this book he made a thorough survey of the available literature, and came to the conclusion that: "our detailed survey of available quantitative evidence has demonstrated that prevalent notions regarding the intimacy of the relationship between physical traits and intellect have been greatly exaggerated. . . . The suggestion is frequently encountered that physical traits may be found associated to a greater extent with temperament than with intellect. Even here, however, little optimism is justified. An intimate connection between body build and temperament has not been disclosed." A good deal of research has been carried on since Patterson's monograph appeared, particularly with respect to body build and its relation to personality, and we must investigate with particular care the validity of the claims advanced by various recent writers that the dearth of positive findings reported by Patterson was due to faulty methods of investigation rather than to a lack of relationship between constitution and personality.

This is not the place to give an historical review of attempts to set up constitutional typologies. We shall merely note the main landmarks and otherwise refer the reader to Table 47, which sets out briefly the various systems advanced by a large number of writers. As is appropriate, the first name in that list is that of Hippocrates who, about 430 B.C., described two antithetical types of body build which he called the *habitus apoplecticus* and *habitus phthisicus*. The former was thick-set, strong, and muscular; the latter thin, delicate, and weak. While many later writers followed this dichotomy, others interpolated a third type intermediate between these extremes, as did, for instance, the Frenchman Rostan (1828), with his digestive, muscular, and respiratory-cerebral type; the German Beneke (1878), with his

318

phlegmatic, athletic, and asthenic-cerebral types; the Italians Viola (1933) and DiGiovanni (1919), with their microsplanchnic, normosplanchnic, and macrosplanchnic types; and the American Wells (1869), with his motive or mechanical system, vital or nutritive system, and mental or nervous system.

TABLE 47

BODY TYPE

Author	Eurymorph	Mesomorph	Leptomorph[1]
Hippocrates (430 B.C.)	Habitus apoplecticus	—	Habitus phthisicus
Halle (1797)	Abdominal	Muscular	Cephalic
Rostan (1828)	Digestive	Muscular	Cerebral-respiratory
Walker (1852)	Nutritive	Locomotive	Mental
Carus (1852)	Phlegmatic	Athletic	Cerebral-asthenic
Wells (1869)	Vital	Motive	Mental
Beneke (1878)	Hyperplastic	Normal	Hypoplastic
Huter (1880)	Food-type	Strength-type	Sensation-type
Virenius (1904)	Connective	Muscular	Nervous-epithelial
Sigaud (1914)	Digestive	Muscular	Cerebral-respiratory
Mills (1917)	Hypersthenic	Sthenic	Asthenic
Viola (1933)	Megalosplanchnic	Normosplanchnic	Microsplanchnic
Stockard (1923)	Lateral	Intermediate	Linear
Bauer (1924)	Hypersthenic	Sthenic	Asthenic
Kretschmer (1948)	Pyknic	Athletic	Leptosome (Asthenic)
Sheldon (1940)	Endomorph	Mesomorph	Ectomorph
Burt (1947)	Pachysome	—	Leptosome
Martiny (1948)	Entoblastique	Mesoblastique	Ectoblastique

Many other writers apart from those mentioned in Table 25 were ringing changes on the same general theme, some of them putting forward hypotheses also regarding the connection between their various physical types with temperament. It was not, however, until Kretschmer (1925) published the first edition of his rightly famous *Körperbau und Charakter* that psychologists and psychiatrists became seriously interested in this general field. Kretschmer took over essentially Rostan's three types, calling the thick-set, round type the

[1] The terms used in the heading of this Table to describe the three main body types were suggested by Rees and Eysenck (1945), and are used here because they are purely descriptive, operationally defined, and do not carry overtones of any particular system. Eurymorph, mesomorph, and leptomorph are defined in terms of observed distributions of body-build indices, calculated according to the Rees-Eysenck formula; "mesomorph" refers to indices lying within $\pm$ 1 S.D. of the mean, "eurymorph" to indices lying more than 1 S.D. in the pyknic direction, and "leptomorph" to indices lying more than 1 S.D. in the asthenic-leptosomatic direction.

pyknic, the thin, lean type the *asthenic* or *leptosomatic*, and the intermediate type the *athletic*. He also added another concept, that of the *dysplastic* type of body build, which essentially denotes an incompatible mixture of different types in different parts of the body.

To this essentially threefold division on the physical side he added an essentially threefold division on the mental side. In the first editions of his book, the temperamental typology was a twofold one based on the two main groups of functional psychoses, the schizophrenias, and the manic-depressive disorders respectively. Schizophrenics were found to be largely leptosomatic in body build, manic-depressives largely pyknic. In later years he has come more and more to regard (on the physical side) the athletic type as not being intermediate between the other two but as being quite separate from them in many ways. Similarly, on the level of personality description, he has taken the epileptic as his third prototype, postulating a special set of traits as characterizing the epileptic personality, and linking this type with athletic and dysplastic body build. Table 48 shows the distribution of some 8,000 cases of schizophrenic, manic-depressive illness, and epilepsy with respect to their body build; while these figures are subject to much criticism (lack of correction for age, subjectivity of body-type ratings, subjectivity of clinical diagnosis, different standards of different investigators), they nevertheless illustrate a conclusion which is forced on the reader after a careful survey of the whole literature (Eysenck, 1947), namely that when all is said and done there is a genuine difference in body build between schizophrenics and manic-depressives; the conclusion with respect to epilepsy is much less certain and is still subject to discussion.

TABLE 48

*Distribution (in per cent.) of Body Type for Schizophrenic,
Manic-depressive, and Epileptic Groups*

	Schizophrenics: 5,233 *cases*	Manic-depressives: 1,361 *cases*	Epileptics: 1,505 *cases*
Pyknic . .	13·7	64·6	5·5
Athletic . .	16·9	6·7	28·9
Leptosomatic .	50·3	19·2	25·1
Dysplastic .	10·5	1·1	29·5
Doubtful .	8·6	8·4	11·0

While the demonstration of the correlation between body build and psychosis might be of interest to psychiatrists, Kretschmer's real contribution to psychology lies rather in his hypothesis regarding the "schizothymia" and "cyclothymia" types as constituting a fundamental dimension of personality, of which the schizophrene and the manic-depressive were merely the exaggerated prototypes. He devoted a great deal of ingenuity and considerable psychological insight to the experimental proof of this proposition. A survey of most of the available material has been published by Eysenck (1950), who draws attention to three main points. In the first place, Kretschmer in his proof is considerably handicapped by lack of statistical sophistication. While most of the experiments reported by him with respect to differences of groups of manic-depressives and schizophrenics, or between normal people of leptosomatic and pyknic body build, give results which are significant when the proper tests are carried out, his overall methods of verifying his general hypothesis are faulty although ingenious, and cannot prove or disprove his case. In the second place, the tests designed by Kretschmer in order to measure the various traits postulated by him to characterize the schizothyme or the cyclothyme respectively are of the very greatest interest and importance and deserve a through investigation by means of more advanced statistical and experimental methods. In the third place, both Kretschmer's hypotheses and his methods have been very much misrepresented in the non-German literature, due perhaps to the fact that no translation has been made of any of the later editions of his book in which he incorporated the experimental evidence as it accumulated and in which he modified his theories and hypotheses accordingly.

The outline of Kretschmer's system was very closely followed by Sheldon (1940, 1942, 1949), who has also incorporated a number of ideas from other writers and has used various novel techniques. The first of the general ideas which characterize Sheldon's scheme is derived from such writers as Bessonet-Favre (1910), Bauer (1923), and Castellino (1927), who try to link up the different types of body build with the three germinal layers in the embryo. As is well known, there are three of these—the ectoderm, endoderm, and mesoderm, to which should perhaps be added the mesenchyme (Hertwig, 1881), which acts as a kind of "packing tissue" between the other germinal layers and gives rise to the connective tissues, the myocardium and the vis- ceral musculature, the endocardium and the endothelium of the blood vessels, the lymph glands, lymph vessels, and the spleen. Body types resulting from over-development of either of these components would correspond approximately to Kretschmer's pyknics (endoderms), athletics (mesoderms), and leptosomatics (ectoderms). Fig. 44 presents such an embryological scheme as developed by Martiny (1948), whose biological arguments are somewhat more plausible than Sheldon's.

In his inspection of some 4,000 male bodies, Sheldon found three extreme types of variants which corresponded closely to Kretschmer's three types. In the first of these, Kretschmer's pyknic type, Sheldon found that "the digestive viscera, especially the gut, held a more or less predominant position in the organic economy. In these people the most manifest external characteristic is a conspicuous laying on of fat, which is an indication of predominance of the absorptive functions—the functions of the gut—over the energy-expending functions." He goes on to say that: "The functional elements of the digestive system are derived embryologically almost entirely from the endoderm, the innermost of the original three embryonic layers. We can quite naturally therefore refer to the extremes of type one as those exhibiting a condition of *endomorphy*."

In a similar way, bones, muscles, connective tissue, and the heart and blood vessels were seen to predominate overwhelmingly in the variants of type two, which correspond to Kretschmer's athletics. This type he therefore called the *mesomorph*, as these functions are derived predominantly from the mesoderm, the second embryonic layer. As regard the third type, Kretschmer's leptosomatic or asthenic type, "the principal derivatives from the embryonic ectodermal layer are the skin itself, hair and nails, sense organs (exteroceptors), and the nervous system, including the brain. Relative to total bodily mass, all these organs are conspicuous in the bodily economy of the extreme variants of type three. . . . Hence, we have named them *ectomorphs* or persons exhibiting ectomorphy".

Having thus adopted the Continental ideas of embryological determination of body type, Sheldon introduces another idea borrowed from Plattner (1938), namely that of considering these three genetic "factors" as components of total body build, each having a certain determinable influence. This influence is rated by Sheldon on a seven-point scale so that each body type may be represented by a set of three numbers denoting respectively the influence of each of the three components. Thus, 117 would be a person characterized by an almost complete lack in endomorphy and mesomorphy, and a complete dominance of the ectomorphy component. All other combinations are similarly described in terms of three numbers. It will be seen that there are 343 theoretical possibilities of deriving

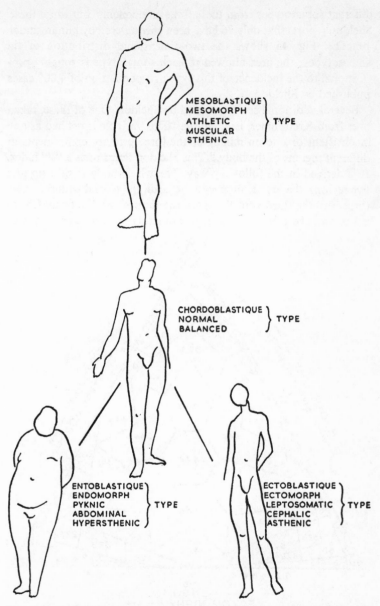

Fig. 44.—Martiny's Diagrammatic Representation of three Main Body Types derived according to the Hypothesis of Embryological Development.

different somatotypes from these three components, but of all these Sheldon reports that only 76 have been encountered by him in actual practice. Fig. 45 shows the two-dimensional distribution of the somatotypes; the area allowed to each somatotype is roughly proportional to the incidence of this type in a population of 4,000 cases published by Sheldon.

Several additional scales are used by Sheldon. One of these, taken over from Kretschmer, is *dysplasia*. "This variable is defined as any inconsistent or uneven mixing of the three primary components in different regions of the body." This Sheldon refers to as a "*d*" index. It is derived in the following way. The whole body is split up into five regions, the first dealing with the head, the second with the trunk (breadth), the third with the arms, the fourth with the trunk (thickness), and the fifth with the legs. Somatotype ratings are made of

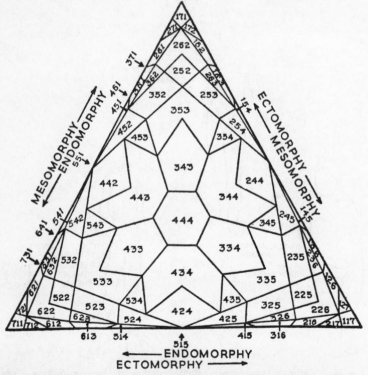

Fig. 45.—Showing a Two-dimensional Distribution of the Somatotypes. The area allotted to each Somatotype is roughly proportional to the incidence of the Somatotype in a population of 4,000 cases.

each of these five regions, and the sum of the disagreements constitutes the "*d*" index.

Another index, the "*g*" index, is concerned with gynandromorphy, i.e. the extent to which a physique presents traits ordinarily associated with the opposite sex. Lastly, yet another index, the "*t*" index, is found, which relates to textual variations among persons, ranging from coarse to fine. The description of this index in Sheldon's work is not at all clear, but Sheldon reports a re-rating reliability on 1,000 cases of ·93.

The only really novel contribution which Sheldon has made to this field is his technique of anthropometric measurement. He makes use of a photographic technique in which each subject is photographed identically posed from three different angles; all measures and ratings are then taken from these standard photographs. There are obvious advantages in this method, although one would like to know a good deal more about repeat reliabilities and correlations of measures so obtained with those derived from more orthodox procedures.

Assessment of Sheldon's contribution so far is difficult. Most of his ideas are derivative rather than original, although there can be no doubt that he has popularized the constitutional type of study in the U.S.A., where this field had been relatively neglected. It is probable that, as far as description of human physique goes, his method, if carefully followed, would give a more accurate and more complete picture than any other yet available. However, a number of questions arise which would have to be answered before his system can be adopted. Most important of these is that of the lack of independence of his three components. On p. 138 of his book, Sheldon gives scatter diagrams showing correlations between his components for 2,000 men and 1,000 women. Correlations between the first and second components are relatively low ($-$ ·32 and $-$ ·11 respectively for the men and the women). Between the third and the first components, correlations are considerable ($-$ ·27 and $-$ ·70). For the correlations between the third and the second components coefficients are again considerable ($-$ ·64 and $-$ ·41). It is quite clear that Sheldon's three types could be described much more parsimoniously in terms of two orthogonal factors, as indeed would seem inevitable in view of the factorial results summarized earlier in this chapter.

This has been shown very clearly by Ekman in two important contributions (1951). As he points out: "Our principal task has been to find out whether Sheldon's morphological system could not be simplified by reducing the dimensions from three to two. It would appear that this question can be answered very definitely in the affirmative." (p. 87.) Ekman goes on to show that a similar simplification is possible in the psychological field, where Sheldon's three dimensions can equally well be reduced to two. He also proves that the correlations between body build and temperament, using Sheldon's material, is not lessened by this transformation. Altogether, Ekman's treatment is much more sophisticated and definite than Sheldon's, and students of the problem of human physique should benefit considerably from a perusal of his contribution.

Similarly, Humphreys (1957) found evidence for the existence of only two independent types of physique in Sheldon's data. Howells (1952) obtained results from a factorial analysis of correlations between persons who were markedly dominant in one of Sheldon's three components, showing that ectomorphy and endomorphy are not independent factors, but are opposite manifestations of one underlying factor. Sills (1950), who correlated somatotype ratings with a number of measurement ratios, also came to a similar conclusion. The facts seem to support Humphrey's (1957) recommendation to the effect that "Research workers, if they want to make use of Sheldon's types, are advised to discard one physical type and the corresponding temperament type. This would result in a saving of measurement time and statistical analysis of data . . . Even if the research worker in this field discards one of the three types, he can still have no confidence in the meaningfulness of the two retained."

This conclusion is subject, of course, to one important proviso. On a purely descriptive basis, two factors may do all that Sheldon's three types can do. If, however, it could be shown that these three types are real derivatives from certain embryological layers and are functionally continuous with these layers, then the observed intercorrelations among the types would be a cheap price to pay for the gain in understanding obtained through this relationship. It would still, of course, be necessary to postulate some causative agency responsible for these intercorrelations, a point completely neglected by Sheldon; nevertheless, no one would deny that wherever there is a conflict between statistical factors and physiological, anatomical, or genetic determination, it is the statistical factor which should be thrown overboard rather than these more palpable influences.

When we look at the evidence presented by Sheldon in favour of his scheme, we find that it is rather unsatisfactory. Apart from neglecting the considerable complexity of the development of the germ layers (the interested reader may refer to Hamilton, Boyd and Mossman, 1945, for a concise account of the known facts regarding embryological development), Sheldon has at no point attempted to make deductions from his hypotheses, which could be used to verify or refute his theory. Many such deductions are suggested by a careful reading of the relevant literature. The ectoderm is concerned with the development of the enamel organ germs of the permanent teeth, various parts of the eye, and the sensory epithelia of the olfactory and auditory organs. It would seem to follow that the ectomorphic person should show measurable differences with respect to quality of teeth, sensory acuity of eye and ear and nose as compared with the other types. Similar deductions could be made for the other somatotypes. It should be possible to make detailed developmental studies on animals, possibly even including genetic changes, which might lead to a verification of this embryological hypothesis. In the absence of such evidence, the whole scheme remains entirely speculative, and must therefore be considered inferior from the point of view of simplicity of description to the factorial one outlined above. Unless the embryological hypothesis can be substantiated and unless some causal factor can be found to account for the negative correlations in the development of the three components, Sheldon's whole system must remain an interesting but speculative attempt to probe beyond the observed interconnections to some hypothetical underlying causes.

Far from supporting Sheldon's concepts, the facts actually seem to be in contradiction to it, if anything. Hunt (1949), to take but one example, has forcibly pointed out the lack of agreement between somatic characteristics and the degree of development of the endodermal, mesodermal and ectodermal derivates.

One remaining question relates to the permanence of the somatotype. In 1940 Sheldon wrote that: "It has been possible to follow the development of several hundred individuals over a period of about a dozen years, and while many have shown sharp fluctuations in weight, we have discovered no case in which there has been a convincing change in the somatotype." In 1949, Sheldon appears to retract what to most readers will be the clear import of that statement by saying: "I have not yet seen a case which seems to present, after careful study, a change in the somatotype, but I have seen cases in which I changed my mind as to how the somatotype should be read. In other words, I have seen later (and earlier) photographs of individuals that seem to introduce new evidence as to the strength of one or more of the primary components, and have thus been led to a revision of a former estimate of somatotype. . . . When I wrote that no case had been discovered in which there had been a convincing change in the somatotype, I meant that in all cases where there *seemed* to be a change I had been convinced on re-examination of both or all photographs that I (or someone) had made an unnecessary error in the first judgment." It is quite clear, then, that the somatotype *as rated* may change, although Sheldon may be right in his contention that the morphogenotype, which he defines as "the three-dimensional trajectory through time along which an organism will travel under basal conditions", does not change. That, of course, is a personal opinion, and he attempts no proof in its favour.

The evidence does not seem to favour Sheldon's opinion. Lasker

TABLE 49

Correlations of Ratings for Male and Female Somatotype between
Ages 12 × 17 × 33

Groups	Endomorphy		Mesomorphy		Ectomorphy	
	12 × 17	17 × 33	12 × 17	17 × 33	12 × 17	17 × 33
Total males (N = 74 at ages 12 and 17, 38 at 33)	·663	·023	·731	·823	·707	·764
Average maturing males (N = 43 at ages 12 and 17, 19 at 33)	·550	− ·025	·723	·966	·681	·753
Total females (N = 78 at ages 12 and 17, 39 at 33)	·668	·247	·832	·787	·843	·717
Average maturing females (N = 43 at ages 12 and 17, 19 at 33)	·515	·051	·682	·773	·848	·690

(1947) found that the somatotype ratings of photographs taken before and after partial starvation are usually very different. Newman (1952) found significant somatotype changes with increase in age in adult men. Tanner (1956), who remeasured and somatotyped as adults aged 25 to 30 years, about two-thirds of a group of children originally measured anthropometrically by Low (1952), found little relationship between birth measurements and later measurements; he did find, however, that the inherent growth characteristics of the children asserted themselves after birth and that correlations between childhood measurements and adult measurements rose sharply.

Hammond (1953) found some degree of constancy of physical types in children over periods of two or three years with correlations ranging from ·65 to ·92 for the different age, sex and racial groups; nevertheless, 18 per cent. of the boys had changed their physical type up to the age of 14, and 12 per cent. of the girls. The evidence suggests that there is considerable stability of somatotypes but that this is by no means as perfect as Sheldon would have us believe.

This conclusion is borne out by the most recent study by Zuk (1958) who correlated ratings of Sheldon's somatotypes on male and female subjects who were measured at aged 12, 17 and 33. His results are given in Table 49. Most of the correlations will be seen to be reasonably high, except those for endomorphy which approach zero. It should be noted, however, that few of the other correlations approximate unity and that in fact not much more than 50–60 per cent. of the variance is common to successive measurements. In part this may be due to the lack of reliability of the ratings; these are much lower than one might have expected. It will be seen from Table 50

TABLE 50

Correlations between Judges' Ratings of Somatotype at
Ages 17 (Males) and 33 (Males and Females)

Groups	Endomorphy		Mesomorphy		Ectomorphy	
	17	33	17	33	17	33
Males (N = 74 at 17, 38 at 33)	·613	·729	·797	·857	·679	·893
Females (N = 78 at 17, 39 at 33)	—	·237	—	·741	—	·832

that the average of these reliabilities is around ·7, with one reliability going down as low as ·237. When it is remembered that exact measures can be taken of body build, it will be realized that reliabilities of this nature are highly unsatisfactory and compare very badly with those achieved by good intelligence tests and questionnaires.

We are now ready to consider correlations between body type, as rated by Sheldon, and temperament type, as rated by him also. 200 young students constituted the sample, as will be remembered from our discussion of Sheldon's rating experiments in Chapter II. The correlations between endomorphy and viscerotonia was ·79; between mesomorphy and somatotonia ·72; and between ectomorphy and cerebrotonia ·83. "These are higher correlations than we expected to find, and they raise some questions of great interest. If we were to regard the product moment correlation as a measure of the degree to which two variables are made up of common elements, correlations of the order of ·8 would suggest that morphology and temperament as we measure them may constitute expressions at their respective levels of essentially common components." Correlations are also given by Sheldon between the three temperamental components and several other bodily indices. Thus, the "g" index (gynandromorphy) correlates ·39 with viscerotonia and ·28 with cerebrotonia, but − ·63 with somatotonia. The "t" index (textural component) correlates ·36 with cerebrotonia, but only insignificantly with the other two components. I.Q. and sexuality also correlate positively with cerebrotonia but hardly at all with the other two components. One might expect from these correlations that the "t" component would correlate with I.Q., which it does (·39), and with æsthetic intelligence (·58) and sexuality (·40).[1]

Much could be said about these results. We have noted in a previous chapter the serious statistical errors apparent in Sheldon's table of correlations from which the temperamental syndromes were derived. We must note here the even more important experimental error of having the same observer rate personality and body build in his subjects when it is almost certain that his hypotheses will influence his ratings. The correlations actually found are much higher than those reported by any other investigators (when corrected for attenuation, on the assumption of any reasonable reliability for ratings, they very closely approach perfection). Such results obviously have to be checked and repeated before very much credence can be given to them. We have encountered only one independent study of Sheldon's claims—that by Fiske (1944). The number of significant findings in this study of adolescent boys is not conspicuously greater than chance expectancy. The use of Sheldon's improved procedure for classifying physique yielded "the same paucity of significant relationships to physique that has been found in earlier studies". This conclusion deserves particular emphasis as the somatotyping of the subjects in this study was done by Sheldon himself, and as a considerable variety of procedures was used for the purpose of personality measurement. In addition, the statistical procedure employed

[1] Perhaps relevant here is the work of Sills (1950) dealing with the relationship between body components and performance of motor skills.

(analysis of variance) was superior to any employed in Sheldon's own studies.

Some support of Sheldon's scheme is given in a comparatively objective study by Child (1950), who used 414 Yale students, who had been somatotyped by Sheldon himself, as subjects. A special questionnaire was constructed for this study based on Sheldon's description of the various personality correlates of his somatotypes and chi-squared analyses made of tables relating body type to questionnaire items. Altogether, 96 predictions were made, based on Sheldon's views. Of the relations empirically observed, 74, i.e. 77 per cent., were in the predicted direction, 20 reached significance at the 5 per cent. level, and 10 at the 1 per cent. level. Of the 21 correlations contrary to prediction, only 1 was significant at the 5 per cent. level, none at the 1 per cent. level. "The three dimensions of physique differed in the confirmation of predictions. The measured difference is that many fewer predictions are confirmed at acceptable levels of statistical significance for endomorphy than for the other two dimensions of physique."

Child also made an attempt to study the magnitude of relationships between physique and self-rated behaviour by constructing scales of viscerotonia, somatotonia, and cerebrotonia, from the most significant items, i.e. those showing the highest correlation with body build. These scales were derived from half of the population and applied to the other half. The resulting correlations are set out in Table 28. As will be seen, the correlations between viscerotonia and endomorphy ($\cdot$13), somatotonia and mesomorphy ($\cdot$38) and cerebrotonia and ectomorphy ($\cdot$27) are in the predicted direction, but are about as low as correlations between body type and temperament have usually been found to be. "It is thus possible but not certain

TABLE 51

Correlations between Dimensions of Physique and Sets of Self-ratings Described in Text.

	Dimension of Physique		
	Endomorphy	*Mesomorphy*	*Ectomorphy*
Self-ratings:			
Viscerotonia .	+ $\cdot$13	+ $\cdot$13	− $\cdot$15
Somatotonia .	+ $\cdot$03	+ $\cdot$38	− $\cdot$37
Cerebrotonia .	− $\cdot$03	− $\cdot$38	+ $\cdot$27

that appropriate measures based on ratings, such as were used here, have quite a sizeable relationship with dimensions of physique. It is reasonably certain that this relationship does not at all approach the magnitude of the relationships reported by Sheldon between dimensions of physique and his measures of temperament."

Scattered investigations by other workers substantiate this conclusion. Thus, Davidson et al. (1957), investigating body build and temperament in a group of 100 seven-year-old children, found symptoms of anxiety and emotional unrest associated with ectomorphy. They also found a relationship between ectomorphy and meticulous, fussy and conscientious traits of personality. In general the correlations between somatotype and psychological attributes were of a low order. Parnell (1957) compared somatotype distributions in 405 healthy students with a group of some 200 students who had sought psychiatric care. Ectomorphs were six times more common in the patient group, mesomorphs five times more common in the healthy group. Smith (1957) studied somatotypes in relation to M.M.P.I. scales in a group of 181 students. Many of his correlations are significant and most of them are in the direction predicted from Sheldon's system. Nevertheless the modal level of his correlation is only between ·3 and ·4, thus falling very short of Sheldon's claims.

One further set of data should be mentioned here, namely that relating to delinquency and criminality. Glueck and Glueck (1950), Sheldon et al. (1949), and Epps and Parnell (1952) have all found a predominance of endomorphic and mesomorphic body build in criminals and a relative lack of ectomorphy. Added to this, we have the interesting demonstration by Hooton (1939), who discovered that pyknics headed the list of crimes for rape, sex offences and assault, but were lowest in murder, whereas the leptosomatics (ectomorphs) had the highest incidence of murder and robbery but only low incidence in crimes such as burglary, assault, rape and other sex offences. Rees (1960) who has presented an excellent summary of all the work on constitutional factors in mental abnormality, concludes that "All these results are in good agreement with the Rees-Eysenck finding of a correlation between extraversion and eurymorph body build, and Eysenck's theory linking extraversion with psychopathy and criminality."

It will be remembered that Sheldon extended his scheme of temperament analysis to include psychotic and neurotic manifestations and a survey of his work in this field can be found in Chapter II. Here we are concerned with the relationship between the morphological components and psychiatric diagnosis, as based on the work of Wittman (1948). 155 psychotic male patients constituted the experimental group and were somatotyped by Sheldon himself. Wittman made a rating for these patients on the traits from her check list,[1] thus obtaining an average rating for each of the primary psychiatric components. This rating procedure apparently had a good deal of reliability, as correlations of her ratings with those of an independent rater averaged ·86. Correlations were then run between these ratings and the morphological components. The first psychiatric component (manic-depressive) correlated ·54 with endomorphy, ·41 with mesomorphy, and — ·59 with ectomorphy. The second psychiatric component (paranoid) correlated — ·04 with endomorphy, ·57 with mesomorphy, and — ·34 with ectomorphy. The third psychiatric component (hebephrenic) correlated — ·25 with endomorphy, — ·68 with mesomorphy, and ·64 with ectomorphy. These correlations are rather high, and as the two parts of the study (psychiatric ratings and morphology ratings) were apparently kept separate, they are of considerable interest.

Sheldon claims that these correlations would be higher still if account were taken of the rather more complex scheme which is presented in Fig. 20, p. 142, in this book. His verbal presentation is by no means clear, but it would appear to be reducible to the following outline.

If we represent the three main body types as the three corners of a triangle, then a line drawn from the centre of this triangle to each of the three corners will represent respectively the viscerotonic component (leading to the endomorph body type), the somatotonic component (leading to the mesomorph body type), and the cerebrotonic component (leading to the ectomorph body type).

Neurosis and psychosis are represented not by the "tonia" of the visceral somatic and cerebral processes respectively, but rather by their "penia", i.e. not by their development but by their absence. Consequently, the three main neurotic and psychotic types will lie in the middle of the three sides of the triangle at opposite ends to the viscerotonic-endomorphic corner (psychasthenia, paranoid schizophrenia), the somatotonic-mesomorph corner (neurasthenia, hebephrenic schizophrenia), and the cerebrotonic-ectomorph corner (hysteria, manic-depressive psychosis). Sheldon attempts to support his hypothesis that the primary psychiatric components are located opposite the morphological poles by means of correlating ratings on primary psychiatric components of the 155 subjects carried out by him while doing the somatotyping, with the same components according to hospital records. These correlations are indeed somewhat larger than those in the Wittman study, but that may be due to the fact that, in addition to body build, Sheldon also had the patients' behaviour to guide him in his ratings. It is difficult, consequently, to accept them as proving his point.

While these studies are experimentally much better controlled than Sheldon's work on normals, they still leave much to be desired. The main outcome, however, is well in line with previous work showing the relationship between manic-depressive psychoses and eurymorph body build, schizophrenia and leptomorph body build, with patients suffering from paranoid delusions being intermediate in body build between the other two, and showing considerable relationship with the mesomorphic body type.[1]

In summary, it may be said that Sheldon's results wherever they are comparable with the work of his predecessors agree fairly well with their conclusions. His studies suffer from methodological and statistical weaknesses which make it difficult to accept some of his claims, particularly in so far as they relate to the size of correlations observed between somatotype and temperament. Correlations with objective tests (Fiske, 1942; Smith, 1949; Janoff et al., 1950) are extremely low, even where they are in the expected direction. In spite of their messianic ring his contributions cannot be dismissed, but neither can they be accepted at face value. They probably contain sufficient truth and insight to be worthy of proper scientific investigation.

Sheldon's analysis is essentially subjective; his types, as are those of Kretschmer and his predecessors, are derived from intuition and theory. It is obviously advantageous to have a more objective approach based on empirical data, and the factor analysis of anthropometric body measurements may be regarded as likely to give rather more scientifically valuable results than those reviewed hitherto. First in this field as in so many others, was Spearman (1927) who analysed some data on body dimensions and anthropological measurements by means of his method of tetrad differences. His conclusion, which has been substantiated by every subsequent research, was that the existence of "type" factors in this field, in addition to a general factor, could not be gainsaid. Later investigators have used more

---

[1] For a direct comparison of the factor-analytic with the Sheldonian approach, the work of Moore and Hsü (1946) may with advantage be consulted.

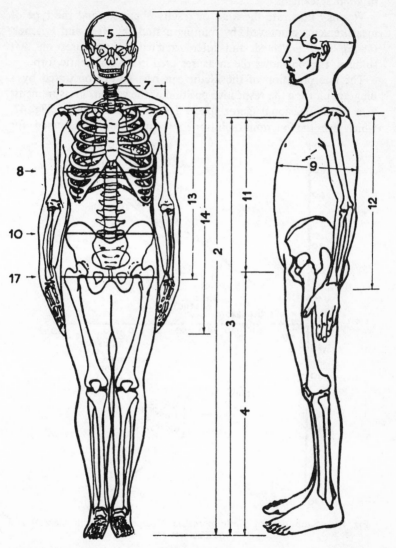

Fig. 46.—Diagram indicating Anthropometric Measurements used by Rees and Eysenck.

advanced methods of analysis and on the whole their conclusions are in good agreement.

We may illustrate the kind of results obtained, and the type of measurements employed, by quoting a study by Rees and Eysenck (1945), who collected and intercorrelated 18 measures on 300 soldiers. Fig. 46 shows the measures used in diagrammatic form.

The interpretation of the factor can best be demonstrated by a diagram plotting the respective position of the various measurements in a two-dimensional factor space. This has been done in Fig. 47, which gives the functional solution for the male sample discussed; for

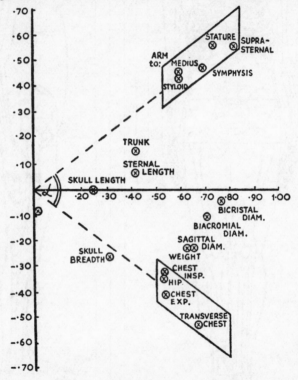

Fig. 47.—Saturation of Anthropometric Measurements with General and Type Factors: Men.

the sake of interest we have also given the results from a more recent analysis by Rees (1950) of 200 women, using very much the same measures (Fig. 48). The similarity between the two solutions will be clear. The first factor has positive correlations with all traits, and is clearly a general factor determining body size. The second factor has

positive saturations for length measurements, and negative saturations
for breadth, width, and circumferential measurements. It is this opposition between the thin, elongated, leptomorph individual and the
thick-set, round eurymorph individual which lies at the base of all
the typologies enumerated in Table 47.

Many other studies are reviewed in detail by Rees (1960) who
concludes that "These findings derived from factorial analysis of
physique in British adult men and women are supported by a large

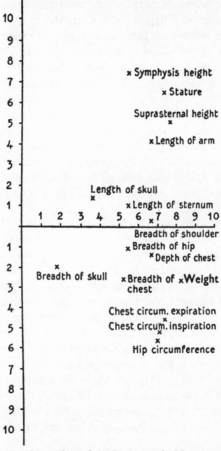

Fig. 48.—Saturation of Anthropometric Measurements
with General and Type Factors: Women.

number of other workers using factorial methods in groups of different ages, racial composition and socio/economic status. This was strikingly shown by Burt (1947) who found from an anthropometric study of 30,000 men of the Royal Air Force that in almost every age group and nationality the same two main factors emerge. Burt (1938) . . . describing factorial analyses of physical measurements in groups of British children and adults, also elicited a well marked general factor and factors making for disproportionate growth in length on the one extreme, and breadth, thickness, girth and weight on the other extreme. Similar factors have been found from factorial studies on groups of different social composition, e.g. Cohen (1941), in a group of 100 Jewish patients in a mental hospital, Hammond (1942) in a group of 100 adult Irishmen, and Burt (1944) in groups of young British and American men." One further study which should here be mentioned, although it is correlational rather than factorial, is the report by the Board of Trade on "Women's Measurements and Sizes" (1957) in which almost 40 measures were intercorrelated for almost 5,000 women. Fig. 4 of this report groups these measurements according to their correlations and it is quite apparent that these measures fall into two independent groups, namely length measurements and width and girth measurements. Within each group correlations are very high, between the groups correlations are low or non-existent.

American studies such as those by Howells (1951), Thurstone (1946) and Heath (1952) usually extract larger numbers of oblique factors and thus may at first sight appear to give different results. However, when second order factors are extracted these usually coincide with the factors found by British workers. Thus Heath (1952) carried out a second order factor analysis on correlations between 29 variables on 4,128 women, with age held constant. Five first-order factors were extracted and interpreted as : A=length of bones, B=cancellous bone size, C=lower body girth, D=girth of extremities, E=upper body girth. Her second order factors X and Y are obviously closely related to the usual length and breadth factors; X has loadings on C, D and E, while Y has loadings on A and B. There is a correlation of ·33 between X and Y interpreted as "an indication of general growth" (page 94). The similarity of this solution to that diagrammed in Fig. 47 is obvious.

All these studies used adults or adolescents. Work on neonates, babies and children is less conclusive. Taking together studies of Carter and Krause (1936), Marshall (1936), Hammond (1957),

McCloy (1940), Mullen (1940), Rees (1950), and Burt (1949), we find that on the whole much the same size and shape factors emerge as with adults, although the picture is not as clear as it is with older subjects. It is interesting to note that factors similar to those describing human body build have also been found in the factorial analysis of body build in cows (Tanner and Burt, 1954), rabbits (Tanner and Sawin, 1953) and rats (Watson, 1956). As Rees (1960) pointed out "The operation of the general and type factors in human physique is strikingly similar to the differential growth ratios determining body forms in the animal kingdom (Huxley, 1932)."

The major outcome of factorial analyses of body build appears to be that we may regard the body as a rectangle which can be described with fair accuracy in terms of two independent dimensions, to wit, height and width. The height factor can best be measured in terms of length of arms, length of leg, total height or other length measures; the width factor can best be measured by chest width, chest circumference or hip circumference. A rectangle or a human body can now be characterized in two ways. If we multiply height by width we get the total size of the rectangle or the body. If we divide the height by the width we get a ratio indicating the shape of the rectangle or body, i.e. whether it is relatively long or relatively squat. Using height as a measure of the length factor and transverse chest width as a measure of the width factor, Rees and Eysenck (1945) have derived two indices of body build which indicate respectively body size and body shape. Both indices are fairly normally distributed in the population (Rees, 1960). Rees and Eysenck (1945) have defined the terms eurymorph, mesomorph and leptomorph as purely descriptive terms denoting types of body build lying 1 S.D. below the mean, within $\pm$S.D. of the mean or 1 S.D. below the mean of the population respectively. Similarly for body size, the population would be divided into macrosomatics, mesosomatics and microsomatics respectively, using one standard deviation from the mean in either direction as a dividing mark. Many other indices have been used in the literature, of course, and their derivation and correlation with the Rees-Eysenck index are discussed extensively by Rees (1960).

We must now turn to comparison of the Kretschmer-Sheldon system and the factorial type of system, because clearly there are marked similarities. The answer is relatively simple and will be found in a paper by Parnell (1957) in which he has calculated the Rees-Eysenck index for some 3,000 subjects who have previously been somatotyped. It can be seen from his Fig. 1 that ectomorphs have high indices of body build, and that indices begin to get lower and lower the more the mesomorph-endomorph direction is approached. We can thus identify Sheldon's ectomorph and Kretschmer's leptosomatic type of body build with leptomorphic body build as defined by the factorial work. It is also clear, however, that the eurymorph end of the factorial typology is sub-divided by Sheldon and Kretschmer into two parts, i.e. the athletic-mesomorphic and the pyknic-endomorphic. What then is the distinction between these two body types? Inspection suggests very simply that it is the distinction between muscle and fat, i.e. that the fat eurymorph will be called endomorphic by Sheldon or pyknic by Kretschmer, while the muscular eurymorph is called mesomorph by Sheldon and athletic by Kretschmer. This factor, therefore, is additional to skeletal body build and may or may not be related to temperament. It seems certain, however, that this fat-muscle component is much more readily modified by environmental influences than is the skeletal component measured by the Rees-Eysenck index; the starvation experiments mentioned before, and the well-known fact that athletes tend to grow fat as they get older, may be quoted in support of this statement (Eysenck, 1959).

More recently still we have the work of Brattgård (1950) and Lindegård (1956). The former used the Strömgren (1937) index on 1,000 cases from a psychiatric clinic and found syntonic personality traits associated with pyknic body build and psychasthenic personality traits associated with leptosomatic body build. Lindegård's results are rather difficult to interpret as he makes use of a rather esoteric system of personality description; on the whole, all his correlations are relatively small.

We must now return to a last problem which was only briefly alluded to in our discussion on Sheldon's work, where it was pointed out that if there was any truth in the hypothesis linking embryological and physiological factors to body build, then ease of description and statistical analysis would have to take second place. Can we say anything about the physiological basis of the factors discovered by factor analysis? For an answer we must turn to the mechanisms of post-natal skeletal growth (Weinman and Sicher, 1947). As is well-known, post-natal development of the skeleton is determined by interstitial growth of either cartilaginous or connective tissue. Bone formations originating from cartilaginous tissue are called endochondral bone formations, and those originating from connective tissue are called appositional bone formations. Endochondral bone formation occurs in the epiphyseal plates, articular cartilage, sternocostal cartilage and cartilage of the base of the skull, among others. In addition, the shaft bones, particularly those of the arms and legs increase in length by endochondral bone formation.

Appositional bone formation starts from periostal or perichondral tissue and causes an increase in the sturdiness of the various bones (Lindegård, 1953).

We thus find that the length of such bones as those in the arms and legs (e.g. radius or tibia) is determined almost entirely by endochondral growth, while their diaphyseal thickness is determined entirely by appositional bone formation. Lindegård (1953) therefore proposed to use the length of the long shaft bones as an index of the *length* factor and the thickness of these bones as a measure of a *sturdiness* factor. This, of course, pre-supposes x-ray measurements of bones, and Lindegård's work is very much concerned with such measurements. The very extensive correlations reported by him suggest strongly that these two factors, derived from physiological and anatomical considerations, correspond closely to the length and width factors of the factor analyst, which thus find strong biological backing. It is also clear from his work that the two measures entering into the Rees/Eysenck body index are well chosen for their purpose as long as we are restricted to measurements taken on the outside of the body. It appears likely that better body type indices could be derived through the aid of Roentgenological analysis. Lindegård concludes his analysis by saying that "the length/sturdiness factors are good mirrors of the general skeletal build of a given individual". To these two factors he adds a muscle and a fat factor, thus ending up with a four-dimensional description of total body appearance. Of all the studies reviewed, his is probably the most advanced and sophisticated on the anatomical and physiological side, and future work will benefit considerably from following up the leads given by him. What is most interesting and impressive, however, is the way in which all the investigations reviewed in this chapter agree on the main underlying descriptive variables and their relations to personality.

How does the body-type factor derived from factor analysis correlate with personality? We have seen that the ectomorph component of Sheldon's corresponds rather closely to the leptomorph factor and accordingly, we would expect leptomorphs to show cerebrotonic, i.e. introverted and neurotic personality traits as compared with mesomorphs and eurymorphs. That this is so is strongly suggested by the characterization Sheldon gives of cerebrotonics. The following traits he mentions are typically introverted:

"love of privacy, socio-phobia, inhibited social address, need of solitude when troubled, introversion". To this list might be added the item "resistance to alcohol, and to other depressant drugs"; evidence on this point is given in a series of papers recently published (summarized in Eysenck, 1957) and in the work of Shagass (1955, 1956) and his collaborators on the sedation threshold. Items characteristic of neuroticism are the following: "physiological over-response, mental over-intensity, apprehensiveness, hypersensitivity to pain, chronic fatigue". Conversely, items characteristic of extra-version and normality (as opposed to neuroticism) are apparent in Sheldon's description of the viscerotonic and the somatotonic types.

What are the facts?

We have already mentioned Sahai's (1931) research, in which he found evidence on the basis of intercorrelational patterns for the existence of a factor of introversion-extraversion. This author carried out a number of physical measures on his subjects, and calculated ratios from these. His data support the existence of a "pyknic" type of body build, and this he found correlated with extraversion to the extent of $\cdot20 \pm \cdot04$, a value which when corrected for attenu-ation reached the respectable size of $\cdot35 \pm \cdot04$. His suggestion that extraverts are somewhat more eurymorph in body build is confirmed by Burt (1937), who found the following correlations of eurymorph body build with temperamental type:

TABLE 52

		General Instability	Extraversion	Cheerfulness
Children	N.			
Abnormal group	131	—·23	·26	·19
Normal group	197	—·11	·08	·17
Adolescents				
Abnormal group	13	—·33	·16	·30
Normal group	100	·04	·18	·14
Adults	180	—·13	·32	·16

Burt's data also suggest that neuroticism or emotional instability is less frequent, and cheerfulness more frequent, in persons of eurymorph build.

Support for the proposition that extraverts are more eurymorph can also be found in the monograph by Sanford *et al.* (1943), to which reference has already been made. Using 18 individual measurements on 48 children, intercorrelations were prepared and subjected to a somewhat unsatisfactory form of cluster analysis. The outcome of this analysis can best be stated in the author's own words: "We have distinguished four syndromes of body build, the first two being based on high positive intercorrelations among the several anthropometric measures, the last two being based on the relationship between the measures on syndromes one and two for the individual subjects:

(1) Wide, heavy build.
(2) Tall, narrow build.
(3) Large build (i.e. tall, heavy, wide).
(4) Short, wide build."

These partly overlapping clusters are awkward to work with and much more unsatisfactory than proper factor measures would have been; however, in spite of this difficulty the results obtained are clear enough. The person of tall, narrow build, i.e. presumably the leptomorphic type, when compared with the person of short, wide, or wide heavy build, i.e. presumably the eurymorph type, is characterized by the following manifest personality syndromes: conscientious work, counter-active endocathection,[1] guilt and remorse, self-sufficiency, orderly production, and sensitive, imaginative creation; all these are introverted qualities. The person of eurymorph body build, on the other hand, is characterized by the opposite qualities to those mentioned above, as well as by good fellowship and social feeling, i.e. particularly extraverted qualities. A similar picture emerges between the physical syndromes and fantasy syndromes derived from the T.A.T. The person of leptomorphic body build is particularly characterized by lack of social themes and lack of love themes; the eurymorph person by self-assertion themes and social and love themes.

Regarding the correlation between physical syndrome and what Sanford calls "family press", i.e. general family background, the main correlations are between leptomorphic body build and tight control, cultural stimulation, and artistic temperament. Those between eurymorph body build and "family press" are mainly with erotic stimulation, lack of tight control, and of cultural stimuli and

[1] The cathection of thought or emotion for its own sake, preoccupation with inner activities.

artistic temperament. Thus, family background again fits in with the general picture of the introvert and the extravert. Correlations between physical syndromes and intellectual abilities show the leptomorph to be characterized by spatial, number, reasoning, comprehension, abstract, manual manipulation, memory, verbal and vocabulary, non-verbal, and all the other abilities measured or rated, whereas the eurymorph is inferior on all of them. This is again in line with a great deal of evidence showing the introvert (and the leptomorph) slightly superior on scholastic tests of general intelligence and knowledge.

In spite, therefore, of the somewhat unsatisfactory cluster technique used by Sanford, we obtain from his very detailed study, which extended over several years and involved a close investigation of all the children along clinical lines, a picture very similar to that described before, namely a marked tendency for leptomorph children to be introverted and for eurymorph children to be extraverted.

These studies have all dealt with normal subjects. Eysenck (1947) extended the scope of this type of investigation to neurotics, again using a hypothetico-deductive approach. If the writers previously mentioned are correct in believing that introverts tend to be leptomorph in body build and extraverts eurymorph, and if Jung is correct in assuming that the hysteric is the prototype of the extravert and the psychasthenic or dysthymic is the prototype of the introvert, then it would follow that in a group of adult neurotics, those of eurymorph body build would be characterized by hysterical symptoms, whereas those of leptomorph body build would be characterized by dysthymic symptoms. Taking a sample of 1,000 unselected neurotics all measured for body type by means of a formula derived from the Rees-Eysenck factorial study, 120 were found to be eurymorphs, 150 leptomorphs, and 730 mesomorphs, i.e. intermediate between the extremes. The following items were found to characterize the eurymorphs as compared with the leptomorphs: hysterical personality, hysterical attitude, hysterical conversion symptoms, diagnosed conversion hysteria, intelligence average or below, muscular tone good. Leptomorphs, on the other hand, were characterized by the items: vocabulary above average, anxious, obsessional, depressed, suffering from headaches, dyspepsia, tremor, irritability, and loss of weight. They also tended to be single and teetotal and to be seclusive.

Most of these differentiations were statistically significant, and in almost every case mesomorphs were found to be intermediate between the extreme groups. It would appear, therefore, that the hypothesis under investigation has been borne out and that hysterics and dysthymics respectively may be justifiably considered to be the neurotic prototypes of the extravert and the introvert respectively.

Rees (1950) carried out a similar study on 60 leptomorph, 77 eurymorph, and 263 mesomorph women using an index of body build derived from his own factorial analysis. Eurymorph women were characterized by hysterical personality, very marked hysterical traits, hysterical motor and sensory conversion symptoms, and backwardness in school; whereas the leptomorph women were characterized by anxiety, depression, irritability, touchiness, suspiciousness, shut-in, weak, and dependent personality, as well as autonomic symptoms, effort intolerance, and above average vocabulary test scores. These results closely confirm those obtained by Eysenck (1947), and leave little doubt that the hypothesis under investigation is at least partly valid. The results are particularly impressive when it is considered that psychiatric diagnoses are notoriously unreliable, particularly on war-time cases, seen only for a limited period of time and under considerable stress of work, and when it is also considered that many of the psychiatrists who took part in this work were relatively inexperienced.

So far we have dealt only with body types relating to the second factor extracted in the variance analysis; obviously, the first factor of body size is also of some interest. Again, it is possible to devise an index based on the factorial studies which would identify the microsomatics (those having a small body), the macrosomatics (those having a large body), and the mesosomatics (those having an intermediate body size). As in the case of the eurymorph, leptomorph, and mesomorph groups, we are dealing of course not with separate types but with a continuous distribution; the extreme groups are simply those who are more than one standard deviation from the mean in either direction.

Eysenck (1947) compared 156 microsomatic, 156 macrosomatic, and 688 mesosomatic male neurotic soldiers, and found the microsomatic person characterized by the following items: unskilled civilian occupation, elementary education, sexually inhibited, narrow hobbies, teetotal, poor physical health, weak and dependent, inert, non-aggressive, anxious, hypochondriacal, depressed, poor muscular tone, low intelligence, poor vocabulary. "Altogether both mentally and physically he is what is popularly called a poor specimen." These results suggest that general body size may be of greater importance for personality than body type, although a repetition of the research would be needed before any such general conclusion could be drawn.

We may conclude on the whole that the work reviewed in this chapter supports the proposition that there exists a correlation of the order of ·3 to ·5 between (*a*) leptomorph body build and introversion and (*b*) leptomorph body build and neuroticism. Both these relationships work in the direction of making the dysthymic individual particularly leptomorph and the normal extravert particularly eurymorph. These generalizations applied equally to the results published by Sheldon and his followers as to those published by the factorial school. In addition, there may be a specific relationship between schizophrenic disorder and leptomorph body build, and/or between eurymorph body build and manic-depressive illness. There may, of course, be further relationships not covered by these generalizations, and it is quite clear that body build is far from having simple and clearcut connections with temperament.

REFERENCES

Chapter IX

BAUER, J. *Vorlesungen über allgemeine Konstitutions-Vererbungslehre*. Berlin: Springer, 1923.

BENEKE, F. W. *Die anatomischen Grundlagen der Konstitutions-anomalien des Menschen*. Marburg, 1878.

BESSONET-FAVRE, A. *La Typologie, Méthode d'Observation des Types Humains*. Paris, 1910.

BOARD OF TRADE. *Women's Measurements and Sizes*, H.M.S.O., 1957.

BRATTGÅRD, S. O. Personality attitude and physical make-up. *Acta Psychiat. Neurol. Scand.*, 1950, **35**, 339–354.

BURT, C. The analysis of temperament. *Brit. J. med. Psychol.*, 1937, **17**, 158–180.

Factor analysis and physical types. *Psychomet.*, 1947, **12**, 171–188.

Factor analysis by sub-matrices. *J. Psychol.*, 1938, **6**, 339–375.

The factorial study of physical types. *Man*, 1944, **44**, 82–86.

Sub-divided factors. *Brit. J. Psychol., Stat. Sect.*, 1949, **2**, 41–63.

CARTER, H. D., and KRAUSE, R. M. Physical proportions of the human infant. *Child Development*, 1936, **7**, 60–68.

CASTELLINO, P. La Costituzione Individuale. La Personnalità. Naples, 1927.

CHILD, I. L. The relation of somatotype to self-ratings on Sheldon's temperamental traits. *J. Pers.*, 1950, **18**, 440–453.

COHEN, J. I. Physique, size and proportion. *Brit. J. med. Psychol.*, 1941, **18**, 323–337.

DAVIDSON, M. A., McINNES, R. G., and PARNELL, R. W. The distribution of personality traits in 7-year-old children. *Brit. J. educ. Psychol.*, 1957, **27**, 48–61.

DI GIOVANNI, A. *Clinical Commentaries deduced from the Morphology of the Human Body.* London: Trans. by Eyre, J. J., 1919.

EKMAN, G. On the number and definition of dimensions in Kretschmer's and Sheldon's constitutional systems. In: *Essays in Psychology dedicated to David Katz.* Uppsala, 1951.

EPPS, P., and PARNELL, R. W. Physique and temperament of women delinquents compared with women undergraduates. *Brit. J. med. Psychol.*, 1952, **25**, 249–255.

EYSENCK, H. J. Cyclothymia-schizothymia as a dimension of personality. I. Historical review. *J. Pers.*, 1950, **19**, 123–153.

Dimensions of Personality. London: Kegan Paul, 1947.

Dynamics of Anxiety and Hysteria. London: Routledge & Kegan Paul, 1957.

The Rees-Eysenck body index and Sheldon's somatotype system. *J. ment. Sci.*, 1959. To appear.

FISKE, D. W. The relation between physique and measures of intelligence. Temperament and personality in superior adolescent boys. *Psychol. Bull.*, 1942, **39**, 459.

A study of relationships to somatotype. *J. appl. Psychol.*, 1944, **28**, 504–519.

GLUECK, S., and GLUECK, E. Unravelling juvenile delinquency. Commonwealth Fund, New York, 1950.

HAMILTON, W. J., Boyd, J. D., and MOSSMAN, H. W. Human embryology. (Prenatal development of form and function.) Cambridge: W. Heffer & Sons, 1945.

HAMMOND, W. H. Measurement of physical types in children. *Human Biol.*, 1953, **25**, 65–80.

An application of Burt's multiple factor analysis to the delineation of physical types. *Man*, 1942, **42**, 4–11.

The constancy of physical types as determined by factorial analysis. *Human Biol.*, 1957, **29**, 40–61.

Physique and development of boys and girls from different types of school. *Brit. J. prevent. soc. Med.*, 1953, **7**, 231–239.

The status of physical types. *Human Biol.*, 1957, **29**, 223–241.

HEATH, H. A factor analysis of women's measurements taken for garment and pattern construction. *Psychomet.*, 1952, **16**, 87–100.

HERTWIG, O. Die Colomtheorie. Jena, 1881.

HIPPOCRATES. The genuine works of: trans. from Greek with preliminary discourse and annotations by Francis Adams. New York: W. Wood & Co., 1891.

HOOTON, E. A. *The American Criminal.* Cambridge, Mass.: Harvard Univ. Press, 1939 (Vol. 1).

Crime and the Man. Cambridge, Mass.: Harvard Univ. Press, 1939.

HOWELLS, W. W. A factorial study of constitutional type. *Amer. J. Physiol. Anthropol.*, 1952, **10**, 91–118.

Factors of human physique. *Amer. J. Physiol. Anthropol.*, 1951, **9**, 159–191.

HUMPHREYS, L. G. Characteristics of type concepts with special reference to Sheldon's typology. *Psychol. Bull.*, 1957, **54**, 218–228.

HUNT, E. H. A note of growth, somatotype and temperament. *Amer. J. Physiol. Anthropol.*, 1949, **7**, 79–89.

HUXLEY, J. S. *Problems of Relative Growth.* London: Methuen, 1932.

JANOFF, I. Z., BECK, L. H., and CHILD, I. L. The relation of somatotype to reaction time, resistance to pain, and expressive movement. *J. Pers.,* 1950, **18**, 454–460.

KRETSCHMER, E. *Körperbau und Charakter.* Berlin: Springer, 1948.

LASKER, G. W. The effects of partial starvation on somatotype. *Amer. J. Physiol. Anthropol.,* 1947, **5**, 323–341.

LINDGÅRD, B. (Ed.). *Body Build, Body Function and Personality.* Lund: Gleerup, 1956.

Variations in Human Body Build. Copenhagen: Munksgard, 1953.

LOW, A. *Growth of Children.* Aberdeen: Univ. Press, 1952.

McCLOY, C. H. An analysis for multiple factors of physical growth at different age levels. *Child Development,* 1940, **11**, 249–277.

MARSHALL, E. L. A multiple factor study of 18 anthropometric measurements of Iowa City boys. *J. exp. Educ.,* 1936, **5**, 212.

MARTINY, M. *Essai de Biotypologie Humaine.* Paris: Peyronnet, 1948.

MOORE, T. V., and HSÜ, E. H. Factorial analysis of anthropological measurements in psychotic patients. *Human Biol.,* 1946, **18**, 133–157.

MULLEN, F. A. Factors in the growth of girls. *Child Development,* 1940, **11**, 27–42.

NEWMAN, R. W. Age changes in body build. *Amer. J. Physiol. Anthropol.,* 1952, **10**, 75–90.

PARNELL, R. W. Physique and mental breakdown in young adults. *Brit. med. J.,* 1957, **1**, 1485–1490.

PATERSON, D. G. *Physique and Intellect.* New York: Century Co., 1930.

PLATTNER, W. Das Körperbauspektrum. *Ztsch. f. a. ges. Neurol. Psychiat.,* 1938, **160**, 703–712.

REES, L. Body build, personality and neurosis in women. *J. ment. Sci.,* 1950, **96**, 426–434.

Body size, personality and neurosis. *J. ment. Sci.,* 1950, **96**, 168–180.

Constitutional factors in mental abnormality. In: *Handbook of Abnormal Psychology* (Ed., H. J. Eysenck). London: Pitman, 1960.

A factorial study of physical constitution in women. *J. ment. Sci.,* 1950, **96**, 619–632.

REES, L., and EYSENCK, H. J. A factorial study of some morphological and psychological aspects of human constitution. *J. ment. Sci.,* 1945, **91**, 8–21.

ROSTAN, L. *Cours Élémentaire d'Hygiène.* Paris: 1828.

SAHAI, M. Circular mentality and the pyknic body build. Ph.D. Thesis. London: Univ. London Lib., 1931.

SANFORD, R. N., ADKINS, M. N., MILLER, R. B., and COBB, E. Physique, personality and scholarship. *Mon. Soc. Res. Child Dev.,* 1943, **7**, Ser. No. 34.

SHAGASS, C., and NAIMAN, J. The sedation threshold, manifest anxiety, and some aspects of ego function. *A.M.A. Arch. of Neurol. & Psychiat.,* 1955, **34**, 393–406.

SHAGASS, C. Sedation threshold: a neurophysiological tool for psychosomatic research. *Psychosom. Med.,* 1956, **18**, 410–419.

SHELDON, W. H. *The Varieties of Human Physique.* New York: Harper, 1940.

The Varieties of Temperament. New York: Harper, 1942.

The Varieties of Delinquent Youth. An Introduction to Constitutional Psychiatry. New York: Harper, 1949.

SHELDON, W. H., HARTL, E. M., and MCDERMOTT, E. *Varieties of Delinquent Youth.* New York: Harper & Bros., 1949.

SILLS, F. D. A factor analysis of somatotypes and their relationship to achievements in motor skills. *Res. Quart.*, 1950, **21**, 424–437.

SMITH, D. W. The relation between ratio indices of physique and selected scales of the Minnesota Multiphasic Personality Inventory. *J. Psychol.*, 1957, **43**, 325–331.

SMITH, H. C. Psychometric checks on hypotheses derived from Sheldon's work on physique and temperament. *J. Pers.*, 1949, **17**, 310–320.

SPEARMAN, C. *The Abilities of Man.* London: Macmillan, 1927.

STRÖMGREN, E. Über anthropometrische Indices zur Unterscheidung von Körperbautypen. *Ztschr. ges. Neurol. n. Psychiat.*, 1937, **159**, 75–81.

TANNER, J. M. Physique, character and disease. *Lancet*, 1956, **2**, 635–637.

TANNER, J. M., and BURT, W. A. Physique in the infrahuman mammalia. A factor analysis of body measurements in dairy cows. *J. Genet.*, 1954, **52**, 37–51.

TANNER, J. M., and SAWIN, P. P. Morphogenetic studies in the rabbit. Genetic differences in the growth of the vertebral columns and their relation to growth and development in man. *J. Anat.*, 1953, **87**, 54–65.

THURSTONE, L. L. Analysis of Body Measurements. Chicago: Psychomet. Lab., Univ. Chicago, No. 29, March 1946.

Factor analysis of body types. *Psychomet.*, 1946, Vol. **2**, 15–22.

VIOLA, G. *La Costituzione Individuale.* Bologna: Cappeli, 1933, 165.

WATSON, R. Unpublished data, 1956: Library of Inst. of Psychiatry, London.

WEINMAN, J. O., and SICHER, H. *Bone and Bones.* St. Louis, 1947.

WELLS, S. R. *How to Read Character.* New York: Fowler & Wells, 1869.

WITTMAN, P. M., SHELDON, W., and KATZ, C. J. A study of the relationship between constitutional variations and fundamental psychotic behaviour reactions. *J. nerv. & ment. Dis.*, 1948, **108**, 470–476.

WITTMAN, P. M., and SHELDON, W. A proposed classification list of psychotic behaviour reactions. *Amer. J. Psychiat.*, 1948, **105**, 124–126.

ZUK, C. H. The plasticity of the physique from early adolescence through adulthood. *J. genet. Psychol.*, 1958, **92**, 205–214.

THE ANALYSIS OF INTERESTS
AND ATTITUDES

[handwritten margin note: Att. is elaboration to interest]

THE TERMS "INTERESTS" and "attitudes" in non-technical usage refer to rather similar concepts. Interests are attitudes having positive valences, or, to put it rather more simply, interests are attitudes held with respect to objects or classes of objects towards which we feel a certain attraction. Lack of interest is usually taken as an indication of a negative or unfavourable attitude; the man who is not interested in women may be regarded as being unfavourably disposed towards them. This simple manner of looking at these two concepts leaves out of account all the complications introduced by such factors as ambivalence, or reaction formation; it is also out of line with the way in which "interest" and "attitude" are being used in contemporary psychology. The former refers almost exclusively to vocational or occupational preferences; the latter to opinions held on social or political matters. The older term "sentiment", introduced by McDougall (1923) to cover this whole area of affective and conative constellations around some central idea, has gone out of fashion; it might perhaps with some advantage be revived to denote what the more recent terms have in common. In the absence of such a unifying term, or of any unified treatment of the data derived from investigations of occupational and socio-political preferences, we must discuss interests and attitudes separately.

Super (1949) points out that "there have been four major interpretations of the term interest, connected with as many different methods of obtaining data". The first type of interest he calls *expressed interest*, which he defines as the verbal profession of interest in an object, activity, task, or occupation; the subject simply states that he likes, is indifferent to, or dislikes the activity in question. The second he labels *manifest interest;* this is synonymous with participation in an activity or occupation. "Objective manifestations of interest have been studied in order to avoid the subjectivity of expressions or to avoid the implications that interest is something static." The third type he calls *tested interest*, using this term to refer to interest as measured by objective tests as differentiated from inventories which are based on subjective self-estimates; the assumption underlying the resulting type of test is that interest is likely to manifest itself in action (e.g. accumulation of relevant information) which can be made objectively measurable.

The fourth type Super calls *inventoried interest;* it "is assessed by means of lists of activities and occupations which bear a superficial resemblance to some questionnaires for the study of expressed interests, for each item in the list is responded to with an expression of preference. The essential and all-important difference is that in the case of the inventory each possible response is given an experimentally determined weight, and the weights corresponding to the answers given by the person completing the inventory are added in order to yield a score which represents, not a single subjective estimate as in the case of expressed interests, but a pattern of interests which research has shown to be rather stable". It is with inventoried interests, more particularly with those obtained by means of the Strong Vocational Interest Blank (1943), that we shall in the main be occupied in this chapter.

This Blank is a device by means of which patterns of interests characteristic of members of different trades and professions may be determined. It consists of 400 items, to each of which the subject responds by indicating whether he likes, dislikes, or is indifferent to that item. One hundred items have reference to occupations; the remainder refer to amusements (golf, fishing), school subjects, activities, and peculiarities of people. Other parts of the Blank call for an indication of most and least liked activities from a given list; preference judgments between alternate choices; and estimates of one's abilities and characteristics. Different forms are used for men and women. Scoring is entirely empirical, weights for a given occupational interest being derived from the actual responses of persons working in that particular field, as contrasted with "men in general". A score "indicates not the *amount* of interest possessed but the *likelihood* that the person has or does not have the interests of men in the given occupation. A high score means that the individual has the interests of the occupation in question, while a low score means that he does not have such interests". In view of the fact that mean raw scores differ considerably from one occupation to another, they are transformed into standard scores, ratings (A, B +, B, B −, C +, and C), or percentile scores.

A superficial cluster-analysis of the intercorrelations of 36 occupations, based on 285 college seniors, led Strong to group occupations into 11 sets. The basis of classification was that each occupation should correlate ·60 or higher on the average with the members of its group, and lower than this with the members of all other groups. (There are three exceptions to this rule, none of great importance.) The resulting classification is produced below, in Table 53. It will be

TABLE 53

Classification of Occupations

Group			Occupation
I	.	.	Artist
			Psychologist
			Architect
			Physician
			Dentist
II	.	.	Mathematician
			Physicist
			Engineer
			Chemist
III	.	.	Production manager
IV	.	.	Aviator
			Farmer
			Carpenter
			Mathematics-physical science teacher
			Printer
			Policeman
			Forest service
V	.	.	Y.M.C.A. secretary
			Y.M.C.A. physical director
			Personnel manager
			City school superintendent
			Minister
			Social science teacher
VI	.	.	Musician
VII	.	.	Certified public accountant
VIII	.	.	Purchasing Agent
			Office worker
			Accountant
			Banker
IX	.	.	Real estate salesman
			Life insurance salesman
			Sales manager
X	.	.	Lawyer
			Author-journalist
			Advertising man
XI	.	.	President of manufacturing concern

seen that four groups contain only one member—production manager, musician, certified public accountant, and president of a manufacturing concern. Interpretation of these clusters is difficult, although many of the relations depicted would be readily acceptable to common sense.

Factorial studies have been carried out by several writers to establish a more fundamental basis of classification. Thurstone (1932) was the first to venture into this new field. His original analysis was· carried out on 18 of Strong's scales. It was found that the observed correlations could be accounted for in terms of four factors, which he labelled (1) interest in science; (2) interest in language; (3) interest in people; and (4) interest in business. A certain amount of argument is centred around the identification of the factors; as we shall see, Strong, in his analysis, has refused to name his factors at all. As Thurstone points out, "this matter of naming the factors is entirely extraneous to the statistical analysis. The statistical work may be correct, while considerable argument might conceivably be made about the naming of the factors . . . when multiple-factor analysis is undertaken there is absolutely no guarantee that the resulting factor loadings will so arrange themselves that they can be readily named". In spite of these warnings, Thurstone's interpretation appears reasonable to the present writer and it is of some interest to see the factorial composition of certain interest scores to illustrate the meaning of these factors. Psychology, for instance, has a loading of ·77 in science, of ·47 in language, of − ·04 in people, and of − ·28 in business. To those who have noted the preoccupation of psychologists with semantic problems and their preference for rats to human beings, the second and third of these correlations will not come as a surprise, just as the average income of psychologists is probably a just reflection on the last of the saturations mentioned. Table 54 sets out in full Thurstone's results, and it can be left to the reader to form his own impression on the correctness of his naming of these factors.

Four further analyses have been carried out by Strong (1943), based on 25, 30, 32, and 36 variables respectively; results from these more extensive later studies show striking agreement with each other, and with Thurstone's original analysis.[1] Only the last and most comprehensive of all these studies will be discussed in detail. Strong presents an unrotated and a rotated solution, both containing four de-

[1] All these studies were carried out on adult subjects. A report by Carter, Pyles, and Bretnall (1935) gives similar results with respect to high-school students.

TABLE 54

Name of Profession	Four Interest Factors				
	I Science	II Language	III People	IV Business	h^2
Advertising	− ·48	+ ·66	− ·21	+ ·22	·76
Art	+ ·45	+ ·70	− ·18	− ·31	·82
Certified public accountant .	− ·04	+ ·32	·00	+ ·56	·42
Chemistry	+ ·98	− ·21	− ·15	+ ·06	1·03
Engineering . . .	+ ·84	− ·36	− ·22	+ ·16	·91
Law	− ·23	+ ·77	− ·12	+ ·44	·85
Ministry	+ ·09	+ ·51	+ ·62	− ·30	·74
Psychology	+ ·77	+ ·47	− ·04	− ·28	·89
Teaching	+ ·36	+ ·15	+ ·68	− ·22	·66
Life insurance . . .	− ·82	− ·02	+ ·27	+ ·45	·95
Architecture . . .	+ ·83	+ ·26	+ ·16	+ ·05	·78
Y.M.C.A. secretary . . .	− ·23	·00	+ ·90	− ·37	1·00
Farming	+ ·71	− ·54	+ ·01	+ ·18	·83
Purchasing agent . . .	− ·05	− ·79	+ ·01	+ ·44	·82
Journalism	− ·15	+ ·84	− ·28	+ ·25	·87
Personnel	− ·30	− ·26	+ ·66	− ·19	·63
Real estate	− ·76	− ·07	− ·06	+ ·58	·92
Medicine	+ ·71	+ ·33	− ·26	− ·09	·69

finite factors and a doubtful fifth factor. Taking the unrotated solution first, we find factor one characterized by the following occupations: Psychologist, Dentist, Mathematician, Physicist, Chemist, Printer, Mathematics-Science Teacher, and Musician. Factor three loads on Strong's original groups III, IV, and VIII, as well as on a masculinity scale. Factor four loads highly on group VI, while factor five has hardly any high loadings. Interpretation of these factors is a little uncertain, but would presumably be in terms of interest in science (factor one), interest in people (factor two), interest in business (factor three), and interest in material things (factor four).

The rotated solution presents a slightly more obscure picture. Factor one is again characterized by interest in scientific subjects; factor four by interest in people. Factor three appears to represent interest in material things (an alternative possibility is that this factor simply groups together low-level occupational interests). Factors two and five are by no means clearly defined, and have no very high saturations to guide in interpretation.

Analyses of female interest patterns have been made by Strong (1943) and by Crissy and Daniel (1939). Both reveal very similar patterns, and Strong has made use of the rotation carried out by Crissy and Daniel on their material. The four rotated factors have been named by these authors: "interest in people", "interest in language", "interest in science", and "interest in male association". Strong "fails to see any gain by naming the factors resulting from rotation . . . naming a factor is largely guessing today". With this remark the present writer would on the whole be in agreement, provided it is confined to factorial studies in the field of interests. There is little trace in these various analyses of any attempt at setting up specific hypotheses regarding the nature of a given factor, and predicting on the basis of such hypotheses the factorial composition of new scales not included in the original analysis. Factor analysis has been used to suggest such hypotheses regarding the classification of interests; what is lacking is any attempt to test the correctness of the hypotheses derived. The design of experiments along such lines would probably be rather complex and difficult, but until the attempt is made the results so far achieved cannot be taken too seriously. From the simple point of view of practical usefulness factor analysis is not likely at the moment to improve on the predictive accuracy of the existing single scales. From the scientific point of view, however, we must formulate some kind of theory to account for the observed intercorrelations, and thus to bring order into an extremely confused field. To refuse to "name" factors may be an act of scientific caution, but clearly the matter cannot be allowed to remain there. Some underlying principles of classification are clearly present in the field of "interests"; until these are found and measured, we can hardly rest content.

Relevant to this general problem of classification of interests is the work of Kuder on his *Preference Record* (1939), although no factorial analyses were carried out by this writer. However, the internal consistency criteria adopted, and the relative independence of the scales which make up the final record, effectively amount to something very similar to a factorial study, and consequently the resulting classification may with advantage be quoted here. Ten main areas are recognized by Kuder: outdoor, mechanical, computational, scientific, persuasive, artistic, literary, musical, social service, and clerical. Intercorrelations between scores in these areas are relatively slight; only three are above ·4 (outdoors versus persuasive $= - ·49$; outdoor versus clerical $= - ·40$; scientific versus persuasive $= - ·42$). There is clearly some overlap with Strong's factors, but Kuder's list would appear rather more comprehensive. Possibly a factor analysis of the correlations between Kuder's 10 areas (which would correspond to primary factors) would result in second-order factors of some interest.

There have been several studies intercorrelating scores on the Kuder test and scores on other tests, particularly the Allport and Vernon Study of Values; there are also a number of correlational studies involving the Kuder and the Strong tests. In addition, of course, the Strong Inventory has been correlated with the Study of Values. Some of these are reviewed below: a general review with original data is given by Stanley and Waldrop (1952).

Much more satisfactory than the purely empirical findings discussed so far is the work to be discussed next. This is clearly based on a definite hypothesis, which can be supported or disproved; it thus follows closely the traditional hypothetico-deductive approach of science. The hypothesis referred to originated with the German psychologist Spranger (1927), who based his typology on the contrasting patterns of interests or values held by his six *types of men*: theoretical (rational, scientific), economic (utilitarian, useful), æsthetic (beauty, harmony), social (people, human relations), political (power, dominance), and religious (unity, communion). Allport and Vernon (1931) constructed a self-administering test of preference-judgments to measure the degree to which respondents were influenced by these various values or interests; this test they called the Study of Values. Use was made in the construction of the different scales of the internal consistency technique, although no factorial study was carried out until Lurie's paper (1937) appeared to make good this deficiency.

This author used 203 students as subjects, all of whom had filled in the Study of Values forms. Tetrachoric correlations were run between 24 scores obtained from the 144 items of the Allport-Vernon test, and a Thurstone-type factor analysis carried out, using oblique factors. Four main such factors are isolated. "Factor I is clearly *social* and altruistic, a factor having to do with the valuing of human relations as such. . . . The second is complex, involving items supposed to correspond to Spranger's economic and political types, and inversely to the æsthetic type; one might call this pattern the *Philistine* type, aggressive, go-getting, utilitarian, anti-cultural. Factor III is plainly *theoretical*. . . Number IV is the *religious* type, probably more closely connected with doctrine and practice than the vague mystical unity with the cosmos that Spranger envisaged." Conformation of the relatively independent existence of these four types comes from a more recent study by Coates (1950), who constructed scales for the measurement of the religious, æsthetic (i.e. opposite to Philistine), theoretical, and social types, and showed by internal-consistency methods the relative independence of these types.

There are obvious connections between these studies and the work of Strong and Thurstone. Lurie's theoretical corresponds to Thurstone's scientific type; Lurie's social corresponds to Thurstone's "interest in people". The Philistine factor probably corresponds to "interest in business". These identifications are merely *a priori*, of course; more solid evidence is provided in some studies by Ferguson, Humphreys, and Strong (1941), Sarbin and Berdie (1940), van Dusen, Wimberley, and Mosier (1939), Duffy and Crissy (1940), Burgemeister (1940), and Tussing (1942). These various authors have shown conclusively that definite trends exist which connect the Strong scoring categories with the Allport-Vernon types. As Strong (1943) points out, "these relationships between the Allport-Vernon values and occupational interests indicate general trends and aid in interpreting both sets of data. Unfortunately they are not high enough to warrant using either test for the other, since scores in one test cannot be transmuted into the other with sufficient reliability for use in individual diagnosis".

An interesting extension of this work on values is presented by Morris (1956), Morris and Jones (1955) and Jones and Morris (1956). These writers constructed thirteen possible "Ways to Live"; these "represent, for the most part, conceptions of the desirable life as embodied in the main religious and ethical traditions". Response categories for each of the thirteen ways to live are presented, ranging from "I like it very much" to "I dislike it very much". Responses were scaled and correlations between the thirteen "ways" obtained from American and Indian students. The American analysis resulted in five main factors called respectively: (*a*) social restraint and self control, (*b*) enjoyment in action, (*c*) withdrawal and self-sufficiency, (*d*) receptivity and sympathetic concern, (*e*) self indulgence. Factors from the Indian analysis were very similar. Factor scores were obtained for various samples of Japanese, Chinese and Norwegian subjects, in addition to the American and Indian ones; these are plotted in Fig. 49.

The thirteen ways to live, and also the five factor scores, were correlated for American students with the Thurstone Temperament Schedule, which gives rise to seven scores (active, vigorous, impulsive, dominant, stable, unsociable, reflective). The results of this study strongly suggest a substantial relationship between the domain of temperament and that of value, especially for values represented by factors (*b*) and (*c*), Enjoyment and Progress in Action, and Withdrawal and Self-sufficiency. Relations are less marked between temperament areas and value factor (*d*) Receptivity, and are much

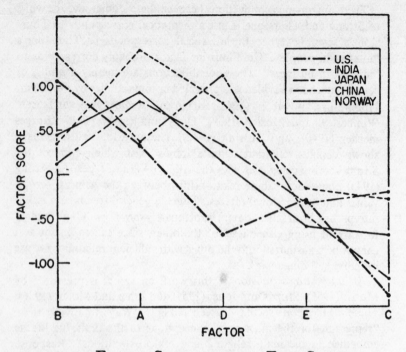

Fig. 49.— FACTOR SCORES OF THE FIVE SAMPLES:
UNITED STATES ANALYSIS

less marked between temperament areas and value of factors (a) and
(e), Social Restraint and Self-Indulgence. The actual correlations are
again below in Table 55.

TABLE 55

*Estimated Value Factor Loadings on Thurstone
Temperament Variables*

Temperament Variable	Value Factor					
	A	B	C	D	E	h²
A	15	24	−06	09	−07	097
V	−27	69	−26	−13	−06	637
I	07	75	−24	−04	13	644
D	17	48	−15	−08	00	288
E	01	06	00	−06	−06	011
S	−02	55	−33	17	00	441
R	06	−20	38	−41	21	400

Rather different from the preceding investigations, although still relevant to the problem of classification of occupational interest, is a recent paper by Vernon (1949). A list of 58 occupations was drawn up by him and given to some 50 judges. These were asked to judge the degree of similarity or dissimilarity of pairs of occupations on a seven-point scale; on the average five judges rated each of the 1,653 possible combinations of two occupations. Correlations were then calculated to show the resemblance of the total pattern of interests in each pair of occupations, and a factorial analysis performed. Four factors emerged:

I. Gregarious versus Isolated.
II. Social Welfare versus Administrative.
III. Scientific versus Display.
IV. Verbal versus Active.

Vernon identifies some of his factors with both Strong's and Spranger's types. Thus factor II he considers to correspond to Spranger's social versus political types; Strong's group 2 he relates to the scientific, 4 to the active, 5 to the social welfare, 8 to the administrative, 9 to the display, and 10 to the verbal type. It is to be noted that Vernon identifies his factors both from the positive and the negative end; this seems a reasonable procedure in a field where negative factor saturations cannot be avoided. Possibly Strong's factors could with advantage be treated in a similar manner. Certainly the impossibility of avoiding bipolar factors makes a simple taking over of methods of analysis and interpretation from the field of cognitive testing somewhat hazardous, and may ultimately lead to new techniques more easily adapted to this type of problem.

Lacking even more in psychological hypotheses than the work of Strong, and even more strongly empiricist in outlook than his, is a study by Adams and Fowler (1946) and Kelley (1946). These writers collected a list of 40 "rubrics" (rather specific interest types) which were then used to construct preference items each of which covered several "rubrics". Correlations were run for 800 men on 35 of these rubrics, and five factors extracted from the matrix. These factors were not rotated or in any way interpreted, but were simply given meaningless names based on the initial letters of the rubrics having high loadings on each factor. As summarized by Vernon (1949), the five factors are:

360 THE STRUCTURE OF HUMAN PERSONALITY

(1) MIMSEC—masculine, mechanical versus social, effeminate.

(2) PEPGAP—persevering, pioneering, economic, practical versus adventurous, physical activity.

(3) PAMRIM—power, aggressive, money, physical activity versus religion, industrious, music.

(4) RODPOD—routine, domestic, religious versus pioneering, outdoor, daring.

(5) NEVCOM—nature-loving, religious, salesmanship versus power, mechanical, spatial, orderliness, verbal, music.[1]

Vernon comments: "So far no convincing examples of the practical applicability of these heterogeneous types have been published, and we are entitled to doubt whether such extreme empiricism actually works." Indeed, it would seem that in this field particularly the use of factor analysis can only be justified if it advances our psychological understanding; as Thomson (1939) has pointed out: "When vocational guidance proceeds by giving to a candidate a number of tests which have previously been given to persons already engaged in the occupations, the use of factor analysis has no mathematical justification whatever."

The most extensive factor study of human interest available has been carried out by Guilford *et al*. (1954). Working on over 1,000 subjects, they factor analysed 95 variables and extracted 24 centroid factors. This work was done independently on two samples to make possible cross-identification of factors. One sample consisted of officers and the other of enlisted men. Seventeen main factors were found in common to these two groups; in addition six other factors were unique to the enlisted men analysis, and five were unique to the officer analysis. For reasons of space only the names of the main factors can be given here; they are mechanical interest, scientific interest, adventure vs. security, social welfare, aesthetic appreciation, aesthetic expression, need for diversion, need for attention, business interest, outdoor work interest, physical drive, precision, thinking, orderliness vs. disorderliness, cultural conformity, clerical interests, aggression and sociability. These factors are certainly not orthogonal and unfortunately no second order factor analysis is given by Guilford. Accordingly, any identification of factors with those mentioned before cannot be undertaken with any reasonable hope of success.

Somewhat different from all the foregoing analyses, both in the activities included in the questionnaire and in the method of analysis

[1] The haunting beauty of these five names recalls Lewis Carroll and Lear.

are two studies by Chisnall (1942) and Hammond (1945). Both deal with leisure-time interests among adolescents attending a Youth Centre, and both agree in finding, first a general factor and then a bipolar factor. "Analysis of the interests showed that some had a very specialized appeal attracting members who showed little interest in other aspects of the Centre (e.g. darts, table tennis, reading), whilst others drew upon a more general interest. This latter kind of interest is the one which is most likely to promote a community spirit." The bipolar factor which followed this general factor "fitted in with the usual idea of an athletic type, interested primarily in physical activities in contrast with a more sedentary type having artistic and intellectual interests". This second factor might be identified with extraversion-introversion, but it might with equal justice be regarded as a sex factor—boys tended towards the athletic, girls towards the artistic pole. Altogether, interpretation in more general terms is difficult of these two researches because of the narrow range of activities included.

One further research may be mentioned which confirmed Chisnall's and Hammond's second factor on an all-male sample of 1,000 Navy recruits. Vernon and Parry (1949) carried out a factor analysis of 20 interest items in a biographical questionnaire, and extracted two general factors, one of which contrasted interests having high cultural loadings (discussion, photography, acting, and reading) with interests in physical activities (boxing, football, metal-work, and cooking). The other general factor was of no interest, as it merely represented a tendency to tick many or few interests. Four group factors were also found, however, after the elimination of the two general factors, which Vernon identified with mechanical, athletic, social, and domestic interest types. The narrow range of items again makes this analysis not quite comparable with those of Thurstone, Strong, and Lurie, although it would not be possible to deny certain similarities.

Altogether, we may agree with Vernon's (1949) conclusion when he writes: "Interests can be classified into groups or types at a rather general level. In spite of the different approaches of different typologists, and the very different kinds of test material analysed by different factorists, there is a fair amount of overlapping or concordance between their results. Similar groupings tend to emerge also whether actual occupational interests or leisure-time pursuits are considered." The amount of agreement found is promising, but it is far from sufficient to make one feel that anything like finality has been reached in these efforts at finding a basis for classification. A parallel might be drawn between the present state of this field and the state of personality questionnaire analysis before the Guilfords' attempt to get away from correlation between *a priori* clusters, and to analyse instead correlations between items. No large-scale study of such intercorrelations between items has yet been carried out, and there is little doubt in the writer's mind that only by such a study, using oblique and second-order factors if necessary, can a really firm

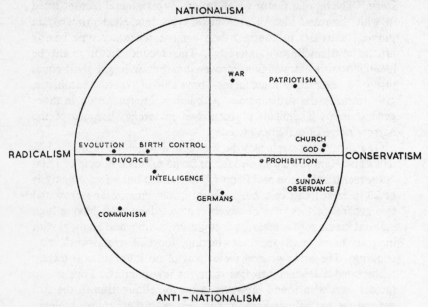

Fig. 50.—Factor Study of Radicalism with Attitude Scales by Thelma Gwinn Thurstone.

foundation be laid for a proper system of classification of interests and values.

After this discussion of the organization of interests and values, we must turn to the problem presented by attitudes. Here, as in so many other fields, the pioneering study is due to Thurstone (1934). Eleven attitude scales were given to almost 400 students, whose scores on an intelligence test were also known. These 12 variables were correlated and two factors extracted from the resulting matrix. Fig. 50 shows in two-dimensional projection the position of the various scales, together with the interpretation of the two factors as given by Thurstone. No detailed criticism of the results of this study need be given here; we may note, however, that the second factor can hardly be identified as a "nationalism" factor in view of the fact that the "patriotism" scale has a higher factor saturation on "conservatism" than on this putative "nationalism" factor, although in ordinary speech these two terms are almost interchangeable. Also it should be noted that the position of the axes is somewhat arbitrary, as there is clearly no simple structure to be derived from this particular analysis. As will be shown later, a slight rotation of this arbitrary axis pattern brings Thurstone's results into good agreement with those of later workers. (A more recent experiment with the Thurstone scales is reported by Diggory, 1953.)

While we may doubt the exact identification of the factors or the precise position of the axes, Thurstone's study must, nevertheless, be regarded as giving strong support to the view, the correctness of which had been adumbrated by Lundberg (1926), George (1925), Likert (1932), and others, affirming the existence of a general radicalism-conservatism factor.[1] Confirmation of his results was given in a study by Kulp and Davidson (1934), who administered a questionnaire containing 108 items on the issues of race, internationalism, national-ism, militarism, and the like to 150 high-school students. Sixty-nine of these items were classified into five categories—15 dealt with racial questions, 17 with national questions, 14 with imperialism, 10 with militarism, and 13 with international co-operation and good-will (internationalism). Intercorrelations ranging from ·22 to ·52 with an average r of ·40 were found between these five groups, and a Spearman-type analysis showed little departure from a two-factor pattern, i.e. a pattern in which all the scores can be accounted for in terms of one general factor and factors specific to each of the separate tests. Saturations of the five groups of items with this general factor of radicalism-conservatism ranged from ·5 to ·8.

At about the same time there appeared another factorial study, in which Carlson (1934) gave five attitude tests and one intelligence test to 215 students. Three factors were extracted, the first of which opposed belief in God to an attitude favourable to pacifism and

[1] Among the earliest attempts to find generality in the field of social attitudes was the study by Lentz, who took six *a priori* groups of questionnaire items: education, religion, government, sex, non-social, and general. There were 190 items in the six groups and 579 college students constituted the sample. Reliabilities for the six sub-tests averaged about ·6 and the intercorrelations between the six sub-tests averaged around ·45, a value which was considerably increased when the correlations were corrected for attenuation. No factor analysis was carried out, but Lentz concludes that his results "argue strongly for the validity of the concept of general conservatism". Cf. also Stagner (1936, 1942).

communism; this factor he called "intelligence" because intelligence was found to correlate positively with attitudes favourable to pacifism and communism. His second factor, *radicalism-conservatism*, opposed belief in God to attitudes favourable towards prohibition and communism; while his third factor opposed belief in God to an attitude favourable towards birth control and was called "*religious*". These groupings, and also the names given to them, could be criticized in detail; the main difficulty seems to be that no convincing interpretation is possible with such a very small number of attitudes. It will be shown later that Carlson's results can be fitted in well with those of Thurstone and later writers, and consequently no further discussion of his data will be given here.

The studies of Thurstone, Kulpe, Davidson, and Carlson were conducted on a relatively small scale. The work of Rundquist and Sletto (1936) on *Personality in the Depression* was carried out on a much larger scale. A considerable number of subjects, including university students, high-school students, and employed and unemployed workers of various types, were used in an effort to study "the effects of the depression on the personality and family life of young people". This purpose dictated the choice of variables. "Loss of morale, development of feelings of inferiority, disharmonic family relationships, increased disrespect for law, economic radicalism, and disillusionment concerning the value of education, are among the effects most commonly alleged to result from unemployment." Consequently, scales were constructed by means of internal consistency techniques, dealing with morale, inferiority, family, law, economic conservatism, and education. Correlations were calculated between these variables on nine different groups containing between 50 and 500 subjects.

No factorial analyses were carried out; the authors relied instead on partial and multiple correlations. Of particular interest here will be the correlations of conservatism with the other scales. Correlations with morale for the various groups are around the ·3 level. With education they tend to lie in the neighbourhood of ·1. With attitude towards the family, correlations are at about the same level as with education, whereas with attitude towards the law they tend to be rather higher, i.e. between ·4 and ·5. On the whole, morale was found most closely associated with the other variables measured, and conservatism least closely associated. "The fourth order partial coefficients between economic conservatism score and score on each of the other scales were computed for 500 men. Their size ranged from

— ·041 (economic conservatism versus family) to ·119 (economic conservatism versus morale). These are obviously not significantly different from zero." It is difficult to interpret this result in the absence of a proper factorial study. If Kulpe and Davidson's findings of a general factor of conservatism could be applied to the present data, then all fourth-order partials would be likely to vanish, so that this particular finding is of no great significance. In addition, the whole study suffers from the fact that what is intercorrelated are not individual items but scales put together partly on an *a priori* basis, although in fairness to Rundquist and Sletto it should be said that the method of internal consistency validation employed by them partly obviates this criticism. Nevertheless, the writer doubts if any general conclusions can be drawn from their work, the importance of which, from the point of view of its primary objection, namely the changes induced in personality by the depression, is, of course, not in question.

The work of Rundquist and Sletto (1936) was followed up by Darley and McNamara (1938, 1940). These authors gave the Rundquist and Sletto scales, as well as four adjustment inventory scales (home, health, social, emotional) and the Minnesota Inventory of Social Attitudes to 100 men and 100 women, calculating correlations separately for the two groups and separately for test and retest applications. Five factors were isolated: factor one, a measure of adjustment to society; factor two, a measure of the individual's effectiveness in social situations; factor three, one of family adjustment; factor four, one of neuroticism; factor five, one of radicalism-conservatism. Correlations between these factors were found to be relatively low, the highest being ·45. New scales were made up on the basis of these findings to measure the factors concerned, but little use seems to have been made of these scales, and the whole analysis does not appear to advance our knowledge to any considerable extent.

More in line with the earlier factorial studies than *Personality in the Depression* is a series of analyses by Ferguson (1939, 1940, 1941, 1942, 1944, 1946). In the first of these studies, Ferguson pointed out that the results of Thurstone and of Carlson "did not yield unequivocal definitions of the factors found to be required for the explanation of the intercorrelations among tests with which they were concerned". Using tests of the equal-appearing interval type for the measurement of attitudes towards war, reality of God, patriotism, treatment of criminals, capital punishment, censorship, evolution, birth control, law, and communism, he administered these instruments to 185 students and factor-analysed the resulting matrix of intercorrelations. He failed to find simple structure with the entire battery of tests, but when scales for the measurement of attitudes towards censorship, law, patriotism, and communism were dropped, he obtained an excellent fit to simple structure and succeeded in locating his axes uniquely.[1] Factor one he found to be characterized by scales dealing with the reality of God, as opposed to belief in evolution and birth control. Factor two was described by scales measuring attitudes towards the treatment of criminals, capital punishment, and war. These two factors he called "religionism" and "humanitarianism", and in his second paper, scales were constructed for the measurement of these two attitudes. In 1941 the experiment was repeated by administering the same scales to another set of 178 students, and the same two factors "religionism" and "humanitarianism" emerged. In 1942 a third factor of "nationalism" was added to the others by re-analysis of the original data so that Ferguson now claims to have established the existence of three "primary social attitudes", as he calls them: religionism, humanitarianism, and nationalism. In 1944 another repetition of the original experiment was carried out, using some 600 cases altogether. In this experiment, Ferguson showed again that the same factors could be extracted from the matrix of intercorrelations. In his other studies, he has tried to relate these various factors to such variables as sex, religion, education, and so forth.

In 1944 Eysenck made an attempt to integrate the findings of Thurstone, Carlson, and Ferguson, as well as those of an analysis carried out by him on some 700 replies to a questionnaire containing 32 propositions. It was found that when the original two centroid axes in each of the various analyses were superimposed on each other, similar items from the different researches fell into the four quadrants. Thus, the first quadrant was characterized by such items as favourable attitudes towards patriotism, war, capital punishment, law, and harsh treatment of criminals. The second quadrant was characterized by favourable attitudes towards evolution, divorce, abortion, birth control, and divorce reform. The third quadrant was characterized by pacifism, anti-ethnocentrism, and favourable attitudes towards sex and race equality, and the fourth by favourable attitudes towards religious issues, such as the existence of God, Sunday observance, church-going, and so forth.

The first axis or factor was interpreted as one of radicalism-

---

[1] This is not a very difficult feat, of course, when almost half the variables have been dropped and only 6 remain!

conservatism; "the *radical* attitudes—communist, favourable towards easy divorce, birth control, and evolution—are opposed to the *conservative* attitudes—patriot, favourable towards religion, capital punishment, law, and so on". The second factor was rather more difficult to interpret. "On the one side we have the practical, materialistic, extraverted person, who deals with the environment either by force (soldier) or by manipulation (scientist). On the other side we have the theoretical, idealistic, introverted person who deals with problems either by thinking (philosopher) or by believing (priest). . . . The *practical* attitude is that of James' "tough-minded" man . . .; the *theoretical* attitude is that of the 'tender minded'."

This interpretation was considered less of the nature of a conclusion but rather as an hypothesis to govern further research, and accordingly an experiment was set up to test the validity of the interpretations made and the reproducibility of the factors isolated. This attempt at validation was governed by two main principles, both of which would appear to contain a methodological advance on previous work: (1) it was considered that confirmation of the correct identification of a radicalism-conservatism factor could only come by reference to a tested criterion, namely an actual survey of opinions held by known conservatives and radicals respectively; (2) it was considered that the nature of the second factor could be clarified most by stating hypotheses regarding its nature and including items which would present a test of the accuracy of these hypotheses. The second of these two principles governed the selection of items, the first determined the sample to whom the questionnaire was given. A set of 40 items was prepared and is reproduced below in Table 56. 750 subjects constituted the sample, which was selected in such a way that 250 were socialists, 250 liberals, and 250 conservatives. Party affiliation was decided on the basis of the vote cast in the last election. Groups were equated for age, sex, and education. Tetrachoric correlations were calculated between all the items, and a factorial analysis carried out which gave rise to two main factors. Fig. 51 shows the distribution of the various items which characterize the two factors. The first factor was called R (for radicalism-conservatism), the second factor T (for tough-minded versus tender-minded).

Proof for the correct identification of the R factor is obtainable by reference to actual attitude statements of the socialist and conservative groups respectively. Differences in item endorsements between these two groups were calculated for each of the 40 items, and the following hypothesis set up. An item having high positive saturation for the R factor should also have a markedly higher endorsement by the socialists as compared with the conservatives. Items having high negative R saturation should show considerably higher endorsement by conservatives than by socialists. Items having zero loadings on the R factor should show no difference in endorsement between the two political groups. Intermediate items should show intermediate differences in endorsement. This deduction can be put to the proof by correlating the column of factor saturations on R with a column of endorsement differences for the 40 items. This correlation turned out to be $+ \cdot 98$, which is sufficiently close to unity to be regarded as adequate proof of the original hypothesis.[1]

Regarding the second factor, unfortunately no such outside criterion was available, and consequently inspection of the variables having high saturations on it becomes necessary. Such inspection, taken together with the provisional hypothesis formed on the basis of the previous tentative identification of that factor, led to the abandonment of the terms "practical" and "theoretical" and to the adoption rather of the terms "tender-minded" (instead of theoretical) and "tough-minded" (instead of practical). The reasons for this renaming will be obvious from an inspection of the items included in Fig. 51.

Scales were constructed from items having high saturations with these factors for the accurate measurement of both R and T. These were found to have almost zero intercorrelation with each other, and to be relatively independent of sex, age, and education. Two exceptions to this general statement may be noted. Women showed a distinct tendency to be more tender-minded, and well-educated subjects showed a distinct tendency towards greater radicalism. Scores on the R factor have on several occasions been found to distinguish at a high level of significance between different political groups, whereas scores on the T factor have usually failed to do so.

One exception should be noted to this rule. In a recent paper, Eysenck (1951) tried to clarify the concept underlying the T factor by putting forward two hypotheses: (1) working-class subjects are

[1] This conclusion may appear to contradict that of Kerr (1952) who carried out a factor analysis on American students for five types of Liberalism/Conservatism, namely, political, economic, religious, social and aesthetic. He concluded from his factor analysis that "Liberalism/Conservatism is shown to be not a unitary dimension of personality but a complex group of relatively independent continuua, five of which are separately identified as political, economic, religious, social and aesthetic." The conclusion does not seem to follow from the data. The question and concepts used by Kerr to define these different varieties of conservatism appear to be so idiosyncratic as to test no widely held theory. This is particularly true of his definition of political liberalism.

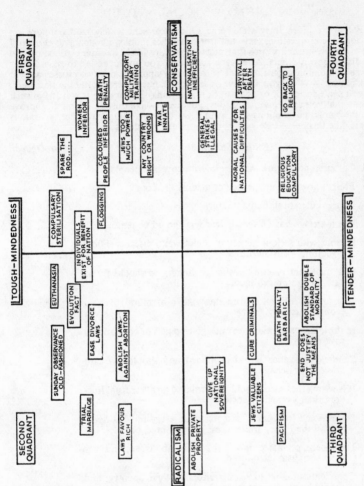

Fig. 51.—Attitudes as related to R and T Factors.

369

TABLE 56

INVENTORY OF SOCIAL ATTITUDES

Below are given forty statements which represent widely held opinions on various social questions, selected from speeches, books, newspapers, etc. They were chosen in such a way that most people are likely to agree with some and to disagree with others. After each statement, you are requested to record your personal opinion regarding it. If you strongly approve, put two crosses after it —like this: + +. If you approve on the whole, put one cross after the statement. If you can't decide for or against, or if you think the question is worded in such a way that you can't give an answer, put a zero—like this; O. If you disapprove on the whole, put a minus sign. And if you strongly disapprove, put two minus signs, like this: — —. Be sure not to omit any questions.

Attitude Statements	*Your Opinion*
1. Coloured people are innately inferior to white people	....
2 Present laws favour the rich as against the poor	....
3. War is inherent in human nature	....
4. The marriage bar on female teachers should be removed	....
5. Persons with serious hereditary defects and diseases should be compulsorily sterilized	....
6. Our treatment of criminals is too harsh; we should try to cure, not to punish them	....
7. Our present difficulties are due rather to moral than to economic causes	....
8. In the interests of peace, we must give up part of our national sovereignty	....
9. Sunday-observance is old fashioned and should cease to govern our behaviour	....
10. It is wrong that men should be permitted greater sexual freedom than women by society	....
11. Unrestricted freedom of discussion on every topic is desirable in the Press, in literature, on the stage, etc.	....
12. Ultimately, private property should be abolished, and complete socialism introduced	....
13. Conscientious objectors are traitors to their country, and should be treated accordingly	....
14. A certain amount of sex education should be given at school to all boys and girls	....
15. The laws against abortion should be abolished	....
16. Only by going back to religion can civilization hope to survive	....
17. Marriages between white and coloured people should be strongly discouraged	....
18. Jews are as valuable, honest, and public-spirited citizens as any other group	....

Attitude Statements   *Your Opinion*

19. Major questions of national policy should be decided by reference to majority opinion (e.g. by referendum) ....

20. There should be far more controversial and political discussion over the radio ....

21. The present licensing laws should be altered so as to remove restrictions on hours of opening ....

22. All human beings are born with the same potentialities ....

23. Divorce laws should be altered to make divorce easier ....

24. Patriotism in the modern world is a force which works against peace ....

25. Modern life is too much concentrated in cities; the Government should take steps to encourage a "return to the country" ....

26. Crimes of violence should be punished by flogging ....

27. The nationalization of the great industries is likely to lead to inefficiency, bureaucracy, and stagnation ....

28. It is right and proper that religious education in schools should be made compulsory ....

29. Men and women have the right to find out whether they are sexually suited before marriage (e.g. by companionate marriage ....

30. The principle "Spare the rod and spoil the child" has much truth in it, and should govern our methods of bringing up children ....

31. Women are not the equals of men in intelligence, organizing ability, etc. ....

32. Experiments on living animals should be forbidden ....

33. The Jews have too much power and influence in this country ....

34. Differences in pay between men and women doing the same work should be abolished ....

35. Birth control, except when medically indicated, should be made illegal ....

36. The death penalty is barbaric, and should be abolished ....

37. There will be another war in twenty-five years ....

38. Scientists should take no part in politics ....

39. The Japanese are by nature a cruel people ....

40. Only people with a definite minimum of intelligence and education should be allowed to vote ....

Personal Details

It would be appreciated if you would fill in the following details:

41. Age........ 42. Sex........ 43. Weekly income (self or husband)......
44. Type of work...

(From Eysenck, 1947)

more "tough-minded" than middle-class subjects; (2) communists and fascists, although at opposite ends of the continuum with respect to the R factor, are both more "tough-minded" than are the socialists, liberals, and conservatives. Both predictions were fulfilled at a high level of confidence. When middle-class socialists, liberals, conservatives, and communists were compared with working-class socialists, liberals, conservatives, and communists, respectively, the latter were found in each case to be more tough-minded than the former. When communists and fascists were compared with members of the other three groups, they were found to occupy positions in the first and second quadrants respectively, i.e. the fascists tended to be conservative and tough-minded, whereas the communists tended to be radical and tough-minded. Both groups were considerably more tough-minded than the three democratic parties of whom the liberals were found to be the most tender-minded.

The analysis of social attitudes into two main factors may thus be regarded as having a considerable degree of validity. It reconciles the data from analyses by all the writers mentioned hitherto, and it appears to be relatively independent of the country in which the analysis is carried out or the particular items or scales employed. Some recently published investigations have shown that a very similar pattern to the one discussed above emerges in such widely different cultures as the American, Swedish, and the German, where the set of questions used in the previous analysis was given to large middle- and working-class samples of nationals in each of these countries respectively (Eysenck, 1953).

One question arises, however, which demands an answer. When the results depicted in Fig. 5 are compared with Ferguson's analysis, it will be found that agreement is striking with respect to the actual position of the various items, but that his two main factors, "religionism" and "humanitarianism", are rotated from R and T through an angle of about 45 degrees. Thus, "humanitarianism" is characterized by the items in the tender-minded-radical quadrant, and "anti-humanitarianism" by the items in the tough-minded-conservative quadrant. Similarly, "religionism" is characterized by the items in the conservative-tender-minded quadrant, and anti-religionism by items in the tough-minded-radical quadrant. Indeed, it would seem that the sets of items in each of these quadrants define a particular type of person. Items in the first (tough-minded-conservative) quadrant define the fascist, and, as pointed out above, when R and T scales are given to members of the fascist party, their scores cluster in this neighbourhood. Similarly, the second quadrant tough-minded-radical) shows a cluster of items characteristic of the communist, and, again, actual experiment has shown that the R and T scores of communists tend to cluster in this quadrant. The third quadrant (radical-tender-minded) is characterized by items which would define members of the Society of Friends, pacifists, members of the Independent Labour Party, and other similar organizations. Items in the fourth quadrant (conservative-tender-minded) all refer to religious beliefs and practices, and would therefore characterize the active church-goer.[1]

There is no absolute preference attached to a description of the relations between attitudes in terms of R and T compared with a similar description in terms of Ferguson's two factors. Both would reproduce the observed correlations with equal accuracy, and both give a psychologically meaningful interpretation. The writer's preference for the R and T solution arises from the social importance of the radicalism-conservatism dichotomy, which enables us to assign a position to the R axis which is quite unique and invariant by simply maximizing the correlation between factor saturations on R and per cent. differences between endorsements for the statements included in the analysis by known socialists and conservatives. On the other hand, it must be admitted that a similarly unique position can probably be assigned to Ferguson's factors by reference to simple structure. There are certain doubts attaching to this possibility, however, as Ferguson worked with a very small number of variables indeed; in analysing a large table of correlations like Eysenck's, it would be much more difficult to reach any form of simple structure. Ultimately, the decision must be made on psychological rather than on statistical grounds, and it is here that the R-T analysis seems to the writer more promising than Ferguson's. It seems more reasonable psychologically to regard communism as a mixture of radicalism

[1] One interesting point should be noted here. The analyses of social attitudes reported bear a striking relation to Lurie's (1937) work on the "study of values". His social-altruistic factor corresponds to the tender-minded radical; his philistine type to the tough-minded conservative; his religious type clearly corresponds to the tender-minded conservative; while the theoretical, scientific factor bears a somewhat less close relation to the tough-minded radical type. This identification is based on the rather remarkable resemblance in description between these various studies; it should be an easy matter to decide by experiment whether such cross-identification is empirically justified.

Of interest here is also a recent paper by Broen (1957) who showed by means of factor analysis that religious attitudes needed two dimensions for their proper description; the first was described as a "Nearness of God" dimension and the other as a "Fundamentalism-Humanitarianism" dimension.

and tough-mindedness, or fascism as a mixture of conservatism and tough-mindedness, than it is to consider radicalism as a mixture of humanitarianism and anti-religionism or conservatism as a mixture of religionism and anti-humanitarianism.

This conclusion agrees well with one of the few factorial studies in the area which were guided by a definite hypothesis. Hatt (1948) was concerned with the problem of ethnic attitudes and elaborated a research design to make possible the study of two frequently mentioned hypotheses. The first of these assumes that attitudes towards ethnic groups are positively correlated with attitudes towards the lower class; this position has found political expression in socialism, communism, and several liberal and progressive movements. Essentially what is implied is a class relationship as the essence of attitude patterns. The other hypothesis maintains that attitudes towards minorities are a function of some universally applicable standard of ethical morality and unrelated to class attitude. This view has often led to the belief that favourable attitudes towards the minority are the expression of a breadth of education likely to be characteristic of the middle and upper classes. However, many who accept this second view do so without any class implication whatsoever. Using three separate groups (university students, high school students, and upper class adults), Hatt constructed and administered six attitude scales measuring antagonism towards the upper class, the middle class, the lower class, Negroes, Jews, and the foreign born. Intercorrelations were run between the six scales for the three groups separately, and a factor analysis, using Hotelling's method of principal components, was carried out. The first principal component accounted for 53 per cent. of the variance, and inspection of its relationship with the several scales revealed at once that it agrees markedly with the hypothesis that attitudes towards minorities vary directly with each other, directly with attitudes towards the lower class, and inversely with attitudes towards the upper class. The types resulting from this factor "represent the polar patterns earlier described as inherent in the first view of the class nature of attitudes towards ethnic minorities; the 'progressive, class-conscious partisan of the lower class', and the 'reactionary and class-conscious upper-class supporter' ".

The second principal component accounts for an additional 20 per cent. of the total variance. "This pattern is definable almost exactly in the terms of the second approach mentioned at the beginning of this paper. It is composed of the same basic inter-class relations as in factor one, the negative correlations of considerable magnitude between attitudes towards upper and lower classes. In this component, however, the association of class attitudes with attitudes towards ethnic groups is reversed. Here antagonism towards the upper and favourable attitudes towards the lower class are associated with antagonism towards the minorities. The other end of this pattern represents a favourable attitude towards minorities associated with favourable attitudes towards the upper class and a negative attitude towards the lower class. This is the syndrome of attitudes which would justify a 'tolerance' approach based upon ethical enlightenment and brotherhood and void of the direct class appeal. In this factor the 'broadly educated, high principled altruist' and 'ignorant, narrow opportunistic bigot' of the second hypothesis are apparent. Both original hypotheses have thus been empirically verified as applicable to the samples, though with different degrees of importance."

The two factors isolated in this admirable study resemble very closely the radical-conservative, and the tough-tender-mindedness factors described previously; as we have shown before, ethnocentrism is correlated both with conservatism (Hatt's first factor) and also with tough-mindedness (Hatt's second factor), which in turn is found much more conspicuously in working-class than in middle-class samples. Here, then, we have another independent proof along quite original lines of the essential soundness of the analysis of social attitudes in terms of the R and T factors.[1]

A striking confirmation of the findings reported by Ferguson, Eysenck, and Hatt is contained in a recent study by Adorno, Frenkel-Brunswik, Levinson, and Sanford on *The Authoritarian Personality* (1950). This brilliant contribution to the study of attitude and personality takes its starting-point from the phenomenon of anti-Semitism. As a first step, five scales were constructed "dealing respectively with imagery (opinions) of Jews as personally *offensive* and as socially *threatening*; with attitudes concerning what should be done to or against Jews; and with the opposing views that Jews are too *seclusive* or too *intrusive* (assimilative)". These sub-scales have reasonable reliabilities and correlate quite highly together, co-efficients ranging from ·74 to ·86; if corrected for attenuation they would all be well over ·9. While no formal factor analysis was carried out these results are in good agreement with a factorial study by

[1] Essentially similar in their conclusion to the R-T studies are a number of papers by Sanai (1950, 1951, 1952). Sanai's main contribution appears to be a renaming of the R and T factors.

Eysenck and Crown (1949) in which 24 statements relating to anti-Semitism were intercorrelated and the resulting matrix factor analysed. A very prominent general factor was found leaving residuals of no more than doubtful significance. A Guttman-type analysis of the scale indicated a reproducibility of 85 per cent. There appears little doubt therefore that anti-Semitism qualifies as a consistent social attitude.

The next step of Adorno *et al.* was the construction of an ethnocentrism scale, referred to as the "E" scale. (The anti-Semitism scale is referred to as the A-S scale.) This E scale is made up of three sub-scales "dealing respectively with Negroes, various other minorities, and patriotism (extra-national groupings)". Correlations between these three sub-scales were again quite high, ranging from ·74 to ·83; if corrected for attenuation, these correlations would all be above ·9. Anti-Semitism was found to correlate ·80 with the total E scale and ·74, ·76, and ·69 respectively with the three sub-scales (Negroes, minorities, and patriotism). "Anti-Semitism is best regarded, it would seem, as one aspect of this broader frame of mind; and it is the total ethnocentric ideology rather than prejudice against any single group which requires explanation."

(In a factorial study of prejudice Hofstaetter (1952) throws doubt on this conclusion by extracting an anti-negro and an anti-semitic factor; however, a glance at his Fig. I will show that these factors are by no means independent.)

Next, a scale of politico-economic conservatism (PEC) was constructed. "No attempt was made, in the construction of the PEC scale, to cover all the forms in which conservatism and liberalism are currently expressed. The main focus was, rather, on some of the more underlying—and therefore more stable—ideological trends which appear to characterize conservatism and liberalism as *contrasting approaches* to *politico-economic* problems." Four main ideological trends were used: (1) support of the American *status quo;* (2) resistance to social change; (3) support of conservative values; and (4) ideas regarding the balance of power among business, labour, and government.

Conservatism was found to correlate with anti-Semitism, to the extent of ·43 (average of four groups totalling 295 subjects). Ethnocentrism and conservatism showed a correlation of ·59 for these groups. This correlation is very close to that obtained for a total of 1,568 subjects ($r = ·57$), and indicates quite clearly the marked relationship between conservatism and ethnocentrism. If conservatives tend to show more prejudice, then we should expect, on the basis of the work previously outlined, to find the more religious also to show more prejudice. This is borne out in fact; it is found that "subjects who profess to some religious affiliation express more prejudice than those who do not".

After these various scales had been constructed, an attempt was made to create yet one further scale for the measurement of implicit anti-democratic trends. "There gradually evolved a plan for constructing a scale that would measure prejudice without appearing to have this aim and without mentioning the name of any minority group. . . . It was clear at the time the new scale was being planned that anti-Semitism (A-S) and ethnocentrism (E) were not merely matters of surface opinion but general tendencies, with sources, in part at least, deep within the structure of the person. Would it not be possible to construct a scale that would approach more directly these deeper, often unconscious forces? If so, and if this scale could be validated by means of later clinical studies, would we not have a better estimate of anti-democratic *potential* than could be obtained from the scales that were more openly ideological?" The items in this anti-democratic or "fascist" scale (called the F scale) include statements such as the desirability of a double standard of morality; that obedience and respect for authority are the most important virtues children should learn; that sex criminals ought to be publicly whipped; and that there will always be war and conflict, human nature being what it is. It will be seen that these items are practically identical with those appearing in the tough-minded-conservative quadrant in Fig. 51; the anti-democratic, or authoritarian, character defined by this scale appears precisely similar to the fascist character outlined there, and as the opposite of Ferguson's" humanitarianism".

It may be interesting to state briefly the explicit generalizations regarding this authoritarian or "force" character which guided Adorno and his co-workers in their selection of items. The variables which they used to make up the basic content of the F scale were conventionalism, or the rigid adherence to conventional middle-class values; authoritarian submission and aggression, i.e. the tendency to be submissive towards ingroup authorities and aggressive towards people who violate conventional values; anti-intraception, defined as opposition to the subjective, the imaginative, the tender-minded; superstition and stereotypy; power and "toughness"; destructiveness and cynicism; projectivity, i.e. the projection outwards of unconscious emotional impulses; and an exaggerated concern with sexual "goings-on".

"These variables were thought of as going together to form a single syndrome, a more or less enduring structure in the person that renders him receptive to anti-democratic propaganda. One might say, therefore, that the F scale attempts to measure the potentially anti-democratic personality." According to this hypothesis, we would expect substantial correlations with the anti-Semitism, ethnocentrism, and conservatism scales, and such are indeed found. The

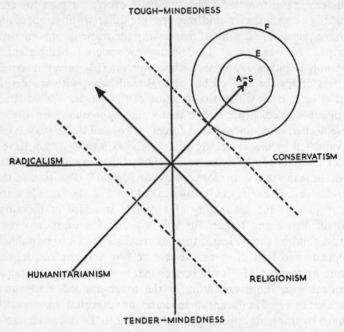

Fig. 52. "The Authoritarian Personality" as related to R and T Factors.

correlation between the F and the A-S scales is ·53; that between the F and the PEC scales is ·52, and that between the F and the E scales is ·73. This last correlation, if corrected for attenuation, would rise to about ·9.

We have already commented on the startling similarity between the results of the study under consideration and those of the studies previously reported, to which, curiously, Adorno, Frenkel-Brunswik, Levinson and Sanford make no reference. That relationship is pictured in Fig. 52. The vertical and the horizontal axes respectively represent the R and T factors; the diagonal lines represent Ferguson's humanitarianism and religionism factor; the concentric circles in the first quadrant represent respectively the anti-Semitism, ethno-centrism, and fascism scales. The PEC scale would be identical with the radicalism axis. Such close agreement between different inves-tigators, using quite different procedures and methods of analysis, is comparatively rare in social psychology, and may be taken as an indication of the firmness with which this attitude-structure is marked in contemporary Western culture.

Criticism of this concept of the "authoritarian personality" will be deferred until after a consideration of the attempt made by the authors of this book to link the concept with a detailed investigation of personality dynamics. In the main, interview procedures were used for the purpose of obtaining more information on personality variables, but projective techniques were also used. The selection of the subjects was determined by their responses on the A-S or the E scale. Most of the interviewees belong either to the uppermost or to the lowermost quartile, the proportions of high-scoring and low-scoring subjects being approximately equal. This basis of choice has been indicated in Fig. 52 by means of two parallel lines drawn at right angles to the humanitarianism factor in such a way that about 50 per cent. of the total population would lie between these lines, with 25 per cent. lying above the upper and 25 per cent. below the lower of the two lines. Comparing these extremes, it was found that certain personality variables appeared to be consistently related to this dichotomy.

These variables in the main appeared to be the following: (1) Repression versus awareness: the prejudiced individual showed a failure on the whole to be aware of unacceptable tendencies and impulses in himself. This failure made it impossible for him to integrate these tendencies (mainly fear, weakness, passivity, sex, impulses and aggressive feelings against authoratitive figures, such as the parents) satisfactorily with the conscious image he had of himself, and led to their being repressed. (2) Externalization versus internalization: as a defence against these repressed tendencies, the prejudiced subject resorts to projection, i.e. that which cannot be accepted as part of one's own ego is externalized. Part of this process of externalization is a tendency towards avoidance of introspection and of insight in general. "Since the energy of the person is in this case largely devoted either to keeping instinctual tendencies out of consciousness or to striving for external success and status, there appears to be relatively little left for genuine libidinization of one's own personal relationships or of one's work as ends in themselves."

(3) Conventionalism versus genuineness: the prejudiced person shows a higher degree of conformity; seemingly he needs external support given by authorities or public opinion in order to find some assurance concerning what is right and what is wrong. Attitudes towards parents, children, and members of the other sex tend to be conventionalized. The unprejudiced person, on the other hand, is not governed in his attitude by conventional approaches to the same extent. (4) Power versus love orientation: the prejudiced person is orientated towards a search for power, "the comparative lack of ability for affectionate and individualized interpersonal relations, together with the conception of a threatening and dangerous environment must be seen as underlying the prejudiced individual's striving for the attainment of power, either directly or by having the powerful on his side". (5) Rigidity versus flexibility: one of the most characteristic aspects of the prejudiced individual is his rigidity. "This must be seen as a consequence of the features discussed so far. In order to keep unacceptable tendencies and impulses out of consciousness, rigid controls have to be maintained, as any loosening of the absoluteness of these controls involves a danger of a breaking through of the repressed tendencies." However, repression does not cause these impulses to lose their dynamic strength; quite on the contrary, abrupt or unsuccessful repression prevents rather than helps in their control and mastery. An ego thus weakened is more in danger of becoming completely overwhelmed by the repressed forces. Greater rigidity of defences is necessary to cope with such increased threat. "In this vicious circle, impulses are not prevented from breaking out in uncontrolled ways. Basically, unmodified instinctual impulses lurk everywhere beneath the surface, narrowing considerably the content of the ego so that it must be kept constantly on the lookout. Rational control extends to a small sector of the personality only."

These descriptions of the authoritarian personality presented by Frenkel-Brunswik with a wealth of supporting detail are extremely convincing, and should be read in full by the student, who may feel that the very abridged summary above does not do justice to the complex theory under discussion. Evidence of the essential correctness of the hypothesized correlation between personality and attitude structure is further given by the fact that after an interview covering the personality aspects only, it was possible, with considerable success, to forecast the attitude-scale scores of the subjects. "The defining criterion of selection, extremely high versus extremely low standing on the overt anti-Semitism or ethnocentrism scale shows a per cent.

agreement of about ·85, with both the overall intuitive ratings and the composite standing on the interview. (This figure is an average of an agreement of about 95 per cent. achieved by one rater, whose material happened to include the most complete interviews, and an agreement of 75 per cent. achieved by the other rater, whose data were more fragmentary.)"

While fully realizing the importance of the contribution made by Frenkel-Brunswik, Levinson, Sanford, Adorno and the other authors of *The Authoritarian Personality*, the writer believes that their work is subject to one very damaging criticism. The proper way to approach a problem of this type would appear to be (*a*) to isolate the fundamental dimensions involved, and (*b*) to investigate the personality correlates of these dimensions. The authors of the book under review started in quite a different manner. Taking their point of departure from one specific issue in the field of social attitudes, they effectively proceeded to construct a dimension which passes through this point without enquiring (*a*) how many dimensions were involved in the field under investigation, or (*b*) enquiring into the proper location of the axes defining this field. Many of their findings, accordingly, are ambiguous. Let us return to Fig. 52. Essentially, Frenkel-Brunswik, in her interviews, compared persons from quadrant one with persons from quadrant three, calling them respectively "prejudiced" and "unprejudiced". In doing so she has unwittingly selected persons who would have high and low scores respectively on Ferguson's "humanitarianism" factor. The outcome, as regards this one factor, is quite clear. The question remains what would happen to the person, say, in the second quadrant, i.e. the person holding communist beliefs. Would he also be contrasted with the prejudiced authoritarian type of person in quadrant one, or would he show many qualities in common with him? Clearly, the existing stereotype of the communist would lead one to assume the second hypothesis. In that case, the characteristics with which Frenkel-Brunswik endows the person in the first quadrant would be shared by the individual in the second quadrant; in other words, the personality pattern painted by her would be characteristic of the tough-minded as opposed to the tender-minded, instead of the "fascist" as opposed to the "humanitarian".

This example may illustrate the importance of a proper dimensional analysis before proceeding further towards the complex inter-relationships obtaining between such dimensions and outside variables. It is possible that Frenkel-Brunswik is right in identifying the authoritarian personality with the tough-minded conservative. Such a belief, however, requires proof and cannot rest on mere assumption. There is much evidence, although in the nature of the case it can only be indirect evidence, in the very pages of *The Authoritarian Personality* to support the view that the authoritarian personality pattern is, characteristic of the tough-minded group as a whole, not only of the tough-minded conservative. It will require a repetition of the work described, with a change in experimental design, before we shall be able to tell definitely what the relations are between personality and social attitudes. At the moment, the evidence is ambiguous, due to disregard of the fundamental requirements of dimensional analysis.

Another very fundamental criticism of this study has been brought forward recently by various authors who have applied the notion of "response-set" to the authoritarianism scales. As was pointed out in a previous chapter, many subjects respond in a stereotyped manner regardless of the content of the question asked (Jackson and Messick, 1958). Thus an acquiescent person might tend to reply with "yes" to all the questions in a questionnaire regardless of their content. As all the items in the authoritarianism scale are worded in such a way that "yes" answers are in the authoritarian direction it is not impossible that the test might measure acquiescence rather than authoritarianism; or indeed, a mixture of the two. This possibility has been investigated by several writers (Bass, 1955; Chapman and Campbell, 1957; Christie *et al.*, 1958; Jackson and Messick, 1957; Leavitt *et al.*, 1955; Cohn, 1956 and Shelley, 1956) and the method employed has usually been that of reversing a number of items in the scale in such a way that now the answer "no" would be in line with the authoritarian attitude. The correlation between original and reversed halves of the test can then be used to infer the presence and extent of acquiescence, the logic being that if all the systematic variance of the original scale were contents variance, i.e. if acquiescence played no part in the response of the subjects, then the original and reversed parts of the test should correlate positively and to a degree determined by their reliabilities. (It is assumed that both halves are scored in such a way that a high score denotes authoritarianism.) If on the other hand all systematic variance happened to be due to acquiescence then the scale should correlate negatively at the level approaching their reliabilities. As Chapman and Bock (1958) point out, "The findings have been that the correlations fall between these two extremes, and from the size and direction of correlation, inferences have been made concerning the presence and relative importance of acquiescence and content variance in the scale." Chapman and Bock, using a rather different method which appears statistically superior, have reanalysed previous studies and came to the conclusion "That for average populations, the content variance in the F scale is around 30 to 40 per cent, and that the remaining reliable variance divides between acquiescence and content-acquiescence covariation, in proportions which depend on the specific population samples." The criticism of the F scale then appears to be well justified and it must be concluded that much of the work done in this field (Christie and Cook, 1958, list over 250 publications through 1956) is now incapable of any definite interpretation.

There have been certain developments in recent years which stem from the general body of theory contained in the *authoritarian personality*. One of these developments is the construction by Jones (1957) of the so-called Pensacola Z Scale. In this he has attempted to free the measurement of the authoritarian tendency from political particularity by using materials as purely personal as possible. The resulting 66 item scale is highly reliable but only correlates ·43 with the original F scale. The scale is by no means unidimensional but contains within it "Four distinct clusters of items, which may be described as "dependency", "rigidity", "anxiety" and "hostility" items.

Another attempt to create a general authoritarianism scale which would not represent primarily *conservative* authoritarianism has been made by Rokeach (1956), and Rokeach and Fruchter (1956). The resulting factor has been called dogmatism. In addition, the authors have created scales for the measurement of what they call "opinionation" which they define as right wing intolerance. In a recent paper Fruchter *et al.* (1958) have reported a factorial study using the dogmatism and opinionation scales as well as the various authoritarianism scales on a group of American students. Three factors were obtained, the first of which is labelled "anxiety", the second one "liberalism-conservatism" and the third one "rigidity-authoritarianism". The pattern of loadings is shown in Table 57.

Rather different is the approach of Livson and Nichols (1957). As they point out, "An implicit, often unrecognized, and sometimes unwarranted assumption underlying the use of any attitude scale (or any test) on a new sample of respondents is that it retains its original built-in statistical characteristics for the new group. Specifically, it is assumed that the scale still satisfies the general criterion—variously

TABLE 57

Scale	Rotated Loadings		
	I	II	III
1. Dogmatism	·68	·10	·48
2. F Scale	·38	·37	·70
3. Anxiety	·72	·03	·27
4. Rigidity	·28	·32	·54
5. Ethnocentrism	·12	·53	·39
6. Political-Econ. Conservatism .	·01	·44	·22
7. Intellectual Rejection . . .	·29	·49	·63
8. Intellectual Acceptance . .	− ·02	·60	·10
9. Opinionation	·35	·53	·13
10. Right-Left Score	·12	·61	·11

defined as homogeneity, internal consistency or unidimensionality, and that the items are sufficiently interrelated to indicate that some common dimension runs from the four sets of items comprising the scale. Turning to the authoritarianism scales, Livson and Nichols pointed out that "The few independent analyses of the statistical adequacy of one or more of these scales in new samples reach uniformly negative conclusions." Going on to their own investigation, the authors carried out a variety of analyses for different adolescent groups and find that "Neither the F nor PEC scales show sufficient evidence of internal consistency in our two samples." Altogether they come to the conclusion that "the results argue strongly that the appropriateness of the E, F and PEC scales for new groups cannot be uncritically assumed".

In a similar vein O'Neil and Levinson (1953) carried out factor analyses of the various authoritarianism scales and came to the conclusion that "Broadly and tentatively it may be stated from this analysis that the Authoritarianism, Ethnocentrism, Religious Conventionalism, and Traditional Family Ideology Scales should not be regarded as comprising four distinct constellations which are internally close-knit. It would appear, rather, that the scales consist of overlapping samplings of ideas located variously on a number of relatively independent dimensions. Speaking less cautiously, it might be suggested that although the scales are relatively unified and distinct at the level of the literal ideological content of items, and although they possess a relatively high degree of internal consistency, they are heterogeneous and overlapping with respect to the underlying psychological dispositions tapped."

Many of the difficulties into which authoritarian personality scales have fallen can thus be seen to be due to the failure of the authors to carry out proper dimensional studies of these scales. This difficulty also attends the report of correlations with personality variables because here also no effort has been made to analyse the dimensionality of the field covered. We must now turn to a series of studies in which an attempt has been made to relate tough-mindedness as a dimension in the attitude field to extraversion in the personality field, i.e. to relate two factorially derived concepts. As most of this work has been summarized in the Psychology of Politics (Eysenck, 1954) no detailed treatment will here be given of the data involved. In part this work attempts to demonstrate relationships between tough-mindedness and some of the value and interest factors discussed previously, and in part it attempts to relate all of these to the personality variables of extraversion. The general hypothesis underlying these studies has been put as follows: "Tough-mindedness is a projection on to the field of social attitudes of the *extraverted* personality type while tender-mindedness is a projection of the *introverted* personality type." The first study to support this hypothesis was carried out by George (1954) using a sample of 500 subjects and administering to them the T and R scales, the Allport and Vernon Value scales and the Guilford R scale as a measure of extraversion, the Guilford S scale as a measure of introversion and the Guilford D scale as a measure of neuroticism. The results of this factor analysis are shown in Fig. 53; it will be seen that the economic and political values are in the tough-minded, conservative quadrant, the religious values in the tender-minded, conservative quadrant, the theoretical value in the tough-minded radical quadrant and the social value in the tender-minded radical quadrant. The neuroticism measures bear no relation to these two factors, but the extraversion measure has a high loading on tough-mindedness. The actual correlation between rhathymia and tough-mindedness is ·41, while social shyness correlates with tough-mindedness −·24.

Along rather different lines is the work of Coulter (1953). She tested groups of Communists, Fascists and a control group, finding, as shown in Fig. 54 that Communists and Fascists both tended to be more tough-minded than the control group and the Fascists were conservative while Communists were radical. She assessed their personality by means of a TAT test especially designed for the purpose and obtained correlations between tough-mindedness and extraversion of ·301 for the Communists, ·297 for the Fascists, and ·307 for the control group.

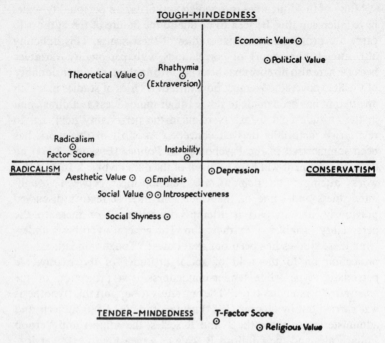

Fig. 53.—Diagram showing the relation between Radicalism, Tough-mindedness, Social Values, and Extraversion Measures.

In a third study, as yet unpublished, Eysenck administered the MPI extraversion scale and the tough-mindedness scale to a random sample of the population consisting of 1,000 men and women. He found a correlation of ·25 between extraversion and tough-mindedness, and he also verified the hypothesis that working class people tend to be more tough-minded than middle-class people. All in all, then, there is evidence from three independent experiments to show that, as predicted, extraversion and tough-mindedness are indeed correlated with each other.

It should be noted that in these more recent studies an improved form of the T and R scales was used which is due to Melvin (1955). This scale is given in full in the Psychology of Politics, pp. 277–279).

To end this section we must note one or two further studies which appear relevant to the general picture emerging. One of these is a study by Evans (1952) who correlated the Allport Vernon values with anti-semitism. As might have been expected, positive correlations were found between anti-semitism and economic and political values

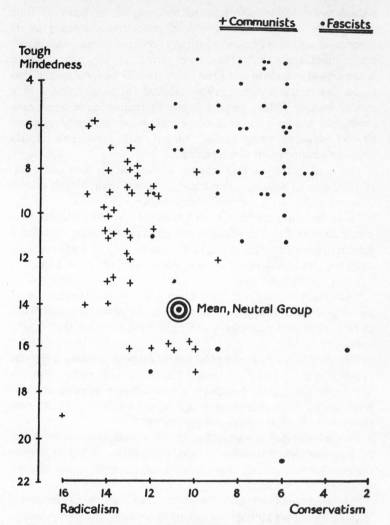

Fig. 54.—Tough-mindedness scores and scores of Radicalism-Conservatism of Communists, Fascists, and Neutral Group.

and negative correlations with aesthetic and social values. Correlations with religious and theoretical values were insignificant.

Of even more interest is a factorial study by Brogden (1952), who intercorrelated sixty of the items in the Allport Vernon Study of Values for 200 students; he then extracted eleven oblique factors from which second order factors were computed. Two of the three second order factors are rejected by Brogden as being of little importance, but the third one is of considerable interest as its description agrees very closely with the notion of tough-mindedness/ tender-mindedness. Brogden's own terms for the two opposed tendencies are idealism and practicality. (It will be remembered that in his first study Eysenck (1944) labelled his second factor in a similar manner, before turning to the alternative set of terms now preferred.) A set of quotations of the items more frequently endorsed by the idealistic/tender-minded subject, will show how closely Brogden's factor resembles Eysenck's:

"He is more interested in reading accounts of the lives and works of such men as Aristotle, Plato, and Socrates; than of such men as Alexander, Julius Caesar, and Charlemagne."

"If he had unlimited leisure and money, he would prefer to make a collection of fine sculptures or paintings; rather than establish a mental hygiene clinic for taking care of the maladjusted and mentally deficient, aim at a senatorship or a seat in the Cabinet, or enter into banking and high finance."

"Assuming that he had the necessary ability and that the salary for each of the following occupations was the same, he would prefer to be a mathematician, clergyman or politician; rather than a sales manager."

"He would prefer a friend of his own sex who is seriously interested in thinking out his attitude toward life as a whole; rather than one who is efficient, industrious, and of a practical turn of mind, one who possesses qualities of leadership and organizing ability, or one who shows refinement and emotional sensitivity."

"He believes that one should guide one's conduct according to, or develop one's chief loyalties toward, one's ideals of beauty; rather than one's religious faith, one's business organization and associates, or society as a whole."

"He would prefer a friend of his own sex who is seriously interested in thinking out his attitude toward life as a whole, one who possesses qualities of leadership and organizing ability, one who shows refinement and emotional sensitivity; rather than one who is efficient, industrious, and of a practical turn of mind."

"He believes that a man who works in business all week can best spend Sunday in trying to educate himself by reading serious books, going to an orchestral concert, or hearing a really good sermon; rather than by trying to win at golf or racing."

"During his next summer vacation he would prefer to write and publish an original biological essay or article; rather than stay in some secluded part of the country where he could appreciate fine scenery, compete in a local tennis or other athletic tournament, or get experience in some new line of business."

"He believes that good government should aim at more aid for the poor, sick, and old; rather than the development of manufacturing and trade, introduction of more ethical principles into its policies and diplomacy, or the establishing of a position of prestige and respect among nations."

"Florence Nightingale interests and attracts him more than Napoleon, Henry Ford, or Charles Darwin."

"He would prefer to hear a series of lectures on the comparative development of the great religious faiths rather than the comparative merits of the forms of government in Britain and the United States."

There is little need to summarize the system of classification arising from the researches reviewed in this chapter, as they appear to agree remarkably well in their broad outlines; although a good deal of filling in at an intermediate level would seem to be required. One point, however, should be raised at this juncture. Regarding the general picture presented, as in the case of personality structure, we are in the case of attitudes dealing with four main and distinct layers. At the lowest level the attitude expressed is entirely specific in its content or is determined entirely by the specific features of the situation. We reach a higher level when such statements of attitude are repeated on separate occasions, thus showing a certain reliability which is the minimum requirement for any kind of organization. Such views, voiced repeatedly in different situations and having a certain degree of repeat reliability, we shall call opinions. Thus, if a person is heard repeatedly in different circumstances to voice a belief that "Negroes ought to be kept down" or "The Government is run by Jews", we may count that as an opinion, whereas an occasional, never repeated exclamation provoked by some unfortunate experience, such as, for instance, "a woman driver, of course!" would not be counted as an opinion but would remain at the lowest level of the hierarchical structure because of its specific nature and its lack of reliability.

When it is shown that certain opinions tend to correlate together, we reach a third level—that of attitude measurement. If, for instance, a set of twenty or thirty statements regarding the Negro or the Jew, all dealing with different aspects of the racial question, are answered in a consistent manner, then we may justifiably speak about an anti-

Negro or an anti-Jewish attitude. Lastly, we reach the highest level when it can be shown that attitudes thus are intercorrelated, thus giving rise to higher order constructs. For instance, as we have seen, anti-Negro prejudice, war-mindedness, favourableness to institutionalized religion, dislike of socialism, dislike of soft upbringing of children, liking for industrial discipline, and many more attitudes are intercorrelated in a conservative pattern; conservatism therefore represents an even wider integration of opinions than does a simple attitude subsumed under it.

Fig. 55 shows this hierarchical structure of attitudes clearly.

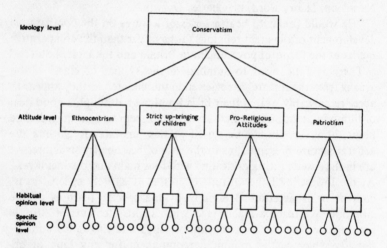

Fig. 55.—Diagram illustrating relation between Opinion, Attitude, and Ideology.

These four stages of organization emerge fairly clearly from current research, although it cannot be gainsaid that intermediate stages are possible. Thus, for instance, the concept of ethnocentrism would be intermediate, in its power to integrate and generalize opinions, between the concept of anti-Negro or anti-Jewish attitude and the higher-order concept of conservatism. However, the general principle of organization from the very large number of low-level verbal statements through the fairly large number of opinions, and the much smaller number of attitudes to the very small number of really high-order general concepts, like conservatism, will be reasonably clear. The technique of factor analysis enables us in a given context to assign to a given statement in a given population the percentage of the total variance contributed by error factors (first level), specific factors (second level), group factors (third level), and general factors (fourth level). Thus we can obtain for any given question or statement an equation setting out clearly the relative importance of the four levels discussed above (Eysenck, 1951).

Factor analysis has been used almost exclusively to derive concepts at the highest level of all; at the level of attitude measurement other forms of consistency analysis, such as the equal-appearing interval scale construction method of Thurstone or Guttman's scalogram analysis, have been used. These methods are plausible alternatives to full-scale factor analysis, but as Eysenck and Crown (1949) have shown, they cannot really replace factor analysis, when the possibility of group factors being present cannot be ruled out.

Research in social attitudes, then, does not essentially constitute an exception to our general finding that a solution by means of oblique primary factors, giving rise to second-order factors, is the most acceptable at the present stage of development of factorial analysis. The stage of obtaining oblique primary factors is usually omitted, either by constructing a scale for each of these primary factors (anti-Semitism, war-mindedness, pro-Church attitude, etc.) by means other than factorial analysis, and then intercorrelating a number of sub-scales (Ferguson) or else by taking one statement from each scale having high correlations with the total scale, and intercorrelating statements of this kind taken from a large number of different scales (Eysenck, 1947). In either case, these "primary factors" show high intercorrelations, and give rise to second-order factors such as R and T, or "religionism" and "humanitarianism".

A last question relates to any further "second-order" factors that may be present in the field of social attitudes. A careful survey of the whole literature covering non-factorial as well as factorial studies fails to reveal any strong claimants, apart from the two factors already discussed, and while, of course, the possibility can never be ruled out that further factors may be found, it is not apparent to the present writer just what ground would be left for these factors to cover. Consequently, it is believed that we have at hand a fairly complete description of the total content of the universe of social attitudes.

REFERENCES

Chapter X

ADAMS, J. K., and FOWLER, H. M. *Report on the Reliability of Two Forms of an Activity Preference Blank*. Washington, D.C.: U.S. Dep. Commerce, 1946.

ADORNO, T. W., FRENKEL-BRUNSWIK, LEVINSON, D. J., and SANFORD, R. N. *The Authoritarian Personality*. New York: Harper Bros., 1950.

ALLPORT, G. W., and VERNON, P. E. *A Study of Values*. Boston: Houghton Mifflin, 1931.

BASS, B. M. Authoritarianism or acquiescence? *J. abnorm. soc. Psychol.*, 1955, **51**, 616–623.

BROEN, W. G. A factor-analytic study of religious attitudes. *J. abnorm. soc. Psychol.*, 1957, **54**, 176–179.

BROGDEN, H. The primary personal values measured by the Allport-Vernon Test "A study of values". *Psychol. Monogr.*, 1952, **66**, No. 16.

BURGEMEISTER, B. B. The permanence of interests of women college students. *Arch. Psychol.*, 1940, No. 255, **59**.

CARLSON, M. B. Attitudes of undergraduate students. *J. soc. Psychol.*, 1934, **5**, 202–212.

CARTER, H. D., PYLES, M. K., and BRETNALL, E. P. A comparative study of factors in vocational interest scores of high school boys. *J. educ. Psychol.*, 1935, **26**, 81–98.

CHAPMAN, L. J., and BOCK, R. D. Components of variance due to acquiescence and content in the F scale measure of authoritarianism. *Psychol. Bull.*, 1958, **55**, 328–333.

CHAPMAN, L. J., and CAMPBELL, D. T. Response set in the F scale. *J. abnorm. soc. Psychol.*, 1957, **54**, 129–132.

CHISNALL, B. The interests and personality traits of delinquent boys. *Brit. J. educ. Psychol.*, 1942, **12**.

CHRISTIE, R., and COOK, P. A guide to published literature relating to the authoritarian personality through 1956. *J. Psychol.*, 1958, **45**, 171–199.

CHRISTIE, R., HAVELY, J., and SEIDENBERG, B. Is the F scale irreversible? *J. abnorm. soc. Psychol.*, 1958, **56**, 143–159.

COATES, T. H. *The Measurement of Adult Interests*. Ph.D. Thesis. London: Univ. London Lib., 1950.

COHN, T. S. The relation of the F scale to a response set to answer positively. *J. soc. Psychol.*, 1956, **44**, 125–133.

COULTER, T. *An Experimental and Statistical Study of the Relationship of Prejudice and Certain Personality Variables*. London: Ph.D. Thesis, 1953.

CRISSY, W. J. E., and DANIEL, W. J. Vocational interest factors in women. *J. appl. Psychol.*, 1939, **23**, 488–494.

DARLEY, J. G., and McNAMARA, W. J. A factor analysis of test-retest performance on attitude and adjustment tests. *J. educ. Psychol.*, 1938, **29**, 652–664.

Factor analysis in the establishment of new personality tests. *J. educ. Psychol.*, 1940, **31**, 321–334.

DIGGORY, J. C. Sex differences in the organisation of attitudes. *J. Pers.*, 1953, **22**, 89–100.

DUFFY, E., and CRISSY, W. J. E. Evaluative attitudes as related to vocational interests and academic achievement. *J. abnorm. soc. Psychol.*, 1940, **35**, 226–245.

EVANS, R. I. Personal values as factors in anti-semitism. *J. abnorm. soc. Psychol.*, 1952, **47**, 249–256.

EYSENCK, H. J. General social attitudes. *J. soc. Psychol.*, 1944, **19**, 207–227.

Primary social attitudes. I. The organization and measurement of social attitudes. *Internat. J. Opin. and Attit. Res.*, 1947, **1**, 49–84.

Measurement and prediction. A discussion of Volume IV of studies in social psychology in World War II. *Internat. J. Opin. and Attit. Res.*, 1951, **5**, 95–102.

Primary social attitudes and the "Social Insight" test. *Brit. J. Psychol.*, 1951, **42**, 114–122.

Primary Social Attitudes as related to social class and political party. *J. Sociol.*, 1951, **2**, 198–219.

Primary social attitudes. II. A comparison of attitude patterns in England, Germany and Sweden. *J. abnorm. soc. Psychol.*, 1953, **48**, 563–568.

Psychology of Politics. London: Routledge & Kegan Paul, 1954.

EYSENCK, H. J., and CROWN, S. An experimental study in opinion-attitude methodology. *Internat. J. Opin. and Attit. Res.*, 1949, **3**, 47–86.

FERGUSON, L. W. Primary social attitudes. *J. Psychol.*, 1939, **8**, 217–223.

The measurement of primary social attitudes. *J. Psychol.*, 1940, **10**, 199–205.

The stability of the primary social attitudes. I. Religionism and Humanitarianism. *J. Psychol.*, 1941, **12**, 283–288.

The isolation and measurements of Nationalism. *J. soc. Psychol.*, 1942, **16**, 215–228.

A revision of the primary social attitude scales. *J. soc. Psychol.*, 1944, **17**, 229–241.

Socio-psychological correlates of the primary attitude scale. I. Religionism; II. Humanitarianism. *J. soc. Psychol.*, 1944, **19**, 81–98.

The sociological validity of primary social attitude scale. I. Religionism. *J. soc. Psychol.*, 1946, **23**, 197–204.

FERGUSON, L. W., HUMPHREYS, L. G., and STRONG, F. W. A factorial analysis of interests and values. *J. educ. Psychol.*, 1941, **32**, 197–204.

FRUCHTER, B., ROKEACH, M., and NOVAK, G. C. A factorial study of dogmatism, opinionation and related scales. *Psychol. Rep.*, 1958, **4**, 19–27.

GEORGE, E. I. *An experimental study of the relation between personal values, social attitudes and personality traits.* London: Ph.D. Thesis, 1954.

GEORGE, R. W. *A comparison of Pressey X-O scores with Liberal-Conservative attitudes.* M.A. Thesis. Columbia Univ. Lib., 1925.

HAMMOND, W. H. An analysis of youth centre interests. *Brit. J. educ. Psychol.*, 1945, **15**, 122–126.

HATT, P. Class and ethnic attitudes. *Amer. sociol. Rev.*, 1948, **13**, 36–43.

HOFSTAETTER, P. R. A factorial study of prejudice. *J. Pers.*, 1952–1953, **21**, 228–239.

JACKSON, D. N., and MESSICK, S. J. A note on "ethnocentrism" and acquiescent response sets. *J. abnorm. soc. Psychol.*, 1957, **54**, 132–134.

JACKSON, D. N., and MESSICK, S. Content and style in personality assessment. *Psychol. Bull.*, 1958, **55**, 243–252.

JACKSON, D. N., MESSICK, S. J., and SOLLEY, C. N. How "rigid" is the "authoritarian"? *J. abnorm. soc. Psychol.*, 1957, **54**, 137–140.

JONES, M. B. The Pensacola survey: a study in the measurement of authoritarian tendency. *Psychol. Monogr.*, 1957, **71**, No. 23.

JONES, L. V., and MORRIS, C. Relations of temperament to the choice of values. *J. abnorm. soc. Psychol.*, 1956, **53**, 345–349.

KELLEY, T. L. *An activity preference test for the classification of service personnel.* Final report. (O.S.R.D., 1944, Publ. Bd. No. 19819), Washington, D.C.: U.S. Dep. Comm., 1946.

KERR, W. S. Untangling the liberalism-conservatism continuum. *J. soc. Psychol.*, 1952, **35**, 111–125.

KUDER, G. F. *Manual to the Kuder Preference Record.* Chicago: Sci. Res. Assoc., 1939.

KULP, D. H., and DAVIDSON, H. H. The application of the Spearman two-factor theory to social attitudes. *J. abnorm. soc. Psychol.*, 1934, **29**, 269–275.

LEAVITT, H. J., HAX, H., and ROCHE, J. H. "Authoritarianism" and agreement with things authoritative. *J. Psychol.*, 1955, **40**, 215–221.

LENTZ, T. F. Generality and specificity of Conservatism-Radicalism. *J. educ. Psychol.*, 1938, **29**, 540–546.

LIKERT, R. A technique for the measurement of attitudes. *Arch. Psychol.*, 1932, **140**, 55.

LIVSON, N., and NICHOLS, T. F. Assessment of the general stability of the E, F and PEC scales. *Psychol. Rep.*, 1957, **3**, 413–420.

LUNDBERG, G. A. Sex differences on social questions. *School and Soc.*, 1926, **23**, 595–600.

LURIE, W. A. A study of Spranger's value-types by the method of factor analysis. *J. soc. Psychol.*, 1937, **8**, 17–37.

McDOUGALL, W. *Outline of Psychology.* New York: Scribner, 1923.

MELVIN, D. *An Experimental and Statistical Study of the Primary Social Attitudes.* London: Ph.D. Thesis, 1955.

MORRIS, C. *Varieties of human values.* Chicago: Univ. of Chicago Press, 1956.

MORRIS, C., and JONES, L. V. Value scales and dimensions. *J. abnorm. soc. Psychol.*, 1955, **51**, 523–535.

O'NEILL, W. N., and LEVINSON, D. J. A factorial exploration of authoritarianism and some of its ideological concomitants. *J. Pers.*, 1953, **22**, 449–463.

ROKEACH, M. Political and religious dogmatism: an alternative to the authoritarian personality. *Psychol. Monogr.*, 1956, **70**, No. 18.

ROKEACH, M., and FRUCHTER, B. A factorial study of dogmatism and related concepts. *J. abnorm. soc. Psychol.*, 1956, **53**, 356–360.

RUNDQUIST, E. A., and SLETTO, R. F. *Personality in the Depression.* Minneapolis: Univ. Minn. Press, 1936.

SANAI, M. An experimental study of politico-economic attitudes. *Internat. J. Opin., Attit. Res.*, 1950, **4**, 563–577.

A factorial study of social attitudes. *J. soc. Psychol.*, 1950, **31**, 167–182.

An experimental study of social attitudes. *J. soc. Psychol.*, 1951, **34**, 235–264.

An empirical study of political, religious, and social attitudes. *Brit. J. Psychol., Stat. Sect.*, 1952, **5**, 81–92.

The relation between social attitudes and characteristics of personality. *J. soc. Psychol.*, 1952, **36**, 3–13.

SARBIN, T. R., and BERDIE, R. F. Relation of measured interests to the Allport-Vernon Study of Values. *J. appl. Psychol.*, 1940, **24**, 287–296.

SHELLEY, H. P. Response set and the Californian Attitude scales. *Educ. Psychol. Measmt.*, 1956, **16**, 63–67.

SPRANGER, E. *Types of Men.* (Trans. 5th German Ed. of Lebensformen by P. J. W. Pigors.) Halle: Niemeyer, 1927.

STAGNER, R. Fascist attitudes: their determining conditions. *J. soc. Psychol.*, 1936, **7**, 438–454.

Fascist attitudes: an exploratory study. *J. soc. Psychol.*, 1936, **7**, 309–319.

STAGNER, R., and KATZOFF, E. T. Fascist attitudes: factor analysis of item correlations. *J. soc. Psychol.*, 1942, **16**, 3–9.

STANLEY, J. C., and WALDROP, R. S. Intercorrelations of study of values and Kuder Preference Record scores. *Educ. Psychol. Measmt.*, 1952, **12**, 707–719.

STRONG, E. K. *Vocational Interests of Men and Women.* California: Stanford Univ. Press, 1943.

SUPER, D. E. *Appraising Vocational-Fitness by Means of Psychological Tests.* New York: Harper, 1949.

THOMSON, G. H. *The Factorial Analysis of Human Ability.* London: Univ. London Press, 1939.

THURSTONE, L. L. A multiple factor study of vocational interests. *Personnel J.*, 1932, **10**, 198–205.

The vectors of the mind. *Psychol. Rev.*, 1934, **41**, 1–32.

TUSSING, L. An investigation of the possibilities of measuring personality traits with the Strong Vocational Interest Blank. *Educ. Psychol. Measmt.*, 1942, **2**, 59–74.

VAN DUSEN, A. C., WIMBERLEY, S., and MOSIER, C. I. Standardization of a values inventory. *J. educ. Psychol.*, 1939, **30**, 53–62.

VERNON, P. E. Classifying high-grade occupational interests. *J. abnorm. soc. Psychol.*, 1949, **44**, 85–96.

VERNON, P. E., and PARRY, J. B. *Personnel Selection in the British Forces.* London: Univ. London Press, 1949.

THE ANALYSIS OF CORRELATIONS BETWEEN PERSONS

ALL THE RESEARCHES discussed so far deal entirely with correlations between tests. In this chapter we shall be concerned with factorial studies in which correlations are run, not between tests but between persons, or, alternatively, even within a single person from one occasion to another. The general possibilities and interrelationships of these different approaches are well illustrated by Cattell's Covariation Chart, which is given below as Fig. 56. This diagram

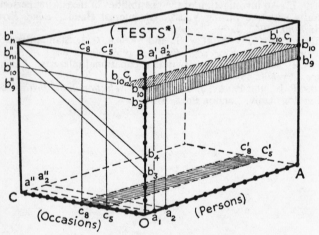

Fig. 56.—Cattell's Covariation Chart.

presents a system of rectangular co-ordinates in three dimensions, arbitrarily truncated. The co-ordinates do not represent continua, but rather a population of points arranged in serial order. Along OA lies a series of persons, a_1, a_2, etc.; along OB lies a series of personality tests, b_1, b_2, etc.; and along OC lies a series of occasions of testing, c_1, c_2, etc.

Cattell discusses in great detail the possible types of correlation to which this general scheme can give rise, but in fact the only three which have been used are correlations between tests, correlations between persons, and correlations between occasions. It is the latter two types of correlations with which we shall here be concerned.

Before turning to a discussion of the various researches employing these methods, it will be necessary to devote a few lines at least to a discussion of the principles underlying these new methods. Such a discussion is necessary in the first place because text-books on statistics hardly ever deal with the possibility of correlating persons or occasions, and, secondly, because a fair amount of difficulty and misunderstanding has arisen in the literature because of failure to appreciate the very simple fundamental points which determine the proper use of these procedures.

Let us begin with correlations between persons. In a typical rating experiment of the type discussed in a previous chapter, we might have a series of persons rated on a seven-point scale on, say, six traits. The results from such a small-scale experiment might then be represented by a rectangular array of ratings as in Table 58. Persons are designated by numbers from 1–9; traits are designated by letters from A–F. For the purpose of this imaginary experiment, we have taken three traits (sociable, humorous, and tactful) which we may consider typical of the extraverted person, and another three traits (ambitious, reserved, and irritable) which we may consider typical of the introverted person. Of our subjects we may consider persons 1, 2, and 3 extraverted; persons 7, 8, and 9 introverted, and persons 4, 5, and 6 to be ambiverted. The meaning of the figures as they stand will be clear. Person 1 is considered to be extremely sociable and tactful and very humorous; he is not at all reserved, nor is he irritable or ambitious. Person 7 is the exact opposite; he is ambitious and irritable and rather reserved; definitely not humorous, and neither tactful nor sociable.

In the ordinary course of events, we would intercorrelate our six traits and find that there were positive correlations between traits A, B, and C, that there were positive correlations also between traits D, E, and F, but that the correlations between these two groups of traits tended to be negative. If we should factor analyse this table of correlations, we would get a very strong bipolar factor, which we would presumably identify with extraversion-introversion.

What would happen if we were to intercorrelate the columns in the table of marks rather than the rows? Let us neglect for the moment any statistical difficulties that might arise and concentrate on the logical meaning of a correlation, which means simply a tendency of two things to vary together in the same direction. Now, clearly persons 1, 2, and 3 are correlated in this sense, because where one has a high rating the others tend to have a high rating, and where one

TABLE 58

Traits	E			A			I		
	1	2	3	4	5	6	7	8	9
A Sociable . . .	1	2	3	1	7	1	5	6	7
B Humorous . .	2	1	1	6	5	2	7	5	5
C Tactful . . .	1	3	2	5	6	7	6	7	6
D Ambitious . .	5	6	7	2	1	6	1	2	3
E Reserved . . .	7	5	5	3	2	5	2	1	1
F Irritable . . .	6	7	6	4	3	4	1	3	2

has a low rating the others tend to have a low rating too: similarly for persons 7, 8, and 9. When we compare these two groups of persons we again find a tendency for covariation to take place, only this time correlations are negative—where persons in the first group have high ratings, persons in the second group have low ratings, and vice versa. Persons 4, 5, and 6 are intermediate between the other two, and would correlate only to a very low degree with either persons 1, 2, and 3 or persons 7, 8, and 9. If we actually calculated the correlations, we would find again a pattern of positive and negative correlations, which would give rise to two groups of people whom we might call extraverts and introverts.

These results are clearly implicit in the set-up of the table, and show that whichever method of approach we use the results reached would be very similar. That, indeed, is as it should be, as in both cases we would be analysing the same table of marks. If we had carried out our analysis of correlations between tests—a procedure which we shall from now on call T analysis—we could have calculated factor scores on our introversion-extraversion factor for the persons, which would have grouped them in the same way as did the factor saturations derived from our table of intercorrelations between persons—a type of analysis we shall call P analysis. Conversely, from the P analysis, factor scores could have been calculated for the traits which would have grouped those in much the same way as did the T analysis.[1]

[1] The question of nomenclature in this field has become rather difficult, several different letters being applied to the various procedures. T analysis (correlations between tests) is called R technique by Burt. P analysis (correlations between persons) is called Q technique by Stephenson, who also used the term "inverted factor analysis". O analysis (correlations between occasions) is called P technique by Cattell, who in turn uses O technique to designate yet another type of correlational procedure, namely the "monovariate correlation of occasions", which he contrasts with "intra-individual covariation", i.e. what we have called O analysis. The position is so confused, the same letter being used for quite different procedures by different writers, that the simplification suggested here seemed to offer the only method of giving a straightforward account of the numerous researches in the field.

So far, then, there seems to be little that is novel in intercorrelating persons. If the correlation between two persons is positive, it means that with respect to the test material used they behave in a similar manner, whereas if the correlation is negative it means that with respect to the test material used they behave in a dissimilar manner. If the test material consists of trait ratings of introversion and extraversion, then clearly extraverts will correlate together, introverts will correlate together, and extraverts will correlate negatively with introverts.

It will be noted that in each example we correlated persons, not with respect to tests but with respect to trait ratings. The reason for this is a very simple one. To calculate a correlation between two persons we must find the average and the standard deviation of each column of figures in Table 38, and this is admissible only if these figures form part of a *metric continuum*. The existence of such a metric continuum cannot be assumed but must be demonstrated. In the case of personality ratings, this can, with some show of reason, be done by assuming with Stephenson (1935) that the traits rated differ for each person with respect to their *significance* for that person. By this is meant that given a universe of traits, some are very representative of a person, others less so, and still others fail to be representative of him in any way. Sociability, sense of humour, and tact would be representative of, or significant for, the typical extravert; ambitiousness, reserve, and irritability would not. For the introvert, the opposite would hold. Consequently, we may reasonably assume the columns in each table of marks to represent a metric continuum, and we would therefore be able to calculate averages, standard deviations, and correlations.

No such assumption could be made if we were dealing with different tests all having scoring systems differing one from the other, and being wholly arbitrary. Thomson (1939) takes as an example a set of four tests—formboard, dotting, absurdities, analogies—for each of which the experimenter has devised some kind of scoring system. In the formboard test he will give a maximum of 20 points; in the dotting test the score might be the number of dots made in half a minute, etc. "To find the average of such different things as this is palpably absurd, and the whole operation can be entirely altered by an arbitrary change, like taking the number of seconds to solve the formboard instead of giving points. . . . This is a very fundamental difficulty, which will probably make correlations between persons in the general case impossible to calculate."

While the existence of a metric continuum may frequently be difficult to prove, there is one method of experimentation which is free from the difficulties raised in this connection, and that is the method of *ranking*. If what we have called the "tests" can be put in some kind of order by each person with respect to significance, applicability, or preference, then we can safely calculate the correlations between persons, and it is indeed with respect to this type of procedure that most of the work in this field has been carried out. The figures in Table 58 are ratings rather than rankings, but it can be seen that they could, without any difficulty, be converted into rankings, and indeed the possibility of such conversion is essential if we are to carry out correlations between persons with any semblance of statistical justifiability. The first research reported in the literature to make use of correlations between persons based upon rankings was carried out by Thomson and Bales (1926), in which correlations were calculated between teachers who marked the essays of schoolboys on a certain topic. Approximations to general factor saturations were calculated by correlating each teacher's ratings with the average of all the teachers. Other workers also used correlations between persons almost from the beginning of correlational study in psychology, but it was not until Beebee-Centre (1933) applied factor techniques to such correlations that the issues relating .o these problems became clarified.

In the fifteen years that followed, a number of papers have been published on this topic, and a number of articles written specifically dealing with methodological questions. Yet all the researches carried out to date, with few exceptions, are merely programmatic or illustrative; they are presented with the intention of showing the possibilities inherent in the method, but they hardly ever go beyond this to actually apply the method so as to release these putative virtues. Illustrations are therefore all that can be given at this stage, and we may begin with studies carried out by Stephenson, who has perhaps made larger claims for P technique than almost any other writer. His terminology is somewhat unusual. He calls the technique of intercorrelating persons either "Q" technique or "inverted" factor analysis, although the latter term has given rise to a good deal of confusion, both logically and mathematically. As Burt (1940) has pointed out, the theorems required for the analysis of correlations between persons are not inversions of those used in analysing correlations between tests, but are identical with them; similarly, the matrix of marks analysed is not the *inverse* of but a *transpose* of that from which correlations between tests are usually derived.

The claims made by Stephenson for "P" technique, although far-reaching, are somewhat difficult to follow. He says: "It is usual to regard factorial analysis as an inductive procedure for surveying the structure of more or less uncharted regions in psychology. . . . Q-technique, on the other hand, is most usefully employed to test psychological hypotheses; it is a system of devices, which . . . serves to affirm the conclusions already reached, but requiring proof. . . . The technique appears to be particularly apposite to the study of personality. It neatly represents the self even if in a statistical fashion. The underlying functions are so complex that probably they can be represented in no other way. It provides, I fancy, by far the best framework into which to fit typology in general, whether Jungian, Freudian, Rorschachian, or any other. . . . It allows us to handle the psychologist's theories about personality, even if, in the last resort, it means studying the psychologists themselves rather than their human subjects." Perhaps a review of some of the studies employing this technique may help us to see to what extent these claims are justified.

In one of his earlier papers, Stephenson (1939) selected 46 men and women, 18 of whom he considered extraverted in tendency, 16 introverted, with the others demonstrating neutral tendencies. "The 46 men and women are in no sense a random sample of individuals; nor is there any methodological reason why they should be, for in work of the present kind, where persons are used as variables, they can be selected on other than purely sampling grounds." These persons were rated by Stephenson himself on a list of 176 traits, according to a standard system of frequency distribution. It appears that not all the correlations between these individuals were calculated. Correlations were run between the 18 supposedly extraverted persons, and also between the 16 supposedly introverted persons. It is not clear from Stephenson's account whether correlations between the extraverts and introverts were run or not, but in any case they are not given in the paper.

What Stephenson shows is that the people whom he considers extraverted, and whom he himself has rated on the 176 character traits, show positive intercorrelations, and that those whom he considers introverted, and whom he himself has rated, again show positive intercorrelations. As, presumably, his ratings and his classifications of people as extraverted and introverted were not independent of each other, it is difficult to see how such a result could have been avoided. In the absence of intercorrelations between the groups, and of intercorrelations regarding the other subjects of the experiment who were neither extraverted nor introverted, it is rather difficult to discover precisely what purpose the analysis serves. From a set of residual correlations left over after the elimination of the general factor, Stephenson claims to have isolated four further sub-factors corresponding to Jung's thinking, intuitive, sensory, and feeling types, but no evidence is presented to justify this identification.

This study brings out extremely well some of the difficulties involved in P analysis. First and foremost among these difficulties must be put the problem of sampling. If we go back to Table 58, it will be clear that there is only a limited number of possible combinations and permutations arising from the attribution of ratings on six traits to a number of persons. Let us assume as a kind of null hypothesis that all these permutations and combinations are equally likely and occur with equal frequency in the total populations. It is obviously of vital importance that the investigator who starts out with a hypothesis that certain traits are correlated in the total population, and thus form a syndrome like extraversion-introversion, should select a strictly random or stratified sample of the population to disprove the null hypothesis. If he selects the people chosen in terms of his hypothesis, i.e. if he selects from all the possible sets of combinations of traits only those which are in conformity with his hypothesis, then clearly his "proof" will be completely worthless. Any other hypothesis could have been proved with equal ease by suitable selection of subjects.

A selection of persons to be tested in accordance with some sampling procedure is essential in all psychological work. It is probably more important in P technique than in any other because of the considerations set out above, and also because in P-technique we usually deal only with a very small number of people, so that our chances of obtaining biased results are very much greater than when the population is comparatively large, as it will usually be in T technique. When, therefore, Stephenson admits that in his study he has "chosen personalities purposely to bring out as clearly as possible the connections between (his) thesis and Jung's typology", any value which his study might have had is clearly lost and when he adds: "The 46 men and women are in no sense a random sample of individuals; nor is there any methodological reason why they should be, for in work of the present kind, where persons are used as variables, they can be selected on other than purely sampling grounds", he seems completely to lose cognizance of the methodological problems involved in disproving the null hypothesis.

Allied to Stephenson's disregard for proper sampling procedures (a disregard shared by Burt and other writers, as we shall see later), is a failure to consider the problem of rotation and simple structure. In considering the correlations between tests, it has always appeared one of the great weaknesses of British writers that they have accepted without question centroid factors as they emerge from the analysis, in spite of the obvious fact that these factors are not invariant but depend entirely on the sample of tests included in the battery. Clearly, the difficulties to which such lack of invariance gives rise must be exacerbated in using correlations between persons, as any change in the composition of the sample group would change the factor saturations, and consequently the actual factors emerging. It might be possible to use the concepts of simple structure or of criterion analysis in order to rotate centroid factors into a more meaningful pattern, but none of the writers who have used this technique has made any attempt to get away from the factor patterns as originally obtained. Indeed, the very existence of this problem has not, to the writer's knowledge, been discussed before.

If the method used by Stephenson is not such as to command confidence, his results are often difficult to understand or to relate to the claims he makes for them. In one study (1939), Stephenson begins with a discussion of the possibility of gaining insight into temperamental and other personality characteristics of an individual, tested by means of incidental information derived from the reaction to the testing process itself. "The psychologist may direct his attention to the subject's general demeanour, his traits, attitudes, and the like, or to the intimate details of the performance itself. Much will be learned about the individual's personality from both these sources." In order to test this hypothesis, Stephenson drew up a list of 60 qualities observed during the test performance of 40 students. He then intercorrelated 16 of the students (again, we note the selection, on unstated grounds, of a much smaller sample from the total one originally tested), and carried out a factor analysis of the correlations. Three factors, or types, were discovered. "There is little that is surprising in the three types: some are superior performers (type one); others average (type two); and others inferior (type three)." It is not clear how people who are good, medium, and inferior can be regarded as different types in any meaning of that term. Nor can we regard this information as adding very much to that given by the straightforward results of the intelligence tests they were performing. If P technique has a separate function to fulfil in psychology, it does not seem possible to deduce it from studies such as this.

In his more recent work, Stephenson (1950) has contributed further studies to illustrate his method. In one of these, he constructed a set of trait names from everyday life, and another one of trait names used in Rorschach interpretation. Ten men constituted the sample and were rated by Stephenson for 100 Rorschach traits and for 400 everyday traits. Lastly, each of the ten men assessed himself on the 400 everyday traits. Correlations were run between persons for each of these three sets of ratings, and factor analyses performed to show a certain degree of concordance observed between the results. This study seems to confirm results reported from the use of T technique that ratings and self-ratings show a certain amount of correlation; apart from that, it does not add very much to our knowledge.

In a second experiment, Stephenson took a number of traits from Jung's book and had seven members of a post-graduate class make self-appraisals and also assess him (Stephenson) himself. In addition, he also made estimates of himself on these traits. Moderate correlations were found between self-estimates and estimates of the experimenter, a conclusion in line with results discussed in our chapter on ratings.

In summarizing Stephenson's contribution, we must note that all the studies reported by him are merely illustrative, and that until a large scale, properly planned and executed experiment is reported, it must be very difficult to assess his claims objectively. In the studies reported, however, there are certain features, both in the experimental design and the statistical treatment, which throw very great doubt on the results. Among these are the practice of only calculating and presenting part of the necessary data, and the failure to use proper sampling techniques, which, in Stephenson's case, is an error not of omission but of commission, as he claims this failure to be a specific virtue of his approach.

The only example of an application of Thurstone's concepts to the analysis of correlations between persons comes in a paper by Moore, Stafford, and Hsü (1947), which contains an excellent and fair review of the history of what these writers call "obverse analysis". Following on the work of Moore (1939, 1941) and of Hsü (1943) on pre-psychotic temperament and its relation to psychiatric syndromes, an attempt was made to confirm the earlier findings of a resemblance between pre-psychotic traits and psychotic syndromes. This study avoids some of the criticisms to which the work of Stephenson and Burt is subject, particularly errors of sampling and failure to rotate the centroid axes derived from the analysis; it may therefore serve as a reasonable example of what may be expected for psychological analysis from P technique.

One hundred and twenty trait items in all were presented to 56 juniors and seniors in a Catholic Women's College, a group very homogeneous in religion, socio-economic status, age, I.Q. level, race, sex, and educational and ecological background. The subjects were asked to check those questions to which they could give a positive answer. Tetrachoric correlations were calculated between individuals, a procedure which is considered justified by the authors on statistical grounds, although it does leave the question of a proper metric curiously undecided. 1,540 correlations were run between the 56 girls; all of these were positive, ranging from zero to ·95. Nine factors were extracted and rotated into simple structure. "There are nine dimensions in this matrix, but only three of them can be readily interpreted." These three factors were identified as follows: Factor one—"a cycloid or extravert type of personality" marked by such traits as preference for tasks clearly outlined and easily worked at, in which one is likely to succeed; dominant interest in things going on around one; plans and wishes mainly concerned with finding someone who can love and be loved, etc. "This factor reveals an easy-going, presumably well-adjusted personality." Factor two—"A somewhat schizoid or introvert type of individual, marked by such traits as life and actions governed by well-defined purposes, preference for tasks that require a great deal of ambition for their accomplishment, reserving one's opinion about a widely admired person, ready to take vigorous steps to carry out one's plans, preference for being alone sometimes, etc. Here there is evidence of tension and nervous energy, as well as of a certain rigidity and idealism of character." Factor three—"A suspicious type of personality, marked by such traits as intense dislike bordering on hatred for someone, life and actions guided by well-defined purposes, preferring music and art to less æsthetic pleasures, craving for love, ready to take vigorous steps to carry out one's plans, made jealous by a number of persons, has accused others of doing a number of things, suspects others of evil intentions, has superstitious practices, has a tired, worn-out attitude, has vivid dreams, tends to worry while laying awake, talks to oneself, easily influenced, has nightmares, etc. This factor is a marked prepsychotic personality with projection as a major outstanding mechanism." (It is interesting to learn that a tendency to be guided by well-defined purposes, to like music and art, to want to be loved, and to be ready to take vigorous steps to carry out one's plans define a pre-psychotic personality!)

The remaining six factors are not readily interpretable. "They form all sorts of combinations and overlapping of traits. They were tentatively interpreted as ambivert or polivert 'types' of traits, less typical than the factors already mentioned. The factors are oblique. When they are further analysed, a super factor is found . . . [which was] identified as the 'fundamental tendency of human traits', and is to be considered basic to later differentiation and specialization of the traits into typical configurations."

A second analysis was undertaken in which all the non-differentiating items were eliminated according to an arbitrary criterion. "Items were discarded if checked by more than 50 or fewer than 6 of the 56 subjects. There were 38 trait items that were discarded according to this criterion." Again, a factor analysis was carried out of the intercorrelations for this new sample of traits and 11 factors extracted. These are quite different from those of the first analysis. "The factors of the second analysis are more clear-cut than those of the first, in the sense that the persons are less similar to each other than before; hence, more typical patterns might be revealed."

It would be futile to go through all these factors in detail. Typical, perhaps, is the second factor, which consists of twelve girls, each claiming the following traits:

"Prefers tasks that are clearly outlined and easy to work at; is dominantly interested in things going on around her in the world in which she lives; plans and wishes mainly concerned with finding someone whom she can love with all her heart; plans and wishes mainly concerned with finding someone who will love her with deep, abiding devotion.

"This seems to be . . . a normal and adjusted factor, with perhaps more of an extravert tendency, as well as a marked trait of wishing to be in love. It may be identified as a romantic factor or 'type' of person."

To the writer it does not appear that the factors emerging, either from the first or the second analysis, are particularly meaningful or easily interpretable. The fact that in two different analyses of the same persons, and largely the same traits, entirely different sets of factors emerge, must make one feel rather uneasy about the meaning of the resulting factors. When we consider the labour involved in

calculating two sets of over 1,500 tetrachoric correlations each, i.e
a total of over 3,000 correlations, as well as the time consumed in
carrying out the factor analyses of two tables 56 × 56, and all the
rotations required to reach simple structure, it seems to the present
writer that the ratio of the worth-whileness of data to the refinement
of statistical treatment is altogether too low. It is his contention that
we have here an abuse of statistical method which cannot be justified
by the very limited increase in psychological knowledge which this
study gives us. P technique may have a contribution to make to
psychology, but if so, hypotheses will have to be stated clearly and
deductions made which can be proved or disproved; the type of
analysis exemplified by Moore, Stafford, and Hsü's paper is not
likely to convince readers of the usefulness of this technique.

One more word should be said about the "super factor" discovered
in this research and discussed at some greater length in another
paper by Stafford and Hsü (1947). These authors link it up with the
super-factor found by Moore (1933), which, it will be remembered,
was extracted from the correlations of the syndromes of both schizophrenic and manic-depressive patients. "This leads immediately to
the interpretation that such a super-factor reflects human personality
traits taken as a whole, the fundamentals of which are in a sense more
basic to psychotic syndromes than the syndromes themselves. A
psychotic syndrome may thus be regarded as something that becomes
more differentiated later in life rather than a basic constitutional
tendency. The super-factor would correspond more properly to such
a basic tendency . . . one would expect to find this same super-factor
in the pre-psychotic personality." The writer cannot follow this
argument, which would appear to identify a super-factor found from
intercorrelations between persons with the super-factor found from
intercorrelations between tests. As will be shown below, the factorial
resolution of a set of marks is unchanged whether that matrix is
analysed by rows or columns, *except* for any general factor between
persons (which would not appear in the correlations between tests),
or the general factor in the intercorrelations between tests (which
would not appear in the intercorrelations between persons). Consequently, it does not seem possible or reasonable to interpret these
two "super-factors" as being identical because by their very method
of extraction they must be interpreted quite differently if, indeed, any
reasonable interpretation of them is possible.

Many other authors have used techniques of this kind in the analysis
of psychiatric patients and their syndromes, among them Tabour

(1958), Williams and Macki (1957), Guertin (1952, 1953, 1954, 1955), Monro (1955). These are rather too specialized and of too little systematic interest to be discussed in detail. Only one study in this category stands out from the rest and demands discussion; reference is to Beck's (1954) Monograph on "The six schizophrenias". Dissatisfied with the usefulness of current nosological conceptions of schizophrenia and its subgroupings, Beck decided to carry out an interdisciplinary study based on psychiatric and psychological assessments of schizophrenics. 120 separate items relevant to psychological defences and ego functions were prepared and sorted for various schizophrenic patients by psychiatrists (on the basis of clinical interviews with the patients), and by psychologists (on the basis of individual Rorschach protocols). Each patient was rated by one psychiatrist and one or two psychologists. A factor analysis was carried out of the matrix of intercorrelations of these various sorts.

Beck, in order to avoid too large a matrix, divided his subjects into an "agreement" group and a "disagreement" group, according to whether psychiatrists and psychologists agreed in their sorts. The exact manner of assigning patients is not altogether clear, and indeed Shaffer as quoted by Conger *et al.* (1956), has pointed out that "The psychiatrists and psychologists seem in better agreement on three of the eight 'disagreement' cases than on three of the twelve 'agreement' ones." However that may be, on the basis of several analyses Beck arrived at five factors which led him to define, "by their juxtaposition", six types or classes of schizophrenic cases.

Conger, Sawrey and Krause (1956) have thrown doubt on the underlying rationale of Beck's procedure. They "question the methodology employed in obtaining Beck's results, and feel that it casts serious doubts on the validity of his conclusions. In the case of each of the above analyses, the group correlation matrix consisted of X individual ratings of Y patients. Thus, each correlation coefficient represents the combination of rater and patient characteristics. In other words, the amount of variance the correlation accounts for is distributed between the two in indiscriminate amounts. Therefore, when this correlation matrix is factor analysed, it is virtually impossible to tell to what extent the factors represent raters or patients."

Conger and his colleagues extracted from Beck's overall matrix the individual intercorrelation matrices for the various raters and factor analysed them separately. Their hypothesis was that "If Beck's factors are in fact due primarily to patient differences, we should then emerge with three quite similar factor patterns". They arrived at the conclusion "(a) That there is disagreement among raters as to the number of factors present in this population of patients, and (b) that there is also disagreement as to which persons identify apparently parallel factors. In the light of this evidence of inter-rater reliability, we do not feel that Beck is justified in his conclusions as to the factors, and consequently the schizophrenic types which characterise his population." It would be difficult to disagree.

It might be thought from these comments that the technique of correlating persons is of comparatively little importance in psychology. That impression would be erroneous. There are certain problems which require a technique of this kind. To take but one example: if we are interested in a study of individual differences in strength of imagery, it would be very difficult to judge the relevant vividness of one person's images as compared to those of another, but it is quite easy for a given person to rank in order of vividness for himself the different types of imagery (auditory, visual, kinæsthetics, etc.), and then to correlate one person with another. An experiment along these lines was reported by Burt (1938), who took 12 persons and subjected them to a questionnaire which required them to grade according to degree of vividness their mental images of about 100 different experiences. Correlations were run between the persons, and a general and three group factors discovered. The general factor shows that there is a tendency for most people's visual imagery to be stronger than their auditory imagery and for their auditory imagery to be stronger than their motor imagery. The three group factors could be identified with visual, auditory, and motor imagery respectively.

While, from the point of view of methodology, this research again exemplifies the error of biased sampling (Burt chose four persons of predominantly visual, auditory, or motor imagery from the total number of students), it does illustrate the possibilities of factorial analysis in connection with correlations between persons when correlations between traits would be difficult if not impossible. It also illustrates another point, which is extremely important, namely the emergence from a matrix of intercorrelations between persons of a general factor which could not have been found in an analysis of inter-correlations between traits.

This last statement requires some explanation. In the hypothetical example given in Table 58, in which an attempt was made to exemplify the kind of problem attacked by Stephenson, the marks in the body of the table were chosen in such a way that a bipolar factor would result from the intercorrelations whether between persons or between tests. In that case, factors are similar, if not identical, regardless of the method of intercorrelation employed. The position is quite different when the first factor to emerge from the marks is a general factor, i.e. a factor having no negative saturations. In that case, this factor is unique to either the matrix of intercorrelations between persons or the matrix of intercorrelations between tests. The general factor discovered by Burt in the above example is specific to the matrix of intercorrelations between persons, and would not have been observed if the tests had been intercorrelated. The reason for this is, of course, quite simple. The meaning of the general factor, psychologically, is that for all persons visual imagery tends to be the strongest and motor imagery tends to be the weakest. When we correlate persons, this factor must appear; when we correlate tests of differences in general vividness of imagery, we start by scoring each test from its own average, thus effectively eliminating the general differences in strength and thereby the general factor which depends on these.

The converse of this general proposition is equally true. If there is a general factor in the intercorrelations between tests, it would not appear if we intercorrelated persons, because again it would be lost in the process of averaging employed in calculating these correlations. Spearman's "g" could never have been found by intercorrelating persons, because in correlating persons the differences in general ability which give rise to "g" are averaged out. Thus, there are factors in the intercorrelations between persons which are not deducible from intercorrelations between tests, and, similarly, there are factors in the intercorrelations between tests which are not deducible from the intercorrelations between persons.

We may say, therefore, that if the process of correlating persons has any major and novel significance in the field of personality study, it must lie in the fact that it gives rise to factors which could not have been discovered in any other way, i.e. general factors describing overall similarities between people's reactions. The only field in which large-scale efforts have been made to apply these principles is that of æsthetic judgment, and a brief description of some of the findings may be of interest in itself, in addition to serving as a clarification of the theoretical discussion given above.

Most of the studies described are very similar in the methodology employed. A number of stimuli (portraits, landscapes, poems, photographs, colours, pictures of statues, vases, pieces of music, etc.) are

ANALYSIS OF CORRELATIONS BETWEEN PERSONS

presented to the subjects, who rank them in order of preference; correlations are then run between these individual orders of preference and the resulting table of correlations is factor analysed. The work of Beebee Center (1933), Stephenson (1935), Williams, Winter and Woods (1938), Dewar (1938), and many others has shown that there appears to exist a general tendency for the individual judges to agree in their rankings, thus giving rise to a general factor in each case. The literature has been reviewed by Davies (1939), who also points out that: "Since in most published investigations an overwhelming proportion of the variance proves to be attributable to the first factor, it is not surprising to find that the saturation coefficients for secondary or specific factors generally have *little* or *no* statistical significance." It follows from this that people in general agree in their preferences, but that it is difficult to discover groups of people sharing special preferences, i.e. types of artistic appreciations. The interest of all this work, then, being mainly concerned with the general factor, we must ask ourselves how this can be interpreted. Burt, under whose direction several of these researches were carried out, appears to consider that they provide evidence for a general factor of artistic capacity or "taste". Such a conclusion, however, does not follow from the results of these studies, there being two main fallacies involved—one methodological, the second statistical.

In the work on which Burt bases his conclusion, the tests employed were of a very heterogeneous nature, ranging from items having very high æsthetic value to items having very little or none at all, like cheap Christmas cards, etc. With tests of this type, it is impossible to rule out the influence of knowledge, teaching, conventionality, and so on, all of which may determine the preference judgments actually expressed by the subjects. Expressed preference for a cheap, pretty-pretty Christmas card over what is known to be an acknowledged work of art requires personality qualities over and above the factor of taste, or rather lack of it, measured by this test. In the absence of experimental proof that such additional factors are not active in the judgments of subjects, we cannot accept evidence from an omnibus test of this kind as giving a true indication of an individual's æsthetic judgment.

The statistical objection to such an identification is even more decisive. As we pointed out before, Spearman's "*g*" could not have been discovered from an analysis of intercorrelations between persons, but only from an analysis of intercorrelations between tests. Similarly, a general factor of taste would be analogous to "*g*" in that it could only be proved to exist by intercorrelating *tests*. All that we can show from intercorrelating *persons* is that with respect to the items under investigation, there is agreement among the subjects in their order of preference; we can go on from there to show that some persons show greater agreement with the majority than do others, or, to put it differently, that some persons have higher factor saturations than others. This, however, will only be equivalent to showing in the cognitive field that some people are better at solving a particular kind of problem than others. It can obviously not establish a general factor of taste, just as little as the demonstration that some people are better than others at a given cognitive task can establish the existence of a general factor of intelligence.

A study designed to obviate these criticisms was carried out by Eysenck (1940, 1941). Eighteen tests altogether were constructed, each consisting of æsthetic objects of a certain type (landscapes, book bindings, vases, masks, Japanese paintings, statues, portraits, etc.). Taking each test separately, correlations were calculated between the rankings by the subjects of the items in the test, and the rankings correlated and factor analysed. The resulting factor saturations for each person were then used as his scores on each test, and the 18 tests intercorrelated and factor analysed. Correlations were nearly all positive, showing that a person who agrees well with the others in one test tends also to agree well with the others in the remainder of the tests, while a person who shows little agreement with the others in one test tends to show little agreement with the others on the remainder of the tests. Thus there does appear to exist a genuine general factor of æsthetic appreciation which is free from the statistical objections raised before. An attempt was also made in this study to obviate the methodological criticism mentioned above. Items in any one of these sets were selected in such a way that none of the subjects could have judged on the basis of prior knowledge of the esteem in which the item was held by persons more knowledgeable than himself. This was achieved in various ways. In some sets (vases, embroidery) knowledge of expert opinion was completely lacking in the subjects, so that it could not have affected their judgment. In other cases, all the items included in the set were by the same artist, e.g. pictures by Claude Lorraine, so that again the name of the artist could not help the subject in discriminating between the items. In these various ways, the factor of knowledge was excluded as far as possible, and it seems that the only conclusion that can be drawn from the data is that there does exist a general factor of æsthetic ability, which was labelled a "taste" or "T" factor by Eysenck.[1]

A similar approach to the above was used in investigating the possible existence of type factors in the æsthetic field. Five tests (two tests using landscape paintings, one using portraits, one using photographs of statues, and one using landscape photographs) were used. Correlations between persons were run for each of the tests, and two factors extracted in each case. Using a person's factor saturations on these factors as his scores on each of the tests, the five tests were correlated for factors I and II separately. The factor I correlations gave rise to the T factor mentioned in the preceding paragraph; the factor II correlations gave rise to another factor which was called "K", and which ran through all the five tests. This factor differentiated those persons who liked modern art, bright sunny photographs, and statues by Kolbe, from those who liked the older masters, cloudy, foreboding photographs, and the statues of Maillol and Barlach. An attempt was made to account for this factor in terms of Hornbostel's work on intersensory perception, in which he found evidence for a "brightness" factor which was apparent in music, vision, and other sense modalities.

The factor K was found to be correlated with extraversion-introversion and with radicalism-conservatism, in the sense that preference for modern art was more prevalent among the extraverts and the radicals. Age was also found to be correlated with the K factor in the expected direction, and when a colour-form test was administered to the same subjects an almost significant correlation was found between liking for modern art and colour preferences. These results, while only tentative, indicate the possibilities inherent in æsthetic preference judgments as indirect measures of personality. Later experiments have verified some of these conclusions (Eysenck, 1947).

Equally promising as tests of æsthetic appreciation appear to be tests of appreciation of humour, where again correlations between persons have been used by several writers, particularly Eysenck (1942, 1943, 1947) and Williams (1945). Essentially, tests used by these writers consist of jokes, limericks, humorous verses, humorous pictures with captions, cartoons, etc., which are ranked in order of "funniness" by the subjects concerned. Intercorrelations among

[1] The correlation between T and intelligence was found to be negligible. A much more detailed discussion of the results, as well as of possible criticism, is given by Eysenck (1942). This paper also relates æsthetic appreciation to more general laws of perception, and summarizes the literature only briefly quoted here.

persons are usually rather low, averaging between ·1 and ·2. Nor can we duplicate the findings from investigations into æsthetic appreciation according to which persons having high-factor saturations on one test also have high saturations on others. When five such tests were intercorrelated by Eysenck (1943), the intercorrelations averaged only ·04. In a similar study by Williams (1945), the first-factor saturations for three tests again only showed insignificant correlations. It would not appear, therefore, that the first or "general" factor is of any great interest or importance in work on the organization of personality.

The position is quite different with respect to a second bipolar factor which emerged from the tests used by both these writers, and which bears an interesting similarity to a factor found by Kambouropoulou (1926) in her analysis of diary entries, joke tests, etc. This factor was considered by her to divide personal from impersonal aspects of humour, i.e. those aspects which are *orectic* (dealing with the affective and conative side of personality) from those which are *cognitive*. The orectic type of humour is largely concerned with jokes dealing with sex, with superiority, and generally which depend on personal empathy of one kind or another, whereas impersonal, or cognitive, jokes depend on incongruity of ideas and quite generally on the more formal aspects of humour. Kambouropoulou (1930) found that "the more extraverted subjects have a greater proportion of the superiority class among the items they find most amusing. Extraversion and preference for the superiority class of humorous items go together."

This suggestion was fully confirmed by Eysenck (1947) and Williams (1945). The former, working on the hypothesis that hysterics could be used as a prototype of extraversion, dysthymics as a prototype of introversion, tested the hypothesis of a correlation between extraversion and preferences for orectic humour by asking 25 male and 25 female hysterics, and 25 male and 25 female dysthymics, to rate 60 cartoons for their funniness. Some of the cartoons exemplified orectic humour, others exemplified cognitive humour, and the results abundantly bore out the original hypothesis. Williams (1945) assessed the temperament of her subjects by means of the Rorschach test and found that "there is here a fairly close correspondence between introversion and impersonality in attitude to humour appreciation, and between extraversion and the personal attitude to humour". These various studies, then, are in excellent agreement on the correlations between type of humour preferred and personality, and we may conclude that here we have a promising tool of research.

In evaluating this work on æsthetic appreciation and sense of humour, however, it should be borne in mind that the factors which were found to be related to personality were not the general factors, which could only have been obtained by means of correlations of persons, but the bipolar or type factors which could have been obtained just as easily by intercorrelating tests or test items. In other words, it is doubtful if these studies can be taken to support the claims made for P technique as a particularly valuable form of methodology in personality research.

On the other hand, these studies do illustrate a point which may lead one to view P technique in a slightly more favourable light. Admittedly the same principles of classification (e.g. personal versus impersonal, or orectic versus cognitive sense of humour) could have been discovered by intercorrelating jokes rather than persons. However, many jokes are not particularly characteristic of the extremes of this bipolar factor, and as the number of jokes which could be intercorrelated is strictly limited, by virtue of the enormous amount of time and energy involved in the calculation and analysis of large tables of correlations, it might easily have occurred that few if any of the jokes included were particularly characteristic of this dichotomy. This would have led, in the end, to a rather inconclusive analysis. The method of intercorrelating persons and including a very large number of variegated jokes appears to be much more likely to suggest profitable divisions in the complex mass of material, and it does so with very much less labour. Also we have the additional advantage of being able to cross-check the hypothesis of factorial identity from one study to another by correlating the factor saturations of our subjects. The division between R and T analysis, therefore, might be made most advantageously in terms of the specific problem which confronts the investigator and the particular stage of development or lack of development of the field which he is investigating. When reasonable hypotheses are at hand, correlations between persons are not likely to be very helpful to him. When the field is very inchoate, however, and the material lends itself to some form of ranking procedure, P technique is a quick and simple way of formulating preliminary hypotheses and going some way towards verifying them. From this point of view, P technique would have a very definite rôle to play.[1]

[1] As a further example of this "suggestive" function of factor analysis, the studies of Eysenck (1940) and Gunn (1951) on preferences for poetry may be mentioned.

We must now turn to an even more recent and novel procedure in the factorial field, in which there is only one subject and where the items correlated are different occasions on which tests were given or ratings carried out. The first suggestion for studies of this kind comes from Baldwin (1942, 1946), who calls his method "personal structure analysis", from Cattell (1943, 1947) and from Primoff (1943). As what is being correlated are different occasions when tests or ratings are being carried out, we shall call this method "O" technique, to bring it in line with "P" and "T" technique.

Baldwin in his paper uses letters written by one subject in the course of her life. His analysis is based on two assumptions. The first is that "the frequency of an item in the case material is a measure of its importance in personality". The second is that "the contiguity of two items, if repeated sufficiently often to exclude the hypothesis that the contiguity is due to change, indicates a relationship in the personality". An analysis of contiguity was therefore carried out, although this was not actually expressed in terms of correlation coefficients but rather in terms of contingency tables, which were tested for significance.

In a later paper, Baldwin (1946) much improved on the crude methods used in his first paper, and employed both correlations and factor analysis in his work. He begins by defining an intra-individual correlation coefficient as "a measure of the relationship between two variables (from time to time) within the behaviour of a single individual". He goes on to say that "by the factor analysis of a table of such intercorrelations, the patterns of variables within the single individual may be delineated. Such an analysis provides an objective method for the integration of behavioural observations into a concept of individual personality structure."

As an example of his intended procedure, he presents a figure (Fig. 57) showing the temporal curves of a hypothetical individual on two variables. It will be seen that the two curves fluctuate together, and are therefore correlated if this correlation is taken over the twenty days of observations. The correlation between A and B within the individual, therefore, would be positive; the contribution of this individual to a group correlation would, however, be in a negative direction because he is above the mean on one variable and below on the other.

Baldwin faces the statistical difficulties raised by the lack of independence of the various observations which comprise his sample. Following statistical procedures worked out, particularly by economists, he removes the temporal trend, which is responsible for this lack of independence by intercorrelating it with the other variables and rotating the axes of the factor analysis in such a manner as to place one of them right through this variable. In this way, all variance due to time trend is taken up by the first factor, and all other factors are independent of it.

We may now describe his actual research. Using the Fels Child Behaviour Scales, he had four children rated every day on the 30 items making up this scale over a period of 20 days. These items were

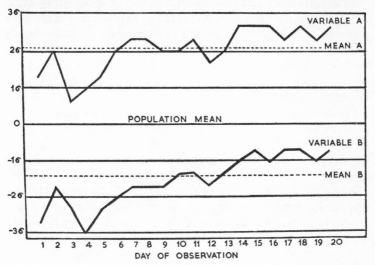

Fig. 57.—Temporal Curves of a Hypothetical Individual on two Variables.

correlated within each individual, thus giving rise to four matrices of intercorrelations (one for each child). These were factor analysed by Holzinger and Harman's "averoid" method, and the factors rotated, as has been explained above, in such a way that the first axis passes through the time variable. Also available were the results of a factor analysis carried out in the usual way, i.e. by correlating the 30 items over a large group of children. (This analysis has already been discussed in a previous chapter.)

The factors isolated were, first of all, a factor of temporal change. The scales which had loadings on this factor were found to include almost all those variables which had high loadings on the factor of *desirability* in the original group analysis. "The factor was labelled 'desirability' because it seemed to express the general concept held by nursery school teachers of the 'good nursery school child'. In view of the high correlation of these variables with time, it would appear that the usual nursery school child goes through an adjustment process, during which time his behaviour tends towards the 'desirable'."

The second factor is also similar for the various children analysed and is labelled "conformity". The existence of such a conformity factor would seem to indicate that the nursery school situation sets up certain standards which the child is expected to meet. He must react to these expectations of conformity, and so he can hardly avoid having a definite personality trait related to the problem of conformity . . . this is a pattern description of conformity; non-conformity appears in the majority of the individual cases and in the group analysis." A third factor was extracted for the various children but showed no similarity between them, and is consequently difficult, if not impossible, to interpret.

Baldwin sums up his work as follows: "This method is devised as a research tool and though as a practical routine method of interpretation it may be too laborious and time consuming for purposes of research, the increased objectivity of the results is worth the increased labour."

With this, the present writer would emphatically agree. The fact that similar factors are found in this "O" analysis as were found previously in the "T" analysis of the Fels Scale (cf. p. 82) might seem to make such separate investigations unnecessary, but the fact that some of the children showed discrepancies from the general pattern which may be quantified in terms of "O" analysis, lends this technique a good deal of additional interest. Some of the statistical questions raised by this method cannot, of course, be said to have received a satisfactory answer. The question of a metric continuum and the question of proper sampling must be regarded as giving rise to a certain degree of uneasiness; the question of rotation into simple structure may or may not be meaningful in this field; the writer is not aware of any discussion trying to justify any of the methods of rotation used in this field, which might establish these methods as firmly as simple structure is established in the fields of T technique. No confident judgment can be made, therefore, of the feasibility or the possible usefulness of this technique.

A much more enthusiastic view of the possibility of this new approach is held by Cattell (1947), who considers it "to have the promise of a systematic new approach, additional to, and perhaps as important as, the familiar 'R' technique, or its successor 'Q' technique". In its main outline his view of this technique is similar to Baldwin's. "Essentially it is a method for applying experimental measurement with co-variational analysis to the single case. This means that one person must be measured on a collection of tests on a series of occasions. The analysis is then made on coefficients obtained from the correlations of traits in which the unit of entry is a day (or hour) of observation." This technique, he considers, "has particular promise in dynamic and clinical psychology, where it can, at least in principle, cope with those problems of discovering unique dynamic structure, which some psychologists have claimed to lie beyond the experimental and statistical approach".

In his approach Cattell adopts an order of importance which to the present writer seems somewhat unusual. "Some theoretical considerations of a narrowly statistical nature remain to be considered in developing this new method, but it would be inappropriate to debate these in any detail until the basic questions have been answered. The latter concern whether the correlations obtained in this way transcend chance error, whether they yield factors having psychological meaning and interest, and whether the factors are of the same general nature as the 'R' technique personality factors." It might be that before a new technique is seriously considered and used, it would be best to clear up such fundamental points as the choice of metric, the lack of independence of the various observations comprising this sample, and the problem of sampling itself. In the absence of such statistical discussion, the meaning of correlations calculated must remain somewhat obscure and doubtful.

In Cattell's first experiment, a normal 20-year-old woman was used as a subject; for 55 days almost consecutively this subject was (1) measured on the same batch of test variables; (2) rated by close observers on personal behaviour; and (3) self-rated on a personality questionnaire. Correlations were carried out in the first place between the objective tests only, and four factors extracted from the table of intercorrelations. These are called (1) emotional abundance versus emotional dearth; (2) physiological ease versus emergency alertness; (3) fatigue versus energy reserve; (4) uncontrolled versus inhibition. These interpretations can be accepted only with some reserve, but the reader must consult the original publication, as a detailed discussion would be too lengthy in this place (Cattell, *et. al.*, 1947).

Scores were next given to each of these factors, and they were intercorrelated in a single matrix with the rated and self-rated personality factors. Five factors were again obtained, which are identified with five factors previously obtained by Cattell in his studies of ratings summarized in a previous chapter. Again the writer feels somewhat doubtful about the interpretations. To give but one example, the first factor obtained from the analysis of the objective tests alone (emotional abundance versus emotional dearth) is characterized by high body sway suggestibility and high P.G.R. deflection; these items, as has been shown in previous chapters, are characteristic of neuroticism. Yet this emotional abundance-emotional dearth test factor now appears in Cattell's second analysis as a factor of "adventurous cyclothymia" versus "withdrawn schizothymia". There is no evidence in the literature that body sway is in any way related to schizothymia-cyclothymia, and in the absence of such evidence identification would seem premature.

Cattell lays great stress on the resemblance of the factors extracted in "O" technique with those extracted in "T" technique. To the present writer there seems to be no very obvious reasons why these factors should be in any way identical. "O" factors are derived from the covariance of traits or tests over a period of time within a single person; the causes which may lead to such covariance, no doubt, are multiform, and may be related to such agencies as general fatigue, physiological changes such as the Menarche, and so forth. It is not unreasonable that in certain chosen batteries of tests, factors corresponding to these causes may be found; on the other hand, if we conceive of a person as having a fundamental neurophysiological constitution, predisposing him to a certain extent towards neurotic breakdown, it is difficult to see why this constitutional factor should be responsible for diurnal covariation. The possibility, of course, cannot be ruled out; during the course of psychiatric treatment, for instance, it is conceivable that a decrease in neuroticism may take place, which would be mirrored in a number of tests defining this factor. If that were to happen, then the same tests which in "T" analysis correlate together to define the factor of neuroticism would perhaps correlate in "O" analysis to define improvement under treatment. Obviously, the whole position is very complex and, in the absence of any sustained attempt to discuss the statistical and theoretical aspects of the matter, little further can with advantage be said.

In a later publication, Cattell and Luborsky (1950) used "O" technique in connection with a neurotic personality. Forty-nine variables were used, including physiological and biochemical measurements, psychological ratings, self-ratings, and objective measures. Fifty-four days constituted the experimental population over which correlations were run between the measures. Nine factors were extracted and rotated into simple structure. The factors extracted are in the main identified with Cattell's primary personality factors, although, again, this identification does not appear to be firmly established to the writer. It is difficult to discuss this research in any detail, as the very large number of variables used and the factors extracted, and the constant reference necessary to previous work, would make such an undertaking a very formidable one indeed.

It will have been gathered that the present writer is less enthusiastic about "P" and "O" techniques than are those who have originated and used them most.[1] Many of the objections which may be brought forward have already been discussed in the course of the text, and it seems that few of them have been answered by the champions of these methods. Neither on the statistical, the methodological, nor the experimental side can any of the published researches be considered faultless. Most of them, particularly those of Stephenson and Burt, were published as examples of the possibilities inherent in such novel techniques; as such they are not at all convincing. Although "P" technique has been in existence for almost twenty years, it has never advanced beyond this stage of giving examples of how useful it might be. In the absence of a properly conducted experiment advancing our knowledge in any respect or throwing some new light on the problems which the technique is supposed to be best equipped to tackle, judgment must be reserved.[2] On the whole, however, the

[1] To the above-mentioned writers we should add Burt and Watson (1951), who analyse one case in detail without adding anything new to the argument, and Hsü (1949), who disapproves of the Baldwin-Cattell methods and substitutes one of his own which cannot readily be considered to be an improvement.

Of very much more interest is a paper by Osgood and Luria (1954) dealing with "A blind analysis of a case of multiple personality, using the semantic differential". Readers who want to see the methods discussed in this chapter used at their best are recommended to consult this paper.

[2] A recent discussion between Stephenson (1952) and Cattell (1952), somewhat reminiscent of an earlier one between Burt and Stephenson (1939), suggests that Cattell and Burt would probably be in agreement with this position. Stephenson still fails to answer the objections to his use of "P" technique, and still makes strong claims for it.

Even more recently Stephenson (1953) has published a book dealing with his techniques. Again he merely quotes small *ad hoc* studies designed to illustrate rather than to prove. His statistical arguments have been criticized rather severely by Cronbach and Gleser (1954) whose detailed arguments should be consulted by anyone wishing to undertake the analysis of correlations between persons. Such readers might also be advised to study another paper by Cronbach (1953) on "Correlations between persons as a research tool". It may be relevant to quote

Continued at foot of next page

422   THE STRUCTURE OF HUMAN PERSONALITY

writer believes that while for certain limited purposes correlations between persons and correlations between occasions may, with advantage, be used, these methods are unlikely to supplant, although they may supplement, the fundamental method of "T" analysis.

REFERENCES

Chapter XI

BALDWIN, A. L. Personal structure analysis: a statistical method for investigating the simple personality. *J. abnorm. soc. Psychol.*, 1942, **37**, 163–183.

Differences in parent behavior towards three- and nine-year old children. *J. Pers.*, 1946, **15**, 143–165.

BECK, S. J. The six schizophrenias. *Res. Monogr.*, No. 6, New York: Amer. Orthopsychiat., Ass., 1954.

BEEBEE-CENTER, J. B. *Pleasantness and Unpleasantness.* New York: Century, 1933.

BURT, C. Factor analysis by sub-matrices. *J. Psychol.*, 1938, **6**, 339–375.

BURT, C., and STEPHENSON, W. Alternative views on correlations between persons. *Psychomet.*, 1939, **4**, 269–281.

BURT, C., and WATSON, H. Factor analysis of assessments for a single person. *Brit. J. Psychol., Stat. Sect.*, 1951, **4**, 179–192.

CATTELL, R. B. The description of personality. *Psychol. Rev.*, 1943, **50**, 539–594.

The Description and Measurement of Personality. London: Harrap & Co. Ltd., 1947.

The three basic factor-analytic research designs—their intercorrelations and derivatives. *Psychol. Bull.*, 1952, **49**, 499–520.

CATTELL, R. B., and LUBORSKY, L. B. P-technique demonstrated as a new clinical method for determining personality and symptom structure. *J. genet. Psychol.*, 1950, **42**, 3–24.

CATTELL, R. B., CATTELL, A. K. S., and RHYMER, R. M. P-technique demonstrated in determining psychophysiological source traits in a normal individual. *Psychomet.*, 1947, **12**, 267–288.

CONGER, J. J., SAWNEY, W. L., and KRAUSE, L. F. A reanalysis of Beck's "Six Schizophrenias". *J. consult. Psychol.*, 1956, **20**, 83–87.

CRONBACH, L. J. Correlation between persons as a research tool. In: O. H. Mowrer (Ed.), *Psychotherapy: theory and research.* New York: Ronald, 1953.

CRONBACH, L. J., and GLESER, G. C. William Stephenson, The Study of Behavior. A review. *Psychometrika*, 1954, **19**, 327–330.

DAVIES, M. The general factor in correlations between persons. *Brit. J. Psychol.*, 1939, **29**, 404–421.

the evaluation of Stephenson's work given by Cronbach and Gleser (1954). They say: "It is imperative to discourage students of personality and social psychology from copying Stephenson's designs as he presents them. . . . We fear that Stephenson's book may misdirect much research effort." There is unfortunately much evidence that the apparent simplicity and attractiveness of these designs has indeed had precisely this effect among research workers of relatively little statistical sophistication.

DEWAR, H. A comparison of tests of artistic appreciation. *Brit. J. educ. Psychol.*, 1938, **8**, 29–49.

EYSENCK, H. J. Some factors in the appreciation of poetry and their relation to temperamental qualities. *Charact. and Pers.*, 1940, **9**, 160–167.

The general factor in aesthetic judgments. *Brit. J. Psychol.*, 1940, **31**, 94–102.

"Type"—factors in aesthetic judgments. *Brit. J. Psychol.*, 1941, **31**, 262–270.

The experimental study of the "Good Gestalt"—a new approach. *Psychol. Rev.*, 1942, **49**, 344–364.

The appreciation of humour: an experimental and theoretical study. *Brit. J. Psychol.*, 1942, **32**, 295–309.

An experimental analysis of five tests of "Appreciation of Humour". *Educ. Psychol. Measmt.*, 1943, **3**, 191–214.

Dimensions of Personality. London: Kegan Paul, 1947.

GUERTIN, W. H. A factor analysis of the Bender-Gestalt test of mental patients. *J. clin. Psychol.*, 1952, **8**, 363–367.

A transposed factor analysis of schizophrenic performance—the Bender-Gestalt. *J. clin. Psychol.*, 1954, **10**, 225–228.

A transposed analysis of the Bender-Gestalts of paranoid schizophrenics. *J. clin. Psychol.*, 1955, **11**, 73–76.

GUERTIN, W. H., and ZILAITIS, V. A transposed factor analysis of paranoid schizophrenics. *J. consult. Psychol.*, 1953, **17**, 455–458.

GUNN, D. G. Factors in the appreciation of poetry. *Brit. J. educ. Psychol.*, 1951, **21**, 96–104.

HSÜ, E. H. The construction of a test for measuring character traits. *Stud. Psychol. Psychiat.*, 1943, **6**, 3–55.

The intrapersonal factor and its clinical applicability. *J. Pers.*, 1949, **17**, 273–286.

KAMBOUROPOULOU, P. Individual differences in the sense of humor. *Amer. J. Psychol.*, 1926, **37**, 288–297.

Individual differences in the sense of humor and their relation to temperamental differences. *Arch. Psychol.*, 1930, **121**, 79.

MONRO, A. B. Psychiatric types: a Q-technique study of 200 patients. *J. ment. Sci.*, 1955, **101**, 330–343.

MOORE, T. V. The essential psychoses and their fundamental syndromes. *Stud. Psychol. Psychiat.*, 1933, **3**, 128.

Psychoses and the prepsychotic personality. *Amer. J. Orthopsychiat.*, 1939, **9**, 136–145.

The prepsychotic personality and the concept of mental disorder. *Charact. and Pers.*, 1941, **9**, 169–187.

MOORE, T. V., STAFFORD, J. W., and HSÜ, E. H. Obverse analysis of personality. *J. Pers.*, 1947, **16**, 11–48.

OSGOOD, C. E., and LURIA, F. A blind analysis of a case of multiple personality using the semantic differential. *J. abnorm. soc. Psychol.*, 1954, **49**, 539–591.

PRIMOFF, E. S. Correlations and factor analysis of the abilities of the single individual. *J. genet. Psychol.*, 1943, **28**, 121–132.

STAFFORD, J. W., and HSÜ, E. H. The super-factor of persons. *J. Psychol.*, 1947, **24**, 63–70.

STEPHENSON, W. Correlating persons instead of tests. *Charact. and Pers.*, 1935, **4**, 17–24.

Methodological consideration of Jung's typology. *J. ment. Sci.*, 1939, **85**, 185–205.

Two contributions to the theory of mental testing. II. A statistical regard of performance. *Brit. J. Psychol.*, 1939, **30**, 230–247.

The significance of Q-technique for the study of personality. In: Feelings and emotions. (Ed. Reymert, M. C.) New York: McGraw-Hill Book Co., 1950.

Some observations on Q-technique. *Psychol. Bull.*, 1952, **49**, 483–498.

The Study of Behaviour: A Technique and its Methodology. Chicago: Univ. of Chicago Press, 1953.

TABOUR, M. H. A factorial isolation of psychiatric outpatient syndromes. *J. consult. Psychol.*, 1958, **22**, 73–81.

THOMSON, G. H. *The Factorial Analysis of Human Ability.* London: Univ. London Press, 1939.

THOMSON, G. H., and BALES, S. The reliability of essay marks. *For. Educ.*, 1926, **4**, 85–91.

WILLIAMS, J. M. *An experimental and theoretical study of humour in children.* Ph.D. Thesis. London: Univ. London Lib., 1945.

WILLIAMS, R. J., and MACKI, V. S. An analysis of interperson correlations among thirty psychotics. *J. abnorm. soc. Psychol.*, 1957, **55**, 50–57.

WILLIAMS, E. D., WINTER, L., and WOODS, J. M. Tests of literary appreciation. *Brit. J. educ. Psychol.*, 1938, **8**, 265–284.

CAUSAL THEORIES OF PERSONALITY STRUCTURE

I N THIS LAST CHAPTER an attempt has been made to bring our picture of the structure of human personality up to date by introducing certain theoretical concepts and experimental techniques which originated in an endeavour to state casual postulates from which the observed behaviour patterns and descriptive factors could be deduced in a more or less rigorous fashion. The factorial literature in the last few years has grown to such an extent that the detailed historical review which we have followed in the preceding chapters could not be maintained, without extending the book to twice its present length; such a detailed review has in fact been presented elsewhere (Eysenck and Eysenck, 1969). The main conclusion which can be drawn from the several hundred recent studies there reviewed, and the original work presented, serve largely to underlines the conclusions derived from the earlier studies discussed in the present volume; results from the different universes of discourse presented by Cattell, Guilford, the MMPI, and many other apparently separate and independent sets of investigations all support very strongly the thesis that two orthogonal personality factors, extraversion-introversion and emotionality-stability, are omnipresent in empirical studies and analyses, and account for a large and important portion of the total variance, for children as much as for adults, and for mentally ill as well as for mentally normal people.[1] Not all investigators are agreed on the nomenclature, of course, and many different terms are still used to designate these major personality variables, but it is now reasonable to say that there is almost complete agreement among experimental investigators that these two factors enjoy a predominant and assured position in the descriptive system of personality measurement.

Such descriptive trait and type systems have an undisputed value, although to some critics they appear tautological and hence of very limited scientific use. Lundin (1961), for instance, likens the notion of traits to that of instincts, and appears to regard their postulation as lacking in any explanatory force. According to him, we *observe* a person behaving in a sociable manner; from this type of observation, many times repeated, we *deduce* the existence of an instinct, or trait, of sociability, only to explain our observation in terms of this hypothetical instinct or trait. This he declares to be a circular and useless process. There is a trace of truth in this often-heard criticism, but it seems to neglect certain aspects of the trait-theory which require to be looked at before the criticisms can be accepted. (1) In classifying behaviour, we are literally faced with millions of separate items, even in a short-term history of a single individual; we must needs have recourse to some form of basic system which enables us to group similar behaviour together. Even if these systems were entirely arbitrary, they would still fill an obvious need; no human discourse about behaviour would be feasible without them. But clearly some systems are better than others, and it is not obviously absurd to look for a system which is optimal according to certain fairly obvious criteria. Factor analysis, as already pointed out in an earlier chapter, provides a model for optimizing certain parameters of such a system.

(2) The system is wrongly criticized for not providing an *explanation* of behaviour; this was never its intention. We would be wrong in saying that a person behaves in a sociable fashion *because* he has a trait of sociability, but then trait psychologists do not usually make this elementary error. They postulate the trait in question simply as a *descriptive* variable, very much in the manner in which physicists elaborated the periodic table of the elements; this is descriptive of certain properties of physical matter, but does not even attempt to explain them. Similarly biologists group together mammals, not because to do so explains why they suckle their young but because descriptively it is useful to group these animals together. Sociability is a useful descriptive concept because it aligns people along a continuum which embraces a large number of separate but clearly related types of behaviour; it does not pretend to explain why some people are more sociable than others. But the causal question could not even be raised unless some answer to the descriptive problem had been found; we cannot ask ourselves *why* Tommy is more sociable than Michael if we do not isolate the continuum of sociability first.

(3) The tautology alleged to exist in trait description is often more apparent than real, or, to put it another way, the relations observed are less logically determined than empirically confirmed. We discover, for instance, that answering "Yes" to a question about

liking to go to parties correlates with sociability as determined either by inventory items, or by actual observation; it might be argued that there is a logical implication such that regardless of empirical observation sociability implies a liking for parties, and vice versa. But this is not true, as can be seen very clearly by looking at the correlations between different sociability items, which fall far short of unity, even when corrected for attenuation. Consider Don Sims, a young man of 21 who had a low N score, a high P (psychoticism) score and a low E score on a personality inventory; his sociability score was low, but he endorsed the "like to go to parties" item. When interviewed he said: "Well, at parties you get free grub, free likker, and a chance to screw some bird, don't you?"—adding, with an angelic smile: "And sometimes you can break up the place, too".

Lundin's criticism is sometimes phrased in another way, e.g. by stating that descriptive theories do not enable hypothetico-deductive methods of confirmation to be made. This criticism is also only partly true. If we look at the personality descriptions given of the choleric and the melancholic, respectively (Figs. 3 and 4), then we may deduce that cholerics (high E, high N) show personality traits similar to those of criminals, while melancholics (low E, high N) show personality traits similar to those of (dysthymic) neurotics. This descriptive similarity would lead us to the deduction that criminals would emerge as emotional extraverts, neurotic patients as emotional introverts. The facts seem to bear out this deduction (Eysenck, 1964; Eysenck and Rachman, 1965); on the whole criminals and neurotics turn out to have high N scores, and to be respectively extraverted and introverted. Nor is this personality description merely a consequence of their status; the status can be predicted from their personality. Burt (1965) studied 763 children, of whom 15% and 18% respectively became habitual offenders or neurotics during the course of a 35 year follow-up; these children had been rated by their teachers for N and E at the age of 10. Of those who became habitual offenders, 63% had been rated as high on N; 54% had been rated as high on E, with only 3% having a low rating on E. Of those who became neurotics, 59% had been rated as high on N; 44% had been rated as low on E, and only 1% as high on E. Thus we see that even the probably not very reliable ratings made by teachers at an early stage of the child's career can predict with some accuracy his later status as criminal or neurotic. Clearly this is an empirical finding, not one which is tautological and constrained by logical implication; purely descriptive systems of personality description can be related by means of the hypothetico-deductive method to areas of conduct originally outside the system.

As another example, consider the report by Moss and McEvedy (1966) of an epidemic of overbreathing among schoolgirls. In a Blackburn school, a few of the girls stated that they were feeling dizzy and peculiar; one or two had fainted. Later in the morning the affection had become epidemic, and "the girls were going down like ninepins"; 85 of the most severely affected were taken to hospital by ambulance. School was closed, but when it was reopened, another epidemic broke out, similar to the first; a week later a third outbreak was reported. No physical cause was discovered. Such epidemics are known psychiatrically to affect mainly hysterical personalities, and the hypothesis was put forward that the girls would have high E— high N scores on the Eysenck Personality Inventory (Eysenck and Eysenck, 1964). Fig. 58 shows the results by class; it will be seen that at all ages the affected girls had higher E and N scores than the unaffected. Here again, then, it is possible to extend a purely descriptive scheme to behaviours originally outside the bounds of that scheme.

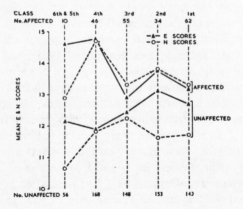

Fig. 58.—E and N scores of affected and unaffected children by school class.

Driving accidents present us with another field to which the personality qualities explicitly associated with our descriptive system can be extrapolated. The careless, impulsive, aggressive qualities of the choleric would suggest that both high E and high N would be found to characterize the accident-prone driver, and studies by Fine (1963), Craske (1968) and particularly by Shaw and Sichel (1970) have verified these descriptive hypotheses. The same personality constellation would lead one to expect persons so endowed to become unmarried mothers (S.B.G. Eysenck, 1961), contract V.D. (Wells, 1969), or show more industrial absenteeism (Cooper & Payne, 1967). There are many fields of social activity where the descriptive concepts of E and N enable one to make verifiable predictions; these fields even include the board-room (successful industrial managers appear to be stable introverts (Eysenck, 1967), and the armed forces (Commando trainees and parachute-jumping volunteers in the Army are almost without exception stable extraverts (unpublished).

On the purely experimental side a descriptive scheme can be tested best through the use of *miniature situations* tests; in other words, the traits supposed to characterize extraverts and introverts, say, or stable as opposed to emotional persons, are embodied in objective laboratory situations which are susceptible to accurate measurement. Most of the tests listed in Table 40 are of this kind. Extraverts are observed to be quick in everyday life situations, but to be less accurate than introverts; hence the speed-accuracy ratio, as determined in the laboratory on specially constructed test equipment, should differentiate between subjects scoring high and low respectively on E. Or one might hypothesize that extraverts, being more sociable, should seek more eye-contact during interview; Mobbs (1968) found that the duration of eye-contacts of introverts was 1.7 sec., that of ambiverts 2.1 sec., and that of extraverts 3.6 sec.; duration of eye-contacts correlated .73 with sociability. These examples may suffice to illustrate the principle involved; many others have been quoted in the course of our discussion, or can be found in the literature. Some studies relate other systems of personality description to the one outlined in this book; often whole systems are constructed on what seems to be just one primary factor in the E or N constellation. Thus Evans (1967) has shown that the concept of field dependence, as expounded by Witkin and his followers, correlates significantly with E scores on the Maudsley Personality Inventory (Eysenck, 1961); this would be expected from the personality description of the extravert as relating more definitely with, and being more influenced by, the external environment.

On the whole, then, it would not seem that criticisms such as those made by Lundin have very much force; trait theories are not just tautological inventions whose usefulness does not extend outside the inscribed circle of their own derivation, but lead to empirical results not logically implicit in their formulation. However, the point remains that science cannot remain content with purely descriptive categories and concepts; it always seeks to proceed to causal theories of one kind or another. Mendeleeff's periodic table of the elements led to the sub-atomic "planetary" theories of Bohr and his successors, so that we now have an understanding of the structure of the elements, and their isotopic variants, which the Table by itself was unable to give us. But of course these modern developments would not have been possible without the descriptive analysis implicit in that Table; description and explanation constantly interact to produce a better understanding of nature. Are causal theories possible in the field of personality?

Eysenck (1957) made an attempt to produce such a theory on the basis of intervening variables taken from the Hullian system; in particular he put forward the hypothesis that extraverts were characterized by high and quickly developing reactive inhibition $(_sI_R)$, while introverts developed inhibition much more slowly. The advantages and disadvantages of such intervening variables have been discussed at length by MacCorquodale and Meehl (1948), Maze (1954) and Ginsberg (1954); the postulates set down in this book, whatever their weaknesses, enabled many deductions to be made which could be tested experimentally. It would not be feasible to describe in detail all the experiments done in support of this theory; the number is too large, and a complete review is available in the book itself. In addition, a more recent theory has superceded the 1957 formulation, so that it would seem more advantageous to concentrate on this later version. Even so, it may be useful to introduce a few selected experiments to illustrate the type of deduction which can be made from a causal theory of the "intervening variable" type; we will then turn to a discussion of the later, "hypothetical construct", type.

According to Hull's theory, inhibition accumulating during massed practice should lead to "blocks" or involuntary rest pauses (IRPs), on the hypothesis that the growth of $_sI_R$, which is conceived of as a negative drive, would gradually make this negative drive equal to D, the total positive drive under which the organism is working; when this point of equality is reached, performance should stop to allow inhibition to dissipate. When enough reactive inhibition has dissipated, performance can begin again, until inhibition builds up again to equal D. An experimental study to test the prediction that extraverts would be more susceptible to the accumulation of inhibition and would consequently show involuntary rest pauses than introverts has been reported by Spielmann (1963). She used as her task simple tapping with a metal stylus on a metal plate. Length

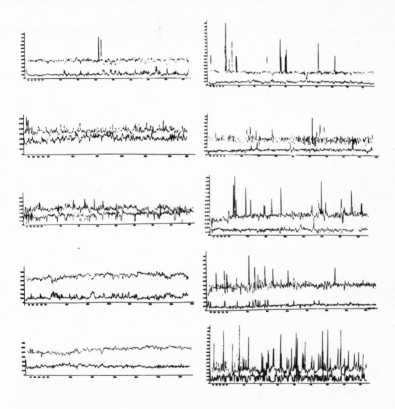

Fig. 59.—Gap and tap time scores for 5 introverted and 5 extraverted subjects on tapping task.

of each tap (duration of contact between stylus and plate) and each gap (duration of movement up and down between taps) was measured very accurately. Confining her analysis largely to the gap lengths, she scored IRPs in terms of discontinuity for any given subject when all his gap times were plotted. Ninety working-class subjects in all were tested, and the five most introverted and the five most extraverted selected on the basis of their M.P.I. scores. Fig. 59 shows the results for 1 min. periods of tapping. The average frequency of IRPs was significantly higher in extraverts than in introverts, the total number of IRPs being 15 times higher in the former than in the latter group. The average onset of IRPs was significantly earlier in the extravert group, and the extraverts produced not only many more, but also longer IRPs. Eysenck (1964) has reported a replication of this study using young apprentices.

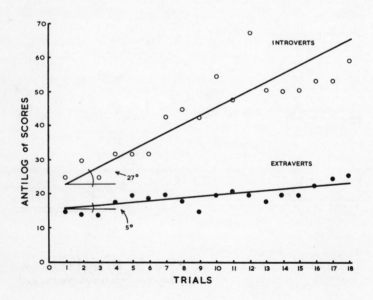

Fig. 60.—Eyeblink conditioning acquisition scores of introverts and extraverts.

Eyeblink conditioning was another type of laboratory experiment which was hypothesized to produce difference between extraverts and introverts under suitable parametric conditions (Eysenck, 1965);

the repetitive nature of the task was predicted to produce inhibition in extraverts which would lower their ability to produce responses and acquire the CR. Fig. 60 shows results from two studies by Franks (1956, 1957) combined and with the scores transformed into antilogs in order to make them more equal in different ranges. It will be seen that the predicted differences appear very much as anticipated, with introverts acquiring the CR much more rapidly. A thorough review of some objections to these and other studies is given elsewhere (Eysenck, 1967). We shall return to both experimental data and theoretical explanations later on.

A third type of prediction was made in relation to pursuit rotor reminiscence (Eysenck, 1956); it was suggested that during massed practice inhibition is built up and interferes with performance, more strongly in extraverts than in introverts; during an interpolated rest inhibition dissipates, and when performance is resumed extraverts and introverts, freed from inhibition, resume at the same level. Because of the greater interference with the performance of extraverts pre-rest they show greater reminiscence. Over two dozen studies have been done to date to put this hypothesis to the test, usually with positive results (Eysenck, 1962); there seems to be little doubt that extraverts do show greater reminiscence when suitable task parameters are chosen (such as adequate pre-rest practice, reasonable rest periods, etc). Again we shall revert to these studies and theories later on; for the moment let us just remind the reader that empirical verification of a theoretical prediction does not necessarily imply the correctness of the theory in question.

These three types of prediction were chosen to illustrate the "intervening variable" type of prediction; the choice was determined not so much by the fact that the experimental results were in line with prediction, but rather because they will furnish us with some sobering food for thought when we turn to the later "hypothetical construct" type of prediction. Intervening variables have no surplus meaning; they have no properties other than those expressed in terms of the theory in question, and no independent existence is asserted. Hypothetical constructs, on the other hand, are concrete and tangible, at least potentially; they have properties of their own, and will usually in psychological theorizing be anatomical, physiological or neurological in character. It is not *necessary* that such hypothetical constructs should be postulated in order to have causal theories which make mediation through the hypothetico-deductive method possible, but it is convenient because it enables some direct tests of the hypotheses in question to be made. Such a theory was suggested by Eysenck (1967), together with a detailed discussion of various types of testable deductions which could be derived from the theory; a large number of such predictions were in fact shown to result in outcomes favourable to the theory. It would be quite impossible to summarize all these studies, or even the larger number since published in the literature, without altering the character of this book; a small number have been selected in order to illustrate certain important generalizations suggested by the evidence.

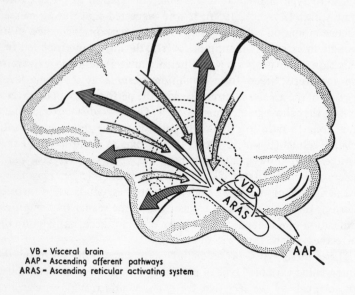

VB = Visceral brain
AAP = Ascending afferent pathways
ARAS = Ascending reticular activating system

Fig. 61.—Diagrammatic representation of anatomical-physiological structures responsible for inherited differences in E (ARAS) and N (VB).

The nature of the theory under discussion can be gleaned from Fig. 61, which shows in diagrammatic form the position of the A.R.A.S. (ascending reticular activating system), which is made responsible for individual differences in extraversion-introversion, and that of the visceral brain, which is made responsible for individual differences in emotionality-stability. We have already discussed the dependence of N on the interplay of sympathetic and parasympathetic innervation in Chapter 8; modern theories of emotion consider that this interplay is actively regulated by the visceral brain, i.e. hippocampal structures, amygdala, cingulum, septum and hypothalamus (McLean, 1958, 1960). This view is not original, and is so widely accepted that we have little to add here to what was said in the previous Chapter, although some further physiological evidence linking N with sympathetic over-reactivity is reviewed by Eysenck (1967). Our main concern will be with the postulated relationship between E and the reticular activating system.

Briefly put, this system is believed to be responsible for producing cortical arousal in response to external stimulation, and our theory postulates that this state of arousal under identical stimulating conditions is higher in introverts than in extraverts; hence behavioural and experimental predictions are predicated upon major differences in degree of arousal, rather than, as in the previous theory, in degree of reactive inhibition. The reticular formation also mediates cortical inhibition (as well as perceptual and motor inhibition; Samuels, 1959), and it is an attractive possibility to consider that extraverts are likely to develop inhibition more readily than are introverts; the new theory would thus incorporate the old one as part of itself. The difficulties inherent in differentiating between active inhibition and lack of arousal, at least in so far as psychological measures are concerned, make the testing of this additional postulate rather awkward. The theory here briefly sketched out is of course much more complex in its full form; in particular it takes into account the important facts that (1) there is a feed-back from cortex to A.R.A.S. initiating arousal or inhibition, and (2) that the visceral brain can also produce arousal, either directly or through the A.R.A.S. These complexities cannot be discussed in detail here; they are fully treated in "The Biological Basis of Personality".

We thus emerge with a system according to which under ordinary (non-emotion producing) conditions introverts are working in a state of relatively high cortical arousal as compared with ambiverts, while extraverts are working in a state of relatively low arousal as compared with ambiverts. This cortical supremacy in introverts produces a constraint on their behaviour, in accordance with conditioned and learned patterns of responses, which leads to the emergence of the particular traits which we have found to characterize introverts; conversely, the relative absence of such supremacy leads to an absence of such constraints, and thus to the emergence of traits characterizing extraverts. Of particular interest in this connection is the mediating role of conditioning; we have already noted that introverts condition better than extraverts, and it seems theoretically inviting to link the neurotic behaviour of emotional introverts with their over-ready conditioning of normally neutral stimuli (Eysenck and Rachman, 1965), and the criminal behaviour of emotional extraverts with their failure to condition the stimuli normally producing socialization in childhood (Eysenck, 1964). Such theories may appear highly speculative, and lacking in direct support; their interest and importance would appear to lie mainly in giving direction to future research, and trying to link together closely studied laboratory phenomena and real-life situations and responses.

Strong emotions are produced in most people only relatively rarely; when they are the visceral brain is spurred into activity and the sympathetic system, or at least some of its sub-systems, are thrown into action. When this happens cortical arousal is produced automatically, and it seems probably that individual differences between extraverts and introverts in respect to arousal are largely washed out. Experiments to differentiate between high and low E scorers should therefore be conducted in such a way that emotions of fear and anxiety are avoided, whether these are produced by the sight of massive electronic apparatus, or by ego-involving test instructions, or in other ways. Similarly, strong emotions are frequently produced in a small sample of people, e.g. neurotics or high N scorers generally; indeed, some neurotics live in a private universe of constant fear and anxiety. For these people a state of low arousal seems almost unattainable and consequently we may expect interaction effects between E and N. Even on personality inventories it has been found that while over most of the range these two dimensions are uncorrelated, in samples characterized by high N scores quite marked negative correlations are found, substantiating the view that in high N subjects high E (low arousal) is almost unattainable (Eysenck, 1961). These complexities must be kept in mind in evaluating the experimental literature; they suggest the routine use of some form of zone analysis, i.e. a splitting of the total universe of the subjects into 4 (high N, high E; low N, high E; high N, low E; low N, low E) or even 9 groups (including medium high E and N scorers as separate groups, in all combinations with high and low E and N scorers). This makes possible the discovery of interaction effects between E and N, as well as the possibility of non-linear trends in one or both variables.

Two examples of such cross-over effects will now be given. The first relates to perceptual defence. Inglis (1960) has put forward the hypothesis that at low levels of stress introverts show suppression and extraverts sensitization, while at high levels of stress this relation is reversed, and has quoted supporting evidence; if we substitute "low N subjects" and "high N subjects" respectively for low and high levels of stress we have here a testable theory of personality-perceptual defence interaction which postulates a cross-over effect. Support for the various parts of this hypothesis has been published by Dodwell (1964), Ehlers (1963, in Eysenck, 1967), Unongo (1967), and Naar (1966). A similar hypothesis may be put forward with respect to the rapidity and extent of motor movement, with introverts showing little movement under low stress and much movement under high stress levels, and extraverts showing the opposite pattern. The work of Venables (1955), Anthony (1960), Rachman (1961) and Wallach and Gahm (1960) supports predictions from this hypothesis. In all these studies no effects related to extraversion would have been observed had N not been taken into account; similarly, no effects related to N would have been observed without paying attention to E. Interaction effects of this kind are so frequent that no study is complete which does not test the outcome by some form of zone analysis, explicitly incorporating in the design the possibility of a cross-over effect.

Another complication in making predictions from this theory arises from the Yerkes-Dodson law, also sometimes known as the inverse-U relation between drive or arousal and performance; according to this law, performance is optimal when drive is neither too high nor too low, and optimal drive is low for complex and high for simple tasks (Broadhurst, 1959). Drive or arousal (the two concepts have been shown to be closely related by Hebb and others) may be either manipulated experimentally (e.g. through ego-involving or task-oriented instructions), or may be determined by subject selection (choice of introverted or extraverted subjects); both methods may be combined to produce a compound design. Or task difficulty may be varied in combination with one or other of the two methods of controlling arousal. Clearly many different experimental designs are possible for investigating predictions outlined from the general theory above. Consider the following examples:

(1) McLaughlin and Eysenck (1967) used an easy and a difficult paired-associates nonsense syllables list on subjects in each of the four personality groups made up by dividing E and N into high and

low scorers; different subjects were used for the easy and the difficult task. Fig. 62 shows the results in terms of the number of errors to criterion, for both lists; the subjects have been ranged along the abscissa according to their hypothetical arousal, i.e. from low (stable extraverts) through neurotic extraverts and stable introverts to high (neurotic introverts). The curves drawn through the four points in each case suggest the nature of the inverse-U relation, with the optimum drive for the difficult list displaced towards the left. It will be seen that as expected the stable extraverts do poorly on the

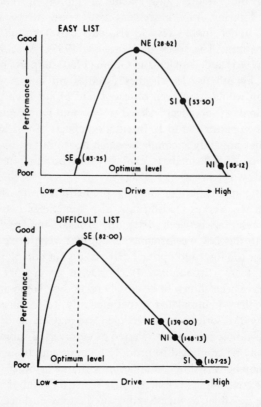

Fig. 62.—Scores of stable extraverts and introverts and neurotic extraverts and introverts on easy and difficult paired associate learning task.

easy list (too low arousal), but do best on the difficult list (optimum arousal). The neurotic extravert group does well on the easy list (optimum arousal) but does poorly on the difficult list (too high arousal). There is of course an arbitrary element connected with the drawing of the inverse-U curve through the performance scores of these four groups, but the investigation will serve to illustrate the theory in question.

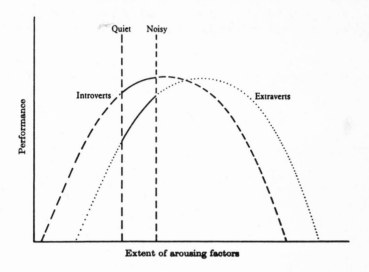

Fig. 63.—Critical flicker fusion thresholds in introverts and extraverts under noisy and quiet conditions.

(2) C. D. Frith, (1967) used the critical flicker fusion threshold as his measure of performance for introvert and extravert groups; additionally he used white noise to increase arousal. His hypothesis is shown in Fig. 63; the abscissa here is not the level of arousal, but the extent of arousing factora, i.e. the intensity of external and internal stimulation. This formulation has the advantage that the units on both axes are measured rather than inferred. It will be seen that the prediction follows from the diagram that under noisy conditions extraverts will improve their performance significantly,

but that introverts will not; that is precisely what Frith did in fact find. Again there is of course some subjectivity in the precise location of the two inverted-U curves, but these details are not too important at this early stage of measurement and verification.

(3) Davies and Hockey (1966) used four groups of extraverts and four groups of introverts to perform visual cancellation tasks under one of two conditions of signal frequency (high or low), and in either noise or quiet (high and low arousal). They made three assumptions: that introverts are more aroused than extraverts, that noise is more arousing than quiet, and that a high signal frequency is more arousing than a low one. The relation between arousal and performance was considered to take the form of an inverted U-shaped curve. Given these assumptions and the further one that adding noise is more arousing than increasing the signal frequency, the eight groups could be ordered in terms of arousal as shown from left to right on the abscissa in Fig. 64. "When the total number of correct detections is plotted on the ordinate the result can be seen to fit an

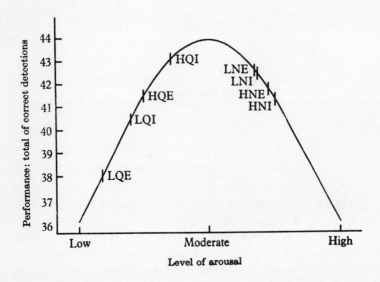

Fig. 64.—Performance of extraverts and introverts under different conditions of signal frequency (high vs. low) and under either noise or quiet.

inverted U. However, no such relation applies to errors of commission or to the total number of responses. Arousal must therefore be envisaged as affecting correct detection in a predictable manner but the way in which it affects the other two response measures, if at all, remains unclear. In any case there is no independent measure of arousal in Fig. 64."

The absence of an independent measure of arousal commented on by Davies and Hockey is not of course an unavoidable weakness; indeed it is the main strength of the theory that direct physiological measures of arousal are available, most notably the EEG which has always played a central part in theories of arousal. Many authors define arousal in terms of certain EEG patterns, such as alpha amplitude or alpha frequency, and it would be expected that extraverts and introverts would differ from each other significantly on one or several of these measures; some early results have already been summarized in Fig. 42. Much work has recently been done in this field, and a good summary is available in Gale, Coles and Blaydon (1969); these authors examine the literature critically and contribute an excellent study of their own. Table 59 is quoted from their paper; it shows that different authors have used different measures of personality, different measures of EEG arousal, and have produced different conclusions. Nevertheless, when all is said and done Gale and his colleagues are able to say, after quoting the statement by Sisson and Ellingson (1955) that "no study has been done conclusively showing a relationship between any feature of the normal adult EEG recorded under standard conditions and any personality trait or variable", "This statement is no longer true." Their own study "confirms the view that there are differences in the EEG characteristics of introverts and extraverts"; these differences, they believe, can best be explained in terms of cortical excitation. It would be wrong to overstate the case; EEG records, even when automatically or computer-analyzed are extremely complex, and interpretation is difficult. Furthermore there are many experimental hazards, and methods of overcoming these are by no means agreed between experts. Perhaps the most that can be claimed is that such data as exist, particularly when we restrict ourselves to those collected under optimal conditions and analyzed with the best equipment available, tend to support the theory in question at a reasonable level of statistical significance. Much further work will be needed before a more positive statement can be made with any confidence.

TABLE 59

STUDIES RELATING THE E.E.G. TO EXTRAVERSION-INTROVERSION

Author	Personality Measure	E.E.G. Measures	Results
Gottlober (1938)	Subjective Rating and Nebraska Personality Inventory N.P.I.	30 sec; eyes closed; per cent time alpha (index); manual scoring	Extraverts have higher alpha index
Henry & Knott (1941)	N.P.I.	300 sec; eyes closed; alpha index i.e. 50% alpha = "high" alpha; 8–12 cps and 7 micro-volts; manual scoring	Introverts have higher index (not significant)
Mundy-Castle (1955)	Primary-secondary function (as measured by a number of tasks)	20 minutes; eyes closed; mean alpha frequency	Alpha frequency correlated with primary function (equated by Eysenck (1953) with extraversion)
Nebylitsyn (1963)	Predominance of excitation or inhibition in dynamism (as measured by a number of tasks)	Derivation unknown; alpha, beta and theta; index, amplitude and frequency	Ss with predominance of inhibition in dynamism have high alpha index and amplitude but low frequency; high beta (amplitude, index and frequency) and high theta frequency. This group could be equated with extraverts (Gray, 1967)
Savage (1964)	Maudsley Personality Inventory (1919)	240 sec; eyes closed; low frequency analysis of 8–13 cps filter; alpha "amplitude"	Extraverts have higher amplitude. Interaction with neuroticism
Glass & Broadhurst (1966)	Either M.P.I. or Eysenck Personality Inventory (1914)	Unknown duration; derived between tasks (arithmetic calculations, Glass 1964); alpha index and rate of change of potential (r.c.p.); opisometric scoring	Extraversion negatively correlated with both r.c.p. and alpha index
Marton & Urban (1966)	Unknown	Alpha index and frequency; manner of derivation unknown	Extraverts have higher index and lower frequency
Fenton & Scotton (1967)	M.P.I.	30 sec; eyes closed; alpha index; mean amplitude; 8–13 cps and 15 micro-volts; manual scoring	Negative (but not significant) correlation between extraversion and both index and amplitude
Hume (1968)	E.P.I.	Duration unknown; manual scoring of output of alpha band filter	Alpha index and extraversion have positive loadings on the same factor
Gale, Coles & Blaydon	E.P.I.	(i) 110 sec; eyes closed; 2–20 cps divided into 9 frequencies; low frequency analysis giving mean integrated output and mean dominant frequency (m.d.f.). (ii) 10 min. eyes open; 10 min. eyes closed; theta, alpha and beta	(i) Extraverts have higher integrated output on all measured frequencies and lower m.d.f. (ii) Extraverts have higher theta, alpha and beta integrated output with eyes open and eyes closed

Other physiological measures than the EEG can of course be used to measure differential states of arousal in extraverts and introverts; several such studies are quoted in Eysenck (1967). It should be remembered, however, that there is no single, direct measure of arousal, and that the principle of response specificity which we encountered in relation to the measurement of emotional activation must also be presumed to be active in relation to the measurement of arousal. It is not possible at the moment to say more about this complex situation; further advances will have to await improvements in the measurement of physiological concomitants of the hypothetical single state of arousal.

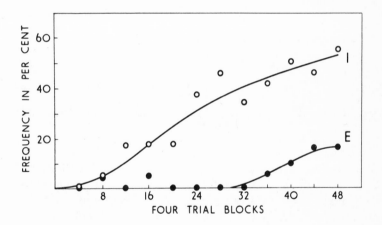

Fig. 65.—Eye-blink conditioning acquisition under conditions theoretically favouring introverts.

Armed with these theoretical considerations and results we may now return to a discussion of some of the experiments noted in connection with the "intervening variable" theory, particularly those relating to eyeblink conditioning. The "reactive inhibition" theory must be replaced by an arousal theory, and it will be seen that this is

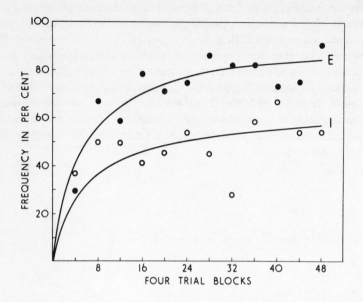

Fig. 66.—Eye-blink conditioning acquisition under conditions theoretically favouring extraverts.

much better able to account for the results, and predict further ones. There is direct experimental evidence that arousal, in both normals and schizophrenics, is positively correlated with eyeblink conditioning; Spain reports values in excess of .6 for normals and of .44 for schizophrenics between level of skin potential and number of CRs. Granted that arousal is greater in introverts, it is possible to deduce not only that introverts should condition more rapidly, but also the parametric conditions which should maximise the differences between them and extraverts. Eysenck and Levy (1967) argued that conditions of partial reinforcement, short CS-UCS and weak UCS would facilitate conditioning in introverts as compared with extraverts, and have published data from experiments using all possible combinations of these three parameters to demonstrate the correctness of their hypothesis. Fig. 65 shows the CR acquisition curve under a combination of conditions favouring the introverts (partial reinforcement, short CS-UCS interval, weak UCS); it will be seen that introverts condition much more readily. Fig. 66 shows the

CR acquisition curve under a combination of conditions favouring the extraverts; it will seen that now extraverts condition better. The reasons for this reversal may be understood best by referring to Fig. 67, which repeats the argument from Fig. 63 and applies it to eyeblink conditioning (performance) and strength of the UCS (arousing factors). The strength of the UCS is measured in terms of pounds per square inch pressure exerted by the puff of air; the weak stimulus was 3 p.s.i., while the strong one was 6 p.s.i. It will be seen that under the former condition performance of introverts is stronger, under the latter performance of extraverts; this of course is just what we have found, comparing strong and weak UCS under all combinations of the other prameters (Eysenck and Levy, 1967)[1].

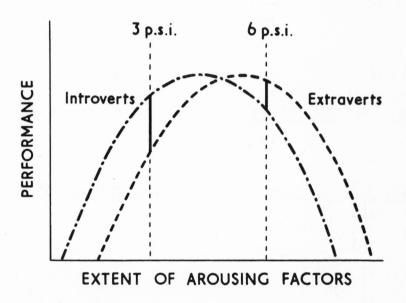

Fig. 67.—Theoretical explanation of findings shown in Figs. 65 and 66, using the same argument as presented in Fig. 63. Degree of arousal in eye-blink conditioning is supposed to be manipulated by varying the strength of the UCS (3 pounds per square inch strength of puff vs. 6 pounds per square inch strength of puff).

Reminiscence, too, would appear to need refurbishing in so far as theoretical accounts go, particularly as later studies, while still showing extraverts as demonstrating greater reminiscence, have failed to support the view that the main difference between extraverts and introverts would be demonstrated in the depressed pre-rest performance of the former; instead the difference was found due largely to the depressed post-rest performance of the latter (Eysenck, 1964; Gray, 1968). An experiment by Farley (1966) shows this quite clearly (Fig. 68); he interposed a 10 minute rest after 30 massed 10 second trials on the pursuit rotor, with another 120 massed 10 second trials after the rest. Extraverts and introverts perform equally before the rest, but the former are superior after the rest. Thus while the prediction of greater reminiscence in extraverts is verified, the theory on which it was based is clearly infirmed. An alternative theory has been put forward by Eysenck (1965) in terms of consolidation of the memory trace; learning is believed to produce mnemonic traces which become available for the improvement of performance only after a period of perseveration or consolidation. This consolidation appears in

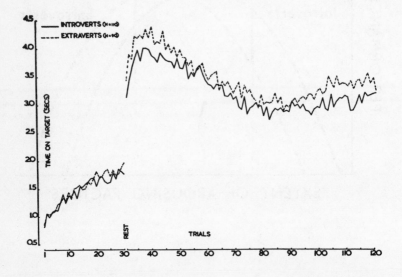

Fig. 68.—Pursuit rotor reminiscene of introverts and extraverts.

performance after rest as reminiscence. Arousal determines the degree of consolidation which takes place, with higher arousal leading to stronger and longer-continued consolidation. It is assumed that physical tasks produce greater arousal in extraverts, mental tasks in introverts; from this it would follow that on physical tasks, like the pursuit rotor, extraverts would show greater reminiscence than introverts, while on mental tasks the opposite would be true.

This latter prediction is subject to one further theoretical proviso. Walker (1958) has put forward the theory, since well-supported by experimental evidence, that during the consolidation process (which may be envisaged as the encoding of short-term reverberating electric circuits into chemical engrams through some form of protein synthesis—John, 1967) the encoded material is not available for reproduction; in other words, *consolidation interferes with reproduction*. From this it would seem to follow that extravert-introvert differences should show a marked interaction effect with time; extraverts should show superior performance for a short period after rest, introverts only an hour or more after rest. This prediction is made on the basis of postulating a longer-continued and stronger consolidation process in introverts, due to their higher arousal level; this would interfere with reproduction on a short-term basis, but would facilitate reproduction over longer periods of time. Howarth and Eysenck (1968) have published a study of paired-associate recall demonstrating this cross-over effect, by having introverts and extraverts learn paired CVC nonsense syllables to a criterion, and then reproduce them at various intervals after learning. (Different subjects were of course used for the different intervals). Fig. 69 shows the results, which show a fully significant cross-over effect, very much as expected. Similar cross-over effects have been found with pursuit rotor reminiscence in some unpublished experiments by F. Farley, but not by Gray, (1968).

The experiments discussed thus far could mostly be explained in terms of the older as well as the newer theory, although the newer theory appears much more powerful in predicting parametric influences; there are also predictions which would not be possible on the basis of the older theory, and the verifications of which demonstrate even more clearly the superiority of the new theory. Chief among these predictions are a series relating to sensory thresholds, and the consequences of differences between extraverts and introverts in such thresholds. It is known from work with animals and humans that arousal lowers thresholds (Gray, 1965); accordingly we would

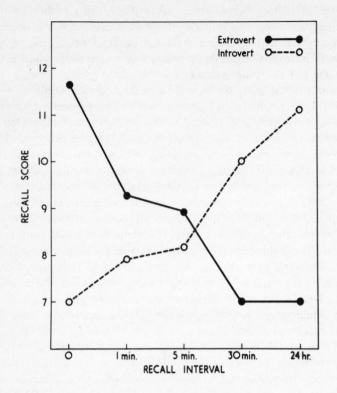

Fig. 69.—Recall of paired associates of extraverts and introverts after different recall intervals.

expect introverts to have lower thresholds than extraverts. Several lines of evidence point in this direction. Smith (in Eysenck, 1967) demonstrated lower auditory thresholds in introverts. Haslam (1967) studied the threshold for radiant-heat induced pain, and found that introverts had markedly lower thresholds. Dunstone et al. (1964) related the thresholds of electrical vestibular stimulation to personality; low-frequency sinusoidal electrical stimulation of the human vestibular apparatus produces lateral sway, and it appears that thresholds for introverts are significantly lower than those of extraverts. Fischer, Griffin and Rockey (1966) found introverts to have lower thresholds for gustatory chemoreceptors, in particular taste thresholds for quinine. Several experimenters have used critical flicker fusion thresholds in correlation with measures of introversion-extraversion; results, as surveyed by Eysenck (1967) suggest greater ability to resolve flickering stimuli in introverts, as expected. All these studies, then, are in general agreement on the point at issue; introverts do seem to have lower thresholds for incoming stimuli than do extraverts.

It may be deduced from this that identical stimuli impinging on the organism would be experienced as a stronger (i.e. farther removed from the threshold) in introverts; as Corcoran (1964) puts it, "if introverts are in general more highly aroused than extraverts, then,

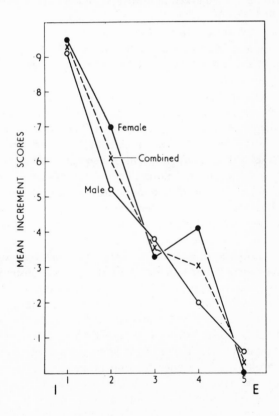

Fig. 70.—Mean salivation increments of 5 groups of male and female subjects, ordered according to degree of introversion, after placing 4 drops of lemon juice on tongue.

assuming that arousal is synonymous with a state of high cortical facilitation, it follows that the output of an effector of an introvert should be greater than the output of an effector of an extravert when both are equally stimulated". He tested this prediction by measuring the increment in salivation during a 20 sec. period following upon the placing of 4 drops of lemon juice on the tongue; introverts as expected showed a greater incrementation than did extraverts, to a very marked degree. Eysenck and Eysenck (1967) have replicated the experiment on 50 men and 50 women, and the results are shown in Fig. 70; the correlation between introversion and salivary output due to stimulation is over .7! Orienting responses, too, would be expected to be more marked in introverts on the same principle, and Dodge (1965) has found this to be so.

A generalized form of this threshold theory has been published by Eysenck (1963) in a form which can best be presented by reference to Fig. 71. This shows the well-established relation between level of sensory stimulation (abscissa) and hedonic tone (liking or disliking); it will be seen that this relation is curvilinear, with high levels of stimulation (pain) disliked, and extremely low levels of stimulation (sensory deprivation) equally disliked. Differences in thresholds displace the introvert curve to the left, the extravert curve to the right, of the ambivert of "population average" curve, suggesting that introverts would be more tolerant of sensory deprivation, extraverts more tolerant of pain. Measures of pain tolerance and of sensory deprivation tolerance have shown that the relation is as hypothesized; a review of the literature is given in Eysenck (1967). An interesting extension of this general theory has been made by Weisen (1965), who compared extraverts and introverts on a test which first equated them in terms of strength of pushing a key against a spring, the strength of the push constituting the behaviour selected for reinforcement. Subjects were sitting in a dark and quiet room, and during the experimental part of the study (i.e. after the operant level had been determined) pushed above a certain strength produced loud jazz music and bright lights for a 3 sec. period; this could be prolonged by further vigorous pushing. Fig. 72 shows the results; as expected extraverts show "stimulus hunger" and press to obtain the sensory stimulation, while introverts lower their strength of pressing in order to escape from the strong stimulation. In another experiment conditions were reversed, pressing produced darkness and quiet for short periods, and now the introverts pressed more vigorously.

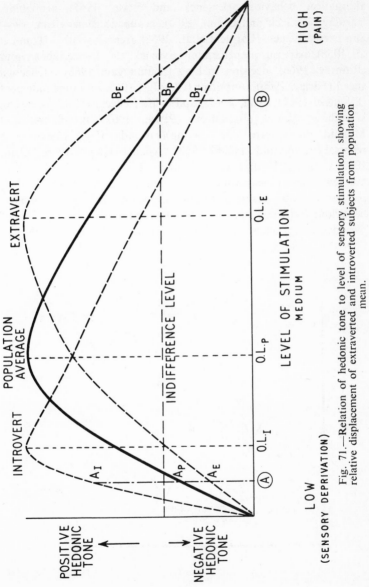

Fig. 71.—Relation of hedonic tone to level of sensory stimulation, showing relative displacement of extraverted and introverted subjects from population mean.

The experiments discussed above are only a small fraction of those which appear in the literature; others deal with such topics as alternation behaviour (Eysenck and Levey, 1965), probability learning (Wallach and Gahm, 1960), group decisions (Rim, 1964) and persuasiveness (Carment et al., 1965), free association (Dunn et al., 1958), extrasensory perception (Eysenck, 1967), speech behaviour (Ramsey, 1966), decision making (Shanmugan, 1965) intellectual speed (Farley, 1966), time error (Claridge, 1960) and time judgment (Eysenck, 1959; Lynn, 1961), spiral after-effects (Holland, 1965), kinesthetic figural after-effects (Petrie, 1967; Broadhurst and Milland, 1969), verbal conditioning (Jawanda, 1966), Necker cube reversal (Franks and Lindahl, 1963), vigilance (Hogan, 1966; Bakan, 1959; Claridge, 1960), and many others. It would appear that there are few areas in experimental psychology in which personality, particularly introversion-extraversion, does not act so as to modify behaviour provided some attention is paid to consideration of parametric variables, and provided that suitable controls are imposed.

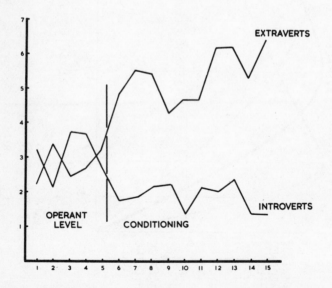

Fig. 72.—Strength of responding of extraverts and introverts when strong sensory stimulation was dependent on strength of response.

This question of controls is more complex than it looks at first; recent research has thrown up findings which suggest that more aspects of the test situation require to be investigated than is usually done. Consider two examples. Using the task of crossing out the letter "e" from printed material, Colquhoun and Corcoran tested extraverted and introverted subjects either in the morning or in the afternoon, and either in isolation or in groups. Both factors were shown to affect performance; Fig. 73 shows the results for the morning vs. the afternoon groups, and Fig. 74 the results for the

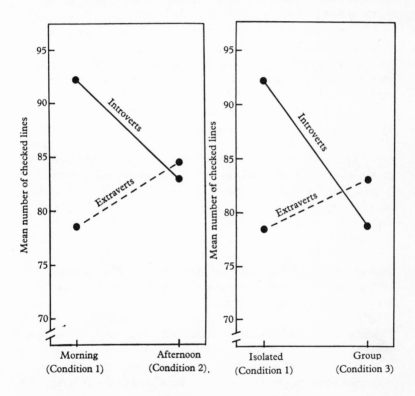

Fig. 73.—Performance on checking task of extraverts and introverts during morning and afternoon sessions.

Fig. 74.—Performance on checking task of extraverts and introverts under conditions of isolation and group performance.

groups vs. isolation conditions. It will be seen that both time of day and testing conditions have a profound interaction effect with extraversion-introversion; the former agrees well with Blake's (1968) finding that introverts and extraverts show different maxima and minima for body temperature according to time of day, suggesting that these are indeed fundamental and physiologically-based phenomena. It would appear that tests which show large differences between introverts in the morning might not do so in the afternoon, or that tests which show discrimination when individually administered fail to do so under group administration conditions. Some of the failures to replicate now in the literature may be due to disregard of these facts.

Implicit in all that has been said in this chapter is the assumption that personality is firmly anchored in physiological and neurological reaction-mechanisms which themselves have a firm anatomical basis; in other words, it is asserted that individual differences in personality, particularly along the E and N dimensions, are largely the product of innate factors interacting with the environment. Observed personality, as measured by Inventory or experimental test, and as demonstrating neurotic or criminal behaviour, is a *phenotype* showing appreciable correlation with the *genotype;* results obtained in the U.K. and the U.S.A. as well as on the European continent suggest that these correlations are not likely to lie below .75 so that we might be justified in saying that some three-quarters of individual differences in personality, in so far as these relate to E and N, are genetically determined. This genetic hypothesis is so strongly opposed to much current thinking which stresses the modifiability of human behaviour that only the most detailed discussion of the evidence could hope to convince most readers of the fact that these propositions are strongly supported by empirical evidence; it would clearly be out of place to append such a discussion at this point. Eysenck (1967) has reviewed the evidence in great detail, and readers must be referred to his book.

It might, however, not be out of place to suggest a possible reason why the notion of genetic causes has been so difficult to accept by most psychiatrists and psychologists. In the first place, of course, it runs counter to the doctrine of "perfectability" of human nature which is so strongly embedded in the manipulative cultures of the U.S.A. and the U.S.S.R.; there is a refusal to admit limitations to the beneficial effects of education and brain-washing. Secondly, there is the more reasonable objection that it is only structure which can be inherited, not function; it is not easily seen how conduct can be determined by heredity. We have seen how the theories incorporated in this chapter can answer this objection; individual differences in the structure of the ascending reticular system and the visceral brain determine differences in the thresholds and functioning of these structures, and these differences, interacting with the environment, largely determine a person's behaviour.

A third objection rises from a partial misunderstanding of what the theory of genetic determination is in fact saying. Psychiatrists in particular often see patients who have been exposed to extreme environmental stresses; they see the palpable effects of these stresses and find it difficult to understand how it can be said that environmental factors do not contribute more than one quarter of the influences that have shaped the behaviour of these individuals. But this of course is an elementary misunderstanding of the statistical statement; the contribution of heredity to individual differences in personality is an average figure covering a particular sample—it does not apply to every person in that sample. Some will have undergone extreme environmental stresses which determine their personalities and responses almost completely, others will have had such an average type of environment that heredity assumes much greater importance in differentiating them from each other than is true on the average. All in all these different types of people and different types of environmental stress average to an overall figure of 75% determination of personality by heredity, but it would be totally wrong to apply this figure to every member of the sample, or to extrapolate it beyond the confines of those countries in which the research was undertaken.

A fourth reason for disregarding hereditary causes lies in the feeling of therapeutic helplessness which is generated by genetic hypotheses; if criminality and neuroses are largely innate, then it is useless to try to prevent or cure them. Natural though such feelings may be, they have no meaning in scientific terms. Consider phenylketonuria, a disease which affects about one child in 40,000 in England. This disorder causes mental defect, and is known to be inherited and due to a single recessive gene. Diagnosis can be made because the urine of children suffering from this disorder yields a green-coloured reaction with a solution of ferric chloride, due to the presence of derivatives of phenylalanine. Apparently these children are unable to convert phenylalanine into tyrosine, and apparently these incomplete breakdown products are poisonous to the nervous system and cause mental deficiency. An almost complete cure is possible by feeding the children on a phenylalanine-free diet, containing however tyrosine; when this is done early enough in life children can grow up without the terrible mental handicap which they would have suffered otherwise. It is precisely by learning about the hereditary nature and mechanisms of this disease that a cure could be found; knowledge of hereditary causes for human behaviour does not imply any kind of therapeutic nihilism. Exactly the opposite is true; only a thorough knowledge of the facts will enable proper therapeutic methods to be employed (Eysenck and Rachman, 1965).

A fifth and less creditable reason for the widespread rejection of hereditary influences is simply ignorance; few psychologists and psychiatrists are sufficiently knowledgeable to find their way around texts involving genetic terminology and formulae, or to be able to judge the validity of an argument or the importance of an experiment. Important new developments, such as the discovery of extra-chromosomal inheritance (Jinks, 1964), are not usually familiar to non-geneticists. Even so, text-book writers not really familiar with the facts, often take it upon themselves to discredit genetic causes, usually by referring to experiments and arguments some 50 years out of date. This is not a good reason for rejecting well-established facts.

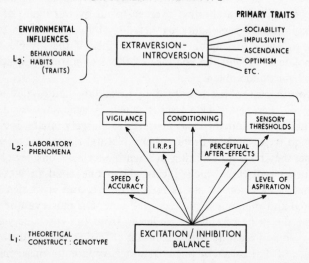

Fig. 75.—Diagrammatic representation of interplay between genotype and environment to produce phenotype of extravert-introvert personality.

The theory here presented may be illustrated by reference to Fig. 75, which shows in diagrammatic form the postulated chain of events. We start with certain physical, anatomic structures, like the reticular formation, the cortex, the autonomic system and the visceral brain, all of which have physiological and neurological significance. Different people differ widely in the precise details of these structures; Williams (1956) has demonstrated the very marked differences which occur in physiological structures and functions in normal samples of human beings. Persons so differentially equipped develop different habitual levels of arousal, and have different thresholds for emotional activation; these can be tested in relatively pure form in laboratory studies of conditioning, sensory thresholds, vigilance and the like. Interacting with the environment, these predispositions produce the various extraverted or introverted, stable or unstable patterns of behaviour which we can analyze through factorial studies, and which can be descriptively isolated as "factors", very much in the manner illustrated in the various chapters of this book. Such personality patterns, expressed through the various traits characterizing them, predispose a person to neurosis, or to criminality, or to accident proneness; there is no inevitability about this, and environment obviously plays an extremely important part. Nevertheless, the predisposition is there; different people react differently to identical circumstances, just as a person may react differently to different circumstances. What we observe is always the phenotype, never the genotype; the latter is a theoretical construct which modern methods of genetic analysis, coupled with advances in psychological testing, can enable us to approach to some extent. The pendulum which had swung so far in the direction of environmental determination is beginning to swing back, but the emphasis on the importance of genetic influences should not lead us to underestimate enviroment; both are inexorably intertwined in their interaction which alone produced observable conduct.

NOTE TO PAGE 425

On p.121 we have cited several studies suggesting the existence of another superfactor provisionally labelled 'psychoticism'. In recent years a certain amount of research has been published in an attempt to validate this concept and demonstrate the existence of such a factor in normal sample of subjects (Eysenck and Eysenck, 1968, 1969). Results have on the whole been in favour of the hypothesis, and a factor 'P' has been found, relatively independent of N and E, both with adults and with children, which could best be interpreted along the lines of the hypothetical psychoticism factor; psychotics on the whole had extremely elevated scores on this factor. Criminals, interestingly enough, also had very high scores, as compared with normals and neurotics. However, little experimental work has been done with this factor, and for this reason no prolonged discussion will be given in this chapter.

NOTE TO PAGE 445

The relations between arousal and growth of CR illustrated in Fig. 67 may also serve to explain why Spence (1964) found positive correlations between N (as measured by the Taylor Manifest Anxiety Scale) and CR frequency, while failing to discover any correlations with E. His method involves procedures for increasing the anxiety felt by subjects on encountering complex electronic equipment, without explanations and reassurance; thus autonomic (sympathetic) reactions are produced which increase cortical arousal, particularly in high N subjects, destroying in this manner the differences between high E and low E subjects in arousal, as explained above. According to this account, the drive involved in the Spence-Taylor type of experiment is still arousal, but it is produced in their case partly through an overspill of emotional (fear) reaction. This accounts for the fact that in our own work, and in that of other American writers who have followed the practice of reassuring subjects and calming their fears, correlations between conditioning and N have usually been zero; it is only under such conditions that a proper test of our hypothesis, linking conditioning with E, can be carried out. This line of argument obviously also has important consequences for the hypothetical link between conditioning and neurosis (Eysenck and Rachman, 1965);

459

REFERENCES

Chapter XII

ANTHONY, S. Anxiety as a function of psychomotor and social behaviour. *Brit. J. Psychol.*, 1960, **51**, 141–152.
BAKAN, P. Extraversion-introversion and improvement in an auditory vigilance task. *Brit. J. Psychol.*, 1959, **50**, 325–332.
BLAKE, M. J. F. Relation between circadian rhythms of body temperature and introversion-extraversion. *Nature*, 1967, **215**, 896–897.
BROADHURST, A., and MILLARD, D. W. Augmenters and reducers: a note on a replication failure. *Acta. Psychol.*, 1969, **29**, 290–296.
BROADHURST, P. L. The interaction of task difficulty and motivation: the Yerkes-Dodson law revived. *Acta. Psychol.*, 1959, **16**, 321–338.
BURT, C. Factorial studies of personality and their bearing on the work of the teacher. *Brit. J. educ. Psychol.*, 1965, **35**, 368–370.
CARMENT, D. W., MILES, C. G., and CERVIN, W. S. Persuasiveness and personality as related to intelligence and extraversion. *Brit. J. soc. clin. Psychol.*, 1965, **4**, 1–7.
CRASKE, S. A study of the relations between personality and accident history. *Brit. J. med. Psychol.*, 1968, **41**, 399–404.
COLQUHOUN, W. P., and CORCORAN, D. W. J. The effects of time of day and social isolation on the relationship between temperament and performance. *Brit. J. soc. clin. Psychol.*, 1964, **3**, 226–231.
CORCORAN, D. W. J. The relation between introversion and salivation. *Amer. J. Psychol.*, 1964, **77**, 298–300.
CLARIDGE, G. S., The excitation-inhibition balance in neurotics. In: H. J. Eysenck (Ed.) *Experiments in Personality*, Vol. 2. London: Routledge & Kegan Paul, 1960.
COOPER, R., and PAYNE, R. Extraversion and some aspects of work behaviour. *Personnel Psychol.*, 1967, **20**, 45–57.
DAVIES, G. R., and HOCKEY, G. R. J. The effects of noise and doubling the signal frequency on individual differences in visual vigilance performance. *Brit. J. Psychol.*, 1966, **57**, 381–389.
DODGE, D. W. Contrasts and similarities in the orienting responses of extraverts and introverts. Purdue University: Unpublished Ph.D. thesis, 1965.
DODWELL, P. O. Some factors affecting the learning of words presented dichotically. *Canad. J. Psychol.*, 1964, **18**, 72–91.
DUNN, S., BLISS, J., and SUPOLA, S. Effects of impulsivity, introversion and individual values upon association under free conditions. *J. Personality*, 1958, **26**, 61–76.
DUNSTONE, J. J., DZENDOLET, G., and HENCKERUTH, O. Effect of some personality variables in electrical vestibular stimulation. *Percept. & Motor Skills*, 1964, **18**, 689–695.
EVANS, F. J. Field dependence and the Maudsley Personality Inventory. *Percept. & Motor Skills*, 1967, **24**, 526.
EYSENCK, H. J. Reminiscence, Drive, and Personality Theory. *J. abnorm. soc. Psychol.*, 1956, **53**, 328–333.
EYSENCK, H. J. The Dynamics of Anxiety and Hysteria. London: Routledge & Kegan Paul, 1957.

EYSENCK, H. J. Personality and the estimation of time. *Percept. & Motor Skills*, 1959, **9**, 405–406.

EYSENCK, H. J. The Maudsley Personality Inventory. London: University of London Press, 1961. San Diego: Educational & Industrial Testing Service, 1961.

EYSENCK, H. J. Reminiscence, drive, and personality—revision and extension of a theory. *Brit. J. soc. clin. Psychol.*, 1962, **1**, 127–140.

EYSENCK, H. J. Experiments with Drugs. Oxford: Pergamon Press, 1963.

EYSENCK, H. J. Personality and Reminiscence—an experimental study of the "reactive inhibition" or "conditioned inhibition" theories. *Life Sciences*, 1964, **3**, 189–198.

EYSENCK, H. J. Crime and Personality. Boston: Houghton Mifflin, 1964.

EYSENCK, H. J. Involuntary rest pauses in tapping as a function of drive and personality. *Percept. & Motor Skills*, 1964, **18**, 173–174.

EYSENCK, H. J. A three-factor theory of reminiscence. *Brit. J. Psychol.*, 1965, **56**, 163–181.

EYSENCK, H. J. Extraversion and the acquisition of eyeblink and GSR conditioned responses. *Psychol. Bull.*, 1965, **63**, 258–270.

EYSENCK, H. J. The Biological Basis of Personality. Springfield: C. C. Thomas, 1967.

EYSENCK, H. J. Personality patterns in various groups of businessmen. *Occup. Psychol.*, 1967, **41**, 249–250.

EYSENCK, H. J. Personality and extra-sensory perception. *J. soc. Psychiat. Res.*, 1967, **44**, 55–71.

EYSENCK, H. J. A theory of the incubation of anxiety/fear responses. *Behav. Res. Ther.*, 1968, **6**, 309–322.

EYSENCK, H. J. and EYSENCK, S. B. G. The Eysenck Personality Inventory. London: University of London Press, 1964. San Diego: Educational & Industrial Testing Service, 1964.

EYSENCK, H. J., and EYSENCK, S. B. G. The Structure and Measurement of Personality. London: Routledge & Kegan Paul, 1969.

EYSENCK, H. J., and EYSENCK, S. B. G. A factorial study of psychoticism as a dimension of personality. *Multivar. Beh. Res.*, Special Issue, 1968, Pp. 15–31.

EYSENCK, H. J., and LEVEY, A. Alternation in choice behaviour and extraversion. *Life Sciences*, 1965, **4**, 115–119.

EYSENCK, H. J., and LEVEY, A. Konditionierung, Introversion-Extraversion und die Starke des Nervensystems. *Zeitsch. f. Psychol.*, 1967, **174**, 96–106.

EYSENCK, H. J., and RACHMAN, S. Causes and Cures of Neurosis, London: Routledge & Kegan Paul, 1965.

EYSENCK, S. B. G. Personality and pain assessment in childbirth of married and unmarried mothers. *J. ment. Sci.*, 1961, **107**, 417–430.

EYSENCK, S. B. G., and EYSENCK, H. J. Salivary response to lemon juice as a measure of introversion. *Percept. & Motor Skills*, 1967, **24**, 1047–1053.

EYSENCK, S. B. G., and EYSENCK, H. J. The measurement of Psychoticism; a study of factor stability and reliability. *Brit. J. soc. clin. Psychol.*, 1968, **7**, 286–294.

EYSENCK, S. B. G., and EYSENCK, H. J. Scores on three personality variables as a function of age, sex, and social class. *Brit. J. soc. clin. Psychol.*, 1969, **8**, 69–76.

EYSENCK, S. B. G., and EYSENCK, H. J. "Psychoticism" in children; a new personality variable. *Research in Education*, 1969, **1**, 21–37.

FARLEY, F. H. Reminiscence and post rest performance as a function of length of rest, drive and personality. Univ. London: Unpublished Ph.D. thesis, 1966.

FARLEY, F. H. Individual differences in solution time in error-free problem-solving. *Brit. J. soc. clin. Psychol.*, 1966, **5**, 306–309.

FENTON, G. W., and SCOTTON, L. Personality and the alpha rhythm. *Brit. J. Psychiat.*, 1967, **113**, 1283–1289.

FINE, B. J. Introversion-Extraversion and motor vehicle driver behaviour. *Percept. & Motor Skills*, 1963, **16**, 95–100.

FISCHER, R., GRIFFIN, F., and ROCKEY, M. C. Gustatory Neuroreception in man. *Persp. Biol. Med.*, 1966, **9**, 549–577.

FRANKS, C. M. Conditioning and Personality: a study of normal and neurotic subjects. *J. Abnorm. soc. Psychol.*, 1956, **52**, 143–150.

FRANKS, C. M. Personality factors and the rate of conditioning. *Brit. J. Psychol.*, 1957, **48**, 119–126.

FRANKS, C. M., and LINDAHL, L. E. H. Extraversion and rated fluctuation of the Necker cube. *Percept. & Motor Skills*, 1963, **16**, 131–137.

FRITH, C. D. The interaction of noise and personality with critical flicker fusion performance. *Brit. J. Psychol.*, 1967, **58**, 127–131.

GALE, A., COLES, M., and BLAYDON, J. Extraversion-introversion and the EEG. *Brit. J. Psychol.*, 1969, **60**, 209–223.

GINSBERG, A. Hypothetical constructs and interview variables. *Psychol. Rev.*, 1954, **61**, 119–131.

GLASS, A., and BROADHURST, A. Relationships between EEG and a measured cortical activity and personality variables. *Electro. enceph. clin. Neurophysiol.*, 1966, **21**, 309.

GOTTLOBER, A. M. The relationships between brain potentials and personality. *J. exper. Psychol.*, 1938, **22**, 67–74.

GRAY, J. A. Pavlov's Typology. Oxford: Pergamon Press, 1965.

GRAY, J. E. Level of arousal and length of rest as determinants of pursuit rotor performance. Univ. London: Unpublished Ph.D. thesis, 1968.

HENRY, C. E., and KNOTT, J. R. A note on the relationship between "personality" and the alpha rhythm of the electroencephalogram. *J. exper. Psychol.*, 1941, **28**, 362–366.

HOGAN, M. J. Influence of motivation on reactive inhibition extra-version-introversion. *Percept. & Motor Skills*, 1966, **22**, 187–192.

HOLLAND, H. C. The Spiral After-Effect. Oxford: Pergamon Press, 1965.

HOWARTH, E., and EYSENCK, H. J. Extraversion, Arousal, and Paired-Associate Recall. *J. exper. Res. in Personality*. 1968, **3**, 114–116.

HUME, W. I. The dimensions of central nervous arousal. *Bull. Brit. Psychol. Soc.*, 1968, **21**, 111 (Extract).

INGLIS, J. Abnormalities of motivation and "ego functions". In: H. J. Eysenck (Ed.) Handbook of Abnormal Psychology. London: Pitman, 1960.

JAWANDA, J. S. Age, sex and personality variables in verbal conditioning and its modification by drugs. Punjab University: Unpublished Ph.D. thesis, 1966. See H. J. Eysenck, 1967.

JINKS, J. L. Extrachromosomal Inheritance. New Jersey: Prentice Hall, 1964.

JOHN, E. R. Mechanisms of Memory. New York: Academic Press, 1967.

LUNDIN, R. W. Personality. New York: Macmillan, 1961.

LYNN, R. Introversion-extraversion differences in judgments of time. *J. abnorm. soc. Psychol.*, 1961, **63**, 457–458.

MacCorquodale, K., and Meehl, P. E. On a distinction between hypothetical constructs and intervening variables. *Psychol. Rev.*, 1948, **55**, 95–107.

McLaughlin, R. J., and Eysenck, H. J. Extraversion, neuroticisms and paired-associates learning. *J. exper. Res. in Personality*, 1967, **2**, 128–132.

MacLean, P. D. Contrasting functions of limbic and neocortical system of the brain and their relevance to psychophysiological aspects of medicine. *Amer. J. Med.*, 1958, **25**, 611–626.

MacLean, P. D. Psychosomatics. In: Handbook of Physiology. Washington: *Amer. Physiol. Soc.*, 1960.

Martin, M., and Urban, Y. An electroencelographic investigation of individual differences in the process of conditioning. Proc. 18th Int. Congr. Exp. Psychol., Moscow, 1966, Vol. 9, 106–109.

Maze, J. R. Do intervening variables intervene? *Psychol Rev.*, 1954, **61**, 226–234.

Mobbs, N. A. Eye-contact in relation to social introversion-extraversion. *Brit. J. soc. clin. Psychol.*, 1968, **7**, 305–306.

Moss, P. D., and McEvedy, C. P. An epidemic of overbreathing among schoolgirls. *Brit. med. J.*, 1966, 26th Nov., 1295–1300.

Mundy-Castle, A. C. The relationship between primary-secondary function and the alpha rhythm of the electroencephalogram. *J. Nat. Inst. Personnel Res.*, 1955, **6**, 95–102.

Naar, R. Perceptual defense, extraversion and stimulus emotionality. Pittsburgh: Unpublished Ph.D. thesis, 1966.

Nibylitsyn, V. D. An electroencephalographic investigation of the properties of strength of the nervous system and equilibrium of the nervous processes in man, using factor analysis. In: Teplov, B. M. (Ed.) Typological Features of Higher Nervous Acitivity in Man, Vol. 3, 47–80. Moscow: Acad. Pedagog., 1963.

Petrie, A. Individuality in pain and suffering. Chicago: Univ. Chicago Press, 1967.

Rachman, S. Psychomotor behaviour and personality with special reference to conflict. London University: Unpublished Ph.D thesis, 1961.

Ramsey, R. W. Personality and speech. Univ. London: Unpublished Ph.D. thesis, 1966.

Rim, Y. Personality and group decisions involving risks. *Psychol. Rec.* 1964, **14**, 37–45.

Samuels, I. Reticular mechanisms and behaviour. *Psychol. Bull.*, 1959, **56**, 1–25.

Savage, R. D. Electro-cerebral activity, extraversion and neuroticism *Brit. J. Psychiat.*, 1964, **110**, 98–100.

Shanmungam, T. E. Personality, severity of conflict and decision time. *Ind. Acad. Appl. Psychol.*, 1965, **2**, 13–23.

Shaw, L., and Sichel, N. S. Accident Proneness. Oxford: Pergamon Press, 1970.

Sisson, B. D., and Ellingson, R. J. On the relationship between "normal" EEG patterns and personality variables. *J. nerv. ment. Dis.*, 1955, **121**, 353–358.

Spence, K. W. Anxiety (drive) level and performance in eyelid conditioning. *Psychol. Bull.*, 1964, **61**, 129–139.

Spielman, J. The relation between personality and the frequency and duration of involuntary rest pauses during massed practice. University of London: Unpublished Ph.D. thesis, 1963.

UNONGO, P. I. Perceptual defence, sympathetic reactivity, and personality. University of Alberta: Unpublished Ph.D. thesis, 1967.

VENABLES, P. H. Change in motor response with increase and decrease in task difficulty in normal industrial and psychiatric patient subjects. *Brit. J. Psychol.*, 1955, **46,** 101–110.

WALKER, E. L. Action decrement and its relation to learning. *Psychol. Rev.*, 1958, **65,** 128–142.

WALLACH, M. A., and GAHM, R. C. Effects of anxiety level and extra-version-introversion in probability learning. *Psychol. Rep.*, 1960, **7,** 387–398.

WALLACH, M. A., and GAHM, R. C. Personality functions of graphic constriction and expensiveness. *J. Person.*, 1960, **28,** 73–88.

WEISEN, A. Differential reinforcing effects of onset and offset of stimulation on the operant behaviour of normals, neurotics, and psychopaths. University of Florida: Unpublished Ph.D. thesis, 1965.

WELLS, B. Personal communication, 1969.

WILLIAMS, R. Biochemical individuality. New York: Wiley, 1956.

SUBJECT INDEX

a, 117, 166
A, 183, 189, 195
abnormality, general factor of, 28, 280
accidents, 428
accident-prone, 429
achievement motivation, 283
activity, 105, 108, 183, 188, 241
activeness, 240
adrenergic personality, 193, 290
aesthetic factor, 410
Ag, 184, 190, 295
anal character, 216
  stage, 31, 218
analysis, component, 39
  confluence, 39
  discriminant, 39
  multivariate, 39
  qualitative, 48
analytic temperament, 55
annoyances, 208
anthropometry, 336
anti-Semitism, 375, 386
antisocial behaviour, 213
anxiety, 246–8, 297, 436
  state, 24, 126, 208
apperceptive mode, 32
arm levitation test, 88
arousal factor, 304, 435, 436, 437, 438,
    439, 443, 447
ascendance-submission, 82, 178, 180
ascending reticular activating system,
    434
assertiveness, 156
asthenic body build, 27
athletic body build, 42, 53–8, 320
authoritarianism, 375–83
attitudes, 350—95
attitude structure, 390
autia, 136, 202
autonomic factor, 292
  functioning, 92
  imbalance, 291, 295
  response specificity, 313–15
axes, rotation of, 49

basic Rorschach score, 278
behaviour, specificity of, 2
Bell inventory, 296

"blocks", 430,
blood pressure, 286, 290
body sway test, 88, 255
body temperature, 454
body type index, 339
bowel training, 216
brain damage, 166
business interest, 354

c, 112, 118, 130, 195, 196
C, 184, 198, 207, 294
C_1, 190
canonical variate analysis, 50, 127, 264
carefreeness, 181
catatonia, 120
cerebrotonia, 138–43, 330
CFF, 60, 68
character, 2
character education enquiry, 227
chemoreceptors, 448
Chevreul pendulum test, 88
choleric temperament, 17, 427, 429
cholinergic personality, 193, 290
Co, 184, 190, 294
co-asthenia, 136, 202
colour-form type, 282
comention, 136, 202
communists, 372, 385
conditioning, 286, 288, 436, 443, 444,
    445
confidence, 137
conformity, 204
conservatives, 372
conservatism, 376
consolidation, 446, 447
control factor, 304
conventionalism, 380
correlation, 9
cortex, 435
co-variation chart, 396
creatinine excretion, 289
criminals, 427, 455
critical flicker fusion, 439
cross-over effect, 437
CS-UCS interval, 444
criterion analysis, 251, 261
  column, 209, 250
cycloid temperament, 25, 119, 192

465

INDEX OF AUTHORS